The
United States and
Latin America in
the 1980s

The United States and Latin America in the 1980s

Contending Perspectives on a Decade of Crisis

Kevin J. Middlebrook *and* Carlos Rico, *Editors*

University of Pittsburgh Press

Published by the University of Pittsburgh Press, Pittsburgh, Pa. 15260
Copyright © 1986, University of Pittsburgh Press
All rights reserved
Feffer and Simons, Inc., London
Manufactured in the United States of America

Library of Congress Cataloging in Publication Data

Main entry under title:

The United States and Latin America in the 1980's.

   (Pitt Latin American series)

   1. Latin America—Foreign relations—United States—
Addresses, essays, lectures.   2. United States—Foreign
relations—Latin America—Addresses, essays, lectures.
3. Latin America—Foreign relations—1948–   —Ad-
dresses, essays, lectures.   4. United States—Foreign
relations—1981–   —Addresses, essays, lectures.
I. Middlebrook, Kevin J.   II. Rico, Carlos, 1950–
III. Series.
F1418.U65 1985   327.7308   85-40359
ISBN 0-8229-3518-X
ISBN 0-8229-6087-7 (pbk.)

Contents

Preface

The structure of this volume reflects both a conviction and a hope. A reassessment of contemporary U.S.–Latin American relations must begin with a better understanding of those issues that constitute the central focus of hemispheric affairs in the 1980s. Yet views on a given question frequently differ sharply between the United States and Latin America, as well as across the political spectrum in a particular country. Thus the principal goal of this volume is to highlight areas of consensus and divergence on major issues by presenting both U.S. and Latin American perspectives on the political economy of contemporary U.S.–Latin American relations, external debt and capital flows, trade relations, democracy, human rights, migration, and security. The principal essays on these topics were commissioned from leading scholars and specialists in the United States, Latin America, and Europe in order to develop contrasting perspectives. Each of the sections on economic, political and social, and security issues also includes paired comments by U.S. and Latin American authors that examine areas of agreement and disagreement among the principal essays. In addition, these comments often draw attention to alternative perspectives on the topic under discussion. We hope that a more balanced appreciation of the range of significant opinion on these different issues will contribute to improved communication and understanding in U.S.–Latin American relations.

We have received invaluable support from several different institutions during the preparation of this volume. Preliminary versions of all but one of the principal essays were commissioned as background papers for the Woodrow Wilson International Center for Scholars' 1982–1983 Inter-American Dialogue. The Wilson Center has provided essential financial and institutional support during all stages of this project. We are particularly grateful to Abraham F. Lowenthal (Secretary of the Wilson Center's Latin American Program, 1977–1983), Louis W. Goodman (Senior Program Associate at the Wilson Center's Latin American Program), and James H. Billington (Director of the Wilson Center). Abe Lowenthal provided valuable suggestions and support during the early stages of the project. Lou Goodman's assistance and advice were important in bringing the book to completion. Finally, the Department of Political Science at

Indiana University-Bloomington and the Center for U.S.-Mexican Studies at the University of California-San Diego provided important support services during the final preparation of the manuscript.

We would also like to express our sincere thanks to a number of individuals who contributed to the preparation of this book. Lisa L. Condit served as rapporteur at the January 1983 authors' conference and commented on the entire manuscript.

Margaret Smith and Enrique Hermosillo skillfully assisted with the organization of the January 1983 conference. Loretta Heyen, Margaret Smith, Jeralee May, Barbara Hopkins, Shirley Garvin, and Terri McArtor provided expert secretarial assistance at different phases of the project, and Jeanne Schaaf proofread the entire manuscript at an intermediate stage. Finally, Frederick A. Hetzel (Director), Catherine Marshall (Managing Editor), and their staff at the University of Pittsburgh Press managed the publication of a lengthy manuscript with great patience, flexibility, and skill.

We jointly commissioned and commented on preliminary versions of the contributions to this volume. Kevin Middlebrook then assumed responsibility for editing and coordinating the publication of this edition; Carlos Rico has assumed responsibility for the publication of the Spanish-language edition.

Kevin J. Middlebrook
Carlos Rico

The
United States and
Latin America in
the 1980s

The United States and Latin America in the 1980s: Change, Complexity, and Contending Perspectives

Kevin J. Middlebrook and Carlos Rico

Events in the early 1980s have revealed dramatically the importance of U.S.–Latin American relations to both Latin America and the United States.* The debt crisis that erupted in 1982–1983 compelled many Latin American countries to reappraise their relations with the United States after more than a decade of efforts to diversify their international economic and political ties. The deep financial and economic crisis that struck Latin America in the 1980s simultaneously underlined the extent to which significant U.S. economic interests and the health of the international financial system depend on the continued economic viability of major Latin American debtor countries. Similarly, the protracted crisis in Central America in the late 1970s and 1980s led to greatly expanded U.S. involvement in the area and widespread debate regarding the United States' military, political, and economic interests in the Caribbean Basin. At the same time, the growing U.S. military presence in Central America sharpened concern throughout the hemisphere regarding U.S. interventionism and future U.S. policies toward the region.

The urgency of these two crises has to some extent disguised the fact that a number of old and new issues in U.S.–Latin American relations have become increasingly interrelated. The linkages between and among such issues as Latin American countries' external debt and financial relations, U.S.–Latin American trade, democracy and the transition from military-dominated authoritarian rule to more open political arrangements in Latin America, the protection and promotion of human rights throughout the hemisphere, migration, and security have

*The term *Latin America* is used in this volume to refer to Mexico, the countries of Central and South America, and the islands of the Caribbean, unless a contributing author or specific context indicates otherwise.

3

become especially salient in recent years. Moreover, economic and political crises in Latin America have blurred traditional distinctions among hemispheric, bilateral, and global problems. Although the contemporary U.S.–Latin American relations agenda certainly is not limited to the issues examined in this volume, these questions are currently at the forefront of public debate and policymakers' proposals regarding hemispheric affairs. Together these issues pose complex challenges for those concerned with the future course of inter-American relations.

Yet there is remarkably little consensus in either Latin America or the United States concerning how these major issues should be addressed, and differences in perspective between Latin American countries and the United States frequently overshadow shared interests and possible bases for cooperative approaches to common problems. The essays in this volume examine central issues in U.S.–Latin American relations in the 1980s in order to illuminate such areas of consensus and divergence. In many cases the essays on a particular topic by a Latin American and a U.S. or European author reflect substantial differences in political and ideological perspectives. This introduction places these essays in a broader context by examining two related questions. First, in what ways have Latin American countries and the United States changed since the 1960s? Second, to what extent have changing realities influenced Latin American and U.S. perspectives on hemispheric relations, and what implications do differing perspectives pose for contemporary U.S.–Latin American relations? The relationship between changing conditions and perceptions of those circumstances is an essential focal point for a reexamination of U.S.–Latin American relations in the 1980s.

This introduction departs somewhat from convention in that it makes no systematic effort to summarize the arguments and conclusions advanced in the essays that follow. The paired comments by both Latin American and U.S. authors at the end of each substantive section evaluate the strengths and weaknesses of individual essays and frequently expand the range of perspectives from which different topics are examined. The fact that this introductory essay addresses the broader context of contemporary U.S.–Latin American relations rather than the content of individual essays in the volume reflects our belief that a synthetic summary of different authors' positions on particular issues could not adequately reflect major differences in perspective in the space available here. Indeed, the purpose of this volume is to highlight rather than mask frequently divergent views on a number of significant issues that together constitute the central focus of inter-American relations in the 1980s.

The Changing Context of U.S.–Latin American Relations

Perspectives on and approaches to U.S.–Latin American relations have shifted over the last two decades in both Latin America and the United States. In Latin America, widespread socioeconomic and political change during the 1960s and 1970s had an important impact on many policymakers' goals and orientations, and substantially increased national capabilities contributed to their efforts to diversify international economic and political ties so as to reduce their countries' long-standing dependence on the United States. Although these attempts at international diversification produced fewer lasting results than originally anticipated, and despite the extent to which the debt crisis of the 1980s has caused a number of Latin American countries to revaluate their relations with the United States, many Latin American groups' continuing commitment to regional cooperation and collective approaches to development problems represent an important departure from an earlier pattern of U.S. leadership in diverse areas of hemispheric affairs.

In the United States, détente with the Soviet Union in the early 1970s, the relative absence of perceived threats to U.S. security interests in Latin America, the internationalization of the U.S. economy, and a critical reappraisal of U.S. foreign policy following the Vietnam war led liberal policymakers to deemphasize traditional military security concerns and a hemispheric approach to Latin America in favor of global perspectives on economic and political issues. The relaxation of East-West tensions created international conditions that facilitated Latin American countries' efforts to diversify their international linkages, and this in turn reinforced the U.S. tendency to evaluate U.S.–Latin American relations in a broader North-South context. However, growing political and military tension between the United States and the Soviet Union in the late 1970s and early 1980s and the rising prominence of revolutionary movements in Central America and the Caribbean led U.S. policymakers to emphasize once again global strategic considerations in U.S.–Latin American relations. The United States' invasion of Grenada in October 1983 and its expanding military presence in Central America demonstrated a renewed commitment to the assertion of its influence in hemispheric affairs, particularly in the Caribbean Basin. As the remainder of this essay will suggest, these developments in both Latin America and the United States hold important implications for the future of U.S.–Latin American relations.

Although much of this introduction examines the changing context of U.S.–Latin American relations, it is important to emphasize at the outset that certain core characteristics of the relationship have remained quite constant over time. First, the United States generally considers Latin

America a secondary foreign policy priority, except when crises involving perceived threats to U.S. security interests erupt in the region. Despite variations over time in the amount of attention that the United States has devoted to hemispheric affairs, U.S. perceptions of Latin America's secondary importance have remained notably consistent throughout different presidential administrations. The United States' position as a global power compels it to evaluate relations with Latin America in terms of international political, military, and economic considerations, and since World War II, U.S. policymakers' views regarding Latin America have been influenced strongly by the character of U.S.-Soviet relations. The primary focus on strategic considerations in U.S. foreign policy since World War II implies that for the most part only perceived security crises such as that in contemporary Central America succeed in moving Latin American issues to the top of the U.S. foreign policy agenda. Latin American countries may be an important focus for specific U.S. policies or may at times challenge particular U.S. interests (with significant variations in the relative importance of individual countries), but in general the region is clearly less important to the United States than are the Soviet Union, political-military and economic ties with western Europe, Japan, and Canada, and perhaps even such strategically sensitive areas as the Middle East.

In marked contrast, the United States is of major importance to Latin America. Although the United States' influence in much of the region has diminished since the 1960s, and although the impact of U.S. policies on different Latin American countries varies considerably, no other country is as important to Latin America across such a wide range of issues. For Mexico and most Central American and Caribbean states, bilateral economic, political, and even military ties with the United States are of great importance. South American countries (especially Argentina, Brazil, and Uruguay, and to a lesser extent Chile, Colombia, Peru, and Venezuela) have more diversified international linkages. Nonetheless, U.S. foreign economic policies regarding trade, capital flows, investment, and the transfer of advanced technology have also had significant consequences for these countries' national economic development strategies. Since 1981 U.S. domestic economic policies (particularly budget deficits and their effect on international interest rates) have had a dramatic impact on many Latin American countries' foreign debt obligations. Even though Cuba's principal economic, political, and military relations are with the Soviet Union and East European states, the United States' quarter-century-old hostility toward the Castro government is a central concern of Cuban foreign policy.

A second enduring characteristic of U.S.–Latin American relations is that Latin American countries' economic and technological dependence on industrialized countries—including, and often particularly, the United

States—constitutes a very real obstacle to national autonomy and development. Rapid economic growth, industrialization, and the expansion of intraregional economic relations during the 1960s and 1970s contributed significantly to Latin American states' resources and capabilities. Nonetheless, the debt crisis of the 1980s dramatically revealed the extent to which they remain vulnerable to economic and political decisions beyond their direct control. Although the terms and degree of external dependency have changed over time for many Latin American countries, the overall asymmetry in power and influence between the United States and Latin America remains a constant in hemispheric relations.

Latin America: Domestic Change, International Diversification, and the Crisis of the 1980s

A discussion of Latin American perspectives on hemispheric relations in the 1980s must begin with an examination of major developments in Latin America since the 1960s. Latin American views of and orientations toward the United States necessarily reflect a long and often difficult history of U.S.–Latin American relations, but rapid socioeconomic and political change in the 1960s and 1970s and many governments' efforts during the 1970s to diversify their international economic and political relations had a particularly significant impact in this regard. Although détente between the United States and the Soviet Union and a general relaxation of international military and political tensions certainly facilitated various Latin American governments' attempts to diversify their international linkages, the marked increase in international activism and in commitment to reducing their dependence on the United States was largely due to expanded national capabilities and resources. It remains to be seen whether the United States' recent aggressive attempts to reassert its traditional influence in the region and the debt crisis of the 1980s will constitute lasting constraints on Latin American foreign policy initiatives and regional cooperation to resolve common development problems.

Socioeconomic and Political Change in Latin America

During the 1960s and 1970s nearly all Latin American countries experienced rapid economic, social, and political change. Their sustained economic growth in part reflected the increased world demand for primary products generated by economic expansion in industrialized countries and the continued inflow of foreign direct investment and loan capital. However, rapid economic growth also resulted from structural reforms and policy initiatives undertaken to promote growth and overcome a broad range of development problems. Between 1960 and 1973, the Latin

American economies grew at an average real annual rate of 5.9 percent. Higher energy costs resulting from international oil price increases in 1973–1974 slowed growth somewhat in most oil-importing countries, but access to external credit and some degree of internal economic adjustment permitted an average regional growth rate of 5.4 percent between 1973 and 1980 (see table 1, columns 4 and 5). Despite continued rapid increases in population, Latin America's real per capita gross domestic product (GDP) rose by an average 3.5 percent and 4.1 percent per year, respectively, during the 1960–1970 and 1970–1980 periods (table 1, columns 6–8).[1]

Although Latin America's overall economic growth during the 1960s and 1970s consistently surpassed the average for developing countries in general,[2] the growth process was characterized by significant limitations and inequalities. Existing problems (such as inflation, balance-of-payments difficulties, and structural unemployment) were sometimes exacerbated, and serious new problems frequently appeared (including urban marginality and environmental pollution). Some economies were particularly dynamic (Brazil, Colombia, Costa Rica, Mexico, Venezuela, the Dominican Republic and Ecuador in the 1970s, Nicaragua until the outbreak of civil war in the late 1970s, Panama in the 1960s, and Paraguay in the 1970s,) but others (Haiti, Uruguay, Argentina in the 1960s, Chile in the early 1970s, and Peru in the late 1970s) lagged behind. Despite remarkably widespread economic growth, some areas (northeastern Brazil, southern Mexico, and the highlands of Bolivia, Ecuador, Guatemala, and Peru) and several countries (Bolivia, Haiti, Honduras, Ecuador, El Salvador, and Nicaragua) remained very poor. Most Latin American countries saw major improvements in such areas as per capita income, literacy, access to education, health care, increased life expectancy, and the overall quality of life. Nonetheless, not all sectors of the population benefited equally from economic growth. The available evidence suggests that the urban middle class and skilled urban workers made the largest per capita gains in real income. There is also considerable evidence to show that rapid growth produced greater income concentration in a number of countries, even though there was general improvement in real income levels.[3]

Important structural shifts in Latin American economies accompanied sustained growth. The data in table 2 show that the most significant change involved the transition from agricultural to manufacturing activities. The production of steel, petrochemicals, machinery, automobiles, electrical products, and other capital and consumer durable goods rose in importance in the more industrialized economies while traditional manufactured items such as textiles, shoes, and clothing declined in significance. This trend was reflected in the changing structure of Latin American exports. Between 1960 and 1979, manufactured goods rose from 3.6 percent to 17.2 percent of regional exports, while the share of exports represented by food, agricultural raw materials, and ores and metals declined.[4] Governmental policies intended to promote manufactured exports were part of Latin American efforts to diversify both the product structure and the geographical destination of export trade.

Here, too, there was considerable variation within Latin America. The shift away from agricultural activities was most dramatic (a total sectoral decline of more than 10 percent between 1960 and 1979) in Costa Rica, the Dominican Republic, and Ecuador. Ten other countries experienced a total agricultural sector decline of between 5 and 10 percent (Bolivia, Brazil, Colombia, El Salvador, Guatemala, Haiti, Mexico, Panama, Paraguay, and Peru). By 1979 the manufacturing sector in four countries (Argentina, Brazil, Mexico, and Uruguay) accounted for at least one-quarter of national GDP.[5] By 1979 three countries together accounted for 62.8 percent of all Latin American manufactured exports (Brazil, 34.3 percent; Argentina, 15.2 percent; Mexico, 13.3 percent).[6]

Economic growth was accompanied by a number of important demographic changes. Latin America's population grew at an average rate of 3.2 percent per year between 1960 and 1970 and 2.6 percent per year between 1970 and 1980 (see appendix A). The urban share of Latin America's total population rose from 49.6 percent in 1960 to 66.2 percent in 1980. Demographic change was a central dimension of Latin America's social transformation, yet it also produced new problems. High birth rates meant a relatively younger population, with increased demands for education and employment. Urbanization produced crowding, slums, and intensified demands on already strained urban support systems (transportation, water, sewage disposal, and so forth).

Many of Latin America's other social characteristics also changed significantly during the 1960s and 1970s. Women entered the work force and the educational system in large numbers. Aggregate measures of population per physician, hospital beds per thousand population, access to potable water and sewage disposal, and so forth showed considerable improvement.[7] As a result, life expectancy at birth increased throughout the region (with the apparent exception of the Dominican Republic) from 59.5 years in 1965–1970 to 61.4 years in 1975–1980 (see appendix A). By the late 1970s life expectancy at birth in Argentina, Costa Rica, Cuba, Panama, and Uruguay nearly equalled that for the U.S. population as a whole (73.3 years in 1978). Average literacy (age fifteen and over) rose from 64.7 percent in 1960 to 74.4 percent in 1980 (data incomplete). The percentage of eligible students enrolled in elementary, secondary, and university education also rose dramatically (see appendix B).

Two of the political changes that accompanied this process of socio-

TABLE 1

ECONOMIC CHANGE IN LATIN AMERICA, 1960–1980

	GDP (Constant US$ millions)			Average Annual Change in GDP (%)		Per Capita GDP (constant 1980 US$)		
	1960	1970	1980	1960–70	1970–80	1960	1970	1980
Argentina	27,896.6	41,967.0	53,713.2	4.2	2.2	1371.2	1767.2	1941.9
Bolivia	1260.0	2048.6	3183.6	5.2	4.8	382.5	477.0	568.5
Brazil	47,056.0	85,560.0	195,846.9	5.4	8.4	650.6	923.9	1651.6
Chile	8558.4	13,241.8	17.664.0	4.5	2.4	1126.7	1414.3	1612.4
Colombia	8240.2	13,712.7	24.126.6	5.1	5.9	478.7	646.8	921.8
Costa Rica	1106.3	1970.1	3406.6	6.5	5.8	838.1	1150.1	1535.9
Dominican Republic	1781.6	2923.0	5700.1	4.5	6.6	513.0	673.0	1033.6
Ecuador	2246.5	3839.6	8316.3	NA	8.8	507.2	645.2	1040.1
El Salvador	1409.3	2439.7	3312.3	5.9	4.1	529.4	681.7	688.2
Guatemala	2855.2	4878.5	8434.2	5.6	5.7	728.2	927.6	1205.1
Haiti	836.6	903.9	1373.6	-0.2	4.0	234.0	213.6	274.3
Honduras	933.3	1545.7	2347.8	5.3	3.6[a]	469.5	570.6	634.0
Mexico	34,994.9	68,928.7	130,613.6	7.2	5.2	975.4	1376.4	1868.6

Nicaragua	981.9	1914.6	2022.9	7.3	0.9	653.3	1003.4	835.2
Panama	1088.5	2341.7	3711.1	7.8	4.0	892.2	1564.3	1958.4
Paraguay	1029.6	1588.7	3629.1	4.2	8.6	525.6	637.8	1145.5
Peru	9454.7	15,450.8	21,202.4	4.9	3.0	910.4	1142.0	1271.3
Uruguay	3963.3	4621.8	6320.6	1.2	3.5	1514.4	1671.5	2183.3
Venezuela	13,605.9	24,633.6	37,060.5	6.0	5.0	1779.5	2295.6	2658.0
Latin America[b]	173,136.6	300,708.9	540,677.3	5.9[c]	5.4[d]	835.7	1128.4	1585.7

Sources: Gross domestic product (GDP) and GDP per capita data are from Inter-American Development Bank, *Economic and Social Progress in Latin America* (Washington, D.C., 1982), table 3, p. 351. Data concerning average annual percent change in GDP for individual countries are from World Bank, *World Development Report, 1982* (New York: Oxford University Press, 1982), table 2, pp. 112–13; data for average annual percent change in GDP for all Latin America are from World Bank, *World Development Report, 1982*, p. 8.

Notes: The reader should note that the GDP percent changes do not correspond exactly to the data presented in the other two categories (for example, see Haiti, 1960-1970).

NA = Not Available

a. Data for 1970–1979.

b. Latin America totals include Bahamas, Barbados, Guyana, Jamaica, Suriname, and Trinidad and Tobago.

c. Data for 1960–1973.

d. Data for 1973–1980.

TABLE 2
LATIN AMERICAN GDP BY ECONOMIC ACTIVITY, 1960–1980
(percentages calculated from constant 1980 US$)

Activity	1960	1970	1980
Agriculture	16.4	13.3	10.3
Mining	4.5	3.8	2.9
Manufacturing	21.1	23.4	24.1
Construction	5.8	5.4	5.9
Utilities	1.1	1.8	2.6
Transportation and communications	6.5	6.8	8.1
Commerce	18.0	17.9	17.6
Financial services	9.9	10.6	11.9
Other services	9.3	9.6	9.4
Government	7.3	7.4	7.1
Total	99.9	100.0	99.9

Source: Authors' calculations based on data presented in Inter-American Development Bank, *Economic and Social Progress in Latin America* (Washington, D.C., 1982), table 8, p. 354. "Agriculture" includes hunting, fishing, and forestry; "mining" includes quarrying; "utilities" include generation of electricity, gas, water; "other services" include community, social, and personal services.

Note: Percentages may not add to 100.0 because of rounding.

economic transformation had particular significance for Latin American domestic and foreign policy. First, the state came to play a more active socioeconomic role in most countries, regardless of the particular characteristics of different regimes. Advocates of broader state involvement often argued that the national bourgeoisie was too small or weak to undertake investments in large infrastructure projects and basic industries and that national sovereignty concerns prevented foreign-owned transnational corporations from doing so; instead, the public sector would take responsibility for essential economic development tasks. Expanded state involvement in national affairs was also perceived to be necessary to resolve the accumulated socioeconomic inequalities that characterized dependent development.

The relative importance of state ownership (principally in the form of state-owned enterprises in basic industries such as oil and petrochemicals, steel, electrical power generation, communications, and some transportation activities; essential raw materials such as copper, iron, tin, and bauxite; and certain mass-consumption activities) and state regulation (for example, setting wage and price guidelines, defining the conditions for foreign direct investment, establishing investment priorities through tax and tariff policies, and so forth) varies considerably among Latin American countries. This variation reflects the impact of diverse historical experiences, competing ideologies (ranging from socialism in Cuba to radical free market experiments in Chile, and to a lesser extent in Argentina and Uruguay, in the 1970s), differences in national objectives and the perceived prerequisites ᴏ. national economic development, and the emergence of a new corps of more technically trained personnel in government ministries and state-owned enterprises. Nonetheless, centralized governmental authority and public sector economic participation took on increasing importance throughout much of the region during the 1960s and 1970s. By the late 1970s the average percentage of central government expenditures devoted to economic activities in sixteen Latin American countries was 23.4 percent (in comparison to 11.4 percent in the United States in 1979).[8] In 1980 total central government expenditures accounted for an average of 22 percent of GDP in twenty-four Latin American countries.[9]

In a number of cases an increasingly statist orientation in national development strategy resulted in more frequent conflict with transnational corporations and intensified demands for fundamental change in Latin America's economic relations with industrialized countries. Some governments' ideological commitment to active state intervention in national economic development appears to have influenced their demands during the 1970s for significant reform in the international economic order, where market forces were perceived to have produced insufficient rewards for developing countries. The foreign policy activism of Chile (until the 1973 military coup), Cuba, Jamaica, Mexico, Peru, and Venezuela concerning international economic issues reflected a parallel domestic commitment to pursue structural economic reform through statist development policies.[10]

Second, widespread socioeconomic transformation and changes in class structure contributed to the emergence of assertive political leadership in a number of Latin American countries. Leaders such as Salvador Allende in Chile, Juan Velasco Alvarado in Peru, Fidel Castro in Cuba, Luis Echeverría in Mexico, Michael Manley in Jamaica, Carlos Andrés Pérez in Venezuela, and Omar Torrijos in Panama, among others, brought new perspectives to national and regional economic, social, and political problems. Although these leaders differed considerably in their political objectives, ideology, development goals, and foreign policy strategies, they acted in the tradition of earlier Latin American nationalists (including Pedro Aguirre Cerda in Chile, Lázaro Cárdenas in Mexico, José Figueres in Costa Rica, Juan Domingo Perón in Argentina, and Getulio Vargas in Brazil, among others) in their efforts to promote national autonomy and redefine relationships with industrialized countries, especially the United States. Their formative experiences included the Cuban revolution of 1959 and the triumph of independence movements in much of Africa and Asia in the 1950s and 1960s and in the Caribbean in the 1960s and 1970s. The lessons drawn from these experiences were not always the same, nor even easily compatible. But in many cases Latin American political leaders in the 1960s and 1970s possessed a new sense of capability in addressing perceived internal and external constraints on national development. They were convinced that socioeconomic development and national autonomy required assertive action and a more equitable relationship with the United States and other industrialized countries. Their preferred instrument for resolving development problems was often an activist state, and they were associated with efforts to diversify the region's international economic and political ties away from dependence on the United States.

Although it is difficult to specify the direct impact of these socioeconomic and political changes on Latin American perspectives on relations with the United States, these developments clearly underpinned widespread Latin American perceptions of the region's "emergence" in the 1970s. Economic and social change contributed to growing national capabilities throughout the region. The emergence of more assertive national elites and an active state sector contributed to regional and international initiatives in diverse economic and political arenas. These changes were well underway by the late 1960s, and they account in part for Latin American countries' willingness to take the initiative in addressing common development problems through statements such as the 1969 Consensus of Viña del Mar, which is discussed below.

Diversification of International Linkages

Latin America's rapid economic growth and expanding industrial capacity and the commitment of many governments to reducing their dependence on the United States led to heightened efforts during the 1970s to diversify the region's international economic and political ties. The larger countries' growing economic capabilities provided the basis for increased participation in the world economy, and they sought new export markets and new sources of capital and technology. The emergence of western European countries, Japan, Canada, and the Council for Mutual Economic Assistance (COMECON) as major economic powers in the 1950s and early 1960s produced an increasingly multipolar international economic order that reduced the relative weight of the United States in the world economy and opened up new economic and political alternatives for Latin American countries. Moreover, Latin America's own economic growth greatly expanded opportunities for intraregional trade. Some countries (especially Argentina, Chile, Uruguay, and some Caribbean states) had long focused their economic relations on western Europe. But for others, the attempt to diversify their economic and political relations away from the United States in order to increase their national autonomy was a significant change.

Although such diversification was evident in several different areas,[11] trade relations showed this change most clearly. In 1961–1963, Latin America sent an average 37.2 percent of its exports to the United States and received 41.8 percent of its imports from the United States. By 1977–1979 these percentages had declined moderately to 35 percent and 32.9 percent, respectively. However, over this same period the importance of the United States as an export market fell more sharply for twelve Latin American countries; the absolute value of this decline ranged from 8.3 percent for Honduras to 26.3 percent for Panama.[12] In the case of Brazil, the European Economic Community (EEC) displaced the United States as the single most important export market.[13] By 1979 Latin America as a whole exported only 25.6 percent of its manufactured products to the United States—less than the share destined either to other Latin American countries (38.8 percent) or to other industrialized countries (26 percent).[14] Intraregional trade, the EEC, and COMECON provided the imports that had previously come from the United States. The process of trade diversification slowed somewhat during the 1970s, and there were some important exceptions to this trend. Indeed, Mexico, Peru, and several small countries in the Caribbean Basin (Barbados, Guyana, Haiti, Jamaica, Trinidad and Tobago) maintained or actually increased their trade dependence on the United States.[15] Nonetheless, the overall decline in the United States' relative position as a trading partner for Latin America was quite evident.

Regional economic integration programs contributed to the diversification of Latin America's economic relations. Beginning with the formation of the Latin American Free Trade Association in 1960, a number of attempts at regional and subregional economic cooperation and/or integration took shape during the 1960s and 1970s. These included the Central American Common Market (1961), the Caribbean Free Trade Association (1967; later the Caribbean Community and Common Market), the East Caribbean Common Market (1968), the Andean Group (1969), and the Latin American Economic System (1975). These experiments varied considerably in their goals, strategies, institutional structure, and the degree of economic complementarity among member states. Regional economic integration programs often contributed significantly to the development of intraregional trade relations. However, regional rivalries, policy disputes, and domestic political instability frequently limited their achievements. In some cases, such problems actually halted cooperation. For example, the 1969 war between El Salvador and Honduras and the 1979 revolution in Nicaragua effectively immobilized the Central American

Common Market. The Chilean military government's implementation of a radical free market economic model after 1973 and Chile's withdrawal from the Cartagena Agreement in 1976 had a similar but less drastic effect on the Andean Group. Yet these programs all represented a deeply rooted conviction that central aspects of underdevelopment and economic dependency should be addressed through collective efforts such as regional cooperation and/or integration.[16]

A number of Latin American countries also sought to strengthen their economic and political ties with other developing countries.[17] Venezuela was a founding member of the Organization of Petroleum Exporting Countries (OPEC). Latin American states joined several other raw material or agricultural commodity producer cartels (including those organized by producers of tin, bauxite, copper, nickel, sugar, and bananas) in the 1970s in the hope of reproducing OPEC's success by increasing the price of traditional export commodities. In 1980 Mexico and Venezuela agreed to provide oil at subsidized prices to a number of oil-importing countries in Central America and the Caribbean. In addition, Latin American countries were important participants in international forums (for example, the United Nations Conference on Trade and Development, the Group of 77, and the Movement of Non-Aligned Countries) organized to advance North-South negotiations for a new international economic order and to strengthen cooperative relations among developing countries. Mexico took a leading role in promoting the Charter of Economic Rights and Duties of States in the early 1970s and hosted the Cancún conference on North-South economic relations in 1981. Between 1979 and 1982 Cuba chaired the Movement of Non-Aligned Countries. Latin American leadership was also important in the development of codes of corporate conduct for transnational enterprises, negotiations concerning the law of the sea (especially the widening of the territorial sea), the indexation of commodity prices, and the elaboration of "fade-out" requirements for foreign direct investment.

Of course, the success of Latin American countries' attempts to diversify their international economic and political ties varied considerably by country, issue, and arena.[18] Different countries' interests and priorities also gave "diversification" quite distinct meanings in different contexts. For example, although a number of countries sought to expand their contacts with such areas as the Middle East, Africa, and eastern Europe, Brazil devoted more effort to this strategy than other countries in the region because of its extreme dependence on oil imports and its pressing need to expand manufactured and agricultural exports in order to compensate for a larger oil import bill after 1973–1974.

More generally, the ability to diversify international linkages during the 1970s depended in part on two other conditions. First, détente between the United States and the Soviet Union and a general relaxation in East-West tensions facilitated Latin American countries' emphasis on economic issues in international affairs and encouraged West European governments and organizations (such as the Socialist International and the World Union of Christian Democrats) to expand their activities in Latin America. Second, the rapid increase in commercial bank lending to the region in the late 1970s permitted Latin American countries to maintain comparatively high levels of economic growth after the 1973–1974 and 1979–1980 oil shocks, even though these credit conditions ultimately proved to be highly unstable. Commercial bank lending to sovereign countries appeared to pose fewer economic and political constraints than foreign direct investment and thus contributed to Latin American countries' self-confidence and assertiveness in international affairs. These conditions proved to be more transient than many Latin American policymakers believed in the 1970s. Nonetheless, many countries engaged in a degree of foreign policy experimentation during this period that contrasted significantly with the more general post-World War II pattern of economic and political dependence on the United States.

Latin American Perspectives on Hemispheric Relations

Latin America's growing economic strength during the 1960s and 1970s, the changing position of a number of countries in the international political economy, and the sustained efforts by some governments to reduce their dependence on the United States significantly influenced Latin American perspectives on hemispheric relations. In many cases Latin American governments questioned an older pattern of U.S. leadership and instead advocated regional initiatives and collective actions to resolve common development problems. Latin American foreign policy positions frequently moved beyond the traditional commitment to nonintervention in relations among sovereign states and the self-determination of peoples as guiding principles in international affairs to include more specific proposals for joint action to promote socioeconomic development.

In this brief evaluation it is impossible to represent fully the variations in perceptions that exist either across the region as a whole or within a particular country. However, two documents—the 1969 Consensus of Vina del Mar (Chile) and the 1981 Declaration of Panama—are indicative of evolving Latin American perspectives on U.S.–Latin American relations since the 1960s. These two statements were written only twelve years apart, yet they show important differences. Although neither document should be viewed as a representative summary of the full range of Latin American opinion on hemispheric relations, these two statements offer useful insights into changes over time.

The Consensus of Viña del Mar was among the first joint Latin American statements concerning the region's relations with the United States.[19] It reflected many governments' growing frustration in the late 1960s with the results of economic and social development programs, especially the limited success achieved through the U.S.-initiated Alliance for Progress. The Consensus sought the implementation of generally accepted principles as a basis for more effective cooperation in inter-American affairs, and it placed special emphasis on resolving the main obstacles to Latin American development in such areas as trade, transportation, external financing and foreign investment, and science and technology.

Two main themes informed the statement's discussion. First, it stressed the importance of those principles that are important to the autonomy of Latin American states both in their internal decisionmaking and in their external political and economic relations, including cooperation, solidarity, respect for national sovereignty and self-determination, and the importance of a more equitable international division of labor. Second, it emphasized the importance of unity and shared Latin American interests in the region's relations with the United States. Given that one of the statement's central goals was to open a dialogue with the United States on development issues, it did not reject the idea of some commonly held hemispheric interests. However, it did note that a clear aim of inter-American cooperation should be the achievement of Latin American goals.

In the context of this discussion of changing Latin American perspectives on U.S.–Latin American relations, it is interesting to note the implicit willingness in the Consensus to accept U.S. leadership in hemispheric efforts to address development problems. As noted above, the Consensus of Viña del Mar was in itself a significant point of departure as a joint statement on the perceived crisis in inter-American relations. It also underlined the value of coordinated action by Latin American countries in various international forums as a means of promoting progress within the region.[20] Nonetheless, the overall purpose of the document was to prompt the United States to realize its various formal commitments to economic and social development in the Western Hemisphere. The signatories acknowledged the importance of U.S. policies regarding trade, investment, foreign economic assistance, and scientific and technological development for Latin America in the post-World War II period. But this orientation also reflected an older heritage of Latin American acceptance of U.S. leadership in many areas.

In this regard the 1981 Declaration of Panama and other documents issued by the Latin American Economic System (Sistema Económico Latinoamericano, SELA) suggest an important shift.[21] Like the Consensus of Viña del Mar, the Declaration of Panama stressed economic and social development issues and such major principles as nonintervention in states' internal and external affairs, self-determination, and national sovereignty. However, the Declaration placed much greater emphasis on national control over economic decisions and the importance of Latin America's own initiatives, policies, and actions intended to address regional problems. It also stressed the global (versus hemispheric or bilateral) context of development issues and Latin America's shared interests with other developing countries in North-South relations.[22] From SELA's perspective, then, Latin American efforts to promote economic and social development should take the form of multilateral initiatives intended to diversify external economic relations and increase the region's negotiating capacity with industrialized countries, particularly the United States. Although the Declaration recognized that specific issues might sometimes require a hemispheric focus, the preferred strategy would involve multilateral initiatives, forums, and programs undertaken by Latin American countries to promote their own economic security.[23]

Finally, both the Consensus of Viña del Mar and the Declaration of Panama agreed that Latin America's interests in hemispheric affairs frequently differ substantially from those of the United States. Although the Consensus signatories sought to promote dialogue with the United States on economic and social development issues, the official Latin American spokesman for the group warned that the region's interests were not necessarily identical to those of the United States; indeed, Latin American and U.S. interests "may even tend to become contradictory in many respects."[24] The Declaration of Panama made the same point even more emphatically by emphasizing Latin America's continuing economic dependence on—and vulnerability to—the United States. This perspective strongly influenced SELA's conclusions regarding the need for coordinated Latin American initiatives to address central issues in U.S.–Latin American relations.

Although an examination of these two Latin American statements on hemispheric affairs is instructive in several ways, it is important to note that the actual policies undertaken by particular governments have not always corresponded closely to the positions outlined in these documents. Capabilities, interests, leadership strategies, and development priorities vary substantially, and these differences often constitute very real obstacles to coordinated action. Moreover, there is evidence to suggest that some governments' private diplomatic positions often departed significantly from those outlined in publicly announced collective statements on issues such as demands for a reformed international economic order.[25] Some analysts have argued that Latin American states' global activities and their strong rhetorical assertion of regional autonomy were part of a strategy intended to compensate for continued weakness and vulnerability in the international system.[26] Nonetheless, an appreciation of changing Latin American views on hemispheric relations in general is a useful starting point for a more detailed examination of Latin American perspectives on major issues in U.S.–Latin American relations in the 1980s.

The Crisis of the 1980s

Several developments in the early 1980s considerably eroded the self-confidence that characterized many Latin American declarations and foreign policy initiatives in the 1970s. The United States' policy toward Argentina during the 1982 Falkland/Malvinas war, its expanding military presence in Central America, and the invasion of Grenada in 1983 all raised serious questions in Latin America regarding the future direction of U.S. policy toward the region and the U.S. commitment to constructive relations among sovereign states. Although shifting domestic political coalitions and changing ideological orientations led some Latin American countries to reduce or curtail their foreign policy activism, U.S. reassertionism in hemispheric affairs and the debt crisis of the 1980s substantially restricted the opportunities and the resources available for Latin American foreign policy initiatives.

The South Atlantic war between Argentina and Great Britain in April–June 1982 over control of the Falkland/Malvinas Islands was among the most dramatic interstate conflicts in the Western Hemisphere in the twentieth century. Whether or not the war ultimately has the lasting impact on inter-American relations that many analysts predicted at the time,[27] in the view of many Latin Americans the conduct of the United States during the conflict underlined the fact that Latin America is of only secondary U.S. foreign policy importance. After the failure of intensive U.S. diplomatic efforts to prevent the outbreak of hostilities, the United States imposed economic and military sanctions on Argentina while offering Great Britain political and limited military support in ending by force Argentina's military occupation of the islands.[28] A number of Latin American governments were unwilling to endorse the Argentine military government's adventurism even though they supported Argentine claims to sovereignty over the islands and condemmed U.S. and EEC sanctions against Argentina, and some observers argued that Argentina's use of force nullified the terms of the Inter-American Treaty of Reciprocal Assistance (the Rio Treaty) that obligate American states to offer each other mutual assistance in the event of an attack by an extracontinental power.[29] Nonetheless, the Reagan administration's support for a North Atlantic Treaty Organization (NATO) ally against a Latin American country distressed many Latin Americans.

Even more significantly, the U.S. invasion of Grenada in October

1983 and the overthrow of its revolutionary regime aroused long-standing concerns regarding U.S. intervention in Latin American countries' internal affairs. The development of one-party rule in Grenada and close political ties with Cuba and the Soviet Union after the 1979 revolution worried governments in some neighboring countries, and several (but not all) eastern Caribbean states endorsed the invasion as a necessary measure to prevent the revolutionary government from eventually engaging in subversive activities in the area. Following the invasion the Reagan administration displayed evidence that after 1980 Cuba and the Soviet Union had supplied the Grenadian government with small arms (which were apparently intended for defense against external and internal attack). The United States also argued that military action was necessary to protect U.S. citizens (principally students at a medical school on the island, many of whom later testified that they began to fear for their physical safety only after the U.S. invasion began) and to prevent the Soviet Union or Cuba from possibly gaining access to an airport under construction with a runway capable of accommodating advanced military aircraft. However, these claims encountered considerable international skepticism. The action was condemned by both the United States' major West European allies (including Great Britain and France) and many Latin American countries (including Mexico and Brazil) as a violation of the Organization of American States (OAS) and United Nations charters.[30]

Similarly, the expanding military presence of the United States in Honduras and El Salvador and its substantial, publicly acknowledged "covert" political and military support for anti-Sandinista opposition forces (the *contras*) further revealed a renewed U.S. commitment to use military force if necessary to shape sociopolitical developments in the Caribbean Basin. By mid-1985, the U.S. military had established forward military supply centers, bases, and support forces in Honduras and Panama that permitted rapid military actions against Nicaragua.[31] The Reagan administration's stated hostility to the Sandinista regime and its apparent unwillingness to support regional peace negotiations contributed to heightened tension in Central America.[32] From the perspective of many Latin Americans, the United States' aggressive efforts to reassert its traditional dominance in Central America and the Caribbean pose grave threats to Latin American countries' national sovereignty and undercut their ability to pursue preferred development strategies and independent foreign policies.

The debt crisis that has confronted Latin America since 1982 also constitutes a serious threat to the region's economic and perhaps political autonomy. The region has not faced such a widespread economic and financial crisis since the Great Depression. It affects nearly all Latin American countries, regardless of their economic size, their degree of openness to the international economy, their national development strategy, or their petroleum resources. The region's aggregate GDP fell by 0.8 percent in real terms between 1981 and 1982 and by another 3 percent between 1982 and 1983. Between 1980 and 1983 per capita GDP declined even more sharply, by 3 percent in real terms. The decline in per capita GDP between 1980 and 1983 ranged from 0.6 percent in Trinidad and Tobago to 22.8 percent in Bolivia, and thirteen countries suffered a decline of more than 10 percent in real terms.[33] In 1984–1985 a number of countries succeeded in slowing or reversing this economic decline by imposing stringent austerity measures and by rescheduling a portion of the interest and/or principal payments due on their foreign debt. Nonetheless, much of Latin America is likely to face difficult economic conditions for at least the remainder of the decade.

The debt crisis has abruptly forced many Latin American countries to revaluate their relations with the United States. The United States plays a key role in the region's economic and financial crisis because U.S.-based commercial banks hold approximately 38 percent of Latin American countries' total outstanding foreign debt; because the United States exercises strong influence over major international financial institutions based in Washington, D.C., such as the International Monetary Fund (IMF); and because U.S. government economic policies concerning such issues as interest rates and trade policy significantly affect the economic situation in Latin American countries. As Laurence Whitehead argues in his essay in this volume, the post-1982 debt crisis dramatically revealed the extent to which sovereign states' foreign commercial borrowing might increase their external dependency rather than expand their opportunities for policy experimentation (which in the 1970s many Latin American borrowers had assumed would be the case). Whitehead also shows that, although the terms of Latin American dependence on the United States in the 1980s are much different than in earlier periods, nearly all Latin American countries' possible alternatives to economic and political dependence on the United States have proved to be much less viable than diversification efforts in the 1970s anticipated. Moreover, their financial dependence on the United States is accentuated to the extent that their foreign debt is denominated in dollars. The need of Latin American debtor countries to reschedule existing repayment obligations, secure additional sources of financing, and gain access to export markets in industrialized countries is a serious economic constraint on both their national development strategies and their ability to promote assertive foreign economic policies. For many governments, relations with foreign creditors necessarily have become the principal focus of national foreign policy.

Indeed, Fernando Fajnzylber's essay in this volume suggests that in the future the international economy may constitute a long-term constraint on economic growth, capacity for technological innovation, and overall national autonomy.

Responses to the economic and political crises of the 1980s have varied considerably both across the region and within individual countries. Confronted by the prospect of enduring financial dependence on external creditors and the United States' commitment to reassert its dominance in areas such as the Caribbean Basin, many Latin American governments have evidenced a more defensive posture in which national ambitions and foreign policy assertiveness are greatly reduced. In some countries, disorientation and disillusionment have characterized domestic political debate regarding appropriate responses to this situation. Moreover, the debt crisis has revealed the extent to which Latin American countries' immediate priorities and future options differ. For example, the maturity structure (short-term versus long-term obligations) and the degree of concentration (several versus many creditors) of external debt, the ability to meet repayment obligations through increased exports, and lenders' perceptions of future creditworthiness vary considerably.

The very volatility of contemporary political and economic crises makes it difficult to predict their ultimate consequences, the variety of approaches that different Latin American countries may pursue to resolve their problems, or the broader lessons that they may learn from their experiences. Even in the midst of great economic difficulty, there is some evidence to suggest that the crisis of the 1980s may demonstrate the utility of collective action to address common problems. For example, in 1983 eleven major Latin American debtor countries met in Cartagena, Colombia, to promote regional cooperation and discuss possible means of confronting the economic difficulties produced by the debt crisis. The "Cartagena Group" sought to strengthen debtor countries' bargaining position vis-à-vis external creditors and to convince industrialized countries and international commercial banks to bear a larger share of responsibility for resolving the debt crisis. In March 1984 Brazil, Colombia, Mexico, and Venezuela provided a joint loan to Argentina to help meet its short-term loan repayment schedule. Shortly thereafter, Argentina, Brazil, Colombia, and Mexico issued a statement calling for more flexible debt repayment conditions that would limit the increase in Latin American debt obligations resulting from unpredictable rises in U.S. domestic interest rates.[34] These initiatives have not led to the formation of a "debtors' cartel," as some observers in industrialized countries initially feared. Instead, each country has generally pursued individual debt rescheduling arrangements with creditor countries and institutions. Joint meetings among major debtor countries and expressions of Latin American solidarity may have a largely symbolic importance, with little practical impact on the countries' economic or political circumstances. Nonetheless, such statements and actions receive close scrutiny both within the region and in international financial circles, and they may prove to be important precedents in the evolution of Latin America's future economic relations with industrialized countries. For example, the July 1985 announcement by the newly elected president of Peru, Alan García, that Peru would limit debt repayments to 10 percent of export earnings and conduct direct negotiations with creditors rather than relying on IMF-mediated discussions, received widespread attention because of its possible demonstration effect in the region.[35]

To the extent that the political and economic crises of the 1980s stimulate coordinated policy initiatives and/or regional action, these experiences may constitute catalysts in the long-term evolution of Latin American foreign policy perspectives. Several earlier events and crises had such an impact on Latin American attitudes regarding the United States. For example, the U.S. invasion of the Dominican Republic in 1965 (reversing a long-standing pledge against unilateral military intervention in the hemisphere) and the covert involvement of the Central Intelligence Agency and U.S. business (particularly the International Telephone and Telegraph Corporation) in the overthrow of Allende's elected socialist government in Chile in 1973 starkly revealed the United States' enduring hegemonic pretensions regarding Latin America. Both events contributed to Latin American countries' growing inclination to act together to prevent U.S. intervention in the hemisphere. For example, a U.S. proposal in June 1979 to send an OAS peacekeeping force to mediate the Nicaraguan civil war (which the Carter administration hoped might reduce Sandinista influence in a post-revolutionary government) was soundly defeated by Latin American member states. Similarly, the abrupt decision by the United States in 1971 to impose a 10 percent tariff surcharge on all imports and the limitations and/or exclusions placed on Latin American exports by the U.S. Trade Act of 1974 highlighted Latin America's vulnerability to external economic events and strengthened some countries' commitment to regional economic development. These U.S. actions later encouraged Mexico and Venezuela to take the lead in organizing SELA in 1975.

In the long run, the crises of the 1980s may encourage some Latin American countries to develop new strategies of regional cooperation and collective action. However, the Contadora Group's recent experience in attempting to negotiate a regional peace agreement in Central America suggests that such efforts may encounter considerable opposition from the United States for some time to come. The Contadora Group (Colombia, Mexico, Panama, and Venezuela) first met in January 1983 on Panama's

Contadora Island in an innovative collective attempt to reach a broadly acceptable negotiated settlement of the expanding Central American crisis. In October 1984 the Nicaraguan government endorsed the Group's draft peace proposal, but the Reagan administration rejected it, arguing that the proposal did not include adequate mechanisms to verify Nicaraguan compliance. At the same time, despite its formal public support for the Contadora process, the Reagan administration reaffirmed its hostility to the Sandinista government and encouraged Honduras, El Salvador, and Costa Rica to raise additional objections to the draft treaty. United States resistance also thwarted bilateral U.S.-Nicaraguan discussions held under Mexico's auspices in Manzanillo, Mexico.[36] In August 1985 the assistant secretary of state for inter-American affairs, Elliott Abrams, summarized the Reagan administration's attitude toward negotiations with Nicaragua by saying, "It is preposterous to think we could sign a deal with the Sandinistas to meet our foreign policy concerns and expect it to be kept."[37] Although Argentina, Brazil, Peru, and Uruguay joined in support of the Contadora Group's efforts in August 1985, regional negotiations remained stalemated. From the Contadora Group's perspective, the Reagan administration's apparent unwillingness to pursue regional peace negotiations in Central America constituted a major obstacle to Latin American initiatives to reduce regional tensions and promote constructive relations in the hemisphere.[38]

The United States: The International and National Context of U.S. Policy Toward Latin America

Three main factors have influenced changing U.S. perspectives on relations with Latin America since the late 1960s: the character of U.S. relations with the Soviet Union and U.S. policymakers' perceptions of security threats in Latin America; the constraints that the shifting position of the United States in the global economy and domestic economic conditions place on foreign policy initiatives; and changes over time in the terms of U.S. foreign policy debate. Of course, these are not the only elements that have shaped U.S. foreign policy perspectives over time; economic interests and ideology have also played an important historical role in determining the focus and content of U.S. policies toward Latin America. Nor is it always possible to disaggregate fully the various considerations that inform a particular U.S. policy or decision. This discussion examines only those factors that appear to account for recent changes in overall U.S. perspectives on U.S.–Latin American relations.

United States perspectives on inter-American relations have undergone two important shifts since the late 1960s. In the first instance, a long-standing emphasis on a "special relationship" with Latin America was replaced by a globalist perspective that focused on broad international economic and political issues and the position of Latin American countries in North-South relations among industrialized and developing countries. The economic and political globalism associated with liberal foreign policy analysts and the Carter administration in the 1970s questioned the value of a specifically hemispheric approach to key foreign policy issues involving Latin America. However, a second change in perspectives in the late 1970s and early 1980s shifted attention from economic and political globalism to strategic globalism. Conservative foreign policy analysts argued that the renewed tensions in U.S.-Soviet relations, the Soviet Union's growing diplomatic, economic, and military presence in the Western Hemisphere, and the emergence of possible threats to U.S. security interests in the region all required increased attention to the strategic dimensions of U.S.–Latin American relations. Reagan administration policies toward Central America and the Caribbean for the most part reflected this view.

None of the perspectives examined here—a hemispheric "special relationship," economic and political globalism, or strategic globalism—necessarily reflected complete uniformity at any given time in U.S. public opinion or U.S. policymakers' views on relations with Latin America.[39] However, each of these major perspectives has been articulated by high-level governmental or nongovernmental special commissions at different times, and all three have had an important impact on the approach of different administrations to U.S.–Latin American relations. An examination of changing U.S. perspectives on inter-American relations is an important basis for a more detailed analysis of U.S. views on central issues in U.S.-Latin American relations in the 1980s.

U.S.-Soviet Relations and Hemispheric Security Crises

Global political and military relations, perceptions of great power rivalry, and possible threats to security interests in Latin America are among the most important considerations influencing the broad contours of U.S. policy approaches toward the region. As the essay by James R. Kurth in this volume shows, U.S. evaluations of and responses to events in the Western Hemisphere since the end of World War II have been shaped predominantly by concerns about the Soviet Union's activities in Latin America and their possible consequences for the global balance of power. The hostility of the United States toward revolutionary movements and radical regimes in the region from the late 1940s to the early 1970s in large part reflected its perceptions of rivalry with the Soviet Union formed during the Cold War.

However, the relaxation of international political and military tensions in the early 1970s eased U.S. fears concerning external threats to the Western Hemisphere. The Nixon-Kissinger strategy of détente with the Soviet Union sought to redefine the U.S. approach to its principal international rival by emphasizing political realism rather than ideological motivations, policy flexibility in pursuit of key goals, and multipolar diplomacy.[40] This policy sought to link the Soviet Union's interest in national economic development to broader accommodation with the United States in international politics. United States policymakers advocated "containment through negotiation" rather than "containment by confrontation."[41] The policy resulted in the 1972 Strategic Arms Limitation Treaty (SALT I), the 1974 protocol on antiballistic missile systems, and the 1975 Helsinki accord, as well as expanded U.S. economic, technological, and cultural exchanges with the Soviet Union and eastern Europe involving both governmental agencies and the private sector. Nixon's rapprochment with the People's Republic of China, symbolized by the 1972 Shanghai Communiqué, sought to guarantee the Soviet Union's interest in dialogue with the United States by opening up the possibility of a Sino-American strategic alliance.

More relaxed U.S.-Soviet relations in the 1970s coincided with the relative absence of perceived threats to U.S. security interests in Latin America. Cuba suspended its active support for revolutionary movements in Latin America after 1968. At about the same time, better-trained and better-equipped Latin American militaries (in part the result of U.S. military assistance and counterinsurgency programs initiated in the early 1960s following the Cuban revolution) succeeded in defeating virtually all major guerrilla movements in the region. The Nixon administration's covert involvement in the military overthrow of Salvador Allende's socialist government in Chile in 1973 dramatically underlined the continued intense hostility of the United States to radical socioeconomic and political change in Latin America. However, the confluence of détente with the Soviet Union and the comparative absence of perceived security threats in the region encouraged liberal U.S. policymakers to discount the possibility of external and internal threats to stability in the Western Hemisphere.

Yet these international and regional conditions proved far less durable than many liberal U.S. policymakers anticipated. By the late 1970s and early 1980s U.S.-Soviet relations had entered a period of renewed tension. The Soviet Union's achievement of overall strategic parity forced the United States to reassess its global military and political position. Soviet and/or Cuban activities in support of revolutionary governments in Angola, Ethiopia, and other countries in the 1970s; the Soviet invasion of Afghanistan in December 1979; and the repression of the Solidarity labor movement in Poland under Soviet pressure in 1980 seemingly revealed the immutably aggressive and authoritarian nature of the Soviet regime. Events such as these disillusioned those advocates of détente who believed that the policy would induce Soviet restraint in developing countries and elsewhere in the world, and critics of détente used these developments to build support for a more hard-line U.S. policy toward the Soviet Union. In retaliation, the Carter and Reagan administrations sought (generally unsuccessfully) to impose an embargo on grain shipments to the Soviet Union, a boycott of the 1980 Olympic games in Moscow, the suspension of construction work on a natural gas pipeline between the Soviet Union and western Europe, and other actions that reversed the tone and content of détente. There was considerable public concern in the United States in the late 1970s and early 1980s regarding the Soviet Union's supposed nuclear superiority vis-à-vis the United States and the dangers posed by a strategic imbalance, and in the end this concern stymied efforts to ratify a second strategic arms limitation agreement (SALT II). Furthermore, the Iranian revolution in 1978 raised doubts in some quarters concerning the costs (symbolized most dramatically when Iranian students held a number of U.S. diplomatic personnel hostage from November 1979 to January 1981) of a more flexible and pragmatic U.S. policy toward regime change in developing countries.

At the same time, rapidly changing circumstances in Central America and the Caribbean further heightened many U.S. policymakers' concerns regarding U.S. security interests in the Western Hemisphere. The Sandinista-led revolutionary coalition in Nicaragua overthrew the Somoza dynasty in July 1979 and eliminated a longtime conservative U.S. ally in Central America. Nicaragua's post-revolutionary diversification of its international political, economic, and military contacts included expanded diplomatic relations with, and economic and military assistance from, Cuba, the Soviet Union, and other socialist countries, which further alarmed conservative foreign policy analysts in the United States regarding the possible expansion of Soviet and/or Cuban influence in the hemisphere. In addition, Cuba renewed its support for revolutionary change in the Caribbean Basin as revolutionary movements and radical regimes assumed greater prominence in the region. Cuba actively supported the overthrow of the Somoza dynasty (as did the governments of Venezuela, Costa Rica, and Panama), and at various times it provided political encouragement and/or material assistance to armed revolutionary movements in El Salvador and Guatemala and leftist governments in Grenada and Guyana.

These developments led many U.S. policymakers in the late 1970s and early 1980s to perceive significant potential threats to U.S. security interests in Central America and the Caribbean for the first time since the early 1960s. As a result, the United States actively sought to slow or prevent the emergence of revolutionary regimes in the Caribbean Basin. The Carter administration's approach to U.S.–Latin American relations initially emphasized questions other than traditional "anticommunist" security issues. In an address given at the University of Notre Dame in May 1977, Carter argued that U.S. foreign policy should not be governed by "an inordinate fear of communism." Nonetheless, the Carter administration maneuvered to reduce the Sandinista presence in the revolutionary government that took power in Nicaragua in July 1979, and Carter authorized renewed military assistance to El Salvador's military government in January 1981 in an attempt to prevent the victory of an armed revolutionary movement. The Reagan administration responded even more aggressively to such perceived security threats in an attempt to preserve U.S. influence in the Caribbean Basin. Although Reagan and other senior U.S. foreign policy officials expressed a reluctance to commit ground forces to combat in Central America,[42] large-scale U.S. military training exercises in Central America (especially Honduras) and the Caribbean and U.S. support (first covert, then publicly acknowledged and defended) for anti-Sandinista guerrillas operating from bases in Honduras and Costa Rica signified an increasingly direct military involvement in the area.[43] Although U.S. public opinion generally continued to oppose such involvement, the invasion of Grenada in October 1983 demonstrated that domestic public opinion would accept—indeed, that it would approve—successful, short-term military actions in the region.[44]

The Economic Context of U.S. Policy Toward Latin America

The United States' changing international and domestic economic situation has also had an important impact on its approaches to hemispheric relations. The increasing internationalization of the U.S. economy and the declining Latin American share of U.S. trade and investment flows to some extent eroded the material basis of the hemispheric "special relationship" that U.S. policymakers frequently asserted until the 1970s. The United States had traditionally been relatively insulated from developments in the international economy, but this changed considerably in the 1960s and 1970s as its global economic predominance declined and Japan, western Europe, Canada, COMECON, and even some newly industrializing countries in Latin America and East Asia came to play a more important international economic role. As late as 1970 exports and imports of goods and services together represented only 12.5 percent of the United States' gross national product (GNP), a substantially lower percentage than in other industrialized countries such as Canada, the Federal Republic of Germany, Great Britain, France, and Japan. But by 1980 international trade constituted 25 percent of U.S. GNP.[45] The United States' growing sensitivity to international economic developments was also underlined by the fact that its share of both total world exports and world financial reserves fell during the 1960s and 1970s.[46]

At the same time, Latin America's share of U.S. trade and investment flows declined as Latin American countries diversified their international economic ties and as U.S. trade and investment linkages with industrialized countries intensified. Thus in 1961 18.5 percent of total U.S. exports (by value) went to Latin America and 24.5 percent of total U.S. imports came from the region. By 1973, before international oil price increases inflated the value of portions of this trade, these proportions had declined to 14.3 percent and 14.7 percent, respectively.[47] Similarly, U.S. direct foreign investment as a share of total Organization for Economic Cooperation and Development/Development Advisory Committee investment flows to Latin America fell from 55 percent in 1970–1975 to 48 percent in 1976–1980. By 1980 only 18 percent of all U.S. foreign direct investment was in Latin America, compared to 26 percent in 1960.[48] The debt crisis of the 1980s dramatically emphasized the fact that economic issues remain at the center of U.S.–Latin American relations, and the economic importance of some Latin American countries for the United States has increased since the 1960s. However, the hemispheric dimension of U.S. international economic policy necessarily became somewhat less salient during the 1970s, and U.S. policymakers increasingly emphasized the global North-South dimensions of U.S.–Latin American economic relations.

One consequence of long-term shifts in the international economic position of the United States was that during the 1970s and 1980s the U.S. economy came under increasing pressure from foreign economic competitors. Manufacturers of products such as automobiles, steel, textiles, consumer electronics equipment, footwear, apparel, and semiconductors were among those most significantly affected. As unemployment and bankruptcies in these activities grew, business and labor groups increased domestic political pressures to implement tariff and/or nontariff barriers to limit the domestic economic dislocation caused by international competition. To some extent these concerns increased in intensity during downturns in the U.S. and international economy during the late 1970s and early 1980s, but protectionist pressures continued to build in the United States even after modest domestic economic recovery occurred. For example, in mid-1985 there were at least three hundred legislative proposals before Congress calling for measures to protect domestic producers from the negative consequences of foreign economic competition. Growing competition from diverse international sources, including newly industrializing countries in Latin America and East Asia, reinforced U.S. perceptions of the United States' relative economic decline and an inability to shape international economic events. Concerns such as these heightened the reluctance of many U.S. political actors to respond favorably to demands by Latin American and other developing countries for structural reforms in the international economic order, including expanded access to markets in industrialized countries such as the United States. Instead, the industrial development of developing countries was increasingly perceived to be a threat to the United States' own economic well-being.

In addition, economic conditions in the United States during the 1970s and early 1980s constituted an important constraint on U.S. foreign economic assistance policy toward Latin America and other developing areas. The United States' real GNP had increased by a compound annual rate of 4 percent between 1963 and 1972, but between 1973 and 1983 real GNP actually declined during four separate years (in 1974–1975 as a result of international oil price shocks, and in 1980 and 1982 as a result of global economic recession and domestic economic readjustment). Only during 1976–1978 did real GNP increase at a rate higher than the 1963–1972 average.[49] The domestic inflation rate averaged 2.9 percent per year between 1960 and 1970, but inflation jumped to an average of 7.3 percent per year between 1970 and 1982; indeed, inflation averaged over 10 percent per year in 1979–1981.[50] Unemployment rates also increased steadily in the late 1970s and early 1980s, rising from an average of 5.4 percent in 1967–1976 to 7.6 percent in 1977–1983.[51] The 1980–1983 global economic recession was the longest since the 1930s, and growing international economic turbulence forced the U.S. government to focus immediate attention on such issues as budget deficits, balance-of-payments deficits, unemployment, and import competition. Persistent domestic economic problems not only increased U.S. policymakers' reluctance to respond to Latin American economic demands on issues such as trade concessions, but they also limited the resources available for foreign economic assistance programs. Moreover, Latin American countries' continued economic growth and their efforts to diversify international economic ties during the 1970s reduced the relative impact of the limited U.S. economic assistance that was available.

The difficulties encountered in enacting the Caribbean Basin Initiative illustrate the extent to which domestic economic problems constrain U.S. trade and economic assistance policies toward Latin America. The Caribbean Basin Economic Recovery Act of 1983 offered a twelve-year exemption from tariffs and quotas to Caribbean Basin countries' exports to the United States. The measure also provided tax incentives to encourage U.S. firms to invest in the area, and it increased the amount of direct economic assistance available to the least developed Caribbean nations.

However, economic recession, budgetary concerns, and protectionist pressures in the United States limited the overall scope of the measure. For example, major Caribbean export products such as textiles, clothing, and shoes were excluded from preferential tariff and import quota treatment. Only the Reagan administration's strong emphasis on the measure's strategic importance in promoting political stability and maintaining alliances in the Caribbean Basin prevented even more extensive restrictions from being added to the measure. Although some U.S. and Asian companies established or expanded production in Caribbean countries in response to trade and tax incentives, larger and more developed countries in the area such as Jamaica, the Dominican Republic, and Barbados reaped the most gains from the Caribbean Basin Initiative. The smaller island countries' lack of transportation and communications limited their attractiveness to foreign investors. As a result, a number of Caribbean governments expressed disappointment with the measure.[52] The Caribbean Basin Initiative thus contrasted dramatically with the resources and initial commitment that the United States devoted to the Alliance for Progress in the early 1960s.

The Changing Terms of U.S. Foreign Policy Debate

The erosion of the post-World War II foreign policy consensus during the 1960s and 1970s and attempts either to establish an alternative basis for foreign policy or to revive key elements of the earlier consensus during the late 1970s and early 1980s also had a significant impact on U.S. perspectives on relations with Latin America. The United States' military and political rivalry with the Soviet Union and ideological concerns regarding "monolithic international communism" and "subversion" dominated much of U.S. foreign policy debate from the late 1940s through the mid-1960s. Strict strategic and ideological bipolarity between the two superpowers focused U.S. foreign policy principally on the containment of Soviet expansion; other goals, issues, and actors were of secondary importance.

Although there was disagreement concerning the most effective means of achieving the goals of containment policy, the widespread public perception that the United States was locked in a protracted life-or-death struggle with the Soviet bloc contributed to the development of a durable bipartisan consensus regarding the appropriate focus of U.S. foreign policy. The belief that "Soviet-controlled international communism" posed a direct and immediate threat to U.S. interests throughout the world imbued foreign policy discussions with an ideological fervor that both assured public and congressional support for presidential initiatives and facilitated policymakers' presentation of the U.S. purpose in world affairs. In addition, the military and economic strength of the United States and its role as political leader of the western alliance permitted policymakers to avoid difficult choices between domestic socioeconomic priorities and foreign policy goals. John F. Kennedy stated in his 1961 inaugural address that the United States would "pay any price" and "bear any burden" in pursuit of its foreign policy objectives.[53]

However, both the international context and the base of domestic political support for post-World War II foreign policy consensus changed over time. The growing international economic and political prominence of West European countries and Japan after the 1950s and détente between the United States and the Soviet Union in the early 1970s contributed to the emergence of a multipolar, more ideologically diverse international system. In addition, ideological divisions, rivalries, and conflicts among socialist countries (particularly between the Soviet Union and the People's Republic of China after the late 1950s) and defections from the Soviet sphere of influence (Indonesia, Egypt, Somalia) made the idea of monolithic international communism increasingly less credible. Changing international circumstances prompted many U.S. foreign policy analysts to question the assumptions of strict strategic and ideological bipolarity that had informed the postwar consensus. In turn, alternative perceptions of the international context encouraged new U.S. foreign policy initiatives; Nixon's rapprochment with the People's Republic of China was a particularly significant departure.

After the normalization of relations with the Soviet Union and the People's Republic of China in the early 1970s, the ideological dimensions of U.S. foreign policy could no longer be taken for granted. In the absence of a simplifying and unifying foreign policy consensus based on strategic tension with the Soviet Union and ideological opposition to communism, U.S. foreign policy debate in the 1970s focused increasingly on the complexity of the international environment (for example, growing economic interdependence among industrialized countries and the turbulence of the international economic system, North-South issues and questions concerning the allocation of global resources, the challenges posed by OPEC and other producer cartels in developing countries, the growing prominence of newly industrializing countries in Latin America and East Asia, and so forth) and the constraints on U.S. leadership in world affairs.

The "lessons of Vietnam" had a particularly strong influence on public perceptions and policymakers' views regarding U.S. commitments in developing countries. As a result of the international and domestic political repercussions of the Vietnam war, U.S. foreign policymakers in the mid- and late 1970s frequently acted in accordance with the lessons they perceived to have been learned during the protracted involvement in

Southeast Asia. Especially from the perspective of liberal foreign policy analysts, the Vietnam war demonstrated the declining efficacy of force in the international system and the fact that security threats in developing countries frequently result from indigenous socioeconomic and political conditions that exist independently of U.S.-Soviet rivalry. The U.S. experience in Vietnam also showed that the domestic political and economic costs of armed intervention either to promote or to frustrate political change in developing countries may be very high, and the outcome of such efforts in Southeast Asia raised new doubts concerning the appropriateness of imposing the U.S. political model elsewhere in the world.[54]

For many U.S. policymakers the Vietnam experience marked the end of the post-World War II foreign policy consensus. The political divisiveness shattered any remaining public agreement regarding the goals of U.S. foreign policy. Congress became more actively involved in foreign policymaking and demonstrated a greater willingness to constrain executive actions abroad; for example, it enacted the 1973 War Powers Act over President Nixon's veto. Disclosures in the mid-1970s of abuses by the Central Intelligence Agency in countries such as Chile substantially increased public opposition to covert intelligence operations. In addition, the Watergate political scandal (which ended with Richard Nixon's resignation in 1974) undermined public confidence in the U.S. political system and increased public confusion regarding the broader national purpose.

The aftermath of the Vietnam war led to a search for a new foreign policy consensus. The Carter and Reagan administrations articulated alternative conceptualizations of the U.S. role in world affairs in an attempt to address the challenges posed by an increasingly complex international system. As the next section shows, these alternative approaches implied significant differences in U.S. perspectives on relations with Latin America.

The Carter administration was intent on restoring both the United States' moral leadership in international affairs and the country's own sense of moral worth in the wake of the Vietnam war and the Watergate political scandal. Carter initially sought to deemphasize the relationship with the Soviet Union as the centerpiece of U.S. foreign policy. Instead, he gave priority to the multilateral management of such global issues as international trade, nuclear nonproliferation, and the law of the sea in an attempt to create a new basis for foreign policy consensus. His human rights policy and efforts to limit weapons sales to developing countries also reflected a concern with issues other than traditional military security. Indeed, the Carter administration's human rights policy attempted to rebuild public confidence in government and foreign policy by appealing to deeply rooted moral and political values. Carter stressed the complexity of international economic and political issues and the United States' need to adjust to the end of its post-World War II preeminence.

Foreign policy analysts noted that the Carter administration's policies were often applied inconsistently and without sufficient coordination. More generally, critics argued that Carter failed to devote sufficient attention either to U.S.-Soviet relations or to U.S. economic strength as a basis for leadership in international affairs. Without an overarching concern similar to the post-World War II focus on U.S.-Soviet rivalry from which to appeal for support from the U.S. public and U.S. allies, Carter's experiment in exercising "leadership without hegemony" led to public perceptions of presidential confusion and indecision.[55]

In contrast, the Reagan administration sought to restore U.S. leadership and authority in international relations by reviving key elements of post-World War II foreign policy,[56] arguing that the decline in U.S. influence during the 1970s resulted mainly from the lack of political leadership and a coherent national purpose. President Reagan proclaimed that "America is back"; his administration accelerated defense spending, implemented economic policies intended to promote inflation-free growth, and focused its attention on resisting the real and/or perceived expansion of Soviet influence in such areas as Central America and the Caribbean. The administration's perception that Soviet-inspired subversion was frequently the source of revolutionary upheaval and security crises in developing countries reinforced the emphasis on containment of the Soviet Union and its allies throughout the world. With the economy in decline in the late 1970s and early 1980s, and in the wake of diplomatic defeats in Iran and Nicaragua and the Soviet invasion of Afghanistan, such simple and decisive foreign policy approaches appealed to broad segments of the public. Growing public distress with the inability of the United States to control international events (symbolized most dramatically by the Iranian hostage crisis of 1979–1981) also increased public support for the use of force to settle crises abroad. However, the absence of a fundamental strategic and ideological bipolarity between the United States and the Soviet Union similar to that which existed in the late 1940s and early 1950s made the restoration of a similar foreign policy consensus much more difficult. And despite Reagan's widespread popularity and skill in political communication, the diffusion of power, information, and political access in U.S. society made executive control of foreign policy much more difficult than in the pre-Vietnam era.

United States Perspectives on Hemispheric Relations

Throughout much of the nineteenth and twentieth centuries the United States asserted a "special relationship" among western hemisphere countries. This long tradition stressed the importance of geographical proximity, common historical experience, and shared ideals, values, and beliefs as the underlying basis of a hemispheric identity that set the Americas apart from Europe.[57] Although the utility of this perspective and the extent to which the United States and Latin American countries actually shared common interests had long been questioned by Latin Americans, as late as 1969 the Rockefeller Commission report on the state of U.S.–Latin American relations argued that "the nations of the Western Hemisphere are not separate entities; they are sovereign peoples indissolubly linked by mutual hopes and needs, mutual interests and common objectives."[58] As earlier sections of this essay have demonstrated, the underlying bases of U.S.–Latin American relations had changed considerably by the late 1960s. Nonetheless, the idea of a "special relationship" linking the United States and Latin America continued to appeal to important sectors of U.S. public and elite opinion.

In many ways the Rockefeller Commission's emphasis on a hemispheric "special relationship" represented the end of an era. It looked backward, stressing the value of historical attitudes shaped during the long period of U.S. predominance in inter-American relations when the United States shaped security relations, trade and investment policies, and even cultural ideals and consumer preferences in much of Latin America. The underlying premises of a hemispheric "special relationship" paralleled the Monroe Doctrine's implicit assumption that the United States should play a leading role in U.S.–Latin American relations.[59] The appeal to hemispheric unity in support of shared objectives complemented well the United States' emphasis on a common front to resist an extracontinental military and ideological foe (first Nazi Germany, then the Soviet Union) from the late 1930s and World War II through the 1960s.

In practice, however, the idea of a hemispheric "special relationship" frequently constituted the basis for unilateral actions by the United States to protect its own economic, military, and political interests in Latin America. Although its position as the most powerful and influential country in the hemisphere has often permitted it to act without significant constraint by Latin American states, the United States asserted the importance of common interests and objectives in order to legitimate such actions. The most dramatic manifestations of this phenomenon were various interventions, both open and covert, in Mexico, Chile, Cuba, and several other Central American and Caribbean states during the nineteenth and twentieth centuries to impose preferences and policies on Latin American countries. Furthermore, critics of U.S. policy toward Latin America argued that the United States espoused a "special relationship" only when a perceived crisis threatened U.S. interests in the hemisphere and it therefore served U.S. interests to do so.[60]

In contrast to this approach, liberal U.S. policy analysts in the 1970s advocated a globalist perspective on U.S.–Latin American relations. For example, the 1974 Linowitz Commission on United States–Latin American relations argued that the context and character of inter-American relations had been considerably redefined by both international events and developments in Latin America.[61] In order to respond to these changing realities, the United States should reject the "special relationship" concept and evaluate its regional and bilateral relations with Latin America in terms of global economic and political concerns: "The issues of primary importance in U.S.–Latin American relations are, in many respects, the main issues of general concern to industrialized and less-industrialized nations. . . . In these areas, the United States cannot, by and large, have one policy for Latin America and another policy for the rest of the world. These problems are global, and they require global policies and global solutions. They are also, nonetheless, particularly critical problems in U.S.–Latin American relations."[62]

A similar perspective informed much of the Carter administration's overall approach to U.S.–Latin American relations, especially during Carter's first years in office before perceived security crises in Iran, Nicaragua, and Afghanistan shifted the predominant focus of high-level foreign policy debate back to such traditional concerns as U.S.-Soviet relations and the potential threats to U.S. security posed by revolutionary movements in developing countries. Although advocates of economic and political globalism recognized the need for close attention to the special characteristics and needs of Latin American countries, they argued that increasingly complex global interdependence (especially in such economic areas as trade, investment, the transfer of technology, and the management of global resources) required that long-standing ties between the United States and Latin America be restructured in terms of general relations between industrialized and developing countries. From this perspective, the appropriate goal of U.S.–Latin American relations was movement toward stable and equitable relations between industrialized countries such as the United States and the developing world, including Latin America.[63]

Jimmy Carter devoted considerably more attention to Latin America than any previous U.S. president since John F. Kennedy, and he moved quickly to address prominent issues that held both real and symbolic importance for Latin America.[64] The renegotiation of the status of the Panama Canal in 1977–1978 was particularly important in this regard. The amount of high-level attention that the Carter administration focused on Latin America in large part reflected the increasing economic and political importance of major countries in the region, including Brazil, Mexico, Argentina, and Venezuela. Richard Nixon and Henry A. Kissinger (assistant to the president for national security affairs, 1969–1975, and secretary of state, 1973–1977) had recognized the need to adjust U.S. policies to the capabilities of emerging powers in Latin America, but Carter's policies toward the region went much further in accepting political and ideological diversity among different countries and regimes.

However, the Carter administration's actions did not always correspond to announced policies. For example, domestic economic constraints and the turbulence of the international economic system undercut an attempt to increase development assistance to Caribbean countries. Similarly, the Carter administration effected little change in economic issues of great importance to major Latin American countries, including expanded access to the U.S. market for Latin American manufactured exports, the transfer of advanced technology to the region, and the stabilization of international commodity prices. Indeed, the Carter administration's emphasis on global policy issues and the international policy context sometimes overshadowed Latin American interests. In some cases U.S. economic policies that conformed to globalist principles harmed the interests of Latin American countries and producers. The Carter administration's rejection of a "special relationship" and paternalism were important departures, but these steps were not sufficient to guaranteee Latin American countries' broader economic and political interests in their relations with the United States.

In the view of liberal internationalists in the 1970s, a predominantly global perspective was necessary to respond to complex foreign policy issues. The perceived promise of détente with the Soviet Union, a relaxation of international political and military tensions, and the relative absence of threats to U.S. security interests in Latin America permitted advocates of this approach to downplay the traditional emphasis on security issues in inter-American relations. Supporters of economic globalism also argued that this approach corresponded to the internationalization of U.S. economic relations and the relative decline of western hemisphere economic transactions in the United States' global trade and investment flows. The Carter administration's emphasis on human rights issues, trade policy, and nuclear nonproliferation in U.S.–Latin American relations corresponded closely to the tenets and assumptions of economic and political globalism.

The strategic globalism articulated by conservative U.S. foreign policy analysts in the late 1970s and early 1980s constituted a markedly different perspective on hemispheric relations. This approach primarily reflected the impact of increased tensions in U.S.-Soviet relations on policymakers' perceptions of potential security threats in the Western Hemisphere. It emphasized both the strategic importance of Mexico, Central and South America, and the Caribbean in the United States' contemporary global military and political rivalry with the Soviet Union and the extent to which the United States' dominant position in the Western Hemisphere historically underpinned U.S. global power. Advocates of strategic globalism argued that the Soviet Union and its allies (particularly Cuba) had become a serious threat to hemispheric security. For example, the Committee of Santa Fe stated this concern bluntly in its 1980 report: "The Americas are under attack."[65] In addition, strategic globalism stressed the relationship between external aggression and internal "subversion" in the Western Hemisphere.

The Reagan administration's primary focus on the perceived East-West dimensions of political and military conflicts in Central America and the Caribbean and the subordination of other considerations to U.S. military security interests corresponded closely to the underlying assumptions of strategic globalism. United States policy toward Caribbean Basin countries after 1981 gave renewed attention to regional security alliances among El Salvador, Guatemala, Honduras, and Costa Rica and among several eastern Caribbean states. The Reagan adminstration also substantially increased military and economic assistance to U.S. allies in the Caribbean Basin in an attempt to promote stability in the area, maintain ideological influence, and subdue armed revolutionary movements. The United States actively assisted in training military and security forces in El Salvador, Honduras, Panama, Costa Rica, and (after 1983) Grenada and several eastern Caribbean states. In addition to its extensive support for anti-Sandinista guerrilla forces based in Honduras and Costa Rica, in 1985 the U.S. government imposed an economic embargo against Nicaragua. The Reagan administration even promoted the Caribbean Basin Initiative (which stressed trade benefits, investment incentives, and foreign economic assistance as necessary U.S. contributions to the area's economic and social progress) to Congress and the public in terms of its value in maintaining internal stability in participating countries and preserving regional security against internal subversion and external threat.

Reagan's forceful efforts to reassert U.S. control in Latin America, particularly in Central America and the Caribbean, reversed the principal focus of U.S. policy toward the region in the mid- and late 1970s. The invasion of Grenada and support for anti-Sandinista guerrilla forces marked a return to an older tradition of U.S. interventionism in Latin American countries' internal affairs. Through these actions the Reagan administration tested the perceived limits that the "lessons of Vietnam" had imposed on U.S. policymakers' use of force to promote foreign policy goals in developing countries. Public opinion polls taken between 1983 and 1985 repeatedly showed that a majority of U.S. citizens opposed the administration's support for efforts to overthrow the Sandinista regime,[66] but in practice public opinion appeared willing to tolerate a variety of aggressive actions that fell short of a large-scale direct military invasion.

The Reagan administration achieved at least short-term success in slowing the process of revolutionary change in Central America and in reasserting a U.S. political and military presence in the Caribbean Basin. However, several factors constrained policymakers' efforts to reestablish U.S. preeminence in hemispheric affairs. Although the administration's apparent reluctance to accept a regionally negotiated peace agreement blocked efforts by the Contadora Group to achieve a political settlement to the Central American crisis, the Contadora countries' commitment to continued negotiations offered persistent Latin American diplomatic resistance to the U.S. emphasis on military approaches to Central American problems. Nicaragua's appeal to the International Court of Justice to prohibit such aggressive actions as Central Intelligence Agency involvement in the mining of a Nicaraguan harbor in 1984 (and the Reagan administration's much-publicized rejection of the court's jurisdiction in the case) focused additional critical international attention on U.S. policies in the area. Latin American regional initiatives and joint statements concerning the debt crisis also suggested that the United States' reassertionist policies in the 1980s would not necessarily restore the underlying political, economic, and ideological conditions that had permitted the United States to act unilaterally on major hemispheric issues only two decades earlier.

In the United States as well, even such dramatic actions as the U.S. invasion of Grenada failed to generate a durable domestic political consensus in support of the Reagan administration's broader military security goals and strategies in the Caribbean Basin. For example, congressional opponents of Reagan's policy toward Nicaragua succeeded in placing important restrictions on U.S. assistance to anti-Sandinista guerrilla forces. Although President Reagan lobbied strenuously in early 1985 to increase military assistance to the *contras* and defended the anti-Sandinista forces as "freedom fighters," the legislation passed in July 1985 authorizing $27 million in additional assistance stipulated that the aid could be used only for "humanitarian" purposes and could not be distributed by either the Central Intelligence Agency or the Department of Defense.[67] United States critics of the Reagan administration's foreign policy toward Latin America argued that the predominant focus on perceived East-West dimensions of the Central American crisis diverted attention from other major countries in the hemisphere and such vital economic issues as long-term measures to resolve the Latin American debt crisis.

More generally, the Reagan administration's perspective on hemispheric affairs and its preoccupation with traditional "anticommunist" military security concerns constituted a sharp contrast to most Latin American countries' foreign policy goals and development priorities. A growing divergence between U.S. and Latin American approaches to major issues in contemporary U.S.–Latin American relations may increase hemispheric tensions and lead to future conflict between the United States and major Latin American countries.

Central Issues in U.S.–Latin American Relations in the 1980s

This essay's examination of changing perspectives on U.S.–Latin American relations indicates both the range of views informing debate on this subject in Latin America and the United States and some of the ways in which international and domestic factors have influenced these perspectives. In addition, the preceding analysis suggests several broader conclusions. First, although major asymmetries in power and resources persist in relations between Latin American countries and the United States, the international and national contexts that influence Latin American and U.S. views on inter-American relations have clearly changed in important ways since the 1960s. Second, a discussion of contemporary U.S.–Latin American relations must begin by disaggregating "Latin America." The process of socioeconomic and political change has assumed distinct characteristics in different countries and subregions, with differing implications for national capabilities and development priorities. Differences in Latin American countries' positions in the international political economy and in the character of their ties to the United States also influence their various national foreign policy goals and orientations. Third, improved relations between Latin America and the United States depend to a considerable degree on a better understanding of certain key issues. Differences regarding such questions as appropriate responses to the Latin American debt crisis and political and military conflicts in Central America may well contribute to increased future tensions between the United States and Latin American countries. Because Latin American and U.S. perspectives on hemispheric relations are often totalizing in their assumptions and approaches, an understanding of the range of significant opinion throughout the hemisphere on major issues is a necessary point of departure for constructive approaches to U.S.–Latin American relations in the years ahead.

The essays included in this volume also suggest that the central topics in contemporary U.S.–Latin American relations do not readily lend themselves to conventional policy distinctions among global, hemispheric, and bilateral issues. Contemporary political and economic crises have established important new linkages among specific issues. Some problems that generally have been considered primarily global have taken on important regional dimensions in this context, and distinct global issues sometimes intersect in ways that give them special significance at the hemispheric level. In other cases, primarily bilateral subjects have been elevated to hemisphere-wide attention as a number of Latin American countries have been confronted by common dilemmas. Given the complexity of current problems, the extent to which key issues are interrelated, the increasing diversity among Latin American countries, and the likelihood that the United States and Latin American countries will approach major issues with different interests, preferences, and ideologies, no single policy approach can satisfactorily address the complex array of issues that now constitutes the focus of U.S.–Latin American relations. Any particular approach must first consider the special requirements of a particular issue and its relationship to other central topics in contemporary inter-American affairs.

The issues examined in this volume illustrate these last points well. For example, access to external financing is a problem that confronts most developing countries, especially those that are highly dependent on oil imports. However, as the essays by Carlos Massad and Richard O'Brien show, Latin American countries hold approximately half of all developing countries' outstanding external debt. Four countries (Brazil, Mexico, Argentina, and Venezuela) account for most of the Latin American total, and these countries frequently dominated discussions of the international debt problem in the early 1980s. In addition, U.S. banks and financial institutions hold approximately 38 percent of Latin American countries' total debt. The management of the debt crisis certainly has broad implications for the international monetary system and for banks and financial institutions in the United States, western Europe, Japan, and other capital-exporting countries, but the coincidence of several Latin American countries' large share of outstanding developing country debt and U.S. banks' high degree of exposure in these same countries necessarily makes the debt problem a major hemispheric concern. The essays by Massad and O'Brien and the comments by Richard E. Feinberg and Roberto Bouzas suggest that whether or not a primarily hemispheric approach to the debt problem is practicable, the U.S. government's sensitivity to the economic burdens that a large foreign debt entails clearly affects U.S. bilateral relations with major Latin American debtor countries. United States domestic economic policies (for example, policies affecting international interest rates and market access for Latin American exports) have a strong impact on these Latin American countries' economic situation. Conversely, Latin America's economic future has direct significance for the United States because of the region's continued importance as an export market for U.S. manufactured goods. Finally, although steps taken to address the debt crisis must include a global reassessment of appropriate forms of development financing, policy initiatives undertaken in a hemispheric context may set important precedents for action on a broader scale.

Trade relations between the United States and Latin American countries raise a similar range of issues. Although their specific interests and policy positions often differ sharply, both the United States and a growing number of Latin American countries are increasingly inclined to view trade as an international issue. United States policymakers must evaluate economic policies toward Latin America on matters such as tariff and nontariff trade barriers in terms of the broader precedent they may establish for overall U.S. foreign economic policy, and many Latin American countries view reform in the international trade regime as a key basis for accelerated national development and the building of a new international economic order. Indeed, decreasing complementarity between the U.S. and Latin American economies may inevitably increase the frequency of conflicts that cannot be resolved in a bilateral or hemispheric framework. Nonetheless, the United States retains an important regional interest in trade relations with Mexico (the United States' third most important trading partner, after Canada and Japan) and the Caribbean (as reflected in the 1983 Caribbean Basin Initiative). Several Latin American countries (Mexico, the Dominican Republic, Haiti, Honduras) also remain highly dependent on bilateral trade with the United States. Furthermore, as the essays by Winston Fritsch and John S. Odell show, the economic viability of the major Latin American debtor countries depends overwhelmingly on increased exports and access to the U.S. market for an expanding range of manufactured goods. Thus the linkage between debt and trade problems to some extent reinforces the hemispheric dimension of U.S.–Latin American trade relations.

The questions of democracy and human rights also defy simple distinctions among bilateral, global, and hemispheric issues. The essays by Howard Wiarda, Guillermo O'Donnell, Rafael Braun, and Margaret Crahan and the comments by Giuseppe Di Palma and Edelberto Torres-Rivas agree, although with different emphases and priorities, that the construction of open, competitive political arrangements and the protection of basic human rights largely depend on decisions taken by national actors. Moreover, in some cases human rights issues have constituted the principal focus of bilateral U.S. diplomatic relations with individual Latin American countries. Yet human rights issues are also the subject of widely endorsed international agreements, including the Universal Declaration of Human Rights (1948), the United Nations International Covenant on Civil and Political Rights (1966), and the United Nations International Covenant on Economic, Social, and Cultural Rights (1966). In addition, these issues have long been a central dimension of hemispheric relations. The dramatic increase in human rights violations in a number of Latin American countries in the 1960s and 1970s became a major concern of inter-American institutions, particularly the Inter-American Commission on Human Rights. The threat that prolonged economic crisis in Latin American countries poses to both established civilian governments and transition processes from authoritarian rule in the region in the 1980s further underlines the hemispheric dimension of these issues.

The issue of migration in the Western Hemisphere raises both bilateral and hemispheric issues. Most crossnational migratory flows in the Western Hemisphere involve the movement of persons from one country to a second, usually contiguous country; in only a few cases (for example, political-economic refugees from El Salvador to the United States) does migration occur across a third, intervening country's national borders. As the essay by Michael S. Teitelbaum and the comment by Gabriel Murillo Castaño note, migration of this kind is predominantly of bilateral or subregional concern to the countries directly involved. However, the magnitude of Latin America's contemporary economic crisis and escalating conflict in Central America have elevated migration issues to the level of hemispheric attention. Migratory flows have become more conflictual than in the past as migrant workers encounter limited employment opportunities in host countries and often return home, only to find their own country in severe economic difficulty. Migration issues also involve a larger number of countries than ever before. The difficulties that most countries have experienced in developing workable national migration policies suggest that migration might be addressed more effectively through a multilateral framework involving the United States and Latin American countries. Moreover, the Central American refugee problem has prompted greater involvement by both international agencies such as the United Nations High Commissioner for Refugees and inter-American institutions. Refugee policy particularly involves hemispheric responsibility. Because regional disparities in the level of economic development are likely to increase and because the political and social crisis in Central America has worsened in recent years, migration will be of growing concern in U.S.–Latin American relations in the future.

Finally, security issues include a number of subjects that vary considerably in their global, regional, and bilateral implications. Cole Blasier's essay analyzes the extrahemispheric dimensions of security issues in U.S.–Latin American relations, particularly the ways in which the United States' global strategic rivalry with the Soviet Union affects U.S. perceptions of approaches to "security crises" in Latin America. Blasier also addresses the nature of U.S., Latin American, and Soviet security interests in the Western Hemisphere. Gregory Treverton's essay on interstate conflict examines both bilateral and/or subregional issues such as territorial disputes between and among neighboring Latin American states and global security problems (for example, nuclear proliferation) that may have special relevance for future interstate conflict in the region. In contrast, Sergio Bitar's essay examines the extent to which U.S. and Latin American interpretations of security issues have differed over time. He draws particular attention to the increasing importance Latin American states attach to regional economic security. The comments by Margaret Daly Hayes and Rafael Hernández analyze both the global and hemispheric implications of security issues in relations between the United States and Latin America.

The issues examined in this volume are of great concern to both the United States and Latin America. The authors of the following essays approach these questions from distinct perspectives that reflect important differences in historical tradition, political and ideological beliefs, and cultural values. Although the views articulated in these essays and comments are not the only possible approaches to the issues analyzed here, they do represent a significant range of opinion on central problems in contemporary U.S.–Latin American relations. A better understanding of major U.S. and Latin American perspectives on these issues is an important basis for improved communications and more effective cooperation between the United States and Latin America in the 1980s.

Notes

We are grateful to Cole Blasier, David Collier, Ruth Berins Collier, Lisa L. Condit, Jorge I. Domínguez, Jeffrey A. Hart, John Lovell, Carlos Massad, Gabriel Murillo Castaño, Gregory F. Treverton, Laurence Whitehead, Van R. Whiting, Jr., and Donald L. Wyman for comments on a preliminary version of this essay. Of course, we alone are responsible for the conclusions and interpretations presented here.

1. Most aggregate data on Latin America's economic performance do not include information on socialist Cuba. Cuba's gross material product increased (in current prices) by an average of 0.4 percent, 6.3 percent, and 4.1 percent per year, respectively, during 1966–1970, 1971–1975, and 1976–1980. Per capita income fell by 1.3 percent per year in 1966–1970 and then increased by 14.5 percent per year in 1971–1975 and approximately 4.1 percent per year in 1976–1980. See Carmelo Mesa-Lago, *The Economy of Socialist Cuba* (Albuquerque: University of New Mexico Press, 1981), table 3, p. 34.

2. United Nations Economic Commission for Latin America, "Balance preliminar de la economía latinoamericana durante 1982" (December 1982) and "La evolución de la economía de América Latina en 1981" (December 1982).

3. For some indicative data from Argentina, Brazil, Colombia, Mexico, and Puerto Rico and a general discussion of these tendencies, see David Felix, "In-

come Distribution and the Quality of Life in Latin America: Patterns, Trends, and Policy Implications," in Aspen Institute for Humanistic Studies, *Governance in the Western Hemisphere* (Washington, D.C., 1982), pp. 439–78; see esp. pp. 443–48.

4. Winston Fritsch, "Latin America's Export Growth Imperative in the 1980s: Can the United States Help Achieve It?" in this volume, table 6.

5. Authors' calculations based on data presented in *Statistical Abstract of Latin America* 22 (Los Angeles: UCLA Latin American Center Publications, University of California, 1983), tables 2305–2323.

6. Fritsch, "Latin America's Export Growth Imperative in the 1980s," table 11.

7. For some indicative data, see *Statistical Abstract of Latin America* 22 (1983), tables 800, 803, 902–903; for comparative purposes, see earlier volumes of the *Statistical Abstract of Latin America*.

8. Authors' calculations based on data presented in ibid., table 2423. "Economic activities" include agriculture, roads, and transportation.

9. Authors' calculations based on data presented in Inter-American Development Bank, *Economic and Social Progress in Latin America* (Washington, D.C., 1982), table 20, p. 362.

10. See Jorge I. Domínguez, "The Foreign Policies of Latin American States in the 1980s: Retreat or Refocus?" mimeograph, Harvard University, Center for International Affairs, March 1984, esp. pp. 6–8, for a more complete statement of this argument. Also see Jeffrey A. Hart, *The New International Economic Order* (New York: St. Martin's Press, 1983), p. 100, and Stephen D. Krasner, *Structural Conflict: The Third World Against Global Liberalism* (Berkeley and Los Angeles: University of California Press, 1985).

11. For example, the United States' importance as a source of foreign direct investment flows into Latin America declined from 55 percent of total Development Advisory Committee flows in 1970–1975 to 48 percent in 1976–1980. (The Development Advisory Committee is composed of Austria, Belgium, Canada, Denmark, France, the Federal Republic of Germany, Italy, Japan, the Netherlands, Norway, Portugal, Sweden, Switzerland, the United Kingdom, and the United States.) The U.S. share of total Organization for Economic Cooperation and Development financing for Latin America fell from 50 percent in 1970 to 40 percent in 1980. See Sergio Bitar, "United States–Latin American Relations: Shifts in Economic Power and Implications for the Future," *Working Papers* 130, Latin American Program, The Wilson Center, Smithsonian Institution (Washington, D.C., 1983), p. 8.

Similarly, by the late 1960s Latin American armed forces relied increasingly on sources other than the United States for weapons and equipment. This change had been accelerated by the U.S. Congress's enactment of legislation in the mid-1960s that prohibited the sale of certain types of weaponry (including advanced jet aircraft) to Latin America. (The legislation sought to limit Latin American countries' use of scarce development resources for the purchase of expensive sophisticated military equipment.) France, the Federal Republic of Germany, the Soviet Union, Great Britain, Spain, Canada, Israel, Italy, and several other countries later emerged as important sources of arms exports to Latin America. Latin American countries' own arms production also increased significantly, particularly in Brazil and Argentina but also in Peru and Colombia. The real value of U.S. military assistance to Latin America also fell considerably between 1970 and 1980. In 1980 only El Salvador, Honduras, the Dominican Republic, Peru, Ecuador, and Bolivia received more than $300,000 in U.S. military assistance. El Salvador received the largest amount in 1980, $5.993 million. *Statistical Abstract of Latin America* 22 (1983), table 1101.

12. The absolute amounts of this decline for the other ten countries were as follows: Bahamas, 16.6 percent; Brazil, 19.4 percent; Chile, 23.2 percent; Colombia, 23.3 percent; Costa Rica, 23.7 percent; Dominican Republic, 9.9 percent; Ecuador, 21.8 percent; Guatemala, 18.6 percent; Nicaragua, 12 percent; Paraguay, 12.8 percent. Authors' calculations based on data in Inter-American Development Bank, *Economic and Social Progress in Latin America* (1981), p. 113.

13. Ibid.

14. Fritsch, "Latin America's Export Growth Imperative," table 10.

15. Inter-American Development Bank, *Economic and Social Progress in Latin America* (1981), p. 113.

16. For a recent attempt to assess the Latin American economic integration process, see Mario I. Blejer, "Economic Integration: An Analytical Overview," in Inter-American Development Bank, *Economic and Social Progress in Latin America* (Washington, D.C., 1984), pp. 5–34.

17. For analyses of Latin American countries' efforts to diversify their international economic and political relations during the 1970s, see Abraham F. Lowenthal and Albert Fishlow, *Latin America's Emergence: Toward a U.S. Response,* Foreign Policy Association Headline Series No. 243 (Washington, D.C., 1979); Elizabeth G. Ferris and Jennie K. Lincoln, eds., *Latin American Foreign Policies: Global and Regional Dimensions* (Boulder, Colo.: Westview Press, 1981); and Roger W. Fontaine and James D. Theberge, *Latin America's New Internationalism: The End of Hemispheric Isolation* (New York: Praeger Publishers, 1976). Hart, *The New International Economic Order,* pp. 89–90, summarizes Latin American activities in support of a new international economic order.

For historical examples of Latin American countries' attempts to diversify international political relations and thus reduce their relative dependence on the United States (for example, through support for the League of Nations and the United Nations), see Gordon Connell-Smith, *The Inter-American System* (London: Oxford University Press, 1966), p. 11, and Arthur P. Whitaker, *The Western Hemisphere Idea: Its Rise and Decline* (Ithaca, N.Y.: Cornell University Press, 1954), chaps. 5 and 6 passim.

18. Laurence Whitehead's essay in this volume, "Debt, Diversification, and Dependency: Latin America's International Political Relations," provides a more detailed assessment of the success achieved by these different diversification efforts.

19. The statement was formulated by ministerial representatives of the Latin American Special Coordinating Commission (Comisión Especial de Coordinación Latinoamericana, CECLA) at its inaugural meeting in Viña del Mar, Chile. The

document was endorsed by representatives of twenty-one Latin American states on 17 May 1969 and presented to then President Richard M. Nixon on 11 June 1969. For a statement regarding the significance of the Consensus, see the address given by Gabriel Valdés S. (then Chile's Minister of Foreign Affairs and president of CECLA) when he presented the document to Nixon; mimeograph (English translation), n.p., 11 June 1969.

Although the Consensus was among the first joint Latin American statements on development issues in U.S.–Latin American relations, individual Latin American governments and statesmen had on numerous occasions sought to define the appropriate character of inter-American relations. See Connell-Smith, *The Inter-American System,* pp. xvi–xvii, 4–5, 22, 30–31, 34–35, and Whitaker, *The Western Hemisphere Idea,* chaps. 5 and 8 passim.

For a brief discussion of earlier Latin American initiatives to promote the region's economic interests in its relations with the United States, see Sergio Bitar, "Economics and Security: Contradictions in U.S.–Latin American Relations," in this volume.

20. "Consensus of Viña del Mar," mimeograph (English translation), n.p., 11 June 1969, p. 4, and Valdés statement, pp. 2–3. For the other points summarized in this discussion, see "Consensus," pp. 2–3, 8.

21. The Latin American Economic System was founded in 1975 primarily at the initiative of Mexico and Venezuela. It reflected Latin America's experience with regional economic integration in the 1960s and early 1970s, and it sought to formulate joint Latin American positions on economic relations with the United States. In contrast to a number of other inter-American organizations, its membership was consciously limited to Latin American states.

22. Sistema Económico Latinoamericano, "Declaración de Panamá," mimeograph, n.p., 1 December 1981, pp. 5–6.

23. Ibid., pp. 6–7, 12. On the question of Latin American collective economic security, see Sistema Económico Latinoamericano, *Las relaciones económicas de América Latina con Estados Unidos* (Mexico, D.F.: Siglo XXI Editores, 1983), pp. 99, 107.

24. Valdés statement, p. 3.

25. Hart, *The New International Economic Order,* p. 91.

26. Domínguez, "The Foreign Relations of Latin American States in the 1980s," p. 52.

27. For a contemporary evaluation of the war's possible long-term impact on U.S.–Latin American relations, see *New York Times,* 1 May 1982, p. 7; 5 May 1982, p. 19; 23 May 1982, p. 1.

28. *New York Times,* 1 May 1982, p. 8; 21 May 1982, p. 1. For an analysis of the Falklands/Malvinas war, see Lawrence Freedman, "The War of the Falkland Islands, 1982," *Foreign Affairs* 61, no. 1 (Fall 1982): 196–210, and Adam Perkal, "Losses and Lessons of the 1982 War for the Falklands," in James W. Wilkie and Adam Perkal, eds., *Statistical Abstract of Latin America* 23 (Los Angeles: UCLA Latin American Center Publications, University of California, 1984), pp. 816–35.

29. For Latin American reactions to Argentina's occupation of the islands and

U.S. and EEC sanctions against Argentina, see *New York Times,* 18 April 1982, p. 18; 25 April 1982, p. 17; 28 April 1982, p. 1; 29 April 1982, p. 19; 30 May 1982, p. 1.

For an analysis of the Rio Treaty's possible relevance to the conflict, see *New York Times,* 20 April 1982, p. 1; 21 April 1982, p. 14; 22 April 1982, p. 30; 27 April 1982, p. 13. The relevant sections of the Rio Treaty are articles 1–3; see *United States Statutes at Large* 63, p. 2 (Washington, D.C.: U.S. Government Printing Office, 1949), pp. 1699–704.

30. This discussion draws on Cole Blasier, "Security: The Extracontinental Dimension," in this volume. See U.S. Department of State and U.S. Department of Defense, *Grenada Documents: An Overview and Selection* (Washington, D.C., 1984) for some of the material that the Reagan administration used to justify the U.S. invasion.

31. *New York Times,* 4 June 1985, pp. 1, 6; 5 June 1985, pp. 1, 4; 13 August 1985, pp. 1, 8; 25 August 1985, p. 3.

32. See Roy Gutman, "Nicaragua: America's Diplomatic Charade," *Foreign Policy* 56 (Fall 1984): 3–23, and *New York Times,* 16 April 1985, pp. 1, 4; 6 June 1985, p. 4.

33. Authors' calculations from data (constant 1982 dollars) presented in Inter-American Development Bank, *Economic and Social Progress in Latin America* (1984), table 3, p. 420. Real per capita GDP increased in only four Latin American countries between 1980 and 1983: the Dominican Republic, 0.8 percent; Jamaica, 2.3 percent; Nicaragua, 2.4 percent; and Panama, 3.4 percent. For an assessment of political responses to the debt crisis, see Robert R. Kaufman, "Democratic and Authoritarian Responses to the Debt Issue: Argentina, Brazil, Mexico," *International Organization* 39, no. 3 (Summer 1985): 473–503.

34. *New York Times,* 31 March 1984, p. 1; 21 May 1984, p. 21.

35. Ibid., 29 July 1985, pp. 1, 4; 30 July 1985, pp. 33, 39.

36. Ibid., 2 October 1984, p. 1; 3 October 1984, p. 1; 18 October 1984, p. 1. See also Rosario Green, "The Permanence of Mexico's Foreign Policy Historical Sources: The United States and Central America," mimeograph, February 1985.

37. *New York Times,* 18 August 1985, pp. 1, 6.

38. Ibid., 22 August 1985, p. 3; 14 November 1984, p. 9. Also see Gutman, "Nicaragua: America's Diplomatic Charade." Tom J. Farer, "Contadora: The Hidden Agenda," *Foreign Policy* 59 (Summer 1985): 59–72, examines the Contadora countries' motives for pursuing regional peace negotiations.

39. One indication of the diversity of U.S. views on contemporary U.S.–Latin American relations is the proliferation of special commission reports on the state of inter-American affairs. See The Committee of Santa Fe, *A New Inter-American Policy for the Eighties* (Washington, D.C.: Council for Inter-American Security, 1980); Inter-American Dialogue, *The Americas at the Crossroads* (Washington, D.C.: Woodrow Wilson International Center for Scholars, 1983), and *The Americas in 1984: A Year for Decisions* (Washington, D.C.: Aspen Institute for Humanistic Studies, 1984); National Bipartisan Commission on Central America (The Kissinger Commission), *The Report of the President's National Bipartisan Commission on Central America* (New York: Macmillan, 1984); and PAACA (Policy

Alternatives for the Caribbean and Central America), *Changing Course: Blue-print for Peace in Central America and the Caribbean* (Washington, D.C.: Institute for Policy Studies, 1984). For a comparison of several different reports on U.S.–Central American relations, see Margaret Daly Hayes, "Prescriptions and Results: Policy Recommendations for Central America in 1984," *Journal of Interamerican Studies and World Affairs* 27, no. 1 (February 1985): 145–59.

40. For a discussion of these issues, see Stanley Hoffman, *Primacy or World Order: American Foreign Policy Since the Cold War* (New York: McGraw-Hill, 1978), esp. chap. 2.

41. Ibid., p. 43.

42. See the transcript of Reagan's speech to a joint session of Congress, *New York Times,* 28 April 1983, p. A12, and Secretary of Defense Caspar Weinberger's address outlining the conditions that should determine the use of U.S. military force in Central America and elsewhere, *New York Times,* 29 November 1984, p. 1.

43. For reports on growing U.S. military involvement in the area, see *New York Times,* 18 March 1985, p. 6; 5 May 1985, section 4, p. 1; 4 June 1985, pp. 1, 6; 5 June 1985, pp. 1, 4; 24 July 1985, p. 1; 28 July 1985, section 4, p. 1; 8 August 1985, pp. 1, 6; 9 August 1985, p. 6; 25 August 1985, p. 3.

44. A *New York Times*/CBS News poll taken shortly after the invasion found that 51 percent of respondents approved the sending of U.S. troops to Grenada (37 percent disapproved). Respondents favoring this action cited their belief that U.S. citizens on the island were in danger (58 percent) and saw it as an action designed to stop the spread of communism (66 percent). However, 51 percent of the respondents agreed that President Reagan "uses [the] military too quickly," and 52 percent "feel uneasy about his approach." *New York Times,* 29 October 1983, p. 9. A subsequent *New York Times*/CBS News poll found that only 30 percent of respondents supported Reagan administration policy in Central America. *New York Times,* 29 April 1984, p. 21.

For evidence concerning the U.S. public's growing reluctance from the mid-1950s to the late 1970s to take an active part in world affairs, see John E. Reilly, "The American Mood: A Foreign Policy of Self-Interest," *Foreign Policy* 34 (Spring 1979): 76. See William Schneider, "Conservatism, Not Interventionism: Trends in Foreign Policy Opinion, 1974–1982," in Kenneth A. Oye, Robert J. Lieber, and Donald Rothchild, eds., *Eagle Defiant: United States Foreign Policy in the 1980s* (Boston: Little, Brown, 1983), pp. 33–64, for an analysis of contemporary U.S. foreign policy opinion that supports these general conclusions.

45. Kenneth A. Oye, "International Systems Structure and American Foreign Policy," in Oye, Lieber, and Rothchild, eds., *Eagle Defiant,* p. 25 (citing *Economic Report of the President,* 1982, table B-2). The comparative data for this point are from John S. Odell, *U.S. International Monetary Policy: Markets, Power, and Ideas as Sources of Change* (Princeton, N.J.: Princeton University Press, 1982), p. 213, n. 45 (based on United Nations and World Bank data).

46. For data on these trends, see Odell, *U.S. International Monetary Policy,* table 5, p. 212, and Robert O. Keohane and Joseph S. Nye, Jr., *Power and Interdependence: World Politics in Transition* (Boston: Little, Brown, 1977),

table 6.3, p. 141 (based on International Monetary Fund, *International Financial Statistics*).

47. Sergio Bitar, "United States–Latin American Relations: Changes in Economic Relations during the 1970s," mimeograph, 1982 (based on United Nations and U.S. Department of Commerce statistics). According to the data Bitar presents, in 1980 Latin America accounted for 17.6 percent and 15.7 percent, respectively, of total U.S. exports and imports.

48. Sergio Bitar, "United States-Latin American Relations: Shifts in Economic Power and Implications for the Future," pp. 5–6 (citing OECD, *International Investment and Multinational Enterprises*, 1981, and U.S. Department of Commerce data). In 1980, 73 percent of U.S. direct foreign investment in developing countries was located in Latin America, although this percentage also showed a steady decline over time, especially after the 1960s. As late as 1975 it was 84.4 percent. Sistema Económico Latinoamericano, "América Latina y Estados Unidos: El papel de las empresas transnacionales," annex III (September 1981), and U.S. Department of Commerce, *Survey of Current Business*, August 1982.

49. International Monetary Fund, *World Economic Outlook* (Washington, D.C., 1982), table 1, p. 143, and *World Economic Outlook* (1984), table 1, p. 29.

50. World Bank, *World Development Report 1984* (Washington, D.C., 1984), table 1, p. 219; International Monetary Fund, *World Economic Outlook, September 1984*, IMF Occasional Paper No. 32 (Washington, D.C., 1984), table 7, p. 33.

51. International Monetary Fund, *World Economic Outlook, September 1984*, table 7, p. 33.

52. This paragraph draws on information in *New York Times*, 20 February 1984, section 4, p. 1; 17 February 1985, section 4, p. 2. Reagan's address to a joint session of Congress announcing the Caribbean Basin Initiative is reproduced in ibid., 25 February 1982, p. 14.

53. *Public Papers of the Presidents: John F. Kennedy, 1961* (Washington, D.C.: U.S. Government Printing Office, 1962), p. 1.

54. For a discussion of these points and other post-Vietnam foreign policy assumptions that came to the fore in the mid- and late 1970s, see Tom J. Farer, "Searching for Defeat," *Foreign Policy* 40 (Fall 1980): 155–74. On the post-Vietnam era in U.S. foreign policy, also see Charles W. Maynes and Richard H. Ullman, "Ten Years of Foreign Policy," ibid., 3–17, and Robert W. Gregg and Charles W. Kegley, Jr., eds., *After Vietnam: The Future of American Foreign Policy* (Garden City, N.Y.: Anchor Books, 1971). For a more general statement of the post-Vietnam "neo-realist" U.S. foreign policy approach, see Richard E. Feinberg, *The Intemperate Zone: The Third World Challenge to U.S. Foreign Policy* (New York: Norton, 1983), esp. pp. 19–25, 230–35.

55. On Carter's foreign policy record, see Stanley Hoffmann, "Requiem," *Foreign Policy* 42 (Spring 1981): 3–26, and Kenneth A. Oye, "The Domain of Choice: International Constraints and Carter Administration Foreign Policy," in Kenneth A. Oye, Donald Rothchild, and Robert J. Lieber, eds., *Eagle Entangled: U.S. Foreign Policy in a Complex World* (New York: Longman, 1979), pp. 3–33. The phrase "leadership without hegemony" is drawn from Marina v.

N. Whitman, "Leadership Without Hegemony: Our Role in the World Economy," *Foreign Policy* 20 (Fall 1975): 138–60.

56. See Kenneth A. Oye, "International Systems Structure and American Foreign Policy," in Oye, Lieber, and Rothchild, eds., *Eagle Defiant*, pp. 3–32, for an initial evaluation of Reagan's foreign policy.

57. See Whitaker, *The Western Hemisphere Idea,* chap. 1.

58. *The Rockefeller Report on the Americas* (Chicago: Quadrangle Books, 1969), p. 133. The commission was organized by Nelson Rockefeller (then governor of New York) at the request of then President Richard Nixon. Its membership was composed of prominent U.S. citizens, many of them representing the private sector and the Republican party.

59. The "Monroe Doctrine" was promulgated in 1823 by President James Monroe. In the aftermath of the Latin American wars of independence from Spain, it warned European powers not to seek colonies or to attempt to impose their political systems in the Americas. The doctrine was subsequently interpreted by the United States as the legitimating basis for unilateral U.S. leadership in inter-American relations. For example, the 1904 Roosevelt Corollary asserted the United States' right to intervene forcibly to maintain domestic order in Latin American countries. For analyses of the origins and implications of the Monroe Doctrine, see Gordon Connell-Smith, *The Inter-American System,* esp. pp. 1–12, and Ernest R. May, *The Making of the Monroe Doctrine* (Cambridge, Mass.: Harvard University Press, 1975).

60. For an early questioning of the underlying assumptions of such a relationship, see Lawrence E. Harrison, "Waking from the Pan-American Dream," *Foreign Policy* 5 (Winter 1971–1972): 163–81. Also see Abraham F. Lowenthal, "The United States and Latin America: Ending the Hegemonic Presumption," *Foreign Affairs* 55, no. 1 (October 1976): 199–213.

61. The Commission on United States–Latin American Relations was chaired by Sol M. Linowitz, a Washington attorney and former U.S. ambassador to the Organization of American States (1966–1969); he later served as co-negotiator of the Panama Canal treaties (1977–1978). The commission was composed of twenty-two prominent U.S. citizens with backgrounds in government, business, and academia. The commission's report and selected background papers were published as *The Americas in a Changing World* (New York: Quadrangle/The New York Times Book Co., 1975).

62. Commission on United States–Latin American Relations, *The Americas in a Changing World,* p. 21. Also see Lowenthal and Fishlow, *Latin America's Emergence,* passim.

63. Commission on United States–Latin American Relations, *The Americas in a Changing World,* pp. 12, 21–22.

64. See Abraham F. Lowenthal, "Jimmy Carter and Latin America: A New Era or Small Change," in Oye, Rothchild, and Lieber, *Eagle Entangled,* pp. 290–303, for an evaluation of the Carter administration's early policies toward Latin America.

65. Committee of Santa Fe, *A New Inter-American Policy for the Eighties,* p. 3. The Committee of Santa Fe (New Mexico) consisted of several conservative

analysts of U.S.–Latin American relations (L. Francis Bouchey, Roger W. Fontaine, David C. Jordan, Gordon Sumner, and Lewis Tambs). Several members of the committee later occupied high-level positions in the Reagan administration.

For a further explication of the strategic globalism perspective on hemispheric relations, see Roger Fontaine, Cleto DiGiovanni, Jr., and Alexander Kruger, "Castro's Specter," *The Washington Quarterly* 3, no. 4 (Autumn 1980): 3–27; Pedro Sanjuan, "Why We Don't Have a Latin American Policy," *The Washington Quarterly* 3, no. 4 (Autumn 1980): 28–39; Jeane Kirkpatrick, "U.S. Security and Latin America," *Commentary* 71, no. 1 (January 1981): 29–40; Constantine Menges, "Central America and Its Enemies," *Commentary* 72, no. 2 (August 1981): 32–38.

66. *New York Times*/CBS News polls showed that 54 percent, 55 percent, and 53 percent of respondents interviewed in June 1983, April 1984, and June 1985, respectively, opposed U.S. support for overthrowing the Sandinistas; *New York Times,* 9 June 1985, section 4, p. 1.

67. Ibid., 16 April 1985, pp. 1, 4; 9 June 1985, section 4, p. 1; 28 July 1985, p. 1.

APPENDIX A

DEMOGRAPHIC CHANGE IN LATIN AMERICA, 1960–1980

	Total Population (in thousands)			Average Annual Population Growth (in %)		Urban Population (as % of total)		Life Expectancy at Birth (in years)	
	1960	1970	1980	1960–1970	1970–1980	1960	1980	1965–1970	1975–1980
Argentina	20,540	23,748	27,710	1.6	1.7	73.6	85.7	67.4	69.4
Bolivia	3825	4780	5600	2.5	1.7	26.8	32.7	45.3	48.6
Brazil	69,730	95,204	118,610	3.7	2.5	46.1	67.6	59.7	63.4
Chile	7683	9717	11,104	2.6	1.4	67.8	81.5	61.5	65.7
Colombia	15,397	22,075	27,090	4.3	2.3	50.9	76.3	58.5	61.0[b]
Costa Rica	1254	1737	2250	3.9	3.0	32.7	45.9	65.4	70.0
Cuba	6826	8585	9830	2.6	1.5	40.3	46.2[a]	71.0	72.3
Dominican Republic	3036	4343	5440	4.3	2.5	30.1	53.1	55.7	55.4
Ecuador	4358	6031	8350	3.8	3.8	34.9	43.5	57.2	60.8
El Salvador	2454	3516	4750	4.3	3.5	38.4	40.3	54.9	59.0
Guatemala	3810	5298	7260	3.9	3.7	34.0	32.3	50.1	57.8
Haiti	3991	5201	5008	3.0	-.4	10.9	25.0	44.5	52.2
Honduras	1849	2553	3691	3.8	4.5	23.1	35.9	49.3	55.5[b]
Mexico	36,046	50,313	69,350	4.0	3.8	50.7	69.0	61.0	65.0[b]

	1411	1970	2730	4.0	3.9	38.4	57.8	50.4	55.2
Nicaragua	1411	1970	2730	4.0	3.9	38.4	57.8	50.4	55.2
Panama	1062	1458	1900	3.7	3.0	41.5	53.8	64.9	69.1[c]
Paraguay	1751	2247	3168	2.8	4.1	35.4	36.5	59.4	64.0[b]
Peru	10,025	13,248	17,780	3.2	3.4	46.2	70.5	53.4	57.2
Uruguay	2540	2887	2910	1.4	0.8	80.8	81.3	69.3	72.0
Venezuela	7349	10,559	13,910	4.4	3.2	66.7	77.7	63.0	66.4
Latin America[d]	208,179	275,470	348,440	3.2	2.6	49.6	66.2	59.5	61.4

Sources: Col. 1. For 1960, *Statistical Abstract of Latin America* 15 (1972). p. 38. Data for Argentina are for 1962. Data for Barbados, Jamaica, and Trinidad and Tobago (in total Latin America) are from Inter-American Development Bank, *Economic and Social Progress in Latin America* (Washington, D.C., 1975), p. 373. For 1970 and 1980, *Statistical Abstract of Latin America* 22 (1983), table 104, and 23 (1984), table 104.

Col. 2. Percentages shown are simple percent change over periods indicated.

Col. 3. Urban population is defined as that share of total population resident in cities and towns of 20,000 or more inhabitants. For 1960 and 1980, *Statistical Abstract of Latin America* 23 (1984), table 104.

Col. 4. *Statistical Abstract of Latin America* 23 (1984), table 104.

a. Data for 1977.
b. Data for 1980.
c. Data for 1975.
d. Latin America totals and averages include Barbados, Guyana, Jamaica, and Trinidad and Tobago.

APPENDIX B
SOCIAL CHANGE IN LATIN AMERICA, 1960–1980

	Literacy (% of population 15 and over)			Students Enrolled in Educational Institutions (% of those eligible in each age group)					
				6–11 years		12–17 years		18–23 years	
	1960	1970	1980	1960	1980	1960	1980	1960	1980
Argentina	91.4	92.6	93.7	91.2	99.9	48.1	72.7	13.2	36.7
Bolivia	36.0	40.0	63.2[c]	45.1	76.6	29.0	54.2	5.0	17.1
Brazil	60.6	66.4	70.3[e]	47.7	76.2	29.6	58.6	4.7	32.0
Chile	83.6	88.3	94.0[f]	76.4	100.0	54.7	86.5	7.2	22.2
Colombia	73.0	78.0	77.6	47.9	70.0	28.8	63.8	4.4	32.9
Costa Rica	84.4	88.4	89.8[e]	74.4	97.5	35.7	54.7	8.0	21.4
Cuba[a]	79.0	87.1	NA	77.7	100.0	43.0	83.4	6.6	29.9
Dominican Republic	64.5	66.9	NA	66.8	82.2	39.4	64.4	3.7	20.6
Ecuador	68.0	73.0	79.0	66.3	80.0	30.3	60.8	5.1	28.5
El Salvador	49.0	56.9	NA	48.7	69.2	40.3	58.1	8.5	18.9
Guatemala	38.0	46.2	NA	32.0	53.3	17.7	33.8	3.6	10.1
Haiti	20.0	24.0	23.0[b]	33.6	41.4	16.4	21.9	1.9	4.3
Honduras	63.0	57.0	40.5	49.5	71.3	24.6	44.7	3.2	14.8
Mexico	65.4	74.2	78.0	58.4	94.2	37.4	67.3	4.7	18.2

Nicaragua	49.6	57.9	NA	42.9	60.8	29.7	53.7	3.6	18.6
Panama	76.7	78.3	NA	68.3	95.7	50.3	83.2	12.7	43.3
Paraguay	74.6	80.2	80.5	69.7	80.0	44.8	51.9	5.8	13.3
Peru	61.1	72.8	79.7[e]	56.7	83.9	43.2	84.0	13.0	32.6
Uruguay	90.0	93.0	89.8	89.9	NA	53.2	67.2	14.1	24.3
Venezuela	65.2	75.9	82.0[d]	68.8	83.2	49.0	60.9	8.6	24.0
Latin America[g]	64.7	69.9	74.4	57.3	82.3	35.4	63.3	6.3	26.1

Sources: Literacy. For 1960 and 1970, *Statistical Abstract of Latin America* 19 (1980), table 1000. Literacy rates calculated by subtracting illiteracy rate from 100. For 1980, *Statistical Abstract of Latin America* 23 (1984), table 106.

Student enrollment. *Statistical Abstract of Latin America* 22 (1983), table 1001.

NA=Not Available

a. Literacy data for Cuba are from Carmelo Mesa-Lago, *The Economy of Socialist Cuba* (Albuquerque: University of New Mexico Press, 1981), p. 164 (based on 1970 population census).

b. Data for 1975.

c. Data for 1976.

d. Data for 1977.

e. Data for 1978.

f. Data for 1979.

g. For literacy rates, Latin America average is mean of the twenty countries above (for 1980, fourteen countries). For student enrollment data, Latin America average includes Barbados, Guyana, Jamaica, and Trinidad and Tobago.

Part I
The Political
Economy of
Contemporary
U.S.–Latin American
Relations

1

The United States, Latin America, and the World: The Changing International Context of U.S.–Latin American Relations

James R. Kurth

The Crisis of the System of 1945

The United States in the 1980s faces fundamental challenges to the pattern of U.S.–Latin American relations that has prevailed for almost half a century. The current armed conflicts in Central America portend either new revolutionary governments or prolonged U.S. involvement and commitment of military advisors and perhaps combat troops to the region. The debt burdens and financial crises of Mexico, Brazil, and Argentina portend major political changes in the largest countries of Latin America and major structural changes in the system of international banking. And the conjunction of these strategic and economic crises makes the challenges confronting U.S.–Latin American relations the gravest since the Great Depression and the international aggressions of the 1930s.

The relations between the United States and Latin America have always been shaped by the relations between the United States and the wider world, by the global international system. In some measure the reverse has also been true: patterns and practices first developed in U.S.–Latin American relations have often been recapitulated by U.S. policymakers in the international arena. But the interconnectedness and the isomorphism of the inter-American system and the international system have been especially pronounced since World War II.

Both in the macrosystem of U.S. relations with the world and in the microsystem of U.S. relations with Latin America, a new era began in 1945 with the United States' awesome victory in World War II. This essay will describe the basic structural features of that era, and it will argue that these features had largely come to an end by the 1970s. However, the central assumptions of U.S. policymakers about the world and about Latin America have remained largely unchanged. It is from this gap between old assumptions and new realities that many of our current problems arise.

Out of the ruins of World War II there emerged a new international system unlike any that had come before. Previous international systems had included several great powers, at least five and often more. Now, in 1945, there were only two, the United States and the Soviet Union. One, the United States, possessed more naval ships and combat aircraft than the rest of the world combined and also held a monopoly of the new nuclear weapons. The other, the Soviet Union, occupied most of the Eurasian land mass with the largest army in the world.

While the international military system was dominated by just two great powers, the international economic system was dominated by only one. The United States produced half the world's industrial goods, possessed most of the world's gold reserves, and held a monopoly of almost all the high technology of the day.

The international system of 1945, then, was historically unique. It was also by its nature historically ephemeral, but this was not clearly seen at the time nor indeed for many years thereafter. It is true that in 1945 some observers thought that Great Britain and France, with their vast colonial empires, would regain their military power and convert the bipolar international system once again into a multipolar one. But this never really happened, encouraging most observers to think that the new bipolar world was in fact the permanent one. In addition, some analysts knew that the United States would eventually lose its nuclear monopoly. This it did in 1949, when the Soviet Union exploded its own atomic bomb—rather earlier than most observers had expected. Later, other states would join the nuclear circle. But the vast bulk (more than 95 percent) of all nuclear weapons are held by the United States and the Soviet Union, once again appearing to confirm the bipolar system of military power.[1]

The eventual transformation of the system of 1945 would come through a quite different route than military power—that is, by the restoration and the diffusion of *industrial* power. The United States' old military enemies (Germany and Japan) first became its political allies by the 1950s and then became its economic adversaries by the 1970s. By the 1970s other countries, the "newly industrialized countries" such as Brazil, Mexico, and South Korea, also became major industrial competitors. But for twenty years after 1945 the United States' economic strengths in the world market went largely unchallenged.

How did Latin America fit into the new international system of 1945? First, the relations between the United States and Latin America before World War II had been something of a prototype for the relations between the United States and much of the wider world after 1945. As "the colossus of the North," the United States had dominated Latin America, much as the United States now loomed over western Europe, the Middle East, and East Asia. Then, as the bipolar conflict—the Cold War—with the Soviet Union sharpened, the United States found it vitally important to consolidate its "own back yard" in the Americas in order to maximize its capacity to lead from "positions of strength" in containing the Soviet Union on the Eurasian land mass.[2] The United States had earlier achieved this consolidation in Latin America on the eve of each of the two world wars with Germany, and it was natural for it to do so again as it confronted the new greatest military power in Europe—and this time in preparation for a conflict that would be sustained over many years. To that end the United States organized a series of major institutions and programs that dealt with a wide range of military, economic, and political relations with Latin America. Some of these institutions and programs, in turn, then became models for similar policies in other, more threatened regions. Thus the Inter-American Treaty of Reciprocal Assistance (the Rio Treaty, 1947) and the Organization of American States (OAS, 1948) were recapitulated in the Atlantic Alliance and the North Atlantic Treaty Organization (NATO, 1949).

Indeed, by the late 1940s U.S.–Latin American relations were institutionalized in a special kind of regional international system—one that has much in common with other systems of relations between great powers and several lesser states that have appeared in other times and other places. Traditional historians and political analysts have often described such systems as areas of hegemony or "spheres of influence." In addition to the United States in Latin America, other major examples of hegemonic systems since World War II have been the Soviet Union in eastern Europe, Great Britain in the Middle East until the 1950s and in the Persian Gulf sheikdoms until the early 1970s, and France in Subsaharan Africa. Relations between the United States and Latin America have had a good deal in common with these other systems of relations between states of unequal power and societies of unequal development. There have also been comparable hegemonic systems in the more remote past.[3] But in many ways, the hegemonic system composed by the United States in Latin America has been the most institutionalized and is thus almost an ideal type.

U.S.–Latin American Relations and Hegemonic International Systems

A hegemonic system is characterized by the following four features:

1. Military alliance: There is a formal military alliance between the great power and the several lesser states (for example, the Rio Treaty,

the Warsaw Treaty, the French agreements with several African states). Often military assistance or protection extends beyond mere alliance to include military weapons, military advisors, or military bases.

2. Economic dependency: The economic relations—trade, investments, economic assistance, or economic advisors—of most small states in the alliance system with the great power are much more intensive than economic relations with any other great power. Often, certain important economic ratios reach the level of 25 percent or more (for example, the small state's exports to the great power as a proportion of the small state's total exports; the great power's investment in the small state as a proportion of the small state's total investment or of its gross national product [GNP]; the great power's grants and loans to the small state as a proportion of the small state's total government budget).

3. Ideological commonality: The political elites of the great power hold a worldview or ideological perspective whose essential elements are also held by the political elites of the lesser states (for example, capitalism, communism, and so forth).

4. Foreign intervention: The great power has intervened—by military, advisory, or proxy means—in the policies of several lesser states in the alliance system. Often there is a general expectation among political elites and counterelites in the states comprising the system that there are certain diplomatic and political limits to a lesser state's behavior, the transgressing of which will provoke the great power to intervene in the offending state. One such transgression is the small state's imminent defection to a competing great power. A related transgression is the imminent displacement of a friendly regime within the small state by an unfriendly one, along with signs that the new regime will move internally toward ideological and institutional forms that are similar to those of a competing great power, thus increasing the probability of the small state's defection to that power. In some cases the great power uses an international organization to legitimize its intervention (for example, the OAS for Guatemala in 1954 and the Dominican Republic in 1965, the Warsaw Treaty Organization for Czechoslovakia in 1968).[4]

The U.S. hegemonic system in Latin America had its origins in the Spanish-American War, but it did not reach its full development and institutionalization in each of these four features until World War II and the Cold War.

Like other great powers in their hegemonic systems (such as the Soviet Union in eastern Europe), the United States in Latin America has been propelled by a strategic logic (although like other great powers, not by that logic alone). The threat of Germany in the 1910s and the 1930s and the threat of the Soviet Union since the 1940s have periodically energized and justified U.S. hegemony in the area.

Of course, the strategic logic has been especially applicable to Central America and the Caribbean. The proximity of this region to the United States and the small size of these countries would have made the region a natural sphere of influence, no matter what the particular economic, ideological, or political character of the "colossus of the North." If somehow either the British, the French, the Germans, or the Russians had established a unified nation on the southern portion of the North American continent by the end of the nineteenth century, they too would have composed a hegemonic system over the states of Central America and the Caribbean and perhaps over Latin America more generally. Indeed, given the style of imperial rule of the time and the actual practice of the British and the French in the Caribbean Basin, the system would probably have been a colonial rather than a hegemonic one.

The strategic logic of hegemony soon worked its way into a political logic. In the first half of the twentieth century, Latin American countries were, of course, exporters of primary commodities. Industrialization had only begun in the region. In other regions of the world with a similar socioeconomic system (such as eastern Europe and the Middle East), the most common political system at the time was traditional monarchy.[5] On the basis of its socioeconomic pattern alone, the natural political system for Latin America might have been the same. But in Latin America the political formula of traditional monarchy had been made wholly impossible both by the role model of the republican United States and by the revolutions of the nineteenth century—first the Latin American wars of independence, then the revolution against the Brazilian monarchy in 1889, and finally the Cuban war of independence culminating in 1898. Accordingly, the political formula chosen by Latin American countries had to be that of a presidential republic. However, given the socioeconomic structure of the region—in other words, its low level of industrialization and its high concentration of land ownership—the political reality had to be something other than a presidential republic as it appeared in the United States (or would later appear in France and several other European states). Within the political form of the presidential republic was the political reality that was most like traditional monarchy—that is, personalistic dictatorship. But the very lack of dynastic legitimacy in Latin America had to be compensated for in some countries by enhanced brutality. Thus it was that by the 1930s the most liberal and democratic of hegemonic powers (the United States) had come to support some of the most brutal and repressive of client regimes (for example, the Dominican Republic, Nicaragua, Guatemala, El Salvador).

Still, personalistic dictatorship had a certain congruence with the socioeconomic structure of most of Latin America until World War II (with the exceptions of Mexico, which had undergone a true social revolution in

1910–1917, and the countries of the Southern Cone, which were the most industrialized countries in the region). When that congruence on occasion broke down, U.S. intervention usually reestablished it—especially in Central America and the Caribbean. Thus conditions of international and internal stability generally prevailed, and U.S. investors found an attractive area for their capital. The political logic of hegemony thus worked its way into an economic logic and an ideological logic of U.S.-supported economic growth in a capitalist framework. By the time of World War II and the Cold War, the U.S. hegemonic system in Latin America was fully developed and institutionalized in its four dimensions.

However, the economic logic of U.S. hegemony continued to unfold. The flow of U.S. investment and access to U.S. markets led to economic development, which in turn produced new social classes and new political strains, conflicts, and crises. In the three decades after World War II, the United States was confronted with the overthrow of several of its client dictatorships (Ubico in Guatemala in 1944, culminating in the crisis of 1954; Batista in Cuba in 1959; Trujillo in the Dominican Republic, culminating in the crisis of 1965; and Somoza in Nicaragua in 1979). These events occurred during roughly the same period and at the same rate that Great Britain confronted the overthrow of its client regimes in the Middle East and the Soviet Union confronted the overthrow of its client regimes in eastern Europe.[6]

The most natural new political formula for some of these countries that overthrew their personalistic dictatorships would have been some form of national-populist military regime. This kind of regime had appeared earlier in Argentina and Brazil and in Guatemala under Arbenz, and similar regimes were then emerging in the Middle East. The political *telos* of these countries, and more generally of other Latin American countries in the early or import-substituting phase of industrialization, was perhaps something like Peronism.[7] But the politics of national-populism in an economy dominated by U.S. direct foreign investment meant a direct political conflict with the United States.

Unlike Great Britain when it confronted nationalism and populism in the Middle East, but like the Soviet Union in eastern Europe, the United States was at times powerful enough, proximate enough, and determined enough to do something about this challenge. The intervention of the Central Intelligence Agency (CIA) in Guatemala in 1954, the military intervention in the Dominican Republic in 1965, and the support of the military coup in Chile in 1973 were all responses to perceived threats to U.S. interests.

In contrast, the botched CIA intervention in Cuba in the early 1960s solidified that country in its authoritarian communism and its alliance with the Soviet Union. That pattern may have been recapitulated in

Nicaragua in the early 1980s. These countries provide a warning about one way in which the U.S. hegemonic system in Latin America could come to an end.

Four Conventional Assumptions of U.S. Foreign Policy

By World War II, the United States' experience in Latin America from the 1900s to the 1930s had already predisposed U.S. policymakers to see international relations in terms of U.S. leadership of a large ensemble of lesser states. The destruction and the defeats brought by that war had the effect of temporarily reducing much of the rest of the world to the level of Latin America. United States policymakers turned easily toward plans and efforts to reshape the wider world as they had reshaped Latin America for the previous two generations.

The 1940s made up the heroic age of U.S. foreign policy, the privileged moment of the United States in world history. The ideas and institutions formed by U.S. policies at that time would have a compelling power (perhaps even a hypnotic quality) in the United States for years to come, long after the material conditions that had generated these ideas and institutions had disappeared. Thus President Reagan in his 1983 address to Congress on the Central American crisis took as his guide President Truman's 1947 address to Congress on the crisis in Greece and Turkey, in which the Truman Doctrine was articulated. Similarly, when the late Senator Henry Jackson sought to solve the Central American crisis in 1983, he called for a new Marshall Plan for the region.

The perceptions and ideas of the 1940s were crystalized into a particular way of looking at the world and the United States' place in it. This worldview contained certain assumptions regarding major dimensions—strategic, economic, ideological, and political—of international affairs. These four assumptions were: (1) the strategic assumption of bipolarity, which held that the world was essentially divided into two opposing alliance systems—that of the United States and that of the Soviet Union; (2) the economic assumption of U.S. enterprise, which held that the principal motor of economic growth in the world was U.S. investment and U.S. markets; (3) the ideological assumption of bipolarity, which held that there were only two significant worldviews in world politics—liberalism (and capitalism) versus totalitarianism (communism); and (4) the political assumption of military regimes, which held that authoritarian military governments were stable and loyal allies of the United States.[8]

These assumptions together formed a set that was coherent, consistent, and comprehensive, and from the mid-1940s to the mid-1960s they more or less corresponded to the conditions of the real world. However,

an opening to China and a policy of détente with the Soviet Union. The neoconservatives of the 1980s often forget that the Republican administrations of the 1970s were the most enthusiastic promoters of U.S.-Soviet détente. Indeed, this is apparently often forgotten by Nixon and Kissinger themselves.

The Conflict Between Old Assumptions and New Realities

In fact, from the mid-1960s to the mid-1970s, each of the four conventional U.S. foreign policy assumptions had become more and more remote from the real world. The strategic assumption of bipolarity and tight alliances confronted the strategic reality of multipolarity and shifting coalitions. The Sino–Soviet conflict (and the earlier Yugoslav–Soviet conflict) demonstrated that communist countries could be anti-Soviet and, indeed, that one of the best instruments with which to contain the Soviet Union was another communist country. The defections of Indonesia, Egypt, and Somalia from the Soviet sphere to that of the United States demonstrated that heavy Soviet influence in a country could be undone and reversed with dramatic suddenness, so long as Soviet troops were not present to protect and preserve that influence. Only in Latin America, where Cuba remained a loyal Soviet ally, did there seem to be no gap between assumption and reality. On the other side of the bipolar assumption, France's independent foreign policy and Ethiopia's defection from the United States to the Soviet Union constituted parallel examples. The overall result was a multipolar balance of power composed of shifting coalitions of states.

The economic assumption of the primacy of U.S. enterprise confronted the economic reality of multipolarity among major industrialized countries. First European and then Japanese investment became a major presence in Latin American economies. Then European and Japanese enterprises became formidable competitors of U.S. enterprises in both Latin American and U.S. markets. More recently, Latin American industrial products (especially from Mexico and Brazil) have begun to compete effectively in the world market, even in the U.S. market. Together these developments marked the emergence of a truly multipolar international economy, in which U.S. investment and U.S. markets played a role of "first among equals."[9]

The ideological assumption of bipolarity between capitalism and communism confronted in many countries the ideological reality of a "third way." In western Europe, this third way was a renewed, strong Social Democratic party (Federal Republic of Germany) or democratic Socialist party (France). In Latin America, similar social-democratic movements received popular support in those few countries in which free elections were permitted (for example, Venezuela and Costa Rica).

In several other Latin American countries, the new moral power was actually the oldest moral power of all, the Roman Catholic church. In its pilgrimage from Vatican II in 1962 through Medellín in 1968 to Puebla in 1979, the Catholic church burst out of and transcended the old bifurcation between capitalism and communism. Guided by their "theology of liberation" and engaged in progressive political action, many Catholics condemned both capitalism and communism as partial solutions and insisted on the best of both—personal freedom *and* social justice (for example, Brazil, Chile, Nicaragua, and El Salvador).[10]

The last of the conventional assumptions to be challenged by new realities was the political assumption of military regimes. But in the mid-1970s, several of these regimes in Central America (in particular in Nicaragua, El Salvador, and Guatemala) demonstrated their growing incapacity to deal effectively with social change and the resulting political conflicts. Indeed, by their very efforts to maintain old systems of economic exploitation and political repression against the force of new social conditions and new social groups, these military regimes actually promoted instability rather than prevented it.[11]

Perhaps most fundamentally, the new economic reality (which reflected a massive change in the structure of the world economy) also spilled over into the new strategic reality, where it eroded the old structure of international politics. By the late 1960s the U.S. economy was no longer able to sustain previous levels of high military spending (about 10 percent of gross national product), including the squandering of resources in military interventions such as that in Vietnam.

In the 1940s and the 1950s, the United States had been extraordinarily competitive in the world market. The United States could sell virtually anything it produced. This situation was in part the result of World War II, which had destroyed most of the United States' industrial competitors. But it was also partly due to a U.S. monopoly of high-technology industries and to U.S. productivity in lower-technology activities. The United States had a handsome surplus in its international balance of trade, and this surplus could in turn finance large-scale expenditures on military forces deployed overseas with U.S. allies (such as in the Federal Republic of Germany and Japan) and on foreign wars (such as in Korea and Vietnam). A productive, competitive, high-employment economy also provided a healthy base for federal taxes and federal spending. In such a happy condition, the United States could maintain a vast system of military alliances and the potential for military intervention—and spend 10 percent of its GNP on defense.

However, the U.S.-protected conditions of peace and prosperity among the United States' West European and Japanese allies led first to the rebuilding of their old industries (textiles, steel, shipbuilding, chemicals), and then to the development of new ones (automobiles, electronics). These new or renewed industries had "advantages of backwardness" in their production processes—that is, lower wages and higher technology than their U.S. counterparts. In the 1960s this led to the successive erosion of U.S. competitiveness in the world market in textiles, steel, shipbuilding, automobiles, and finally even electronics.[12] Both quantitative and qualitative U.S. superiority in these industries had been the basis for the United States' victory in World War II.

Had the United States' West European and Japanese allies built up there own militaries at the rate that they developed their industries, some current U.S. defense and industrial problems would have been solved (or indeed might never have arisen). But the allies did not. Indeed, by the 1970s there developed a rough inverse correlation between military spending as a percentage of GNP and industrial competitiveness in the world market. A continuum went from high military spending and low market competitiveness to low military spending and high market competitiveness, in a sequence composed of the United States, Great Britain, France, the Federal Republic of Germany, and Japan. But this difference in the pattern of military spending between the United States and its allies was not the only, or even the major, reason for declining U.S. competitiveness. Many other factors were also at work, including the allies' advantages of backwardness such as lower wages and newer production technologies.[13]

By the 1970s, then, the United States' military allies in world politics had become its industrial adversaries in the world market. The allies were undercutting the economic base of the United States' military defense of them. And with the consequent rise of protectionist pressures in the United States, the allies were also undercutting the political base of U.S. alliances with them. The economic and political bases of U.S. military commitments abroad were being eroded by the relentless workings of the world market.[14]

By the mid-1970s newly industrializing countries such as Brazil, Mexico, South Korea, and Taiwan joined these other industrial competitors. The newly industrializing countries were even better able to exploit the advantages of backwardness and to out-compete the United States in major industrial markets. Because of these industrial advantages, newly industrializing countries (especially Brazil and Mexico) appeared to offer excellent prospects for massive loans when international commercial banks were awash with petrodollar deposits in the late 1970s. And so by the early 1980s, these countries' rapidly increasing debt burdens made it even more essential for them to capture export markets in the world economy—and particularly in the United States—in order to generate foreign exchange earnings.

The diffusion of industrial power to major Latin American countries meant a great expansion in U.S. economic interests in the region. United-States-owned multinational firms and international banks had a broader and deeper interest in Latin America than ever before. But a further consequence of this development was a substantial increase in the threat of Latin American competition to industrial products manufactured in the United States. United States industrial labor and taxpayers now have a greater hostility than ever to Latin American access to U.S. markets and U.S. government guarantees for international bank loans to the region. As U.S. economic interests in Latin America have expanded, the domestic political coalition to support those economic interests—and to support economic internationalism more generally—has weakened.

In the late 1970s some U.S. policymakers recognized a number of these historic shifts in the structure of the international system and attempted to compose foreign policies based on the new realities, particularly with regard to policies toward Latin America.

Like Roosevelt with Mexico, the Carter administration recognized in the Panama Canal issue the value of a satisfied Panama still nestled within a wider U.S. strategic and economic framework, and thus it brought about the new Panama Canal treaties of 1978. Like Truman with the Bolivan revolution, the Carter administration also recognized that the Nicaraguan revolution did not need to become a long-term threat to the United States, and it reached an accommodation with the Sandinistas in 1979. Like Kennedy with the Alliance for Progress, the Carter administration recognized the inherent instability—the "pyrrhic victory"—of military regimes from the viewpoint and the values of the United States, and it suspended military and economic assistance to the most brutal Latin American torture-states. And as an integrating principle for the new foreign policy, U.S. policymakers articulated the standards of human rights. The human rights policy allowed the United States to reach out to the growing professional middle class in Latin America, a class that was often the victim of military regimes' torture and terror (as in Argentina, Chile, and Uruguay).

These policies together constituted the most extensive reform ever of the U.S. hegemonic system in Latin America. Indeed, it could be argued that with the conjunction of new Latin American realities and new U.S. policies, the U.S. hegemonic system had reached its end and had been transformed into a new inter-American system whose central tendency was coequality.

But as had often happened before, the macrocosm of global events, filtered through U.S. congressional and electoral politics, overwhelmed the microcosm of Latin American policy. The establishment of formal diplomatic relations with China in 1978 and the conclusion of the strategic arms limitation negotiations (SALT II) with the Soviet Union in 1979 were both salutary recognitions of new strategic realities. But these initiatives expended virtually all of the political capital in Congress for dealing with communist states, probably made it impossible to undertake a diplomatic opening toward Cuba, and indeed probably contributed to the reckless rhetoric in September 1979 concerning the dangers of a Soviet army brigade in Cuba. More fatal events were the revolution against the shah of Iran and the taking of the U.S. embassy hostages, the Soviet invasion of Afghanistan, and the related shocks to an already troubled U.S. economy. Together these developments provided the opportunity for the 1980 electoral successes of conventional conservatives, and these electoral victories brought in their train the restoration of all the old foreign policy assumptions in their purest form.

Yet most of these events should have confirmed that the old assumptions no longer fit real conditions. In particular, the revolution against the shah illustrated how erroneous it can be to assume the stability of military regimes, and the taking of the embassy hostages underlined the disasters that ensue when the United States becomes identified with a torture-state.

Alternative Assumptions for U.S. Foreign Policy: A New Realism

A different set of assumptions would comport better with the new real world. The new strategic, economic, ideological, and political assumptions might resemble the following:

1. A strategic assumption of multipolarity: The United States would continue to contain the Soviet Union's *military* expansion, but it would do so as the "majority leader" of shifting coalitions of states. Most of these states will be the familiar U.S. allies. But some might be Marxist or even communist states that are willing to pursue cooperative relations with the United States (following, for example, the models of Yugoslavia, China, and Rumania).

The history of the past twenty years shows that when Soviet influence in a country is based on military aid, economic assistance, ideological affinity, political clients, or even all of these elements combined, it is still reversible—and indeed often has been reversed (China, Indonesia, Egypt, Somalia). It is only when Soviet influence is based on military protection against the United States (Cuba, Vietnam) that it becomes irreversible. Thus the United States should continue to contain the military expansion of the Soviet Union, including deterring the placement of

Soviet military bases in other countries. But in carrying out this venerable policy of containing Soviet military expansion, the United States could at times find Marxist or even communist countries to be very effective allies, and allies that are less costly than unstable "conservative" military regimes that in fact are capable of conserving nothing at all.

In Latin America, however, several generations of Marxists have come to perceive the United States as their central and consistent opponent. Conversely, for them the Soviet Union is far away and hardly appears to pose a threat. Thus in this region it may be too much to expect Marxist movements that might come to power to be allies of the United States. However, they would constitute a threat to U.S. strategic interests only if their fears of U.S. intervention drove them into a long-term alliance with the Soviet Union and the acceptance of Soviet military bases.

2. An economic assumption of multipolarity: The United States would continue extensive trade and investment ties with Latin America, but it would do so as "first among equals" in a system of many industrialized and newly industrializing countries.

The multipolar industrial system can contribute enormously to the principal U.S. interest in the containment of the Soviet Union. The old assumption of U.S. enterprise inevitably meant that from time to time there would be economic conflicts between a Latin American government and U.S. corporations, conflicts that would quickly escalate into conflicts between that government and the U.S. government. The U.S. government felt compelled to defend the interests of these corporations and thus to oppose particular policies of Latin American governments, such as nationalization of important enterprises. This happened in Guatemala and Cuba in the 1950s; Brazil, Peru, and Bolivia in the 1960s; and Chile in the 1970s. Sometimes this conflict was even mandated by congressional legislation; for example, the Hickenlooper Amendment directed the U.S. government to cut off economic assistance to countries that expropriated U.S. investments without sufficient compensation. And at times these conflicts drove the Latin American government in question to seek the protection of what was until recently the only other great power around, the Soviet Union, as with Guatemala in 1953–1954 and Cuba in 1959–1960.

However, in the new multipolar industrial system, such conflicts between Latin American governments and U.S. corporations will arise less often, or at least they will be buffered by similar conflicts with western European or Japanese (or even Brazilian) corporations. And in the cases where the dispute escalates to a conflict with the U.S. government, the Latin American government in question will find it in its interest to seek aid not from the Soviet Union but from some other western industrialized country, as Nicaragua did from France in the early 1980s. For example, a possible revolutionary regime in El Salvador or Guatemala could turn for assistance to France, the Federal Republic of Germany, Spain, or perhaps even Mexico.

3. An ideological assumption of multipolarity: The United States would follow the leads of contemporary social democracy and contemporary Catholicism (which have positioned themselves as moral forces between capitalism and communism) in Latin America.

In most Latin American countries, Catholicism is now the more relevant of these two forces. Contemporary Catholicism is the worldview that has the greatest likelihood of meeting the material and moral needs of large numbers of Latin Americans without being opposed to the basic interests of the United States. Capitalism and communism each offer partial, divisive, and therefore unstable solutions to the problems of Latin American societies because each exalts some classes to the destitution or the destruction of others. Catholicism can speak to people in each and every class, and it seeks to call the social parts into a social whole.

Contemporary progressive Catholicism also asserts the primacy of labor over capital (for example, Pope John Paul II's 1981 encyclical, *On Human Work*). This focus may lead to a variety of conflicts between Catholic-inspired governments and U.S. corporations. But this Catholicism, like that of earlier generations, will never become an ally of the Soviet Union.

4. A political assumption that, in general and in the future, the best U.S. allies in Latin America will be centrist-party regimes (in the more industrialized countries) or national-populist regimes (in the less industrialized countries), rather than conservative military ones.

At first glance the military governments in the Southern Cone of South America (which political scientists refer to as "bureaucratic-authoritarian" regimes) appear to have been very stable indeed. They held power in Brazil from 1964 to 1985, in Chile since 1973, in Uruguay from 1973 to 1985, and in Argentina from 1976 to 1983. However, many factors are combining to present a rather different picture for the future. For example, military regimes in these countries have faced economic crises as deep as those that helped bring about the military coups that earlier overturned civilian regimes. The stagflation of the advanced industrial world in the 1970s became the deep economic recession—indeed, the depression—of the early 1980s. And the impact of depression in the advanced industrial countries is amplified in the newly industrializing or underdeveloped ones.

In the Great Depression of the 1930s, most Latin American regimes were thrown out of power, and successor regimes often adopted radically different policies. There is every reason to believe that the unfolding world economic crisis (brought about in part by the United States' economic policies in the early 1980s) eventually will have brought down most of the military regimes in Latin America. If these regimes have been identified with the United States (and the United States with them), their successors are likely to be, at least for a time, hostile to the United States.

It would be far wiser for the United States to work for the establishment of centrist-party regimes in the more industrialized Latin American countries, where the social conditions for such governments probably exist (Argentina, Chile, Uruguay, and Brazil). It would also be wiser to work for the establishment of populist regimes in the region's less-developed countries (much of Central America). These centrist-party or populist regimes' support for a more equitable distribution of political power and economic goods would be more capable of establishing enduring stability than existing repressive and regressive military regimes.

One model for Latin America in the 1980s might well be Latin Europe in the 1970s, particularly Spain and Portugal. Authoritarian regimes in these countries were followed by center-right democratic governments (in Spain directly, in Portugal after a few years). But the Franco and Sálazar-Caetano regimes in their last decade or so were no longer torture and terror systems. It is rare for an authoritarian regime to give up power peaceably, as happened in Spain and to a degree in Portugal. It is especially difficult for a torture-system to give up power without great violence and chaos, because the members of the regime know that they will be the first targets of revenge. Political transitions are inevitable, but torture-systems make a smooth transition almost impossible. At a minimum the United States would be wise to once again pressure Latin American military regimes to eliminate torture and terror, to move from being like Franco in 1950 to being like Franco in 1970.

Together, these four new assumptions—strategic, economic, ideological, and political—recognize that today and in the years to come the United States will not be the only source of strength in support of basic U.S. national interests. Now there are many such sources: other capable states interested in containing Soviet military expansion, other industrialized economies interested in participating in Latin American economic development, other moral forces interested in opposing totalitarianism, and, as a result of these, other potential political leaderships in Latin America capable of cooperation with the United States. The ultimate meaning and the real legacy of the four old assumptions has been to bring into being a new world that can do on its own what only the United States could do before.

U.S.–Latin American Relations in the 1980s

What will be the actual course of U.S.–Latin American relations in the late 1980s? A review of hegemonies in other times and other places suggests a number of different possible paths, rather than a simple and inevitable recapitulation of the past history of U.S. hegemony in the region. These different paths might be termed reassertion, dissolution, devolution, and transformation.

1. Hegemonic reassertion: The first path could be the reassertion of U.S. hegemony in Latin America, including a systematic and sustained effort to use U.S. military advisors and perhaps combat troops to contain and suppress revolutionary movements in El Salvador, Guatemala, and possibly elsewhere. Here the closest comparison would be to the Soviet Union in eastern Europe. The likely costs and consequences of this path for both the United States and Latin America are well known and would be severe.

2. Hegemonic dissolution: A second path could be a dissolution of U.S. hegemony, a disengagement of U.S. power from local political conflicts, perhaps undertaken by a Republican administration whose credentials and reputation would otherwise be impeccably conservative. This path would be comparable to de Gaulle's withdrawal from Algeria in 1962. It also would have some similarities to Eisenhower's withdrawal of support from the French in Tonkin in 1954 and from Batista in Cuba in 1958, and to Nixon's withdrawal from Indochina in 1973. Unfortunately, the actual events that followed these earlier U.S. disengagements do not inspire confidence in the effectiveness of dissolution.

3. Hegemonic devolution: A third path could be a devolution of U.S. hegemony to other countries in the region capable of establishing their own miniature hegemonies. In war-torn Central America this might mean Mexico and Venezuela, which have grown into substantial if problem-ridden economic powers. This path would be comparable to the devolution of British hegemony (and of U.S. influence) in the Persian Gulf to Iran and Saudi Arabia in the early 1970s. The fate of these particular "twin pillars" (as they were called by Henry Kissinger) or "regional influentials" (as they were called by Zbigniew Brzezinski) does not in itself inspire confidence in devolution as a solution. Nor does the current troubled condition of Mexico and Venezuela inspire confidence in their capacity to play this role.

4. Hegemonic transformation: The path that would best conform to the new U.S. foreign policy assumptions outlined above would blend both the second and third paths and go beyond them. It would, like devolution, recognize the strengths of other countries in the Americas in helping to bring about an inter-American order characterized by both mutual

security and social justice. It would also recognize that what on occasion appears to be a case of dissolution need not in fact be a case of defeat. Rather, it can be merely a moment at the extreme end of a swing, a station on the way to renewed equilibrium—one now shaped and ordered by many states that are both industrial democracies and strategic allies of the United States. In particular, hegemonic transformation would remove two features of hegemony (ideological commonality and foreign intervention) while retaining the essence of the other two, the prohibition of a Soviet military presence and the continuation of extensive economic ties. A prototype would be U.S. relations with Mexico since the 1930s.

The actual path that the United States takes in Latin America in the 1980s will be primarily a function of political and economic logics within the hegemonic power itself. This path will be the result of conflicts and coalitions among major economic interests, bureaucratic organizations, and social groups in U.S. society. Two major coalitions will be discussed here, one now favoring a reassertion of U.S. hegemony in Latin America and another potentially in favor of a diminution or transformation of U.S. hegemony in the region.

The Hegemonic Coalition

The cluster or coalition of interests and organization supporting a reassertion of U.S. hegemony—in particular, intervention in Central America—is composed of three major elements. These are: (1) industries that have direct investments in Central America, a rather small group; (2) industries that are no longer competitive in the wider world market, a very large group indeed; and (3) a mass base that subscribes to conventional definitions of patriotism and anticommunism.

Industries that have direct investments in Central America have an obvious interest in preventing revolutionary regimes in the region. Even noncommunist revolutionary regimes may give rise to instability and unpredictability, especially regarding the labor force's working conditions and wages in these industries' factories and plantations. The firms by themselves would not be a significant political force. However, they can be joined by the more numerous and more substantial firms with large direct investments in South America and Mexico, which may come to fear a domino effect from revolutions in Central America.

The more interesting group is composed of industries that are no longer competitive in the world market. They have an interest in somehow creating in Latin American markets de facto preferences for their goods over the goods of European, Japanese, or even Brazilian and Mexican competitors, a kind of "imperial preference" system. In the British colonial system, colonial administrators gave de facto preference to British goods by utilizing a network of government purchases and regulations, even though until 1932 the empire de jure was supposedly governed by free trade and an absence of trade barriers. Similarly, in the U.S. hegemonic system in Latin America, an authoritarian military regime with long-established ties to U.S. government agencies and the local American Chamber of Commerce is far more likely to give preference to U.S. goods than would a populist or revolutionary government. The interest of U.S. industries in a system of de facto preferences will almost certainly grow in the next several years as these industries face more intense competition in a stagnant or depressed world market.

The southern states of the United States assume a special place in the hegemonic coalition. The South is the region nearest to Latin America, and for this reason alone it would be most sensitive to events there. In addition, some of the uncompetitive industries mentioned previously (most notably the textile industry) are located in the southeastern states. Moreover, the South was long the region that was most labor intensive in both its agricultural and industrial production and that has been most hostile to labor organizations and to ideas that sound like Marxism (or, for that matter, Catholicism).

It is natural, then, that in Congress the major opponents of the Panama Canal treaties in 1978, the principal backers of Somoza to the end in 1979, and the primary supporters of increased U.S. military intervention in El Salvador since 1980 have been southern senators and congressmen. When President Carter undertook his 1980 reelection campaign, he was forced to recognize this massive political reality. This largely explains his shift toward more anti-Marxist policies in 1980 and his inability to allow El Salvador to go the way of Nicaragua. Any presidential candidate in the 1980s, Democratic or Republican, will face this same reality. The "new South" is a two-party South, and it is now the largest electoral swing-bloc in the nation. Thus presidential candidates in the 1980s will be under heavy and continuous pressure to be anticommunist in general and anticommunist in Central America and the Caribbean in particular.

The Potential for a Nonintervention Coalition

At present there is no cluster or coalition of interests and organizations that is both opposed to the various modes of intervention—military, advisory, and proxy—and comparable in strength and persistence to the hegemonic coalition. However, it is possible to envision some potential members of such a coalition whose wider interests may lead them to oppose U.S. intervention in Latin American countries and, thus in effect, to support some form of hegemonic dissolution or devolution.

One economic group worth considering here is made up of the major international commercial banks. Of course, banks do not look forward to populist or revolutionary regimes in Latin America. But the nature of banks' economic interests (for example, loans or indirect investments in preference to direct investments) makes them less exposed to nationalization than the multinational firms in the hegemonic coalition. International banks are also sensitive to sharp increases in the dollar's inflation rate and U.S. budget deficits, and they would prefer not to have additional major increases in U.S. military spending produced by a new military intervention. Finally, and most important, international banks are sensitive to the positions and reactions of the governments of West European states and the largest newly industrializing countries, such as Mexico and Brazil. Systematic and sustained opposition to U.S. intervention in Central America by countries such as the Federal Republic of Germany, France, and Mexico could well be translated into a degree of opposition by the international banks.

Mexico's reaction could also be an especially important consideration to the large U.S. multinational corporations with major direct investments in that country. These firms will not want to see their investments become the target of repeated anti-U.S. demonstrations by Mexican groups protesting Yankee intervention "in their own back yard."

It is interesting to note that the relatively accepting or passive attitudes of major U.S. businessmen at the time of the Cuban and Nicaraguan revolutions played a significant role in the success of these revolutionary movements. In both Cuba by 1958 and Nicaragua by 1978, most members of the local business class had withdrawn their support from the dictatorial regime, making it reasonable for U.S. businessmen and U.S. officials to withdraw their support, too. In both Cuba and Nicaragua the revolutionary leadership seemed at the time more populist than communist. In each case, this conjunction of populist movement with local business support temporarily gave rise to hopes among U.S. policymakers for a viable third way between a personalistic dictatorship (which no longer fit a new social structure) and a revolutionary communist regime—which might fit this new social structure so well that it could do without U.S. investments and U.S. influence. This is one major reason that the United States did not intervene to prevent the revolutionary movements from taking power.

But in Cuba, in the end, the political conflict over U.S. direct investment followed its logic and destroyed the option of a postrevolutionary populist regime. Moreover, the very fate of the Cuban revolution tended to deter the business class in other Latin American countries from pursuing such populist adventures in later years. The fate of the Nicaraguan revolution may do the same, as it seems to have in El Salvador and Guatemala. If so, the path that leads away from hegemonic intervention directly to hegemonic dissolution is likely to remain unattractive to U.S. businessmen for some time to come.

However, the path of hegemonic devolution could be an attractive alternative for some U.S. businessmen, especially the international banks and multinational firms discussed above. Given their strong presence and (on occasion) influence in Mexico, Venezuela, and Brazil, they could find the shift from U.S. government intervention to more active involvement by the Mexican, Venezuelan, or Brazilian governments to be a feasible and manageable change, and one in which they could continue to preserve their interests.

The Roman Catholic church in the United States could constitute another major member of this coalition by providing a mass base for nonintervention. The recent statements and activities by the U.S. National Conference of Catholic Bishops concerning El Salvador are a prefiguration of what could be. In addition, since 1981 the opposition in Congress to U.S. military aid to military regimes in Central America has come primarily from senators and congressmen from northeastern states with large Catholic populations (especially Massachusetts, Connecticut, Pennsylvania, and Maryland). Of course, in these states opposition to such military aid is grounded in a broad coalition of different groups (such as liberal professionals, labor unions, and poor people) that includes non-Catholics as well as Catholics. Nevertheless, the Catholic church may give this opposition a coherence, continuity, and weight that it might not otherwise have. Finally, because it is part of an international institution—one even more universal than international banks and multinational firms—the Catholic church in the United States has its own contacts in countries such as Mexico, Venezuela, and Brazil. Thus U.S. Catholics could also find the path of hegemonic devolution to be especially attractive.

Hegemonic Transformation and Industrial Transformation

In the longer run, the transformation of U.S. hegemony in Latin America into a more advanced inter-American relationship will probably depend on the transformation of the U.S. economy into a more advanced industrial structure. This would provide the basis for a more prosperous and less threatened U.S. economy, which would be both more open to Latin American manufactured exports and more capable of sustained lending to Latin American countries. With a more advanced industrial structure (one centered on high-technology industries and services), the United States would become again a successful exporter in the world market and a generator of balance-of-trade surpluses. Latin American exporters then could become efficient suppliers of the more traditional industrial products (for example, textiles, steel, and even automobiles) to the U.S. market. A more advanced U.S. industrial structure would also be a successful innovator of high-technology weapons systems (such as precision-guided munitions), which would provide the basis for a more effective and more confident—and therefore less frantic—containment of Soviet military expansion. Furthermore, a more advanced U.S. industrial structure, with its attendent economic growth and optimistic national mood, would provide the basis for a more generous spririt in U.S. domestic politics and for more sustained support for human rights in Latin America.

It is not inevitable that a once-leading industrial power lose its competitive edge in the world market to new industrial powers (which have the advantages of newer plants and newer production methods) and sink into industrial decline. This did happen to Great Britain in the late nineteenth century in relation to Germany and the United States, and then from the 1950s to the 1970s in relation to virtually all of western Europe.[15]

However, another industrial path is possible, one that was followed by Germany and by the United States itself in earlier times. In the late nineteenth century, Germany and the United States did not merely equal and then overtake Great Britain in the production of the leading British industries (steel, railroad equipment, and shipbuilding). They went even further and developed entire new industrial sectors, such as the chemical and electrical industries at the end of the nineteenth century and the automobile and aviation industries in the early twentieth century. In these new industries, Germany and the United States have remained consistently ahead of Great Britain down to the present day.

More than any other country, the United States has a long history of successive and successful industrial transformations, of moving out of old industries and into new ones (as Japan has been doing in the last decade). New industrial sectors could provide the United States with a renewed industrial base and a renewed competitive lead in the world market. This renewed competitive lead would reduce the pressures in the United States for protective tariff barriers against less-advanced industrialized and industrializing countries—especially Mexico and Brazil, but also Latin America more generally. For example, it is much more likely that the duty-free trade provisions of the recent Caribbean Basin Initiative would have been accepted by the Congress in such an environment.

The new industrial sectors in the U.S. economy would probably include semiconductors, computers, telecommunications, and robotics in the 1980s, and biotechnology, lasers, and "space industrialization" in later years.[16] Although the United States will face stiff competition from Japan in some of these sectors, it has considerable comparative advantages in them. These competitive assets include: the massive U.S. defense budget, which can provide a base for research, development, and initial orders for large-scale production; the largest complex of scientific research institutions in the world; and the largest and most flexible capital market in the world, which can channel investment to the new industries.

There could also be new high-technology niches in older industries, such as steel industry "minimills" that have higher productivity than large integrated steel mills, numerically controlled machine tools, special chemicals, and certain advanced automobile components. These niches could provide a place for many workers in older industries who are now in danger of displacement and unemployment.

Conversely, the United States could then readily absorb imports of manufactured products from Mexico, Brazil, and other Latin American countries, such as basic steel and many major automobile components. New industrial sectors and a renewed competitive lead in the world market could also provide the economic and political bases for renewed lending by the United States to Latin America.

Much of this industrial transformation could come about through the normal operation of the market by itself. But it could either be facilitated or impeded by U.S. government policies. What political coalitions are likely to cluster around the policy issues of industrial transformation?

The economic interests most in favor of policies favoring industrial transformation are, of course, firms and employees in the new industries themselves. But by definition, these are new and therefore relatively small in number compared with those in older industries.

Government policies facilitating industrial transformation would not be attractive initially to some other groups, some of which were identified earlier as members of a potential nonintervention coalition. In general, international banks and multinational firms are wary of industrial policy (that is, government policies directed at selected industries). They fear that such policies will increase governmental intrusion in their freedom of operation in the market. The Catholic church will also be wary of government policies that encourage the decline of older industries and an increase in unemployment. There is a considerable overlap between blue collar labor and Catholic laity. Thus some of the major groups that might join a coalition opposing U.S. intervention in Latin American political conflicts are also likely to join a coalition opposing the industrial transformation of U.S.–Latin American economic relations.

It will not be easy to resolve these potential contradictions, but it is possible for creative political leadership to do so. International banks and multinational firms could come to understand that U.S. government policies intended to facilitate industrial transformation would also facilitate the continued openness of the U.S. market to Latin American exports and the continued repayment of Latin American debts. Catholics in the

United States could come to understand that policies such as these would also facilitate self-confidence and interdependence between two great pillars of the Catholic world, North America and Latin America. These broadened understandings could be facilitated by political leadership that itself understands and articulates how the disparate parts within the United States and Latin America fit into the whole of inter-American relations.

It is at this point that a renewed U.S. foreign policy can be seen to draw its strength from a new national industrial policy, which in turn will draw its strength from a new domestic politics in the United States. Fifty years ago, in the depths of the last great world depression, the United States under the leadership of Franklin Roosevelt innovated both a Good Neighbor policy for Latin America and a New Deal for the United States. So, too, in a new time of troubles, the surest reform of U.S. policy in Latin America will probably begin with reform in the United States.

Department of Political Science
Swarthmore College

Notes

1. On the impact of nuclear weapons on the international system, see Michael Mandelbaum, *The Nuclear Revolution: International Politics Before and After Hiroshima* (Cambridge: Cambridge University Press, 1981); John H. Herz, *International Politics in the Atomic Age* (New York: Columbia University Press, 1959).

2. On the origins and development of containment, see John Lewis Gaddis, *Strategies of Containment: A Critical Appraisal of Postwar American National Security Policy* (New York: Oxford University Press, 1982); Walter LeFeber, *America, Russia, and the Cold War, 1945–1980,* 4th ed. (New York: Wiley, 1980).

3. These include Austria in the German states from 1815 to 1866 and in the Italian states from 1815 to 1859, and Germany in southeastern Europe from 1934 to 1945. On German foreign economic policy in that region, see Albert O. Hirschman, *National Power and the Structure of Foreign Trade,* rev. ed. (Berkeley and Los Angeles: University of California Press, 1980).

4. A useful comparative analysis is Edy Kaufman, *The Superpowers and Their Spheres of Influence: The United States and the Soviet Union in Eastern Europe and Latin America* (New York: St. Martin's Press, 1977).

5. See Hugh Seton-Watson, *Eastern Europe Between the Wars, 1918–1941,* 3d. ed., rev. (New York: Harper & Row, 1967); Robert L. Wolff, *The Balkans in Our Time* (Cambridge, Mass.: Harvard University Press, 1956).

6. See Adam B. Ulam, *Expansion and Coexistence: Soviet Foreign Policy, 1917–1973,* 2d ed. (New York: Praeger, 1974); J. B. Kelly, *Arabia, the Gulf and the West* (New York: Basic Books, 1980).

7. On the politics of import-substituting industrialization, see David Collier, ed., *The New Authoritarianism in Latin America* (Princeton: Princeton University Press, 1979). I have discussed comparisons between Latin American and European development in my essay in the Collier volume, "Industrial Change and Political Change: A European Perspective," pp. 319–62.

8. The perceptions and ideas of U.S. policymakers in the 1940s are discussed in Gaddis, *Strategies of Containment*.

9. Tom J. Farer, "Searching for Defeat," *Foreign Policy* 40 (Fall 1980): 155–74.

10. The evolution of the Roman Catholic church in Latin America is discussed in Daniel H. Levine, ed., *Churches and Politics in Latin America* (Beverly Hills, Ca.: Sage Publications, 1980); Joseph Comblin, *The Church and the National Security State* (Maryknoll, N.Y.: Orbis Books, 1979).

11. This development is analyzed in several of the background essays in Richard E. Feinberg, ed., *Central America: International Dimensions of the Crisis* (New York: Holmes & Meier, 1982).

12. I have discussed the evolution of U.S. industries in the world market in "The Political Consequences of the Product Cycle: Industrial History and Political Outcomes," *International Organization* 33 (Winter 1979): 1–34.

13. A comprehensive analysis of the causes of U.S. industrial decline is given by Ira C. Magaziner and Robert B. Reich, *Minding America's Business: The Decline and Rise of the American Economy* (New York: Harcourt Brace Jovanovich, 1982); Robert B. Reich, *The Next American Frontier* (New York: New York Times Books, 1983).

14. David P. Calleo, *The Imperious Economy* (Cambridge, Mass.: Harvard University Press, 1982).

15. See especially Correlli Barnett, *The Collapse of British Power* (New York: Morrow, 1972); Robert Gilpin, *U.S. Power and the Multinational Corporation: The Political Economy of Foreign Direct Investment* (New York: Basic Books, 1975), sections on Great Britain.

16. Reich, *The Next American Frontier;* also the special issue of *Business Week* on "America's Restructured Economy," 1 June 1981, especially pp. 94–98.

2

Debt, Diversification, and Dependency: Latin America's International Political Relations

Laurence Whitehead

Latin America's Faltering "Emergence"

During the 1970s liberal observers commented on what they called Latin America's "emergence" as a more assertive and self-confident presence in the international arena. They urged policymakers in the United States to recognize the momentum and durability of this process and to respond to it creatively rather than defensively. Some traditional U.S. assumptions about the region ("the hegemonic presumption") would have to be revised or discarded, and some delicate adjustments would be required in certain areas of mutual sensitivity (for example, the status of the Panama Canal). But in the long run, the United States' interests would best be served by the negotiation of a more mature relationship. The growing autonomy and diversity of the major Latin American republics would eventually force the United States into conceding greater pluralism within the Western Hemisphere.

A growing awareness of the limitations of U.S. power pointed to the same conclusion. However, liberal analysts argued that Latin America's emergence would not necessarily undermine U.S. strength provided that a readjustment of the relationship was handled with skill, tolerance, and foresight. A more sophisticated and self-confident generation of Latin American leaders would prove harder to "control" in the traditional sense, and they would doubtless make inconvenient demands and would enter into troublesome liaisons. But they were also likely to prove more responsible and realistic than many of their predecessors, whose lack of real autonomy had often translated into unpredictability and impulsiveness. Strengthened Latin American ties with western Europe, Japan, or the Middle East might result in some inconvenience for U.S. policymakers, and these relations could run counter to a long-standing U.S. tradition of "Monroism." Nonetheless, these prosperous U.S. allies would also find themselves drawn into assuming a greater responsibility for the costly task of addressing Latin America's development problems.

This "liberal" approach to inter-American relations has a long pedigree, but the relative ascendancy it achieved among U.S. policymakers in the mid- to late 1970s was unusual. Elsewhere in this volume James R. Kurth examines the secular trends that have reduced the United States' relative power in the world since 1945, and he argues that official perceptions responded to these underlying processes only after considerable time.[1] If this was the case, the mid-1970s witnessed a number of traumatic events (notably in Southeast Asia and the Middle East and within U.S. domestic politics) that sharply diminished U.S. self-confidence and assertiveness just at the time that Latin America's emergence was being most emphasized. Indeed, one central concern of this essay is to distinguish between two processes that became conflated in the literature on "emergence." The first of these is a secular shift in the relative importance of the United States and Latin America that is underway regardless of current economic and political conjunctures. (Fernando Fajnzylber's essay in this volume analyzes this process, which is most simply illustrated by a statistic: between the middle and the end of the twentieth century, the United States' population will fall from over half to under one-third of the total population of the Americas.) The second process is more subjective and potentially reversible. It concerns the United States' willingness to accommodate a more assertive Latin America and to give priority to those initiatives that would strengthen Latin American self-confidence and independent control over national resources. This disposition among U.S. policymakers reached a peak in the late 1970s and has been in headlong retreat since the early 1980s. This essay will consider the part that the debt crisis of the early 1980s played in the change in U.S. outlook as opposed to more voluntaristic explanations. It will also assess whether Latin America's emergence merely faltered in the early 1980s or whether it suffered a more lasting setback.

The Latin American gains of the 1970s were striking enough, even if the term "emergence" implies a degree of innovation unwarranted by the historical record. In many countries bilateral dependence on the United States—political, economic, and even military—was sharply reduced during the decade, and Latin America's international and intraregional ties were greatly extended and diversified. The remarkable pace at which international commercial banks made loans to sovereign states was an important factor facilitating these developments throughout the region. Sovereign lending adds to a debtor government's margin for maneuver because it carries with it less economic conditionality than loans from official multilateral sources and less political obligation than bilateral assistance from a "patron" government. It also avoids the economic, and perhaps political, constraints that may develop from reliance on direct foreign investment as a major source of external capital. The major drawbacks of this type of financing from the standpoint of those seeking increased national autonomy are that servicing costs are variable and may seriously mismatch revenue and that periodic "rollovers" of borrowing will be required—not always in conditions of credit laxity.

However, during most of the 1970s these limitations appeared to be quite theoretical because worldwide inflation (especially dollar inflation) conferred windfall gains on debtors, and successive rollovers proceeded with apparently ever greater ease. These conditions lasted long enough to entice almost all Latin American countries—large and small states, oil exporters and importers, *cepalistas* (those favoring public sector participation in national economic development) and "friedmanites" (those favoring free market economies), democracies and authoritarian regimes, and even Cuba—into extensive commitments with international commercial banks. One feature of these commitments that acquired special importance later on was that, even when the banks supplying the loans were not U.S.-based, the overwhelming bulk of sovereign lending to Latin America was denominated in dollars. This was not an inevitable feature of the process. Many debtor countries would have been granted loans in yen or deutschemarks if they had so desired. But from habit and because the dollar was so weak compared with other major currencies, Latin American debtors borrowed in U.S. currency far more than the country composition of their foreign trade would have warranted. They thus placed themselves at the mercy of U.S. domestic monetary authorities.

Although some broad generalizations apply to Latin America as a whole, the realities facing the region's major countries were of course markedly diverse. Probably the most striking illustration of Latin America's "emergence" was provided by Mexico, the major country that was—and, paradoxically, remains—the most heavily dependent upon its bilateral ties with the United States. Huge new oil discoveries in the mid-1970s unleashed a period of economic and foreign policy assertiveness (most notable with regard to Central America) that forcefully underlined the relevance of the liberal diagnosis outlined above. Yet Mexico was also the most spectacular casualty of the 1982 debt crisis, and its experience can also be interpreted as a vindication of those who argue that the "emergence" thesis mistook rhetoric and opportunism for maturity and emancipation. Brazil, without oil and without Mexico's many-stranded involvement with the United States, may have provided a more valid illustration of the liberal thesis. During the 1970s Brazil progressively loosened its political ties with the United States (most strikingly when it recognized the Cuban-backed government of Angola in 1975), diversified its economic links, and asserted itself as an autonomous regional power and a nation capable of impressive internal political development. In the adverse conditions of the early 1980s (examined in more detail below), Brazil's emergence suffered some serious, but not as yet fatal, reverses.

The case of Argentina is, as always, sui generis. Ever a rival rather than a dependency of the United States, Argentina has long practiced autonomy and assertiveness in the international arena, and it has always cultivated a great variety of international ties. The best case for Argentina's "emergence" could have been made in the early 1970s, but by 1975 the country's deep and unresolved internal political problems overwhelmed any promise it might have shown in the international arena. Indeed, its internally driven crisis propelled it along a distinctive path (which included close economic links with the Soviet Union, although without any of the political or military consequences that these ties supposedly entail) until the war with Great Britain over the Falkland/Malvinas Islands in 1982.[2] Since then Argentina has returned to a pattern more consistent with the "emergence" thesis, but its response to the debt crisis could prove as distinctive as its earlier history.

In another highly distinctive case, Cuba's international policies during the 1970s could also be characterized as confident and assertive. The U.S.-directed boycott of Cuba crumbled during that decade, and the Castro regime gained a degree of regional acceptance without having "reformed" its conduct from the U.S. point of view (and without diminishing its dependence on the Soviet Union). From the U.S. perspective, this was by far the most unwelcome variant of Latin American "emergence," and one that most U.S. policymakers were determined to contain or reverse rather than to live with.

It would be possible to cite still other examples that add to the range of outcomes subsumed in the liberal diagnosis (for example, Guatemala asserted its autonomy by persisting in gross violations of human rights and dispensing with U.S. military aid). Nevertheless, the common factors that affected the whole region—particularly the availability of commercial bank credit—provided an objective basis for interpretations of Latin America's "emergence."

As the 1970s progressed, it became increasingly accepted by many observers that Latin America was indeed achieving at least a partial emancipation from earlier conditions that can be characterized loosely as "external dependency." In particular, many Latin American governments were thought to be achieving a greater degree of autonomy and self-assertion in their relations with the United States. Beyond these very general points of agreement, however, lay some fundamental divergences of interpretation. Some analysts emphasized the limited and conditional nature of this apparent emancipation and the ways in which it served mainly the interests of a restricted class of Latin Americans with good reasons of their own for preserving an essentially inequitable status quo. Other observers distinguished between certain Latin American countries that were pursuing approved paths of development (which were therefore progressively freeing themselves from past conditions of subordination) and other countries that through misfortune or misrule were failing to do so. Rival schools of thought promoted rival examples of enlightenment or misgovernment, but most analysts shared an underlying assumption in the probability of progress.

With the benefit of hindsight, it is easy to see that this assumption was insecurely based. The long post-World War II expansion of world trade clearly lost its momentum after the mid-1970s, and the credit conditions that permitted a resumption of Latin America's economic growth after 1975 were unhealthy, if not inherently unsustainable. In addition, the self-doubt and uncertainty of direction that characterized U.S. foreign policy in the late 1970s were unlikely to become stable and continuing features of the international scene. Any underlying tendency toward a more autonomous and self-assertive Latin America was likely to encounter more testing conditions. Yet few observers could have anticipated the speed and completeness with which the supportive conditions of the late 1970s would be reversed by the early 1980s. Even fewer analysts would have guessed that virtually all Latin American countries would experience difficulties of similar acuteness, regardless of their great differences in political and economic philosophy and in external orientation.[3] Moreover, the sharp reversal of international conditions that occurred in the early 1980s shows unexpected signs of persisting for as long, and of operating as powerfully, as the earlier processes that precipitated this shift.

Since 1982 the task of securing additional increments of external finance has become the most pressing necessity (and has proved an extremely costly, protracted, and uncertain process) confronting almost all Latin American governments, virtually regardless of their political orientation. All the major Latin American countries have found themselves in urgent need of external economic assistance and support. They also have found, as this essay attempts to show, that most of their alternatives to political dependence on the United States have withered on the vine. In the short run these countries' autonomy is diminished and their assertiveness curbed to an extent that few observers would have imagined possible until very recently. Moreover, in this case the "short run" is apt to stretch out over a considerable period of time, during which lasting shifts in the international balance of forces can be expected.

The mid-1984 negotiations to restructure Mexico's external debt provided one small but by no means insignificant illustration of this point. These negotiations resulted in lower interest rate margins and a postponement of debt-principal repayments until the 1990s. However, they also gave commercial banks and the International Monetary Fund (IMF) a role in periodic monitoring of Mexican economic policy throughout the rest of the 1980s. The IMF's agreement with Mexico was to expire in 1985, but the rescheduling plan stated that only if *commercial* bankers were satisfied with Mexico's economic performance at the end of *1987* would they agree to postpone the $17 billion of principal repayments falling due between 1988 and 1990. As the *Wall Street Journal* explained, "Bankers fear that Mexico's President . . . might go on a spending spree before his term of office expires in 1988."[4] This plan was a substantial break with past precedents, under which Mexico pledged to meet certain quantitative economic targets set by lenders for a predetermined emergency period (up to three years, but no longer). This time a Mexican president may be required to concede a significant degree of external control over key internal economic variables not only during his own term of office, but also well into his successor's term. Episodes such as this indicate how far the climate of confidence, assertiveness, and autonomy that prevailed in Latin America in the 1970s has given way to a new, more defensive atmosphere in which national ambitions are drastically reduced, and there is a reluctant acceptance that for the foreseeable future *economic* autonomy will be substantially constrained. It is still unclear to what extent *political* autonomy will also be affected, but it would be naive to suppose that this area could remain basically unchanged.

An acute scarcity of foreign exchange (particularly dollars) produces a very direct and immediate form of "dependence" upon potential suppliers. Latin American economies have in general become more "open" over the past decade, and their structural dependence upon imports of capital goods and intermediate inputs has, if anything, increased rather than decreased as a consequence of their import-substituting industrialization policies. In times of prosperity these economies have access to various sources of foreign exchange, but in times of hardship many of these suppliers disappear. The residual foreign exchange sources are still located mainly in Washington (this includes not only the U.S. government but also the international financial agencies based in that city). And in the conditions likely to prevail throughout most of the 1980s, the economic policies adopted by the U.S. government may have a greater impact on Latin America's immediate economic well-being than anything that Latin American governments themselves may attempt.

The experiences of the early 1980s raise several analytical issues that will be addressed in this essay. Is the financial crisis that surfaced in 1982 simply a severe cyclical jolt, or should it be viewed as a secular shift in the balance of economic power that has permanently damaged hopes of Latin America's "emergence"? To what extent was the region's apparent success in consolidating its autonomy and diversifying its international ties in the 1970s a product of its internal evolution, and to what extent was it made possible merely by political disorientation and monetary laxity in the United States—conditions that are perhaps unlikely to be repeated in the foreseeable future?

The relationships among debt, dependency, and diversification have proved more complex than perhaps initially expected. The traditional notion that heavy foreign borrowing would probably involve a substantial loss of national autonomy was replaced in the 1970s by the widespread belief that sovereign lending by commercial banks might offer an easy escape from "dependency." How should this relationship be evaluated, given the conditions prevailing in the world economy in the 1980s? Of course, the answer depends largely on how the borrowed resources were used, but here too some traditional assumptions may require reevaluation. For example, reformist economists have long recommended that Latin American governments use their margin of maneuver to strengthen economic ties within the region and with nontraditional trading partners outside the Western Hemisphere. To a significant extent Latin American countries followed this advice in the 1970s, and foreign borrowing was used to support extensive programs of international integration and economic diversification. Yet diversification of this kind has proved to be a very disappointing defense against the debt crisis and the reappearance of an acute economic dependence on Washington. Under what circumstances, then, does diversification contribute to increased autonomy? Was the error simply a failure to diversify out of *dollar* indebtedness (in accordance with other steps taken), or was the underlying strategy more deeply flawed?

The following section considers the erosion of U.S. leadership in the Western Hemisphere during the 1970s and its at least partial reversal since then. Following a review of Latin America's attempts at international diversification during the 1970s and an evaluation of subsequent setbacks, the essay examines some of the connections between Washington-based policy decisions and the recent unfolding of the regional foreign exchange crisis. Finally, the concluding section evaluates prospects in the medium term (that is, to the end of the 1980s) for the evolution of the region's foreign exchange constraint. The analysis also considers the implications this constraint may have for Latin American politics, for the development of inter-American relations, and for the prospects of Latin America's much-heralded "emergence."

The Erosion of U.S. Global Leadership

For reasons discussed by James R. Kurth in a companion essay, the United States no longer exercises the same degree of regional hegemony that it did in the 1940s or even at the time of the Alliance for Progress. Although the recent dollar scarcity and decline in world trade may have at least temporarily renewed Latin America's economic dependence on the United States, the terms of that relationship are quite distinct from those of earlier periods. This section outlines some of the long-term trends contributing to the erosion of the United States' *global* leadership position. It also briefly considers recent U.S. efforts to counteract this process. This analysis suggests that the apparent success that these efforts have achieved so far may not prove sustainable in the longer run because the basic determinants of U.S. power continue to weaken. The concluding section of this essay relates this view of the United States' position to Latin America's medium-term economic and political prospects.

In *relative* terms, U.S. power has been gradually receding for the past thirty years. The United States' problems with the Soviet Union and the international economy can only be properly understood if placed in this long-term context. Great Britain's experience with a much longer process of relative decline indicates that domestic opinion tends to lag, only becoming aware that things are not as they were during intermittent episodes of crisis. It is the essence of "relative decline" that change occurs gradually, almost imperceptibly, in the leading country, and that the citizens of that country are rather well placed to insulate themselves from uncomfortable truths about the outside world. What causes the relative decline is not a stunning defeat or an internal collapse in the leading country; instead, it is simply that other countries change faster, perhaps making greater sacrifices and striving harder to catch up. Great Britain's awareness of being overtaken by Germany after the heyday of Victorian ascendancy came in sudden, belated, and perhaps badly judged bursts of alarm that occasionally broke through ingrained popular complacency. There is no need to dwell here on the analogies to, for example, U.S.-Japanese relations over the past generation. The essential point is that successive bursts of concern (in 1971, 1975, and 1983—that is, at the bottom of each downturn in the U.S. and international economy) must be viewed as awakenings to a secular process of relative decline, not merely as conjunctural episodes.

The essential cause of the United States' relative decline is quite straightforward and not dissimilar to the cause of Great Britain's relative decline after the mid-nineteenth century. The advantages accumulated at the starting point were simply so exceptional that any sustainable form of international expansion or progress was bound to require a large element of "leveling up." Thus the United States' overwhelming lead in military power was bound to be diluted as other countries (with U.S. assistance) recovered from the devastation of World War II. Some 52 percent of the world's merchant shipping was U.S.-owned in 1947, not a proportion that could be sustained in peacetime. Similarly, with only 6 percent of the world's population in 1945, the United States produced and consumed some 40 percent of the world's output. By 1950 this declined to 33 percent, and by 1970 it had fallen to 25 percent. In 1980, with under 5 percent of the world's population, the U.S. share of world output had declined to some 23 percent (which is still a high proportion). Likewise, the United States' share of world manufacturing value-added fell from 57 percent in 1948, to 34 percent in 1958, to 21 percent in 1980. It was this military and economic base and the confidence it inspired (together with the accumulation of world gold reserves in Fort Knox as a result of European capital flight in the 1930s and 1940s) that underpinned the international role of the dollar. In 1948 the U.S. government held 74 percent of the total world stock of monetary gold. By 1958 this share had fallen to 54 percent, and by 1968 to 25 percent—a proportion that has remained generally stable since then.[5]

The statistics on international trade tell a similar story. In 1948 the proportion of U.S. exports in total world trade was, of course, abnormally high at 22 percent. By 1963 this share had fallen to 15 percent, and the relative decline continued steadily thereafter (reaching 11 percent in 1980). The subsequent severe overvaluation of the dollar almost ensures that this share will be further eroded during the current decade.

Another crude indicator of relative economic power is even more telling: in 1940 the United States produced 63 percent of world oil output, with a large surplus available for export. In addition, U.S. companies operating in Latin America accounted for another 15 percent of world oil output, and Latin America's surplus for export amounted to 11 percent of world output. In 1950 the United States still produced 52 percent of world output with a surplus for export, and the Latin American export surplus was equal to 14 percent of world output. But in 1960, U.S. output had fallen to only 34 percent of world production, with little surplus for export. The Latin American export surplus had declined to 11 percent. By 1970 the United States had become a substantial net importer of oil, producing only 20 percent of world output, while the Latin American surplus had fallen to 6 percent of world output. The Americas as a whole became a net importer of oil during the 1970s, a condition that seems certain to persist throughout the 1980s even if there is a great expansion of Mexican output. United States production is currently only about one-sixth of world output, whereas the United States still accounts for about 30 percent of world oil consumption. It was this structural shift that made the Organization of Oil Exporting Countries (OPEC) so powerful in the 1970s. Although OPEC's power weakened significantly in the early 1980s under the impact of world economic recession, energy conservation efforts, and the development of non-OPEC supplies, the United States will continue to require a substantial volume of imported oil for the foreseeable future. Indeed, the U.S. oil deficit appears likely to exceed the Latin American oil surplus for the remainder of the 1980s.

Thus by the 1970s the United States had become much less preponderant in the international economy than it had been two decades earlier. The United States clearly remained the largest and strongest single power in the world, but it was no longer in such a dominant position that it could more or less automatically secure the acquiescence of its allies on any matter that it regarded as sufficiently important. However, U.S. public opinion was slow to accept this changing relative position, and the U.S. policy-formation process was not at all well adapted to negotiating with allies on the basis of full parity. It is difficult enough to steer a policy past the gamut of domestic veto groups and special interests without then having to reconsider the whole matter in the light of external reactions. In any event, there were and are many unresolved issues of alliance politics that almost inherently require leadership from a single power center.

Monetary policy is one major area in which a single leadership center may be unavoidable. The international position of the dollar is similar to the preponderant role that the pound sterling played in world finance before 1914, despite the prior decline of Great Britain's domestic industries. An overvalued exchange rate, a tendency to keep interest rates relatively high, and the loss of competitiveness by many of Great Britain's basic industries were all caused by the need to maintain the international role of sterling before 1914 and (even more so) by efforts to reestablish that role in the 1920s. Yet despite the urgency of these problems, Great Britain was in no position to disregard the requirements of the international economy—of which it was still such an essential pivot and beneficiary. At the time, no other country was capable of taking over Great Britain's international economic responsibilities, even after its material capacity to fulfill this role had been fatally weakened by World War I. Charles Kindleberger has gone so far as to relate the 1929–1933 world depression to Great Britain's inability either to carry out its traditional stabilizing role or to transfer its international financial functions to some other power.[6] The analogies to the present condition of the dollar are quite striking.

Today's circumstances are, of course, in many respects far different from those of the interwar period. Yet the parallels demand consideration. For example, in the 1970s (as in the 1920s) nearly all Latin American countries experienced quite rapid economic growth based on an increased "opening" of their economies to international trade. Between 1970 and 1980 total trade as a percentage of gross domestic product more than doubled in Argentina, Brazil, Chile, Ecuador, Mexico, Panama, and Venezuela, and it substantially increased in all other Latin American countries. Thus the region proved highly vulnerable to a downturn in world trade. The same trend has also affected the United States, which has paid little attention to the international dimensions of its economic processes. Total trade rose from under 11 percent of U.S. gross domestic product in 1960 to 24 percent in 1980.[7] As in the 1920s this rapid trade expansion was related to a liberalization of finance that proved unsustainable. After a long period in which credit was made available at a low cost (ex post facto) and from a variety of sources that were often none too severe in their imposition of conditions, an acute liquidity squeeze now threatens to impose high real interest rates for several years, even on those relatively favored borrowers that retain access to new funds. Developing countries that "normally" supplemented their domestic savings with foreign capital inflows now find themselves abruptly compelled to generate export surpluses to repay capital to their industrialized country creditors—and, in effect, to finance the U.S. budget deficit. This obligation arises precisely when world trade is most depressed, when commodity prices are at a deep cyclical low, and when protectionist sentiment is growing in industrialized countries. Because debtor countries have been unable to raise their exports enough, they have instead been forced to slash all their imports ferociously, thereby depressing demand for U.S. exports and adding to the problems of the U.S. economy.[8] The net resource transfer from Latin America to the industrialized countries (in fact, overwhelmingly to the United States) was estimated at $20 billion in 1982 and $30 billion in 1983. These totals did not include unrecorded capital flight, which was probably of comparable dimensions. The decapitalization of Latin America continued during 1984, driven by the lure of high U.S. interest rates and political insecurity and rampant inflation in Latin America.

Perhaps the single most remarkable indicator of the long-term erosion of the United States' international economic position is the decline in its status as a net creditor nation. Before World War I, the United States was, of course, a net capital importer (supplied mostly by London capital markets as Great Britain accumulated a large foreign investment surplus). Great Britain's net creditor status was undermined by World War I and eliminated by World War II. In contrast, the United States has held a net creditor position since 1918, and it accumulated massive overseas investments between the 1940s and the 1970s. However, by the end of 1983 the United States had an estimated international net creditor position of only $125 billion. It suffered a current-account deficit of about $100 billion in 1984. Thus by mid-1985 the United States became a net debtor country for the first time in over half a century, and it will almost inevitably continue to accumulate substantial net foreign debt for the rest of the decade because of U.S. currency overvaluation and prospective budget deficits.[9]

There has been a sea change affecting the United States' military leadership role and the cohesion of its alliance system. Symptomatic of this change is a series of episodes, no one of them providing conclusive evidence but cumulatively very striking: the United States' paralysis over the Iranian revolution and the subsequent hostage crisis; its uncertain role in southern Africa as white supremacists gradually slip into wider and more overt conflict; the painful "necessity for choice" between warring allies in the 1982 South Atlantic conflict over the Falkland/Malvinas Islands; and the inability to restrain an Israeli invasion of Lebanon that deeply compromised U.S. policies in the Middle East. In all these areas of international life, events have delivered a sharp rebuff to traditional assumptions underpinning the United States' world role. Moreover, it has become harder to envisage effective conflict resolution by means of peaceful cooperation.

Note that all the growing difficulties mentioned above concern tension *within* the U.S. sphere of influence rather than conflict between the U.S. and Soviet spheres. This is not to suggest that the Soviet Union and its allies are unaffected by, or uninterested in, the tendency toward a breakdown of the U.S.-based liberal international order. But their role is secondary. Indeed, their alliance system faces problems not all that dissimilar from (and certainly not milder than) those afflicting the U.S.-led group of countries. Far from presenting a successful challenge to the international capitalist system, the communist world has shown signs of succumbing to many of the same failings, compounded by special problems of its own (especially in food production). Even on the military front, the Soviet bloc displays many signs of vulnerability: a draining rivalry with China; great difficulty in stabilizing its defense perimeter in Poland and Afghanistan; inability to shape events in the Middle East or Asia; and only a very limited capacity to aid its sympathizers and clients farther afield. Neither in material nor in ideological terms can the Soviet system be plausibly presented to U.S. allies as anything like the overriding threat to a U.S.-led world order that it may perhaps once have been (for example, at the height of the Korean War). Of course, the East-West conflict is still active and dangerous. In fact, the danger of nuclear war may be greater than it has been for a generation. But the United States' view of the source of this danger is not shared by all its allies. Foreign opinion leaders who once accepted the official U.S. worldview now increasingly consider that some of the major forces dislocating the liberal international order in the 1980s have their origins essentially within the "western" or "capitalist" world. A strategy of increased confrontation with the Soviet Union might serve to distract temporarily *U.S.* public attention from the real sources of dislocation, but if anything it widens the gulf in public perceptions between the United States and many of its allies, thereby contributing in the longer run to the further erosion of the United States' leadership position.

The commercial, financial, and military difficulties outlined above interact to undermine the U.S.-led post-World War II order. All these tensions ultimately acquire an expression at the political level. However, their causes are structural, not just narrowly political. Over the past generation the United States' material ascendancy in the western alliance has been substantially diminished, and its ideological basis has been weakened. Moreover, political leaders throughout the noncommunist world (not just in the United States) have responded to these difficulties by turning inward, looking to the national policy instruments available to pursue their objectives and showing less willingness to listen to the viewpoints of their international partners.

Since the 1980 general election, the United States has tried to reassert its leadership through an act of will, and at least in the short run it has achieved some degree of success in this enterprise. Although it seems hardly possible to reverse the above-mentioned long-term decline in the United States' relative strength, it is argued by some that a clear and sustained U.S. commitment to a few sound basic principles will at least restore the United States' authority and cause its friends to rally round once more. The aim has been to restore a strong and respected United States based on resolute hostility to the Soviet system and a commitment to sound money and market freedom. From this point of view, the United States' recent disarray is to be explained by lack of resolution in economic management and by gullibility and confusion regarding the nature of the Soviet challenge, rather than by any reluctance to adapt to a necessarily reduced ascendancy in world affairs.

From this perspective, it follows that firm and consistent U.S. leadership focusing attention on the East-West dimension of all international political issues can and will restore cohesion and effectiveness to the western alliance. The Reagan administration's key idea regarding world politics was that an inherently expansionist and totalitarian Soviet regime has profited from U.S. nervelessness and western disarray to shift the military balance in its favor. This perspective views the Soviet system as inherently flawed, so that its only source of superiority is its capacity for military expansion and regimentation. This is taken to mean that the Soviet Union responds to internal setbacks by increased militarization and additional acts of external aggression (either overt or disguised). In this schema, the Soviet Union is credited with an outstanding capacity for duplicity, so that it can orchestrate an enormous range of apparently disparate opponents of U.S. policies, from the European peace movement to Iranian mullahs, to the Palestine Liberation Organization, to the Indians of highland Guatemala.

This perspective excuses the United States from giving much weight to the bewildering array of apparent grievances expressed by its many critics and opponents. Moreover, it affects U.S. negotiations with the Soviet Union by generating a climate of mutual distrust and casting doubt on the wisdom (indeed, the morality) of making concessions to the Soviet Union, no matter how strong the apparent advantages to both sides. For from this perspective, only by making the United States much stronger and by forcing fundamental change on the Soviet Union can any great-power compromise or settlement be envisaged.

This determination to view virtually all international issues from an inflexible Cold War viewpoint may yield some short-term dividends because it does impose a very clear and familiar pattern of priorities. Over the longer term, however, it may expose U.S. leadership to two main risks. First, it is always dangerous either to overestimate the threat from an antagonist or to underestimate the recklessness of one's allies, for both these errors increase the risk of conflict by miscalculation. (Argentina and Israel both illustrated this point in 1982.) Second, a lasting reassertion of U.S. leadership would require the United States' allies not merely to acquiesce to the currently prevailing U.S. view but to identify fully with underlying U.S. assumptions. This cannot be achieved in any durable sense unless the central power's worldview takes into reasonable account the genuine preoccupations and distinctive viewpoints of its associates and allies. The U.S. reassertionism of the early 1980s was achieved largely by turning a deaf ear to discordant views from overseas and by concentrating on the reaffirmation of a somewhat nationalistic form of domestic unity.

Many of these generalizations also apply to U.S. relations with Latin America in the 1980s, which contrast markedly with the liberalism and self-doubt of the mid-1970s. However, this is not simply a straightforward contrast between Republican and Democratic administrations. A key turning point probably came near the middle of the Carter presidency, after a narrow Senate vote in 1978 to ratify the Panama Canal treaties had exhausted the liberal lobby's political capital. Subsequently, the Nicaraguan revolution and more restrictive U.S. monetary policy after October 1979 paved the way for much that has been claimed by, and attributed to, the Reagan administration. Moreover, the Reagan administration never entirely abandoned the earlier U.S. assumption that in the longer run most major Latin American countries are "coming of age." It endorsed the corollary that approved behavior should receive U.S. support—although the category of "approved" countries was redefined to give more emphasis to probusiness solutions, and the threat of "misrule" was specified in simplified anti-Soviet terms. However, major countries such as Brazil, Mexico, Venezuela, and Argentina received far less attention under Reagan than the ministates of Central America. For the most part the United States' concern with these key states focused on their alignment regarding the isthmian confrontation. Until the 1982 debt crisis, the Reagan administration also implicitly assumed an increased autonomy and assertiveness on the part of larger Latin American countries.

Central America was excepted from this instance, and U.S. attention has been concentrated on the area in which external vulnerability was at its greatest and traditional forms of subordination to the United States were most characteristic. The United States' allies came under strong pressure to accept Central America as a test case of agreement with U.S. views. However, this proved to be a quite unpromising issue on which to persuade U.S. allies that all the blame lies with the Soviet Union and Cuba, especially since U.S. domestic opinion remains divided on this question.[10] Even in the short run it remains unclear whether the reassertion of U.S. power in Central America is producing the required results. But to establish the United States' long-term credibility on this issue would require the consolidation of stable and respectable pro-U.S. governments in the area. Unless that can be achieved, the use of Central America as a test case will tend to undermine, rather than to reinforce, the United States' reasserted leadership.

The restoration of sound money and market freedom constituted the Reagan administration's other main strategy for reestablishing a strong United States. Here too some short-term dividends were obtained from the adoption of firm policies. But the incidental costs have been higher than expected, and the longer-term effects on the United States' international position remain doubtful. A tight monetary policy greatly strengthened the dollar and helped bring down U.S. inflation, albeit at a high cost in lost output and employment. Countries such as Mexico and Brazil, facing desperate dollar shortages, felt obliged to fall more into line with the United States on a number of disputed issues because of their urgent needs for U.S. financial assistance. But what the United States can secure is acquiescence rather than any change of heart, and it is evident that this tight money policy produced more severe consequences in Latin America than its authors had anticipated. When (rather belatedly) it became apparent how much U.S. bankers, U.S. investors, and U.S. exporters stood to lose from a liquidity squeeze of such severity, Washington policymakers abruptly changed tack. On this front as well, the current administration's efforts to reassert the U.S. position may not persuade U.S. allies of the rightness of its diagnosis, and such efforts may not produce the improvement in material conditions that is a prerequisite for a restoration of U.S. leadership.

For the next several years nearly all Latin American countries will have to scramble for access to U.S. markets in order to bolster their export earnings. They must also placate U.S. commercial banks and Washington-based international financial institutions in order to obtain further credit. However, even in the case of short-term economic transactions, the old conditions of U.S. leadership no longer obtain. U.S. policies regarding trade and finance are so constrained by domestic considerations that little room is left for measures specifically intended to alleviate Latin American economic difficulties. There have also been such significant changes in the economic structure (particularly the industrial structure) of both the United States and Latin America that adjustment to a relationship of greater parity appears to be inescapable in the longer run. In addition, although economic necessity may have strengthened the United States' position in the hemisphere, there is now far less convergence of political outlook between the United States and Latin America than formerly pre-vailed. Latin America's recently renewed dependence upon the United States must be attributed mostly to the falling away of other international partners as a consequence of the global recession rather than to any long-term reestablishment of the conditions for U.S. preponderance. This final point is developed in the next section.

Latin America's Efforts at Economic and Political Diversification .

Throughout the 1970s Latin America increasingly diversified its inter-national links and acquired a more assertive and autonomous presence in world arenas. One measure of this diversification is the region's pattern of external trade. In 1970 under 1 percent of Latin America's total trade was with the Middle East, but by 1980 this share had risen to 6 percent. Similarly, trade with Africa (including South Africa) rose during this period from a little over 1 percent to nearly 4 percent of total regional trade. (In both cases Latin America's imports from these regions consid-erably exceeded the value of its exports to them.) Trade *within* the Latin American region also rose as a proportion of total trade, from under 17 percent to over 19 percent between 1970 and 1980. Developing country markets (including OPEC) absorbed only 18 percent of Latin America's exports in 1970, but this proportion had risen to 25 percent by 1981. Instead of supplying 21 percent of Latin America's imports in 1970, by 1980 developing countries supplied 40 percent of regional imports.[11]

The diversification of Latin America's international ties may still be a long-term trend, but this process was abruptly interrupted in 1982–1984. The economic crisis pushed the political goal of diversification into the background; most Latin American countries must judge their external policies in terms of their urgent need for foreign exchange. The diversified links they sought to develop for the most part have proven to be unexpectedly fragile—in part because of the economic and political crises afflicting the rest of the world. For most governments other than the United States, Latin American economic problems are in practice a rather low priority.

Indeed, between 1970 and 1980 Latin America's importance as a trading partner declined for industrialized countries other than the United States. The Latin American share of Japan's total trade declined from 6 percent to 5 percent over this period, and the Latin American share of western Europe's total trade slipped from 4 percent to 3 percent. Latin America's importance as a trading partner rose for Africa and the Middle East between 1970 and 1980 (from approximately 1.5 percent to 4.5 percent, and from approximately 1.5 percent to 4 percent, respectively), but its share of these regions' total trade remained marginal. In contrast, Latin America's share of total U.S. trade rose from under 15 percent in 1970 to approximately 16.5 percent in 1980. Nevertheless, the region's economic problems attract high-level attention only intermittently even from the United States—and then mainly when Latin America's difficulties impinge on powerful domestic interests such as banks or the steel industry. Assuming that the debt problem remains acute for much of the 1980s, Latin America's relationship with the United States and the international financial agencies based in Washington will be so urgent that they are bound to overshadow the region's links with the rest of the world.

Latin America's hopes of diversifying its international links have already encountered a long list of disappointments and frustrations. There are special factors that explain some of the setbacks, notably the 1982 South Atlantic conflict. But worldwide problems of trade and finance provide the essential explanation. Although most acute in Latin America, similar constraints have operated throughout the world, causing generalized retrenchment and risk aversion. Disentanglement from costly and speculative Latin American ventures has been widespread because of a loss of confidence in Latin America's capacity to service its huge external debt; because U.S. reassertionism and bilateralism raised doubts about the persistence of most-favored-nation trade practices in the region; because the strong appreciation of the dollar compared with European and Asian currencies increased the financial weight of U.S.-based enterprises in the region compared with their competitors; and because the appreciation of the dollar made "dollar-zone" developing countries' exports more costly compared with those of their nondollar-zone competitors. Most of Latin America's new partners have felt a lack of leverage in the region when things go wrong.

Similarly, Latin American countries have also encountered difficulties because of their attempts at diversification. Adverse experiences arising from links outside the Americas, together with a common sense of vulnerability to the United States and exclusion from Washington policy circles, have caused Latin American governments to draw close together to some extent. But the limited comfort and solidarity they offer each other is mainly psychological. For the most part, the practical assistance they need is not available from within Latin America, especially because the debt crisis was diffused so uniformly across the region. So at least in the short run, Latin American countries will have to turn to Washington. Although the "Cartagena Club" of Latin American debtors has attempted to forge a common outlook and promote regional solidarity, in practice each country is engaged in essentially bilateral negotiations with its creditors.

Thus far "Latin America" has been considered as a single unit. In reality, of course, there are several quite distinct subregions with different levels of economic development, contrasting trade orientations, and diverse geopolitical interests. Brazil had undertaken the most ambitious and wide-ranging attempts at diversification. Much of what is said below concerning links to Africa, the Middle East, eastern Europe, and Japan applies largely to Brazil and rather little to other countries. Similarly, Argentina's efforts at diversification are sui generis because of its economic rivalry with the United States (both countries export temperate foodstuffs), its political rivalry with Brazil, and its trade links with the Soviet Union. The countries that once formed the Andean Pact obviously have a disposition toward Pacific Basin initiatives, with less interest in Africa or the Middle East. The countries of the Caribbean Basin have generally made relatively little progress in diversifying away from the United States because geographical considerations and economic convenience pull them so strongly toward it. There are a number of small exceptions to this generalization (notably the French territories of Martinique and Guadeloupe) and one very major exception—Cuba, which faces quite different problems of diversification. Finally, Mexico presents another special case. Mexico is overwhelmingly oriented toward its northern neighbor, yet it has the aspirations and potential to become a middle-rank power in its own right. Thus "diversification" clearly has a variety of meanings for these different subregions. Yet under the present conditions, they all face rather similar frustrations and constraints. A brief survey of the main alternatives to dependence upon the United States will show how all of these countries have been adversely affected by the debt crisis.

The Soviet Union and the Council for Mutual Economic Assistance (COMECON)

The Soviet bloc accounted for about 6 percent of Latin America's total trade in both 1970 and 1980. However, this statistic largely reflects

Soviet bloc trade with Cuba, a full member of COMECON since 1972. For other Latin American countries, COMECON represented only between 1 and 2 percent of total trade during the 1970s. However, the key point is that eastern Europe went bankrupt (in terms of hard currency) a year before Latin America. Significant Latin American interests were among the losers. For example, Poland owed Brazil $1.6 billion that cannot be paid in the hard currency Brazil so urgently needs. Poland offered coal, sulphur, and an icebreaker in lieu of cash, but Brazil has threatened to halt exports of iron ore and agricultural products unless Poland meets its obligations in full. Brazil was found to have the second largest exposure to Polish debt on a per capita basis because, long after more cautious exporters had retrenched, Brazilian companies eager to penetrate new markets continued selling on credit to Poland. This was one reason for Brazil's disappointing export figures in 1983.

What Latin America most needs is hard currency. But of the COMECON countries, only the Soviet Union (through its sales of oil and gold) generates a substantial hard currency income. As the international price of oil falls, Soviet foreign exchange resources are increasingly overstretched. Cuba is very expensive to the Soviet Union in terms of dollar earnings foregone, and there is now strong pressure in the eastern bloc to add to its Latin American commitments by shoring up the Nicaraguan revolution.

Apart from Cuba and Nicaragua, Soviet links with Latin America are limited by differences in political perspective, a lack of economic complementarity, and the complications that may arise from U.S. hostility toward any such convergence. Argentina is a major exception in this regard because its grain surplus so neatly matches Soviet import requirements and because Argentina is relatively resistant to U.S. pressure on such matters. Argentina refused to participate in the grain embargo against the Soviet Union declared by President Carter in January 1980, with the result that by 1982 about three-quarters of the grain it exported went to eastern bloc markets. Although the U.S. embargo has since been lifted, the Soviet Union seeks to strengthen its ties to alternative suppliers, especially because Argentina has been willing to commit itself to a five-year grain agreement that guarantees a high minimum annual rate of delivery. On the other hand, there are few eastern bloc goods that Argentina wishes to purchase (in 1982 Soviet merchandise exports to Argentina were under $30 million, or no more than 2 percent of the value of Argentine imports), in part because payment is required in scarce hard currency. The Soviet Union is therefore anxious to offset its trade deficit with Argentina. It has taken a strong interest in Argentine plans to build nuclear power stations, reportedly selling heavy water for the reactors and significant quantities of enriched uranium. Soviet turbines are also used in Argentina's ambitious hydroelectric schemes, and presumably the Soviet Union responds sympathetically to requests for arms supplies. However, during the South Atlantic conflict the Soviet Union was careful to keep a low profile. And although the Argentine military was disappointed by the United States' posture during that conflict, there are major ideological obstacles to any serious convergence with the Soviet Union on political matters. Moreover, since the restoration of democracy in Argentina in 1983, the Argentine market for either Soviet armaments or capital goods has contracted sharply, while the Soviet Union has reverted to North America as a major grain supplier.

Mexico and the Soviet Union negotiated ambitious trade agreements in the mid-1970s, but these agreements produced relatively modest practical results. As with the rest of Latin America, the Soviet Union encountered large trade deficits with Mexico (with Soviet imports from Mexico exceeding exports by more than three to one). The COMECON trade fair in Mexico City in November 1984 (Camexport, the largest such fair ever held outside a COMECON member state) was a major effort to overcome these difficulties. After the United States imposed protectionist measures against Mexican steel exports in 1984, the Soviet Union sought to increase the volume of bilateral barter trade. Mexico was willing to exchange specialty steels for the petroleum industry for Soviet steel technology.

However, in the present climate of intensified East-West conflict and renewed economic vulnerabilty, the prospects for other Latin American countries' political or economic collaboration with the Soviet bloc are distinctly limited.[12]

Africa

In this region, too, Brazil took a leading role in developing new ties and new markets. African countries may not explicitly have defaulted on loans in the same way as Latin America and eastern Europe, but that is because they were never so creditworthy and their administrative machinery was always less developed. Nevertheless, Brazil took the risks and again inflated its export figures, at a severe cost in resulting bad debts. Nigeria was Brazil's most important market in Subsaharan Africa, and it became one of the OPEC members most adversely affected by the oil glut. Brazil exported about $800 million worth of goods to Nigeria in 1981, but this total fell to only $400 million in 1982 and to below $200 million in 1983. Future trade will depend largely on barter arrangements that circumvent Nigeria's shortage of cash. In early 1985 an ambitious countertrade deal was announced that could raise Brazil's exports to around $1 billion in 1985, making it the largest exporter to Nigeria.

Angola, a Portuguese-speaking nation directly across the Atlantic, was a commitment of both political and commercial interest to Brazil. This involvement may produce benefits in the long term, but for the present Angola is a deeply troubled country and an uncertain trading partner. A large contingent of Cuban troops has been stationed there since 1975, when they served to repel a South African incursion. Tension between Angola and South Africa remains extremely high because of the unresolved status of Namibia and the civil strife within Angola. Cuba has stated that despite external pressure, it will not withdraw its troops unless the Angolan government requests it. So far the Angolan government has not done so (its own survival might be at risk), and so the Cubans stay on. However, Cuba is forced to pay an increasingly heavy price for this involvement.

On the other side of the ideological divide, right wing groups in the Argentine, Brazilian, and Uruguayan military showed some interest in the formation of a South Atlantic organization linking them with South Africa. But the 1982 South Atlantic conflict and the trend toward civilian government in South America have brought that proposal into discredit. In summary, therefore, Latin America's links with Africa suffered considerable setbacks in the early 1980s, and the prospects for sustained recovery are uncertain.

The Middle East

In this area the prospects looked exceptionally good in 1980 and 1981. Latin America's economic complementarity with this region was strong, and Middle Eastern markets were expanding faster than markets elsewhere. Furthermore, Latin American countries all have significant communities of "Turcos" or "Sirios" who speak Arabic, retain family ties in the Middle East, and are indefatigable traders, financiers, and middlemen. Venezuela, of course, had important ties to the Middle East dating back to 1960, when it encouraged Arab countries to join together in the founding of OPEC. Both Mexico and Brazil shifted away from earlier support for Israel following the 1973 Middle East war, and so they could collaborate with Middle Eastern governments at the United Nations and in developing country forums. Arab businessmen have also shown an increasing interest in investments in Latin America. For example, in 1977 the Arab Latin American Bank (Arlabank) was established with 60 percent Arab and 40 percent Latin American participation. One declared purpose of the bank was to channel Middle Eastern funds into Western Hemisphere investments. The bank grew rapidly, and by 1982 it had established a presence throughout the region. However, following the 1982 debt crisis, Arlabank began to retreat from the Latin American market. It moved its headquarters from Peru to Bahrain, and it has since concentrated on Middle East-based trading and commerce.

There have also been other substantial setbacks in Brazil's ties to the Middle East. Following the Iranian revolution, Brazil turned to Iraq as its major supplier of crude oil. Under a wide-ranging agreement signed in 1980, Iraq gave Brazil important oil supply guarantees and trading preferences in return for Brazilian iron ore exports, construction contracts, technical assistance from Petrobrás (the state-owned Brazilian oil company), and particularly supplies of Brazilian armaments. Shortly thereafter, Iraq launched an attack on Iran that led to a prolonged war and crippled the trade agreement with Brazil. Subsequently, there were signs of friction between Brazil and Libya, which had purchased several hundred million dollars worth of Brazilian exports (mostly armaments). In the wake of the debt crisis, Brazil entered into barter arrangements with various oil suppliers (including Iran and Algeria), offering commodities and manufactured goods as payment in lieu of dollars. However, these agreements have not proved very satisfactory. For example, the 1984 agreement with Iran provided for the supply of $400 million in Brazilian goods in exchange for a commitment to buy $600 million of Iranian oil. But doubting Brazil's word, the Iranians required confirmed letters of credit from western banks before they would dispatch the oil. In October 1984 Brazil reached an agreement with Saudi Arabia for the exchange of military personnel and the eventual production of Brazilian armaments there. Saudi Arabia was particularly interested in Brazil's rockets, training aircraft, and tanks, and it has a large trade surplus with Brazil.

Latin America's relationship with Israel has also undergone a series of jolting transformations. Following the shah's downfall in Iran and the return of the Sinai oilfields to Egypt, Mexico became Israel's largest supplier of crude oil, accounting for nearly half of all its oil imports. Latin America had traditionally been a very marginal market for Israeli exports, but in 1980 Israel launched a serious export drive in the region. Its comparative advantage lies in agribusiness, electronics, solar energy, construction, and especially armaments. In 1982 the United States relaxed its embargo on the export from Israel of Kfir fighter planes, and the Israeli invasion of Lebanon provided a rich booty of Soviet-made weapons available for resale. Accordingly, Israel's military exports to Latin America have risen to record levels, with the conflicts in the South Atlantic and in Central America providing some especially promising opportunities. Israel's defense minister paid a visit to Honduras in early 1983, underscoring the importance of Israel's new links in the region and highlighting the political as well as the commercial dimensions of this relationship. However, the fragility of these Israeli initiatives is quite apparent.

Japan

In the long term, Japan's highly advanced economy and low production costs make it a very attractive trading partner for Latin America. During World War II the Japanese communities on Latin America's Pacific coast were often dispossessed, interned, and even deported, but a very large Japanese colony in Brazil survived and achieved great economic success. Japan's capital-rich but land- and natural-resource-scarce economy is highly complementary with the Brazilian economy. Moreover, Japan's growing financial strength has offered an alternative source of credit for Latin American development.

In due course these long-term realities will undoubtedly reassert themselves. But in the early 1980s, Japan's economic growth slowed sharply and its currency weakened very markedly. Consequently, Japan's demand for raw material imports from Latin America fell sharply, as did its willingness to invest in grandiose development projects (for example, iron ore mines to supply its steel industry). Latin American purchasers have found Japanese exports extremely competitive, but Japanese importers mostly have regarded Latin America as no more than a useful, but secondary, source of supply. Before the debt crisis Latin America purchased about 6 to 7 percent of Japan's exports and accounted for around 4 percent of Japan's imports. Indeed, in 1981 major Japanese exporters saw Latin America as a safety-valve outlet for products placed under trade restraint in European and North American markets. Japanese automobile exports to Latin America rose 40 percent in 1981 alone. However, Japanese importers resisted Latin American demands to act as a safety valve for their exports (for example, diverted Mexican oil exports). Thus Japan enjoyed a large trade surplus with the region until the debt crisis abruptly curtailed Latin America's capacity to import.

Recognizing the severity of their trade imbalance with Japan, various Latin American governments have long urged Japan to offset its export surplus with increased investment. Mining and vehicle assembly projects were the favored sectors. Before the 1982 debt crisis, various Japanese companies showed an interest in the major Latin American countries. Brazil, the favorite before 1975, was displaced by Mexico as the preferred operating base. Japanese banks showed similarly poor timing, emerging as the most active lenders in the Eurodollar market in the first half of 1982 and therefore stepping into the gap left as U.S. and European banks reined in such lending. Consequently, when the debt crisis struck, Japanese banks found themselves saddled with a $10 billion exposure to Mexico and a $9 billion exposure to Brazil. Although Japanese governmental authorities have some responsibility for this situation (they liberalized the

rules governing foreign lending just before the bubble burst), they have
made few concessions to help their most seriously affected banks. For
example, in Japan no tax relief is available on debt losses. After the bitter
lessons of 1982–1983, it may be some time before either Japanese investors or bankers recover an interest in Latin American ventures. Indeed,
at a time of adversity and contraction, Japan is likely to give priority to
markets and suppliers in the Far East and reduce its exposure in Latin
America.

Western Europe

For Latin America in general, the major alternative to the United
States—in either commerce or politics—must be western Europe.
Strengthened ties with the European Economic Community (EEC) would
provide a solid and respectable counterweight to dependence upon the
United States. Conscious of this reality and of the reorientations that
might follow from the accession of Portugal and Spain to the EEC in
1986, Latin American countries have sought to cultivate new links with
Brussels to supplement their long-standing presence in the major European capitals. Acknowledging this, the European Parliament voted to
establish a Europe–Latin America Institute to act as a clearing house,
information center, and focus of research. Unfortunately, however, these
developments are less promising than they appear, and Latin America
can expect relatively little from the EEC either in terms of economic
assistance or expanded market opportunities until progress is made in
resolving the EEC's severe internal difficulties.

About three-quarters of EEC resources are currently devoted to the
Common Agricultural Policy, which cushions West European farmers
from world market conditions and therefore stimulates overproduction
and the stockpiling of food surpluses. These surpluses not only exclude
Latin America from potential West European outlets for its food exports,
but they also force down prices in third-country markets when surpluses
are dumped at a loss. Latin American countries derive little benefit from
such dumping, and they sometimes sustain substantial losses either directly (for example, in the case of cane sugar displaced by West European
beet sugar) or more often indirectly through market distortions. In areas
other than agriculture, the EEC has proved a feeble bulwark against
protectionism. Indeed, the protectionist aspects of EEC policies partially
explain why the EEC market accounted for only 17 percent of Latin
America's total trade in 1980, down from 25 percent in 1970. Since then
unemployment in western Europe has soared, further reinforcing the protectionist impulse.

The EEC does devote significant resources to aid developing countries, and it has followed a fairly enlightened policy toward Latin America in the terms established for such assistance. But the principal aid beneficiaries are former European colonies in the southern Mediterranean, Africa, and Asia. It is doubtful that much heed will be paid to Latin American demands for economic assistance while the existing beneficiaries of EEC programs remain in severe difficulties. Although it is true that the accession of Spain and Portugal to the EEC may shift the internal balance of power in a direction more favorable to Latin America, that step remains problematic because of the demands the Iberian Peninsula will add to the EEC's overloaded agenda. Although accession has taken place on schedule, a number of years will elapse before Spain and Portugal will be sufficiently well integrated into the EEC to press for any significant assistance to Latin America. Admittedly, recent West European thinking has been closer than that of the United States to the Latin American viewpoint concerning necessary responses to the international economic crisis (for example, on the appropriate size of IMF quota increases). But this coincidence of perspective depends on the complexion of individual governments, which change according to the will of the electorate, just as in the United States.

Although the EEC may have little to offer Latin America in terms of economic concessions, it might perhaps offer an important alternative source of political support. This is possible in principle, and indeed the European Parliament has been increasingly assertive in international affairs, including human rights questions and the promotion of democracy.[13] But the powers of the Parliament are still strictly circumscribed, and most EEC decisions are reached by consensus among the member governments. Hence the EEC leadership can take the initiative on very few foreign policy issues. (The embarrassment over sanctions against Argentina during the South Atlantic conflict illustrates the difficulties.)

The joint meeting of EEC foreign ministers with their Caribbean and Central American counterparts in San José, Costa Rica, in September 1984 was a potentially significant exception to this generalization. This was the first meeting of EEC governments held in Latin America, and its symbolic importance was underlined by the fact that the Europeans appeared to resist pressure from the United States to treat Nicaragua like a pariah. However, its practical consequences are likely to be fairly modest. The foreign ministers offered only a token amount of economic assistance (a small fraction of the aid provided by the United States), and they warned that Central America could not expect to receive any of the "Lomé Convention" economic benefits that the EEC extends to former European colonies.

Thus in practice the prospects for a Latin American convergence with western Europe still depend heavily on the individual outlook of the major European countries. Under Chancellors Brandt and Schmidt, the West German government followed a quite active policy in Latin America—encouraging the Socialist International to increase its activities there, supporting Brazilian nuclear energy projects in the face of U.S. opposition, and offering limited support to the Sandinista government in Nicaragua. However, even at the moment of greatest apparent disagreement with the United States over Latin America, the Federal Republic of Germany was never disposed to press its viewpoint too hard against firm U.S. resistance; most Latin American issues were simply too peripheral to justify more than a very limited commitment. Since November 1982 the Kohl government has been much less likely to dissent from the United States' viewpoint or to pursue an activist policy in Latin America.

Since 1980 France's socialist government (recently reinforced by the González government in Spain) has represented the main source of encouragement to those Latin American countries seeking to diversify their international ties. In political terms, it offers an alternative to the United States—as exemplified by the Franco-Mexican initiative on Central America and France's decision to supply helicopters and minesweepers to Nicaragua. France has stepped up its independent intelligence-gathering activities in Latin America, and it has sought to expand its arms supplies to the region. France has also proposed a more expansionary and development-oriented approach to the international economic crisis. As a source of ideas and encouragement, these initiatives are important. This approach is more a French nationalist stance (recalling General de Gaulle's Latin American rhetoric of the 1960s) than a distinctly socialist position. But to make some real difference to a debt-burdened region, France must achieve success in its domestic economic management; it must free resources for its Latin American ventures; and it must liberalize its imports. First and foremost, President Mitterrand must show that he can provide practical assistance to the fragile democracy in Spain—no easy task. France must also convince the other western powers that its own economic and political doctrines are in the best interests of the whole western alliance, not simply postures taken by a "free rider." Most Latin American governments understand the limitations of the French position, and at least in the short run they expect more comfort from France than real help.

In 1982 Great Britain, after generations of disinterest in Latin America and withdrawal from the Caribbean, became unexpectedly involved in a major battle over—of all improbable issues—the sovereignty of the Falkland/Malvinas Islands. The aftermath of that episode overshadows all other Latin American issues as far as the British government is concerned. To restore its authority over eighteen hundred islanders, Great Britain incurred £700 million in direct war expenses and several hundred casualties. It is estimated that the full cost of recapturing and garrisoning the islands for four years will be £2,560 million, or over £1.5 million per islander. Locked into a "fortress Falklands" policy, the Thatcher government has little scope for other initiatives that might aid Latin America to resolve its economic difficulties and to reassert its autonomy. In any case, the British government has been most reluctant to dissent from the United States regarding the management of the debt crisis. Great Britain has also given the United States strong support in its emphasis on resisting Soviet-Cuban expansionism, although the October 1983 U.S. invasion of Grenada surprised the British government and took place against its advice.

Similarly, Italy has its own special reasons to avoid additional Latin American commitments. In the South Atlantic conflict, Italy felt obliged to go along with EEC sanctions against Argentina, but this was strongly resisted by Italians with family ties to Argentina. Central America raises other issues that are highly divisive within Italy. Finally, the failure in June 1982 of Italy's largest private bank, the Banco Ambrosiano, was apparently linked to its huge illegal operations in Latin America. The full story of this scandal (which culminated when the managing director of the bank apparently hanged himself from Blackfriars Bridge in London) may never be unraveled. However, enough information has been uncovered to show the deep involvement of the Vatican's top financial advisers, a Freemason's lodge (called P2) involving leading members of the extreme right in Argentina and Uruguay, and senior political, military, and banking officials in Italy. Banco di Italia inspectors making enquiries in South America have generally met with obstruction, and on occasion they have been treated like criminals. As further testimony emerges concerning the activities of P2, the taint of scandal extends into the furthest reaches of the political and business elites of both Italy and Argentina.

Christian Democracy

Diverse nongovernmental organizations based in western Europe have taken an active interest in Latin American affairs and have encouraged the region's attempts at diversification. These organizations' social, cultural, and humanitarian influence may at times be quite important, but under present economic conditions they are mostly on the defensive. The Christian Democrat and Socialist Internationals are exceptions to this generalization because of their ties, respectively, to the international Roman Catholic church and to the West European labor movement and leading political parties. However, western Europe's Christian Democrats must be disappointed by the performance of their protégé parties in various parts of Latin America and in Spain. Christian Democratic parties are a major force only in Venezuela, Chile, Guatemala, and El Salvador, and severe difficulties confront the movement even in those countries.

Perhaps reflecting the World Union of Christian Democrats' problems, Pope John Paul II has taken an increasingly direct and personal role in promoting Catholicism in Latin America, most notably through his visits to Brazil and Central America. He has also sanctioned a strong line against "theology of liberation" doctrines that enjoy a considerable following in various parts of the Latin American church. Such direct pontifical activism overshadows the activities of local Christian Democratic parties. Of course, this type of action must be mainly religious in form, with the political and economic objectives kept in the background. Nevertheless, it is fairly clear that the Pope has tried to curb Catholic radicalism and strengthen anti-Marxist currents of opinion in Latin America. The Vatican may sometimes have a significant mediating role to play (as in the Argentine/Chilean boundary dispute over the Beagle Channel, and perhaps in the Central American conflict.) But as an external prop to Latin American autonomy and international pluralism, it can only exercise an indirect moral influence.

The Socialist International

At its founding in 1951, the Socialist International had an overwhelmingly European membership and outlook. It was initially concerned primarily with the fate of democratic socialists in eastern Europe, where the popular front movements of the early post-World War II years had been replaced by the most rigid forms of Soviet-imposed communism. The Socialist International was also concerned with the fate of Spanish and Portuguese socialists still suffering repression under what it regarded as a "fascist" form of government, despite the Axis defeat. But between 1955 and 1959 the organization conducted a relatively vigorous and successful campaign to extend its activities into South America, operating from a secretariat in Montevideo. But after 1959 the Socialist International's presence in Latin America went into eclipse. This was in part because the political freedoms needed for socialist organization proved short lived. However, it also reflected the fact that the Cuban revolution produced quite different reactions among European and Latin American socialists. The established leaders of the European socialist parties had strong reservations regarding a country that had taken the "wrong" side in the Cold War. In contrast, Latin American socialists were often attracted to the revolutionary romanticism they associated with the Cuban example.

The Nixon administration's efforts to destabilize the Allende government in Chile and the subsequent tragic destruction of Chilean democracy produced a strong impact among West European socialists. Although many of the established party leaders regarded Allende's policies as far more radical than they themselves would endorse, they were bound to express solidarity with both his general aims and his apparent reliance on democratic methods. Allende's fate revived memories of Europe's struggles against fascism, and it reignited distrust of U.S. foreign policy priorities. It was particularly disturbing to the French, Italian, and Spanish Socialist parties, which had considered the popular front tactic of alliance with Communist parties in order to expand their electoral strength.

In the late 1970s the Socialist International's principal European leaders (Palme, Kreisky, Mitterrand, Schmidt, Shimon Peres, Soares, and González) supported an effort to enlarge the organization and increase its activities outside Europe, particularly in Latin America. At the Socialist International's 1979 congress in Vancouver (Canada), over thirty parties—including seven from Latin America and the Caribbean—were listed as full members. In addition, eighteen other Latin American parties sent observers. These included Mexico's governing Institutional Revolutionary Party (PRI), Peru's American Revolutionary Popular Alliance (APRA), Argentina's Radical Civic Union (UCR) and Montoneros, Nicaragua's Sandinistas, and Grenada's New Jewel Movement. The keynote speakers at the Vancouver meeting included Carlos Andrés Pérez (former president of Venezuela), Francisco Peña Gómez (secretary of the Dominican Republic's governing party), Leonel Brizola (subsequently elected governor of Rio de Janeiro), and Edén Pastora (the Nicaraguan guerrilla leader who subsequently broke with the Sandinistas). The congress created a permanent committee for Latin America under the presidency of Peña Gómez.

However, as with the Socialist International's temporary success in Latin America in the late 1950s, the favorable climate existing in 1979 did not last long. The crisis in Central America significantly changed the environment in which the Socialist International operated in the region, and it confronted the organization with a difficult and potentially destructive task of self-definition. What kind of "democracy" and "socialism" did it seek to promote in Latin America? In 1979 the Socialist International could readily support the Sandinistas (a broad opposition front promising, among other things, political pluralism and free elections) against the Somoza dynasty. But it could exert only a modest influence over Sandinist Nicaragua, where the drive to consolidate an imperiled revolution soon clashed with the commitment to observe conventional democratic practices. As these dilemmas became sharper, the Spanish Socialist party adopted a typically cautious stance, promising that relations with the Sandinistas would remain cordial "for as long as the original plan for the revolution remains in force." At the Socialist International's conference in Rio de Janeiro in October 1984, strenuous efforts were made to forge a compromise between the Sandinistas and their non-*somocista* opponents that would permit a reasonably democratic election to be held in Nicaragua in November 1984, but reconciliation was not achieved. The Socialist International (like the Vatican) can sometimes play a mediating role, and it exercises some moral influence over its Latin American affiliates. But its real influence is only contingent and indirect.

Self-Reliance

If Latin American countries wish to strengthen their autonomy and avoid renewed dependence upon the United States, but can only obtain rather uncertain and limited external support from other sources, at least in principle they have the alternative of increased self-reliance. In fact, intraregional trade has been one of the most dynamic elements in Latin America's export performance over the past decade, and a number of regional organizations exist to promote international cooperation within the region. Unfortunately, these arrangements have also been affected by the current economic climate. The Central American Common Market has suffered the worst setbacks, but the Andean Pact and other organizations for regional cooperation have also encountered severe problems. The momentum of regional integration has been lost, and the debt crisis has even disrupted many purely bilateral exchanges between Latin American countries. For example, Brazil's export drive has been hampered by the collapse of major markets in Argentina and Chile. Despite Mexico and Venezuela's sale of oil on concessionary terms to the oil-importing countries of Central America and the Caribbean, there have been delays in payment and interruptions of supply. Liquidity shortages have even hampered trade relations between the major Latin American economies (for example, for a time Brazil and Mexico were forced to rely upon unsatisfactory barter arrangements because of payment difficulties).

During 1984 the major Latin American governments came together in the so-called Cartagena Club to strengthen regional solidarity and promote a common outlook on the economic difficulties afflicting the region. This effort was never likely to develop into a "debtors' cartel" as some western commentators feared, but it did contain the potential for a significant degree of cooperation vis-à-vis these countries' creditors. However, this initiative never really pointed in the direction of increased self-reliance. The goal was to achieve a stronger external bargaining position through collective agreement. Although it appeared as if a large area of common agreement had been defined, in practice each separate government made its own arrangements with the international financial community. There was insufficient community of interest or solidarity of outlook to offset the immediate centrifugal consequences of the debt crisis.

In summary, this section has argued that none of the external links cultivated by Latin American countries during the 1970s proved durable sources of support during the crises of the early 1980s. Nor was regional solidarity a significant source of strength. With the relative failure of these efforts at diversification, the consequence of the debt crisis was to renew Latin America's economic dependence on its traditional suppliers of external financing, especially in the United States. However, before evaluating the region's medium-term prospects, it is necessary to consider briefly the interrelationships between short-term U.S. economic policies (especially those of the U.S. Federal Reserve Board) and the development of the debt crisis in Latin America.

The Debt Crisis of 1982

It is now possible to see that some serious financial breakdown had become almost unavoidable in Latin America several years before the Mexican default in August 1982. For example, Ricardo Ffrench-Davis has noted that Latin America's commercial debt grew at such an unsustainable pace in the late 1970s that the only way to avoid severe dislocation as old debts matured was to allow gross indebtedness to continue to grow far faster than export earnings or economic output. Thus events such as the Falklands/Malvinas war and the Mexican default were only symptoms or detonators of a problem that was bound to manifest itself in some form. Ffrench-Davis also argues that even the U.S. Federal Reserve Board's switch to a policy of severe monetary restraint in October 1979 was insufficient to explain the depth and persistence of the debt crisis.[14] However, although some severe shock was to be expected for the reasons cited by Ffrench-Davis, it is striking how much clearer this appears with hindsight than it did at the time. Moreover, the particular form of the debt crisis and the severity and duration of the aftershocks owe much to the policy choices made in the United States—choices that were by no means mandated in advance.

From October 1979 (during the Carter administration) until at least autumn 1982, the U.S. Federal Reserve Board pursued a policy of severe monetary restraint. This policy was intended to counter the inflation unleashed (or at least exacerbated) by the 1979 oil-price shock and to restore confidence in the dollar as an international reserve currency. The Reagan administration argued from the outset that the United States' most important contribution to world development would be the pursuit of "sound economic policies" at home. In February 1982 it asserted that "both the United States and the rest of the world would benefit from a stronger and more stable dollar." Both within the United States and abroad, strong emphasis was to be placed on "the superiority of market solutions" and the priority of combating inflation. Some countries, industries, and regions would, of course, find the transition to noninflationary and private sector-led growth painful, but "market forces, rather than government bail-outs, will be relied upon to make appropriate adjustments."[15] The Reagan administration apparently believed that existing international provisions were fully adequate to resolve developing country financing problems.

However, by late 1982 most of Latin America was in virtual default. The world's leading finance ministers (encouraged by the U.S. Federal Reserve Board) were soon engaged in strenuous negotiations to expand the IMF's resources, maintain credit flows to developing countries, and reduce dollar interest rates. Unexpected developments in Latin America played a key role in producing this change of heart.

In August 1982 Mexico, by then the largest oil producer in Latin America, ran out of foreign exchange. Initially the Mexican government announced a ninety-day moratorium on the repayment of principal due on its external public debt. Soon thereafter the moratorium was extended into 1983, and Mexico was forced to take a series of drastic remedial measures—severe devaluation, unprecedented exchange controls, an "unthinkable" nationalization of the private banks, and of course, an emergency agreement with the IMF. For a short period immediately after the bank nationalization, it even appeared that the Mexican government intended to include these banks' interbank debt in the official moratorium on repayments. This step would have been a shattering blow to confidence in the world's short-term international money markets because it was not customary for international bankers to distinguish among the national origins of such assets and liabilities— let alone to assess bank fees according to perceptions of sovereign risk. In any event, Mexico was persuaded to exclude interbank transactions from the moratorium. But merely suggesting this possibility greatly aggravated other Latin American countries' liquidity problems with internationally active private banks.

An investigation by Joseph Kraft into the decision-making process during the August 1982 crisis concludes that Mexican governmental authorities were forced to create an international crisis in order to focus the U.S. Department of the Treasury's attention on their debt problems. This lack of attention may have been caused partly by poor Treasury staff work, but the Kraft study singles out "the basic strategy of the Reagan administration in foreign, and especially foreign economic, matters. The emphasis is on a negative approach—veto power. The perception is that since structures are shaky, the United States can exercise maximum influence by not going along, by hanging tough, and making others plead for the support of Washington. . . . Thus the Treasury, as a matter of moderate policy, did not want to help the Mexicans until a true emergency presented itself."[16]

As the repercussions of the Mexican moratorium spread, it became obvious that a true emergency *was* at hand. It then became apparent in the United States that the Latin American debt crisis threatened both the solvency of the U.S. banking system (Mexican debt alone accounted for 44 percent of the nine largest U.S. banks' capital) and the prosperity of many U.S. exporters.[17] At this point there was a marked change in U.S. policy, including a major relaxation of the U.S. Federal Reserve's restrictive monetary policy. The Latin American debt crisis could not be averted by this means, but it could perhaps be contained.

By early 1983 Mexico had both imposed a moratorium on its international creditors and extracted a "forced loan" from them. With the IMF's approval, international commercial banks were required to increase their net dollar exposure to Mexico by 7 percent in 1983 in order to secure a rescheduling agreement. Further "involuntary lending" to Mexico was required in 1984. Mexico's credit crunch was certainly the most dramatic financial event in 1982, but in reality the financial crisis extended far beyond Mexico—and, indeed, beyond the oil-exporting economies. Latin America as a whole was severely affected. Even before the Mexican crisis, Argentina was in technical default for reasons that were only partly related to the South Atlantic conflict of April–June 1982. By the end of the year, Brazil had moved far down a path similar to that of Mexico. Under pressure to find new sources of foreign exchange, Brazilian private banks had accumulated heavy liabilities on the interbank market. Thus they suffered severe side effects from the Mexican nationalization. In addition, Brazil's exports were hampered by the international recession, and its large external debt implied a heavy balance of payments cost when interest rates rose. Venezuela, Chile, and Peru are all engaged in comparable negotiations, together with many of the smaller Latin American countries. Indeed, virtually every country in the region is either openly renegotiating its foreign debt obligations or on the brink of doing so.

The New York Federal Reserve Bank has reviewed previous such episodes and concluded that: countries that do not promptly meet their contractual debt-servicing commitments subsequently experience substantial periods of time during which the rate of lending declines; once problems in a borrowing country become sufficiently serious for widespread payment delays to occur, they are likely to persist for some time (for example, of nineteen countries in payment arrears in 1978, fifteen were still in arrears in 1981); the time and resources needed to negotiate a rescheduling agreement are considerable. The short-term gain that the debtor country achieves by lowering its debt-service payments may be outweighed by a heavy loss in income over an extended period when bank lending falls and the domestic economy is forced to contract.[18]

It is clear that the policy of severe monetary restraint launched by the U.S. Federal Reserve Board in 1979 had within three years succeeded in curbing U.S. inflationary expectations and strengthening the dollar, albeit at a heavy cost in foregone economic output. In the wake of the debt crisis, this policy was temporarily relaxed. But once the most acute phase of the international crisis had passed, domestic considerations (especially the growth of the United States' structural budget deficit) once again took precedence, and monetary restraint was reimposed. Restrictive monetary policy works by pricing or rationing credit out of reach of the weakest borrowers. Who these borrowers may be is not known with certainty in advance. In this case, U.S. monetary authorities were apparently surprised to discover that the weakest borrowers for the most part proved to be Latin America's "sovereign" borrowers rather than U.S. corporations (which can use tax write-offs to offset their interest payments). These countries were vulnerable because most of their debt was denominated in dollars and carried variable interest rates. Tight U.S. monetary policy reduced domestic inflation (and thus Latin America's dollar export earnings) without reducing nominal interest rates. The resulting increase in "real" interest rates paid to dollar creditors accentuated the flight of private capital out of Latin America. Moreover, it raised the value of the dollar against all other currencies, which further depressed the dollar value of many Latin American exports. Since 1982 Latin America has shifted from being a net importer of foreign capital to a substantial net exporter of savings to the United States. These savings have helped finance the persistent and increasingly structural U.S. budget deficit. In the short run this net capital inflow into the United States had a positive counterpart from the Latin American standpoint in that the U.S. trade deficit rose to unprecedented proportions largely because of rising U.S. demand for foreign-produced goods. In 1984 some major Latin American countries began to record unheard-of trade surpluses, attributable not just to a compression of imports but also to a rapid increase in their exports to the United States. Unfortunately, although such a trade surplus may ease Latin American countries' international payments problems, its counterpart has been severely disturbed and depressed domestic economies threatened by hyperinflation.

The final section of this essay considers whether this short-term trend can produce a medium-term resolution of the debt crisis. What must be noted here is that as the U.S. trade deficit soars, foreign access to the U.S. market necessarily becomes highly politicized. Unless U.S. officials can find some market-determined method to slow and then reverse the growth of the trade deficit, politicians will feel obliged to do so by legislative means.

Economic dependence can take many forms. In the past some Latin American countries have been dependent upon official U.S. aid, and others have complained of dependence upon inflows of private investment channeled through multinational corporations. In the 1970s Latin America relied upon a new form of external dependence that seemed comparatively benign—commercial bank credit to sovereign lenders. Since 1982, however, Latin American dependence increasingly has taken another form. Trade access to industrialized country (especially U.S.) markets on favorable terms may be the most urgent requirement for many countries in the region, and in order to secure or preserve such access, Latin American governments may be asked to meet increasingly stringent conditions. Some of the required conditions will be purely technical and economic, but there could also be a political price to pay. At one extreme, Nicaragua faces exclusion from the benefits of the United States' Caribbean Basin Initiative for political reasons. At the other extreme, some governments are in such good standing with the United States that they can aspire to discriminatory free-trade agreements. In between these two extremes, the majority of Latin American governments will have to compete against each other for reasonably open access to the U.S. market. Just as the growth of Latin American debt in the late 1970s proceeded at a pace that was clearly (with hindsight) unsustainable, so the post-1982 growth in U.S. imports from Latin America proceeded at a pace too fast to continue. A significant degree of closure in U.S. market access would have severe consequences for Latin American exports and, consequently, would worsen the region's debt problems.

Medium-Term Prospects for Latin America

There are in principle just three ways in which Latin America's acute short-term foreign exchange problem can be resolved. Each has quite different implications for inter-American relations over the medium term. A broad and sustained recovery of the international economy might, with some time lag, produce a satisfactory solution based on market forces. In the interim, Latin American governments would confine themselves to the implementation of "sound" stabilization policies. This is, of course, the outcome advocated by the U.S. government and generally favored by private bankers. The second alternative is along lines envisioned by the Brandt Commission. An unassisted recovery will be too slow and too weak, and it will demand crippling and destabilizing sacrifices of foregone economic growth by debtor governments. Recognizing this, western policymakers might agree on some concerted program of economic stimulus and financial assistance, roughly similar to the post-World War II Marshall Plan. The third alternative has fewer advocates, but it may be the most probable. In the absence of either a strong "spontaneous" recovery or a successful package of emergency measures, Latin America's immediate foreign exchange problem will be "resolved" through some combination of deflation and internal economic restructuring that reduces the demand for convertible currency until it equates with a permanently reduced supply. Whether this represents a satisfactory, or even a sustainable, "solution" in any broader sense remains highly questionable.

In practice, these three solutions are all likely to operate to some degree, the proportions varying substantially from country to country. Whichever of the three alternatives preponderates, the immediate acute scarcity of foreign exchange can be expected to ease in most Latin American countries. (For example, by late 1984 Brazil and Mexico—the two largest debtors—had made considerable progress in rebuilding their foreign exchange reserves and rescheduling their debt-servicing obligations.) When that happens, the initial condition of extreme financial vulnerability will give way to some new pattern of relationships in which Latin American governments will recover at least some limited room for maneuver. Which of these three methods of financial "adjustment" (a deceptively neutral term) prevails will make a great difference to the quality of inter-American relations over the medium term.

A sound market-based recovery would presumably originate in the industrialized countries (probably in the United States) and only revive Latin America's growth prospects after a substantial time lag. As interest rates fell and most export prospects brightened, some major countries (probably led by Brazil) would find it easier to service their foreign-debt obligations and attract new capital. It is not clear whether such a recovery would most strongly benefit newly industrializing countries or the exporters of traditional commodities whose terms of trade have been badly squeezed. Unable or reluctant to incur too much additional debt, Latin American countries as they recovered might turn instead to direct foreign investment as a source of external capital, thus inviting the prospect of a large expansion in the role played by multinational corporations. With a strong dollar, U.S.-based corporations would be well represented, although Japanese and West European firms would also be attracted. Inflation will remain a severe problem throughout Latin America whatever else happens, and public enterprise would be reined in and social spending held down so as to maintain fiscal discipline and provide tax incentives for enterprise. Some time would elapse before imports returned to pre-1982 levels, and it would take even longer before former levels of employment and real wages could be restored. Firm government would be needed in the meantime (not necessarily authoritarian, but resolute in the pursuit of "sound" policies even if democratic in form), and recovery would come fastest in those countries in which policymakers wholeheartedly pursued this strategy. These would also tend to be the United States' most loyal allies on general international issues, and so they might receive some supplementary financial assistance on that basis. This assistance would, however, play only a small part in the recovery. The main incentive offered would be the prospect of unhindered access to the U.S. market for Latin American exporters.

The future would be different for those countries that discourage foreign investment, vacillate over the pursuit of trade surpluses, or resort to fiscal stimulation to restore earlier levels of employment—that is, for those that are not wholehearted in the pursuit of "sound" policies. A "spontaneous" recovery would reach them later; their difficulties with foreign finance and the supply of imports would last longer; and in the meantime little help could be expected from the United States either in the form of financial assistance or trade concessions. The prospects would be even worse for those countries that also dissent from the U.S. line on other international issues (not only anticommunism, but also, for example, willingness to suppress narcotics trafficking). In this case, recovery would clearly tend to reinforce an inter-American system structured along traditional lines, with pro-U.S. and pro-private-sector Latin American governments in the ascendant. However, it is also apparent even from this brief sketch that there would be many obstacles along the way. Even if the U.S. economy performed as required, several years would elapse before even the best-placed Latin American countries could recover the levels of employment and consumption achieved at the beginning of the decade.[19] In the meantime, "sound" policies would produce many losers and only a limited range of rather visible beneficiaries. This may be particularly difficult to accept in the newly restored and still fragile democracies of Brazil and Argentina, among others. It is overly optimistic to assume that many governments will proceed firmly and wholeheartedly along this route, especially if the industrialized countries remain in doubt concerning the breadth and durability of their recovery prospects.

Skepticism regarding the market-based solution has fed demands for a "new Marshall Plan," a "new Bretton Woods," or some other variety of concerted international program to ease the debt burden and boost development prospects in developing countries. There is no single alternative to be considered here, but the various schemes put forward all have several basic characteristics in common. For example, they all require a negotiated agreement among major western governments—a stringent condition considering the inability of the United States and its allies to reach consensus on the many other issues that divide them. In practice, it is only with Washington's approval that any such scheme could be launched. This applies to developing countries in general, but above all to any scheme for aiding Latin America. (Indeed, the Caribbean Basin Initiative was launched more or less unilaterally by the United States with only token assistance from its allies.) Therefore, various major U.S. domestic lobbies would have to be persuaded that an emergency assistance package for Latin America had something to offer them. In fact, U.S. bankers and exporters do have substantial interests at stake in Latin America, and no doubt the security dimension could be emphasized.[20]

A brief consideration of the conditions that would have to be met in order to secure U.S. endorsement of some Marshall Plan-type aid program for Latin America makes clear what sort of inter-American system it would serve. Instead of rewarding "sound" policies, support would go primarily to those countries of greatest strategic importance to the United States or in greatest danger of collapse. Aid would come with conditions required by U.S. exporters, labor unions, bankers, evangelists, and whoever else could muster votes in Congress. It would probably tilt inter-American relations toward bilateralism and away from multilateralism. Enlightened policymakers would certainly try to promote nondiscriminatory assistance along the lines favored by Brandt or Schmidt, and some of their arguments might eventually prevail. But the public mood in the United States and other industrialized countries is not conducive to such efforts.[21] Unfortunately, therefore, the second alternative route to recovery is likely to be possible (if at all) only on conditions that are opposed to Latin America's desire for autonomy and self-assertion and that are bad for the development process.

The most likely prospect is that neither the market-based solution nor any concessionary aid program will prove swift or strong enough to resolve the foreign exchange difficulties faced by most Latin American countries in the medium term without creating potentially unmanageable economic and political conflicts and without sacrificing the possibilities for future growth. Therefore, economic adjustment will be brought about mainly through deflation and/or internal restructuring. Adjustment can take many forms, and it can be accompanied by a variety of international orientations (as Latin American experiences of the 1930s can testify). In general, however, this adjustment process will add to the problems of maintaining regional cohesion and respect for constituted authority.

Such a statement does not necessarily endorse the alarmist predictions that sometimes follow. Neither social upheaval nor outright default can be excluded as *possible* developments in contemporary Latin America, but these are far from being the most *probable* outcomes. If it proves necessary to administer repeated doses of austerity to a restless populace,

Latin American regimes will generally prove capable of doing so. Similarly, they are quite unlikely to turn away from the existing international economic system, even when the penalties for attempting to participate seem unduly harsh. The most likely outcome is that the major Latin American governments will reluctantly acquiesce to external requirements that lack their consent. Dominant opinion will be that this outcome is unjust but inescapable.[22]

If most Latin American countries do not experience a satisfactory economic recovery during the rest of the 1980s, many will believe that the responsibility for this failure lies more in Washington than in national capitals. This view is not confined to Latin American politicians. For example, Rudiger Dornbusch has argued that "the regulatory and macroeconomic policies of the United States continue to aggravate the debt problem. . . . The commercial policies of the United States and American criticism of the trade policies of the debtor countries are entirely inconsistent with a satisfactory solution to the debt problem. . . . In sum, American policy has been to try and do the impossible: be good neighbors, protect the bad loans of banks, and protect domestic employment. The United States cannot achieve all these targets at the same time."[23] Dornbusch fears that good neighborliness may prove the most expendable of the three priorities.

Over the medium term, then, Latin America's economic prospects and even its political future will depend heavily on policy decisions taken in Washington and defined mainly in terms of U.S. perceptions and priorities. U.S. government policymakers striving to halt or reverse the long-term erosion of U.S. ascendancy in the world must contend with deep-seated forces that move in the opposite direction. In these circumstances, Latin America's aspirations for both economic recovery and political autonomy are unlikely to be satisfied, even in part. It is possible that a sustainable recovery in the industrialized countries will provide a context in which Latin American countries, with much effort, can regain by the end of the decade the income levels first achieved in 1980. However, it is not difficult to envision developments in the U.S. economy that would deprive the region of even this degree of recovery. In any event, it is unlikely that the United States will resume within the next five to ten years its pre-1982 role as a net supplier of capital to finance Latin American development. On the contrary, the United States may remain a net importer of capital for most of the 1980s. If this is the case, Latin America will find its economic and political well-being heavily dependent upon access to the U.S. market for its export products. Trade dependency of this kind could prove just as constraining as traditional variants of dependency mediated through foreign aid, arms flows, and the activities of multinational corporations.

This discovery of renewed dependence on the United States and the frustration of hopes for a more pluralist international order are bitter blows to many Latin Americans. Both the material and psychological climate will make it more difficult for their governments to negotiate with the United States, with other international power centers, or with each other on the basis of self-confidence and mutual cooperation. No clear prediction follows of some inevitable upheaval or confrontation. But the inter-American system, like the international community of nations as a whole, has been performing poorly for some time. The medium-term economic prospects for Latin America can only add to its burdens.

Nuffield College
Oxford University

Notes

1. This raises an interesting question of symmetry that cannot be resolved here. As Latin America's relative position in the world improved, did the official perceptions of Latin American policymakers also lag behind? The available evidence tentatively suggests the opposite. Latin American leaders more typically anticipate a degree of strength and autonomy that their countries have yet to attain. But there are undercurrents of pessimism and uncertainty in the official perceptions of both rising and relatively declining powers. Latin American overconfidence in the 1970s masked a sense of anxiety that has been amply vindicated in the early 1980s.

2. For a discussion of the Soviet-Argentine rapprochement occasioned by the U.S.-initiated grain embargo against the Soviet Union in 1980, see Nikki Miller and Laurence Whitehead, "The Soviet Interest in Latin America: An Economic Perspective," in Robert Cassen, ed., *The Soviet Union and the Third World* (London: Chatham House, 1985).

3. It is both salutary and ironic to reread the political-risk evaluations of Latin America that were paraded with such solemnity before the debt crisis broke. Both *Euromoney* and *Institutional Investor* ranked Mexico as the most creditworthy sovereign borrower in Latin America in 1980. Argentina was ranked third.

4. *Wall Street Journal,* 30 August 1984.

5. Ronald I. McKinnon, *An International Standard for Monetary Stabilization,* (Washington, D.C.: Institute for International Economics, 1984), provides a striking interpretation of the evolution of what he calls the "world dollar standard" and its increasing instability. In the 1960s "visions of a continually dwindling American gold stock kept presidents Eisenhower, Kennedy, and even Johnson awake at night. This strengthened the conservative bias in American monetary policy toward stabilizing the domestic price level. . . . After 1970, only the Federal Reserve System—at the center of the world dollar standard—conducted monetary policy without reference

to the foreign exchanges. . . . the American cycle of boom and bust of the past dozen years is primarily due to instability in the demand for dollar assets . . . and [to] the failure of the Fed to accommodate these demands by adjusting U.S. money growth toward stabilizing the exchange rate. . . . The world economy suffered major price inflations in 1973–74 and 1979–80, and a major deflation in 1982–83. Each of these episodes followed one of the sharp depreciations or appreciations of the U.S. dollar. . . . That these fluctuations in the American and world price levels were mainly monetary in origin, and not primarily due to exogenous changes in the price of oil, is established empirically (below)" (pp. 8, 10, 5).

McKinnon argues that U.S. monetary authorities acting alone can no longer effectively stabilize these worldwide cycles of inflation and deflation, even if they shift from what he criticizes as their narrowly insular analyses. Regulating the "world money supply" in the 1980s would require systematic collaboration between several major central banks. For illustrative purposes he suggests an international monetary standard as follows: 45 percent dollars, 35 percent deutschemarks, 20 percent yen. These proportions illustrate how U.S. economic ascendancy has diminished since the early postwar years.

Although McKinnon's economic reasoning is very sophisticated, his political assumptions are quite innocent. There are deep-seated reasons why U.S. policy-makers are unable to achieve consistency between monetary and fiscal policies even on a national basis, quite apart from tailoring a viable international standard. This is not simply a problem of false economic analysis. His proposed solution would drastically affect internal and international power relationships, as can be seen from the following: "The monetary base of the new international standard would be under the joint control of the Bundesbank, the Bank of Japan, and the Federal Reserve System. And . . . the U.S. would cede some autonomy in determining the supply of dollars in order better to stabilize the demand for them" (pp. 75–76).

6. Charles Kindleberger, *The World in Depression, 1929–1933* (London: Penguin, 1973), p. 28. "The depression was so wide, so deep, and so long because the international economic system was rendered unstable by British inability and U.S. unwillingness to assume responsibility for stabilizing it in three particulars: (1) maintaining a relatively open market for distress goods; (2) providing counter-cyclical long-term lending; and (3) discounting in crisis" (pp. 291–92).

7. According to an official U.S. government estimate, one of every six U.S. jobs now depends on exports. Sales to developing countries rose from 29 percent of all U.S. exports in 1970 to 39 percent in 1982. *Wall Street Journal*, 28 March 1983.

8. The *Economic Report of the President* (Washington, D.C.: U.S. Government Printing Office) transmitted to Congress in February 1984 states, "Mexico alone accounted for 7.6 percent of U.S. exports in 1981. Seven of the most indebted Latin American countries together accounted for 13.9 percent of U.S. exports. . . . The U.S. bilateral trade balance with Mexico alone . . . registered a decline of $12 billion between 1981 and 1983. The U.S. loss in net exports to Latin America was about $21 billion. . . . Exports of U.S. industries such as farm and construction machinery have been particularly hard-hit" (p. 47).

9. Governor Wallich of the U.S. Federal Reserve Board testified to the U.S. Senate on this process on 23 March 1984, pointing out that eventually the United States might "find itself in the position of having to earn a surplus on the trade balance to cover a deficit on investment income." *Federal Reserve Bulletin* (Washington, D.C.) (April 1984): 295–96. This was the predicament that caused so much strain in the post-World War II British economy, which was accustomed to its *rentier* status.

10. For an evaluation of U.S. policies in Central America through May 1983, see Laurence Whitehead, "Explaining Washington's Central American Policies," *Journal of Latin American Studies* 15 (November 1983): 321–63. An updated version through mid-1984 appears in *Politica Internazionale* (Rome) (Autumn 1984).

11. Increased trade with OPEC countries accounted for about two-thirds of the rise in total Latin American trade with all developing countries. These percentages were calculated from *United Nations Yearbook of International Trade Statistics, 1981,* 1 (New York: United Nations, 1983), special table C. They refer to "developing countries of the Americas," a category embracing all of Latin America (including Cuba and former European colonies in the Caribbean, even the French overseas departments of Guadeloupe and Martinique).

12. For a fuller discussion focusing on the cases of Cuba, Chile, Argentina, and Nicaragua, see Miller and Whitehead, "Soviet Interest."

13. I discuss this in "International Aspects of Democratization," in Guillermo O'Donnell, Philippe Schmitter, and Laurence Whitehead, eds., *Prospects for Democracy: The Transition from Authoritarian Regimes* (Baltimore: Johns Hopkins University Press, 1986). The permanent head of the EEC delegation to Latin America, Dr. Manfredo Macioti, recently made a rather visionary appeal for western Europe and Latin America to join together in a strategy to roll back recession and relaunch the world economy. In somewhat more practical terms, he also called upon the EEC to support those Latin American programs for economic integration that are rooted in respect for parliamentary democracy and human rights.

14. Ricardo Ffrench-Davis, *Deuda externa y alternativas de desarrollo en América Latina* (Santiago, Chile) (Apuntes CIEPLAN, June 1984), p. 2.

15. *Economic Report of the President* (Washington, D.C.: U.S. Government Printing Office, 1982), pp. 167, 169, 189.

16. Joseph Kraft, *The Mexican Rescue* (New York: Group of Thirty, 1984), p. 12.

17. "Debt crises were a major factor in reducing U.S. sales in 1983 to at least six Latin American debtor countries. The combined 1982–83 loss in U.S. exports to them totalled nearly $15 billion, equally over one-half of the total drop in U.S. exports in 1982 and 1983." *U.S. Trade Performance in 1983 and Outlook* (Washington, D.C.: U.S. Department of Commerce, June 1984), p. 29.

18. "Bank Lending to Developing Countries: Problems and Prospects," *Federal Reserve Bank of New York Quarterly Review* (Autumn 1982): 27–29.

19. "How long will it take for world recovery, accompanied by IMF-approved stabilization plans and continued lending, to restore [Latin America's]

growth and improve debt servicing capability? Even with good luck it will probably take most of the decade. A base-case forecast made on these assumptions puts real GDP in the seven major Latin American countries only 6 percent higher in 1987 than in 1982, a 7 percent drop in per capita income." Thomas O. Enders and Richard P. Mattione, *Latin America: The Crisis of Debt and Growth* (Washington, D.C.: Brookings Institution, 1984), p. 3.

From another perspective, Albert Fishlow casts doubt on the assumption "that economic recovery of the industrialized countries will give such a large boost to trade that debtor-country imports will not have to continue to bear the full burden of adjustment, permitting growth to resume comparatively soon. This picture is simply too rosy on two major counts. One is the overstatement of the responsiveness of developing-country exports to income growth in the industrialized countries. The other is the possibility that global development in the future will be less trade-intensive than in the last two decades." Albert Fishlow, "The Debt Crisis: Round Two Ahead?" in Richard E. Feinberg and Valeriana Kallab, eds., *Adjustment Crisis in the Third World* (Washington, D.C.: Transaction Books, for the Overseas Development Council, 1984), p. 40. William R. Cline, *International Debt and the Stability of the World Economy* (Washington, D.C.: Institute for International Economics, September 1983) contains the optimistic projections queried by these authors.

20. Enders and Mattione, *Latin America,* p. 56, resort to a sophisticated variant of this approach: "When the crisis in some countries drags on with per capita incomes below 1980 levels, as they may be for much of this decade, and without credible promise of relief, it is easy to imagine resentment and frustration exploding and turning against governments when they fail to persuade the U.S. and other industrial countries of the need for more generous terms. Not only would the current broad but weak trend toward democracy fail, but public order and national security could also be at risk. And it is worth remembering that after a generation of often failed national security governments, military intervention may no longer be the plausible alternative it was in the 1960s and 1970s. . . . The degree of danger . . . is sufficiently great to justify every effort to manage the crisis through facilitating trade, adjusting exchange rates, promoting capital reforms, and providing additional funds."

21. Both advocates and opponents of such a strategy agree that public opinion is not ready. Thus John Williamson considers that current conditions in Latin America make a new "Marshall Plan" as appropriate as it was for western Europe in the late 1940s: "A rather similar international initiative could play an equally constructive role in rekindling growth and promoting the emergence of democracy in Latin America. It is nonetheless a fact, however tragic, that the present-day leaders of the Western world show absolutely no signs of responding to the contemporary crisis in Latin America with leadership of the calibre provided by President Truman and George Marshall. Given that political fact, it is pointless to discuss responding to the debt crisis in terms of grandiose plans for restructuring international debts. A major international initiative of this sort is conceivable only after a profound change in Northern political attitudes, or else in the wake of a

crisis that would first produce further deterioration in the Latin American position." John Williamson, "The Debt Crisis in Perspective," *The Journal of International Affairs* (special issue on global debt) 38, No. 1 (Summer 1984): 21.

Federal Reserve Chairman Paul A. Volcker, in an August 8, 1984, statement to the Foreign Affairs Committee of the House of Representatives, acknowledged the slowness and some of the strains and injustices of the current adjustment process. However, he stated that proposals for "some sweeping new initiative to settle the problem decisively and 'across the board' . . . seem to me based on unrealistic assumptions—typically on an expectation that someone else is prepared to assume large new burdens. I do not sense, in that connection, any willingness on the part of the U.S. Congress, or other parliaments, to provide massive new financial assistance for countries that, in the economic hierarchy of developing countries, are among the most advanced. . . . Countries are not in the same position, in terms of their own resources and in terms of the efforts they have made to place their own economies on a sounder footing, and it would be difficult—even perverse—to provide the same terms and conditions for all."

22. Fishlow puts this well: "If it were not for past stabilization experiences that proved unsuccessful, and a respectable literature skeptical of orthodox policy, dissent would not run so deep. What has been added this time is the further conviction that the debtor countries are being forced to bear the cost unfairly. In their view they were not alone in erring by borrowing excessively. Banks also loaned too much. . . . Inappropriate fiscal policy in the U.S. that contributes to high interest rates may be criticized by the IMF, but it goes unpunished and undebited for the difficulties it has imposed on the adjustment of others" ("The Debt Crisis," p. 47). Widespread dissent is probable, but default or uncontrollable upheaval is less likely.

23. Rudiger Dornbusch, "On the Consequences of Muddling Through the Debt Crisis," *The World Economy* (London) 7, No. 2 (June 1984): 146, 160. On the origins of the crisis he writes: "The lending (and borrowing) may have been unsound in the first place, but it certainly became so when the monetary-fiscal policy mix in the U.S. increased rates of interest sharply and caused the dollar to appreciate and commodity prices to decline. The combination of these three 'shocks' is devastating on countries whose debt is largely denominated in dollars. There is no question that the present debt problem is in good measure due to the failure of the U.S. to pursue sound fiscal policies. It is therefore absurd, and indeed outright cynical, that American Treasury officials should travel to the debtor countries preaching belt tightening" (p. 151). He justifies placing so much emphasis on U.S. policies as follows: "The macro-economic policies of the U.S., as the largest developed economy, determine the environment for developing countries not only directly but also via the indirect effect on other developed countries" (p. 145).

3

Democratization, Endogenous Modernization, and Integration: Strategic Choices for Latin America and Economic Relations with the United States

Fernando Fajnzylber

This essay pursues two main goals. First, it draws attention to some of the major challenges that Latin America will face in the next decade. These include: imbalances in the domestic productive structure and accumulated social needs; the fact that the international market, which in the past encouraged and supported growth, is becoming (at least in the short- and medium-terms) an obstacle to domestic economic dynamism; and the possible implications that industrial and technological restructuring under way in industrialized countries may have for Latin America. Second, this essay argues that the concepts of "democratization" and "endogenous modernization" constitute bases, starting from the present economic and political crisis, for articulating new development strategies that will make it possible for Latin America to meet the grave challenges facing the region in the next decades. These developments hold important implications for the future of U.S.–Latin American relations.

A necessary point of departure for this analysis is an understanding of the specific characteristics of both the present international situation and relations between Latin America and the United States. Forecasting economic relations between the United States and Latin America is a significant intellectual challenge even in normal circumstances. If the task is approached with a minimum of rigor, it is necessary to formulate assumptions in at least the following five areas: (1) the domestic political-economic evolution of Latin American countries and the United States; (2) the foreseeable evolution of East-West relations, both in advanced capitalist states and among Latin American countries; (3) the evolution of the world economy; (4) the principal technological trends at the international level; and finally (5) the impact of developments in each of these areas on economic relations between Latin America and the United States.

This intellectual challenge is now substantially more difficult because the present situation constitutes, in each of the different aspects mentioned above, a point of inflection for trends experienced during the post-World War II period. Under present circumstances, the extrapolation of trends is an unsuitable methodological approach. In order to make projections, it is necessary to interpret, and in order to interpret, one must work on the basis of a viable theory. But at present, in both politics and economics, perplexity and theoretical impotence have to a considerable extent replaced the credibility and consensus that at other times emanated from accepted scientific proofs.

In the political field, this perplexity is expressed in the upsurge of alternative manifestos in which a vocation for social engineering predominates over political sensitivity. On the one hand, there are proposals that seek to reconstruct the social and political conditions prevailing in the golden decades of the nineteenth century, when a group of Schumpeterian businessmen led the transformation of economy and society. Other proposals invite western Europe and the United States to emulate the Japanese "miracle," adding to it the technologies of the twenty-first century. Yet it is unlikely that the welfare state constructed over the last several decades can be so easily dismantled in these countries so long as democratic practices remain in force. Neither is it easy to imagine a politico-cultural shift that would lead the workers of Ford, Renault, or Phillips to assemble every Monday morning to sing their respective firm's anthem—even if the ministries of industry and trade in each country were transformed into a copy of Japan's Ministry of Trade and Industry (MITI). History and comparative experiences are without doubt a fertile source of inspiration for conceiving utopias, particularly in moments of crisis. But it is indispensable that the cultural and political particularities of the societies in question be incorporated into these discussions. The "Manchesterian" and "Japanese-technological" utopias described above do not fully meet this requirement.

Nor is the future of East-West relations likely to present easy alternatives. From an optimistic perspective, recent developments suggest that the arms race will continue indefinitely. But from a pessimistic point of view, these same events mean that humanity may be approaching what could be its final mistake.

In the economic field, the increasingly somber vision offered by quantitative indicators is accentuated by the inability of available economic theory to provide a clear interpretation of what is happening and, consequently, plausible ways of overcoming the current crisis. Moreover, there is a widespread conviction that the international financial system requires modifications as substantial as those that national financial structures experienced in the 1930s. There is also a growing consensus that the international economic system is currently experiencing a transition toward a new technological-industrial pattern in which the relative weight of different sectors, countries, organizational frameworks, and productive modes will be substantially modified. This panorama may explain the melancholy of successive economic projections that international organizations have offered for the next decade. Recent trends suggest that the most pessimistic scenario may well be the most probable.

For the first time since 1945, the gross domestic product fell throughout Latin America in 1982. The majority of Latin American countries were unable to pay their external debt, regardless of the size of their domestic market, the availability of oil and other natural resources, or their strategies for penetrating the international market. Latin America experienced zero-order economic growth during the period from 1981 through 1984, resulting in a 9 percent decrease in per capita gross domestic product (GDP) and further aggravating already high levels of urban and rural poverty. The domestic social implications and the international financial dimensions of these trends are obvious, and they explain why a consensus is beginning to emerge that Latin American countries should reformulate and significantly redefine the development strategy they have followed over the last several decades. At this juncture, the international crisis and the accumulation of domestic economic imbalances in different Latin American countries converge.

If this discussion has accurately described the current international situation, it is obvious that future U.S.–Latin American economic relations can pose only limited and modest objectives. In addition to recognizing the fundamental perplexity of the current situation, this essay examines three dimensions of U.S.–Latin American economic relations: the domestic economic challenges that gave rise to the development strategy Latin American countries have followed in the last several decades; the outlook for the international economy, which played a positive role in Latin America's past growth but which will constitute an important future constraint; and the principal international technological trends. The conclusion synthesizes these domestic and external challenges, and it suggests directions for new development strategies. Democratization and endogenous modernization are possible axes for a new development strategy in Latin America.

Latin America's Disjointed Industrialization and the Problem of Accumulated Social Needs[1]

Latin America's industrialization has without doubt played a decisive role in the region's precarious and peculiar modernization during the last several decades. This industrialization process differed from country to country depending upon the structure and orientation of the traditional export sector, the size and degree of heterogeneity of the domestic market, and the character of international economic ties. Industrialization began in some Latin American countries at the end of the nineteenth century; it intensified during the Great Depression and after World War II. From the 1930s through the 1950s, the significance of industrialization extended well beyond particular sectors. To a considerable extent it constituted the center of gravity for development strategies. Moreover, industrialization became the banner for various social movements that, despite national particularities, shared a commitment to modernize their countries (Aguirre Cerda in Chile, Cárdenas in Mexico, Haya de la Torre in Peru, Perón in Argentina, and Vargas in Brazil).

Following this period of rapid industrial growth accompanied by accelerated urbanization, the 1970s witnessed growing frustration with the consequences of industrialization for national development. This in turn produced an inclination to address the deficiencies of industrialization by rejecting it entirely. In this sense, industrialization is passing from a privileged position in Latin America to one of widespread reexamination. A better understanding of the specific characteristics of Latin American industrialization helps explain this shift in perceptions.

An examination of Latin America's past economic performance shows that three groups of countries reflect the heterogeneity of conditions and strategies in the region. The countries also constitute a basis on which to delineate central elements of the debate concerning future development strategies, particularly industrialization strategies. These groups of countries are: Brazil and Mexico; Argentina, Chile, and Uruguay; and the members of the Central American Common Market.[2]

During the past three decades, Latin America grew at a more rapid pace than the world economy as a whole (5.5 percent and 4.9 percent annual growth of GDP, respectively, between 1950 and 1977), surpassing both the United States and western Europe (3.6 percent and 4.3 percent, respectively). Only Japan and the centrally planned economies experienced more dynamic growth (8.6 percent and 7.3 percent, respectively). However, when one considers population growth, the region's relative position in terms of per capita output eroded significantly; its annual per capita growth rate over this same period was slower than that of the world economy as a whole (2.6 percent and 2.9 percent, respectively), and it lagged behind both western Europe (3.6 percent) and Asia (2.7 percent).

Rapid population growth is a peculiarity of Latin American development. Between 1950 and 1975 Latin America's population grew more rapidly than that of any other region in the world. It doubled in twenty-five years, whereas world population grew less than 60 percent, and the population of the industrialized countries increased only slightly more than 30 percent. In 1963 Latin America's population was approximately 20 percent more than that of the United States; in 1979 this ratio had risen to 60 percent, and by 1995 the region's population is expected to be more than double that of the United States.

As in other regions, the industrial sector in Latin America has grown at a more rapid pace than the economy as a whole.[3] The relative weight of the manufacturing sector rose from 18 percent of the region's GDP in 1950 to 24 percent in 1977, a level similar to the 25 percent observed in the United States. During this period of rapid expansion, the industrial sector transformed itself internally and modified other productive activities in terms qualitatively similar to industrialization processes in other regions. It absorbed labor from the agricultural sector and contributed inputs and equipment for agricultural modernization; it encouraged the development of service activities necessary for the production, marketing, and financing of industrial goods, which acted as a further incentive to industrial expansion; it urbanized and modified the transportation and communications infrastructure; and it influenced (both directly and indirectly) the orientation and growth of the public sector—directly through its physical and educational infrastructure requirements and indirectly through the social transformation produced by economic growth (expressed in terms of the development of trade unions, political parties, consumer organizations, and other social groups that influenced the expansion and orientation of the public sector).

The industrialization process assumed different dimensions and forms in different Latin American countries. Brazil and Mexico experienced the most rapid industrialization in the region (8.5 percent and 7.3 percent annual growth in industrial production, respectively, in comparison with 6.8 percent for the region as a whole). Argentina, Chile, and Uruguay (4.1 percent, 3.7 percent, and 2.7 percent, respectively) stand at the other extreme. These latter three countries—whose industrialization was initially advanced and later frustrated—generated 41 percent of Latin America's total industrial output in 1950, but in 1978 their share fell to 20.5 percent. Brazil and Mexico, large countries undergoing rapid industrialization, increased their share of Latin America's industrial output from 42.1 percent to 61.8 percent during the same period. Whereas in 1950 Brazil and Mexico generated an industrial output similar to that of Argentina, Chile, and Uruguay combined, in 1978 the industrial output of these latter countries represented only one-third that of Brazil and Mexico.

Argentina, Chile, and Uruguay have a significantly lower rate of demographic growth and a higher degree of urbanization than other Latin American countries. Consequently, a smaller proportion of their population is engaged in agricultural activities. Despite a slower rate of growth (which is also reflected in the fact that their investment coefficient was consistently lower than the regional average between 1960 and 1978), estimates for 1970 indicate that there was comparatively less poverty in these countries than in the rest of Latin America. Indeed, whereas some 26 percent of the region's total urban population was below the "poverty line" in 1970, the corresponding proportions for Argentina, Chile, and Uruguay were 5 percent, 12 percent, and 10 percent, respectively. Similarly, some 62 percent of Latin America's rural population was below the poverty line in 1970, while only 19 percent was in Argentina, 25 percent in Chile, and practically none in Uruguay.

The contrast between these three countries' premature development and then arrested industrialization and Brazil and Mexico's post-World War II industrial dynamism is remarkable. Brazil, whose economic transformation and industrial modernization lead the region, suffers from some of the most severe poverty in all of Latin America: 35 percent of Brazil's urban population was below the poverty line in 1970, whereas the proportion was 26 percent for the region as a whole. This proportion was 73 percent in rural Brazil versus 62 percent for the whole region. In Mexico, the same poverty indicators were not far below the regional average. No matter how much Brazil and Mexico may have improved living conditions during the 1970s, it is clear that a significant percentage of the population has received little benefit from industrial modernization.

The economic dynamism of the small countries that comprise the Central American Common Market is striking. Between 1950 and 1978 their economic growth rate was higher than that of the region as a whole and comparable to that of Brazil, Mexico, and Venezuela. Despite the reservations and qualifications that apply to GDP growth as an economic indicator, this fact does qualify somewhat the stereotypes that are generally held regarding Central America. The prevalence of such uninformed views in part accounts for the perplexity caused at the international level—and even in Latin America—by recent social and political movements in Central America.

One manifestation of Central America's disjointed and precarious "modernization" (though, in the final analysis, still modernization) is the region's rapid urbanization. The region's urban population grew from 16 percent to 43 percent of the total population between 1950 and the late 1970s. In 1980 Nicaragua was the most urbanized (54 percent) country in the region. Costa Rica, the most urbanized country in Central America in 1950 (26 percent), increased its urban population to 46 percent in 1980.

During the same period the proportion of economic output stemming from the primary sector in Central America dropped from 38 percent to 27 percent for the region as a whole. Secondary activities raised their share of regional output from 15 percent to 24 percent, with the highest proportions being reached in Costa Rica (28 percent) and Nicaragua (27 percent). During this period of rapid industrial growth, there was also a significant increase in life expectancy, development of transportation and energy infrastructure, and a decline in illiteracy from 61 percent to 43 percent for the region's population as a whole. The most dramatic example was Costa Rica, where illiteracy fell to only 10 percent in 1975.

Growth, urbanization, and precarious industrialization in Central America coexist with urban and rural marginality. These developments fostered the expansion of middle-class sectors tied to a burgeoning state bureaucracy and commercial and professional activities. They also produced a new urban bourgeoisie with interests in modern agro-industrial activities, industry, trade, banking, and real estate, as well as an industrial proletariat limited in size but well aware of both its relative leverage and the persistence of powerful agricultural interests in traditional export sectors. Central American society has thus undergone important changes in recent decades that were not reflected in national political structures. The contradiction between increasing social complexities, the magnitude of accumulated needs, and closed political structures (Costa Rica is the exception) called forth the symbiotic alliance between powerful economic groups and the armed forces. These tensions became increasingly intense over time, until they finally burst to the surface in the late 1970s.

In addition to relatively rapid industrialization, Latin America has experienced sectoral shifts within manufacturing activities that are apparently similar to those observed in industrialized countries, including the increased importance of consumer durables, chemicals, and light engineering products. Thus Latin America formally reproduced those trends that proved functional to the transformation of production in industrialized countries: in these countries, the satisfaction of basic consumer needs for nondurable goods encouraged the expansion of durable-goods industries and their increasing diversification; the scarcity of natural resources, combined with access to cheap oil, fostered the substitution of synthetic products for natural ones, which in turn stimulated the rapid growth of the chemical industry; the intensification of international competition and the pressure of trade unions on wages encouraged automation and increased the demand for machines and equipment. Ironically, then, Latin America—a region with significant unsatisfied basic needs, a generous endowment of natural resources, and abundant and unemployed labor—has pursued an industrial pattern that was congruent with conditions prevailing in industrialized countries.

This development strategy has been largely dysfunctional in terms of the needs and potentialities of Latin American countries. Among its most striking consequences is income concentration, which has reached critical levels in the more advanced countries in the region. The most revealing cases in this regard are Brazil and Mexico, where economic dynamism, domestic market size, and diversification of production reached their highest levels in Latin America. After three decades of rapid economic growth in these two countries (which will be difficult to reproduce in the future), the top 10 percent of the population controls five times the wealth of the lowest 40 percent. Indeed, the industrialization-urbanization process has raised the income of a significant proportion of the population while holding a high proportion of the agricultural and marginal urban sectors at former income levels. Therefore, the distance between the two extremes has become wider. This may be due more to the specific characteristics of industrialization in these countries and its precarious articulation with the agricultural sector than to any inherent tendency of industrialization to concentrate income.

Rapid population growth and historically inequitable patterns of income distribution in Latin American countries have undoubtedly affected the results of the industrialization process. However, these factors do not themselves explain its essential characteristics. The discussion that follows attempts to explain why the effects of industrialization in Latin America have been so different from those in the advanced countries.

As noted above, Latin America's industry is precariously and asymmetrically linked to agriculture. In contrast to the industrialized countries' development pattern, the production of basic foodstuffs for the domestic market in Latin America—and the peasant population on which this production is based—have been subject to systematic political and economic neglect. With the exception of Argentina and Uruguay (where the principal export products are also basic foodstuffs for domestic consumption), this neglect has resulted in the systematic erosion of the foreign-trade surplus generated by the agricultural sector and a growing external deficit in industrial machinery and other inputs required for agricultural production. These problems have coincided with an expanding external deficit in the industrial sector in precisely those activities experiencing most rapid growth: automobiles, chemical products, and capital goods. These activities are all dominated by the transnational firms that in their home countries generated the trade surplus in these manufactured goods that advanced countries enjoy.

In addition to the problems associated with a precarious articulation between industry and agro-industry, energy programs in Latin America often have been dysfunctional in terms of the resources available to the region. Although only one Latin American country has been an important oil exporter in the past several decades (Venezuela), the region has relied on this energy source to a greater extent than other areas of the world. In 1925 liquid fuels represented 13 percent of world energy sources, while in Latin America this proportion had already reached 57 percent. By the end of the 1960s, the proportion had risen to 40 percent in the world, while in Latin America it exceeded 70 percent.

One of the clearest expressions of a disarticulated economic structure and the absence of creative development strategies in Latin America is the relatively small size of the capital-goods sector. Even though there is significant production of capital goods in the larger Latin American countries, the "endogenous creativity" of such goods is minimal. The backwardness of the capital-goods sector is largely responsible for the industrial sector's trade deficit, and it is the principal structural component of the region's current financial crisis. For Latin America as a whole, capital-goods and transportation-equipment activities accounted for almost half of the manufacturing sector's external deficit in 1955; that proportion rose to 62 percent by the end of the 1970s. In the specific case of Mexico, the trade surplus generated by petroleum exports between 1978 and 1982 was less than the capital-goods sector's trade deficit.

The backwardness of the capital-goods industry is closely linked to the overall characteristics of Latin America's pattern of industrialization in recent decades. Indeed, a central element in Latin American countries' industrialization policies has been large-scale but indiscriminate investment. Such investment required a setting in which the cost of investment was as low as possible, which was achieved in part by encouraging capital-goods imports. The objective of this policy was to encourage the production of nondurable consumer goods first, and later the production of intermediate goods. But to do this, national production of machinery and equipment (which in its initial phase would have meant higher investment costs) was sacrificed. The available data show that the level of tariff protection granted to the capital-goods industry is significantly lower throughout Latin America than that for other industrial activities.

This situation was further aggravated by the characteristics of demand and supply in the capital-goods industry. On the demand side, it is useful to distinguish among public enterprises, the subsidiaries of transnational corporations, and private national firms. Financial considerations have constrained public enterprises in the acquisition of domestically manufactured capital goods. Public sector decentralized firms in much of Latin America run a deficit in their capital account because of the structural fact that public enterprises' pricing policies are intended to subsidize the purchase of the goods and services they produce. This deficit in the capital account is balanced by access to international financing, which experience shows is often associated with the import of capital goods. Consequently, structural and financial elements have limited the public sector's opportunities to play a dynamic role in the promotion of locally produced capital goods. This role is fundamentally different from that played by public enterprises in the growth of the capital-goods industry in industrialized countries, where there has been close commercial and technical collaboration between public enterprises' demand requirements and the supply of manufactured products by large private firms, often on the grounds of national interest. This has been the case, for example, in the energy, communications, and transportation sectors and the armaments industry. Collaboration of this kind has been a central characteristic in the development of these industries.

The subsidiaries of transnational corporations are major consumers of capital goods in Latin American countries. Their acquisition of machinery and equipment generally corresponds to the corporation's global policy in this area. In certain cases the equipment and machinery they use is specially designed for them and patented by the user firm (for example, in the automobile, food processing, and pharmaceutical sectors). The importation of capital goods is one means of actually making direct investment in the host country. Moreover, because subsidiaries are often responsible for products in the final phase of the production cycle, the machinery and equipment required for their production are transferred from industrialized countries to developing nations. For reasons such as these, demand by transnational corporation subsidiaries does not constitute a major incentive for the local production of capital goods, despite the fact that these firms represent a high proportion of total demand for such goods. This situation contrasts sharply with the role that these firms play in their home countries.

Finally, because local firms are generally small- and medium-sized enterprises, the financing available to them for the acquisition of capital goods becomes a decisive factor in determining their demand for such products. Financing arrangements offered by local capital-goods manufacturers are generally significantly less attractive than those available on the international market. Thus domestic private firms' overall demand for locally produced capital goods is substantially reduced.

On the supply side, it is also important to distinguish between national and foreign producers. Foreign producers initially exported capital goods from manufacturing plants located in their home countries to the Latin American market. As long as that possibility was open, producers' motivation to establish manufacturing facilities in Latin American countries was limited because of local industrial policies, the frequent absence of adequate technical infrastructure, and the fragmentation of limited local markets among a large number of international suppliers. However, as some Latin American markets began to close because of rising local protectionism and the decision by some firms to establish plants in the host country (usually expanding from the local repair installations that are indispensable in this sector), other firms felt compelled to safeguard their market position by making a similar move. These firms sought to limit the effects of this policy on their export market by producing locally only the simplest kinds and smallest sizes of equipment. For foreign producers, local manufacture made sense only when access to markets was at risk.

For national producers the capital-goods sector constituted one of several investment opportunities. The factors mentioned above also meant that such investment was less profitable and more exposed to international competition and that it focused on more demanding buyers encouraged by structural factors to make their purchases abroad. These considerations, combined with the apparently greater technological complexity of this sector, encouraged private national capital to seek investment opportunities in other sectors. The production of capital goods is thus of relatively marginal interest to firms whose main commitments are in other activities.

Even though limited market size in the smaller Latin American countries has constrained the manufacture of mass-produced capital goods, this is a minor factor in explaining the backwardness of capital-goods production in the region. First, similar problems exist in countries whose domestic market is significantly larger than that of the smaller western European countries, which are major producers in the international capital-goods market. Second, minimum plant size and economies of scale are relatively low for a wide range of nonserial capital-goods activities established in different Latin American countries, including cement, iron and steel, petrochemical products, automobiles, synthetic fiber textiles, and various agro-industrial products. Third, regional industrial projects in small (Central America) and medium-sized (the Andean group) Latin American countries have larger economies of scale than those required by the majority of capital-goods manufacturing processes.

Instead, the factors that explain the weak development of the capital-goods sector in Latin America have to do with the general pattern of industrialization and the structural and institutional factors already mentioned. These factors channel potential demand toward other countries and discourage potential suppliers from undertaking local production. From this perspective, it is highly significant that the capital-goods import coefficient increased during the period of rapid economic growth in Brazil and Mexico, when official economic policy gave high priority to the development of this sector. Given the technological innovation that is associated with the capital-goods industry, the technological backwardness of many Latin American countries is to a large extent due to the failure to develop this sector. It is unlikely that this problem can be solved merely by formulating measures intended to encourage research and development activities at the level of the firm and to regulate the transfer of technology from abroad. Rather, change must occur in those factors shaping the overall character of industrialization.

In addition to the growing external deficit generated by "disjointed" industrialization and the systematic erosion of the agricultural sector's surplus (which in countries such as Mexico has actually become a deficit), Latin America has suffered since 1973 from a huge bill for petroleum imports. This burden is associated with the productive structure, and thus with development strategy. It is aggravated by debt-servicing obligations contracted in an effort to compensate for structural deficits and the financial drain associated with direct foreign investment. Ironically, direct foreign investment has played a leading role in those rapidly growing industrial sectors that define the domestic production profile. Its dynamism reflects the relative weakness of national industrial entrepreneurs.

The presence of foreign firms in national industry is not limited to Latin America. What is unique to the region is the magnitude of that presence, the inefficiency of the productive structure that foreign investment has shaped, and these firms' use of manufacturing processes that lack technological complexity. In short, foreign firms' local actions reflect little input from domestic actors. They are motivated principally by microeconomic considerations and a spirit of conquest. They are concentrated in the most dynamic economic activities, just as they are in their home countries. However, the effects of their presence in Latin America are quite different. Whereas transnational firms are the main source of trade surplus in their home countries, in Latin American host countries they often account for a large share of the country's trade deficit.

There is a second important difference between these firms' performance in Latin America and in their home countries. When firms compete in industrialized countries on the basis of product differentiation, the "destruction" of existing commodities and its effect on the use of productive resources are offset by the "creation" of new commodities, designs, production techniques, equipment, and marketing mechanisms. All these activities help maintain the dynamism of the productive process; the process of "creative destruction" described by Schumpeter is fully developed. The subsidiaries of these corporations operating in Latin America also employ new products, processes, equipment, and advertising techniques. However, with very few exceptions (which do not necessarily include advertising), the creative phase of these activities is not carried out locally. Whereas the leading oligopolistic firms generate technological innovation in their home countries, in Latin America their subsidiaries utilize (and therefore amortize) research expenditures made several years before in their home countries.

This argument does not overlook the existence of national private and public sector enterprises in Latin America that have shown that they possess all the "Schumpeterian attributes," including the potential for technological innovation. These firms exist, and some of them have become well known internationally. The essential point is that their industrial initiatives have not been decisive, as they were in several southeast Asian countries, especially Japan.

This "finding" obviously does not explain the cause of this phenomenon. Such an explanation would require detailed analyses of the historical origins of different social formations in Latin America and of the roles played by different social and economic agents in the formation and development of nation-states in the region. The fragility of the drive for industrialization refers specifically to the content and weakness of the "endogenous nucleus" of Latin American industrialization. Different countries in the region have given priority to industrialization since the 1930s and 1940s, and the results achieved are well known. What has been lacking is a strong industrial vocation—effective leadership capable of developing an endogenous industrial potential so as to adapt, innovate, and compete internationally across a significant range of economic sectors. Latin Americans who blame the inadequacies of the industrialization process on transnational corporations overlook the responsibility shared by the national business sector (public and private) and other social forces that, in their formulation of domestic policies in different periods, have failed to establish effective bases for Latin American industrialization.

One example is the high tariff protection accorded to industrial activities in Latin America. In Japan, the country that has achieved the most notable success in post-World War II industrialization, high protective barriers fostered a learning process by national business groups linked to the state. Industrial strategy focused on those chemical and light engineering activities that enjoyed dynamic growth in demand. Imports were first replaced by local products. Then, as innovations were made, Japan undertook selective integration of national industry and prepared to penetrate international markets. Its targeted export markets included the United States, the main source of technological inspiration. In other words, protection served an industrialization strategy oriented toward the future conquest of the international market; it was a "learning" protectionism. In Latin America, on the other hand, domestic protection sheltered an indiscriminate, small-scale reproduction of industries found in advanced countries. These activities were disjointed in their capital-goods components. Moreover, they were led by subsidiaries of transnational firms whose perspective was alien to local conditions and whose innovations were not only made principally in their home countries but were also of limited utility beyond their own narrow requirements. This might be called "frivolous" protectionism.

It is obvious, then, that domestic protectionism alone cannot explain differences in industrialization patterns between Latin America and countries such as Japan. Although these two strategies shared high levels of protection, they differed substantially in terms of their conceptualization of industrialization, the agents that led the process, and the application of selectivity and temporal perspectives. The weakness of Latin American industrialization is due to a more complex set of factors. High indiscriminate tariff protection and the large-scale presence of transnational corporations reflect the weakness of the national business sector rather than cause the inefficiency that characterizes this group. The elimination of protectionist barriers will not in and of itself produce efficiency.

The level of domestic protection in Latin America has largely been determined by the rate of profitability obtainable in activities not exposed to international trade, such as construction, trade, and finance. The most powerful private national business groups concentrated their investments in these activities. When they sought to diversify into industry, it was perfectly rational for them to seek equally high profit margins. This would explain the paradoxical situation that industrial sectors whose leading firms were transnational enterprises (which one could hardly justify protecting by the "infant industry" criterion) for decades enjoyed high, indiscriminate levels of protection. Excessive protection encouraged the fragmentation of the productive structure and subsequently became necessary to guarantee its survival. Thus it is understandable that economies sheltered by frivolous protection failed to produce industrial exports in proportion to growth in total output.

It follows that an analysis of Latin America's present financial crisis must consider both external factors (examined in more detail in the following section) and the structural characteristics of the industrialization strategy followed to date. Specifically, the weakness of the external sector is closely linked to the dominant pattern of industrialization: the precarious leadership of the automobile industry, plus shortcomings in the production of capital goods; the asymmetrical relationship between industry and agriculture; and dysfunctional patterns of energy use. These factors explain the external deficit and, consequently, the cause of external indebtedness. Overcoming these external weaknesses will necessarily require the transformation of the industrial sector, its relationship with agriculture, the pattern of energy consumption, and the financing mechanisms on which it is based.

Thus the pattern of Latin American industrialization—far from being a temporarily distorted image of industrialization in advanced countries—suffers from serious limitations. It does not address the needs of a large share of the population, and it is incapable of taking full advantage of creative opportunities and abundant natural resources. The neoliberal response by Southern Cone countries is a compulsive search for a "Manchesterian utopia." It seeks to address the problems of Latin American industrialization by questioning its existence and withdrawing to an international division of labor in which Latin American countries would be resigned to the simple export of natural resources. Not only does this approach fail to resolve accumulated social needs, it also intensifies them by structurally discouraging national creativity.

The International Market and Latin America: A Source of Past Dynamism and Future Constraint

There is little doubt that the transformation of production in Latin American countries—especially in those whose rapid economic growth permitted them to penetrate industrialized countries' markets for manufactured goods in the 1960s and early 1970s—contributed to the expansion in global industrial production (at an average annual rate of 6.1 percent) between 1950 and 1975. This transformation also contributed to the growth in international trade (8.8 percent per year) and the accelerated increase in direct investment (slightly over 10 percent per year) during the same period. These developments were soon followed by the internationalization of financing activities and, after 1974, by the recycling of petrodollar surpluses. These shifts in financing made it possible to prolong Latin American countries' economic dynamism beyond what growth in industrialized countries, international trade, and domestic savings would have allowed. Necessary domestic structural reforms were replaced by external indebtedness.

The magnitude of Latin America's contemporary financial crisis and the desperate search for short-term solutions have apparently reduced analysts' interest in understanding the link between the erosion of the industrial dynamism of the 1950s and 1960s and the crisis of the 1970s. The first section of this essay examined some of the structural factors that tied the development strategy pursued in Latin America in recent decades to current imbalances in the foreign trade sector. This section discusses the relationship between the "exhaustion" of developed countries' industrialization process in the late 1960s and the economic crisis of the 1970s.[4]

Among those factors explaining developed countries' rapid industrial growth in the post-World War II period, the most important are: the availability of a technology stock produced between the 1920s and World War II; the influence that the U.S. model of consumption and industrial organization exerted on the other industrialized countries; the availability of a skilled labor force and business capacity that, despite the partial physical destruction of industrial assets, remained present in these countries (especially in Japan and the Federal Republic of Germany); the "pull" factor that the spread of consumer durable goods and the substitution of synthetic products for natural ones projected throughout the industrial system; the response of the capital-goods sector, which incorporated, multiplied, and diffused technical progress throughout the whole productive apparatus; access to energy sources whose already low relative prices actually declined during this period; and the modernization of the agricultural sector and its integration into the industrial structure. During these decades of rapid economic growth, the "growth–technical progress–international trade–growth" cycle acquired particular dynamism. This had an especially invigorating effect on the capital-goods sector.

These countries' loss of economic dynamism in the late 1960s was due to the weakening of the factors discussed above as well as to the appearance of obstacles or barriers caused by that growth. For example, labor scarcities began to appear in the 1960s as a result of rapid economic growth. This situation strengthened the position of trade unions, whose national unity was further favored by international détente and the fact that wages had begun to rise more rapidly than productivity. All the industrialized countries experienced this shift, although with differing degrees of intensity.

The imitative spread of consumer durable goods and automobiles also began to show inevitable signs of market saturation. Pessimistic predictions concerning the future consumption of automobiles contrast sharply with the dynamic forecasts of the earlier period. Similar changes occurred with the replacement of natural products by synthetic ones. Together with the increasing relative weights of wages and taxes (associated with public sector expansion during the period of rapid growth), the market saturation of those sectors that sparked the industrialization process produced declining profits. This pressure intensified because of technological change that, accompanied by modifications in the sectoral structure of industry, was expressed in a fall in output-capital ratios.

From the moment that economic dynamism began to slow, productivity growth also declined. This situation varied in intensity from one country to another, but the same trend appeared in several industrialized countries after 1969. This tendency, plus the fact that the sectoral heterogeneity of industrial productivity is greater than the range of wages, reinforced the trend toward wage increases rising more rapidly than productivity, thus fueling inflationary pressures. The slowdown in economic growth and the drop in productivity increased idle capacity and discouraged innovation, thereby consolidating the trend. These tendencies and the precarious outlook for future economic growth encouraged the appearance of protectionist pressures, which reduced the stimulating impact of international trade and its feedback effect on growth. The brief 1971–1973 recovery of the international economy did not produce any significant change in these structural factors. However, it did produce an additional harmful effect in the form of speculation in commodity prices, which exerted further pressure on profit rates and the inflationary process.

In the financial area, the rapid industrial growth of the earlier period was accompanied by growing indebtedness on the part of households, firms, and governments. Individual consumers' indebtedness was to some extent associated with the greater burden of acquiring consumer durables such as automobiles and housing. It was therefore a reflection of a transformation in the industrial structure. For firms, increasing indebtedness stemmed from both demand and supply factors. Declining output-capital ratios produced additional needs for financial resources in order to create a compensating expansion in capacity. At the same time, declining profitability also made it necessary to rely on external sources of financing. This change in firms' financial structure became apparent throughout the industrialized countries as external financing assumed an increasingly prominent role. Along with labor legislation and trade union pressures for job stability, this made firms' cost structures more rigid by increasing the proportion of fixed costs, because interest payments and remunerations did not decline as output fell. In those sectors characterized by an oligopolistic ownership structure (such as the leading industrial activities), cost pressures were transferred to prices. Moreover, wage increases in these activities served as a reference point for other sectors. These factors further intensified the inflationary process.

Public sector indebtedness was associated with increasing social demands to neutralize somewhat the backwardness of less-favored groups, sectors, and regions, which had been accentuated during the period of rapid economic growth. Borrowing also took place because of an increase in the already high capital-output ratio that characterizes public sector investments. The ability of leading industrial, commercial, and financial activities to avoid significant fiscal pressures through sectoral diversification and internationalization constituted an additional source of inflationary pressure.

The general phenomenon of growing indebtedness encouraged the rapid internationalization of private banking, first by major U.S. banks and later by European and Japanese financial institutions. This trend started in the late 1960s, and it led to the creation of the Eurodollar market, which was outside government control. By 1978 this market already represented some $860 billion. In addition to its clear implications for the autonomy and effectiveness of different national governments' monetary and fiscal policies, the existence of these massive financial resources encouraged speculative processes such as those affecting commodity prices between 1971 and 1973. Speculation became more pronounced as inflation rates climbed. Thus the quadrupling of oil prices in

1973 undoubtedly had a significant inflationary impact, but it in fact reinforced and intensified pressures that had already surfaced.

This discussion suggests that the exhaustion of the developed countries' industrial model contributed substantially to present global stagflation. The expansion of international liquidity associated with the rapidly growing U.S. balance-of-payments deficit and increasing global indebtedness (which originated both in the transformation of the real economy and in the speculation that arose as a consequence of recession) intensified the inflationary process.

The relative economic weight of different industrialized countries also shifted as a result of rapid growth during the 1950s and 1960s. Perhaps the most significant aspect of this change was the erosion of the United States' position and the rise of Japan and western Europe, a phenomenon that also held important implications for U.S.–Latin American bilateral relations. Indeed, there has been a notable decline in the relative weight of bilateral economic exchanges in the United States' and Latin America's foreign economic relations, especially in trade, direct investment, and external financing. This trend toward the diversification of Latin America's foreign economic relations away from the United States acquired more intensity the farther away the country was (the extreme cases being Brazil and the Southern Cone countries of Argentina, Chile, and Uruguay). It reflected the diversification of Latin America's productive structure as well as the diversification of the region's international political relations and the strengthening of intraregional ties.[5] Furthermore, the erosion of the United States' relative position in growth and international trade vis-à-vis western Europe and Japan from the 1950s through the early 1970s contributed to the development of Latin America's economic relations with these other industrialized countries. This was also the period in which Latin America began to expand its economic ties with socialist countries, although these exchanges remained at a relatively low level.[6]

Future Directions

The industrialized countries' partial economic recovery in 1975–1978 attenuated somewhat the fears of an international depression similar to that of the 1930s. However, the second oil shock in early 1979 resulted in prolonged recession. Recession has had an especially damaging impact on developing country exporters of manufactured goods. The World Bank's outlook for developing countries in the 1980s is summarized in a single sentence: "For developing countries, the most salient features of an unfavorable international outlook for the 1980s are less aid, continued weakness in commodity prices, deteriorating export opportunities, and poor prospects for commercial borrowing."[7] This view is based on the recent behavior of the international economy, the outlook for growth in industrialized countries, the level of indebtedness reached by developing countries, the lending limits and country concentration of private commercial banks' loan portfolios, and the implications these factors have for growth in developing countries.

This section examines probable future economic trends in those developing countries with a relatively high degree of industrialization, which the International Monetary Fund (IMF) describes as "major exporters of manufactures." These include Brazil and Argentina in Latin America.[8] There are two main reasons for focusing on these countries. First, future economic projections for them are more favorable than for other oil-importing countries in Latin America; in this sense they constitute borderline cases, below which one would expect to find other countries in the region. Second, Brazil and Argentina have pursued furthest the development strategy adopted by other Latin American countries. Thus they illustrate the external constraints that other countries may face if they continue these same policies without introducing significant modifications.

As a basis for this discussion, it is useful to summarize basic data concerning recent international economic trends.[9] First, the financial surplus generated by oil-exporting countries from 1979 to date corresponds roughly to non-oil-producing developing countries' deficit. With the exception of 1980 (in which their current account deficit reached $45 billion), industrialized countries managed to balance their current account during this period. Second, the principal exporters of manufactured goods account for more than one-third of the current-account deficit of non-oil-producing developing countries. Since 1978 the terms of trade for exporters of manufactured goods have been systematically negative because of the combined effects of the post-1979 increase in oil prices and declining prices for all agricultural commodities and mining exports. Similarly, the volume of developing country exports has fallen since 1978 because of a slowdown in international trade and the growth of protectionism in industrialized countries.[10] Imports from industrialized countries also decreased dramatically after 1980 as a result of external constraints on domestic economic growth.

Third, from 1977 to 1982 the external debt of "major exporters of manufactures" rose from $83 billion to $194 billion, and external debt as a share of their combined GDP rose from 19.5 percent to 24.9 percent. Debt-servicing obligations (interest payments and amortization) as a share of total exports of goods and services rose from 13.5 percent in 1977 to 20.1 percent in 1982. More important, interest payments as a share of exports nearly doubled, rising from 4.2 percent to 8 percent during this same period. This change was largely due to the doubling of international interest rates between 1978 and 1981.

Finally, an important characteristic of this group of developing countries is that their external financing comes principally from private international banks. In 1973 private banks provided 54 percent of these countries' external borrowing, while in 1982 this share had grown to 68 percent. Private banks' increasing importance as a source of financing for developing countries' balance-of-payments deficits was accompanied by a reduction in maturity periods and a rise in interest rates, which were incompatible with the terms of maturity or profitability rates required of investments in developing countries. For example, of the $200 billion in oil-importing countries' external debt held by private banks in 1979, nearly 70 percent consisted of loans with maturity periods of three years or less. As the international recession continued, developing countries increasingly used bank loans to cover emergency imports of oil and foodstuffs, to finance budget deficits, and above all, to repay outstanding debt. By 1985 as much as two-thirds of total new borrowing was used to cover existing external debt.

For all these reasons, it is clear that international trade and finance no longer constitute positive supports for Latin America's economic growth. To the contrary, during the 1980s the international market is likely to constitute an important constraint on domestic economic growth, necessary transformations in the productive structure, and the satisfaction of accumulated basic social needs that were postponed or ignored during the preceding period of rapid growth. For this reason it is useful to examine 1982 IMF projections for economic growth in industrialized countries and their implications for developing countries.[11]

The basic IMF hypothesis is that those developing countries with a strong external imbalance (which is the case for the majority of Latin American countries) will suffer restrictive growth policies. The following is a summary of the assumptions implicit in this forecast:

With respect to policies, a crucial assumption is that countries that are confronted with serious external imbalances will implement comprehensive programs of adjustment. Most such programs will have to include fiscal reform leading to a reduction in excessively high rates of growth of the monetary aggregates; adoption of a realistic exchange rate, combined with a change in domestic prices so that they reflect world market prices; and attenuation of government controls and regulations, including more realistic pricing policies by official marketing agencies, and interest rates that are allowed to reflect real rates of return.[12]

Based on these assumptions regarding domestic policy and likely international economic conditions, the IMF projects two probable scenarios for developing countries that are major exporters of manufactured goods.[13] In scenario A (the intermediate hypothesis), during the period from 1984 to 1986 these countries will experience a 0.5 percent per year decline in the terms of trade. The current-account deficit will rise from $32 billion in 1982 to $37 billion in 1986. Domestic economic growth will average 5 percent per year between 1984 and 1986. In scenario B (the pessimistic hypothesis, but the more likely outcome), these countries will experience a 1 percent per year decline in the terms of trade from 1984 through 1986, and the current-account deficit will rise to $56 billion. Domestic economic growth will average only 4.5 percent per year. Although the growth rates projected in these scenarios are well below historic levels in these countries (8.1 percent per year in 1968–1972 and 5.9 percent per year in 1973–1978), they may still be too high given the IMF's assumptions regarding restrictive domestic economic policy.[14]

Even to obtain the results summarized in these two scenarios, other important conditions will be necessary. The IMF's assumptions in this regard reveal well the constraints the international economy is likely to impose on developing countries.

(1) Real interest rates in international financial markets are gradually reduced, bringing the three-month London interbank rate to about two percent in real terms by 1986; (2) oil prices are assumed to stay constant in real terms at their 1983 projected levels; (3) the trade restrictiveness of the industrial countries toward the exports of the non-oil developing countries is assumed to remain about the same as it is now; (4) official development assistance is projected to be maintained in real terms from 1981 through 1986.[15]

Thus even in the most favorable foreseeable circumstances (scenario A), the prospects for developing countries' economic growth during the 1980s are gloomy. If actual events more closely approximate scenario B, the international financial system will hardly be in any condition to provide the stimulus necessary for developing countries' growth. The IMF study concludes tersely: "In the circumstances which are characterized by scenario B, the possibility of an adequate response by the market to the financing needs of the developing countries would become problematic."[16] Prolonged recession is likely to lead to greatly increased social tensions in some Latin American countries, where expectations produced during the period of rapid growth clash with an economic recession that has already lasted several years and (according to these IMF projections) may well persist for several more.

By the mid-1970s, external financial imbalances had reached significant levels in several Latin American countries. The recycling of petrodollar surpluses after 1975 made it possible to neutralize—and to some extent ignore—the structural factors producing this imbalance. However, these imbalances resurfaced in unprecedented magnitudes in 1980 and became particularly severe from 1981 through 1983. The convergence of external and internal factors produced a decline in GDP per capita in most Latin American countries. Regional GDP *fell* by 1.0 percent in 1982 and 3.1 percent in 1983, rising to only an estimated 2.6 percent in 1984. Per capita GDP fell continuously from 1981 through 1983, with a cumulative decline of 8.9 percent from 1981 through 1984. Urban unemployment and inflation increased significantly throughout Latin America. Indeed, the average annual inflation rate for the region reached 175.4 percent in 1984. Latin America's terms of trade fell by 21.7 percent from 1981 through 1984, and the region experienced a net transfer of capital to industrialized countries totaling $77 billion from 1982 through 1984.[17]

Studies by the United Nations Economic Commission for Latin America indicate that in order to absorb growth in the labor force and gradually decrease existing levels of unemployment, Latin America must sustain an economic growth rate of approximately 7 percent per year during the next decade. Under the most optimistic circumstances, it is likely that unemployment will become much more severe throughout the region. But what will happen if future developments are closer to scenario B, described above? One possibility would be that shortfalls in external financing will force a drastic slowdown in the pace of domestic economic growth. Latin American countries may also attempt to ease the external burden by suspending debt servicing. Alternatively, access to additional resources through the IMF might make it possible for these countries to renegotiate external indebtedness. Recent developments suggest that increased efforts will be made to expand IMF resources so as to allow it to respond adequately to an emergency. Although this strategy would hypothetically safeguard the interests of creditors, it obviously does not respond to the domestic challenges facing developing countries.

Given the accumulated social needs in Latin America, the expectations produced in the period of rapid economic growth, the need to absorb imbalances in domestic production, and the challenges posed by technological-industrial restructuring in industrialized countries, priority should be granted to those measures that stimulate economic growth in the region. One should not underestimate the dynamic effect that Latin American growth during 1975–1980 had on the United States. Indeed, the United States' current-account surplus with Latin America rose from $1.5 billion in 1970 to $3.4 billion in 1975, $15.6 billion in 1980, and $21.5 billion in 1981.[18]

There is general agreement in international circles that recent U.S. economic policy intensified the 1981–1983 recession and that world economic recovery is to some extent dependent on modifications in that policy. Latin America would particularly benefit from strong growth in the United States. Approximately one-third of the region's foreign trade is linked to the United States, and this proportion increases significantly the farther north one goes in Latin America. However, the analysis set forth in the first two sections of this essay demonstrates that world economic recovery is a necessary but not sufficient condition for overcoming Latin America's domestic production imbalances and accumulated social needs. The linear prolongation of conventional development strategies that a dynamic international economy might make possible would only delay necessary modifications in Latin America's pattern of development. Significant economic and political reforms remain an unavoidable national responsibility.

Technological-Industrial Restructuring in Advanced Countries: Challenges and Opportunities for Latin America

The speed and effectiveness with which industrialized countries adapted to post-1973 energy conditions is an important (but partial) reflection of a more complex process of profound technological-industrial restructuring now underway in these countries. In 1982 the major industrialized countries used 16 percent less energy and 26 percent less oil per unit of output than in 1973.[19] The political will to adapt to a challenge of this magnitude, combined with the flexibility to modify social behavior and innovate technologically, indicates the importance of endogenous creative capacity.

The particular political and social value that industrialized countries attach to scientific and technological activities in the context of rapid change is clearly reflected in the following statement by the Organization for Economic Cooperation and Development (OECD):

Far more than previously, the policies of the OECD governments towards science and technology now flow from economic, foreign and social policy concerns. Inflation, unemployment, lack of economic growth, the necessity for adjustment policies, the inexorably rising costs of energy imports, uncertain availability of crucial raw materials: such problems largely determined the policy-agendas of most governments. Current developments in science and technology policies have to be understood principally as the attempt to harness the potential of research to the challenge which these problems pose.[20]

Quite apart from institutional and rhetorical differences in the emphasis placed on public sector intervention, industrialized countries have systematically attempted to develop and incorporate the most advanced technology into national production as a means of responding to crisis conditions. There is a consensus that comparative advantages in international trade during the next several decades will be based on precisely this kind of "voluntarist" and "interventionist" action at the national level.[21]

The technological-industrial shift implied by this approach is particularly apparent in energy and leading technological sectors. However, it also has major implications for the production of a wide range of goods and services. These include:[22]

1. Consumer durable goods. These products include mainly automobiles and electric household appliances, which have been the basis for expanding consumption in both industrialized countries and developing areas such as Latin America. This sector has undergone significant technological change because of a series of factors that appeared in industrialized countries in the 1970s: a tendency toward saturation of demand for traditional products, growing concern with environmental problems, a sharp rise in energy prices, competition from developing countries, labor pressures to increase job satisfaction, and opportunities for the large-scale application of technological innovations from electronics and computing. In the manufacture of automobiles, these changes have produced a restructuring of production arrangements on an international scale: increasing automation (including the use of robots) at the plant level; the introduction of lighter materials, new designs, and electronic controls; a rise in energy efficiency; the search for new fuels; and a reduction in pollutants. The production of electric household appliances (as well as electronic games), which was previously relatively labor-intensive, has become more capital-intensive because of increased automation. This shift was prompted largely by increasing competition from newly industrialized countries.

2. Intermediate goods. Intermediate goods include a wide range of materials used in the manufacturing process, such as cement, iron and steel, basic petrochemicals, paper, and glass. This sector grew rapidly during the 1950s and 1960s (particularly chemical products), which made it possible to take advantage of economies of scale. Low costs for energy and other raw materials permitted the introduction of major innovations in both products and production processes (again, especially in chemicals). However, this situation changed dramatically in the 1970s. In addition to slower general economic growth, the sector was shaken by price increases for energy and other raw materials, pressures from environmentalists, and competition from several developing countries where large basic-processing projects based on the availability of abundant natural resources had begun to mature. Further innovations in this sector are likely to be concentrated on marginal improvements in products, the search for new product applications, and marginal increases in the efficiency of the overall production process (such as saving energy and reducing pollution). Principal attention has turned to the search for alternative energy sources, such as coal, natural gas, agricultural and urban waste,

and various agricultural products. Recent developments in the nuclear energy field also point in this direction.

Technical innovation in these continuous production manufacturing activities is also moving toward the development of sophisticated, technology-intensive products that incorporate higher value-added. In the iron and steel industry, the shift toward the production of specialty steel is now well advanced. In the chemical industry, emphasis is now placed on pharmaceuticals, pesticides, and other sophisticated chemical products.

3. Capital goods. It is likely that in the near future, wage pressure as a stimulus to technological innovation in industrialized countries will be replaced by intensified export competition from other developed countries and (in some cases) from newly industrialized countries. Pressures to reduce the role of labor in the production process will thus persist. However, changing energy conditions and technology somewhat constrain the introduction of major modifications in the design of capital goods and complex plants. As a result, issues such as energy efficiency, safety measures, and environmental effects (including noise pollution) have become decisive features in determining the competitiveness of capital goods.

Technological change has also had a major impact on the capital-goods sector. For example, in the machine-tools industry there is a steady trend toward the introduction of digital controls. This control format originated in the aerospace industry's production requirements and then spread to machine tools in general. The idea that computing techniques can be used in industrial design (including the manufacture of capital goods and operational control of integrated processes, machine tools, and entire plants) now appears to be much closer to reality than to science fiction.

The direct application of science and technology to manufacturing in the capital- and intermediate-goods sectors lays the basis for further diffusion of technological innovation to the production of more general goods and services. For example, the rapid increase in agricultural productivity in advanced countries is to a significant degree due to innovations in the chemical industry and in the manufacture of agricultural machinery. Innovations in communications, computing, and electronics have greatly affected financial transactions and commercial and public administration. These innovations are also likely to have a growing impact on education and health. The decreasing cost of communications materials will also produce changes in personal transportation, and this development may open up new possibilities for the geographical decentralization of production. Such a shift toward a new technological-industrial model is the most visible expression of deeper transformative processes that may well affect the overall functioning of society.

4. Biosciences and biotechnology. Some observers argue that the in-

novative potential of biotechnology is comparable to that of microelectronics. In agriculture, for example, the biosciences have already made it possible to shift the focus of research from fertilizers to the process of fertilization. Agriculture is likely to move increasingly from reliance on conventional chemistry to the use of plant physiology, molecular biology, and genetic engineering. In the pharmaceutical field, significant progress has been made in understanding the causes of illnesses, thus permitting greater emphasis on preventive rather than corrective medicine. In the health field in general, the application of microelectronics to analysis and the design of instruments will complement the contribution of biotechnology to understanding and preventing illnesses.

The Latin American Response to Technological Restructuring in Industrialized Countries

These developments hold important implications for Latin America. First, given the prospects for a relatively long period of slow growth in the world economy, industrialized countries are undertaking a transition toward a new model of industrial technology that may lead to a new growth cycle. Latin American countries will thus face an international context that offers them little stimulus for growth in the short and medium terms. Indeed, policies undertaken by industrialized country governments to strengthen their relative positions in this transition process may create a new ranking in the international political economy that further disadvantages developing countries. Long-term technological change in industrialized countries may also allow Latin American countries to create a new productive structure on an international scale, but national productive structures will need to be transformed if they are not to become obsolete. Some of the industries that are most important in Latin American countries (such as automobiles, petrochemicals, and capital goods) are precisely those sectors in which major technological transformations may take place at the international level in the years ahead.

Second, these changes underline the decisive importance of regional cooperation to incorporate up-to-date projections of future technological change in international negotiations in different industrial sectors. Unless this occurs, Latin American countries may only acquire equipment and production processes that are already outmoded in industrialized countries (as has sometimes been the case in the past). Errors of this kind in the development of Latin America's leading industrial sectors would seriously affect national growth in the decades ahead.

Some of the highly labor-intensive activities in which Latin American countries have concentrated their industrial export efforts may experience significant changes over the next several years as labor costs rise. Industries such as textiles, clothing, and electronic parts may become much less competitive. Thus it is clear that Latin America must make a major effort to develop advanced-technology industries. This is an area in which regional cooperation can be extremely valuable. However, the fields in which technological innovation can be most appropriately applied in Latin America may differ from those in industrialized countries, reflecting the region's own needs and resources.

Which are the most appropriate areas for future development in Latin America? Here it is useful to distinguish among three different fields: (1) the broad range of advanced technologies in which future technological-industrial restructuring will occur at the international level; (2) those areas in which some Latin American countries have succeeded in developing advanced industrial activities with sufficient critical mass and sufficiently close integration with the productive apparatus to enjoy some degree of international competitiveness; and finally (3) those areas in Latin America that are clearly backward both in scientific-technological infrastructure and in their integration with the productive apparatus as a whole.[23]

Because advanced technologies represent the long-term basis for international comparative economic advantage, Latin America cannot completely ignore developments in these activities. It would be extremely short-sighted to do so because scientific-technological change will affect not only international trade but also the forms in which society and the satisfaction of its needs are organized.

Although there is widespread international agreement on the importance of incorporating science and technology into productive activity, countries differ widely in their reasons for sharing this conviction. In the United States, in the Soviet Union, and to a lesser extent in Great Britain, France, and China, military and geopolitical considerations clearly play a significant role. But in Japan it is the almost total lack of natural resources that makes international competitiveness in the manufacturing sector the basic element of survival. Japan has concentrated on translating progress in advanced science and technology into new products, processes, and production techniques that strengthen its international position in consumer durables and capital goods. In India, the historical trauma of successive conquests by external powers produced a strong emphasis on military self-sufficiency, especially nuclear energy and weapons production. Among East European countries, labor shortages and low labor productivity complement military considerations and a desire to compete in the international market as motivating factors.

Latin America must consider carefully its strategic options in science and advanced technology. Considerations such as natural resource and labor shortages are not relevant. Fortunately, geopolitical factors are for the moment limited to very few cases. And although international competitiveness in manufacturing is a generally shared goal, the weakness of national industrialists and transnational corporations' dominance in the industrial sector constitute significant long-term obstacles to achieving it. Under such circumstances it is pointless to attempt to reproduce in Latin America the "Japanese model," which stresses the incorporation of science and technology in the development of new products, processes, and techniques destined for individual consumption and international trade. Latin America must clearly undertake sustained efforts to strengthen national industrial businesses in both the public and private sectors, to rationalize the productive structures of different industrial sectors, to modernize technology for national industry, and to raise national industry's international competitiveness.

However, these efforts do not imply that international competitiveness must be the only goal toward which advanced technologies and society in general are focused. In Latin America, the linkage between advanced technologies and society must rest on a different central axis than in industrialized countries. It must take into account the following considerations: accumulated social needs in basic services such as education, health care, transportation, communications, housing, and food production; the existence of relatively solid institutional experience and an institutional infrastructure that attempts to address these needs within each country; and the fact that the need to satisfy these demands with limited budgetary resources requires a dramatic increase in productivity in different economic sectors. Because the demand for basic social services is essentially satisfied in industrialized countries, increased productivity necessarily results in higher unemployment, with its consequent sociopolitical effects. Thus efforts to incorporate advanced technologies into the productive apparatus concentrate on individual consumer goods that can be traded on the international market rather than on basic social services. Latin American efforts to apply advanced technology to basic services would place the region in a vanguard position internationally. This would open up an enormous potential for cooperation with other developing countries, with far-reaching implications in international politics and economics.

These considerations suggest that Latin America's most viable future strategic option lies in the application of advanced technologies to the provision of basic social services. The development of a scientific, technological, engineering, and production apparatus should be based on a dynamic nucleus of national firms—including both public and private firms and joint ventures with trasnational corporations. This strategy would involve projects such as the application of genetic engineering techniques to health care provision and food production and expanding the use of mass media in education, both in pedagogical method and in content. The fact that more than half of Latin America's population is under fifteen years of age represents an enormous challenge. But at the same time it offers a potential for learning and creativity that may be particularly relevant in this period of transition toward a new technological-industrial model at the international level. It is for this reason that the education-science-technology trilogy acquires particular significance. It is vital to utilize advances in science and technology to structure an educational process that is compatible in content and technique with national particularities and that simultaneously accelerates the diffusion of technical knowledge and scientific methods throughout society.

The development of computer software, large-scale instruction in programing methods in both urban and rural areas, the use of information-processing equipment designed and produced locally in accordance with national requirements (such as low cost, simplicity, and compatibility with a democratic educational process), and a national job training program would all be part of this new educational effort. Such a policy would serve multiple goals. For example, it would constitute a powerful motivation for a predominantly young population, expand the educational training process, increase productivity, and develop an industrial-technological capacity in which some Latin American countries could take an international lead in some specific applications.

In the health care sector, the use of electronic medical equipment and information-processing systems is just beginning at the international level. Given Latin American countries' specific conditions (public health systems with varying degrees of coverage and the limited availability of trained medical personnel), it is necessary to define a specific functional strategy that, on the one hand, makes it possible to utilize advances in electronic medical equipment for communications and computing so as to increase the efficiency of the health system and, on the other hand, favors national development of the corresponding "hardware."

Because of Latin America's geographical size and the degree of national economic integration induced by public sector initiatives, a number of complex industrial systems are already in place in communications, transportation, petroleum and petrochemicals, the generation and distribution of electricity, aviation, railroads and subways, and telecommunications. Although these systems differ in their specific requirements, they share requirements for "hardware" and "software" capable of regulating and controlling complex operational systems (including the training process for technical personnel). The magnitude of this demand, the accumulated institutional experience in these different sectors, and the technological opportunities open in these activities are all factors that suggest that this area be given high priority in the development of technological-industrial capacity. These complex industrial systems offer an opportunity to develop an integrated program for national producers of advanced electronic goods. At the same time, efforts should be made to conceive and implement an extensive software-development program linked to the design and production of industrial equipment. International experience suggests that the boundary between hardware and software is becoming increasingly blurred; a country's progress in one field ultimately requires expertise in the other as well.

There are also areas in which Latin American countries should emphasize the development of consolidated technologies. Agronomy, some energy-linked activities, and civil engineering are possible candidates. All of these activities evidence a sound technological base, some integration with productive structures, and some indication of international competitiveness. Future efforts in these areas should concentrate on reinforcing the existing technological base and increasing the application of technology to production, although through different institutional mechanisms in each case. In the agricultural sector, the link between research activity and production requires expanded activity by national and regional development banks in order to integrate agriculture and industry more closely. In the energy sector (a captive market served mainly by public enterprises in Latin American countries), technological change should focus on the development of specialized activities, perhaps in joint ventures with transnational engineering firms that have access to advanced technologies. This would then be a basis for diffusing technological innovation to the productive apparatus as a whole. In all three fields—agronomy, civil engineering, and energy products—systematic efforts should be made to tie domestic developments to the international level. In doing so, consideration should be given to Latin American countries' international policies and their economic and commercial linkages to the world market.

As noted in the first section of this essay, Latin America's greatest technological backwardness is in the industrial sector. Within this sector, future development strategy should give top priority to foodstuffs, chemicals, and capital goods. These are all areas in which linkages between the productive apparatus and the technological infrastructure are extremely weak. This problem is especially severe because these are priority sectors for long-term economic development. In each of these areas, it will be necessary to formulate local, national, and regional programs for scientific-technological infrastructure development. Programs of this kind should take into account the scientific infrastructure already available, the extent of national business involvement, and the potential support that private firms might receive from public enterprises that are either suppliers or major users in these sectors. It is essential that the preparation of these sectoral technological development programs (which would specify priorities, necessary resources, and appropriate institutional mechanisms) include active participation by businesses, consumers, suppliers, academic experts, engineering firms, and officials from the different governmental agencies relevant to the activity under consideration.

Conclusions

Over the next several years, Latin American countries must confront a series of challenges: imbalances in domestic productive structures and accumulated social needs (which were postponed in the period of rapid economic growth but which are now surfacing); an international economy that in the past constituted a stimulus for domestic growth but that at least in the short and medium terms will constitute an obstacle to domestic economic dynamism; and industrial and technological restructuring in industrialized countries that may drastically erode the international competitiveness of some sectors in different Latin American economies. Latin America's particular model of development and industrialization is to a large extent inherited from the Great Depression of the 1930s. However, the above considerations suggest that the present crisis will require important modifications in this development strategy. A new approach is necessary to respond to domestic and international conditions in the years ahead.

In Latin America's recent political evolution, two aspirations have become increasingly generalized: democratization and modernization. These two ideas constitute a basis for the elaboration of a new development strategy. The intensity and form in which these aspirations are expressed differ throughout the region, but they provide an axis on which to base a variety of specific development proposals. In those Latin American countries in which authoritarianism and political exclusion represent a historical constant, as well as in those countries in which long-established democratic political arrangements have been recently interrupted, one now perceives a deep appreciation for those forms of social organization that make it possible to address societal aspirations and anxieties through democratic processes.

A similar change has taken place in views concerning modernization. In recent years some Latin American countries have experienced an initially attractive process of "showcase modernization," in which traditionally austere societies entered into sudden and indiscriminate contact with modern goods and services developed and produced in other contexts. These goods and services were imported to replace "inefficient" local production, which disappeared when exposed to international competition during a recessionary period when "dumping" practices and export subsidies were the norm. This showcase modernity supplanted the irrationality of preexisting domestic production with an even more irrational import structure, which quickly led to increased unemployment, a decline in previously accumulated technological capacity, and unsustainable demands for external financing.

Consequently, endogenous modernization should be the key point of reference in a future development strategy. Efforts should be made to integrate scientific and technological advances into national productive structures so as to achieve real assimilation. This integration will require the political will to achieve high rates of economic growth that reinforce the search for equity. Large-scale labor training programs will also be necessary to produce this kind of modernization.

The alternative for Latin America is passive insertion into the international economy in accordance with industrialized countries' needs. This is also "modernization." However, modernization of this kind is transplanted physically to Latin American countries without being incorporated into domestic productive structures. It does not enrich or promote national capacity for technological innovation. It is an alien "modernity" whose internal dynamics are determined by distant and often unknown actors and objectives, which are frequently opposed to Latin American countries' national interests. Instead of showcase modernity, Latin America requires a development strategy that makes its population a decisive factor in its own destiny.

From this perspective it is clear that Latin America's strategic options are not—as it is sometimes fallaciously asserted—either to encourage exports or promote import substitution. The real options are very different: either to create an endogenous nucleus capable of sustaining the technological dynamism necessary to penetrate successfully the international market, or to surrender to external agents the responsibility for determining Latin America's present and future productive structure. This latter alternative involves both the export of natural resources for as long as they are in demand or until they are exhausted and the manufacture of obsolete products that by definition hold little opportunity for future growth.

Given the future constraints posed by the international economy and the need to formulate new development strategies, it is likely that the concept and practice of regional economic integration will acquire much greater importance in Latin America. Recent political and economic changes in the region open up opportunities for regional collaboration that closed political regimes fear out of concern that cross-national contacts would encourage social unrest. Authoritarian regimes' inherent insecurity causes them to distrust initiatives for regional cooperation that expand interchanges among national societies, even when these include national business communities. The legitimacy of democratic governments emerging now and in the next several years, together with their will to develop human and natural resources, should make it possible to foster cooperation programs in areas such as health care, education, transportation and communication infrastructure, energy, international marketing, and applied scientific and technological research.

This does not deny the limitations and obstacles that exist to regional economic integration. However, the purpose here is to emphasize those implications that democratization and endogenous modernization may hold for future regional cooperation. The problems encountered by different integration processes in Latin America since the 1960s reflect largely the limitations of national development strategies adopted in the past. Endogenous modernization, by diversifying the productive structure and stimulating domestic creativity, creates opportunities for regional cooperation that are limited by productive structures oriented toward the export of raw materials.

The debate on new development strategies in Latin America should address a number of important issues. First, future development proposals must combine growth, efficiency, and creativity. The lack of attention to creativity in past development strategies has resulted in development patterns dysfunctional to Latin American needs and capabilities. Second, more attention must be given to required changes in national productive structures, both within the industrial sector itself (such as modifications in business leadership and the degree of integration) and in relations between industry and agriculture, industry and the energy sector, and industry and finance. Third, there must be closer coordination between national planning and the market in order to make sectoral strategies more compatible with the decentralization of day-to-day decisions. Finally, more emphasis must be devoted to the character of the social base that sustains a new development strategy.

Including creativity as an essential component of efficiency is a specific functional requirement of the political perspective articulated above. If meeting popular needs were not an important goal in Latin America, simply importing products, techniques, organizational methods, patterns of food consumption, and models of education, health, housing, communication, and recreation would be sufficient. The historical record shows that Latin America can grow without developing its own creative potential. However, the inevitable result is that a high proportion of popular needs and aspirations is sacrificed, postponed, or repressed. A development strategy devoted to the exportation of raw materials and the importation of "showcase modernity" obviously does not need to emphasize creativity; indeed, it would seek to root out those expressions of national creativity that might question the underlying premises of the model.

Thus the importance of creativity in future approaches to development reflects both the need to overcome accumulated social needs and the process of technological transition now under way in industrialized countries. Microprocessors, genetic engineering, laser rays, optical fibers, and new energy sources are the basis for future comparative economic advantages. Moreover, these new technologies offer innovative ways of addressing problems as fundamental as mass education, nutrition, cultural integration and development, the decentralization of decision making, and the industrialization of agriculture. In those countries that succeed in restructuring and reinforcing an endogenous capacity for technological innovation, a young, adaptive, and inquisitive population can become the basis for the progressive transformation of both the economy and the society.

The goal of economic growth must also be part of Latin America's future development strategy. Growth is, of course, an essential requirement for addressing the region's accumulated social needs. However, growth is also required for the development of creativity. As long as the productive system expands, it is possible for it to transform itself by developing new products, processes, and techniques and by experimenting with new ways of organizing production and the labor force. As previously noted, growth does not always contribute to the development of creativity. For that to occur, specific attention must be given to the "content" of economic growth—the role of different actors in the productive process and their linkages with society at large.

Assuming that democratization and endogenous modernization can become the basis for achieving Latin America's development goals, the future character of U.S.–Latin American economic relations depends in large part on the extent to which U.S. policies support this strategy. The history of the United States' own economic transformation suggests that it would support a Latin American development strategy based on values that are the very core of its own success. However, if future U.S. foreign policy toward Latin America identifies itself with strategies that combine authoritarianism and showcase modernity (as has occurred in the past), the medium- and long-term result is likely to be gradual economic and political separation between Latin America and the United States. This is likely to occur despite the heterogeneity of conditions in Latin America and possible short-term increases in financial and commercial transactions with the United States. United States policy toward Latin America must comprehend that the region's social tensions are of predominantly domestic origin and that they derive primarily from social and economic structures that do not correspond to the needs and aspirations of large sectors of the population. United States policies toward the region should reflect those values that inspire the United States' own society and polity. Policies that support authoritarian regimes and showcase modernity are ethically questionable and politically risky in both domestic and international terms. Moreover, the continuation of such policies will only aggravate the challenges that the international economy and accumulated domestic social needs pose for Latin America—with the risk that the political conflicts now raging in Central America will spill over into the larger and more complex nations in the region.

At the same time, the United States should appreciate the dynamic effect that Latin America can produce if its future development strategy is articulated in terms of values such as democratization and endogenous modernization. With a population that will soon be twice that of the United States, Latin America has the potential to contribute significantly to world economic growth. Conversely, the United States is in a position to make an enormous contribution to Latin America's future economic, scientific, technological, and cultural development. The net transfer of resources necessary would very probably be less than those military expenditures required if social and political conflicts in the region intensify sharply.

United Nations Economic Commission for Latin America
and United Nations Industrial Development Organization
Santiago, Chile

Notes

The opinions expressed in this essay are the author's exclusive responsibility and in no way compromise the organizations with which he is associated.

1. This discussion of Latin America's recent development strategy is drawn from Fernando Fajnzylber, *La industrialización trunca de América Latina* (Mexico, D.F.: Editoral Nueva Imagen, 1983), chapter 3.

2. Ibid., chapter 1.

3. The exception here is the United States, where growth in the industrial sector has been similar to that of the economy as a whole.

4. Fajnzylber, chapter 1.

5. See Sergio Bitar, "América Latina y Estados Unidos: Relaciones económicas en los años 70," *Estudios Internacionales* 58 (April–June 1982).

6. Comisión Económica para América Latina, "Las relaciones económicas externas de América Latina en los años 80," *Colección Estudios e Investigaciones* 7 (September 1981).

7. World Bank, *World Development Report, 1981* (Washington, D.C.: 1981), p. 2.

8. This definition would also apply conceptually to Mexico. However, the IMF classifies Mexico as a "net oil exporter."

9. See International Monetary Fund, *World Economic Outlook, 1982;* Tony

Killick, ed., *Adjustment and Financing in the Developing World: The Role of the International Monetary Fund* (Washington, D.C.: International Monetary Fund and Overseas Development Council, 1982); David Ibarra Muñoz, "El entorno financiero del desarrollo," mimeograph, July 1982.

10. Shailendra J. Anajaria et al., *Trade Policy Developments in Industrial Countries* (Washington, D.C.: International Monetary Fund, 1981).

11. International Monetary Fund, *World Economic Outlook, 1982,* pp. 19–20.

12. Ibid., p. 21.

13. The IMF study summarized here also offers a third, "optimistic" scenario. However, the IMF judges that these countries' actual performance will fall somewhere between scenarios A and B.

14. International Monetary Fund, *World Economic Outlook, 1982,* tables 34 and 36.

15. Ibid., p. 21.

16. Ibid., p. 23.

17. Comisión Económica para América Latina, *Balance preliminar de la economía latinoamericana durante 1984* (Santiago, Chile, 1985), tables 2, 3, 4, 5, 6, 7.

18. Inter-American Dialogue, "Working Group Report on Economic and Financial Issues," mimeograph, Woodrow Wilson International Center for Scholars, Smithsonian Institution, Washington, D.C.: January 1983, p. 79.

19. Organization for Economic Cooperation and Development, *OECD Economic Outlook* (July 1982): 8. Also see Hollis B. Chenery, "Restructuring the World Economy: Round II," *Foreign Affairs* 59 (Summer 1981): 1102–20.

20. Organization for Economic Cooperation and Development, "Science and Technology Policy for the 1980s," 1981.

21. For an example of the extent to which there is substantive agreement on this point (despite formal institutional differences), one need only compare the advanced technology programs of Japan's MITI and the United States' Department of Defense. See R. B. Reich, "Making Industrial Policy," *Foreign Affairs* 60, No. 4 (Spring 1982): 852–81. For a contrasting perspective, see Bruce R. Scott, "Can Industry Survive the Welfare State?" *Harvard Business Review* 60, No. 5 (September–October 1982): 70–84.

22. Organization for Economic Cooperation and Development, "Science and Technology Policy for the 1980s"; "Technical Change and Economic Policy," 1980; "Project Interfutures" (sectoral studies for the automotive and electronics sectors), 1978–1980.

23. These subjects are developed further in Fajnzylber, chapter 5.

Part II
Economic Issues in
U.S.–Latin American
Relations

4

External Financing in Latin America: Developments, Problems, and Options

Carlos Massad

The difficulties that Latin American countries experienced in obtaining many products from abroad during World War II contributed to the stimulus already provided by the Great Depression to develop domestic economic production in many areas. By the end of the war, Latin American countries had accumulated foreign exchange reserves that under normal conditions would have facilitated a policy of opening up their economies to world trade. However, external markets were in practice limited to the United States. Western Europe and Asia were in no position to import Latin American products actively or to offer a varied supply of goods to the region. Latin American countries thus found it necessary to improve the organization of their productive efforts through economic planning and selective policies that emphasized industrial expansion as the main engine of growth. Foreign trade and exchange rates were strictly controlled.

For a time, previously accumulated foreign exchange reserves provided the financing necessary to cover the trade imbalances that resulted from rapid industrial growth. But their depletion in some cases and the postwar recession of the late 1940s demonstrated that domestic savings were insufficient to finance the desired rate of economic growth. Thus an important role appeared for foreign savings. Different countries' policies varied within this general context, particularly with respect to official attitudes toward government deficits and domestic price stability. Changes in a country's terms of trade and in national fiscal equilibrium probably explain most of the problems in the foreign trade imbalances and domestic inflationary pressures that surfaced during this period.

At the time, private banking had no role in international finance except in the form of trade-related, short-term operations. Medium- and long-term financing was undertaken principally through official institutions (mainly government-to-government credit) and direct foreign investment. Government-to-government loan operations typically involved fixed, subsidized interest rates and long maturities, so neither interest rates nor amortization periods raised particular problems. Direct investment was strictly linked to the exploitation of mineral resources (copper, oil, tin, iron, and so on) and the production of agricultural commodities (coffee, fruits, sugar, cocoa, and so forth).

Several years after World War II, direct foreign investment began to flow at a rapid rate into Central America, Venezuela, and Ecuador. These countries then opened up their economies and followed a development model that emphasized the exportation of primary products and the importation of a wide variety of manufactured goods. Because of domestic political problems, exchange controls, and/or less favorable treatment of foreign investment, other Latin American countries did not become important recipients of foreign capital. They continued to pursue a development strategy based on relatively high protection for domestic industries and specific stimuli to some sectors of the economy, placing greater emphasis on foreign borrowing than on foreign investment.

By the mid-1960s most Latin American countries evidenced rapid rates of economic growth, so their attractiveness as borrowers was substantially enhanced. At the same time, foreign investment in Latin America began to ebb as new investment opportunities appeared in other areas and nationalization became a real risk. Moreover, as Latin America's per capita income levels came to exceed substantially those of other developing areas, both international organizations and industrialized countries shifted their concessional resources toward other regions. Within the World Bank this process became known as "graduation," and through it some developing countries found their access to the Bank's resources increasingly limited. The U.S. government's growing skepticism regarding both foreign assistance and U.S. contributions to international and regional organizations stimulated and sustained this general tendency.

At the same time, world private financial markets developed rapidly in the late 1960s and early 1970s. Foreign investment lost its importance in the financing of current-account imbalances and reserve increases in Latin America, and foreign borrowing in the form of loans from private sources grew rapidly. By the mid-1970s, direct foreign investment as a share of total net capital inflows had dropped to 17 percent, compared to 44 percent ten years earlier. Table 1 shows the size and composition of Latin America's foreign debt from 1970 to 1983.

In early 1984 the total foreign debt of Latin American countries probably exceeded $340 billion. This figure includes both private and public debt from all sources, covering all maturities. The $337 billion reported in table 1 is an estimate that excludes several kinds of debt: nonpublicly guaranteed suppliers' credits, loans from banks other than those reporting

TABLE 1

LATIN AMERICAN AND CARIBBEAN FOREIGN DEBT, 1970–1983[a]

(outstanding and disbursed at end of each year; all amounts in US$ billions)

	Total Debt	Official Sources		Private Sources[b]	
		Amount	% of Total Debt	Amount	% of Total Debt
1970	23	8	36	15	64
1971	26	9	36	17	64
1972	30	10	34	20	66
1973	40	12	28	28	72
1974	56	14	25	42	75
1975	75	16	22	59	78
1976	98	18	18	80	82
1977	116	21	18	95	82
1978	152	25	16	127	84
1979	184	27	15	157	85
1980	229	31	14	198	86
1981	280	34	12	246	88
1982	314	39	12	275	88
1983[c]	337	47	14	290	86

Sources: International Bank for Reconstruction and Development, *World Debt Tables,* 1982–1983; Bank for International Settlements, *Annual Report,* various years; Inter-American Development Bank, *External Debt and Economic Development in Latin America,* Washington, D.C., 1984.

a. Estimates include long-, medium-, and short-term debt, as well as unguaranteed debt with financial institutions that report to the Bank for International Settlements. Unguaranteed debt with other financial institutions and unguaranteed suppliers' credits are not included. Latin America and the Caribbean include the following countries: Argentina, Barbados, Bolivia, Brazil, Colombia, Costa Rica, Chile, Dominican Republic, Ecuador, El Salvador, Guatemala, Guyana, Haiti, Honduras, Jamaica, Mexico, Nicaragua, Panama, Paraguay, Peru, Suriname, Trinidad and Tobago, Uruguay, and Venezuela.

b. All short-term debts are assumed to be from private sources.

c. Preliminary estimate.

to the Bank for International Settlements, and some direct firm-to-firm loans. This figure also excludes foreign-owned nonbank deposits in Latin American banks.[1]

The estimated $340 billion of foreign debt equalled approximately 47 percent of total Latin American gross domestic product, and interest payments equalled some 35 percent of Latin American exports in 1983. Table 2 provides data on these two indicators for several groups of Latin American countries based on published (but underestimated) figures. There are practically no exceptions to the finding that both foreign debt and interest payments have grown substantially in the last five years in relation to these indicators.

TABLE 2

INDICATORS OF INDEBTEDNESS FOR LATIN AMERICA AND THE
CARIBBEAN, 1983

	Total Debt as % of Gross Domestic Product	Interest Payments as % of Goods and Services Exports
All Latin America (24 countries)	47	35
Argentina, Brazil, Mexico	46	41
Chile, Colombia, Peru	50	31
Smaller countries[a]	47	24
Six oil-exporting countries[b]	48	31
Non-oil-exporting countries[c]	46	39
"Open" economies (Argentina, Chile, Uruguay)	65	50

Sources: U.N. Economic Commission for Latin America, *Balance preliminar de la economía latinoamericana en 1983;* International Monetary Fund, *Balance of Payments Yearbook,* 1983; World Bank, *Informe sobre el desarrollo mundial,* 1984.

a. Includes all Latin American countries except "large" (Argentina, Brazil, Mexico) and "medium-sized" (Chile, Colombia, Peru) countries and Venezuela.

b. Bolivia, Ecuador, Mexico, Peru, Trinidad and Tobago, and Venezuela.

c. Includes all other Latin American countries that are not significant oil exporters.

The remainder of this essay explores the main reasons for the recent increase in debt levels in the region, considering both the demand and supply sides of the issue. The essay also examines the impact of increased indebtedness on Latin American countries' domestic policies and economic stability, and the prospects for future resource transfers to the region. It also evaluates the terms-of-trade, interest rate, and foreign-financing conditions that would make high and growing debt levels bearable. Finally, the essay examines the domestic and international policy options that are available to debtor and creditor countries if these conditions are not fulfilled.

Why Did Latin America's Foreign Debt Grow So Fast?

With practically no exceptions, foreign indebtedness to private sources increased very rapidly in Latin America in the 1970s. Debt levels increased both in countries that opened up their economies by reducing barriers to trade and capital movements and in countries that did not follow policies such as these. Debt increases were registered in oil-exporting countries as well as in non-oil-exporting countries. With very few exceptions, both large and small Latin American countries showed rapid growth in overall indebtedness.[2] A systematic examination of this generalized phenomenon must begin by considering those "demand" and "supply" elements that gave impetus to increases in indebtedness.

Demand Elements Influencing Foreign Indebtedness

Demand for foreign borrowing is not necessarily connected to a country's foreign trade operations. Of course, an increase in imports and/or exports necessitates increased use of short-term, trade-related commercial credit. But increases in regional imports and exports accounted for a relatively small proportion of the total increase in Latin America's demand for foreign debt in the 1970s. More important factors included interest rate differentials between domestic and foreign capital markets and deficit spending in some sectors of the Latin American economies.

There are two aspects to the problem posed by interest rate differentials. First, differences between domestic and foreign rates persisted over a prolonged period. Second, domestic rates tended to be higher than foreign ones, in some cases reaching unprecedented levels.

Most theoretical analyses assume that interest rate differentials among countries are rapidly eliminated by capital movements. However, empirical evidence does not support this assumption. Interest rate differentials tend to persist even among industrialized countries that permit substantially free capital movements. (This is the case after allowing for expected changes in exchange rates as measured through foreign-exchange futures markets or covered rate differentials.) Latin America is no exception to this situation, and in several countries domestic interest rates (expressed in terms of foreign exchange equivalents) have deviated substantially from foreign rates. Table 3 provides indicative data regarding domestic and foreign interest rates (both expressed in terms of dollars) in Argentina, Chile, and Uruguay during the period from 1977 through 1982.

Two hypotheses have been advanced to explain the origins of this phenomenon in Latin America (apart from the usual one of capital movement regulation): financial market segmentation and tradable versus nontradable securities. Segmented domestic financial markets emerge because not all those seeking credit have access to foreign borrowing. In practice, it is the larger enterprises and those involved in foreign trade that have such access. Most other credit demanders have access to foreign loans only through domestic intermediaries. These intermediaries effectively prevent foreign and domestic interest rates from coming together by capturing all or most of the differences in rate. Because most borrowers have no direct access to foreign borrowing, they are unable to act through this market mechanism to force a reduction in the spread between domestic and foreign rates. Thus market segmentation in part explains the failure of domestic and foreign interest rates to converge rapidly under conditions of free (or nearly free) capital movements.[3]

Interest rate differentials also exist because of controls on capital outflows and inflows. The maintenance of such controls encourages the

TABLE 3

SELECTED LATIN AMERICAN DOMESTIC AND INTERNATIONAL INTEREST
RATES, 1977–1982

(annual rates, %)

	Domestic Interest Rate[a]			International Interest Rate[b]
	Argentina	Chile	Uruguay	LIBOR[c]
1977	10.0	58.4	22.4	6.4
1978	37.2	51.1	33.4	9.2
1979	34.5	40.5	37.8	12.1
1980	45.6	46.9	40.7	14.0
1981	−30.3	51.9	38.2	16.8
1982	−65.8	−12.1	—	13.6

Sources: Roberto Zahler, "Recent Southern Cone Liberalization Reforms and Stabilization Policies: The Chilean Case, 1974–1982," *Journal of Inter-American Studies and World Affairs* (November 1983): 509–62; International Monetary Fund, *International Financial Statistics,* April 1983; Central Bank of Argentina, lists of financial data, series 484; U.N. Economic Commission for Latin America, *Estudio Económico: Uruguay 1981,* November 1982.

    a. Domestic interest rate in U.S. dollar equivalent.

    b. LIBOR for operations in U.S. dollars; rate for 180 days, London.

    c. London Inter-Bank Offered Rate.

issuing and trading of securities that are not tradable internationally (because of the nature and form of the securities, the risk involved, or simply inadequate or costly information about them). Domestic securities do not become tradable instantaneously as capital controls are dismantled. Because there are costs involved in this shift, the process is likely to take some time, perhaps years.[4]

Of course, market segmentation and the nontradability of securities are related. Market segmentation exists only insofar as some domestic securities cannot be sold to foreign lenders (that is, insofar as some domestic borrowers are precluded from borrowing abroad). Both market segmentation and the existence of nontradable securities explain why domestic interest rates may *diverge* from foreign rates even under conditions of free capital movements. But other factors explain why domestic rates in Latin America have been *higher* than foreign rates during recent years, thus providing an incentive to borrow abroad. This differential resulted from both short-term and structural economic policies and from the behavior of important groups of large, interrelated enterprises.

The first factor was the generalized counterinflation effort pursued in Latin America in the 1970s. As external inflation accelerated during this period, so did domestic inflation rates. Governments necessarily gave high priority to resisting this trend. In an environment such as this, policies favored monetary restriction, which produced higher interest rates and/or excess demand for credit. As domestic rates increased relative to foreign rates, the incentive to borrow abroad grew. At the same time governments reduced restrictions on such borrowing, with obvious consequences.

Interest rate differentials also persisted because of structural economic policies in the region. During the last decade, several Latin American countries undertook policies intended to effect major changes in economic structure and incentives. Argentina, Costa Rica, Chile, Mexico, Peru, Uruguay, and Venezuela all deregulated trade, capital movements, and financial systems, and they introduced important changes in tax and/or social security systems. Apart from their long-term implications, these reform policies changed short-term relative prices and encouraged the movement of resources from activities whose relative prices decreased to those that registered an increase. Although imports provided some cushion, in those sectors in which relative prices rose, there was still a stimulus to expand domestic production that implied additional demands for credit. Those activities that were expected to contract did so only slowly, in the expectation that policy changes would be transitory. Businesses in these sectors were willing to borrow in the meantime, even at high real rates of interest, to maintain some minimum level of operations until circumstances changed. Therefore structural economic reforms increased the total demand for credit (domestic or foreign), thus pressing domestic interest rates upward without an overheating of the economy.

In many cases this tendency was accentuated by links between domestic banks and nonfinancial firms. Where these ties exist, there is no independent evaluation of nonfinancial firms' policies, and their mistakes do not necessarily result in their being rationed out of the financial market. Moreover, these firms may not be required to provide as much collateral for loans as other firms, thus allowing them to work with a higher debt-to-capital ratio. The higher this ratio, the lower the risk for the firm's owners, and hence the higher the interest rate they are willing to accept (insofar as they can finance it) to stay in business in difficult times.

Foreign-exchange policy also contributed to interest rate differentials. If the exchange rate is fixed in nominal terms when inflation is rapid, nominal domestic interest rates (which tend to reflect expected inflation rates) may become extremely high in dollar terms.[5] For example, a nominal domestic interest rate of 25 percent per year with an annual domestic inflation rate of 25 percent is equivalent to a real domestic interest rate of zero but to a dollar rate of 25 percent because the price of the dollar is fixed. Under these conditions, a foreign interest rate of 15 percent per year would imply a gain of 10 percent per year for a borrower who obtains financing abroad rather than from domestic sources. A situation of this kind has prevailed in several Latin American countries (Argentina,

Chile, Uruguay, Mexico, and Peru). Of course, a similar but less extreme incentive to borrow abroad exists when the exchange rate moves at slower speed than the domestic inflation rate. This was the case for some time in Brazil and Colombia.

A second major cause of Latin America's growing external debt in the 1970s was excessive spending by the public and private sectors. The problem of excessive public sector spending is well known, and it has been carefully examined by economists and international financial institutions. The public sector, under pressure to improve living conditions, expands its expenditures until they exceed current receipts, and the difference is financed through foreign and/or domestic borrowing. Foreign borrowing produces a direct increase in official foreign debt, while domestic borrowing results in less direct growth in foreign indebtedness.

When the public sector borrows domestically, money (and/or "quasi money") is created over and above the quantity in demand. The excess supply of money has a counterpart in an excess combined demand for goods and services and securities. This excess demand is satisfied through a deficit in external payments, which results in the depletion of international reserves. Government financial officials' policy response is to borrow abroad, and thus the official external debt increases.

Excessive spending by the private sector explains cases of rapid increase in indebtedness in those Latin American countries in which the public sector maintained equilibrium (or near-equilibrium) in its own accounts. Most analysts have assumed that private sector spending can be effectively regulated by government control over the expansion of domestic credit. However, if alternative sources of financing are available abroad, the private sector can also overspend.

Insofar as excessive private sector spending is concentrated in tradable goods (that is, goods that can be imported or exported), it will be reflected in a current-account deficit in the balance of payments and financed by a corresponding inflow of capital as the private sector borrows abroad. If there is also excess demand for nontradable goods, part of the external borrowing will produce an increase in reserves, and the prices of nontradable goods will rise relative to the prices of tradable items—which is equivalent to a revaluation of the currency.[6] Private sector expectations might then accelerate the pace of foreign borrowing. With fixed exchange rates, the nominal prices of tradable goods will remain stable while the prices of nontradable items continue to rise. Domestic price indexes will reflect a higher inflation rate. Nominal domestic interest rates remain inflated and become extremely high in dollar terms, thus encouraging further borrowing abroad. As a result, foreign debt increases as a component of the economy's liability structure.

This chain of events will produce the need for adjustment in the balance-of-payments current account at some point, in much the same manner that excessive public expenditures eventually require adjustment. However, this unorthodox case of excessive spending is more difficult to detect. Its symptoms are all considered to be positive indicators: increased capital inflow, larger reserves, and perhaps rapid rates of economic growth. But because there is insufficient investment, this process is as unsustainable as that generated by excessive public spending.

In cases in which excessive private spending dominates the picture, most of the increase in foreign indebtedness can be traced to the private sector. In cases in which excessive public sector spending predominates, official debt is usually the principal component in total foreign indebtedness.

Foreign Lending: The Supply Side

The demand for additional external borrowing in Latin America during the 1970s coincided with an increased supply of foreign credit. The oil shocks of 1973–1974 and 1978–1979 generated large current-account surpluses for oil-exporting countries. A significant share of these surpluses was deposited in private banks that operate actively in the international financial market, thus expanding substantially the available resources of the international banking system.[7] At the same time, oil-importing countries registered large balance-of-trade deficits that required increased foreign borrowing.

Because Eurocurrency deposits are not subject to reserve requirements, the capacity of this market to expand is quite substantial.[8] In fact, the total supply of credit in this market is essentially determined by the demand for it. The total foreign assets of banks reporting to the Bank for International Settlements (net of interbank deposits) grew at an average annual rate of 20 percent between 1974 and 1982.

The financial commitments of U.S. banks to Latin American countries also grew rapidly during this period. These loans represented substantial proportions of the banks' total equity (net worth), which became a source of some concern to U.S. comptroller authorities. Table 4 shows the "exposure" of a number of large U.S. banks in Brazil, Mexico, and Venezuela.

Consequences of Increasing Indebtedness and Changing Debt Composition

Both demand and supply factors contributed to Latin American countries' growing indebtedness during the 1970s. The main sources of loans were private banks, particularly U.S. banks. Thus as indebtedness increased, the relative importance of debts owed to private banks rose. This

TABLE 4

DEBT EXPOSURE IN SELECTED LATIN AMERICAN COUNTRIES FOR TEN U.S.
BANKS

(outstanding loans in US$ billions)

	Brazil	Mexico	Venezuela	Total of 3 Countries	Total as % of Bank's Equity
Citicorp	4.4	3.3	1.1	8.7	180
Bank of America	2.3	2.5	2.0	6.8	148
Chase Manhattan	2.4	1.7	1.0	5.1	183
Manufacturers Hanover	2.0	1.7	1.1	4.8	174
Morgan Guaranty Trust	1.7	1.1	0.5	3.3	122
Chemical Bank	1.3	1.5	—	2.8	143
Bankers Trust	0.9	0.9	0.5	2.2	143
Continental Illinois	0.5	0.7	0.5	1.6	96
First Interstate	0.5	0.7	—	1.2	64
Security Pacific	0.5	0.5	—	1.0	68

Source: The American Banker, quoted in The Economist, 30 April 1983, p. 13.

change in debt composition had several important implications. First, debt became more expensive, and repayment periods were shortened as the relative significance of concessional loans declined and commercial terms became the norm. Second, the number of creditors increased substantially, making negotiations more complicated in the event of a debt crisis. Third, interest payments were increasingly based on floating rates whose changes affected the total debt stock rather than just the flow of new borrowing. Fourth, lenders' "exposure" became a major concern, and "country-risk" analysis attracted increasing attention. Finally, because there is no established market in which lenders can liquidate their portfolio assets, a market valuation of these assets cannot be made. Portfolio classification thus becomes an exercise that requires the active participation of the national comptrolling authority.

The changing composition of foreign debt also has other dimensions. Private bankers are not expected to be politically motivated in their decisions to lend—at least insofar as total indebtedness does not exceed lenders' perceptions of reasonable limits, measured in proportion to borrowers' gross domestic product and export earnings. As debt levels rise relative to borrowers' economic size and foreign-exchange resources, the risk of default increases, and lenders become more and more interested in the borrowing country's macroeconomic policies. This is particularly true for very large lenders, which in the case of Latin American countries are mainly U.S. banks.

This situation affects Latin American countries in three major ways, although the consequences are less severe for those countries that have used foreign borrowing to increase significantly their productive and export capacity. First, the level of indebtedness and its maturity structure impose restrictions on domestic policies. The shorter the average maturity of the debt stock, the larger the share that matures each year. Unless a country is willing to accept a transfer of real resources abroad by reducing its foreign debt, these maturities must be financed. If the transfer of resources is to favor the debtor country, total indebtedness must rise—further taxing the country's capacity to borrow. Because banks evaluate a country's creditworthiness on the basis of indicators such as foreign-exchange reserve levels, the balance of trade, and the ratio of debt-service obligations to export earnings, a country is bound to adopt policies that produce positive effects on those indicators. This implies that monetary policy, exchange rate policy, interest rate policy, fiscal policy, and so forth are in fact constrained even if banks do not place formal restrictions on a country's domestic policies. Obviously, the higher the level of indebtedness for any given maturity structure, the greater the amount of gross new borrowing that is required each year. Interest payments also require financing, and they are determined not only by overall indebtedness but also by foreign interest rate levels.

A second consequence of higher indebtedness is the increased probability of an eventual (reverse) transfer of real resources from borrowers to creditors. As an external loan is drawn upon, the borrowing country receives a transfer of real resources. These resources are repaid in the form of interest and amortization payments. However, if new borrowing exceeds amortization and interest payments, the borrower continues to receive a net transfer of resources. As indebtedness grows in relation to standard indicators such as a country's gross domestic product and export earnings, the probability of obtaining new net loans decreases, and the likelihood of being forced to transfer real resources abroad increases. The magnitude of this transfer is linked to variables such as interest rates, terms of trade, and external inflation.[9]

Third, the increasingly commercial character of debt stocks establishes a new mechanism for the transmission of external shocks to Latin American economies and thus increases their vulnerability. As debt from private sources grows, the proportion of the total debt stock that is subject to floating interest rates increases. Changes in interest rates then become an important source of current-account imbalances. For Latin America as a whole in early 1983, a 1 percent rise in interest rates over the course of a year implied additional interest payments of about $2.4 billion. Of course, interest rates may rise or fall. But the main point is that interest rate fluctuations introduce a new source of instability in the balance-of-payments situation when the level of indebtedness is high. They join terms of trade, export volumes, the effect of interest rates on domestic expenditures and investment, and exchange rate fluctuations as vehicles for the transmission of international disequilibria to Latin American economies.

A further complication arises because interest rate fluctuations are often associated with shifting terms of trade and changes in the exchange rate value of an intervention currency vis-à-vis other currencies that are important in international trade. Changes in these different areas require adjustment policies that work in the same direction so that their effects reinforce each other. Moreover, fluctuations in interest rates tend to affect the quality of lending bank portfolios. Higher interest rates erode portfolio quality because investments made on the basis of lower interest rates become unprofitable, and borrowers' debt burden becomes less bearable. Conversely, lower interest rates improve the quality of bank portfolios. Thus changes in interest rates affect banks' willingness to lend in a way that reinforces the destabilizing effects described above.

Can Current Levels of Indebtedness Be Sustained?

Over the long run, foreign savings will have an important role to play in the economic development of Latin American countries. United States Department of Commerce figures show that the average yields of U.S. investment in Latin America are more favorable to investors than those in other areas of the world.[10] This finding suggests that a portfolio-composition model applied to countries that are net suppliers of savings would result in a sustained capital inflow to Latin America. Such a model also indicates that even if yield and variability were equal all over the world, capital movements would still produce a net inflow into those areas with a smaller capital stock.[11]

However, foreign investment and foreign debt differ in their political and economic implications for Latin America. Although the political dimensions of this issue will not be developed here, investment and debt differ in the kind of foreign presence they imply in a country. Foreign investment, particularly when it is important in relation to the size of the economy or the particular sector involved, stimulates foreign attention to micropolicies and the exercise of power. Foreign debt is generally free of these characteristics.

From an economic perspective, foreign investment usually involves foreign ownership of real assets, while external debt by definition involves foreign ownership of financial assets. Direct foreign investment provides the investor with a flow of income that can only be estimated with some probability and that is subject to economic fluctuations in the sector concerned. In contrast, debt provides the lender with a flow of interest payments at a rate that is either fixed at the beginning of the operation or that floats in relation to some reference rate in international markets or in the lender's domestic market. Investment profits can usually be remitted abroad as they are generated. These remittances tend to vary, *ceteris paribus,* with the relative success of the business involved. Interest payments, however, are not subject to such variations except in the extreme case of the borrowing enterprise's failure if the loan is not guaranteed. An inflow of resources in the form of direct foreign investment is directly connected to capital expenditures, while an inflow of resources in the form of debt may not be directly related to an increase in a country's productive capacity. On the other hand, loan principal remittances are made on a previously agreed schedule, while capital investment remittances are usually not subect to such limitations. In practice, though, capital remittances from direct investment take time because they require that the investment itself be liquidated.

As previously noted, over the last decade the bulk of foreign capital flowing to Latin America has been in the form of debt. Given the region's continuing development needs, net additional flows of foreign capital will be required if Latin America's economic growth rate is to recover to the level of the 1970s. The debt-servicing problems that a large number of Latin American countries have encountered since 1982–1983 underscore the need to examine the circumstances that would make possible a sustained transfer of real resources from abroad through foreign borrowing.

A level of indebtedness that increases over a long period of time can be sustained so long as creditors perceive that they will eventually be repaid. If this perception is widely held, creditors have no inclination to demand the payment of outstanding principal. Indeed, their main concern is with maintaining a secure flow of interest payments. For this reason, increasing indebtedness is acceptable so long as: the borrowing country's productive capacity continues to expand; this expansion produces an increased volume and value of exports relative to imports; interest payments do not place an excessive burden on the balance-of-payments current account; and foreign financial markets develop relatively smoothly. In short, increasing indebtedness is sustainable insofar as the current-account imbalance is not greatly disproportionate to exports and gross domestic product.

To what extent does foreign borrowing expand the debtor country's productive capacity? Medium- and long-term borrowing from official multilateral sources usually goes to investment projects that include both foreign and domestic financing, so that increased borrowing abroad also implies the commitment of additional domestic resources to investment. Under these conditions, foreign borrowing constitutes an addition to domestic savings, and the borrowing country's debt-servicing capacity increases along with its total investment. However, when private foreign banks become the principal source of foreign credit, the link between external borrowing and domestic investment weakens.

Of course, the debtor country's domestic economic policies are crucial to the determination of the investment rate and the growth of productive capacity. But world economic conditions also play an important role, especially in decisions such as the allocation of resources to the production of tradable versus nontradable goods. A vigorous world economy and expanding international trade provide the basis for increased export volumes and more stable export prices. Raw material exports are more susceptible to sharp price fluctuations than manufactured products because their supply is generally quite inelastic in the short run, while their demand is determined by demand for final products. A global economic downturn negatively affects developing countries' terms of trade, in part because raw materials constitute a major proportion of their total exports. Thus if the world economic growth rate declines, there is first a sharp drop in developing countries' terms of trade, which recover somewhat later on as the world economy stabilizes at a new, lower level. Similarly, if the international economy's growth rate increases, developing countries' terms of trade improve sharply and then deteriorate to a new, stable level. Fluctuations in the terms of trade introduce substantial instability in developing countries' balance of payments, which are more severe the more important raw materials are in a country's total exports.

Part of this effect in recent years has resulted from protectionist tendencies in industrialized countries that are associated with declining world economic growth and slowing international trade. Furthermore, the deterioration in non-oil-exporting Latin American countries' terms of trade has coincided with increases in nominal (and real) external interest rates. Both declining terms of trade and rising external interest rates have increased borrowing countries' debt burden.[12]

Given the size of the U.S. economy, the influence of U.S. domestic policies on the world economy is far stronger than that of any other individual country. Indeed, U.S. economic policy is perhaps the single most important factor in determining economic conditions the world over. For this reason, the United States' economic policies are a matter of great interest for debtor countries regardless of the source of their external financing.

To what extent do developments in international financial markets affect debtor countries' capacity to borrow? For any given maturity structure, gross financing requirements increase with the total debt stock. Debtors need additional amounts of foreign financing just to prevent their debt stock from falling. As indebtedness grows, more and more resources must be devoted to repayment if the level of debt is ever to be reduced. Interest payments also increase with additional borrowing, unless interest rates fall at a faster rate than the growth in overall indebtedness. For all these reasons, as the level of indebtedness rises it becomes increasingly important for debtor countries that international financial markets expand smoothly. Any serious market dislocation might cause major problems for debtor countries. In turn, these problems are likely to reverberate through international financial markets in a vicious circle.

The above discussion shows that foreign borrowing is sustainable insofar as it contributes to the expansion of debtor countries' productive capacity and export potential; as long as growth rates and other conditions in the world economy facilitate export expansion and reasonably stable terms of trade; and if international financial markets continue to supply funds on a regular basis. To what extent are these conditions likely to be fulfilled for Latin America during the 1980s? Recent information indicates that trends in all three areas are unfavorable to future external borrowing. First, a preliminary U.N. Economic Commission for Latin America (ECLA) study of nine Latin American countries over a twelve-year period shows that in five cases, foreign savings were substituted for domestic savings so that available investment resources grew less than the debt stock.[13] Further analysis is required to determine whether foreign and domestic savings are substitutable or complementary. However, the ECLA study clearly indicates that growing indebtedness has in several cases been associated with major increases in consumption. In these cases higher debt levels have improved at least some groups' present welfare, but without contributing to the expanded productive capacity that is necessary to sustain future consumption and debt repayment.

Second, terms of trade have recently moved strongly against Latin American countries. Here it is necessary to distinguish between the region's oil-exporting and non-oil-exporting countries. Until 1980 terms of trade moved against non-oil-exporting countries and in favor of oil exporters. But during 1981–1983, terms of trade deteriorated for both groups of countries, showing only a slight recovery in 1984. Real interest rates increased at the same time, and the combined negative effects have been substantial for all Latin American countries.

Table 5 shows the effects of deteriorating terms of trade and rising interest rates on the current-account balances of eighteen non-oil-exporting Latin American countries. If the terms of trade had been those prevailing in 1965–1969, and if interest rates had been at 1978–1979 levels, the total current-account balance for this group of countries would have been a surplus of over $3 billion rather than the actual deficit of $15.5 billion. Of course, if terms of trade and interest rates had been different, other conditions might also have changed. Nonetheless, these data pro-

TABLE 5

ESTIMATES OF THE EFFECTS OF TERMS-OF-TRADE AND INTEREST RATES
ON THE CURRENT ACCOUNT BALANCES OF EIGHTEEN
NON-OIL-EXPORTING LATIN AMERICAN COUNTRIES, 1975–1983
(US$ billions)

	Current Account Balance	Terms-of-Trade Effect[a]	Interest Rate Effect[b]	Adjusted Current Account
1975	−10.6	−3.6	.1	−7.1
1976	−7.1	−1.7	.3	−5.7
1977	−5.4	.9	.5	−7.0
1978	−8.2	−1.9	−.5	−6.8
1979	−14.3	−4.7	−.5	−9.1
1980	−24.0	−9.5	−1.4	−13.1
1981	−28.1	−15.8	−4.6	−7.7
1982	−27.5	−17.7	−5.5	−4.3
1983	−15.5	−15.6	−3.1	3.2

Sources: U.N. Economic Commission for Latin America (on the basis of IMF data), *Balance of Payments*, April 1984; and International Monetary Fund, *International Financial Statistics*, April 1984.

a. Estimated by comparing effective trade balance with 1965–1969 priced trade balance multiplied by Organization for Economic Cooperation and Development (OECD) countries' consumer price index.

b. Estimated on the basis of the coefficient: net interest paid to net overall debt (includes long-, medium-, short-term debt minus debtor countries' deposits in banks reporting to the International Bank for Settlements). The coefficient was considered "normal" in the period 1978–1979; any values over that average have negative effects.

vide some indication of the relative importance of terms of trade and interest rates in current-account imbalances and the affected countries' need for additional financing.[14]

How much of the existing imbalance should be eliminated through adjustment policies and how much should be financed are open questions. If at least some of the factors producing terms-of-trade and interest rate problems are transitory rather than permanent, financing might be more reasonable than adjustment. Furthermore, protectionist tendencies are proliferating in industrialized countries. Even though they have not yet had a major impact on Latin American exports, these pressures discourage the allocation of additional resources to export activities and thus affect future export growth rates.

Finally, several factors have introduced instability in international financial markets in recent years: the behavior of smaller banks, which tend to be relative newcomers to international business; the sharp fluctuations in the price of oil; and the deterioration of private banks' asset portfolios. Large private banks increased their capacity to lend abroad as the international financial system expanded in the 1970s. They improved

their methods of evaluating country risk, and they expanded their network of branch offices and correspondent banks so as to establish closer
ties with prospective borrowers. As interest rate spreads grew, smaller
banks also found foreign lending attractive. However, because they were
not able to establish their own country-risk evaluation capacity, and because they were not in close contact with prospective clients, these
smaller banks generally entered the market in the footsteps of larger
banks. They increasingly participated in syndicated loans. As a result, as
table 6 shows, both large and small banks substantially increased their
international commitments between 1972 and 1982.

However, smaller banks' exposure in foreign lending is sufficiently
reduced to permit sharp reactions to changing economic and political
conditions. Whereas a bank that is highly exposed would have to consider
its own interest very carefully before curtailing sharply its foreign lending,
a bank with limited exposure can withdraw unilaterally without serious
consequences for its own portfolio. Smaller banks generally do not have
the necessary staff or the required information to evaluate the overall
consequences of such an action. When danger signs appear, smaller banks
curtail their lending at the same time without considering the impact that
this pursuit of narrow self-interest may have on international financial
markets.

Apart from the attitudes of lending banks, the global economic recession of the early 1980s reduced the supply of savings and credit available
in international financial markets. World demand for petroleum contracted sharply, producing serious difficulties for oil-exporting countries
because of the size and allocation of production quotas. The oil supply
cartel could not be sustained effectively, and petroleum prices dropped
rapidly. This price decline altered the distribution of current-account surpluses and deficits in the world. Oil-exporting countries' surpluses disappeared, and an important source of additional liquidity in international
financial markets dried up.

Global recession and high real interest rates in the early 1980s also
eroded banks' domestic and foreign asset portfolios. Although national
authorities can take steps to support domestic firms in financial trouble
(thus indirectly strengthening domestic banks' assets), firms located in
foreign countries are usually beyond their jurisdiction. The only real
means of responding to a probable weakening in banks' external assets is
to regulate the foreign exposure of domestic banks. Bank comptrolling
authorities in the United States thus became stricter in their evaluations
in an effort to limit the consequences of economic problems in other
countries.

These events—the withdrawal of smaller banks from the international
lending market, the reduction and elimination of oil-exporting countries'

TABLE 6
GROWTH OF INTERNATIONAL PRIVATE BANK LENDING, 1972–1983[a]

	1972		1973		1974		1975		1976		1977	
	$[b]	%[c]	$	%	$	%	$	%	$	%	$	%
Banks in Western Europe	182.2		244.4	34.1	279.4	14.4	329.9	18.1	385.6	16.9	466.2	20.9
Banks in Japan & Canada	24.0		29.4	22.5	34.5	17.4	34.2	−.9	39.0	14.1	39.9	2.3
Banks in United States	9.2		15.2	65.2	34.7	128.3	48.3	39.2	69.6	44.1	92.6	33.0
Offshore Branches of U.S. Banks	9.4		23.5	150.0	36.1	53.6	51.1	41.6	74.9	46.6	91.1	21.6
Total Banks Reporting to Bank for International Settlements	224.8		312.5	39.0	384.7	23.1	463.5	20.5	569.1	22.8	689.7	21.2

Sources: Bank for International Settlements, *Annual Report,* June 1977 to 1983, and *Review,* April 1984.

a. Refers to banks operating in Belgium, Luxembourg, France, Federal Republic of Germany, Italy, Netherlands, Sweden, United Kingdom, Canada, Japan, the United States, and Switzerland, and offshore branches of U.S. banks in the Caribbean and the Middle East. These figures contain considerable double-counting because of interbank transactions within the respective areas. This amount may be as much as 40 percent of the total. However, this amount has not been deducted here, nor has the author estimated debt obligations excluded from totals shown.

b. Billions of U.S. dollars at end of each period.

c. Annual rate of growth.

current-account surpluses, and the deterioration of banks' asset portfolios—created an environment conducive to a drastic reduction in the flow of additional resources to financial markets. This situation is dramatically clear in table 6. These events significantly affected developing countries, particularly Latin America.

Can Latin American governments do anything to alter this situation? Of the three conditions described here as necessary for Latin American countries' continued foreign borrowing, only the first is partially within the purview of Latin American governments. Incentives to increase productive capacity and to allocate additional resources to the production of

1978		1979		1980		1981		1982		1983	
$	%	$	%	$	%	$	%	$	%	$	%
611.4	31.1	776.0	26.9	903.0	16.4	998.4	10.6	1022.8	2.4	1027.2	0.4
56.1	40.6	71.0	26.6	101.2	42.5	122.8	21.3	129.7	5.6	150.9	16.3
119.2	28.7	136.4	14.4	176.8	29.6	256.6	45.1	363.4	41.6	396.0	9.0
106.5	16.9	127.6	19.8	141.0	10.5	172.0	22.0	172.9	0.5	179.8	4.0
893.1	29.5	1111.0	24.4	1321.9	19.0	1549.7	17.2	1688.8	9.0	1753.9	3.8

tradable goods are basically linked to domestic policies and to the stability of such policies. However, developments in the international economy also exert an influence on these questions. Foreign interest rates influence domestic ones, and export expansion is linked to the growth rate of the world economy and to trade policies in the main markets. The availability of foreign financing also influences domestic investment levels. However, all these factors are of secondary importance in comparison with the domestic allocation of resources between investment and consumption. In this area, domestic policies predominate. This is not merely a question of investment as a proportion of gross domestic product; the efficient evaluation of alternative investment projects and their efficacious completion are also required.

Current Approaches to the Debt Crisis

The conditions necessary to sustain current-account deficits through substantial capital flows to Latin America are unlikely to be fulfilled, and there are now significant pressures to eliminate or reduce substantially these deficits rather than to finance them. Latin American countries' adjustment efforts and costs have already been substantial: the region as a whole ended 1983 with an even lower per capita income than in 1982, and in several cases income per capita fell by more than 7 percent. (In the case of Chile, per capita income fell in 1982 by nearly 23 percent.) Unemployment levels in many countries reached record highs.[15]

Too much emphasis on adjustment presents several dangers. First, the costs of very strong adjustment policies are likely to be sufficiently high to discredit policy approaches pursued since the mid-1970s (including an opening up of trade and financial relations), with important long-term consequences. Second, the current economic recession in Latin America, if accentuated by excessive emphasis on adjustment policies, is likely to produce a feedback effect on the world economy that will slow global economic recovery. This effect may be particularly pronounced in the United States. Rapid adjustment generally involves a decline in imports that is faster than the increase in exports, at least in the short run. Latin American imports from the United States amount to $40 billion per year and are concentrated in machinery and transportation equipment, which together are nearly 50 percent of Latin America's total imports. Third, excessive emphasis on adjustment will further erode the value of lending banks' asset portfolios, giving further impulse to a retrenchment in foreign-bank lending to the region.

Finally, it is not clear that adjustment policies alone are an adequate response to present difficulties. At least some of the factors that have contributed to the current crisis are transitory in nature. For example, there are good reasons to believe that the world economy has already begun to recover. Interest rates are likely to return to more customary levels, although some time may elapse before they do so, and terms of trade cannot be expected to remain at present levels indefinitely. Thus one might argue that excessive emphasis on adjustment policies is not only deleterious but also unnecessary.

However, one factor shaping the present crisis is lasting: the level of indebtedness. For this reason, strategies to address the debt crisis should involve both adjustment and financing as part of a multifaceted approach intended to cope with both transitory and long-term elements.

The International Monetary Fund (IMF) plays a leading role in promoting adjustment policies as a condition for additional financing. Countries request IMF assistance when their own reserves cannot sustain a balance-of-payments deficit. Under normal circumstances, adjustment policies in deficit countries attempt to expand exports, reduce imports, and stimulate net capital inflows without significantly affecting either other countries or the world economy. The burden of adjustment falls on the deficit country, whose own "misbehavior" and errors are assumed to be the sources of the problem. The IMF has no means other than moral suasion to induce balance-of-payments surplus countries to adjust. If financing were amply available, the asymmetry in IMF actions—strong stimuli for debtor countries to implement adjustment policies, and only moral suasion on creditors—would not be very important because countries could finance rather than adjust a large share of their deficits. But when additional financing is not readily available from the market, the situation is quite different. IMF powers are decisive in influencing debtor countries' policies because the resources available to the Fund can be essential in smoothing out the adjustment process. Unless these financial resources are easily accessible in sufficient amounts, adjustment costs become unbearable. This is what has happened as world economic recession, the interruption of financial markets' expansion, and the shortage of IMF funds have all coincided.

The IMF has been quite conscious of this dangerous coincidence of events. Faced with widespread liquidity problems, IMF authorities have given strong backing to debt renegotiation efforts in countries such as Mexico, Argentina, Brazil, and Chile. This support has included prodding major banks not only to reschedule debt maturities but also to increase their net lending to the countries involved. However, these initiatives have emerged as part of a debtor country's commitment to pursue adjustment policies above and beyond those adjustment efforts already underway.

The Fund has found its own resources severely stretched. As a result, IMF authorities requested an increase in the size of member quotas. Member states approved an increase of 47.5 percent after protracted bargaining between the United States and most of the other countries. This increase means that by 1984 the IMF had about $15 billion in additional loanable resources—which is equivalent to only 15 percent of the 1981 current-account deficits for all non-oil-exporting developing countries. Continued severe resource constraints will probably constitute an incentive for the Fund to promote very strict adjustment policies that place a heavy economic burden on debtor countries. The recessionary bias in such policies and the concentration of the adjustment burden on debtor countries are clearly reflected in the conditionalities attached to IMF loans. This situation is likely to continue to result in mounting resistance by debtor countries to accept, or to abide by, IMF prescriptions.

Apart from the resources that are available to debtor countries, Fund financing is especially important because private banks believe that IMF evaluation and policy prescriptions substantially improve the creditworthiness of borrower countries. Indeed, a pattern seems to have emerged in recent debt renegotiations. The IMF provides its seal of approval for the debtor country's adjustment policies, and it agrees to provide additional financial resources on the condition that private bank creditors do likewise. The creditor banks agree to be represented by a committee composed of the largest institutions, whose task is to reach agreement with the debtor country on the general conditions for debt rescheduling and additional financing. Further negotiations are then necessary between the country and individual creditors to formalize the agreement. Amortization payments are not made while negotiations are going on, in a kind of "moratorium by mutual agreement" between debtor and creditors. The whole process takes several months to complete, but a liquidity crisis is thus averted.

Renegotiation has become a costly process for debtor countries in both political and economic terms. In political terms, debt negotiations are a burden because it usually takes a relatively long time for an agreement to materialize, while public opinion closely follows the negotiating process. In economic terms, until early 1984 renegotiations usually increased the debt burden because banks used the opportunity to increase interest rate spreads and to add other commissions—on top of real interest rates that in the early 1980s were the highest in more than fifty years. Increased spreads and other debt costs after renegotiation might be justified by arguing that a country that must renegotiate its debt constitutes a greater risk for creditors. However, if renegotiation involves the extension of government guarantees to portions of the debt that were not previously so covered (as has often been the case for Latin American countries), this justification is weakened or invalidated. Moreover, a risk premium was included in the cost of all previous borrowing, and it is not clear why that premium should be increased when the event covered by such payments actually occurs. Fortunately, the tendency to increase debt burdens during renegotiations abated in 1984.

Borrower countries' perceptions of debt costs also increase the likelihood of future problems as high interest rates persist. Although individual banks may not be aware of this phenomenon, private banks as a group should realize the dangers that this situation presents, especially if they exercise their bargaining power jointly. Actions that increase the economic burden for debtor countries are self-defeating in character. In fact, the quality of lenders' asset portfolios is closely and directly linked to borrowers' debt costs, because an increase in the debt burden implies a reduced probability of eventually repaying creditors. In practice, then, debt burden and the quality of asset portfolios are two sides of the same problem on which the interests of borrowers and lenders coincide.

Bases for a Possible Solution to the Debt Problem

A long-term strategy to resolve the debt crisis must include both financing and adjustment measures because both transitory and permanent factors are involved. Care should be taken that short-term policies support longer-term responses. To begin with, the problem of short-term liquidity should involve three different steps: the renegotiation of debt maturities coming due during the current crisis period and in the near future; IMF borrowing under terms that take into account recessionary pressures in the world economy; and additional borrowing from private creditors already involved in debtor countries. These three measures are closely interrelated and should be undertaken simultaneously. It does not seem practical to search for new, longer-term sources of financing under emergency conditions.

Reactivation of the World Economy

As previously noted, world economic recovery would in itself do much to resolve present problems of foreign debt. Sustained growth in the United States, western Europe, Japan, and socialist countries would improve terms of trade and reduce real interest rates. To facilitate such growth, action should be undertaken in three areas. First, a substantial new allocation of IMF special drawing rights (SDRs) would increase world liquidity and redistribute somewhat the adjustment burden among countries. Since private financial markets are not expected to expand substantially in the near future, SDRs take on renewed importance as a source of additional liquidity.

Second, a more symmetrical adjustment process would contribute significantly to the reactivation of the world economy. Forcing the adjustment burden on debtor countries alone will prolong recessionary tendencies. However, if creditor countries pursue more expansionary domestic economic policies, adjustment will occur in a more balanced fashion. International institutions can play an important role in achieving this goal, even though they can use little more than moral suasion as an instrument.

Third, domestic economic policies in creditor countries could also make other contributions to global economic recovery. By altering the domestic policy mix so as to reduce interest rates, these countries could reduce the debt burden on borrower countries without sacrificing their own goal of price stability, while at the same time strengthening the quality of lending banks' asset portfolios. By giving additional support to their own banking systems, creditor countries would contribute to a steady, even (though somewhat reduced) flow of private resources to financial markets. This support could take the form of liquidity insurance systems that would recognize that present portfolio problems are not due to mismanagement or misbehavior but rather to factors that affect the world economic system as a whole. Also, bank comptrollers could carefully review their portfolio classification criteria so as to take into account IMF agreements and World Bank or regional development bank support for debtor countries.

Debtor Countries' Economic Policies

Debtor countries' long-term policies must recognize that debt levels have reached a point at which interest rate fluctuations are highly significant in provoking changes in their current-account balance. Although short-term adjustment policies negotiated with the IMF can help avert a liquidity crisis, long-term policies must be devised to reduce the debt burden in the future. For example, domestic savings must play a larger role in capital formation than they have in the recent past. Incentives for domestic saving should be reviewed with this goal in mind. Perhaps the single most important factor in this regard is fiscal policy, in its double role of stimulating savings and discouraging consumption.

Similarly, external constraints to excessive spending (whether private or public) have become more severe as debt levels have risen. Recourse to foreign borrowing to finance public or private sector imbalances will no longer be as easy as it was before 1981. The effects of excessive spending will henceforth need to be managed within national borders, and thus they will appear mainly as domestic inflationary pressures. If rapid inflation is to be avoided in the future, domestic spending must be held in check. It is important to emphasize that this restraint must apply to both the private and public sectors.

More financial resources must also be allocated to the tradable goods sector so as to improve the balance-of-payments current account and reduce the burden placed on the capital account. Realistic exchange rates that reflect these goals are probably the single most important means of achieving this end.

Latin American countries' efforts to manage external debt should strive to prevent the concentration of loan maturities in particular periods and to take advantage of possible reductions in interest rates or interest rate spreads. As part of these efforts, it would be useful to promote periodic exchanges of information and points of view among bank comptroller authorities in both creditor and debtor countries so as to improve their mutual understanding of portfolio-classification systems and loan-review techniques. Debtor countries could also expand the exchange of information among themselves, and they might even consider establishing some means of coordinating their activities in financial markets.

In particular, debtor countries should seek to alter the composition of their external liabilities by increasing the relative share of borrowing from official sources. In this way the cost and variability of borrowing could be limited and the repayment periods lengthened. In addition, the relative share of direct foreign investment in debtors' external liabilities should be increased. Profit remittances abroad might be induced to move in such a way as to have a countercyclical effect in the host country. Imaginative efforts will be needed in this area to limit the political and economic frictions between investors and host countries that in the past have led to nationalizations.

Finally, debtor countries should also take better advantage of regional markets for trade expansion. Regional economic integration and financial cooperation can save foreign exchange without misallocating resources. Regional cooperation could also be extended to improve debtor countries' bargaining power on trade issues. This is particularly important because protectionist tendencies in industrialized country markets may limit the success of export promotion in the tradable-goods sector.

Institutional Changes

The debt problem will remain a challenge, though perhaps not in such a dramatic form as in the early 1980s. Some adaptations in international financial institutions will therefore be necessary. These adaptations will, unavoidably, involve greater official participation in the management of external debt. First of all, a substantial increase in total IMF resources is advisable. Even after the quota increase approved in 1983, the IMF's resources as a proportion of total world trade were about one-fourth of what they were in its first years of operation. Moreover, only about half of IMF quotas provide currencies that can be used to support its various programs and facilities. An expanded IMF will be able to provide better support to countries in debt-repayment difficulties. As a result, other creditors will be more inclined to continue lending. The World Bank and regional development banks should also play a larger role in transferring savings to the developing world, thus contributing to debtor countries' efforts to alter the composition of their external financial liabilities.

Even though measures may be taken to reactivate the world economy and to reduce borrower countries' debt burden, fluctuations in world economic activity will not disappear. Thus it is likely that another debt crisis will appear at some time in the future. For this reason it seems advisable to consider the institutionalization of debt-renegotiation arrangements.

At present two types of organizations are involved in debt renegotiations: "clubs" and "committees." In club-type organizations (the best known of which is the "Paris Club"), creditor governments meet with the debtor-country government to reschedule official loans. The "club" appoints a chairman to act as host and coordinator of the negotiations, and all creditor governments participate. The general bases for rescheduling are agreed upon, usually with the participation of the IMF and (at times) the World Bank. The debtor country then approaches each official creditor individually to renegotiate its corresponding debt obligation within the framework of the general agreement. Private creditors are excluded from the agreement. The club-type organization is most useful in managing problems associated with debts from official sources because the number of creditor governments involved is small.

Only private creditors participate in committee-type organizations. These are ad hoc committees composed of the larger individual creditor banks and chaired by the largest creditor, which acts as coordinator. International organizations do not participate in the committee. However, the IMF has played a very active role in stimulating negotiations and in providing a "certificate of good behavior" after an evaluation of the debtor country's adjustment program, which serves as the basis for private banks to refinance or reschedule outstanding debt. The Institute for International Finance has been established in Washington, D.C. (financed by contributions from a large number of banks) to provide information concerning debtor countries and facilitate the exchange of data and creditors' viewpoints. The "committee" is most appropriate for debt negotiations involving private credit sources. However, these organizations may contribute to the formation of a creditors' cartel, which would have negative political and economic consequences for developing countries.

The major international financial organizations also have an important role to play in debt renegotiations by bringing together both private and official creditors in an organized fashion in a context that takes into account national and international dimensions of the problem. A debt-refinancing facility undertaken jointly by the IMF and the World Bank might be one way of addressing this problem. Access to the facility could be established on the basis of certain objective indicators, while the amount and terms of assistance could be determined on a case-by-case basis. The resources necessary to finance such a facility could be drawn from several sources, including additional borrowing from the original private lenders to the country involved. Financial resources could also come from a new allocation of SDRs. The proceeds accruing to creditor countries could be placed at the disposal of the facility without cost, as a means of reducing the debt burden on borrowers.

In this regard it is important to recall that market mechanisms for distributing debt burdens between creditors and debtors no longer operate as they did in the 1930s. At that time, foreign borrowing usually took the form of bonds placed in international markets. As debtor countries began to experience the effects of worldwide depression, the price of these bonds fell to a fraction of their original market value. Debtor countries could then buy back their own debt, thus forcing part of the adjustment burden on creditors. The only way to produce a similar effect under present circumstances would be to establish a secondary market for bank portfolios, an idea that does not seem practical unless such a market were to be supported by government authorities in creditor countries. If a debt-refinancing facility were established, it could create an early-warning system so that countries and institutions involved in difficult cases could act before the situation worsened.

Another necessary institutional change involves the creation of a means of cushioning the economic impact of international interest rate changes on debtor countries. International interest rates reflect the economic policies of industrialized countries, over which the IMF has no effective influence. Debtor countries should be at least partially insulated from interest rate changes that are of great importance to them but completely beyond their control. There are two possible ways of mediating the effects of interest rate fluctuations: as part of a jointly operated IMF and World Bank debt-refinancing facility, through which low-cost financing could be provided to debtor countries to cover interest payments over and above certain limits; or as a separate arrangement through which debtor countries make interest payments to creditors up to some maximum annual limit. Amounts exceeding this limit would be postponed until market interest rates decline.

Several other proposals have also been put forward to redistribute the debt burden between borrowers and creditors.[16] All these proposals demonstrate that there are currently no market mechanisms in place to effect the desired result. Initiatives such as these will be unnecessary if the world economy revives soon, if terms of trade become more favorable for debtor countries, if real interest rates return to their customary levels, and if private banks and official financial institutions resume lending at regular rates. However, even the proposals made so far may be insufficient if these conditions do not appear. The assumption that time works in favor of borrower countries' ability to repay their debts, although reasonable, may be proved wrong. The safest approach is one that emphasizes policy and institutional adaptation rather than good luck.

Conclusion

It is unlikely that an action program as all-inclusive as the one suggested here can be implemented. Some of these proposals are conflictual in the sense that they do not necessarily serve the perceived interests of all debtors and all creditors. The policy-making coherence required at both domestic and international levels to implement a comprehensive approach to the debt problem is not present in existing institutions. Public discussion of the debt crisis is dominated by fears and misgivings rather than by objective analysis.

It is worth considering in more detail the kind of conflicts that these suggestions may produce. For example, although it is generally agreed that the reactivation of the world economy will benefit all parties involved, there is considerable debate regarding the best way of promoting global economic recovery. A new allocation of SDRs has been opposed by the United States on the grounds that it is likely to have inflationary effects. This effect would probably be negligible in an environment characterized by unemployed resources and very slowly expanding private bank liquidity. However, a more symmetrical adjustment process would force part of the adjustment burden onto creditors, who will naturally resist it. Similarly, debtor countries' efforts to allocate additional resources to the tradable-goods sector are likely to clash with protectionist tendencies in industrialized nations, which are the principal markets for the resulting additional output. Even efforts by debtor countries to increase commercial and financial cooperation among themselves may be perceived as dangerous, as has happened in the past.

It is also unlikely that increasing international institutions' financial resources (which must come largely from creditor countries) will find ready support, as demonstrated by recent U.S. attitudes regarding increased resources for the IMF and the Inter-American Development Bank. Moreover, the institutionalization of debt-rescheduling mechanisms involving official international institutions or officially supported private institutions, or other means of supporting debtor countries or private creditors, is likely to be attacked in creditor countries as a "bailout" paid for with taxpayers' money.

Most of these conflicts are more apparent than real, and in some cases short-term conflicts may be resolved in the long run. Given the level of indebtedness reached in the early 1980s, it is clearly in the interest of both debtors and creditors to achieve a more symmetrical adjustment process in which the burden is shared by all parties involved. It is also in the different parties' common interest to avoid sharp fluctuations in world liquidity and to provide for more orderly liquidity growth. Similarly, all parties would benefit from debtor countries' restructuring of external liabilities so as to increase the relative importance of borrowing from official creditors.

More substantive conflicts of interest are involved (at least in the short run) in the distribution of the debt burden, the kind of adjustment process involved, and the consequences of debtor countries' eventual insolvency. In all these cases, however, creditors must recognize that an excessive economic burden on debtor countries is not politically tolerable and that political tolerance will set limits on the adjustment policies acceptable to debtor-country governments. Official support for debtors and creditors is not simply a "bailout" when the failure to provide that support could have global negative consequences. Debtor countries are in no position to absorb the combined effect of deteriorated terms of trade, high real interest rates, contracting or slowly growing world trade, and retrenchment in the banking system. Latin American debtor countries have already undertaken major adjustment programs, and pressures for further adjustment may produce domestic political consequences that will certainly be reflected in these countries' attitudes toward creditors.

Policy-making coherence at both the domestic and the international level has certainly not been enhanced by developments since the mid-1970s. Exchange rates have been more volatile than expected, and (perhaps as a result) so have interest rates. Sharp shifts in the worldwide distribution of current-account imbalances and a decline in the relative financial weight of international institutions also indicate decreasing capacity to manage international economic problems. Recent negotiations in the General Agreement on Tariffs and Trade (GATT) have been a disappointment for developing countries, and the 1983 meeting of the U.N. Conference on Trade and Development (UNCTAD) also produced few results.

More specifically, borrower countries' efforts to establish an agreed-upon general framework for debt negotiations should not be perceived as a menace to creditors. Rather, these efforts are a clear indication that debtor countries' limits of political tolerance have already been reached. Because U.S. banks are Latin American countries' and firms' principal creditors, there is ample room for action by U.S. governmental authorities to both stimulate and support U.S. public and private financial institutions to reach workable (that is, politically feasible) agreements concerning interest and amortization payments on outstanding debt. These agreements should include means of redistributing the adjustment burden between debtors and creditors.

As with any new and acute problem, the first reactions to the debt crisis have been characterized by fears and misgivings. More effort has been devoted to attributing blame than to finding solutions. Typically, too, the importance of the problem will eventually quell these initial reactions, and analysis will take the place of quarreling. All the actors involved in the debt problem will continue to exist in the same world, so it is important for all those concerned to realize that confrontation will in the long run be more costly than cooperation. Given the nature and magnitude of the debt issue, Latin American debtor countries must certainly be part of any solution, not just part of the problem. Despite the difficulties involved in implementing a multidimensional strategy for addressing the debt problem, this is the most realistic approach. The danger of the debt crisis becoming intractable is too great, and the ensuing consequences too far-reaching, for such a strategy to be ignored. It is perhaps in this negative sense that the debt problem can be viewed as having produced a new kind of interdependence.

United Nations Economic Commission for Latin America
Santiago, Chile

Notes

The original version of this paper was written in 1983 while the author served as a consultant to the U.N. Economic Commission for Latin America; it has since been revised and updated. The author gratefully acknowledges the comments and suggestions made by Hector Assael, Roberto Zahler, and Tatjana Montes, as well as by the editors of this volume. The opinions expressed here are the author's and are not the responsibility of the insitutions with which he is affiliated.

1. These figures are not net of Latin American deposits in banks outside the region. Unguaranteed and short-term debt figures for off-shore financial centers in the region (such as Panama) are excluded on the grounds that an important proportion of these totals might already be accounted for in the debts of other countries in the region.
2. Perhaps the most notable exceptions are Colombia and Paraguay. Because foreign investment flows were substantial in Paraguay, the country's external debt did not reach significant levels.
3. Roberto Zahler, "Monetary and Real Repercussions of Financial Opening-Up to the Exterior," *CEPAL Review* 10, U.N. Economic Commission for Latin America, Santiago, Chile (April 1980): 127–53.
4. Carlos Massad, "Movimientos de capitales en América Latina," Segunda Conferencia sobre América Latina y la Economía Mundial, Instituto Torquato di Tella, Buenos Aires, Argentina, August 1980.
5. Domestic interest rates will reflect both inflation and devaluation expectations.
6. Because demand for nontradable goods is expressed in domestic currency, part of the foreign exchange proceeds generated by external borrowing is converted into domestic currency, thus increasing foreign exchange reserves.
7. Because oil-producing countries had a higher preference for liquid assets than industrialized countries, the change in the distribution of surpluses is not simply a redistribution of liquidity.
8. Eurocurrency deposits are deposits in banks in financial centers. They are denominated in currencies other than the currency of the host country, and they are usually not subject to regulations as restrictive as those applicable to deposits in domestic currency.

9. Carlos Massad and Roberto Zahler, "Dos estudios sobre endeudamiento externo," *Cuadernos de la CEPAL* 19, Santiago, Chile (October 1977); Carlos Massad, "The Real Cost of the External Debt for the Creditor and for the Debtor," *CEPAL Review* 19, U.N. Economic Commission for Latin America, Santiago, Chile (April 1983): 153–67.

10. Carlos Massad, "Cartera de inversiones de los paises exportadores de petróleo: diversificación orientada hacia América Latina," *Estudios de Economía* 12, Universidad de Chile, Departamento de Economía, Santiago, Chile (1978): 147–72. An updated version of this paper is "Oil Exporting Countries' Investment Portfolio: Diversification Towards Latin America" in Femhy Saddy, ed., *Arab-Latin American Relations* (New Brunswick, N.J.: Transaction Books, 1983), pp. 99–125.

11. Herbert G. Grubel, "Internationally Diversified Portfolios: Welfare Gains and Capital Flows," *American Economic Review* 58 (December 1968): 1299–314.

12. Massad, "The Real Cost of the External Debt."

13. Unpublished ECLA study.

14. Carlos Massad, "Aspectos principales del financiamiento externo," *Gaceta Internacional* 1, No. 1, Caracas, Venezuela (July–September 1983): 33–38.

15. U.N. Economic Commission for Latin America, *Preliminary Balance of the Latin American Economy in 1983*, Santiago, Chile, January 1984.

16. See, for example, Norman Bailey, David Luft, and Roger Robinson, "Exchange Participation Notes: An Approach to the International Financial Crisis," Georgetown University, Center for Strategic International Studies, CSIS Significant Issues Series, 5, No. 1, Washington, DC, 1983; Peter B. Kehen, "A Bailout for the Banks," *New York Times*, 6 March 1983, F3; Richard S. Weinert, "Banks and Bankruptcy," *Foreign Policy* 50 (Spring 1983): 138–49; Minos Zombanakis, "The International Debt Threat: A Way to Avoid a Crash," *The Economist*, 30 April 1983, pp. 11–14.

5

External Debt and Capital Flows in Latin America

Richard O'Brien

This essay examines the Latin American debt crisis and its implications for U.S.–Latin American financial affairs. The essay first considers the debt crisis in its hemispheric context. This analysis shows that although the debt crisis in Latin America may well be addressed by the United States as a hemispheric policy issue, the U.S.–Latin American debt problem is in many respects part of the global issue of developing countries' commercial-bank debt. The second section traces the buildup to the recent debt crisis in the region, with particular emphasis on events in six countries: Brazil, Chile, Peru, Venezuela, Argentina, and Mexico. Although common external factors shaped the debt problem in these countries, all six countries reached a common position of deep recession and debt/financial crisis while pursuing quite different economic policies. Third, the essay considers in detail one of the most important aspects of Latin America's debt crisis—the buildup of excessive short-term debt by the major borrower countries. Excessive short-term borrowing has inflated these countries' debt-service burdens. Debt-rescheduling efforts will ease the cash flow impact of excessive short-term debt, but rescheduling will do little to reduce interest costs. The fourth part of this analysis examines the exposed position of U.S. commercial banks in Latin America (with reference to the ratio of outstanding loans to the banks' total capital), focusing particularly on the smaller U.S. banks that have played a more active role in bank lending to Latin American countries than to other developing country borrowers. Finally, the last section considers some of the policy implications of the debt crisis.

Latin American Debt and the United States: A Hemispheric Issue?

Latin America's total external debt at the end of 1983 was estimated to be at least \$336 billion, including short-term debt.[1] This amount is equivalent to half the debt owed by all developing countries. Moreover, several Latin American countries dominate the international debt scene: four of the five largest developing country debtors are located in the region. Some two-thirds of Latin America's total external debt ($240 billion) is owed to international commercial banks, and some $85 billion of this amount (38 percent) is owed to U.S. banks. In turn, Latin America holds 61 percent of all debt owed to international commercial banks, and the largest Latin American debtor countries once again dominate the picture. From the lending side, U.S. banks play a predominant role in Latin America. Their share of all commercial bank loans to the region (38 percent) is more than that of any other national banking group. This share is slightly above U.S. banks' share of international bank lending to developing countries in general (35 percent).[2]

These data to a considerable degree reflect the sheer economic size of Latin America and the major Latin American debtor countries compared with other developing regions. Similarly, the prominence of Latin American countries in U.S. banks' loan exposure, and the prominence of U.S. banks in the region's financing, reflect mainly the importance of U.S.–Latin American trade and economic relations compared with those between the United States and other developing countries.

The aspect of the U.S.–Latin American financial relationship that cannot be easily explained by the region's economic size is the intensity of the debt problems that Latin American countries now face. By early 1983, six major Latin American countries were in the process of rescheduling part of their bank debt, and only one major country (Colombia) was fully up-to-date on its interest and principal payments. The region's size also fails to explain why, in a ranking of seventeen major developing country borrowers' ratio of debt interest payments to current-account earnings, Latin American countries head the list (see table 2 below). Seven of the eight developing countries with the highest ratios are in Latin America. Nor does size alone explain why Latin American borrower countries more frequently have excessive levels of short-term debt.

Yet Latin America's economic size does substantially explain the extent of the debt burden in the region. In an international economy in which external borrowing has suddenly become an expensive exercise (compared with the relatively cheap source of credit it was in the 1970s), and at a time when international trade has slumped, it is not surprising that larger debtor countries dominate discussions of the debt problem. Indeed, it is because Latin American countries were thought to be more creditworthy than many other developing countries that the region has suffered more acutely from a loss of creditworthiness following debt-servicing difficulties. All developing countries have faced deteriorating trade and financing conditions in the past several years. The poorer countries were unable to postpone their adjustment process because their immediate balance-of-payment imbalances could not be financed. Because Latin American economies are larger, more developed economically, and more creditworthy than those of most other developing countries (with only a few Asian exceptions), they have been able to attract foreign capital and credit and to use foreign savings extensively. Many African countries face no less difficult financial problems than Mexico, but rather than borrowing abroad to finance desired imports, these poorer countries have had to curtail imports sharply. Now that many Latin American countries are no longer creditworthy, *their* imports must also be cut severely—at the same time that interest costs associated with financing high import levels in the past reduce the amount of current account earnings that might otherwise be spent on imports.

For a variety of business reasons, U.S. commercial banks have played a key role in satisfying Latin America's demand for credit. As United States-based businesses traded with the region, their bankers supported their corporate clients with financial services and credit. United States banks later followed up these opportunities and tried to maximize profits and capitalize on their growing knowledge of the region by venturing abroad with their own offices. The majority of U.S. banks' developing country branches are in Latin America. Where U.S. bank branches hold local banking licenses, local financing funded by local deposits provides an important source of revenue. This banking business was expanding long before the Eurodollar credit boom of the 1970s. Similar banking business opportunities also exist elsewhere in the world, but except for selected Asian countries and western Europe, these opportunities have been fewer or more recent.

The relationships surrounding the financing of U.S. businesses that invest in and trade with Latin America are important in two respects. First, these relationships provide income to banks and banking services to developing countries without a massive accumulation of debt. Second, these relationships can also provide developing countries with a means of accumulating debt without having to raise medium-term syndicated credit.

With an existing reason to be involved in Latin America, it was a relatively straightforward and logical step for U.S. banks to extend the relationship to the provision of cross-border dollar credit. Indeed, where a bank had built extensive trade financing relationships, developed a correspondent banking network, and pursued corporate-client links, the opportunities and pressures to participate in the foreign-lending boom of the 1970s were very great. Where a bank had a market share or perhaps even a banking license to protect, even a narrow profit margin on dollar credit was acceptable given the overall profitability of its business with that country. In the extreme case, it could be argued that new dollar lending was similar to a "loss leader"—lending at a small marginal profit to protect existing profits, as a business might offer a "loss leader" to attract future business. Marginal lending under these circumstances, in fact, can be more easily justified than a loss leader, given that the protected business is already established and the total relationship is already profitable, whereas there is less certainty that a loss leader will actually lead to future profit. The only complication is that the marginally profitable business (in this case, dollar lending at small interest rate spreads) may prove to be unprofitable as a result of major credit losses.

There are also important supplementary reasons that explain the important role that U.S. banks have played in financing in Latin America. Some of these considerations are not specific to U.S.–Latin American economic relations. United States banks were generally pioneers in the international syndicated credit market. The international dominance of U.S. multinational businesses required international banking services. Moreover, in the 1960s overseas lending offered more attractive growth prospects to U.S. banks than domestic financial markets because of regulatory limitations on interstate banking and restrictions on expansion into nonbanking services. United States banks' relative dominance of the market declined only as other banks (especially British, Japanese, German, and Arab banks) entered the market. As pioneers, U.S. banks built up larger portfolios in developing countries generally. With U.S. banks leading the international banking industry and with Latin American countries among the leading developing country borrowers, the two trends combined to place the U.S.–Latin American financial relationship at the forefront of discussions concerning relations between international commercial banks and developing countries.

The corollary to this conclusion is that the global developing country debt problem is a U.S.–Latin American problem writ large. Similarly, the U.S.–Latin American financial crisis is the international bank–developing country debt problem in microcosm (albeit in rather large microcosm).

Of course, Latin America's financial crisis had its own regional catalyst: the April 1982 war between Argentina and Great Britain. The resulting political crisis was a crisis for U.S.–Latin American relations, and the resulting financial embargoes against Latin America were a severe blow to the Eurocredit market (in much the same way that Poland's earlier debt and political crisis led to a crisis in East-West financial relations). The speed with which the Falklands/Malvinas war produced a domino effect on curtailing bank credit to Latin America once again led to charges that international banks (and not just U.S. banks) were motivated by "herd instinct." To understand the reasons behind the domino effect and the apparent "herd instinct" of the banking community, one must consider both the nature of banks' attitudes toward risk and the brief historical experience of the Eurocredit market.[3]

Banks, like all businesses, seek to achieve economies of scale. This orientation results in a tendency to specialize in certain businesses, both to justify the initial basic costs of the business and to maximize profits thereafter. Sovereign country borrowers have been perceived as having certain specific characteristics, and thus an international bank generally regards its sovereign loans as one homogeneous part of its portfolio in the same way that it would regard its shipping or property loans as another homogeneous part.

Having decided that the nature of a given business is acceptable (lending done with a ship or property as security, lending to a country, and so forth), a bank's natural defense against risk for each portfolio will be to diversify names within the portfolio. But this diversification process clearly does little to reduce risk if the attractiveness of the total business (for example, shipping, balance-of-payments financing, and so forth) goes into decline. At that point a bank will seek to reduce its portfolio commitment in that type of business as soon as possible—notwithstanding that there are sound and unsound shipping companies, or sound and unsound sovereign borrowers. During the retrenchment period, a bank will attempt to keep the better parts of the portfolio and sell the high-risk portions. Other banks in a similar position will respond in the same way.

Once serious questions have been raised concerning a major client in the portfolio, growing risk aversion will lead a bank to question other clients' financial positions. Two cases in the sovereign country risk/Euromarket experience illustrate this point. In 1979 the oil-rich Islamic state of Iran became a credit risk. Bankers then immediately (and prudently) began to examine their exposure to other oil-rich Islamic countries. In 1980 national political crisis led to a collapse of Poland's socialist, centrally planned economy. Bankers (and economists) asked, "How stable is the socialist, East European-satellite economic system?" As a result, the financial circumstances of Rumania, Hungary, and other East European countries were all reexamined in a more critical light. And so it was with Latin America after the Argentine-British war. Where renewed scrutiny revealed financial weakness, the dominoes fell. If Latin American countries had been financially sound, they would have withstood bankers' reappraisals. But where reexamination revealed weaknesses in a country's financial condition, lending was curtailed. The recent Asian experience provides further support for this conclusion: following the Philippines' debt moratorium in late 1983, banks reexamined the creditworthiness of other Asian borrowers (especially Indonesia and South Korea). Because their financial and economic situation contrasted very favorably with that of the Philippines, there was no regional domino effect on bank lending.

There is also a second aspect of this issue. For a time the South Atlantic war severed British-Argentine economic relations, and other European Economic Community (EEC) countries followed suit. It is assumed in the Eurocurrency market (especially in multinational loan syndicates) that all lenders will be treated equally. If this assumption proves false, as it threatened to do on this occasion, a crisis results. Such a crisis can occur in various ways. For example, an Argentine borrower may wish to embargo interest payments to a British bank, but a U.S. bank may be the syndicate's agent bank with responsibility for collecting interest payments from the borrower. The agent bank has no authority to treat syndicate members differently. If the full interest payment is not received, the agent bank must withhold a portion of all member banks' receivables regardless of bank nationality—even though this was not the intent of the borrower. The position of a British agent bank acting on behalf of banks of other nationalities would be even more problematic in this situation.

Similar problems occur when bank deposits are frozen for political reasons, as occurred when the United States moved to freeze Iranian bank deposits during the 1979–1981 U.S.-Iranian crisis. Courts must ultimately determine the legality of such actions, but at the time the sudden doubt raised concerning Iran's loan payments caused considerable confusion. The turmoil surrounding Iranian bank deposits reduced banks' confidence that they would be paid on time. It is clear that banks' confidence in other borrowers or depositors who show solidarity with the borrower/depositor in question may also suffer.

National governments have long criticized the influence of multinational business because it complicates a world of sovereign states. The Eurocurrency market is no exception in this regard. However, because money is fungible, financial embargoes are difficult to enforce effectively and cannot be maintained indefinitely. Moreover, their imposition strikes at the very heart of the international financial market's operational system and principles, which assume that all lenders are treated equally unless laws or tax regimes (but not embargoes) stipulate otherwise at the outset.

Thus the elements for a regional debt crisis were well in place by early 1982. The net flow of external funds to Latin America had already slowed in 1981. The South Atlantic war was the first catalyst, followed shortly thereafter by Mexico's financial crisis in August 1982. These two episodes gave a special hemispheric feature to the global debt crisis. The Argentine factor affected all U.S.–Latin American relations, and Mexico continues to be the most important example of how closely U.S.–Latin American economic and financial relations are intertwined.

The regional or hemispheric nature of the debt problem is thus important. But it should not be overdrawn. This latter observation is significant not just because Latin America is only part of a global problem, but because there are very large country-by-country differences concerning the common debt problems within the region. In practice, an analysis of debt issues is best conducted primarily on a country-by-country basis, with due regard to any regional aspects that may apply.

Nonetheless, there are four major arguments for a regional approach (in addition to global and country analysis) to the debt problem. First, because the global debt crisis is largely manifested in Latin America with U.S. banks in the vanguard (see table 1), it is very important that U.S. policymakers accord high priority to the Latin American debt problem. Second, because almost all major Latin American countries face a debt problem (with almost all major U.S. banks involved), it makes sense from a policymaker's "economies-of-scale" perspective to consider a hemispheric approach. Third, because the region's financial crisis is se-

TABLE 1
U.S. BANKS' EXPOSURE IN LATIN AMERICA AND OTHER DEVELOPING
COUNTRIES
(June 1982; US$ billions)

	U.S. Banks	Eurocurrency Market	U.S. Bank Share as % of Total
Argentina	8,612	25,305	34.0
Brazil	18,886	55,300	34.2
Chile	6,259	11,757	53.2
Colombia	2,730	5,473	49.9
Ecuador	2,179	4,674	46.6
Mexico	24,926	64,375	38.7
Peru	2,363	5,216	45.3
Venezuela	11,046	27,249	40.5
Other Latin America	4,342	10,141	42.8
Total Latin America	81,343	209,490	38.8
Indonesia	2,531	8,155	31.0
South Korea	8,622	19,994	43.1
Philippines	5,576	11,365	49.1
Taiwan	4,506	6,427	70.1
Other Asia	6,786	16,253	41.8
Total Asia	28,021	62,194	45.1
Middle East and Africa	13,068	71,858	18.2
All developing countries	122,432	343,542	35.6
Latin America as percentage of all developing countries	66.4	61.0	—

Sources: United States Federal Reserve Country Lending Survey and Bank for International Settlements data.

vere at a time when U.S.–Latin American political relations are themselves at a crucial juncture, the region's debt problems are a high-priority issue for the United States.

Finally, as the debt crisis has evolved, the difference in the positions of U.S. banks and banks of other nationalities has become more obvious. In many cases, U.S. banks have made fewer provisions to protect their loans to sovereign countries than European banks, and U.S. banks' exposure as a percentage of total equity is often higher than that of European banks. Differences such as these affect the strategic and tactical options open to U.S. banks and banks of other nationalities in debt reschedulings. Similar differences also exist among various banks in the United States with major loan commitments in Latin America. These differences in banks' positions mean that some banks have little choice but to lend more money to borrower countries to help them make interest payments, while other banks can more easily afford to write off outstanding debts and avoid new exposures.

A qualification is necessary here. These four reasons for a hemispheric treatment of the debt issue could be more accurately described as reasons that the Latin American debt problem is a high financial, economic, and foreign policy priority for the United States. It does not necessarily follow that policy responses should be predominantly hemispheric rather than global. However, if the region's debt problems (or even those of Argentina, Brazil, Mexico, and Venezuela) could be solved, then the more global developing country debt problem would be much less of a threat to the international financial and economic system. If a coherent regional approach can be engineered (and for political reasons, the arguments for this approach might be more appealing), then a regional strategy should be encouraged.

Debt reschedulings in Latin America have so far been dominated by U.S. actors. United States banks head most of the bank steering committees established to address problems in a given country, and the U.S. Department of the Treasury organized government support loans for Argentina in early 1984 in conjunction with other Latin American central banks (specifically those in Brazil, Colombia, Mexico, and Venezuela). The U.S. Federal Reserve Board is also in a position to shape U.S. monetary policy, and the U.S. Congress may shape the U.S. federal budget so as to alter the debt-servicing burdens that debtor countries face as a result of changes in dollar interest rates deriving from U.S. monetary and fiscal policy. Finally, as an example of U.S. actors' central role in the Latin American debt crisis, it should be remembered that Mexican government officials went first to Washington and New York in early August 1982 to lay out the extent of Mexico's financial difficulties.

Common External Factors and Contrasting Domestic Characteristics in Latin America's Financial Crisis[4]

There were two common, largely external factors behind the onset of the economic and financial crisis in Latin America in late 1982 and early 1983. The first was Latin American countries' substantial use of foreign private credits in the years up to 1982 and the subsequent sudden contraction of capital markets during 1982. The second was the impact of the world economic cycle, which during 1981–1983 produced falling commodity prices, weak export markets, and high international interest rates. The impact of this cyclical change was perhaps intensified by Latin American countries' shift away from import substitution toward export orientation and by their increased dependence on foreign credit.

Apart from these common external elements that affected the whole region, it is much more difficult to identify shared causal factors in the origin of the debt crisis, either in the specific policies pursued or in the economic experiences of Latin American economies. Most countries in the region enjoyed a relatively high growth rate in 1979 and 1980. Data from the United Nations Economic Commission for Latin America show an average regional growth rate of 6.5 percent and 5.9 percent respectively, about the same as the average rate for the 1970–1978 period. For some countries (for example, Peru and Chile) this continued economic expansion derived from buoyant commodity exports. For others (such as Brazil and Mexico) growth continued as a result of expansionary economic policies coupled with large capital inflows. In contrast, Venezuela followed a deliberately cautious policy that produced economic stagnation despite higher petroleum export earnings. Brazil's growth stopped abruptly in 1981 when the economy moved into recession, while the Mexican oil boom continued into early 1982.

Exchange rate management has been a highly visible factor in the economic problems of many Latin American countries. After defending a particular exchange rate by various means (including combinations of high domestic interest rates, foreign exchange intervention, foreign exchange controls, and exhortations) governments in Argentina, Mexico, Chile, and Venezuela have all eventually been forced to devalue. Devaluations result in economic difficulties for dollar debtors and in protracted negotiations regarding measures to help private sector debtors meet their external obligations. The immediate effect of devaluation is to disturb relative prices and discourage imports. Only when a new parity or "crawling peg" exchange rate can be established, and when speculation or further devaluation risks have subsided, can capital flight be reversed. In the interim, domestic interest rates may rise rather than fall, bringing increased distress to domestic currency debtors and worsening recession and unemployment. Exports increase only after a lag of at least several months. These problems have arisen throughout Latin America.

However, the causes of exchange rate problems have varied. During the 1970s Mexico's and Venezuela's currencies were buoyed by petroleum exports, which unfortunately undermined the competitiveness of the non-oil economy (the so-called Dutch disease). When the oil prop suddenly disappeared in 1981, the economic and political costs of moving to a lower exchange rate (particularly given the possibility that the international petroleum market would stabilize again) encouraged a delay in policy response. This delay eventually made adjustment more difficult, especially because debt was high and reserves lower after the struggle to maintain parities. In Venezuela the current account was in small deficit in 1982, but outflows on the capital account eventually made devaluation imperative.

In contrast, in Chile, Argentina, and Uruguay, fixed exchange rate policy was the centerpiece of economic programs intended to win the long-running battle against inflation. Other countries (for example, Brazil) have used a crawling peg arrangement for many years, although they have had only limited success in avoiding the same problems of high real interest rates and, now, recession. Nevertheless, the crawling peg strategy did at least prevent massive overvaluation, which inevitably produced major economic convulsions in Chile, Argentina, and Uruguay when correction was attempted.

Fiscal policy has also varied widely among Latin American countries. For example, Chile and Uruguay achieved near balance in public sector finances, while other countries continued to run significant deficits. Several countries adopted vigorous policies of trade and investment liberalization, while others (notably in the Southern Cone) continued import-substitution policies.

The overall diversity of economic policies among different countries in the region is therefore striking. Perhaps the only common policy element in most Latin American countries during the 1970s was the substantial use of foreign capital. Up until 1979 foreign borrowing was cheap because real interest rates lagged behind inflation. Indebtedness therefore made good sense. Oil-exporting countries used the opportunity to borrow to develop petroleum resources and related industries, pursuing what in retrospect was an overly bullish view of future oil prices. After 1979 foreign borrowing became increasingly necessary for most Latin American countries as oil import bills rose while export revenues fell. Borrowing (particularly at short maturities) increased sharply during 1980–1981, bringing about the cash flow shortage that triggered the debt crisis. If the world recession had ended in 1981, all might have been well, but by

1982–1983 most countries were unable to weather another year of recession without major adjustments.

The experiences of six Latin American countries—Brazil, Chile, Peru, Venezuela, Argentina, and Mexico—illustrate both the diversity of domestic economic policies and the common external shocks that led up to the region's debt crisis.

Brazil[5]

Between 1963 and 1981 Brazil's real gross domestic product (GDP) grew at an average rate of more than 8 percent per year, making it one of the fastest-growing countries in the world. Growth slowed to an average 7 percent per year after the 1973–1974 oil shock, and foreign borrowing increased substantially to maintain the balance of payments despite higher import payments (especially for crude oil). At the end of 1978, total external debt stood at $49 billion, just over half the end-1982 total of $86 billion.[6] The second oil price shock in 1979–1980 coincided with an increase in real international interest rates and placed severe strain on the balance of payments. Calculations suggest that from 1979 to 1982 the "excess" interest costs due to higher than normal interest rates totaled $6 billion, while "excess" payments for oil imports reached $18 billion.[7]

The Brazilian government's initial response to this situation was to borrow further and maintain economic growth. In 1980 the current-account deficit exceeded $12 billion (or about 4.5 percent of GDP) and was financed partly by drawing down foreign exchange reserves. The pricing of new loans was a major source of contention that year because international banks were unwilling to consider large new lending without higher interest rate spreads.[8] The government drew down exchange reserves as an alternative measure.

The government also undertook adjustment measures in 1979–1980, including a tightening of fiscal and monetary policy, a maxidevaluation, and a liberalization of foreign trade. Nonetheless, economic growth accelerated in 1980 to 8 percent and only slowed in 1981, registering a 1.9 percent decline. Commercial bank financing expanded again in 1981 with the recognition that economic adjustment was under way and in response to interest rate spreads that were much higher than for most other newly industrialized countries. Financing was thus secured for the still substantial current-account deficit of $11 billion.[9] The 16 percent boost in exports was particularly encouraging, bringing the trade account from a deficit of $3 billion in 1980 to a surplus of $1 billion in 1981. But Brazil typically runs a nonfinancial services deficit of $2 to 3 billion per year even before net interest payments are included. By 1981, as a result of increased indebtedness and high U.S. interest rates, the net financial services deficit reached $9.2 billion—up from $6.3 billion in 1980 and more than triple the 1978 figure.

In 1982 the balance of payments deteriorated sharply, and the current account finished the year with a $14.4 billion deficit. Continuing high interest payments, declining exports due to lower commodity prices, and shrinking foreign markets (particularly some of the developing country markets that had been so successfully penetrated in 1981) were the main factors producing this downturn. This increased deficit could not be financed in foreign credit markets. During 1982 only $5.5 billion of the total deficit was covered by net capital inflows, leaving nearly $9 billion to be financed from a loss in net international reserves.

Chile

Two themes dominate any assessment of the Chilean economy's performance in recent years: copper prices and economic policy. In 1982–1983 copper accounted for 40 to 50 percent of total exports, down from the peak levels of the early 1970s. However, there was still substantial price volatility. In 1982 copper exports earned about $1.7 billion, down from $2.1 billion in 1980 despite an increase in export volume.

Government economic policy until mid-1982 followed a relatively pure version of free-market economics inspired by University of Chicago-trained economists. The government eliminated its deficit, substantially reduced import protection, and (perhaps most controversially) pegged the peso at thirty-nine to the dollar from spring 1979 onward. These policies produced two direct results. First, inflation was dramatically reduced from over 400 percent per year in the mid-1970s to less than 10 percent per year in early 1982. Second, the peso became increasingly overvalued until 1982. This situation produced very high domestic interest rates and, consequently (because the government promised to maintain the peso parity), large-scale foreign borrowing by the private sector. Simultaneously, noncopper exports declined after 1980 while imports tripled between 1977 and 1981, bringing large trade and current-account deficits— the counterpart to this capital inflow. Interest payments also increased very substantially between 1979 and 1982 because of growing indebtedness and higher international interest rates.

Economic adjustment began in 1981 as economic growth slowed and imports began to contract. Financial difficulties grew, particularly in tradable-goods industries facing foreign competition and in companies with large peso debts. Weaknesses began to emerge in a financial structure that had earlier been geared to survive high inflation and in some domestic banks linked closely to conglomerate companies. In early 1982, the strains resulting from real interest rates of over 40 percent per year, increasing bankruptcies, and growing unemployment forced the government to devalue the peso. With copper prices at two-thirds the 1980 level and capital inflows slowing, there was little hope of relief. The only alternative to devaluation was to wait for the peso's overvaluation to dissipate by maintaining a lower inflation rate than in the United States. But with U.S. inflation back below 10 percent, this would have been impossible without devastatingly high peso interest rates. The peso was initially devalued by 18 percent in June 1982, and in August it was allowed to float. By the end of 1982 the peso had been devalued by about 100 percent.

The initial effects of devaluation were inevitably destabilizing. Dollar debtors were largely unprepared for the sharp increase in the peso cost of their debt, and peso debtors gained little benefit because domestic interest rates remained high as expectations of further devaluation increased. Moreover, continuing tight fiscal policy and the domestic recession kept inflation at around 20 percent in 1982 despite the substantial devaluation. This meant that the change in the real exchange rate was unusually large. Most economies inflate rapidly after a major devaluation, thus diminishing the degree of realignment in the exchange rate.

The worst of the adjustment probably came in 1982. Chile's GDP fell by 14.3 percent, and imports in the second half of the year were less than 50 percent of the 1981 volume. Although imports had undoubtedly been inflated by the economic boom and inventory accumulation, this fall was nothing short of drastic. Unemployment increased to 25 percent (double the 1981 level), and there were widespread corporate bankruptcies and state interventions of banks.

Peru

In 1979–1980 oil export revenues raised Peru's export earnings substantially as increased oil production coincided with higher prices. Export earnings peaked in 1980 at $3.9 billion, compared with only $1.9 billion two years earlier. Along with the stabilization and liberalization measures introduced in 1978 as part of an International Monetary Fund (IMF) program, these developments moved the current account into surplus in 1979 and, despite higher imports, close to balance in 1980. Foreign debt (which had been rescheduled) was repaid on the original schedule, and Peru was able to borrow further from international credit markets.

However, after 1980 the prices of Peru's commodity exports began to drop sharply almost without exception. Copper, silver, zinc, and lead prices all fell, followed in 1981 by a decline in oil prices. Real export prices fell an average weighted 50 percent from their previous levels. Of course, 1980 had been an exceptional year for metal prices, but by spring

1982 Peru's commodity prices (excluding oil) were at their lowest level in real terms in post-World War II history.

In 1982 Peru implemented a stabilization program to reduce the current-account deficit and stabilize the domestic economy. The principal elements in this program were a reduction in the public sector deficit to 4.2 percent of GDP and limitations on external borrowing. The deficit fell significantly, although the overall public sector deficit declined to only 6.6 percent of GDP. Imports were cut by $300 million (about 8 percent), but export earnings remained constant and interest payments rose. Overall, the stabilization program trimmed the current-account deficit by only about $100 million, to $1.4 billion. Meanwhile, economic growth slowed to 0.7 percent per year, and unemployment and underemployment became an increasing problem. Bankers' confidence that Peru was moving in the right direction enabled the government to continue borrowing in 1982, although often at short maturities. With uncertainty rising in the absence of any imminent improvement in commodity prices, the Peruvian government had to maintain this short-term exposure.

Venezuela

Venezuela's difficulties had three sources: declining oil export revenues, excessive short-term debt, and currency management problems. Oil revenues rose from $8.6 billion in 1978 to a peak of $18.9 billion in 1981 and then fell to $16 billion in 1982. The volatility of oil revenues did not in itself pose a major problem. Venezuela ran a current-account surplus of $4.4 billion in 1981, and even in 1982 the deficit was only $2.2 billion. This figure compared with Central Bank foreign exchange reserves of $7 billion at the end of 1981, plus up to another $15 billion in reserves held by state enterprises.

However, Venezuela's second problem—that of a large short-term public debt—made its cash flow position much weaker than a balance-of-payments analysis would suggest. At the end of 1981 commercial banks reported to the Bank for International Settlements that Venezuela had $16.6 billion in loans due in 1982, of which approximately $14.4 billion probably had an original maturity of less than one year. Several attempts during 1980–1982 to refinance much of this debt at longer maturities failed as a result of disagreements over price and coverage. As uncertainty grew about Latin American risks in general (and about oil exporters in particular), this reliance upon short-term debt left Venezuela's cash flow position weak. This situation, together with calculations showing that on a purchasing power basis the *bolívar* had become overvalued since being pegged to the dollar in 1976, fueled speculation that devaluation was imminent. The result was a massive capital outflow between early 1982 and February 1983.

With reserves falling to close to minimum prudential levels, the government had to choose between capital controls and/or devaluation. But with the prospect of a large current-account deficit in 1983 unless imports were curbed, there were doubts whether this could be financed in the more difficult lending markets then prevailing. Moreover, with reserves insufficient to meet a large shortfall, the moment for capital controls had probably passed. Devaluation or partial devaluation was necessary to help cut imports and restore confidence in the *bolívar,* and thereby to encourage some capital to return.

In March 1983 the Venezuelan government announced a three-tiered exchange rate system that required foreign debt repayments and essential import transactions to be made at the old exchange rate (4.3 *bolívars*/dollar); established an exchange rate of 6 *bolívars*/dollar for another list of important imports; and set a free-market rate for other imports. General uncertainty regarding Venezuela's financial situation left little choice but a moratorium on public sector debt repayments for three months, pending refinancing of much of the short-term debt. Venezuela simultaneously opened discussions with the IMF for financial support.

Argentina

Economic policy in Argentina in recent years has been less coherent than in most other Latin American countries, with frequent changes both in substance and in emphasis. The principal aim of the post-1976 military government was to reduce inflation, which had reached over 400 percent per year in the early 1970s. On at least two occasions, the exchange rate was used as the principal instrument to achieve this end. For example, in December 1978 the government initiated a new policy of announcing the nominal exchange rate in advance. The idea was to set the rate of devaluation below the inflation rate so that world price levels would force a slowing of domestic inflation. However, without other important supporting measures—particularly substantial reductions in the public sector deficit—this approach proved unworkable. Moreover, in its initial stages this policy encouraged foreign borrowing because it guaranteed a high rate of return on loans, while in its later stages capital outflow was controlled only by high domestic interest rates.

Exports grew significantly from 1977 to 1981 because of price increases for beef and wool and larger volumes of other export commodities, particularly corn and hides. Total export earnings grew by an average of 13 percent per year. However, imports grew even more rapidly, largely because of tariff liberalization policies that reduced the average tariff from 95 percent to below 40 percent. The total cost of imports almost tripled from 1977 to 1980 and took the trade account into deficit. Imports of services almost quadrupled over the same period, reflecting high interest payments on foreign debt.

Argentina's debt totaled $34 billion by the end of 1981, making Argentina one of the most heavily indebted countries in relation to total export receipts. As a result of economic stagnation, imports began to fall in 1981 and continued to do so thereafter. Export earnings stopped growing as falling prices offset higher volumes. Nevertheless, the current-account deficit narrowed in 1981 and finished 1982 at only $3.1 billion.

At the beginning of 1982 there was some optimism regarding Argentina's future economic situation primarily because the new finance minister, Juan Alemánn, received strong backing from President Galtieri to take stiff measures to reduce the public sector deficit, a prerequisite for controlling inflation. However, the South Atlantic war froze financial relationships and effectively cut off new credits to Argentina. With the subsequent ouster of General Galtieri and Alemánn, renewed government policy instability and great political uncertainly discouraged new bank lending. Following Mexico's liquidity crisis in late 1982, Argentina was soon caught up in the regional credit problem.

Mexico

Between 1960 and 1972 Mexico's annual economic growth averaged 6.8 percent, with an average annual inflation rate of 3.8 percent. Then between 1973 and 1976, budgetary and monetary policies produced accelerating inflation that made the peso increasingly overvalued and eventually led to an 80 percent devaluation in 1976—the first modification in Mexico's exchange rate since 1954. Economic growth was only 4.2 percent in 1976 and 3.4 percent in 1977. The discovery of oil (or rediscovery, since Mexico has produced oil since 1904) on a substantial scale offered the opportunity for rapid investment-led growth.

Oil exports rose from just over 200,000 barrels per day (bpd) in 1977 to 500,000 bpd in 1979; oil revenues quadrupled to $4 billion per year during the same period. The value of proven oil reserves increased from $80 billion in 1976 to $898 billion in 1979, and to over $2 trillion in 1982. The prospect of continued large oil-export revenues led to a massive upscaling of investment plans in both the public and private sectors. The public sector concentrated on investments in infrastructure and basic industries such as ports, iron and steel, and petrochemicals, as well as the necessary investments in petroleum production.

Although some observers raised doubts regarding the orientation of these investments, development planners were undoubtedly motivated by a long-term vision of Mexico as an industrial giant rather than by short-term calculations of returns from different investments. The public sector deficit averaged 7.7 percent of GDP from 1976 to 1980, while the current-account deficit averaged 3.1 percent of GDP. With oil exports building up slowly, albeit steadily, a substantial part of this deficit was financed by foreign borrowing. In 1976 public sector foreign debt (excluding private banks nationalized in 1982) totaled $19.6 billion. By the end of 1981 this total had reached $53 billion. Private sector debt rose from $4.9 billion in 1976 to $14.9 billion in 1981.

The emergence of a world oversupply of oil in 1981 was a surprise to most observers. In 1981 Mexico had planned to export 1.5 million bpd of its total production of 2.3 million bpd, thus earning about $20 billion. In fact, Mexico sold an average of only 1.1 million bpd at a price well below the $36 per barrel initially anticipated. The $5.5 billion shortfall in oil earnings inflated the current-account deficit from $6.8 billion in 1980 to $13 billion in 1981. This deficit, plus a substantial private outflow on the capital account as devaluation fears increased, was financed by foreign borrowing. Total external debt thus increased almost 50 percent, reaching $74.9 billion. Of the $24.2 billion net total borrowed, $9.3 billion consisted of new public sector short-term debt.

Some attempts were made to restrain public sector spending and control the current-account deficit. But the oil glut was thought to be only a temporary phenomenon, and the government therefore avoided major policy changes. Flows into dollars (the peso was fully convertible) increased in late 1981 and early 1982. The shortfall in oil earnings and the consequent balance-of-payments disequilibrium were evident, and the peso became increasingly overvalued in terms of purchasing power. Estimates based on wholesale prices indicated a one-third decline in competitiveness since 1977. Imports surged ahead while non-oil exports and tourist income languished. In February 1982 speculation finally forced a devaluation, and the peso rapidly moved from twenty-six to forty-five to the dollar.

During the early months of 1982, concern over the direction of the economy mounted both in Mexico and abroad. Following the February 1982 devaluation, the government granted compensatory wage increases of approximately 60 percent for the year, which made higher inflation inevitable. Domestic confidence had reached a low ebb. Many companies with predominantly peso revenues had borrowed in dollars and now needed relief. Investment fell off sharply, and real economic growth did not exceed 2 percent in 1982. Oil export earnings were little higher than in 1981. Debt amortization totaling $7.1 billion in public sector medium-term debt and $10.7 billion in outstanding short-term debt was due in 1982 (based on total debt at the end of 1981).

It was in this environment—with the growing belief that the world oil glut would persist in the short run, and with many international banks approaching prudential limits in their lending—that new bank loans be-

gan to dry up. Mexico's policy of maintaining relatively low foreign exchange reserves (averaging less than two months' imports) then brought
on the debt crisis very suddenly.

In 1983 most Latin American countries faced a period of austerity and
economic adjustment as they struggled to reduce dependence on foreign
capital inflows in the context of world recession. As this section has
shown, the origins of the debt crisis lie partly in policies specific to each
country and partly in external events. Virtually the whole range of economic policy instruments has been used in the region. But this diversity
did not prevent most Latin American countries from reaching a common
position of deep recession and debt/financial crisis.

In response, a patchwork of international support emerged, consisting
of debt rescheduling, maintenance of short-term credit lines, as well as
IMF financing with policy conditionality. But it has been clear that these
rescue packages could not offer much more than temporary alleviation of
the region's financial squeeze. Long-term adjustment depends crucially
upon an upturn in the world economy to produce more favorable commodity prices and to reopen export opportunities in processed and manufactured goods. Some further decline in interest rates was also necessary
to ease the debt-servicing burden. By mid-1984 some external conditions
had improved, reflected most dramatically in relatively rapid economic
growth in the United States, economic recovery in Japan, and a more
modest recovery in western Europe. The United States' recovery in particular helped countries such as Brazil to expand exports. However, interest rate changes remained a problem, provoking renewed discussion of
the need for an upper limit on the extent to which increased interest rates
could inflate the size of borrower countries' debt-servicing obligations.
IMF austerity plans remained in place in several Latin American countries, but there was increasingly general recognition that the region's
economic recovery is imperative.

Aspects of Latin American Debt

Measurement of the Debt-Service Burden

Latin America's debt-servicing requirements are very onerous. In
1983 three countries (Argentina, Mexico, and Brazil) faced the prospect
of using more than 30 percent of current-account earnings for the payment of interest alone, and four other countries (Colombia, Chile, Ecuador, and Peru) were due to use more than 20 percent of current-account
earnings for this purpose. This interest burden is not eased by the rescheduling of principal; indeed, higher interest rate spreads on rescheduled

loans may even increase the burden. Latin American countries lead and dominate the "league table" of interest burdens (see table 2).

Debt-service ratios must also take into account principal repayments (see table 3). Latin America again leads the list of major debtor countries in this regard. Because all debts are being rescheduled only with great difficulty, short-term repayments must also be included in a full cash flow debt-service ratio. However, doing so increases the ratios to such a degree that such debt servicing clearly will not take place. Nonetheless, some attempt to include excessive short-term credits in these ratios (that is, short-term debts in excess of a reasonable level of trade financing) is instructive (see table 4). The first column in table 4 (Debt Service Ratio A) indicates the total debt-service burden after excessive short-term debts have been successfully rescheduled. Ratio B indicates (where different from Ratio A) the debt-service burden prior to any such rescheduling. Reschedulings improve the burdens significantly, although all these Latin American countries' ratios remain above the traditional 20 percent mark once thought to be a maximum prudential level.

TABLE 2
INTEREST PAYMENTS AS PERCENTAGE OF 1983 CURRENT-ACCOUNT EARNINGS FOR MAJOR DEBTOR COUNTRIES[a]

Argentina	35.1
Mexico	33.0
Brazil	32.0
(Ivory Coast)	27.6
Colombia	23.6
Chile	23.3
Ecuador	23.3
Peru	23.0
(Turkey)	17.8
(Philippines)	17.8
Venezuela	13.8
(Algeria)	12.4
(S. Korea)	11.0
(Nigeria)	9.5
(Thailand)	9.4
(Indonesia)	9.2
(Malaysia)	8.1

Source: The AMEX Bank Review, London, March 1983, 5.

a. Estimates for 1983, using current account earnings for 1982.

TABLE 3
AMORTIZATION
PAYMENTS AS
PERCENTAGE OF 1982
CURRENT-ACCOUNT
EARNINGS FOR MAJOR
DEBTOR COUNTRIES[a]

Argentina	52.8
Brazil	33.2
Chile	28.4
Peru	23.3
(Algeria)	22.7
(Indonesia)	18.6
Mexico	17.1
Ecuador	14.6
(Ivory Coast)	14.4
Colombia	12.1
(Philippines)	11.6
(Turkey)	10.4
(S. Korea)	9.5
(Thailand)	9.3
(Nigeria)	8.8
Venezuela	8.7
(Malaysia)	3.0

Source: Author's calculations based on American Express Bank data.

a. Medium-term debts due in 1982 as percentage of 1982 current-account earnings. This table assumes that excessive short-term credits are successfully rescheduled.

Trade Financing, "Excess" Short-Term Debt, and Rescheduling

A great deal of international bank lending activity has traditionally been of a short-term nature, especially in the form of 90- to 180-day financing for a country's export and import trade. Thus even before medium-term lending became fashionable, countries readily built up short-term exposures and continually rescheduled some debt. However, the sharp buildup of—and reliance upon—short-term credits in Latin America after 1980 in several cases went well beyond levels acceptable by trade financing standards, even when the boom in imports at the time is taken into account.

Table 5 provides data on major debtor countries' short-term debt to banks at the onset of the debt crisis and its equivalent in months of

TABLE 4
EFFECT OF SHORT-TERM DEBT
RESCHEDULING ON DEBT-SERVICE
RATIOS FOR MAJOR DEBTOR
COUNTRIES, 1983

	Ratio A^a	Ratio B^b
Argentina	87.9	150.6
Brazil	65.2	80.4
Chile	51.7	67.0
Mexico	50.4	107.9
Peru	46.3	53.4
(Ivory Coast)	42.0	42.0
Ecuador	37.9	72.6
Colombia	35.7	35.7
(Algeria)	35.1	35.1
(Philippines)	29.4	58.0
(Turkey)	28.2	28.2
(Indonesia)	27.8	27.8
Venezuela	22.5	54.8
(Thailand)	18.7	18.7
(S. Korea)	18.5	18.5
(Nigeria)	18.3	18.3
(Malaysia)	11.1	11.1

Source: The AMEX Bank Review, London, March 1983, 5.

a. After rescheduling excessive short-term debt obligations.

b. Prior to rescheduling excessive short-term debt obligations. Both ratios represent debt-service burdens as a proportion of total current-account earnings.

imports. The countries are listed according to the ratio of short-term debts to imports as of June 1982. The table includes both Latin American and selected other developing countries for comparative purposes. Latin American debtor countries dominate the list dramatically; all of them have much more short-term debt than might be expected for a country using 90- to 180-day trade financing. (The rolling float of short-term trade finance might "normally" be expected to lie somewhere between three and six months' imports equivalent.)

What do these data suggest concerning the management of the debt crisis in Latin America? First, the data in table 5 confirm that the growing emphasis on short-term maturities pushed short-term outstanding debt well beyond expected norms. For the eight Latin American countries listed in table 5, in June 1982 some $38.9 billion (or 50 percent of these countries' short-term debt of $77.8 billion) could be termed "excess"

TABLE 5

SHORT-TERM DEBT TO BANKS AND TRADE FINANCING IN MAJOR
DEBTOR COUNTRIES, 1982[a]

	Short-Term Debts to Banks (US$ billions)	Measured as Months of Imports	"Excess" Short-Term Debt (US$ billions)
Argentina	11.05	16.1	6.93
Mexico	28.75	14.9	17.17
Venezuela	12.68	12.3	6.49
Ecuador	2.10	10.7	0.92
(Philippines)	6.48	9.8	2.51
Brazil	14.68	8.0	3.67
Chile	4.19	7.7	0.93
Peru	2.17	6.8	0.26
Colombia	2.20	5.5	0.0
(S. Korea)	10.29	5.1	0.0
(Ivory Coast)	0.65	3.9	0.0
(Thailand)	2.34	3.1	0.0
(Nigeria)	3.49	2.4	0.0
(Indonesia)	2.60	1.9	0.0
(Malaysia)	1.55	1.6	0.0
(Turkey)	0.72	1.1	0.0
(Algeria)	0.73	0.9	0.0

Source: The AMEX Bank Review, London, March 1983, 5. Calculations are
based on Bank for International Settlements reports.

a. Short-term debts as of June 1982, expressed in months of imports (for year
to December 1981).

short-term debt. Only one major debtor country outside the Latin American region (the Philippines) faced excess short-term debts, and only one
Latin American country (Colombia) had held short-term debts below the
equivalent of six months' imports. Second, the data imply that some
rescheduling of excess short-term debt makes sense for countries in which
this debt exceeds the equivalent of six months' imports. (In fact, all the
countries in this position finally sought to reschedule this debt.) For four
of the eight countries above this level, the amount of excess short-term
debt due exceeded the amortization of other debts due during 1982.
Third, the impact on the debt-service burden can be assessed by calculating the impact of rescheduling any excess short-term debts.

Finally, the amount of excess short-term debt can be compared with
the banks' existing medium-term exposure in order to gauge the impact of
short-term debt rescheduling on the banks' asset maturity structure. Rescheduling excess short-term debt would increase banks' term exposures
by 80 percent in the case of Mexico and by 50 percent in the case of
Argentina. These short-term loans are already on banks' balance sheets,

so there is no increase in their overall lending exposure. But term increases will quickly absorb any remaining term lending capacity, and this change might substantially reduce banks' inclinations to loan to the countries in question. An unanticipated 50 percent increase in term loans in one year is a shock to any bank, even though the rescheduling makes a dramatic improvement in the borrower country's debt-service ratios.

By distinguishing the amount of excessive short-term debt from reasonable, trade-related short-term borrowing, it is possible to identify the amount of short-term lines of credit that (in a calmer market environment) borrowers might expect to reestablish with their bankers (for example, a six-month equivalent level). But in the present crisis, banks seek to minimize all exposures, making even "normal" trade financing credit difficult to obtain.

The Position of U.S. Banks

Bank Exposure

The most significant aspect of U.S. banks' exposure in Latin America concerns their levels of exposure as a percentage of bank equity (see table 6). Of the top twenty U.S. banks (ranked by total assets), in 1982 ten banks had loans to Mexico and Brazil combined that were equivalent to

TABLE 6

DISTRIBUTION OF TOP TWENTY U.S. BANKS' LOAN EXPOSURES TO MAJOR LATIN AMERICAN BORROWERS, 1982

Total Loans as Percentage of Bank Equity Capital, 1982	Mexico	Brazil	Venezuela	Three Borrowers Combined
90 to 100		1		1
80 to 90		1		1
70 to 80	1	1		2
60 to 70	3	2	1	6
50 to 60	4	5		9
40 to 50	4	2	1	7
30 to 40	5	2	4	11
20 to 30	2	3	5	10
10 to 20[a]	1	(0–3)	(1–9)	(2–13)
Less than 10[a]	0	(0–3)	(0–8)	(0–11)
Total	20	20	20	

Source: Based on data compiled by *The American Banker* using U.S. Securities and Exchange Commission records.

a. Specific data are not available at these lower levels because of bank reporting requirements.

total bank capital. Although no bank in this group had its entire capital exposed in any one country in the region, and although there were only seven cases in which country exposures exceeded two-thirds of equity, there were twelve country exposures that were more than 50 percent of equity. All twenty banks had more than 10 percent of their capital in Mexico; seventeen had more than 15 percent of their capital in Brazil; and at least twelve banks had more than 15 percent of their capital in Venezuela. At these exposure levels, the losses that would be associated with outright default by any one of these three countries would seriously damage the capital bases of U.S. banks.

In practice, however, a bank's capital base can be damaged well before any formal default on principal payments might occur. A bank is required to maintain certain reserves and to make specified loan-loss provisions according to the quality of its assets. Whenever interest payments are not made on outstanding loans within a certain grace period (now up to ninety days), a bank must declare these loans as "nonperforming." Nonperformance not only reduces interest income (bank earnings), but it also requires that provision be made against the possible loss of principal (since the nonpayment of interest is deemed to be an indication that principal payments may also be in doubt). Such provisions must inevitably come from profits or capital, and if profits are insufficient to allow for these provisions, then bank capital must be reduced. In order to keep the bank financially sound, additional capital must be raised from investors—who are less likely to provide that capital (that is, to buy the bank's stock) if earnings are poor.

These considerations make it very important to banks that debtor countries keep interest payments current, even if this requires the banks to arrange new loans so that interest can be paid. Loan reschedulings, new loans, and borrower countries' adjustment policies have so far offered banks a reasonable chance of improving the quality of outstanding loans (and borrower countries' creditworthiness). Under these circumstances, loan reschedulings on commercial terms have proved to be the most attractive strategy for lending banks.

The Role of Smaller U.S. Banks

The actions of smaller U.S. banks have received a great deal of attention during the debt crisis.[10] These banks play an especially important role in Latin America for several reasons. First, if smaller banks choose to withdraw from the market (and for reasons discussed below, this option is more likely to be open to them), the burden of rescheduling and new lending is placed on the larger banks. Second, insofar as smaller banks have a significant loan exposure, the effect of the debt crisis is felt more widely throughout the U.S. economy. Third, the absence of the smaller banks now would not only add to the larger banks' burden but also remove one source of growth from the credit market. Finally, the smaller-, regional-bank aspect of the debt crisis is a phenomenon particular to the United States. Elsewhere in the Eurocredit market, smaller banks have not engaged in international lending to a significant degree. These banks provide up to one-quarter of the total loans to major Latin American country borrowers (led by Mexico at 26.6 percent; see table 7); to some extent their share rises as the size of the country's debt increases. Smaller banks' exposures tend to be more heavily weighted toward loans to banks in Latin American countries than to other kinds of borrowers. Conversely, loans to the public sector and private nonbanking borrowers are less significant for smaller banks than for larger banks. Given the generally lower credit risk in interbank transactions, smaller banks that are less active in international lending are inclined to prefer bank loans rather than loans to public sector or corporate borrowers with more uncertain credit risks.

Smaller U.S. banks' share of all Euromarket exposures in all loan categories is generally greater for Latin American borrowers than for major Asian borrowers (especially in the case of loans to banks). Thus small banks' involvement in debt rescheduling has been more of a Latin American than a global phenomenon. Smaller banks' share of the market (in all loan categories) is largest in Mexico. Indeed, smaller banks had regarded Mexico as a special case that did not pose country-risk issues. When Mexico's 1982 economic and financial crisis erupted, smaller banks' realization that this was a faulty assumption produced a particularly strong adverse reaction against further loan commitments to Latin American borrowers.

What do these observations suggest regarding the relationship between U.S. banks and Latin American debtor countries? The most obvi-

TABLE 7
SMALL BANKS' SHARE OF U.S. BANK LOANS TO MAJOR DEBTOR
COUNTRIES, 1982
(as % of total)

Total Loans		To Banks		To Public Sector		To Private Nonbank Sector	
Mexico	26.6%	Mexico	33.4%	Mexico	22.5%	Mexico	27.0%
Chile	25.2	Chile	32.7	Chile	20.4	Venezuela	19.2
Brazil	18.7	Brazil	29.9	(S. Korea)	16.1	Chile	15.2
(S. Korea)	17.6	Argentina	26.5	Argentina	11.6	Argentina	13.8
Argentina	16.7	Venezuela	25.7	Brazil	11.4	(Philippines)	11.9
Venezuela	16.5	(S. Korea)	24.6	Venezuela	9.7	Brazil	9.7

Source: U.S. Federal Reserve Board, *Country Exposure Lending Survey,* June 1982.

ous fact is that smaller banks' contributions are notably greater for Mexico than for the other major debtor countries; among other Latin American debtors, only Chile comes close to this level of dispersion of exposure among banks. Thus in recent rescue operations it has been particularly important to keep smaller banks involved in Mexico. This, in turn, has made it important to keep debt servicing current, because smaller banks' lower exposures give them greater flexibility to accept losses on outstanding loans and to refuse to contribute new money. Smaller banks' deep involvement in Mexico also means that a Mexican default on outstanding loans would be particularly damaging to U.S. banks and to the U.S. economy—which underlines the importance of the debt crisis as a major U.S. financial policy issue.

The high degree of dispersion among banks' loans to Mexico undoubtedly stems from two factors. First, as Mexico's total financing needs rose above other countries' needs, the larger banks were compelled to sell down a larger portion of these assets to smaller banks. Second, a wider range of U.S. banks has found lending to Mexico acceptable, given its location and banks' other business connections there. Just as U.S. banks generally have had greater incentives to lend to Latin America than to other regions, so Mexico represents that "natural" relationship in a more intense form.

Policy Implications

Given the prominence of the Latin American debt issue during 1983–1984, it is not surprising that the crisis has held important implications for U.S. policy. Indeed, the United States' policy regarding interest rates has at times appeared to give greater attention to the impact of dollar interest rate increases on Latin America than on the United States itself. Latin American complaints concerning high interest rates have probably received greater attention from U.S. policymakers than similar protestations from western Europe and other regions.

The most important economic and financial policy questions concerning the Latin American debt crisis fall into two categories: policies to change the ways in which capital and credit flow to Latin America, and policies to alter the ways in which private banks lend money overseas to large borrowers. The focal point of the first category has been U.S. policy toward the IMF and the World Bank. The Reagan administration has generally been lukewarm in its support of the Bretton Woods institutions. Although the Reagan administration has supported IMF policy conditionality and efforts by major borrower countries to reach an agreed-upon policy position with the Fund, it has reduced U.S. funding to these institutions and favors some reduction in the IMF's lending power (through a reduction in the high percentage of members' quota contributions that the IMF has been able to use in making loans). Nevertheless, the overall shift in recent U.S. policy toward multilateral financial institutions may offer more to Latin America than to other developing countries. For example, the shift in U.S. emphasis away from the International Development Association (IDA, concessional lending) and toward the International Finance Corporation (IFC, private sector financing) should offer new opportunities to the Latin American private sector while taking away few concessional funds, especially as far as the region's largest debtor countries are concerned.

The principal thrust of recent U.S policy toward private bank lending to Latin America has been to tighten bank lending procedures, especially procedures regarding country risk related loan-loss provisions (that is, how much money banks should set aside against sovereign country loans in case of default). There has been no formal government intervention to set the price of such loans, but U.S. government officials have often stressed the need to ensure that new loan conditions are sustainable and that bank fees for rescheduled loans are reasonable.

The nature of the U.S. response to Latin America's debt crisis (case-by-case rescheduling) has focused debate on how to reach satisfactory solutions to each country's difficulties rather than on establishing new procedures or institutions to resolve the debt problem. At the same time, Latin American debtor countries have sought solutions through increasing cooperation. Nonetheless, a series of meetings involving various Latin American countries has not produced any radical solution or reaction to the debt crisis, although these meetings undoubtedly helped highlight the urgency of the region's problems. However unlikely the prospects of a debtors' cartel (and Latin American countries have made great efforts not to threaten action through such a cartel), discussion of this approach has raised Latin American participants' consciousness of the need to identify viable long-term solutions to the problem. Loan reschedulings are now for longer periods of time with some control over banks' fees, and the IMF's practical influence over policy in countries such as Mexico is visibly waning. Efforts to resolve the debt crisis have focused principally on restoring order and ensuring that the lessons of the current crisis are not forgotten, while essentially allowing future credit flows to be channeled to Latin American borrowers in the same way as before. To the extent to which international commercial banks are less enthusiastic lenders than before, capital imports must be reduced and foreign savings must play a less important role in Latin America's economic development than in the past.

Of course, U.S. policy could be radically different. A massive "Marshall Plan" for Latin America could be beneficial for U.S.–Latin American political relations whatever its economic or financial rationale. But to the extent that debt rescheduling resolves much of the region's cash flow problem; insofar as recent economic growth in the United States has boosted Latin American exports to the U.S. market; and to the extent that individual countries' policies have achieved some degree of economic adjustment, such a large-scale U.S. assistance program should not be necessary. However, a serious problem may arise within Latin America in the future. As countries relax austerity measures, it will be difficult to curb public sector deficits and contain inflation. Neither continued austerity nor rising inflation will assist in maintaining political stability. An increase in political instability in the region would produce new challenges for U.S. foreign policy.

American Express Bank Ltd.
London, England

Notes

1. Inter-American Development Bank, *External Debt and Economic Development in Latin America* (Washington, D.C., January 1984). Throughout this essay, short-term debt refers to credits with an original maturity of less than one year; medium- and long-term credits have maturities of more than one year. "Long term" is rarely used to describe credits with maturities of less than ten years.

2. Author's calculations based on data presented in Bank for International Settlements, "The Maturity Distribution of International Bank Lending," mimeograph, July 1984; Federal Financial Institutions Examination Council report, "Country Exposure Lending Survey," mimeograph, May 1984.

3. The Eurocurrency market consists of deposits and loans in banks in financial centers that are denominated in any freely tradable currency. These deposits and loans are usually not subject to regulations as restrictive as those applicable to deposits and loans in the domestic financial market.

4. I am indebted to my colleague John Calverley (economist, American Express Bank Ltd.) for the preparation of this section.

5. Unless otherwise specified, the data cited in the six country profiles are from the International Monetary Fund's *International Financial Statistics* series.

6. Banco Central do Brasil sources.

7. *The AMEX Bank Review* (London) (March 1983): 1–3.

8. The interest rate spread is the margin paid over the LIBOR (London Inter-Bank Offered Rate). This is a bank's profit on a loan (that is, the interest paid to the bank over its marginal funding costs). LIBOR is the basic Eurocurrency lending rate, which is itself marginally higher (usually about one-eighth of 1 percent) above the deposit rate. Brazil had been borrowing at spreads of from five-eighths to three-quarters of 1 percent. This spread later moved up to over 2 percent.

9. Brazil almost applied to the International Monetary Fund for assistance in late 1980. However, the policy changes that the government implemented were understood to be broadly in agreement with policies that the IMF would have requested.

10. This analysis concentrates on a comparison between nine money-center banks and those banks smaller than the top twenty-four banks (in terms of assets). The role of the intermediate fifteen banks is assumed to be approximately somewhere in between these two groups.

A money-center bank is a general term used to describe the large U.S. banks in the large U.S. money centers, notably New York, Chicago, Los Angeles, and San Francisco.

especially the potential U.S. role in a collective effort to alleviate the painful effects inflicted on most of the United States' southern neighbors by the wide and frequent fluctuations in primary-commodity prices. On the other hand, there are also issues related to the effects of U.S. trade policy on Latin American exports. Of particular relevance in this context is the problem of how to prevent U.S. trade restrictions from cutting short the region's increasing trade diversification toward manufactured exports. This is a central issue in a longer-term view of U.S.– Latin American trade relations, and much ultimately will depend upon the United States' ability to adjust to a changing international division of labor that relocates an increasing (and presently sizable) share of high-productivity world industrial capacity to former primary-product exporters in Latin America.

This essay addresses this second set of issues. The kinds of questions discussed here surpass the framework of bilateral negotiations. Indeed, they do not differ from those that already are—and will most certainly continue to be—present on the agenda of North-South economic diplomacy. However, given the imperative of satisfactory export performance for macroeconomic stability in most Latin American countries during the rest of the decade, the importance of U.S. trade policies for Latin America cannot be underestimated: the United States is still by far the largest single market for Latin American products, accounting for about a third of the region's overall exports and a quarter of its non-oil sales abroad.

This essay is divided into four sections. The first briefly surveys the main post–World War II economic trends and the present commodity composition and direction of Latin American trade. It is followed by two sections on recent trade-policy issues (with special emphasis on trade relations with the United States) and a concluding section. The reader should bear in mind that this essay is no exception to the rule that any work dealing with Latin American economic questions at a general level is bound to be simplified because of the large number of countries involved and especially because of the enormous differences among them in economic size and output structure.

Post-World War II Trends and the Present Structure of Latin American Trade

One of the outstanding achievements of postwar global economic development was the reconstruction and accelerated expansion of a multilateral trade network after over a decade of rampant trade restrictions, bilateralism, and war. World trade not only grew very fast by past standards (over 7 percent per year from 1948 to 1973, compared to 0.5 percent per year between 1913 and 1948), but trade volume also rose an average 2 percent per year faster than output.

Until the mid-1960s, however, the growth of world trade was not equally shared among industrialized and developing nations. The value of industrialized countries' exports increased by 345 percent between 1950 and 1965, but that of developing countries rose by only 198 percent.[1] In the same period, the Latin American share of world exports fell continuously from 11.3 to 6.9 percent, as shown in table 1.

Developing countries' comparatively poor export performance was to a large extent a result of profound transformations in the direction and commodity composition of world trade—away from the traditional prewar division of labor between primary- and manufactured-good exporters that accompanied the post-World War II trade boom. Until the mid-1960s, trade among industrialized economies grew at a much faster rate than that among other regions, and trade in primary products decreased steadily as a proportion of global trade as the terms of trade for these goods continuously deteriorated after the Korean War boom.

However, especially in the case of Latin America, poor export performance in the two decades following World War II was also related to the widespread adoption of industrial and foreign economic policies aimed at rapid import substitution by the region's larger economies. Some Latin American countries had already begun to follow this development strategy in the 1930s as a result of external constraints imposed by the depression. After World War II, recurrent foreign exchange problems, the grim

TABLE 1
LATIN AMERICA, 1950–1979:
SHARE IN WORLD EXPORTS OF SELECTED COMMODITY GROUPS (in %)

	1950	*1955*	*1960*	*1965*	*1970*	*1975*	*1979*
Total exports	11.3	10.0	7.9	6.9	5.7	5.5	5.2
Food	NA	20.5	17.4	16.1	15.9	14.6	14.8
Agricultural raw materials	NA	8.9	7.0	7.9	5.9	4.7	4.5
Minerals and ores	NA	14.5	14.6	15.1	15.2	13.2	14.0
Non-ferrous metals	NA	14.4	11.8	12.8	12.2	10.0	9.1
Fuels	NA	27.4	25.6	20.5	15.1	10.8	9.2
Manufactured goods	NA	0.7	0.5	0.6	1.0	1.3	1.5
Chemicals	NA	2.0	1.7	1.6	2.3	2.8	2.3
Iron and Steel	NA	0.7	0.6	1.1	1.1	0.8	1.9
Machinery and Transport Equipment	NA	0.1	0.1	0.1	0.4	0.7	0.9
Other manufactured products	NA	0.6	0.6	0.9	1.2	1.7	2.1

Sources: United Nations Conference on Trade and Development, *Handbook of International Trade and Development Statistics* (New York, 1979), and *Supplement* (1981), tables A.1 to A.10.

NA = Not Available

outlook for trade in primary products, and national strategic considerations turned import-substitution industrialization into a major policy objective in several countries.

The instruments used to enforce import-substitution industrialization (overvalued exchange rates plus import controls or high levels of protection for competing imports, multiple exchange rates, subsidized credit for and government participation in import-substituting projects, among others) varied among different Latin American countries. Nevertheless, the common result was to shift profitability in favor of activities geared to domestic markets. In most countries (with the possible exception of Mexico) these policies not only curbed the growth of traditional primary exports; they also inhibited the development of manufactured exports from long-established branches of industry.

From the mid-1960s onward the outlook for Latin America's exports and balance-of-payments position began to change rapidly. Faster growth rates in industrialized (Organization for Economic Cooperation and Development, OECD) countries led to a sizable increase in world demand for primary products. The value of industrialized countries' imports of primary goods, which had risen at an average rate of 3.3 percent per year between 1955 and 1963, grew by 5.8 percent per year during 1963 through 1968 and 19.1 percent per year in 1968 through 1973.[2] This substantial improvement in primary-commodity trade was accompanied by a sharp increase in international capital flows to the region in the forms of both direct investment and, increasingly, money loans. For example, by the end of the 1960s many Latin American countries were already regular customers in Eurocurrency markets.

These changes lifted the traditional foreign exchange constraint on Latin American economies, with two important consequences. First, the secular compression of imports' share of gross domestic product (GDP), which had fallen by a third since the early 1950s, was arrested and reversed. This shift allowed industrial capital formation and activity levels to proceed at faster rates, pushing import substitution into broad areas of intermediate and capital goods in the larger countries, as table 2 shows. Second, these developments encouraged a progressive change in exchange rate regimes, leading to a more favorable treatment of export activities through measures such as exchange rate unification and frequent devaluations aimed at offsetting the usually large differentials between domestic and world inflation rates.

However, the removal of the antiexport bias implicit in previous economic policies was not restricted to these measures. Toward the end of the 1960s there was a growing belief in Latin America that as a consequence of high OECD growth, recent General Agreement on Tariffs and Trade (GATT) tariff-liberalization rounds, and the eventual success of

TABLE 2
LATIN AMERICA, 1950–1974:
MANUFACTURING INDUSTRY OUTPUT STRUCTURE (in %)

	1950	*1960*	*1974*
Industrialized countries[a]	100.0	100.0	100.0
Nondurable consumer goods	63.8	51.5	36.2
Intermediate products	23.5	28.9	35.2
Durable consumer and capital goods	12.7	19.6	28.6
Medium-sized economies[b]	100.0	100.0	100.0
Nondurable consumer goods	64.8	54.7	49.5
Intermediate products	28.3	30.2	33.0
Durable consumer and capital goods	6.9	15.1	17.5
Other[c]	100.0	100.0	100.0
Nondurable consumer goods	79.3	76.8	68.1
Intermediate products	14.2	16.5	23.8
Durable consumer and capital goods	6.5	6.7	8.1
Latin America	100.0	100.0	100.0
Nondurable consumer goods	65.5	54.1	40.3
Intermediate products	23.3	28.2	34.1
Durable consumer and capital goods	11.2	17.7	25.6

Source: United Nations Economic Commission for Latin America, *América Latina en el umbral de los años 80*, Doc. E/CEPAL/G. 1106 (Santiago, Chile, 1979), table 32.

a. Argentina, Brazil, and Mexico.

b. Colombia, Chile, and Peru.

c. Bolivia, Dominican Republic, Ecuador, Panama, Paraguay, and Central American Common Market countries.

Generalized System of Preferences (GSP) negotiations started in 1964, there would be increasing room for the region's manufactured exports in the world market. Thus economic policy in the industrializing countries of Latin America also came to incorporate a battery of incentives for manufactured exports, such as fiscal subsidies, drawbacks, low interest rate export and preexport credit lines, and so forth.

The effects of these measures at a time of rapid expansion in world trade were impressive. From 1965 to 1973 total Latin American exports rose by 10.8 percent per year, in contrast to a growth rate of 3.6 percent per year during the previous fifteen years. Latin American manufactured exports soared at an astonishing 26.5 percent per year, while world trade in manufactured goods grew by only 16.4 percent per year during this period. The larger and more industrialized countries (Argentina, Brazil, and Mexico) responded faster to this changing environment of expanded world trade and new domestic policies, and they were responsible for the largest part of the growth in Latin American manufactured exports, as evident in table 3.

Just as the prospects for the growth and diversification of Latin

TABLE 3
LATIN AMERICA, 1965–1973: MANUFACTURED EXPORTS
(in US$ millions and in %)

	1965	1970	1973
Manufactured exports			
Argentina	144	420	978
Brazil	237	580	1,672
Mexico	183	444	1,200
Others[a]	386	731	1,275
Latin America	950	2,175	5,125
Share of manufactured exports in total exports of:			
Argentina	5.1	12.3	19.0
Brazil	7.5	9.7	17.9
Mexico	13.0	30.0	40.8

Source: United Nations Economic Commission for Latin America, *América Latina en el umbral de los años 80,* Doc. E/CEPAL/G. 1106 (Santiago, Chile, 1979), p. 60.

   a. Includes other members of Latin American Integration Association; members of Central American Common Market and Caribbean Free Trade Association/Caribbean Community; Panama; Dominican Republic.

American exports brightened, the Latin American economies were challenged by the 1973–1974 oil shock and its sequels of recession in the major industrialized countries and global economic instability. However, managing the large deficits that this sudden oil price rise and the subsequent 1974–1975 slump in world trade produced in Latin American non-oil exporters' current accounts did not prove as difficult as initially expected. The substantial levels of foreign long-term lending that these countries were able to attract allowed external adjustment to be spread over a longer period, thus preventing the need to reenact trade and foreign exchange restrictions in the fashion of the 1950s.

Increased foreign indebtedness was not unique to Latin America. It was a phenomenon common to almost every non-oil developing country as a necessary result of the rapid recessive adjustment of industrialized countries' current-account deficits and the resilience of Organization of Petroleum Exporting Countries (OPEC) surpluses. Foreign indebtedness was immensely eased by the accommodating behavior of world financial markets. This, in fact, turned large-scale foreign borrowing into part and parcel of the growth strategy adopted after 1973 in several Latin American countries. Because the long-term feasibility of this strategy depended crucially upon maintaining a good export performance—on the basis of which creditworthiness was ultimately assessed—it reinforced the trend toward export-promoting policies established during the mid-1960s.

However, after 1973 good export performance by developing countries did not depend on wise domestic policies nearly to the extent it did under the favorable economic conditions prevailing before the 1973–1974 oil shock. Of course, these policies were still a necessary condition. But the much greater instability in world trade caused by uncertainty over the future paths of key exchange rates and, especially, sharp cyclical fluctuations and protectionist measures in industrialized countries played a far more important role in determining the behavior of Latin American exports.

Latin America's non-oil primary exports, which still accounted for about one-half of total export earnings, felt the impact of this unstable economic environment most severely. As indicated in table 4, their prices experienced very large fluctuations (both by past standards and in comparison with manufactured goods) as a result of the markedly cyclical demand pattern in industrialized countries and of the slump in the prices of tropical beverages (which have a large weight in the region's non-oil primary exports bill) in 1978.

In contrast to the unsettled behavior of primary commodities, Latin American manufactured exports followed a much more stable and predictable path after the world trade setback of 1974–1975. Their performance relative to that of other regions varied across different sectors, as even the gross disaggregation presented in table 5 shows. These differences reflected not just productivity differentials but a variety of other factors as well. Among the most important influences were: (1) the sectorally uneven distribution of fiscal incentives; (2) the degree of excess capacity created by the deceleration in Latin America's output growth in the second half of the decade; and (3) the presence of multinational corporations, since intrafirm transfers account for about 40 percent of the region's trade in manufactured goods.[3]

Nevertheless, the aggregate performance of manufactured exports was good. Although expansion was slower than in the booming early 1970s, manufactured exports' total value rose rapidly after 1975—at 23.2 percent per year, compared to 17.1 percent per year for world trade in manufactured goods (see table 5). This reestablished the trend toward an increasing share of manufactured goods in total exports, as shown in table 6.

The combined effects of rapid import-substitution industrialization, the growth of manufactured exports, and the oil crisis were not limited to changes in the commodity composition of exports and imports. There were also important alterations in the direction of Latin American trade, as tables 7 and 8 show. In this respect, one striking development was the steady and large fall in the proportion of Latin American non-oil exports absorbed by industrialized countries, while the share going to other areas—particularly intra-Latin American trade—increased substantially (see table 9). This shift was partially the result of higher rates of growth in developing countries (compared with industrialized countries) after

TABLE 4

LATIN AMERICA, 1973–1981: INDICATORS OF PRIMARY EXPORTS PERFORMANCE

(% change in the year shown)

	1963–72	1973	1974	1975	1976	1977	1978	1979	1980	1981
Gross domestic product growth of major trading partners	5.0[a]	6.2	0.1	-1.2	5.2	4.5	4.0	4.0	3.3	0.8
Unit value of:										
World manufactured exports	3.0	17.7	21.8	12.3	—	9.0	14.7	14.5	11.0	-5.0
Latin American non-oil primary exports	4.3	47.4	20.9	-12.5	23.0	27.3	-13.6	14.2	14.0	-14.7

Source: International Monetary Fund, *Direction of Trade Yearbook, 1981* (Washington, D.C., 1981), tables 9, 14, and 76.

a. Refers to 1968–1972.

TABLE 5

LATIN AMERICA AND THE WORLD, 1975–1979:
YEARLY RATES OF EXPORT GROWTH FOR SELECTED GROUPS OF
MANUFACTURED PRODUCTS (in %)

	Latin America	*World*
Chemicals	14.0	19.7
Iron and steel	38.3	11.5
Machinery and transport equipment	23.5	15.9
Textiles	16.3	17.4
Others	26.0	19.7
Total manufacturing	23.2	17.1

Source: United Nations Conference on Trade and Development, *Handbook of International Trade and Development Statistics, Supplement* (New York, 1981), tables A6, A7, A9, A10, A11. Textiles are defined as including SITC classes 26, 65, and 84.

TABLE 6

LATIN AMERICA, 1960–79: COMMODITY COMPOSITION OF TRADE (in %)

		EXPORTS				
	1960	*1965*	*1970*	*1973*	*1975*	*1979*
Food	42.6	42.8	41.3	40.0	35.1	33.5
Agricultural raw materials	9.5	9.1	6.0	5.5	3.3	3.6
Ores and metals	12.5	13.9	17.5	1.2	9.6	9.5
Fuels	31.8	28.4	24.4	26.3	38.2	35.7
Manufactured goods	3.6	5.8	10.4	14.5	13.2	17.2
		IMPORTS				
	1960	*1965*	*1970*	*1973*	*1975*	*1979*
Food	12.6	13.6	11.0	12.5	10.0	10.2
Agricultural raw materials	3.7	3.8	3.0	2.7	1.8	2.1
Ores and metals	2.0	3.0	3.0	2.7	2.3	2.7
Fuels	14.3	12.9	11.7	15.7	23.0	21.1
Manufactured goods	67.4	66.7	69.1	64.3	60.6	59.4

Sources: United Nations Conference on Trade and Development, *Handbook of International Trade and Development Statistics* (New York, 1979), tables A.1 to A.5, and *Supplement* (1981), tables 3.2A, 3.2B and A.7.

Note: Commodity groups defined as follows: Food (SITC $0+1+22+4$), agricultural raw materials (SITC $2-22-27-28$), ores and metals (SITC $27+28+68$)), fuels (SITC 3) and manufactured goods (SITC $5+6+7+8-68$). Totals do not add to 100 because of rounding.

1973. To a greater extent, however, it was a reflection of the general trend toward an increased proportion of manufactured goods in Latin American exports to the region's principal markets, as shown in table 10.

Table 10 also demonstrates that Latin American manufactured exports to industrialized countries are not composed simply of technologically simple goods produced with cheap labor. This is largely due to the

TABLE 7

LATIN AMERICA, 1960–1979: EXPORTS BY AREA OF DESTINATION

(in US$ millions FOB and % of total)

	1960		1970		1979	
	$	%	$	%	$	%
World	10,170	100.0	17,707	100.0	85,378	100.0
Developed market economies	8,004	78.7	13,221	74.7	56,027	65.6
United States	4,020	39.5	5,818	32.9	29,405	34.4
European Economic Community	NA		4,554	25.7	15,941	18.7
Japan	265	2.6	974	5.5	3,295	3.9
Others	3,719[a]	36.6	1,875	10.6	7,386	8.7
Developing countries	1,860	18.3	3,366	19.0	22,963	26.9
Latin America	1,680	16.5	3,035	17.1	18,733	21.9
Africa	105	1.0	119	0.7	1,642	1.9
West Asia	28	0.3	37	0.2	1,290	1.5
Others	47	0.5	175	1.0	1,298	1.5
Socialist countries	306	3.0	1,120	6.3	6,388	7.5

Source: United Nations Conference on Trade and Development, *Handbook of International Trade and Development Statistics* (New York, 1979), and *Supplement* (1981), table A.1.
NA = Not Available
a. Includes the European Economic Community.

TABLE 8

LATIN AMERICA, 1960–1979: IMPORTS BY REGION OF ORIGIN

(in US$ millions FOB and % of total)

	1960		1970		1979	
	$	%	$	%	$	%
World	10,040	100.0	18,623	100.0	98,215	100.0
Developed market economies	7,843	78.2	13,909	74.7	59,292	60.4
United States	3,870	38.5	6,477	34.8	27,728	28.2
European Economic Community	NA		4,425	23.8	17,257	17.6
Japan	315	3.2	1,112	6.0	6,320	6.4
Others	3,665[a]	36.5	1,895	10.2	7,988	8.2
Developing countries	1,950	19.4	3,684	19.8	34,036	34.7
Latin America	1,680	16.7	3,035	16.3	18,733	19.0
Africa	44	0.4	237	1.3	2,872	2.9
West Asia	61	0.6	234	1.2	10,013	10.2
Others	165	1.6	178	0.9	2,418	2.5
Socialist countries	247	2.5	1,030	5.5	4,887	5.0

Source: United Nations Conference on Trade and Development, *Handbook of International Trade and Development Statistics* (New York, 1979), and *Supplement* (1981), table A.1.
NA = Not Available
a. Includes the European Economic Community.

TABLE 9

LATIN AMERICA, 1960–1979: NONFUEL EXPORTS BY AREA OF DESTINATION
(in US$ millions FOB and % of total)

	1960 $	1960 %	1970 $	1970 %	1979 $	1979 %
World	6,930	100.0	13,384	100.0	54,872	100.0
Developed market economies	5,999	86.6	10,364	77.4	34,532	62.3
United States	2,840	41.0	3,981	29.7	12,713	23.2
European Economic Community	NA		4,179	31.2	13,937	25.4
Japan	259	3.7	938	7.0	3,219	5.9
Others	2,900[a]	42.0	1,266	9.4	4,663	8.5
Developing countries	625	9.0	1,900	14.2	13,968	25.5
Latin America	530	7.6	1,642	12.3	10,660	19.4
Africa	37	0.5	90	0.7	1,058	1.9
West Asia	24	0.3	37	0.3	973	1.8
Others	34	0.5	131	1.0	1,277	2.3
Socialist countries	306	4.4	1,120	8.4	6,372	11.6

Source: United Nations Conference on Trade and Development, *Handbook of International Trade and Development Statistics* (New York, 1979), and *Supplement* (1981), tables A.1 to A.10.

NA = Not Available

a. Includes the European Economic Community.

TABLE 10

LATIN AMERICA, 1979: COMMODITY COMPOSITION OF EXPORTS BY AREA OF DESTINATION
(as % of total in each commodity group shown)

	United States	Other Industrial Countries	Latin America	Other Developing Countries	Socialist Countries	Total Value (US$ millions)
Food	23.8	41.9	10.8	5.8	18.1	28,604
Agricultural raw materials	10.9	48.4	18.3	9.1	12.8	3,038
Ores and minerals	20.7	55.4	15.3	2.6	7.8	8,104
Fuels	54.7	15.1	24.5	3.0	—	30,506
Manufactured goods	25.6	26.0	38.8	7.0	2.4	14,668
Chemicals	23.6	31.5	37.7	5.7	2.2	2,910
Iron and steel	21.0	32.5	31.9	7.2	6.3	1,341
Machinery and transport equipment	23.4	19.0	45.5	11.8	0.2	4,131
Textiles	15.7	42.5	23.8	6.7	11.1	3,600
Other	29.0	26.6	36.5	4.4	3.0	6,286

Source: United Nations Conference on Trade and Development, *Handbook of International Trade and Development Statistics, Supplement* (New York, 1981), tables A.1 to A.10.

massive presence of multinational corporations in the larger Latin American countries' leading high-technology export sectors, which can be noted by comparing the composition of selected manufactured exports shown in table 11 with data referring only to intrafirm trade in selected manufacturing groups presented in table 12. Table 11 also calls attention to the very high country concentration of Latin American manufactured exports, especially in the modern capital goods industries in Argentina, Brazil, and Mexico.

Trade in Manufactured Goods and the "New Protectionism"

The structural changes in Latin American trade since the mid-1960s that have been outlined above began and were consolidated in times of unprecedented global trade expansion and growing trade liberalism among industrialized countries. The so-called Dillon (1960–1961) and Kennedy (1963–1967) tariff reduction GATT negotiations gave new impetus to trade liberalization; for a group of eight OECD countries, the average tariff level (which was still over 25 percent by the end of the 1950s, after having fallen from above 50 percent in 1950) was reduced to 18 percent after 1961 and to about 9 percent after 1967.[4] Tariffs for light manufactured goods of special interest to industrializing countries (such as textiles and clothing) were not significantly affected by these measures. However, following the 1964 United Nations Conference on Trade and Development (UNCTAD) developing country pressures for preferential access for their manufactured and semiprocessed products to industrialized country markets began to have some effect. After long negotiations they were successful, and GSP schemes were implemented by the European Economic Community (EEC) and Japan in 1971. The limited actual benefits conceded by these schemes will be evaluated below. However, the fact that these schemes were implemented in contravention of GATT principles of nondiscrimination and generalized most-favored-nation treatment is illustrative of the general trend toward freer trade in industrialized countries at the time.

This mood had already begun to change toward the end of the pre-oil crisis trade boom. As the result of far-reaching post-World War II changes in developing countries' economic-output structure (examined with regard to Latin America in the preceding section), penetration by developing country manufactured goods in industrialized country markets rose quickly. By 1973 the share of these goods in industrialized countries' total manufactured imports reached 20 percent, compared with only 11 percent a decade earlier.[5] The sharp decline in industrialized countries' demand and the rise in their unit labor costs after the 1973–1974 oil shock

TABLE 11

LATIN AMERICA, 1979:

SELECTED COUNTRY SHARES IN TOTAL MANUFACTURING AND SELECTED MANUFACTURED EXPORTS (in %)

	Total Manu-facturing	Chemicals	Textiles	Clothing	Footwear	Iron and Steel	Transport Equipment	Electrical Machinery	Non-electrical Machinery	Other
Larger industrial-ized countries	62.8	36.5	66.2	48.7	81.5	73.0	90.1	81.1	93.1	54.5
Argentina	15.2	10.2	6.1	19.0	8.4	13.9	26.6	9.1	21.0	17.7
Brazil	34.3	10.6	46.1	22.8	67.4	45.1	55.5	58.5	61.3	21.0
Mexico	13.3	15.7	14.0	6.9	5.7	14.0	8.0	13.5	10.8	15.0
Medium-sized economies	10.7	8.2	14.2	11.3	—	3.7	5.4	2.7	3.7	19.1
Chile	4.1	4.4	—	—	—	3.7	1.2	1.0	1.1	8.9
Colombia	5.2	3.0	10.1	11.3	—	—	1.9	1.7	2.6	8.3
Peru	1.4	0.8	4.1	—	—	—	3.3	—	—	1.9
Oil-exporting countries	3.1	12.6	1.8	1.5	—	2.3	0.6	0.7	0.9	3.8
Others	22.4	42.7	18.8	38.5	18.5	21.0	3.9	15.5	2.3	22.6
Latin America	100.0	100.0	100.0	100.0	100.0	100.0	100.0	100.0	100.0	100.0

Source: United Nations, *Yearbook of International Trade Statistics* (New York, 1980), *passim.*

TABLE 12

U.S. RELATED-PARTY IMPORTS OF SELECTED MANUFACTURED GOODS BY
COUNTRY OF ORIGIN, 1979

(as % of total U.S. imports of each manufactured good for country shown)

	Textiles	Clothing	Footwear	Nonelectrical Machinery	Electrical Machinery
Argentina	0.5	2.9	0.8	39.1	76.1
Brazil	9.2	18.0	0.5	59.9	95.3
Mexico	9.6	68.0	60.9	87.7	95.6

Source: G. K. Helleiner and R. Lavergne, "Intra-Firm Trade and Industrial Exports to
the United States," *Oxford Bulletin of Economics and Statistics,* vol. 41 (1979), p. 307.

led to renewed efforts by industrializing countries to stimulate their
manufactured exports, which reinforced antiliberal feelings and triggered
defensive protectionist reactions in industrialized countries.

Although bound by GATT rules not to resort to "old" tariff protectionism, industrialized countries developed a series of very effective nontariff barriers aimed at selective market closure (permitted by the GATT
articles concerning abnormal situations) to stop the tide of developing
countries' manufactured export competition. Some of these barriers are
unilateral and formal, such as quantitative restrictions or countervailing
duties charged specifically to compensate for subsidies granted to exports
in the country of origin. Other barriers (the so-called orderly marketing
agreements) result from bilateral negotiation. They enforce quotas and
permissible rates of growth for particular imports from individual countries under the threat of formal action. These barriers are usually informal, "voluntary" agreements, but they are equally effective safeguards
against rapid import penetration.

The United States was no exception to the trend toward protectionism
in industrialized countries. The Trade Act of 1974, which empowered the
U.S. executive to monitor trade and enforce nontariff barriers in case
"grave injury" was done to a domestic industry by high import growth,
led to a large increase in the application of those measures. During the
life of the Trade Act, which extended from January 1975 to December
1979, at least 111 subsidy and 119 antidumping countervailing duty cases
were filed.[6] According to an Organization of American States Secretariat
document, effective application of these measures by the U.S. government rose from sixteen in 1971–1974 to sixty-two between 1975 and September 1978.[7]

The increase in new U.S. protectionism can also be detected in the
U.S. Generalized System of Preferences scheme, which began operation
in January 1976. On the one hand, the system introduced "competitive
need" criteria according to which GSP duty-free tariff treatment is phased

out if exports of a particular product from a beneficiary country become larger than 50 percent of total U.S. imports of that product or larger than a dollar limit (fixed initially at $25 million annually) that varies according to growth in U.S. gross domestic product. For countries with a limited degree of export diversification or large exports of semiprocessed primary goods (as is the case with several Latin American countries), this can mean exclusion from the benefits of the GSP for their principal export products. In fact, of the total $3.5 billion in Latin American exports to the United States eligible in principle for duty-free treatment under the GSP in 1978, only $1.5 billion actually received this benefit.[8]

On the other hand, about seven hundred tariff items corresponding to "import-sensitive" manufactured goods—that is, those competing with low-productivity, noncompetitive branches of U.S. industry benefiting from government relief schemes—were not included in the GSP. This was tantamount to excluding from preferential treatment items such as textiles, clothing, footwear, and iron and steel—all products of special interest to several Latin American countries (see table 13) that in general enjoyed high rates of tariff protection.

The restrictions placed on access to the U.S. preference scheme greatly diminished its advantages to Latin America. On the basis of 1971 trade data, the trade-diversion and trade-creation benefits derived by Latin American countries from its application were estimated at $74.6 million—that is, just 1.2 percent of the region's total exports to the United States in that year.[9]

However, despite the reduced significance of the GSPs, there was much concern at UNCTAD—where Latin American countries traditionally have a strong voice—when the "donor" (industrialized) countries initiated meetings in Tokyo in 1973 for a new round of GATT most-favored-nation (MFN) tariff reductions.[10] The worries of the "beneficiary" (developing) countries stemmed from their fears of the effects of further industrialized country tariff reductions on the preferential margins enjoyed by them under the GSPs.

These concerns appear unjustified, at least as far as the effects of the erosion of preferential margins resulting from the Tokyo Round (concluded in 1979 and enforced between 1980 and 1985) on Latin American trade with the United States are concerned. Table 14, based on pre-Tokyo Round tariff rates and 1974 trade data, shows that the weighted average U.S. MFN tariff rate on Latin American manufactured goods is below 10 percent, even if only the non-oil-exporting countries are taken into account. Although these averages may give a distorted view of the rates actually paid on some manufactured goods (as suggested by table 15), they are quite low. If one considers that between 1974 and 1980 the average real exchange rate of Latin American currencies appreciated by

TABLE 13

LATIN AMERICA, 1977: COMMODITY COMPOSITION OF MANUFACTURED EXPORTS

(as % of total manufactured exports by each of the countries shown)

	Chemicals	Textiles	Clothing	Footwear	Iron and Steel	Transport Equipment	Electrical Machinery	Nonelectrical Machinery	Others
Large exporters of manufactured goods									
Argentina	11.3	9.9	3.9	3.8	7.6	13.0	7.6	17.4	26.0
Brazil	13.0	3.7	6.2	1.6	6.0	15.0	3.5	16.1	34.9
Mexico	6.0	12.5	3.3	5.7	8.6	14.6	9.9	21.0	18.4
	23.1	9.8	2.5	1.2	6.9	5.4	5.9	9.6	35.6
Medium-sized economies									
Colombia	15.3	12.5	5.3	—	2.3	5.5	1.5	4.1	53.5
Chile	11.5	18.2	10.8	—	—	3.4	1.9	5.9	48.3
Peru	21.3	—	—	—	5.9	2.7	1.4	3.3	65.4
	11.8	27.9	—	—	—	21.8	—	—	78.5
Oil-exporting countries	60.1	2.0	1.9	—	3.7	1.4	1.0	2.9	27.0
Others	36.9	10.9	8.5	2.4	6.1	1.1	4.0	1.1	30.5
Latin America	19.5	10.1	5.0	2.9	6.6	9.0	5.9	11.7	30.0

Source: United Nations, Yearbook of International Trade Statistics (New York, 1980), passim.

over 20 percent against the dollar (because of macroeconomic management problems caused by very high inflation rates and large capital inflows), the GSP-erosion effects of the Tokyo Round do not appear
menacing.[11] In fact, the impact of the five-year phased tarriff reductions
included in the Tokyo agreements could have been countervailed by not-
too-large real exchange rate devaluations.

The Tokyo Round negotiations concerning codes of conduct regulating the application of nontariff barriers were of much greater relevance to
U.S.–Latin American trade relations.[12] The outcome of these talks effectively hurt Latin American trade for at least two reasons. First, preferential treatment for developing countries in those clauses regulating the use
of export subsidies and the application of countervailing duties (such as
longer periods over which to spread the abolition of subsidies, and lighter
countervailing duties) was granted in exchange for the concept of "graduation" or the "enabling clause" among GATT rules. This clause pre-
scribes that preferential treatment conceded to any country is temporary
and conditioned on the members' judgment regarding its stage of development. The introduction of this clause in the agreement was the result of
pressure by U.S. negotiators at Tokyo. It was the price paid by developing countries for the formal acceptance by the GATT of discriminatory
treatment in their favor. Needless to say, the logic and fairness of this
two-tiered classification in a world in which only five countries account
for over 50 percent of world non-oil exports have been strongly criticized
in Latin America, especially in the larger countries.[13]

Second, the price paid by the Carter administration to have the Tokyo
agreements approved by the U.S. Congress was to allow the authority to
implement U.S. trade policy to be "shifted from the relatively free-trade
oriented Treasury Department to the Commerce Department."[14] This
change may be of significance because the Tokyo negotiations left considerable room for discretionary nontariff barriers to be erected against
developing country exports to the United States after they failed to reach
an agreement on a code of conduct concerning the sensitive issue of
safeguards against disruptive imports. Thus Latin American exporters are
still liable to arbitrary exclusion from U.S. markets for products that, as
indicated above, are of particular interest to their future trade growth.

On occasion, some country or product may receive special treatment
for international or domestic political reasons.[15] However, the bargaining power of the adversely affected country in orderly marketing agreements with the U.S. government is usually quite low. Moreover, as
latecomers, the large Latin American exporters usually face markets
already regulated by safeguards erected against the Asian newly industrializing countries.

TABLE 14

INDICATORS OF U. S. TRADE BARRIERS AGAINST LATIN AMERICA[a]

	Value of Total Imports (US$ millions)	Imports Subject to Most-Favored-Nation Treatment		Imports Under Generalized System of Preferences (GSP)		Value of Imports Subject to Nontariff Barriers (US$ millions)	
		Value (US$ millions)	Weighted Average Tariff Rate	Value (US$ million)	Weighted Average Tariff Rate	Export Restraints	Licensing plus Quotas
All Goods							
Latin America[b]	17,999	15,853	2.2	1,767	0.0	382	7,922
Non-oil-exporting countries[c]	10,465	6,558	4.1	1,731	0.0	377	1,497
Major exporters of manufactured goods[d]	5,402	4,080	5.2	1,322	0.0	255	765
Primary Products							
Latin America	14,592	13,611	1.4	978	0.0	20	7,922
Non-oil-exporting countries	5,388	4,327	2.7	958	0.0	19	1,497
Major exporters of manufactured goods	2,882	2,269	3.7	613	0.0	16	765

Manufactured Goods						
Latin America	3,407	2,242	7.4	789	0.0	362	0
Non-oil-exporting countries	3,281	1,773	9.3	774	0.0	359	0
Major exporters of manufactured goods	2,521	1,811	7.1	709	0.0	239	0

Source: Computed from Alexander J. Yeats, *Trade Barriers Facing Developing Countries: Commercial Policy Measures and Shipping* (London: Macmillan, 1979), pp. 216–20.

a. Compiled using 1974 trade data and 1977 trade regime.

b. Includes Argentina, Bahamas, Brazil, Chile, Colombia, Costa Rica, Dominican Republic, El Salvador, Guatemala, Haiti, Honduras, Jamaica, Mexico, Netherlands Antilles, Peru, Trinidad and Tobago, and Venezuela.

c. Latin America, excluding Venezuela, Trinidad and Tobago, Bahamas, and Netherlands Antilles.

d. Brazil, Argentina, and Mexico.

TABLE 15

U.S. MOST-FAVORED-NATION (MFN) TARIFF INCIDENCE ON LATIN
AMERICAN EXPORTS

(in % of total exports of each of the country groups shown)

	Free	Low	Medium	High
Major exporters of manufactured goods	40.9	28.5	21.8	8.1
Oil-exporting countries	7.7	92.2	—	—
Non-oil-exporting countries	50.0	40.9	4.3	4.5
Total	22.7	68.3	6.2	2.8

Source: United Nations Conference on Trade and Development, *Handbook of International Trade and Development Statistics* (New York, 1979), table 7.3.

Note: Country classification as in table 14.

Long-Standing Issues Concerning Trade in Primary Products

New U.S. protectionist measures are of interest to Latin America mainly because of their effect on exports of manufactured products. However, despite the progressive export-diversification experienced by Latin American countries in the recent past, conditions affecting trade in primary products are still of even greater concern to them. This is the case not just because of the greater size of these countries' trade in commodities but also because of a few products' continuing importance to their export bills (see table 16).

Setting aside the controversial issues related to long-term trends in commodity terms of trade (which occupied a substantial part of post-World War II economic literature), Latin Americans have traditionally emphasized two factors that adversely affect the performance of the region's primary exports. The first is the level and structure of the tariffs applied by industrialized countries to crude and semiprocessed food and raw materials. The second (not strictly related to trade policy but, nevertheless, of utmost importance to Latin America) is the great instability of foreign exchange earnings to which primary producers are frequently subject as a consequence of fluctuations in commodity prices.

Industrialized country tariffs on primary products have been criticized mainly for their progressive escalation against items with higher degrees of processing. This characteristic of the tariff structure of industrialized countries can be detrimental to primary exporters for both static and dynamic reasons. On the one hand, this system may affect the distribution of value-added in the chain of food and raw-materials processing between trade partners, as well as developing countries' potential foreign exchange earnings. The latter can be substantial. According to an UNCTAD study, adding one stage of processing to a group of ten basic raw products before export would have brought an additional $27 billion in gross export earnings to developing countries in 1975—about 25 percent of non-OPEC developing countries' total exports in that year.[16] On the other hand, more extensive elaboration of primary products could give a sizable push toward industrialization in more backward areas without provoking the allocational distortions that have occurred in more closed and inward-looking post-World War II industrialization experiments.

In assessing the effects of tariff escalation on primary exports, both nominal and effective rates of protection should be considered. The latter take into account the fact that nominal tariff rates are poor indicators of the impact of protection in industries relying heavily on dutiable imported inputs. They measure the effect of protection on value-added per unit of output in the importing country's affected industry. Effective protection is thus a better indicator of how the tariff structure of industrialized countries affects resource allocation in the processing of crude materials on a world scale.

Table 17 provides some indication of the effects of the post-Kennedy-round U.S. tariff structure on primary products at different stages along the processing chain for a sample of twenty-one major non-oil commodities.[17] It shows that although nominal U.S. rates are not high—indeed, except for Stage 1 goods, they are lower than those charged on average by the EEC and Japan—they do escalate against more elaborated products, and that effective rates of protection at the more advanced stages of processing can be two or almost three times higher than nominal rates because of higher value-added coefficients at those stages. If one considers that by the mid-1970s, 73.5 percent of Latin American non-oil exports to OECD countries were composed of Stage 1 commodities,[18] the effect of the U.S. tariff structure on Latin American trade may be perverse, because the United States absorbs almost 40 percent of the region's food and raw-materials exports to OECD countries.

For more elaborated products, the problem of tariff escalation is closely tied to the more sensitive issues concerning nontariff barriers discussed above. In this sense, Latin American trade in primary products could gain considerably from a general liberalization of trade. Estimates of the effects of a 50 percent across-the-board cut in tariffs and quantifiable nontariff barriers on OECD agricultural imports alone, from a sample of fifty-seven developing countries, indicate that it would cause a 5 percent increase in *total* exports for the six Latin American countries included in the sample. These estimates also show that these Latin American countries would reap over half of the resulting increase in world agricultural exports.[19]

Frequent and violent commodity price fluctuations are another factor hampering Latin America's export performance and the benefits the re-

TABLE 16

EXPORT DIVERSIFICATION INDICATORS FOR SELECTED LATIN AMERICAN AND INDUSTRIALIZED COUNTRIES

	Diversification Index[a]					Number of Commodities Exported[b]		Product Concentration 1977[c]
	1962	1968	1972	1976	1978	1968	1978	
United States	.349	.335	.335	.394	.359	179	179	—
Federal Republic of Germany	.439	.355	.315	.376	.324	177	179	—
Japan	.548	.453	.423	.502	.464	165	165	—
Latin America								
Brazil	.806	.758	.682	.667	.586	123	154	39.2
Argentina	.805	.766	.762	.686	.669	129	155	26.6
Mexico	.690	.663	.537	.542	.549	136	146	40.3
Colombia	.831	.767	.715	.742	.758	90	110	70.7
Chile	.868	.863	.864	.861	.812	61	113	59.4
Uruguay	NA	.915	NA	.795	.778	25	94	48.0
Peru	.831	.867	.933	.892	.825	53	96	45.1
Ecuador	.913	.915	.951	.783	.771	26	53	78.4
Guatemala	.893	.734	.723	.760	.769	91	99	64.7
Nicaragua	.879	.795	.745	.774	.776	71	90	61.9
Costa Rica	.931	.750	.769	.763	.756	78	95	64.1

Paraguay	.903	.882	.885	.902	.919	26	33	60.8
Panama	.915	.886	.882	.856	.832	26	50	66.7
Trinidad and Tobago	.853	.820	.811	.759	.775	74	82	93.2
Dominican Republic	.912	.882	.910	.900	.900	36	63	70.5
El Salvador	.866	.728	.738	.778	.753	86	91	74.3
Honduras	.873	.793	.846	.848	.855	60	60	68.3
Bolivia	.926	.893	.923	.764	.824	20	37	69.0
Venezuela	NA	.882	NA	.790	.807	61	82	94.9

Sources: 1962 and 1972 data are from Alexander J. Yeats, *Trade Barriers Facing Developing Countries: Commercial Policy and Shipping* (London: Macmillan, 1979), pp. 43–44. All other data are from United Nations Conference on Trade and Development, *Handbook of International Trade and Development Statistics* (New York, 1980), table 4.3D, and *Supplement* (1981), table 4.5.

NA = Not Available

a. Absolute deviation of country shares from world trade structure as follows:

$$S_j = \frac{\sum_i (h_{ij} - h_i)}{2},$$

where h_{ij} is the share of commodity i in total exports of country j, and h_i is the share of commodity i in total world exports. The index ranges from 0 to 1, with the latter representing maximum commodity concentration. For some countries, the fourth year reported is 1975.

b. Number of products exported at the SITC three-digit level (182 products). This figure includes only those products that accounted for more than 0.3 percent of the country's total exports *or* that exceeded US$ 50,000 in 1968 and US$ 80,000 in 1979.

c. Share of three leading products (at the SITC three-digit level) in total exports, in percent.

TABLE 17
POST-KENNEDY ROUND U.S. PROTECTION
AGAINST CRUDE AND PROCESSED RAW
MATERIALS

Degree of Processing	Nominal Rate	Effective Rate
Stage 1	3.9	3.9
Stage 2	7.3	14.7
Stage 3	7.6	20.6

Source: Alexander J. Yeats, *Trade Barriers Facing Developing Countries: Commercial Policy and Shipping* (London: Macmillan, 1979), pp. 83 and 89.
Note: Degree of processing rises from Stage 1 to 3. Of the 21 products included in the sample, only 7 had less than 3 identifiable stages.

gion derives from trade in primary goods. The usual policies aimed at minimizing the short- and medium-term effects of such fluctuations are either direct buffer-stock stabilization schemes or the operation of special funds to compensate countries for their effect on export earnings. Large-scale commodity stabilization programs date back to the Brazilian coffee valorization scheme of 1907. Since then they have been applied with varying degrees of success to certain primary products by individual producing countries or, more commonly since World War II, through international commodity agreements involving both producers and consumers. At least a formal international consensus on the far-reaching consequences of the problem of commodity price instability was achieved when this concern was explicitly included among the leading issues in the report approved at the first UNCTAD session in 1964, which called for a world trade system more responsive to developing country needs.

Although the accelerated recovery of primary-product prices that followed UNCTAD's 1964 conference somewhat eroded developing countries' enthusiasm for ad hoc international action promoting stabilization, tremendous post-1974 commodity price instability revived the issue at the 1976 UNCTAD meeting in Nairobi, which passed a resolution creating the Integrated Programme for Commodities (IPC). The main objective of the Programme was to stabilize the prices of eighteen primary products (with special attention to ten "core" commodities) through buffer stock management and other auxiliary devices. Its basic difference with respect to existing international commodity agreements was its broader product coverage and the overall reduction of financial needs and risks resulting from greater product diversification.

Negotiations concerning the operational details of the common fund to finance stockpiling and, especially, the political issues related to the amounts, country distribution of contributions to the fund, and voting rights in the management of the Programme dragged on after the first working committee met in March 1977. Agreement was eventually reached at the end of 1979 on the size of the fund, but at levels clearly insufficient to be effective.

There is still some academic debate concerning the magnitude of financing needed to achieve effective primary-product price stability and the benefits to be derived from it—especially whether there is a trade-off between an increase in producers' revenues and price stability. However, there is some evidence that an effectively implemented IPC could be of great significance to Latin America, which between 1975 and 1979 was responsible for 26.3 percent of world exports of the ten core commodities it covers.[20] In fact, recent simulations of an UNCTAD-type integrated scheme for six commodities of particular interest to Latin America over a thirteen-year period show that, provided there are adequate financial resources and buffer stocks to keep fluctuations within a 15 percent band around 1950–1975 price trends, the discounted value of export revenue gains for Latin American producers would be about $4.5 billion—some 16 percent of yearly average exports between 1970 and 1975.[21]

Although potential gains to Latin American primary exporters are not negligible, the major benefit of commodity price stabilization to both exporters and importers would come from stability itself. As far as exporters are concerned, the main benefit would result from the possibility of dampening balance-of-payments fluctuations and their negative effect on macroeconomic stability. In the case of Latin America, where minerals and tree crops (products with longer investment leads and larger proportions of fixed costs to total costs) account for a large share of total commodity exports, one could argue on a priori grounds that such a change would be particularly beneficial. In fact, this may explain why commodity price stabilization has traditionally ranked high among regional priorities and why Latin Americans have usually played a leading role in the organization of international commodity agreements.

It might be argued that these benefits could be achieved directly by export-earnings stabilization funds. Indeed, industrialized countries seem to favor this approach; witness the drawings allowed by the International Monetary Fund under the Compensatory Financing Facility or the European Economic Community's STABEX fund, which is open to less-developed former European territories. However, access to these funds usually occurs post factum, which of course does not prevent price fluctuations from occurring. In contrast, successful commodity-price stabilization prevents violent price explosions and can have important additional benefits in terms of global macroeconomic stability. The international experience of the past ten years has shown that the cost-induced impact of sudden upsurges in primary-product prices on industrialized countries' price levels triggered nonaccommodating adjustment policies that, through their depressive impact on aggregate demand for commodities, caused the spectacular price collapses of 1974–1975 and 1981–1982.[22] These developments had grave consequences for world economic stability.[23]

Medium-Term Policy Choices and Urgent Needs

The two preceding sections showed that two broad trends influence the context of contemporary U.S.–Latin American trade relations. The first is the irreversible tendency toward greater trade diversification and the increasing participation of manufactured and semimanufactured goods in Latin American exports, resulting from the post-World War II structural changes undergone by several national economies and spurred by these economies' growing internationalization since the mid-1960s. The second trend, which ultimately results from the decreased complementarity between the U.S. and Latin American economies and which accompanied the above-mentioned processes, is the clear shift in U.S. trade policy toward greater protectionism in recent years.

However, it is unlikely that the conflicts that inevitably arise from these trends can be resolved within the framework of bilateral negotiations. These conflicts are not a special feature of Latin America's economic relations with the United States; rather, they are one aspect of a much broader problem involving all the world's major trading areas. Moreover, the continuous decline in U.S. world economic hegemony since World War II has eroded the United States' political power to enforce a genuinely liberal world trading system as well as its will to move alone in this direction.

Therefore, from a Latin American perspective, a realistic dialogue with the United States on trade issues should begin by defining how U.S. action in international organizations could be conducive to better prospects for Latin American trade. The U.S. position at the GATT can have decisive influence on the future of Latin American trade, given the urgent need to remove barriers now encumbering the growth of the region's manufactured and semimanufactured exports. The U.S. position regarding negotiations on the elaboration of a special code to prevent disruptive imports is especially important. This is the area in which conflict is most certain to arise because, in the end, these issues involve a painful and lengthy adjustment in the productive structures of mature industrialized economies. However, because in the future the United States is bound to continue to face competition from ever more complex manufactured products (as forcefully argued in the Watkins and Karlik study for the U.S.

Congress Joint Economic Committee), and because present U.S. trade barriers overtly penalize the most successful exporters, the unfairness and inefficiency of these barriers must be faced squarely.[24]

The most promising negotiated approach toward freer trade in "sensitive" products seems to be long-term arrangements providing for progressive trade liberalization in areas in which existing barriers prove to be most detrimental to the growth of Latin American exports. The gains from negotiated long-term arrangements are many, including longer periods over which to spread adjustment in the United States and a correct signaling of export opportunities to Latin American countries. Moreover, this targeted liberalization could be negotiated, either collectively or by individual countries, in contrast to the phasing-out of present preferential treatment conceded to Latin America under the GSP or in the GATT's countervailing duties code.[25] If this negotiating strategy is pursued, the choice of products and the speed with which subsidies are to be withdrawn would be of importance to Latin America because of the danger of trade diversion to other competitors, especially in some light manufactured goods such as textiles and clothing.

The other area in which a more sympathetic U.S. approach to Latin American trade problems could bring lasting benefits is in negotiations concerning the implementation of UNCTAD's commodity price stabilization program. The United States has up to now been at the forefront of opposition to the effective implementation of the scheme, even though the benefits that would accrue to both Latin America and the world economy from the operation of the IPC appear to be substantial.

It should be noted that better market access for Latin American exports of manufactured goods and the expected benefits from commodity-price stabilization—although undeniably important from a long-term perspective—are not nearly as important for Latin America's immediate trade prospects as the urgent need to reverse both the recession in world trade visible since 1981 and the more recent contraction in the flow of long-term capital to the region. The domestic macroeconomic effects of the recessive balance-of-payments adjustment policies now being implemented in response to these adverse exogenous shocks are truly alarming. Latin America's per capita income fell more than 5 percent in 1983, after having declined more than 3 percent in 1982. This situation is unprecedented in the region's post-World War II history, and it is a source of increasing social and political tension.

In conclusion, it should be stressed that restoring growth in world trade and averting trade conflicts are not unrelated issues. The adjustment required in industrialized countries to minimize present conflicts with developing country exporters and the reforms needed to impart greater stability to commodity markets would be substantially eased in an environment of sustained global trade growth. However, the restoration of Latin American trade growth to a large extent also presupposes solving the financial difficulties faced by several countries in the region, especially the larger ones. The severe adjustment problems created by the sharp recent decline in international long-term bank loans to Latin American countries, superimposed on a world trade recession, led to the generalized adoption of extremely severe deflationary adjustment policies that are bound to affect substantially the growth of intraregional trade.

The reversal of present trends in world trade and financial markets is thus an urgent necessity if Latin American countries' ability to continue policies leading to greater integration into the world economy is to be preserved. To help achieve this goal is a direct challenge both to the United States and to the multilateral institutions governing global economic cooperation that the United States decisively helped to shape in the post-World War II period.

Departamento de Economía
Pontifícia Universidade Católica do Rio de Janeiro
Rio de Janeiro, Brazil

Notes

The author gratefully acknowledges the comments made by participants in the January 1983 Inter-American Dialogue Workshop, as well as the research assistance received from Beny Parnes, Demosthenes M. do Pinho Netto, and Renata de La Rovere. The reader should be aware that this essay makes no reference to Cuba, given the long-lasting embargo imposed on its trade with the United States.

1. International Monetary Fund, *Direction of Trade Yearbook* (Washington, D.C., 1980), pp. 62–63.

2. General Agreement on Tariffs and Trade, *Networks of World Trade by Areas and Commodity Classes: 1955–1976*, GATT Studies in International Trade, No. 6 (Geneva, 1978), table A.6.

3. Inter-American Development Bank, *Economic and Social Progress in Latin America: The External Sector* (Washington, D.C., 1982), p. 134.

4 These include the United States, the United Kingdom, West Germany, Japan, France, the Netherlands, Belgium, and Sweden; see United Nations Economic Commission for Latin America, *América Latina en el umbral de los años 80*, Doc. E/CEPAL/G. 1106 (Santiago, 1979), p. 121.

5. Albert Fishlow, Jean Carriere, and Sueo Sekiguchi, *Trade in Manufactured Products with Developing Countries: Reinforcing North-South Partnership*, Report of the Trilateral Task Force on North-South Trade of the Trilateral Commission, The Triangle Papers No. 21 (New York, 1981), p. 19.

6. J. M. Finger, "The Industry-Country Incidence of 'Less than Fair Value' Cases in U.S. Import Trade," in Werner Baer and Malcolm Gillis, eds., *Export Diversification and the New Protectionism: The Experiences of Latin America* (Champaign: National Bureau of Economic Research and University of Illinois Press, 1981), p. 265.

7. Organization of American States, *Presiones proteccionistas en los Estados Unidos que afectan a los países de América Latina* (Washington, D.C., 1978), p. 2.

8. Organization of American States, *Generalized Systems of Preferences of the U.S. in 1979,* Doc. CIES/CECON/175 (Washington, D.C., 1980), quoted in Rachel McCulloch, "Gains to Latin America from Trade Liberalization in Developed and Developing Countries," in Baer and Gillis, eds., *Export Diversification and the New Protectionism,* p. 243.

9. R. E. Baldwin and T. Murray, "MFN Tariff Reductions and Developing Country Trade Benefits Under the GSP," *Economic Journal* 87 (March 1977): 39.

10. See, for instance, United Nations Conference on Trade and Development, *Operation and Effects of the Generalized System of Preferences,* Doc. TD/B/C.5/15 (New York, 1974).

11. The data on Latin American exchange rates are from Inter-American Development Bank, *Economic and Social Progress in Latin America: The External Sector* (Washington, D.C., 1982), p.44.

12. For example, until 1979 the U.S. government was not bound to prove that grave injury was inflicted on a domestic industry before taking retaliatory action under the 1974 Trade Act.

13. See, for example, Roberto Abdenur and Ronaldo Sardenberg, "Notas sobre las relaciones Norte-Sur y el Informe Brandt," in *Estudios Internacionales* 14, No. 54 (April–June 1982): 166–200.

14. Rachel McCulloch, "Gains to Latin America from Trade Liberalization in Developed and Developing Nations," in Baer and Gillis, eds., *Export Diversification and the New Protectionism,* p. 245.

15. A good example of this special treatment is the restriction the United States applied in 1977 to footwear imports from South Korea and Taiwan. In 1981, with expiration due, the International Trade Commission recommended extension of these quotas for only two years and for Taiwan alone. However, despite "pressure for harsher limits by Congressional representatives from affected districts, the Reagan Administration has gone further and allowed the quotas to lapse. . . . South Korea and Taiwan figure importantly in the national security strategy of the Administration, the more so because of continuing ties to China. The New England region most affected by shoe imports is also heavily Democrat, unlike the textile South." Fishlow et al., *Trade in Manufactured Products,* p. 54.

16. United Nations Conference on Trade and Development, *The Processing Before Export of Primary Commodities: Areas for Further International Cooperation* (Geneva, 1978), p. 14. The products included in the list are cotton, coffee, cocoa, natural rubber, jute, tropical woods, leather, copper, bauxite, and phosphates.

17. Of course, the Tokyo Round negotiations slightly affected these values.

For an estimate of overall OECD effects, see Fishlow et al., *Trade in Manufactured Products,* p. 61.

18. United Nations Economic Commission for Latin America, *América Latina en el umbral de los años 80,* p. 37. This figure is based on a sample of the seventeen chief primary exports of Argentina, Barbados, Brazil, Colombia, Costa Rica, Guatemala, Guyana, Honduras, Mexico, Trinidad and Tobago, and Venezuela.

19. Alberto Valdes, "Trade Liberalization in Agricultural Commodities and the Potential Foreign Exchange Benefits to Developing Countries," (International Food Policy Research Institute, February 1979), quoted in McCulloch, "Gains to Latin America," p. 251.

20. United Nations Conference on Trade and Development, *Handbook of International Trade and Development Statistics, Supplement* (New York, 1981), p. 220.

21. Jere R. Behrman, *International Commodity Agreements: An Evaluation of the UNCTAD Integrated Commodity Programme* (Washington, D.C.: Overseas Development Council, 1977).

22. The effects of commodity price instability on industrialized country price levels are not negligible. According to one estimate, 45 percent of the 1973 rise in the U.S. consumer price index occurred as a result of large non-oil commodity price increases above trend values. Moreover, because of the downward inflexibility of industrial prices, these inflationary upsurges—induced directly or indirectly by food and raw-material price explosions—can have a significant permanent "ratchet" effect. On this point see Joel Popkin, *Commodity Prices and the U.S. Price Level,* Brookings Papers on Economic Activity 1 (Washington, D.C.: Brookings Institution, 1974).

23. For a fuller discussion of the propagation mechanisms implicit in the preceding argument, see Nicholas Kaldor, "Inflation and Recession in the World Economy," *Economic Journal* 86 (December 1976): 703–14; Lance Taylor, "Back to Basics: Theory for the Rethoric in the North-South Round," *World Development* 10, No. 4 (April 1982): 327–35.

24. Stephen B. Watkins and J. R. Karlik, *Anticipating Disruptive Imports* (Washington, D.C.: U.S. Government Printing Office, 1978), *passim.*

25. In more general terms, this proposal has been presented in McCulloch, "Gains to Latin America."

7

Growing Trade and Growing Conflict Between Latin America and the United States

John S. Odell

Disputes between the governments of Latin American countries and the United States over international trade have become much more frequent and more intense since the 1960s. At the same time, however, the United States and Latin America have also increased their cooperation through trade in some important respects. The economic-crisis years of 1982 and 1983 badly squeezed hemispheric commerce, but U.S.–Latin American trade rebounded in 1984. An analytical review of this experience suggests several reasons for these changes and some factors that will determine the future course of trade relations between Latin America and the United States.

Growing Conflict Over Trade

There were some U.S.–Latin American trade conflicts before 1970. Most Latin American leaders were suspicious of free-trade theories emanating from the United States after World War II. It was obvious, in their view, that free competition between large, technologically advanced companies from industrialized countries and young, weak industries in Latin America would simply permit the former to devour the latter. Students of history knew that England had practiced protectionism for the first eighty years of its own industrial development, before attaining a dominant world position and then advocating free competition. The United States had clung to strong protection even longer; indeed, it was only after World War II that the United States felt comfortable enough to begin to lower its own tariff barriers. To many Latin Americans it seemed likely then (and still does today) that such free-trade advice was offered not honestly but as a device of U.S. business for undermining potential new foreign competitors and thereby promoting its own interests.

As a result, Latin American governments were often critical of the

U.S. emphasis on free markets and trade liberalization. They attempted (generally in vain) to persuade the United States to support the formation of international commodity organizations in order to improve their terms of trade. Raúl Prebisch of the United Nations Economic Commission for Latin America (ECLA) argued that developing countries' terms of trade tend to deteriorate steadily over the long run. During the 1950s, prices of several Latin American commodities did trend downward, putting pressure on copper exporters such as Chile and coffee sellers in Brazil, Colombia, Mexico, and Central America.

From time to time U.S. restrictions on particular imports provoked protests from Latin American trading partners. Andean states were angered by U.S. quotas on lead and zinc imports in the late 1950s. In 1959 the United States raised quota barriers to Venezuelan oil, while at the same time exempting Canadian oil from this new restriction. Venezuela then helped found the Organization of Petroleum Exporting Countries (OPEC). Quotas and sanitary restrictions on meat imports have rankled Argentina for years. Developing countries also object to the "escalation" in the tariff structures of most industrialized countries, which discriminate against imports of raw materials in processed (as opposed to crude) form. During the 1960s the United States, after compelling Japan and Hong Kong to limit their cotton textile exports to the U.S. market, turned the same demands on Brazil, Mexico, and other Latin American countries. After some acrimony, they too complied. Finally, there was at least one conflict over U.S. export subsidies: Mexican cotton exporters protested U.S. subsidies to domestic cotton farmers during the 1950s.

The United States, on the other hand, was flush with monetary reserves during the early post-World War II period and enjoyed an overall export surplus every year until 1971. To the extent that U.S. officials were concerned with Latin America, the issues involved were generally matters of politics, investment, or aid, rather than trade. Some U.S. officials were frustrated by Latin American reluctance to join fully in their plans for a multilateral, free-trade world. Indeed, the trend in Latin America was toward higher protectionism at a time when the United States was lowering tariffs. Thus U.S. government leaders felt they were being generous in not raising tariffs against Latin America to the same degree. In 1966 U.S. producers of instant coffee protested Brazil's practice of charging a tax on green coffee exports to them while selling green coffee without the tax to Brazilian processors.

Many of the trade complaints before the 1970s had some validity. But in general they were isolated events during a period of rapid growth in world trade, at least in comparison with the post-1970 period.

U.S. Complaints Since 1970

After 1970 the United States began to devote somewhat more attention to Latin American trade policies. In 1972 coffee-exporting countries and the United States failed to agree on prices and quotas under the International Coffee Agreement, and so the Agreement's effective provisions lapsed. The United States felt that the exporters' price demands were excessive. Soon thereafter coffee prices climbed steeply. United States alarm and irritation touched off by the oil price increases of 1973–1974 were directed in part at Venezuela and Ecuador. These two countries were initially denied access to the benefits of the U.S. Generalized System of Preferences (GSP) for developing country products, which was enacted two years later. Both countries were finally admitted to GSP in 1980.

In 1974 U.S. companies and the U.S. government began to act against export subsidies by developing country governments. For decades U.S. law had allowed citizens to file complaints against foreign trade practices regarded as unfair, including government subsidies to exporters. Such subsidies are used by many countries, including the United States (most commonly on behalf of farmers). But the General Agreement on Tariffs and Trade (GATT) is hostile to subsidies (particularly for manufactured and semiprocessed goods), and international rules permit any importing country to impose countervailing duties to remove the presumed distortion of free competition if the imports cause or threaten injury to national industry. However, U.S. agencies had not imposed countervailing duties on imports from developing countries prior to 1974.

But beginning in the late 1960s, Brazil and other Latin American countries began more active export-promotion programs. During the same period a number of U.S. industries experienced stronger import competition, often much more from industries in other industrialized countries than from developing countries. Nonetheless, U.S. labor unions began to object strongly to the idea that highly competitive companies in countries such as Brazil should be considered deserving of official encouragement indefinitely. The U.S. government had entered into international agreements to fix or lower its tariffs, and so U.S. industries under pressure reached for other means to combat competition from imports.

In 1974 the U.S. footwear industry filed complaints against Brazilian and Argentine programs paying subsidies to shoe exporters. The U.S. Treasury demanded that the two governments rescind the subsidies or face a countervailing duty. Although the Latin American products had captured only a tiny share of the U.S. market, the outcome of these two cases foretold a pattern that was to spread in subsequent years. The

Brazilian Minister of Commerce and Industry denounced the shoe investigation as "an aggression," fearing that this was the beginning of a war on programs essential for national industrial development. International trade became a sensitive public issue. Brazil refused to rescind its subsidies, and the United States imposed a 5 percent countervailing duty. Argentina, illustrating the second type of response, complied with the U.S. demand to abolish its subsidy on shoe exports to the United States.

Since 1974 the U.S. government has decided that certain Latin American exports have benefited from net subsidies ranging in amount from zero to 77 percent of the products' values. These products have included leather goods other than shoes, as well as wool, textiles, clothing, iron, steel, scissors, ceramic tiles, and cut flowers. Before 1979 Washington assessed countervailing duties even when U.S. producers were not injured by the imports in question. In that year the United States agreed to assess duties only in cases of injury, but this concession was extended only to governments that accepted a new GATT code restricting the use of export subsidies. In Latin America only Brazil, Chile, and Uruguay had accepted this code as of August 1984. In addition, Venezuela, Paraguay, Honduras, and El Salvador benefited from this injury test by virtue of agreements in force prior to 1979. Mexico received the benefits of this provision in 1985 by making bilateral commitments to the United States to avoid export subsidies. Subsidized exports from other Latin American countries remained vulnerable to countervailing duties regardless of injury.

The number of antidumping complaints against Latin American producers also rose after 1970. "Dumping" is selling in a foreign market at a price lower than that charged for comparable products in the company's home market (with or without subsidies from its home government). International rules have long recognized dumping as another unfair trade practice justifying counteraction if it results in injury to producers. Historically, the U.S. government has dismissed most specific domestic requests for antidumping duties, either on the grounds that sales were not in fact taking place at "less than fair value" or because dumping did not cause injury to U.S. producers. Although the filing and investigation of a complaint often attract press attention, most such accusations are dismissed. In a celebrated 1980 case, the U.S. Department of Commerce held that Mexican winter vegetables were not being dumped. However, the United States did impose antidumping duties on Mexican sulphur in 1972, Chilean sodium nitrate in 1983, and certain steel products from Brazil in 1983 and 1984.

In the U.S. official view, antidumping and antisubsidy duties are not protectionism, in the sense of unjustified barriers to imports. They are regarded as enforcement of internationally recognized rules that are available to all countries. It is argued that, in the absence of action against violations of global rules, the politically likely alternative would be irresistible pressure for true, legislated protectionism. (Latin American responses to this argument are discussed below.)

How widespread have these U.S. administrative measures been? One recent study done in the United States examined the value of U.S. imports of products subject to antidumping and antisubsidy complaints during the period 1975–1979. Virtually all the targets were manufactured goods. Complaints were filed against only 0.8 percent of all manufactured imports from Latin America, and duties were actually imposed on only 0.4 percent of these imports.[1] Corresponding data for the subsequent period are not available.

During the multilateral Tokyo Round trade negotiations in 1978, the United States made an example of generous Brazilian subsidy programs, attempting to persuade Brazil that they were also a costly disincentive to efficiency in Brazil itself. The Brazilian government agreed to phase out its two most prominent subsidy programs by 1983, in exchange for U.S. agreement to apply an injury test in future complaints against Brazilian subsidies. In 1982 the United States complained that Brazil was reneging on this commitment, and frictions continued. The subsidies were eliminated in early 1985. The United States also objected to a new Uruguayan subsidy program as a violation of a similar commitment.

Until very recently the U.S. government and U.S. companies expressed far fewer complaints about access to Latin American markets than Latin Americans expressed about access to the U.S. market. This has been the case even though tariff rates are much higher, and quotas, licensing requirements, and exchange controls much more widespread, in Latin America. The reason may be that many U.S. companies have simply not been oriented toward exporting. But the U.S. government has already reacted to U.S. trade deficits by demanding more concessions from other countries, and the future is likely to bring more U.S. complaints concerning Latin American trade barriers.

There have also been frictions between the United States and Latin American countries over other specific practices. Latin American policies requiring companies to increase their purchases of local inputs and expand their exports will, if implemented, conflict with exports from other countries. The United States has protested such policies established in Mexico. The United States wanted Mexico to join the GATT, even if membership was accepted with many qualifications, and it was disappointed with President José López Portillo's 1980 decision not to join.

In recent years U.S. businesses and government officials have begun to press for reductions in foreign barriers to U.S. exports of services, such as construction, engineering, banking, insurance, air and sea transportation, motion pictures, and data processing. The United States is the world's strongest exporter of services, a sector in which trade has grown much faster over the last decade than total world trade. The United States has a large surplus in services trade. But U.S. firms are frustrated by many forms of restriction overseas, including outright prohibitions and quotas and discrimination in taxation, government procurement, and access to domestic facilities. Few international rules covering services trade have been negotiated, and U.S. negotiators have been promoting the idea of a major multilateral negotiation toward this end. Quite predictably, other states are much less enthusiastic. Developing countries, led by Brazil and India, have resisted this idea in the GATT.

Latin American Complaints Since 1970

Declining terms of trade have continued to aggravate many developing countries' economic problems. Terms of trade are defined as export prices divided by import prices. However, this is a complex issue. Apparent trends for a single country are highly sensitive to the points in time chosen for comparison, and countries' experiences vary sharply, depending upon which products they import and export. Table 1 shows trends for twenty-one western hemisphere countries using 1960, 1975, and 1980 as the observation points. The terms of trade for eight of these countries were higher in 1975 than in 1960; after 1975, four of these continued to rise while the other four slumped. Three other countries' terms of trade declined during 1960–1975 but recovered during 1975–1980. The remaining nine countries (including the United States) indeed saw their terms of trade deteriorate over the period 1960–1980. The most dramatic price change during this period—and the one with widest effects—was that of petroleum.

Another long-standing complaint by Latin American countries has been the typical deficit in their trade with the United States, which they have viewed as evidence that the overall trade relationship is unfair to them. Several countries in the region continue to make this argument. For several well-known reasons, a bilateral trade balance can be quite misleading as a guide in formulating policies. Country A's imbalance in trade with country B is often partially offset by country A's imbalances in the opposite direction with other trading partners. Furthermore, the overall trade balance is only one component of the balance of payments; a trade imbalance may be offset or magnified by payments for tourism, remittances by migrants, capital movements, debt service, and other items. Moreover, a trade imbalance alone is not an adequate measure of the distribution of welfare gains from trade between two countries. Nevertheless, trade deficits are quite relevant in politics. As a guide for explaining and predicting policies, they are not so misleading.

TABLE 1

TERMS OF TRADE OF WESTERN HEMISPHERE COUNTRIES
(1975=100)

	1960	*1975*	*1980*
Long-term increase			
Venezuela	46	100	160
Bolivia	56	100	159
Ecuador	89	100	147
Colombia	96	100	132
Rise and recent decline			
Dominican Republic	47	100	40
Jamaica	85	100	83
Peru	89	100	87
Mexico	97	100	94
Trinidad and Tobago	100	100	99
Decline and recent recovery			
El Salvador	109	100	110
Guatemala	126	100	113
Costa Rica	132	100	107
Long-term decrease			
Argentina	109	100	73
Nicaragua	112	100	92
Brazil	114	100	72
United States	115	100	82
Paraguay	116	100	76
Panama	117	100	77
Honduras	119	100	83
Chile	126	100	73
Uruguay	132	100	92

Source: World Bank, *World Development Report 1982,* table 8.

In any case, the recent U.S.–Latin American experience has been extremely mixed. Table 2 again shows the dangers of discussing international economic relations only in regional terms. During the period from 1979 to 1981, eleven Latin American states had deficits in their trade with the United States on average, while in fourteen other cases it was the United States that experienced the deficit. The largest deficits on the Latin American side (in proportion to the country's exports to the United States) were registered by Argentina, Barbados, Chile, Colombia, and Panama.

After 1981, severe debt-servicing problems forced many Latin American governments to slash imports and push exports even harder. The debt crisis helped reverse the aggregate hemispheric trade balance. What had been a 1981 U.S. surplus of $3 billion on merchandise trade with Latin

TABLE 2
LATIN AMERICAN BILATERAL BALANCES OF TRADE
WITH THE UNITED STATES, 1979–1981
(+ indicates average Latin American surplus, − indicates deficit)

	Average Imbalance (US$ millions)	Average Imbalance as Share of Average Exports to U.S. (%)
Argentina	−1,356	154
Bahamas	+1,106	74
Barbados	− 56	70
Bolivia	+ 32	16
Brazil	+ 214	5
Chile	− 667	118
Colombia	− 467	40
Costa Rica	− 5	1
Dominican Republic	+ 111	13
Ecuador	+ 184	18
El Salvador	+ 80	20
Guatemala	− 98	23
Guyana	+ 19	17
Haiti	− 23	9
Honduras	+ 128	27
Jamaica	+ 49	12
Mexico	−2,136	19
Nicaragua	+ 32	15
Panama	− 388	129
Paraguay	− 12	12
Peru	+ 200	15
Suriname	+ 21	14
Trinidad and Tobago	+1,505	72
Uruguay	− 36	29
Venezuela	+ 971	17

Source: International Monetary Fund, *Direction of Trade Statistics Yearbook 1982,* table for United States.

America became Latin American surpluses of $4.9 billion in 1982 and $16.4 billion in 1983.[2]

In the view of many Latin American countries, the 1970s brought an increasing tempo of specific new U.S. measures making their trade situation worse. The decade opened with a dispute between the United States and Mexico over access to the U.S. market for winter vegetables. Florida growers and the U.S. Department of Agriculture imposed restrictions on rising imports of Mexican tomatoes. In 1971 President Richard Nixon imposed a 10 percent duty surcharge on all dutiable U.S. imports during the exchange rate dispute with Japan and western Europe, provoking cries of outrage from Latin America. This surcharge was removed four months later after a realignment of major currencies had been negotiated. In 1974 the U.S. Congress refused to renew the traditional sugar program. This action meant the end of quota restrictions on access to the U.S. market, but sugar-exporting countries complained of being forced to compete without the preferential access to high prices they had secured under the quota program.

Passage of the U.S. Trade Act of 1974 also elicited strong criticism in Latin America. In this law the U.S. Congress authorized the President to negotiate further tariff reductions, and the United States belatedly adopted the GSP, allowing duty-free entry for imports from developing countries. But the GSP program was hedged with numerous limitations. Some of the products in the production of which Latin America has a comparative advantage (such as garments and shoes) were excluded outright. A "graduation" clause provided that preferential treatment on eligible products would be withdrawn from a particular country if its exports of that item to the U.S. market exceeded a certain value or a certain share of U.S. imports. Since 1974 the U.S. government has periodically added new products to the list and removed certain countries' exports of other items. The latter action has often provoked charges of protectionism.[3] Latin American countries were also disturbed by new provisions in the Trade Act giving the President wider authority to take administrative action against imports believed to be injurious to the U.S. economy.

The Trade Act of 1974 enabled the United States to participate in the multilateral trade negotiations that were concluded in 1979. Latin American analysts later expressed great disappointment with the results. They regarded the GATT negotiations as an exercise among the economically powerful for their own benefit and a continuation of an indefensible effort to impose rules on weaker countries that prevent them from becoming strong competitors. Developing countries demanded and received a general commitment to provide them with "special and differential treatment" in international trade. But Latin American representatives worried that tariff reductions in industrialized countries would in practice erode their preferences under the GSP.[4]

Latin American countries were equally disappointed with GATT negotiations regarding nontariff barriers. They viewed the new code on subsidies and countervailing measures as a prominent example of an effort by industrialized countries to dismantle key programs necessary for their development. Many Latin American countries saw the general "graduation" clause demanded by the United States and others—pressing countries at Brazil's level of economic development to forego their special treatment and abide by the same trade rules as the leading industrialized countries—as particularly one-sided and irritating.

A study done for ECLA later found that the United States imposed nontariff barriers on products whose 1976 imports were worth $2.9 billion, and that in the Tokyo Round the United States offered to modify nontariff barriers covering less than 10 percent of the affected imports.[5] Developing countries were keen for agreement on a new code regulating the increasing use of such "safeguard" measures to prevent their use against only selected exporters. Largely because of firm opposition from the European Economic Community (EEC), no agreement was reached on this question.

Nontariff barriers to U.S. imports of textiles and clothing have a particularly long history, and they began to affect Latin American companies in the 1960s. The United States has imposed such restrictions, and then lifted them after a few years, in the cases of Argentina, Barbados, Belize, Costa Rica, El Salvador, Honduras, Jamaica, Nicaragua, Peru, and Trinidad and Tobago. During the 1970s earlier restrictions were maintained against Brazil, and protection spread to exports of new textile products from Colombia, Haiti, Mexico, and the Dominican Republic. Restrictions were reimposed on Jamaica.[6] On the other hand, a number of Latin American and other countries have had trouble filling their textile and apparel quotas.[7]

The upsurge of U.S. administrative measures to restrict imports (including complaints about export subsidies) has led to nearly continuous frictions with Latin American exporters. Latin American defenders of export-subsidy policies maintain that economic development requires such actions, that the U.S. government has helped its own industries to further similar goals, and that in any case these policies are a matter of national sovereignty. Sophisticated analysts further note that Latin American exchange rate policies often discriminate against their own exports, so that financial subsidies to exporters should be viewed as compensation for this discrimination rather than as new distortions of free competition. Some also object that denying the injury test to countries that refuse to sign the subsidies code is discrimination inconsistent with the U.S. obligation under the GATT to give the same treatment to all GATT members.

Latin American countries suspect that the measurement of dumping and injury is subject to influence by powerful U.S. domestic groups, so that the technical, legal nature of the proceedings is more apparent than real. They note that in many cases the same industries that file such complaints about Latin American trade practices also apply for most other available protective measures against imports, thus ostensibly showing that the cause of these conflicts is not an increase in unfair export practices but a true increase in U.S. protectionism. Latin

American exporters view these measures as a form of harassment that can affect business even if the complaints are eventually dismissed by U.S. agencies. When products from a given country are under administrative review, U.S. buyers may well turn to other sources to reduce uncertainty.[8] In this sense, the importance of such actions cannot be measured adequately by the size of trade affected at the time of the complaint. More fundamentally, a climate of protectionist threat in the United States can deter Latin American investors from expanding production in both the industries affected and in other activities not yet attacked, thus suppressing future trade that would have arisen in the absence of the threat.

Two recent studies done in the United States also suggest that the U.S. market is less open than U.S. policymakers generally believe. United States leaders often argue that the U.S. market is one of the most open in the world. To support this position they cite the fact that imports of manufactured goods from developing countries have grown more rapidly in the United States than in other industrialized countries. However, William R. Cline has found that identifiable nontariff barriers affect as large a share of U.S. imports as they do imports of any of the major industrialized countries.[9] Another study examined the 100 leading South American export products to the United States. It found that in late 1982, fifty-seven of these products faced serious actual or potential access problems because of either high tariffs, removal of GSP benefits, other administrative measures, or possible protectionist legislation.[10]

In order to keep these examples of increasing conflict in perspective, it is important to note that western hemisphere governments have also continued to sign trade agreements. During the 1930s Latin American countries were among the first to reach bilateral agreements with the United States under the reciprocal-trade program. Fifteen Latin American countries are members, with the United States, of the multilateral GATT, and they have reached many more bilateral agreements within its framework. For example, thirteen Latin American countries concluded new pacts with the United States during the Tokyo Round negotiations in the 1970s. (The agreement between the United States and Mexico did not take effect because it was contingent upon Mexico's joining the GATT.) More recently, Latin American countries and the United States have established mutual arrangements regarding particular products. By mid-1984 twenty Central American and Caribbean countries had arranged to be designated beneficiaries of the United States' new Caribbean Basin Initiative. A central feature of this program is a U.S. grant of duty-free treatment for these countries' exports to the U.S. market (with specified product exceptions) for twelve years.

Growing Cooperation Through Trade

Despite the increase in official conflict over trade issues during the 1970s, the people of the Americas at the same time increased cooperation through trade. To be sure, import restrictions in both the United States and Latin America prevented trade in some sectors from reaching levels it would have attained otherwise. But some evidence indicates that the "new protectionism" of the 1970s had less effect on trade flows than is often supposed.

Consider the growth of Latin American exports to the United States between 1974 and 1981, as shown in table 3. During this period the world economy suffered from oil price increases, payments imbalances, exchange rate fluctuations, recessions, and rising protectionism. World export expansion slowed by half, in comparison with the boom of the preceding decade. Even so, Latin America as a whole increased the value of its exports to the United States by 117 percent, or by an annual average of 16.7 percent between 1974 and 1981. Of course, inflation eroded the purchasing power of the dollars earned through these exports (by an average of 9.9 percent per year if measured by the U.S. gross national product implicit price deflator). But clearly it would be inaccurate to think that real expansion of exports had been choked off.

However, this export growth did not represent much change in the aggregate Latin American share of the U.S. import market. The Latin American share of U.S. imports (excluding Venezuela) was 11.6 percent in 1974 and 11.8 percent in 1981. In contrast, developing countries in Asia and oil-exporting countries did increase their share of total U.S. imports. There was also little growth in Latin American penetration of the U.S. domestic market as a whole. Although Latin American exports rose by 117 percent, the U.S. gross national product grew 105 percent. Latin America managed to maintain its position as the U.S. economy expanded, but not much more.

Table 3 also shows that Latin American countries varied greatly in their export performances. Exports to the United States from Uruguay, Mexico, Honduras, Argentina, Panama, Brazil, Haiti, and Costa Rica boomed. However, exports from Bolivia, Colombia, El Salvador, Guatemala, and Jamaica essentially stagnated in real terms, and those of Nicaragua and Venezuela fluctuated downward in real terms.

During the same seven-year period, the United States increased its exports to Latin America by 165 percent, or by an annual average of 23.6 percent in nominal terms. The most rapid advances in U.S. exports were to Argentina, Mexico, Paraguay, and Chile. The slowest (or negative) growth took place in U.S. trade with El Salvador, Jamaica, Brazil, and Nicaragua. (Two appendices to this chapter show the leading products in

TABLE 3
GROWTH OF BILATERAL TRADE BETWEEN LATIN AMERICA AND THE
UNITED STATES
1974–1981 (in US$ millions)

	Latin American Exports to U.S.			U.S. Exports to Latin America		
	1974	*1981*	*Average Annual Change*	*1974*	*1981*	*Average Annual Change*
Argentina	409	1,214	28.1%	597	2,192	38.2%
Bahamas	1,025	1,306	3.9	253	441	10.6
Barbados	34	82	20.2	38	149	41.7
Bolivia	109	184	9.8	105	189	11.4
Brazil	1,825	4,852	23.7	3,089	3,798	3.3
Chile	329	661	14.4	452	1,465	32.0
Colombia	553	900	9.0	659	1,771	24.1
Costa Rica	183	426	19.0	232	373	8.7
Dominican Republic	504	977	13.4	410	772	12.6
Ecuador	509	1,103	16.7	326	854	23.1
El Salvador	171	270	8.3	202	308	7.5
Guatemala	226	384	10.0	240	559	19.0
Guyana	88	119	5.0	66	106	8.7
Haiti	120	287	19.9	125	301	20.1
Honduras	162	493	29.2	159	349	17.1
Jamaica	249	399	8.6	337	479	6.0
Mexico	3,610	14,013	41.2	4,855	17,789	38.1
Nicaragua	104	152	6.6	200	184	−1.1
Panama	117	329	25.9	364	844	18.8
Paraguay	23	52	18.0	30	108	37.1
Peru	651	1,277	13.7	647	1,486	18.5
Suriname	79	199	21.7	73	138	12.7
Trinidad and Tobago	1,361	2,269	9.5	192	688	36.9
Uruguay	18	165	116.7	42	163	41.2
Venezuela	5,014	5,800	2.2	1,768	5,445	29.7
Total	17,473	37,913	16.7	15,461	40,951	23.6

Source: International Monetary Fund, *Direction of Trade Statistics Yearbook, 1981* and *1982,* table for United States.

bilateral trade between the United States and Latin American countries in 1980.)

Trade in manufactured products is of particular interest to all governments. A recent study by the World Bank attempted to estimate the effects of protectionist measures by industrialized countries on developing countries' manufactured exports by examining the expansion of those exports and their shares in industrialized country markets from 1970 to 1980. Some of the results are surprising. Developing countries as a group increased their manufactured exports to the "North" by nearly 11 percent per year in real terms. This was accomplished partly by diversifying into new product markets, some of the most important of which are chemicals, metal products, and machinery (including electronic products). But the textile, apparel, and leather industries also managed to raise their export volumes by no less than 13 percent per year, despite the extent and expansion of protectionist measures directed at them. Equally interesting is the fact that East Asian developing countries—the targets of many of these protectionist measures—not only maintained but sharply increased their share of developing country manufactured exports. Southeast Asian exporters also made important gains in this regard. These relative gains came largely at the expense of Latin American countries, which lost ground in competition with other developing countries.[11]

The same World Bank study also examined developing countries' share of domestic consumption of manufactured goods in industrialized countries. In 1970 developing countries had penetrated only 1.7 percent of these markets (1.3 percent in the United States); by 1980 their share had increased to 3.4 percent (2.9 percent in the United States).[12] During the 1970s industrialized countries allowed imports from all sources to penetrate further into their economies, and penetration by developing countries was faster than the average. A handful of developing countries accounted for most of this gain; most countries have hardly participated. Market penetration of this kind would surely have been faster in the absence of any protectionist barriers. However, these results suggest that existing protection has left some room for trade expansion.

Even if two countries increase their cooperation through trade in comparison with the past, this does not mean that they necessarily increase the share of their trade that they conduct with each other rather than with third parties. In this sense the United States and Latin America have diversified away from each other to a limited extent, at least with respect to imports in Latin America. The U.S. share of aggregate Latin American imports fell from 42 percent in 1961–1963 to 33 percent in 1977–1979.[13] EEC countries have also lost much ground in Latin America. The sharpest relative gains have gone to the Middle East, reflecting petroleum price increases. But other Latin American exporters and Japan have also enlarged their shares of Latin American import spending.

In other respects, however, trade diversification does not seem to have been dramatic. Latin American exports as a whole shifted away from the United States, but only from 37 percent in the early 1960s to 35 percent of Latin American exports in the late 1970s. Brazil and many smaller Latin American countries did reduce their dependence on the U.S. market, but Argentina and Venezuela did not. Mexico and several island countries actually increased their trade dependence on the United

States during this period. In the aggregate, the main relative gain was in exports to other countries in the region, which rose from 8 to 16 percent of Latin American exports.[14] In the future, "South-South" trade may offer further attractive possibilities for expansion.[15]

Just as Latin America's reliance on the United States to purchase its exports has remained substantial in the aggregate, so too does the United States continue to send roughly the same share of its own exports to Latin America as it did in the early 1960s. The combined Latin American share of U.S. exports was 16 percent in 1961–1963 and fifteen percent in 1977–1979. The only major decline during this period was in the share going to Argentina (down from 1.5 to 0.8 percent); the only notable expansion involved Mexico, whose share of U.S. exports rose from 3.8 to 4.8 percent over this period.[16]

The United States remains far less dependent on trade with Latin America than vice versa, especially when specific bilateral trade patterns are considered. The bilateral disparity is enormous in cases such as Mexico, which relied on its northern neighbor to buy 68 percent of its exports in 1977–1979. Even Argentina, Chile, and Uruguay (which send between 8 and 14 percent of their exports to the U.S. market) are many times more dependent on the United States than vice versa. Although most Latin American countries have reduced their dependence on the United States as a source of imports and finance, the fundamental inequality remains large.

The Crisis Years 1982–1983

However one interprets the trade growth of the 1970s, it had come to a halt by 1982—a year of deep commercial and financial crisis in many parts of the world. The United States' gross national product declined by 1.9 percent in real terms, following two previous years of severe slump. Unemployment rose steadily, reaching 10.8 percent—the highest level since 1940—by the end of 1982. Trade and current-account imbalances worsened, and the trade deficit exceeded the largest in U.S history up until that time. However, the U.S. economy began to recover in 1983 and grew by 3.3 percent. This was accomplished despite a severe deterioration in the overall trade deficit (from $42.6 billion to a new record of $69.3 billion in 1983).

Domestic economic conditions were more severe still in Latin America during 1982–1983. Latin America was accustomed to substantial aggregate growth, but in 1982 the region suffered "its worst economic recession in the entire post-war period and probably the most serious since the years of the Great Depression," according to ECLA. For the first time in four decades, the region's overall gross domestic product declined (by 0.8 percent), and its gross domestic product per capita fell by more than 3 percent.[17] Unemployment soared, massive capital flight occurred, and new foreign lending fell off sharply as Latin American countries interrupted their debt repayment. Several Latin American countries (Argentina, Uruguay, Bolivia, Costa Rica, Guyana, and especially Chile) suffered economic declines in 1982 much worse than the regional average, while Panama managed to continue moderate growth. In contrast to the United States, the domestic situation in Latin America deteriorated much further in 1983. Aggregate gross domestic product declined another 3 percent in real terms as governments struggled to brake inflation and reduce external deficits. Bolivia, Guyana, and especially Peru experienced worse than average economic hardship during 1983, while economic conditions improved somewhat in Argentina, Jamaica, the Dominican Republic, and Nicaragua.[18]

Latin American exports to the United States declined with the U.S. economy in 1982, falling by 1.7 percent in nominal value. United States inflation during that year also reduced the purchasing power of the dollar by 6 percent. But as the U.S. economy recovered in 1983, Latin American exports to the U.S. market rebounded even more strongly, by 10.1 percent in nominal value. Several countries departed from this overall pattern, however. Mexico, Chile, Uruguay, Ecuador, El Salvador, and Haiti managed to expand their exports to the United States during both 1982 and 1983. In contrast, Argentina, Paraguay, Guyana, Trinidad and Tobago, and Jamaica sold far less to the U.S. market in 1983 than in 1982.[19]

The United States' export sales to Latin America suffered an almost unbroken decline during 1982–1983. United States exports were greater in nominal value in 1983 than in 1981 only to Trinidad and Tobago, Haiti, and El Salvador. During this period Latin America as a whole slashed its imports from the United States by no less than 40 percent.

Inter-American commerce improved sharply during 1984. Latin American exports to the United States increased in value by approximately 17 percent over 1983. During the first half of 1984 the United States absorbed about three-fourths of the increase in Latin America's exports to the world market. United States exports to Latin America also grew by about 14 percent in 1984.[20] However, several factors created uncertainty concerning future improvements in this area, including the world balance-of-oil supply and demand, fiscal deficits in the United States and the high value of the dollar, persistent inflation in Brazil and runaway inflation in Argentina, and pressures to change national trade policies.

Reasons for Trade Conflict in the 1970s and 1980s

To the extent that western hemisphere countries would benefit from an expansion of mutual trade, it is important to understand the causes of barriers and interstate conflicts that threaten trade expansion. These conflicts result in part from factors that can be changed, but in some measure they are caused by conditions that are not subject to much policy control. First, some degree of friction between the United States and Latin America on trade issues is rooted in true conflicts of national interest. If early industrialization requires protection and state subsidies, while more mature industries benefit from open world markets, then to some degree the stage is set for dispute even though two trading partners also may have other interests in common.

Second, the recent past has been a period of change in the distribution of world economic power. Power shifts of this kind are likely to produce frictions, at least during the transition period if not over a longer period of time. The United States' shares of world production and world exports have declined in the aggregate, although these shares are still large and even rising in some sectors. Some Latin American countries have improved their relative position considerably, but others (like the United States) have slipped back in world competition. When an industry first experiences stiff international competition, and therefore faces low profits and employment layoffs, it is likely to appeal to its government for trade protection, at least temporarily until the industry is either rejuvenated or left to its fate. Some international frictions may accompany shifts in international competitiveness simply as part of the transition, even if the most farsighted policy measures are taken.

Many of the United States' trade conflicts have arisen with Japan and other industrialized countries in the first instance, reflecting the rise of Japanese rather than Latin American industry. Yet once a domestic campaign to protect an industry is established and begins to persuade political leaders, there is a tendency to operate against all imports in that sector in order to frustrate efforts to circumvent the barriers.

Third, economic disputes are exacerbated by the presence of conflicting ideologies or long memories of past conflict, neither of which can be greatly influenced in the short run. If a laissez faire ideology is deeply held in Washington, while various more-statist visions of development are held with equal conviction in other capitals, then one should not be surprised to see periodic differences between countries over international economic exchanges, as long as the countries involved rely to some extent on world markets. Past conflicts have left Latin America suspicious about the United States, and some actors in the United States hold similar feelings regarding Latin American countries. These suspicions continue to affect contemporary trade relations.

But not all economic disputes represent genuine conflicts of national interest. Many stem from domestic politics, producing outcomes that on the whole are less than optimal for the countries involved. For example, the laws and institutions governing administrative regulation of trade in the United States provide remedies for U.S. producers seeking relief from import penetration. But some of these procedures do not authorize the agency in question to take into account the costs of protection for other U.S. interests—including those of consumers, other businesses, or U.S. foreign policy. In protecting the interests of one sector of society, administrative mechanisms can damage other U.S. interests and at the same time touch off an international dispute.[21]

Particular industries vary in their domestic political strength, which explains in part why there are more international trade frictions in some sectors than in others. In the United States, the sector with the greatest success in winning trade protection is the textile/apparel complex. But this well-known coalition of industries is unusual; its labor force is huge, dwarfing even that in automobiles or steel. As a result, it can muster widespread support in the U.S. House of Representatives that is capable of blocking even key bills of national concern. Even determined Presidents have found it difficult to avoid this roadblock.

Shoes and sugar provide contrasting examples. They show that anti-protectionist coalitions can also be organized and that these coalitions do not always lose. For years the U.S. footwear industry has suffered from equal or greater import penetration, unemployment, and firm closings than the textile/apparel complex. Yet U.S. trade policy has been much less protective of shoes. Protectionist bills have been introduced in Congress since the 1960s, but none has been approved. In the 1970s the International Trade Commission twice found that imports caused injury to the U.S. footwear industry, and it recommended steep increases in protection. But large retail companies and consumer organizations mounted a vigorous lobbying effort to oppose new import barriers, and the cabinets of Presidents Gerald Ford and Jimmy Carter were deeply split on the issue. Both Ford and Carter declined to implement the Commission's recommendations. The Carter administration negotiated four-year export restraints with South Korea and Taiwan, leaving Latin American and other exporters unaffected. In 1981 President Ronald Reagan rejected pleas to extend those two restraint measures. The U.S. shoe industry, although sizable in terms of employment, is only one-tenth the size of the textile/apparel complex. Its Washington lobby was slower to organize and is less well financed. Therefore its legislative support is less broad. Nonetheless, some form of nontariff shoe protection may be restored in the future, given that import penetration exceeds 70 percent of the domestic market.

The case of the U.S. sugar industry also shows that trade policies (and thus international trade relations) shift in response to changing domestic political conditions, which are in turn subject to some policy influence. The sugar industry in the United States is quite small, and yet for decades it was able to secure passage of quota restrictions on sugar imports. Imports have typically supplied about half of domestic sugar consumption. However, in 1974 the world sugar price shot up to extreme heights. Industrial users and consumer groups then organized a strong antiprotection coalition, headed by suburban members of Congress. Industrial users such as the Coca-Cola and Pepsico companies made electoral campaign contributions to offset those of sugar growers. Through the efforts of this coalition, the traditional quota program was dismantled, opening the U.S. market to free import competition. Since then, the world price has tumbled again, and the growers have succeeded in reestablishing a price-support program and import quotas.

Similarly, changing domestic political conditions in Latin American countries account for variations in international trade relations. Mexico's negotiations with the GATT are a clear example of this phenomenon. Mexican President José López Portillo proposed these negotiations in 1979, and an agreement was reached and initialed at the end of that year. The Mexican delegation made a number of tariff and other commitments, but it also rejected major concessions sought by GATT members. The agreed-upon protocol of accession thus contained broad loopholes. For example, Mexico reserved the right to protect its agriculture and to take whatever measures it felt were necessary to promote industrialization, including reimposition of some import quotas. As part of this agreement, the United States and other countries agreed to lower some tariffs on Mexican products.

President López Portillo then invited a broad, national debate on the GATT question. During this remarkable *consulta popular,* small- and medium-sized industry, academic analysts, and opposition political leaders organized vocal protests against the agreement. Other interests were in favor of adhering to the GATT, and a majority of the President's economic cabinet recommended ratification. But the most powerful ministries recommended against ratification.[22] In the end, López Portillo felt compelled to reject the agreement that he himself had initiated.

Domestic political processes in Latin America and in the United States have also produced industrial policies that are themselves additional fundamental determinants of international trade relations. Policies that facilitate a national economy's smooth adjustment to global changes reduce the incidence of interstate trade disputes. Yet many governments have in fact established industrial policies that retard international adjustment, or at best fail to encourage it. In the United States, current industrial policy is a combination of laissez faire rhetoric, actual reliance on market-driven adjustment to some extent, and a host of regulations and tax and spending programs that intervene in industry in many ways. These measures have been imposed at different times for many different reasons, and the lack of coordination among them results in some self-inflicted wounds. Market forces do move some capital and workers out of industries that are losing their international competitiveness and into other sectors. There have been isolated cases of successful comprehensive, coordinated adjustment. But the steel, textile, color television, and automobile industries have also sought and received import protection. In the United States (but not in all countries) protection is almost always granted without including conditions that require the industry involved to restructure itself or undertake specific measures to increase its competitiveness. Thus in many cases the industry's problem is not solved by protection. Similarly, the U.S. tax code promotes the mobility of capital, but it does not give companies incentives to retain their former employees or to help their surrounding communities to adjust to industry changes. Financial assistance and retraining programs for displaced workers have been notoriously ineffective in promoting adjustment. Predictably, then, workers in declining industries mount political campaigns for measures that will freeze the industrial structure—measures that often hurt industries abroad.

At the same time, the U.S. government has also spent enormous sums to promote the development of emerging industries, including semiconductors, communications equipment, advanced aircraft, and plastics. This spending is mostly administered by the Pentagon and the National Aeronautics and Space Administration according to military criteria, rather than to promote international commercial adjustment. Very little effort is made either to determine whether military and other industrial policies are consistent with each other or to improve their congruence. This hodgepodge of partly contradictory actions and inactions makes international trade conflicts more likely than is necessary.

Latin American industrial policies are also causes of international friction. Some of these tensions are probably unavoidable, but national industrial policies sometimes cause unnecessary problems for the country in question. For example, many developing countries have pursued urban industrialization as an end in itself, assuming that its benefits would trickle down to their poorest citizens, who tend to be subsistence farmers in the countryside. It is now widely acknowledged that policies such as these have in fact discriminated heavily against rural areas, leaving deep internal inequalities.

In addition, some of these countries have also encouraged the development of industries beyond their international comparative advantage. The result is that inefficient companies unable to compete in world markets must be subsidized indefinitely from strained national budgets, as well as by other domestic companies and consumers paying unnecessarily high prices. Inefficiency thus spreads through the economy. When governments are unable to resist pressures for excessive protection and fail to phase out such policies after industries leave infancy, then these governments risk avoidable conflicts with other countries. Too-hasty industrialization may bring costs both at home and abroad that exceed its benefits.[23]

Colombia and Mexico offer examples of Latin American industrial trade problems that are partly self-inflicted. A recent World Bank study tried to determine why Colombia had been so much less successful in exporting garments than Hong Kong, South Korea, and Taiwan. The investigation found that wages were not lower in East Asia, that government subsidies there were less than or equal to those in Colombia, that Colombia had an advantage in lower transportation costs, and that foreign quotas did not limit most categories of its garment exports.

But labor productivity was much lower in Colombia, a problem attributed especially to its factory managers. Another important price difference derived from the fact that East Asian clothing manufacturers had access to fabric at world prices, while Colombian competitors had to pay fabric prices 50 to 100 percent above world levels because Colombian fabric producers enjoyed high tariff protection. Buyers in the United States also complained that Colombian deliveries were less punctual and of less reliable quality than Asian exports. The study suggested that Colombian managers (with some exceptions) gave less attention to quality, punctuality, and productivity because they were accustomed to selling only on the domestic market, where they have been sheltered from foreign competition by government trade policy. Yet the Colombian government is also eager for exports. Colombia is quite representative of Latin America in this respect. Similar policies and problems would likely appear in studies of other countries and industries in the region. Indeed, many Latin American countries have been much less successful than Colombia at exporting manufactured goods.[24]

Mexico's industrial exports are much larger in volume than those of Colombia, although they remain much smaller in per capita terms than those of East Asia. Many of these Mexican goods are made in the northern border zone, where companies enjoy exemptions from some of the restrictions that prevail in most of Latin America. A World Bank team evaluated the efficiency of Mexican industry as a whole during a 1976 visit, finding that it compared fairly well with other large import-substituting developing countries but not so well with more open, specialized economies. They also found wide variations; for 13 percent of the products studied, the domestic prices charged were more than 50 percent above international levels.[25] This is part of the cost of protectionist industrial policy.

Finally, trade conflicts have been exacerbated by recession, balance-of-payments deficits, debt-servicing crises, and disequilibrium exchange rate policies in various countries. The recent international recession certainly intensified pressures for closing national markets. So too did the rise in the value of the U.S. dollar, even while U.S. trade and current-account balances were deteriorating. The rising dollar made imports more attractive in the United States and thus increased the pressure on the depressed economic sector—and thus on Congress. Exchange rate policies in Latin America have often put similar pressure on producers there, reinforcing their interest in protectionist trade measures.

Implications for Future Developments

This analysis offers some guides for the future. First, although conditions vary from sector to sector and from country to country, some generalizations are valid regarding future U.S.–Latin American trade relations. In the short run, countries suffering from rapid inflation will need to control it in order to lay a foundation for economic recovery and international trade negotiations. Exchange rate adjustments (in the United States and elsewhere) can be expected to make a positive contribution to this goal after a lag period. However, the greatest imperative for an improvement in hemispheric trade and financial cooperation is further improvement in economic growth rates, which increase trade flows even without any reductions in trade barriers.

Second, over the longer term, governments throughout the hemisphere must work toward more efficient alternatives to trade protection and expensive subsidization. In the United States, better-coordinated and more imaginative industrial policies can help workers and companies adapt to changing domestic and international economic conditions. In Latin America as well, more selective efforts to create new comparative advantages can reduce the domestic and international costs of current industrial policies. Improvements in domestic policies would lay the basis for reductions in both trade barriers and complaints about other countries' trade practices. Without such improvements, the future will be characterized by trade disputes that could have been avoided. Indeed, without improvements in national industrial policy, *both* the United States and many Latin American countries may see other countries forge ahead of them economically.

Similarly, those who seek to maintain a relatively open world trade system must work to form domestic political coalitions that support both alternatives to protectionist trade policy and trade policies that favor an open international system. There is evidence that these coalitions can be politically effective in the United States. In Latin America, too, Brazil's 1978 decision to phase out export subsidies illustrates an effort to change trade policy in ways that can help the country itself while simultaneously reducing strains in the international system. If the immediate financial crises are surmounted, there will be space for other such efforts. In Latin America as well as in the United States, domestic political projects of this sort may eventually permit a lowering of some remaining trade barriers.

Fourth, the experiences of the 1970s (despite relative economic stagnation during the decade) showed that international market forces can be turned to advantage. Farmers, workers, and investors have provided examples of trade expansion in every country in the Western Hemisphere. There is reason to expect that the 1980s will offer more such examples if policies are aimed at encouraging trade cooperation.

Finally, it is only realistic to assume that some conflict on trade issues is likely even in the best of conditions. The strong and the weak have different interests, and shifts in their relative positions can increase sources of friction. If in the 1980s some parties are also determined to impose unwelcome ideologies on their trading partners, or feel compelled to sacrifice opportunities for joint gains, then future international economic conflicts could become more intense. But if most parties exercise tolerance and patience, these disputes might be limited.

School of International Relations
University of Southern California

APPENDIX A
Leading Products in Latin American Exports to the United States, 1980[a]
(US$ million)

Argentina

Meat in airtight containers, NSPF	124.2
Sugar, syrups, molasses, honey	89.5
Petroleum products	76.4
Leather	73.1
Gold, nonmonetary, except ores and concentrates	47.2
Total exports to U.S.	740.8

Bahamas

Petroleum products	1,270.0
Organic chemicals and related products	27.7
Medicinal and pharmaceutical products	22.9
Special transactions, NSPF	16.9
Lime, cement, fabricated building materials	12.1
Total exports to U.S.	1,381.8

Barbados

Sugar, syrups, molasses, honey	37.5
Electronic components and parts thereof	13.8
Parts of office machines and automatic data processing machines	8.5
Undergarments, knit	7.9
Electrical apparatus, resistors, printed circuits	7.5
Total exports to U.S.	95.6

Bolivia

Tin and tin alloys, wrought and unwrought	95.9
Ores and concentrates of base metals	34.5
Sugar, syrups, molasses, honey	14.2
Petroleum products	12.0
Wood, shaped or simply worked	5.1
Total exports to U.S.	181.9

Brazil

Coffee	1,053.8
Sugar, syrups, molasses, honey	414.8
Footwear, new	244.2
Cocoa	197.4
Iron or steel plates and sheets	103.6
Total exports to U.S.	3,714.6

Chile

Copper and copper alloys, wrought and unwrought	278.3
Gold, nonmonetary, except ores and concentrates	39.6
Fruits and nuts, NSPF, prepared or preserved	34.9
Precious metal ores, concentrates	31.8
Nonferrous waste and scrap, NSPF	18.2
Total exports to U.S.	515.0

Colombia

Coffee	780.5
Sugar, syrups, molasses, honey	102.5
Vegetable materials, NSPF, crude	70.1
Precious and semiprecious stones, pearls, NSPF	58.0

Fruits and nuts, NSPF, prepared or preserved	40.1
Total exports to U.S.	1,240.5

Costa Rica

Fruits and nuts, NSPF, prepared or preserved	99.1
Coffee	60.6
Meat, fresh, chilled, or frozen	60.2
Sugar, syrups, molasses, honey	37.4
Undergarments, knit	20.9
Total exports to U.S.	356.4

Dominican Republic

Sugar, syrups, molasses, honey	259.8
Coffee	87.6
Pig iron, etc., and ferro-alloys	75.8
Gold, nonmonetary, except ores and concentrates	57.6
Cocoa	55.0
Total exports to U.S.	785.9

Ecuador

Crude petroleum	288.6
Cocoa	106.0
Coffee	104.3
Petroleum products	98.6
Fruits and nuts, NSPF, prepared or preserved	95.2
Total exports to U.S.	861.6

El Salvador

Coffee	264.3
Electronic components and parts thereof	42.7
Sugar, syrups, molasses, honey	21.5
Shellfish, fresh, frozen, salted, dry	18.4
Electrical machinery and apparatus, NSPF	15.7
Total exports to U.S.	427.3

Guatemala

Coffee	196.9
Sugar, syrups, molasses, honey	97.3
Fruits and nuts, NSPF, prepared or preserved	32.3
Meats, fresh, chilled, or frozen	27.8
Crude petroleum	19.6
Total exports to U.S.	435.0

Guyana

Ores and concentrates of base metals	52.9
Sugar, syrups, molasses, honey	36.3

Shellfish, fresh, frozen, salted, dry	16.2
Gold, nonmonetary, except ores and concentrates	3.8
Outer wearing apparel, women's, girls', and infants'	3.0
Total exports to U.S.	119.8

Haiti

Baby carriages, toys, and sporting goods	42.0
Undergarments, knit	20.2
Outer wearing apparel, women's, girls', and infants'	17.7
Electrical apparatus, resistors, printed circuits	14.1
Electrical machinery and apparatus, NSPF	13.4
Total exports to U.S.	251.7

Honduras

Fruits and nuts, NSPF, prepared or preserved	127.5
Coffee	73.7
Meat, fresh, chilled, or frozen	60.3
Sugar, syrups, molasses, honey	43.7
Shellfish, fresh, frozen, salted, dry	24.9
Total exports to U.S.	418.8

Jamaica

Ores and concentrates of base metals	309.5
Sugar, syrups, molasses, honey	27.7
Beverages, alcoholic	13.8
Tobacco manufactures	7.5
Undergarments, knit	4.9
Total exports to U.S.	383.0

Mexico

Crude petroleum	5,926.6
Gas, natural and manufactured	551.2
Telecommunications equipment, NSPF, and parts	412.6
Shellfish, fresh, frozen, salted, dry	325.4
Vegetables, fresh, chilled, frozen, or preserved	316.5
Coffee	311.5
Television receivers	291.6
Total U.S. exports	12,519.5

Nicaragua

Meat, chilled, fresh, or frozen	61.1
Coffee	35.0
Sugar, syrups, molasses, honey	31.7
Shellfish, fresh, frozen, salted, dry	30.2
Fruits and nuts, NSPF, prepared or preserved	21.0
Total exports to U.S.	211.1

Panama

Gold, nonmonetary, except ores and concentrates	92.5
Sugar, syrups, molasses, honey	78.1
Shellfish, fresh, frozen, salted, dry	49.8
Fish, fresh, chilled, or frozen	21.1
Fruits and nuts, NSPF, prepared or preserved	17.3
Total exports to U.S.	329.5

Paraguay

Coffee	35.2
Gold, nonmonetary, except ores and concentrates	21.4
Sugar, syrups, molasses, honey	7.1
Essential oils, perfumes, cosmetics	3.7
Silver, platinum, unworked or partly worked	2.6
Total exports to U.S.	81.1

Peru

Crude petroleum	540.4
Silver, platinum, unworked or partly worked	221.3
Precious metal ores, concentrates	141.6
Coffee	114.0
Copper and copper alloys, wrought and unwrought	111.5
Total exports to U.S.	1,386.2

Suriname

Ores and concentrates of base metals	100.3
Shellfish, fresh, frozen, salted, dry	4.0
Special transactions, NSPF	3.1
Hides, skins, except furskins, undressed	0.5
Wood, shaped or simply worked	0.5
Total exports to U.S.	108.8

Trinidad and Tobago

Crude petroleum	1,495.5
Petroleum products	801.9
Inorganic chemical elements, oxides	40.3
Special transactions, NSPF	13.1
Organic chemicals and related products	7.4
Total exports to U.S.	2,378.3

Uruguay

Fish, fresh, chilled, or frozen	15.3
Clothing and accessories of leather, fur, textile materials, rubber, or plastics	14.0
Outer wearing apparel, women's, girls', and infants'	13.0
Gold, nonmonetary, except ores and concentrates	12.6

| Leather manufactures, NSPF | 7.5 |
| Total exports to U.S. | 97.2 |

Venezuela

Petroleum products	3,200.6
Crude petroleum	1,692.2
Gas, natural and manufactured	89.4
Iron ore and concentrates	81.0
By-products of coal, petroleum, etc.	73.5
Total exports to U.S.	5,297.1

Source: U.S. Bureau of the Census, *U.S. General Imports*, FT 155/Annual, 1980.

a. Products are defined at the three-digit level. Values are f.a.s. NSPF=Not Specially Provided For. Totals include products not shown.

APPENDIX B
Leading Products in U.S. Exports to Latin America, 1980[a]
(US$ million)

Argentina

Aircraft, spacecraft, and parts thereof	214.6
Civil engineering and contractors' equipment	121.7
Trucks and special-purpose motor vehicles	106.9
Organic chemicals and products, NSPF	102.6
Automatic data processing machines	79.8
Total U.S. exports	2,452.5

Bahamas

Medicinal and pharmaceutical products	19.7
Meat, fresh, chilled, or frozen	17.9
Passenger motor vehicles	15.4
Organic chemicals and products, NSPF	13.8
Furniture and parts thereof	11.9
Total U.S. exports	391.5

Barbados

Meat, fresh, chilled, or frozen	5.2
Wood, simply worked; railway ties, wood	5.2
Telecommunications equipment, television and radio equipment, parts	4.3
Electronic tubes, semiconductors, microcircuits, parts	4.3
Corn or maize, unmilled	3.7
Total U.S. exports	134.1

Bolivia

Wheat, unmilled	23.3
Civil engineering and contractors' equipment	15.6
Aircraft, spacecraft, and parts thereof	7.9
Trucks and special-purpose motor vehicles	7.0
Internal combustion engines (nonpiston) and parts	6.2
Total U.S. exports	168.6

Brazil

Aircraft, spacecraft, and parts thereof	377.2
Wheat, unmilled	363.4
Fertilizers and fertilizer material, NSPF	319.0
Corn or maize, unmilled	249.6
Organic chemicals and products, NSPF	247.3
Total U.S. exports	4,306.3

Chile

Wheat, unmilled	172.7
Civil engineering and contractors' equipment	81.3
Corn or maize, unmilled	56.4
Fertilizers and fertilizer material, NSPF	47.8
Aircraft, spacecraft, and parts thereof	45.4
Total U.S. exports	1,388.7

Colombia

Wheat, unmilled	99.2
Parts of road vehicles and tractors, NSPF	95.8
Aircraft, spacecraft, and associated equipment	82.3
Organic chemicals and products, NSPF	80.2
Civil engineering and contractors' equipment	75.5
Total U.S. exports	1,708.4

Costa Rica

Paper and paperboard	32.1
Synthetic resins, rubber and plastic materials	30.7
Wheat, unmilled	21.1
Aircraft, spacecraft, and associated equipment	15.8
Organic chemicals and products, NSPF	14.1
Total U.S. exports	493.6

Dominican Republic

Fertilizers and fertilizer material, NSPF	43.5
Fixed vegetable oils (soft), crude or refined	32.9
Wheat, unmilled	28.4
Synthetic resins, rubber and plastic materials	28.1

Corn or maize, unmilled	24.9
Total U.S. exports	786.8

Ecuador

Wheat, unmilled	58.7
Trucks and special-purpose motor vehicles	47.2
Paper and paperboard	37.4
Parts of road vehicles and tractors, NSPF	32.8
Synthetic resins, rubber and plastic materials	32.5
Total U.S. exports	851.2

El Salvador

Electronic tubes, semiconductors, microcircuits, etc.	29.6
Wheat, unmilled	20.3
Electrical machinery and apparatus, NSPF	16.0
Fertilizers and fertilizer material, NSPF	12.8
Synthetic resins, rubber and plastic materials	12.3
Total U.S. exports	268.2

Guatemala

Synthetic resins, rubber and plastic materials	32.4
Organic chemicals and products, NSPF	30.2
Fertilizers and fertilizer material, NSPF	26.5
Civil engineering and contractors' equipment	25.6
Wheat, unmilled	21.6
Total U.S. exports	548.4

Guyana

Civil engineering and contractors' equipment	17.0
Wheat, unmilled	8.8
Inorganic chemicals and products, NSPF	4.6
Animal feeding-stuff	4.4
Parts of road vehicles and tractors, NSPF	4.3
Total U.S. exports	95.7

Haiti

Baby carriages, toys, and sporting goods	24.2
Wheat, unmilled	19.9
Fixed vegetable oils (soft), crude or refined	15.0
Electrical machinery and apparatus, NSPF	12.0
Underwear, etc., knit, and bras, corsets, etc.	9.4
Total U.S. exports	303.8

Honduras

Paper and paperboard	31.0
Synthetic resins, rubber and plastic materials	17.0

Wheat, unmilled   13.3
Parts of road vehicles and tractors   12.8
Organic chemicals and products, NSPF   8.6
Total U.S. exports   373.7

Jamaica
Inorganic chemicals and products, NSPF   30.9
Corn or maize, unmilled   20.2
Oilseed and oleaginous fruit for soft oils   15.9
Synthetic resins, rubber and plastic materials   11.2
Meat, fresh, chilled, or frozen   9.0
Total U.S. exports   302.1

Mexico
Parts of road vehicles and tractors, NSPF   1,128.3
Corn or maize, unmilled   681.4
Aircraft, spacecraft, and associated equipment   402.6
Organic chemicals and products, NSPF   392.6
Oilseed and oleaginous fruit for soft oils   384.0
Total U.S. exports   14,884.8

Nicaragua
Fertilizers and fertilizer material, NSPF   17.3
Organic chemicals and products, NSPF   13.9
Parts of road vehicles and tractors   13.1
Fixed vegetable oils (soft), crude or refined   11.6
Vegetables, fresh, etc., dried leguminous vegetables   11.2
Total U.S. exports   247.3

Panama
Television receivers and combinations   34.3
Medicinal and pharmaceutical products   29.4
Paper and paperboard   28.3
Tobacco manufactures   27.2
Petroleum products, refined   21.5
Total U.S. exports   688.5

Paraguay
Tobacco manufactures   12.9
Aircraft, spacecraft, and associated equipment   9.7
Telecommunications equipment, television and radio
  equipment, parts   6.1
Manmade fabrics, woven, except narrow fabrics   5.8
Trucks and special-purpose motor vehicles   3.8
Total U.S. exports   103.2

Peru

Civil engineering and contractors' equipment	139.1
Wheat, unmilled	117.0
Corn or maize, unmilled	73.9
Parts of road vehicles and tractors	56.6
Organic chemicals and products, NSPF	43.6
Total U.S. exports	1,160.6

Suriname

Inorganic chemicals and products, NSPF	19.1
Residual petroleum products, NSPF	6.1
Parts of road vehicles and tractors, NSPF	5.1
Animal feeding-stuff	3.9
Nonelectric parts, NSPF, for machinery	3.8
Total U.S. exports	134.0

Trinidad and Tobago

Aircraft, spacecraft, and associated equipment	80.4
Civil engineering and contractors' equipment	38.2
Wheat, unmilled	20.5
Pumps, NSPF, compressor, filter equipment, etc.	20.3
Animal feeding-stuff	19.6
Total U.S. exports	673.6

Uruguay

Fertilizers and fertilizer material, NSPF	20.1
Aircraft, spacecraft, and associated equipment	7.8
Parts of road vehicles and tractors, NSPF	6.8
Synthetic resins, rubber and plastic materials	6.4
Telecommunications equipment, television and radio equipment, parts	5.8
Total U.S. exports	180.5

Venezuela

Parts of road vehicles and tractors	272.9
Civil engineering and contractors' equipment	225.8
Corn or maize, unmilled	154.9
Wheat, unmilled	134.9
Internal combustion piston engines and parts	114.1
Total U.S. exports	4,512.8

Source: U.S. Bureau of the Census, *U.S. Exports: World Area by Commodity Groupings,* FT 455/Annual, 1980.

a. Values are f.a.s. NSPF=Not Specially Provided For. Totals include products not shown.

Notes

The author is grateful to Jorge I. Domínguez, Kevin J. Middlebrook, David Mares, and Carlos Rico for suggestions on this essay; to the Ford Foundation for supporting his research on related subjects; and to Michele Boucher for able research assistance.

1. J. M. Finger, "The Industry-Country Incidence of 'Less than Fair Value' Cases in U.S. Import Trade," in Werner Baer and Malcolm Gillis, eds., *Export Diversification and the New Protectionism: The Experiences of Latin America* (Champaign: National Bureau of Economic Research and University of Illinois Press, 1981), pp. 260–79. An exception was Uruguay, 32 percent of whose exports to the United States were subject to such duties. Cases not resulting in such duties include those in which the exporting country rescinded its subsidies in order to avoid them.

2. Calculated from International Monetary Fund, *Direction of Trade Statistics Yearbook 1984* (Washington, D.C., 1984), table for the United States, using the twenty-five countries included in tables 1–3 in this essay.

3. The original legislative authority for the Generalized System of Preferences expired in January 1985. The Trade and Tariff Act of 1984 renewed the program through mid-1993.

4. However, estimates by the Organization of American States and others indicated that losses due to eroding preferences would be more than offset by export gains due to reductions in tariffs on other products. See *Business Latin America,* 16 May 1979 and *passim.* Also see Bela Balassa, "The Tokyo Round and the Developing Countries," *Journal of World Trade Law* 14 (March/April 1980): 93–118; John Mathieson, *The Tokyo Round Trade Agreements: What Effect on the Developing Countries?* ODC Communique 1979/3 (Washington, D.C.: Overseas Development Council, 1979).

5. P. I. Mendive, "Ronda de Tokio: Evaluación de los resultados alcanzados en las negociaciones comerciales multilaterales al 30 de octubre de 1979," B/CEPAL/1.218 (n.p.: Economic Commission for Latin America, April 1980), table 20. Total U.S. imports in 1976 exceeded $124 billion.

6. U.S. International Trade Commission, *The History and Current Status of the Multifiber Arrangement,* USITC Publication 850, 1978, pp. 41–58; International Monetary Fund, *Developments in International Trade Policy,* Occasional Paper No. 16, November 1982, table 21.

7. See David Morawetz, *Why the Emperor's New Clothes Are Not Made in Colombia: A Case Study in Latin American and East Asian Manufactured Exports,* World Bank Staff Working Paper No. 368 (Washington, D.C., 1980).

8. There is some quantitative evidence supporting this fear. Finger, "The Industry-Country Incidence," 274, finds that an increase in complaints brings a reduction in an industry's import growth rate.

9. William R. Cline, *Exports of Manufactures from Developing Countries: Performance and Prospects for Market Access* (Washington, D.C.: Brookings Institution, 1984), chapter 2.

10. Stephen Lande and Craig VanGrasstek, "United States-South American Trade Liberalization Prospects" (Washington, D.C.: Manchester Associates, 1982), p. 38.

11. Helen Hughes and Anne O. Krueger, "Effects of Protection in Developed Countries on Developing Countries' Exports of Manufactures" (Washington, D.C.: World Bank, January 1983).

12. Ibid.

13. Inter-American Development Bank, *Economic and Social Progress in Latin America: The External Sector* (Washington, D.C., 1982), table 9. The only exceptions were Jamaica, Barbados, Trinidad and Tobago, and Guyana.

14. Ibid., table 8.

15. See Albert Fishlow, "Making Liberal Trade Policies Work in the 1980s," in Roger D. Hansen et al., eds., *U.S. Foreign Policy and the Third World: Agenda 1982* (Washington, D.C.: Overseas Development Council, 1982), pp. 65–67.

16. Calculated from International Monetary Fund, *Direction of Trade, 1961–1965 Annual,* and International Monetary Fund, *Direction of Trade Statistics Yearbook 1982,* tables for the United States.

17. Organization of American States, *CECON Trade News* 8/1 (January 1983): 6.

18. Preliminary estimates by Inter-American Development Bank.

19. International Monetary Fund, *Direction of Trade Statistics Yearbook 1984,* table for the United States.

20. U.S. Department of Commerce, *Business America,* 20 August 1984, p. 24.

21. It is also true that such institutions in the United States require more public disclosure and more open debate than in many countries, so that opposing interests routinely have opportunities to raise objections about the producers' arguments. Thus this problem may be less severe in the United States than in most countries.

22. *Análisis Político* (Mexico), 12 November 1979 and 3 December 1979; *Uno Más Uno,* 16 March 1980; *Excelsior,* 17 March 1980; interviews in Mexico City, 1980 and 1982. See also Dale Story, "Trade Policies in the Third World: A Case Study of the Mexican GATT Decision," *International Organization* 36 (Autumn 1982): 767–94.

23. By the same token, liberalization imposed "cold turkey"—without supporting programs to foster the development of new skills and the creation of new industries to replace the inefficient activities—can also involve unnecessary costs.

24. Morawetz, *Why the Emperor's New Clothes.*

25. International Bank for Reconstruction and Development, *Mexico: Manufacturing Sector: Situation, Prospects, and Policies* (Washington, D.C., 1979).

8

COMMENT: Debt and Trade in U.S.–Latin American Relations

Richard E. Feinberg

North Americans and Latin Americans of widely differing political persuasions share much common ground when the subject turns to international economics. There is broad agreement on the virtues of economic interdependence; the growing importance of economic exchanges between North and South; the fact of Latin America's increased integration into the global economy; and the strong linkage between financial and trade issues. These widely shared views are reflected in the four essays on economics in this section.

Massad, O'Brien, Fritsch, and Odell concur on the advantages of global interdependence. They view favorably the decisions of many Latin American governments in the 1960s and 1970s to become more "open"— to increase exports and imports more rapidly than their growth in gross national product (GNP) and to finance a portion of investment through external capital inflows. Consequently, they are alarmed at the threats that current global economic crises pose to interdependence. Trade has contracted, and the ability of Latin American countries to meet their external debt obligations is in doubt. In response, each author presents policy recommendations directed at recreating the conditions for renewed growth and increased international flows of commodities and capital.

The four essays also share a globalist perspective. The authors recognize that, although U.S.–Latin American economic relations are intense, they are enmeshed in a larger system. Today, hemispheric traders and financiers scan a global horizon. The rules (such as they are) that govern international trade are determined in the Geneva offices of the General Agreement on Tariffs and Trade (GATT), while monetary matters are the purview of the International Monetary Fund (IMF). Intra-Latin American or hemispheric initiatives may sometimes be possible, but their potential should not be overstated, and their designers must be cognizant of the larger global system. Carlos Massad notes that intra-Latin American trade can provide significant markets, but he intends this outlet to complement rather than replace North-South trade. Richard O'Brien notes that although Latin America accounts for over half of commercial bank debt, many other developing countries face similar debt problems. O'Brien suggests that a hemispheric approach to the debt crisis might be useful, but he cautions that the region is only one part of a larger global financing problem. He does not suggest what a regional solution might look like. The authors' enthusiasm for globalism is well founded, but it has blinded them to the resurgence of regionalism in U.S. economic relations with the small countries of the Caribbean Basin.

If there is general accord on the value of interdependence and the reality of globalism, the authors do not always agree when discussing the central concern of all four essays: how best to manage the international financial and trading systems. They devote some space to discussing the implications of the global crisis for outward-oriented development strategies, but they pay less attention to its impact on political institutions. This subject will be addressed in more detail below.

International Finance

Nowhere is the increased interdependence between the United States and Latin America more marked than in international finance. Latin American countries have experienced rising ratios of external debt and debt service to GNP. The U.S. banking system (itself in a phase of very rapid technological innovation and geographic expansion) has become increasingly intermeshed with Latin America.[1] As O'Brien points out, for ten of the top twenty U.S. banks, loans to Mexico and Brazil equal their total capital. In the 1970s lending to Latin America increased much more rapidly than other aspects of bank business and bank capital. The excitement of lending to Latin America was pervasive not only in the major banks in New York, Chicago, and San Francisco (and London, Paris, and Tokyo); bankers in Detroit, Cleveland, and Phoenix also opened lines of credit to Latin American clients.

Massad and O'Brien fundamentally agree on the basic causes behind this boom in bank lending. The reasons boiled down to bankers' calculations of risks, profits, and opportunities. The risks in international lending were considered to be low. Bankers often repeated that "countries cannot go bankrupt or disappear," and many bankers believed that in the worst case, the U.S. government would bail them out. Generally, the United States would try to keep friendly governments solvent on "national security" grounds. In the unlikely event that a country should actually default, the Federal Reserve Board would act in the interests of domestic financial security to minimize the impact on the U.S. banking system. Presumably this might require an injection of government funds into the wounded banks.

This perceived low risk compared very favorably with the perceived opportunity and the lack of other good alternatives. The sharp increase in international oil prices after 1973 severely unbalanced the current accounts of oil-importing developing countries. The actions of the Organization of Petroleum Exporting Countries (OPEC) thus created a tremendous demand for external finance, and the banks—themselves suddenly flush with deposits from the rich oil-exporting nations—were the only source with sufficient funds to fill the financing gap. Nor were the banks tempted by alternative borrowers, since loan demand in industrialized countries was weakened by slow growth in production and (in some countries) increased corporate ability to finance operations through internal profits or to borrow on nonbank capital markets. Thus developing countries' demand for funds was met by a ready response from willing commercial banks. Increased international lending was considered a positive-sum game.

To these economic causes for increased bank lending, both O'Brien and Massad add another: the competitive structure of the banking system. Both note the "herd instinct" in banking circles. Driven partly by the fear of losing market shares and partly by mood (Keynes's "animal instincts"), the banking system can undergo periods of enthusiasm and rapid expansion, as occurred in the 1970s. But these same herd instincts can also produce panic and rapid retrenchment, as in fact occurred in 1982–1983 in lending to Latin America.

Both authors comment on this sudden and drastic retrenchment, which saw lending contract so rapidly that interest payments from Latin America to the international banking system began to surpass new loans. Latin America thus became a net exporter of capital to the banking system, and to U.S. banks in particular. The contradiction of lending reflected deterioration in the creditworthiness of countries trapped by a global recession and a debt burden suddenly inflated by dramatically increased interest rates. But the banks' own behavior contributed to the crisis by first providing the loans that enabled many countries to continue to maintain living standards and avoid adjustment to a worsening global economic environment and then by very suddenly reducing the rate of new lending. Although some reduction in lending growth rates was inevitable and desirable, the sharp cutback itself created problems. The resulting economic contraction—and in some cases, virtual chaos—in debtor countries further hurt their creditworthiness. The cutback in lending also made it impossible for countries to meet their debt-service obligations, since the practice had been to finance old loans with new loans. The result was a rash of emergency and forced loan reschedulings.

That the system has continued to function at all is impressive, given the depth of the global recession and the magnitude of the debt crisis. The banks demonstrated flexibility in their willingness to reschedule debt. The major banks were able to organize both themselves and the hundreds of smaller banks that had extended loans to developing countries into committees that made it possible to avoid technical defaults and prevent dramatic breakdowns. For their part, many developing country governments—especially in Latin America—proved capable of "adjusting" (that is, depressing living standards) more rapidly and dramatically than many had thought possible.

The IMF's alacrity and boldness in preventing a systemic collapse were also impressive. The IMF noted that the banks' "herd instinct" threatened to render debtor countries illiquid. Although it appeared rational from the perspective of each individual bank to reduce exposure, if all banks attempted to do so, no bank could be repaid. The IMF also feared there would be a public outcry if its own loans appeared to be funneled immediately into the coffers of retreating banks. Because the U.S. Congress was considering a large increase in funding for the IMF, the Fund was especially anxious to avoid the appearance of "bailing out" the banks. For these reasons, the IMF conditioned some of its own credit upon banks themselves putting up new money. Thus banks made "involuntary" loans to Mexico, Brazil, and other countries. Although banks chafed under this official coercion, many bankers recognized that had the IMF not stepped in to steady credit markets, the system might have collapsed. At least in the short run, the financial markets proved to be susceptible to destabilizing and self-destructive behavior. There was a need for an official coordinating or regulating mechanism.

Although the IMF took the lead in most cases, the U.S. government was generally supportive—despite the Reagan administration's promarket, anti-intervention stance. Reality and self-interest triumphed over ideology. In the cases of Mexico and Brazil, the U.S. government itself extended short-term lines of credit to help alleviate liquidity crunches. The Federal Reserve Board was especially active in working with U.S. banks, the IMF, and officials from key debtor countries to prevent the financial system from tearing itself apart.

Many observers considered the policies of the banks, the IMF, and the U.S. government too ad hoc, too "patchwork" (in O'Brien's phrase) to restore the international financial system to good health. Despite the IMF's arm-twisting, the net increase in new lending remained lower than interest payments. The "unnatural" state of developing countries transferring capital to more industrialized countries continued. Latin American countries were compelled to mount trade surpluses in order to generate the foreign exchange to finance the outflow. Some observers, especially in

Latin America, noted that if this net outflow were to continue, the costs and benefits of remaining current on debt service would shift. Default could become a "rational" calculation. Bankers might protest that it is incorrect for debtors to measure the value of their relationship with the banks in terms of current flows, because the debtor country should benefit from increased production created by the original loan. Moreover, a defaulting country might suffer sanctions, such as the impounding of its financial assets and exports. Nevertheless, if a "transfer of real resources from borrowers to creditors" (in Massad's phrase) came to be perceived as a secular trend, attitudes in Latin America toward commercial banks would be likely to shift. Increased tensions would result.

Massad and O'Brien agree on several measures that would help to alleviate the debt crisis. Certainly the resources of official institutions (notably the IMF and the World Bank) should be augmented significantly. The mix of official and private finance should shift somewhat toward official flows. The resulting ratio of official to private flows might not return to pre-1973 levels, but the balance would be more even. The industrialized countries that control the IMF concur with this prescription, and in 1983 they voted to expand its resources. However, no major decision on future World Bank activity levels has yet been reached.

Massad and O'Brien also agree that commercial banks should continue to reschedule debts flexibly and extend new loans—at least when the debtor country has agreed to appropriate austerity measures, generally in coordination with an IMF stabilization program. The two authors also emphasize the importance of global economic recovery for creating a more favorable environment for new lending and for strengthening markets for Latin American exports. The implication is that an aborted global recovery would have dire consequences. However, so long as recovery occurs, the international financial system appears manageable, albeit at some cost to Latin American countries.

The Reagan administration would agree with most of these points. Although it hesitated at first to expand the resources of an institution that some officials considered similar to domestic welfare programs, the administration eventually supported an increase in IMF resources and influence. It also came to accept the frequency of debt reschedulings as well as IMF (and Federal Reserve) pressure on banks to make new loans—despite the administration's distaste for official prescriptions for how private institutions should allocate their resources. The Reagan administration also placed strong emphasis on the need for developing countries to adjust their own economies and for industrialized countries to lead a global recovery. Although Massad recognizes the inevitability of austerity in Latin America, he places greater emphasis on more financing and other reforms. In contrast, the Reagan administration (and O'Brien to a degree) see adjustment as playing a larger role in establishing a new equilibrium.

However, both O'Brien and Massad remain uncomfortable with these measures alone. O'Brien seems uncertain as to whether they will be sufficient. He hedges on whether the problem (at least for some countries) is one of liquidity (and therefore short-term and solvable by a financial injection) or one of more fundamental solvency, although he does conclude with an expression of faith in the resource potential and economic strength of the major debtor countries.

Massad believes that the international financial system could be considerably improved, and he suggests a number of reforms. He would introduce measures to force industrialized countries to bear more of the burden of global adjustment ("adjustment symmetry"), and he recommends that industrialized countries (presumably mainly the United States) reduce their fiscal deficits so as to permit a more relaxed monetary policy and lower international interest rates. Massad urges bank comptrollers to smooth the "boom-and-bust" cycles in international lending by creating a "liquidity insurance system" and by favoring loans to countries under IMF stabilization agreements. That a Latin American chooses to address himself to what might be considered U. S. domestic economic policies illustrates the great stake that Latin America now has in U.S. fiscal and monetary policy, as well as in banking regulation. Massad also offers recommendatons for Latin American governments: better management of external debt and enhanced domestic savings and foreign equity investment to offset the lesser availability of commercial bank credits.

O'Brien, Massad, and the Reagan administration agree on one other fact: that a rapid expansion of Latin American exports is absolutely necessary if the debt crisis is to be alleviated. There is a clear link between trade and finance.

Trade Issues

United States exports to Latin America tumbled almost 40 percent during 1982–1983, from their 1981 high of $40 billion.[2] During 1982 the nearly $9 billion drop in U.S. merchandise exports to Latin America accounted for over 40 percent of the total decline in U.S. exports that year and a loss of about 250,000 jobs. Much of this decline in Latin America's import capacity was caused by the contraction of international capital markets. The retrenchment of U.S. banks hurt the manufacturing sectors in both Latin America and the United States.

Latin America's future ability to purchase U.S. products will depend on both its access to international credit and its ability to earn foreign exchange by exporting. Winston Fritsch and John Odell share the belief that expanding international trade benefits both the United States and Latin America, but they differ on the degree to which protectionism in the United States has slowed Latin American exports. Fritsch perceives a "new protectionism" that arose during the 1970s. Odell recognizes that U.S. trade policy historically has discriminated against the processing of raw materials and food in the producing country by escalating tariffs against processed goods. He also concedes that Latin American exports would have been higher had the United States eliminated all trade restrictions. However, Odell contends that even though the number of trade disputes involving Latin American products has increased and protectionist rhetoric is louder, the actual erection of trade barriers has not been great. Data showing a continuing expansion of Latin American exports to the U.S. market (by 117 percent between 1974 and 1981) would seem to support his case. In this debate on the intensity of U.S. protectionism, Odell (an American) and Fritsch (a Brazilian) take predictable sides. Perhaps just as predictably, this American writer finds more merit in the argument that, all things considered, the U.S. market remains one of the most open in the world. It should further be noted that, whereas in 1978 trade between the United States and Latin America was approximately in balance, by 1983 Latin America enjoyed a massive surplus of about $15 billion. Latin American exports, after a small dip in 1982, resumed their upward trend in 1983 and 1984 as the U.S. economy recovered, while U.S. exports to Latin America declined sharply.

Odell further notes the increasing pressures in the United States for trade "reciprocity"—for Latin American countries to reduce their own barriers against U.S. products. Latin American countries certainly tend to be much more protectionist than the United States, as (they would argue) befits their stage of development. In earlier stages of industrialization, the United States also protected its infant industries. Some Latin American governments unilaterally reduced trade barriers in the 1970s as part of broader economic liberalization strategies. However, the financial pressures of the 1980s have sparked a resurgence of measures aimed at allocating foreign exchange through official intervention. Indeed, the timing would hardly seem propitious for a reduction in protectionism in Latin America. Nor would it seem to be worth very much to U.S. exporters, at least in the short run. Latin American imports are limited less by tariffs, licensing, and quotas than by the lack of foreign exchange. Trade distortions change the mix of imports more than the total amount. Financial constraints rather than trade policy set the outer bounds on Latin America's import capacity.

But what of the future? Odell worries that if Fritsch was wrong to see a protectionist wave in the 1970s, the 1980s may yet justify his fears. Fritsch and Odell agree that a recovery of U.S. and global economies is absolutely crucial if protectionist pressures are to be dampened. They also note that growth of the U.S. market, more than specific trade policies, will determine the rate of growth in Latin American exports. In other words, the income effect of a rising GNP swamps the price effect of trade-distorting tariffs and other measures.

Odell also briefly discusses U.S. industrial policy. Latin American governments are not the only ones that intervene in the market place in order to affect the competitiveness of their firms. As Odell notes, the U.S. government also has an industrial policy—a mixture of fiscal incentives, credits, government procurement policies, official support for research and development, and so forth. Some critics of industrial policy argue that government intervention is bound to be inefficient, politicized, and protectionist. They fear that declining firms and unions would successfully petition any centralized agency in charge of industrial policy for protective barriers against imports, to the detriment of domestic consumers and developing country producers. But other analysts, including Odell, would respond that the United States already has industrial policies and that the choice is between ad hoc and counterproductive policies or more explicit policies that seek to rationalize and upgrade U.S. industry, help displaced workers to find new jobs, and assist firms to move into other lines of production. In this way, government policy can cushion the inevitable dislocations that accompany international trade, and affected workers and firms will be less eager for official protection against imports. Ironically, an interventionist industrial policy may be necessary at home if freer trade is to be maintained across borders. Latin American exporters could benefit from an adjustment-oriented industrial policy in the United States.

Development Strategies

By the late 1970s development economics had largely been taken over by a trade theory that emphasized the virtues of lower tariff barriers, openness to international competition, and properly aligned exchange rates. These reforms were intended to provide incentives for greater efficiency in production and export-led growth. The Asian "gang of four" (Taiwan, South Korea, Singapore, and Hong Kong) were held to be shining examples of export-oriented success stories. Ironically, many Latin American intellectuals and policymakers accepted this perspective at exactly the moment when the necessary international conditions for its success were placed in jeopardy. An export-led growth strategy depends upon buoyant international markets, and although this condition obtained in the 1960s and during part of the 1970s, it no longer held in the early 1980s. The four authors in this section all hope that a global economic recovery will reinflate world trade and again create markets for expanded Latin American exports.

Throughout Latin America, the liberal experiments of the 1960s and 1970s are threatened or in shambles. As all the authors note, the sudden contraction of external markets for trade and finance in the early 1980s dramatically eroded the bases of a development strategy that relied on export opportunities and foreign capital inflows. O'Brien perceptively remarks, "The impact of this cyclical change was perhaps intensified by Latin American countries' shift away from import substitution toward export orientation and by their increased dependence on foreign credit."

Although it would be foolish to blame any single government for the 1980–1982 global recession, Reaganomics certainly contributed to this problem, especially to sustaining high interest rates. Only those who believed in the extremely optimistic assumptions of the supply-side school failed to predict that the mix of tax cuts and heightened military spending would result in a widening U.S. fiscal deficit. The Federal Reserve Board feared that if it accommodated the fiscal deficit with any expansionary monetary policy, inflation would accelerate. Thus the Federal Reserve sought to counter loose fiscal policy with tight monetary policy. The inevitable result was high interest rates.

The Reagan administration apparently paid little attention to the international implications of its policy mix. Had its initial optimism (that the stimulus of tax cuts would bring a rapid recovery) proved correct, the adverse impact abroad might have been short-lived. But because the U.S. economy failed to respond promptly to supply-side medicine, the adverse international consequences of tight money worsened.

In a world of closely integrated capital markets and a huge volume of outstanding debt, high U.S. interest rates had a profound effect. As O'Brien notes, interest payments now absorb well over 20 percent of the seven major Latin American debtor countries' export earnings. Massad calculated that the rise in interest rates worsened the current-account balance of eighteen non-oil exporting Latin American countries by $4.6 billion in 1981, $5.5 billion in 1982, and $3.1 billion in 1983.

In addition to sharply increasing the service charge on debt, high interest rates in the United States drained developing countries of their own financial resources. The net increase in foreign assets in the United States rose from $38 billion in 1979 to $78 billion in 1981.[3] Over half of the latter amount came in the form of short-term bank deposits ("hot money"), with $30 billion originating in Latin America. To stem this hemorrhaging of liquid capital, many countries were forced to raise their own interest rates. The setting of positive, real interest rates was a desirable development in some countries where holding down interest rates had discouraged savings and hindered the efficient allocation of investment. But the sudden, sharp rise in interest rates added another contractionary element to the problems of a depressing debt overhang and a recessionary global economy.

The international environment was the main force that threw Latin American economies into near chaos. O'Brien describes the considerable variation in economic policies pursued by the major Latin American countries, and he finds that the results were depressingly similar— balance-of-payments and debt crisis, IMF stabilization programs, and severe austerity. However, despite the evidence he convincingly marshalls, O'Brien hesitates to pin the blame for the hemisphere-wide crisis on economic management in the United States, concluding blandly that "the origins of the crisis lie partly in policies specific to each country and partly in external events."

Mistakes by Latin American governments certainly did exacerbate their problems. Several of them postponed cuts in government spending and real wages in the hope that the global recession would end quickly, or (in Mexico's case) that oil prices would rapidly rebound. Attempts to maintain income levels in the midst of a deteriorated international economic environment led to a rapid accumulation of more debt, the disappearance of foreign exchange reserves, and the forced adoption of "shock" treatments when access to international credit suddenly dried up.

Overvalued exchange rates were another disequilibrating factor in several countries' balance of payments. As Massad cogently argues, a fixed exchange rate in several countries, when coupled with high local interest rates, attracted large inflows of short-term capital. Overvalued exchange rates also worked against exports and hurt domestic producers. But governments hesitated to devalue for fear of the inflationary and contractionary consequences.

The IMF and the World Bank have urged Latin American countries to increase their integration into the international economy. No matter, as O'Brien and Massad both note, that the increase in interdependence in the 1970s intensified the shocks of the early 1980s. There are several explanations for this apparent contradiction betwen experience and prescriptions. First, the IMF and the World Bank tend to identify the causes of countries' problems not in the liberalization of the 1970s but in the remaining elements of government intervention: in exchange rates, prices, and fiscal policy. Second, the IMF and World Bank are committed by their constitutions and belief systems to an open international order. Third, international financial institutions have tended to project a relatively optimistic scenario with regard to global recovery, thus providing a framework for future export growth in developing countries. The strong performance of the U.S. economy in 1983–1984 and the resulting surge in U.S. imports from developing countries lent credence to this analysis. Finally, the economists working in these institutions (and in the industrialized country government bureaucracies that heavily influence them) have great difficulty in conceiving of alternative, feasible approaches. In this they are not alone. Latin American governments tend to accept IMF prescriptions partly because they need the associated finance, but also because they basically cannot envision another set of measures that responds to severe balance-of-payments problems and recognizes the constraints under which policy must be made.

A neo-Keynesian might advocate increased fiscal spending as the way out of recession. A policy of fiscal stimulation could be part of a more inward-looking strategy built around an expanded domestic or regional market. The U.N. Economic Commission for Latin America (ECLA), where Carlos Massad works, once housed advocates of such a strategy. But the greater openness of many Latin American economies and their serious balance-of-payments problems raise questions about the relevance of an inward-looking strategy. Rather than providing clear means for improving the trade account, a strategy such as this would probably tend to worsen the trade balance by stimulating imports and directing producers toward domestic consumers rather than the international market.

Perhaps a more promising approach lies in a possible synthesis of import-substitution and export-promotion strategies.[4] A selective import-substitution policy that directs resources toward industries that save foreign exchange and attain productive efficiency could complement an export-promotion strategy that seeks to improve the trade account. However, much more work needs to be done to test the practical feasibility of such a "balanced-growth" synthesis.

Massad, abandoning his neo-Keynesian forebears at ECLA, urges that governments adopt conservative fiscal policies to generate increased domestic savings. His motivation lies in the external constraint: with the prospect of reduced foreign credit, Latin American countries must generate more of their own capital for investment. Also contrary to earlier ECLA distaste for devaluation, Massad urges the adoption of realistic exchange rates to stimulate exports and improve the current account. This change in ECLA perspective partly reflects shifting ideological winds in the Southern Cone (Argentina, Chile, and Uruguay), but it also responds to a different and more demanding international environment.

Political Economy Issues

The four papers in this section give only passing attention to the political implications of economic trends. Admittedly, it is difficult to demonstrate strict causality between economic development paths and politics. Based on the experience of Europe and some Latin American countries in the 1930s, analysts have frequently associated economic decline with the emergence of political authoritarianism. However, more contemporary experience in Latin America suggests that the relationship between economic pressures and politics may be more complex and less predictable. In several countries (including Peru, Bolivia, Brazil, Argentina, Chile, and Uruguay) economic problems have *increased* pressures for political liberalization. Whereas in the 1930s some democratic regimes were held responsible by their populations for economic decline, more recently authoritarian regimes had the bad luck to be in power when economies turned sour. Recent experiences in Latin America have linked economic contraction with political liberalization, turning conventional wisdom on its head.

In the longer run, however, democracy certainly has a better chance to survive amidst sustained economic growth. Pressure groups will compromise more readily when each can claim a share of expanding economic resources. Conflict can mount when groups struggle to preserve existing living standards in the face of austerity measures. For those interested in the democratization of Latin America, the global recession was an unexpected blessing. However, once democracy has been restored, renewed global growth will be of great importance.

Central America is another subject largely absent from the four papers. Given the relatively small size of the Central American economies (the combined annual gross national products of the five countries equal about $20 billion), this omission is understandable. Events in Central America barely make a dent in the economic statistics for Latin America, much less the global economy. Nevertheless, for strategic reasons U.S. foreign economic policy is now paying attention to Central America.[5] The Caribbean Basin Initiative, which provides one-way free trade for exports from Central America and the insular Caribbean, became U.S. law in 1983. United States aid to Central America has also been increasing, and it may rise dramatically in the future. Although Mexico and South America have largely outgrown hemispheric preferences and entered the more mature world of global interdependence, the more traditional approaches of bilateralism, concessional aid flows, and special regional relationships may still be valid for the small, less-developed nations of Central America.

Overseas Development Council
Washington, D.C.

Notes

1. For a discussion of recent trends in banking, see Lawrence J. Brainard, "More Lending to the Third World? A Banker's View," in Richard E. Feinberg and Valeriana Kallab, eds., *Uncertain Future: Commercial Banks in the Third World* (New Brunswick, N.J.: Transaction Books for the Overseas Development Council, 1984), pp.31–44.

2. "U.S. 'Costs' of the Third World Recession: They Lose, We Lose," Overseas Development Council *Policy Focus* 2 (1984).

3. U.S. Department of Commerce, *Survey of Current Business* (Washington, D.C.: U.S. Government Printing Office, June 1982), table 1, line 56 and table 10, lines 72–73.

4. For a more extensive discussion of alternative development strategies, see Richard E. Feinberg and Valeriana Kallab, eds., *Adjustment Crisis in the Third World* (New Brunswick, N.J.: Transaction Books for the Overseas Development Council, 1984).

5. See Richard E. Feinberg and Robert A. Pastor, "Far from Hopeless: An Economic Program for Post-War Central America," in Robert S. Leiken, ed., *Central America: Anatomy of Conflict* (New York: Pergamon Press, 1984), pp. 193–217.

9

COMMENT: U.S.–Latin American Economic Relations: Perspectives for the 1980s

Roberto Bouzas

Economic relations between Latin America and the United States are now experiencing the most severe strain in several decades. It is difficult to predict their future evolution for at least two reasons. First, in order to resolve the principal existing conflicts it is necessary to move beyond the realm of marginal adjustments and enter the barely explored territory of substantial revision of prevailing economic policies, established mechanisms of international economic interaction, and patterns of integration into the world economy. Second, there is an evident lack of perception in the United States (mainly in the U.S. government) concerning both the international consequences of domestic U.S. economic policies and the extent of the challenges faced by the world economy,

A useful starting point for this comment is to indicate which positions are shared—implicitly or explicitly—by Carlos Massad, Richard O'Brien, Winston Fritsch, and John Odell. These common perspectives are of the utmost importance, and by themselves they draw attention to the chasm existing between the gravity of challenges now facing U.S.–Latin American economic relations (and the international economy more generally) and the precarious, casuistic economic-policy approaches that have dominated public debate and actions on these issues in recent years.

All four essays in this section concur that U.S.–Latin American economic relations are at present influenced by a combination of both long-term tendencies and conflicts and short-term pressures caused by the depth and length of the 1981–1982 economic recession in the United States and U.S. domestic economic policies implemented in the early 1980s. These analytically (but not historically) divisible factors deepen strains in U.S.–Latin American economic relations and aggravate their more conflictual aspects. A sustained U.S. and world economic recovery would certainly improve the global environment. However, it remains to be seen whether the cyclical upswing that the U.S. economy began in early 1983 will be sufficiently powerful and lasting to make a significant

309

contribution to resolving the problems of slow economic growth, diminishing or stagnating trade flows, external disequilibria, and deep financial crisis now affecting the international economy and (particularly) Latin America. If this does not happen, these problems can no longer be considered "short-term" phenomena. Therefore the only alternative to increasing conflict and disintegration is a broad, integrated policy response. Although all four authors emphasize the importance of U.S. economic recovery as a means of reducing conflict in U.S.–Latin American economic relations, they fail to examine likely future scenarios. This is a necessary basis for evaluating the evolution of U.S.–Latin American economic relations during the remainder of the decade.

All four essays also note that the dilemmas present in U.S.–Latin American economic relations are not unique to the Western Hemisphere. Recent experience has shown that conflicts in trade, monetary, and financial matters pervade the whole contemporary international economy. This has important implications for regional versus global policy approaches. The rapid economic growth and trade expansion that industrialized countries experienced during most of the post-World War II period slowed in the 1970s and gave rise to increasing competition and conflict. At the same time, the U.S. economy became more vulnerable to external factors. The progressive erosion of its postwar hegemony reduced its flexibility and increased the costs of adaptation. Indeed, one could envision the United States pursuing a regional economic policy as a consequence of increasing disintegration in the industrialized world and the emergence of relatively independent economic blocs.

Finally, all the essays in this section share the view that trade and financial matters (which are hardly separable under stable conditions) are inextricably linked in the context of economic crisis. Indeed, barring the unlikely possibility of rapid recovery in international private capital markets or an equally implausible substantial increase in official aid flows, the heavy indebtedness of Latin American countries makes amortization and servicing dependent upon generating trade surpluses. Stagnation or slow growth in world trade and the trend toward increasing protectionism in industrialized countries limit the scope for an increase in exports, leaving import reductions as the main focus of economic adjustment. Recent experience has shown dramatically that significant import restraint has an immediate negative impact on the level of domestic economic activity. The social, political, and economic implications of maintaining import restraint for an extended period are cause for considerable misgivings in Latin America regarding the merits of this approach.

This summary of the positions shared by the four essays in this section does not exhaust the discussion of the causes of the present crisis or viable policy responses. Some alternative views are presented in the observations that follow.

U.S.–Latin American Financial Relations in the 1980s: From Disequilibrium to Disarticulation?

The papers by Massad and O'Brien offer a broad perspective on recent developments in, and the present state of, U.S.–Latin American financial relations. Financial issues have traditionally been an important question on the agenda of hemispheric economic affairs, but in the early 1980s they became a top priority. This is both a consequence of the debt crisis in which Latin American countries have been submerged and a reflection of the implications that an aggravation of the present situation would hold for the United States and the international financial system.

As Massad and O'Brien point out, the rapid increase in Latin American countries' external debt in the past fifteen years is the result of a number of factors. Indebtedness is a generalized phenomenon, regardless of differences in policy instruments and/or development models favored in different Latin American countries. However, it is important to emphasize two additional considerations. First, to understand the origins of external indebtedness, one must explore in more detail both the role played by international banks and prevailing conditions in the financial sector, including the latter's relationship with productive activity in the industrialized economies (particularly in the United States). Second, regardless of differences in policy instruments and development programs implemented in different Latin American countries, the region as a whole has undergone closer integration of domestic financial markets into the international economy. Massad and O'Brien may be referring to this phenomenon when they note that an active role for foreign capital is a common characteristic of recent Latin American economic development experiences. However, emphasizing the integration between domestic and world financial markets is a more relevant point of departure for analytical as well as policy-oriented purposes.

One common interpretation purports to explain Latin America's present external debt problem as the result of balance-of-payments disequilibria produced by the 1973–1974 and 1979 oil shocks. "Mistaken" or "irresponsible" economic policies are often cited as another cause of rapid debt accumulation. As both Massad and O'Brien emphasize, these factors undeniably played a role. External disequilibria and prevailing economic policies in Latin America created a market for—and increased the profitability of—an influx of foreign financial resources into these economies, stimulating a process of rapid indebtedness increasingly dependent upon money markets ("hot money").

However, both authors fail to note another dimension that is an essential basis for understanding the present situation and posing effective alternatives. The rapid growth in Latin America's external debt is only part of a more general expansion of the financial sphere relative to productive activities.[1] In the last two decades, the industrialized economies—and particularly the U.S. economy—have experienced increasing indebtedness in the personal as well as the corporate sector. Whereas in the period 1961–1965 the ratio of liquid assets to short-term debt for the U.S. nonfinancial corporate sector was 1.54, by 1976–1980 it had fallen to 0.70. Similarly, corporate interest payments as a percentage of profits rose from 9.5 percent to 31.7 percent over the same period.[2] In the personal sector, total outstanding consumer installment credit plus outstanding mortgage debt on nonfarm/noncommercial properties as a percentage of personal disposable income rose from 70 percent in the 1960–1964 period to 81 percent in 1977–1981.[3]

This tendency emerged in a context of stagnant real productive investment and economic growth. Indeed, beginning in the late 1960s and early 1970s, there was a marked decline in the growth rate of real productive investment in the industrialized economies.[4] Thus the rapid increase in Latin American external debt must be regarded as part of a broader process of financial investment and speculation taking place in the context of relative stagnation in productive investment in industrialized countries. It was the result not only of banks' calculations or relative profitabilities and risks and of the availability of abundant liquidity, but also of a more general pattern of financial speculation. This point has important consequences for analytical and policy-prescription purposes. As a result, one could argue, for example, that both Massad and O'Brien overemphasize the potential role that foreign direct investment might have played in recent Latin American economic development—and may play in the future—as a substitute for financial capital.

O'Brien and Massad are correct in drawing attention to the considerable differences in policy instruments and development models pursued in Latin America. There is no doubt that in the last decade the three Latin American countries with the highest absolute levels of external indebtedness went through quite different development experiences. Beginning in 1976, Argentina underwent an impressive process of deindustrialization accelerated by rapid liberalization of trade, financial, and exchange rate policies. Brazil, deeply affected by two successive oil shocks, continued its process of rapid industrial growth, import substitution, and manufactured exports promotion in the context of foreign-exchange controls and selective import protection. Mexico, in turn, saw its external debt increase very rapidly in a period characterized by "petrolization" of its economy within a regime of strict exchange rate freedom and progressive trade liberalization. If emphasis on differences among Latin American countries' economic policies is taken to the extreme, the conclusion that "supply factors" (as Massad labels them) promoted external debt accumulation would be strengthened.

However, there are some similarities in these different national experiences that cannot be dismissed. O'Brien notes that one common theme in these different contexts is the role that foreign capital has played in Latin American economies. But what should be stressed is the more profound relationship that has been established between domestic and international financial markets, making domestic economic policies in Latin America very dependent upon external capital flows. Integration of this kind did not necessarily arise from the presence of international banks in local financial markets (for example, Mexican legislation prohibits the presence of foreign financial institutions). Rather, it resulted from the subordination of domestic monetary, fiscal, and exchange rate policies to the need to obtain external financial resources. In all these cases, the consequences included abrupt devaluations; a general deterioration of domestic currencies' role as media of exchange, units of account, and reserves of value; and a "dollarization" of the economies.

It became evident in the mid-1970s that the rate of increase in Latin America's external debt was not sustainable in the medium term. External debt grew much faster than either borrowing countries' net exports or creditor banks' available capital. Moreover, a number of countries had already entered into the "vicious circle" of contracting new debt to pay for the amortization and service of old commitments. International banks—seduced by investment opportunities generally guaranteed by sovereign states, stimulated by abundant liquidity and scarce investment alternatives in industrialized countries, and encouraged by competitive behavior ("herd instinct") directed toward maintaining shares in a rapidly expanding market—increased their exposure without paying much attention to underlying economic tendencies and indicators of financial health. After the second oil shock in 1979, the rapid deterioration in the main debtor countries' financial position and the shift in the prevailing mood in international capital markets led to an increase in the proportion of short-term credit to total loan credit and to higher spreads in interest rate charges.

Although these disequilibria in Latin America's external indebtedness were not sustainable in the medium term, they were significantly aggravated by international economic conditions in the early 1980s. Indeed, it is difficult to overestimate the impact that U.S. domestic economic policies have had on the world economy and, more specifically, on Latin

America. The Reagan administration's Economic Recovery Program produced sizable fiscal imbalances that, combined with the restrictive monetary policy implemented by the U.S. Federal Reserve Board, led to a rapid rise in interest rates, record unemployment levels, and a sharp, lasting recession in the U.S. economy. Rapid disinflation produced extraordinarily high real interest rates, which multiplied deflationary pressures. These tendencies were transmitted to the world economy through changes in trade flows and in the cost and availability of capital, making the U.S. Economic Recovery Program a proposal for global deflation.[5] Rising real interest rates, deteriorating terms of trade, and shrinking export markets made the Latin American economic situation unsustainable. The "speculative" financing of the 1970s was suddenly interrupted, radically changing the assumptions and behavior of private international financial markets.[6] At the same time, international banks' "herd instincts" worked perversely, leading to efforts to reduce as quickly as possible each bank's exposure and potential losses. Substantial "involuntary" bank lending followed as a result of pressures from the International Monetary Fund (IMF) and central banks. However, a radical change in the state of the market had taken place.

Additional flexibility in U.S. monetary policy and an increase in IMF resources will not be adequate to resolve the dramatic situation faced by high-debt Latin American economies. Because such policy responses are predominatly short-term in scope and conventional in nature, they are poorly suited to address the consequences of a decade of economic imbalances. Latin American countries now confront a future of recurrent external crises in the context of domestic economic stagnation (or even negative real economic growth), increased poverty, and the progressive dismantling of domestic industrial structures. These points will be developed further in the last section of this comment.

U.S.–Latin American Trade Relations: Is Conflict Avoidable?

The essays by Fritsch and Odell provide a useful discussion of recent developments and key conflicts in U.S.–Latin American trade relations. Each author represents accurately the perceptions predominant in the United States and Latin America on trade issues. Although Odell attempts to provide an overarching analysis of U.S. and Latin American complaints and positions on trade questions, his interpretations are understandably influenced by his North American perspective. Indeed, at times it is difficult to square Odell's impressionistic interpretation of Latin American positions on trade matters with Fritsch's sober arguments.

Trade clearly constitutes a key aspect of U.S.–Latin American economic interactions. As both Fritsch and Odell point out, this has been an area of increasing misunderstanding and conflict since the 1970s. These tendencies are rooted in the processes of economic diversification that have prevailed in Latin America during the last two decades and in the structural adjustments occurring in the U.S. economy in the last ten years. Fritsch notes explicitly that Latin America and the United States have reduced their economic complementarity. Regardless of individual country differences, there has been a general trend toward economic diversification and growth in Latin America. This process has been paralleled in the United States by increasing pressures for structural adjustment to the new realities of world trade and changing patterns of relative competitiveness. To evaluate properly future tendencies in U.S.–Latin American trade relations, these two dynamics must be further analyzed. To appraise the potential for conflict and cooperation in this area, this section delineates some general ideas concerning the overall environment in which hemispheric trade relations will develop in the future.

Even if it once was, Latin America is no longer homogeneous in its economic structures or its foreign trade composition. Primary commodities still play a central role in the export pattern of many Latin American countries, but economic diversification has occurred rapidly—though not uniformly—in most of the region. The larger economies have developed relatively important industrial sectors. The main issues associated with these changes are well known, and Fritsch's essay summarizes them well. This comment, therefore, will concentrate on questions associated with trade in manufactured goods, since this area has the highest potential for growth and is the basis of any redefinition of Latin America's role in the world economy.

It is useful to begin this discussion by examining some long-term tendencies in the U.S. foreign trade sector that influence the general framework of U.S. trade policy and trade performance. In the last fifteen years, the United States' external sector has undergone important transformations.[7] Although traditionally regarded as a closed economy, during the 1970s the United States experienced a significant opening to foreign trade. The share of exports in the gross national product rose from 3.9 percent in the late 1960s to 7.6 percent in the late 1970s. Similarly, imports as a proportion of final sales more than doubled from 8 percent to 21 percent during the same period.[8] Beginning in 1971, the U.S. trade balance exhibited a consistent tendency toward deficit (especially after the 1973-1974 oil shock). Growing surpluses in agricultural trade were insufficient to compensate for the deterioration in energy trade. Trade in manufactured goods closely followed cyclical variations in economic activity, while at the same time increasing the range of its fluctuations. Trade in manufactured goods registered deficits in 1972, 1973, 1978, and 1982—

unprecedented developments in the post-World War II period. The current-account balance also showed strongly cyclical behavior.

These developments were associated with the emergence of an "external constraint" on the U.S. economy, as a result of which any sustained economic expansion in the United States would face a marked deterioration of trade and current accounts. Insofar as the international monetary system worked *smoothly* on the basis of a de facto dollar standard, these problems could be compensated for by creating international liquidity in the form of dollars, with a relatively minor impact on the level of domestic economic activity. However, in the 1970s this response became less viable because of the emergence of flexible exchange rates and the expanding array of liquid asset alternatives to the dollar. As a result, a significant deterioration in the U.S. current account places pressure on the dollar (as happened in 1977 and 1978, forcing President Carter to mount a "dollar rescue operation" in November 1978). This is a crucial relationship, given the likelihood of large and increasing U.S. trade and current-account deficits in the mid-1980s. These developments, in turn, will have a significant impact on the value of the dollar, the future course of U.S. monetary policy, and the prospectives for a strong, sustained economic recovery in the United States. These tendencies suggest that the ability of the U.S. economy to act as an individual agent of international economic expansion has been substanially eroded.[9]

The second point to be stressed here—concerning the competitiveness of the U.S. economy, especially the manufacturing sector—is no less controversial than the first. It is well known that the U.S. share of world manufacturing trade has contracted significantly since World War II. At the same time, imports have increased substantially as a proportion of domestic consumption, particularly in certain categories of manufactured goods.[10] After 1974 the U.S. economy was unable to compensate for the large deficit in energy trade through expanded surpluses in manufacturing trade, as the Federal Republic of Germany and Japan did. Thus it should be no surprise that debate regarding "industrial policy" and "reindustrialization" has become increasingly active in the United States in the past several years.[11] Whatever the final outcome of this discussion, it is not unreasonable to believe that some type of adjustment policy intended to "accelerate" or "channel" the transfer of resources from declining activities into fast-growing industries will be implemented. Because it is unlikely that economic growth will be rapid enough to make this adjustment less traumatic and more "automatic," any such adjustment policy will have important implications for Latin America.

These comments may seem to be a digression, but in fact they are of crucial relevance to Latin America. The United States' casuistic and pragmatic approach in its trade policy is closely related to the fact that some central dilemmas of domestic economic and industrial policy remain unresolved. Insofar as these key issues are not addressed explicitly and coherently, one must expect continued ad hoc trade practices resulting from pressures exerted by labor or business sectors affected by specific circumstances. And despite free-trade rhetoric, there is no indication that protectionist pressures and practices will decline in the near future. As Odell correctly notes, shifts in relative competitiveness in the international marketplace in a context of slow economic growth or stagnation are an inevitable source of protectionist pressures.

Whether the United States formulates an articulated industrial policy or continues to pursue ad hoc trade policies, one can safely anticipate increasing restrictions on Latin American access to the U.S. market for manufactured goods. Pressures for "reciprocity" legislation, local minimum content requirements, increased rigidity in the application of "graduation" criteria, and the debate over the continuation or phasing-out of the Generalized System of Preferences (GSP) in 1985 clearly show the direction of this trend. Even optimistic macroeconomic projections for U.S. economic growth in the next several years anticipate relatively high levels of unemployment, with clear implications for protectionist pressures. The fact that the U.S. economy is undergoing a process of structural adjustment in the context of slow growth cannot be neglected in any evaluation of future prospects for U.S.–Latin American trade relations.

In the past three decades Latin America and the United States have undergone a process of mutual trade de-linkage.[12] Over the period 1950–1980, Latin America's relative importance as a market for U.S. exports fell 37 percent. The Latin American share of total U.S. imports declined by 66 percent during this same period. Similarly, the U.S. share of total Latin American exports fell by 30 percent, and the U.S. share of total Latin American imports declined by 40 percent.

According to the data presented by Odell (table 3), the value of U.S. imports originating in Latin America increased by 117 percent between 1974 and 1981—an amount substantially lower than the 155 percent increase in the value of all U.S. imports. When Mexico's rapidly growing oil exports to the United States are excluded from the regional total, this difference is even more striking: Latin American exports to the United States grew by only 72 percent in value. Although there has indeed been growth in the absolute magnitude of U.S.–Latin American trade, a different interpretation emerges when relative amounts are considered.

In contrast, Latin America recovered part of its importance as an outlet for U.S. exports between 1974 and 1981. Whereas total U.S. exports grew by 137 percent during this period, U.S. exports to Latin America increased by 165 percent. Given this development, the severe contraction in Latin American economic growth and import demand in the early 1980s has important implications for the U.S. economy.

The data presented here lead to two important conclusions. First, the process of trade de-linkage between the United States and Latin America is much more important for the Latin American share of the U.S. market than for any other variable. This tendency was interrupted somewhat in the 1970s because of Latin American oil exports to the United States. Second, Latin America as a whole faces a long-term tendency toward trade deficits with the United States. This is particularly clear regarding trade in manufactured goods: according to U.S. Department of Commerce data, whereas in 1970 the U.S. trade surplus with Latin America reached $4 billion (the equivalent of 127 percent of the total U.S. trade surplus in manufactured goods), by 1979 this imbalance had reached $17 billion (the equivalent of 313 percent of the total U.S. trade surplus in manufactured goods). This tendency toward Latin American trade deficits was sustainable because of the existence of credit market conditions that provided the necessary balance-of-payments financing. The United States (as well as other industrialized countries) benefited greatly from this process. Obviously, Latin America also profited from higher rates of economic growth.

As Odell correctly notes, in a multilateral trading system, bilateral trade balances are not a reliable indicator for policy purposes. However, in the context of generalized deterioration in Latin America's trade and current-account balances, a general increase in import barriers is to be expected. So far the overall reduction in economic activity has been the main factor restricting Latin American imports. Of course, one might also argue that under the present circumstances Latin American countries are likely to increase protection in order to save badly needed foreign exchange. Slow growth is anathema to trade liberalization. This is a point of departure that cannot be overemphasized.

In conclusion, the diversification of Latin American exports, the process of structural adjustment in the U.S. economy, and the role that the United States and Latin America play as markets for each other have substantially increased trade conflicts. The shift from complementarity to competitiveness has been particularly dramatic because of slow growth and economic stagnation. Unless these conditions substantially change, it is unlikely that conflict in U.S.–Latin American trade relations will diminish.

International Trade and Finance: Adjustment or Reform?

The Latin American economies have been able to overcome external constraints on growth because of credit market conditions that permitted a rapid accumulation of debt. Both Latin American and industrialized countries benefited from this process—the former through higher rates of economic growth and the latter through an increase in foreign demand that became an important force in maintaining domestic economic activity. Global economic performance in the 1970s would have been much poorer if developing countries had not had recourse to external indebtedness. From a Keynesian perspective, high-debt Latin American economies were important sources of effective demand for industrialized countries.

The sudden interruption of this process of debt accumulation because of both long-term and conjunctural factors placed the world economy under great strain. Latin American countries must now generate enough foreign-exchange earnings to amortize and service a huge external debt. Notwithstanding multiple reschedulings, in 1982 Latin American countries began to transfer real resources to the rest of the world. This is obviously an unsustainable situation. Domestic economic adjustment in debtor countries has been the principal strategy used so far to address the international economic crisis.

As previously noted, economic stagnation in Latin America adversly affects industrialized countries by removing one of the most dynamic sources of effective global demand.[13] Adjustment through import restraint is a self-destructive approach that will not only create social, economic, and political pressures of unknown magnitudes in Latin America but will also worsen U.S.–Latin American relations and adversely affect the economic interests of the United States.

Latin American countries have considerable experience with the effects and consequences of IMF-style stabilization programs. The costs of deflationary adjustment policies have increased substantially under the present conditions of acute disequilibrium. Mexico, frequently identified as an example of successful adjustment, was able to meet IMF conditions only by accepting an estimated 5 percent decline in gross national product in 1983, a substantial increase in unemployment, and a general deterioration in living conditions. Most projections indicate that Mexico faces bleak prospects for the rest of the decade.[14] As a result of its inability to fulfill domestic economic targets, Brazil has signed an average of three letters of intent with the IMF each year since 1982. Argentina's newly elected civilian government confronts the challenge of reconciling popular demands with IMF and international bank inflexibility.

What is at stake is both the survival of these countries as modestly diversified economies and the promotion of democratic political regimes throughout Latin America. Some observers may believe that it is possible for Mexico to survive on oil exports or for Brazil to depend on soybean exports. But this is unrealistic in either economic or political terms. Latin American countries must continue to try to build modern, efficient industrial sectors that can profit from comparative advantages in labor costs and/or the availability of raw materials. However, this cannot be achieved by relying upon generalized import-substitution policies. Creative and future-oriented industrial policies must also be elaborated. This can only occur in a context of economic growth.

Insofar as economic growth is restricted by short-sighted adjustment policies, domestic and international conflicts will increase. The political consequences of internal turmoil in Latin American countries will be felt for years, and the United States has little to gain in the long run from such a situation. Catastrophic predictions are rarely accurate, and flexibility and adaptability are two of the strongest characteristics of Latin American societies. Nevertheless, the potential for conflict cannot be ignored. The international economy and U.S.–Latin American economic relations are now beset by a wave of contradictory objective interests. The future costs will be high if these strains are aggravated by short-sighted policy approaches.

Facultad Latinoamericana de Ciencias Sociales
Buenos Aires, Argentina

Notes

1. See María da Conceição Tavares, "A crise financeira global," *Revista de Economía Política* 3, No. 2 (São Paulo) (April–June 1983): 15 and ff.

2. See Henry Kaufman, *National Policies and the Deteriorating Balance Sheets of American Corporations* (New York: Salomon Brothers, 1981).

3. *Economic Report of the President, 1983* (Washington, D.C.: U.S. Government Printing Office, 1983), p.242 and ff.

4. Bank for International Settlements, *Annual Report 1979* (Basle, Switzerland) (June 1979), p. 28.

5. Roberto Bouzas, "La política económica de la administración Reagan (Bases para un desorden futuro)," in Helio Jaguaribe et al., eds., *La política internacional de los años 80: una perspectiva latinoamericana* (Buenos Aires: Ed. de Belgrano, 1982), pp.138–40.

6. André Lara Resende, "A ruptura do mercado internacional de crédito," in Persio Arida, ed., *Dívida externa, recessão e ajuste estrutural* (Río de Janeiro: Ed. Paz e Terra, 1982), p. 44 and ff.

7. W.H. Branson, "Trends in U.S. Trade and Investment since World War II," in Martin S. Feldstein, ed., *The American Economy in Transition* (Chicago: University of Chicago Press, 1980), p. 195 and ff.

8. *Economic Report of the President. 1983*, pp. 164–65.

9. See C. Fred Bergsten, "Can We Prevent a World Economic Crisis?" *Challenge* 25, No.6 (January–February 1983): 4–13.

10. Ira C. Magaziner and Robert B. Reich, *Minding America's Business: The*

Decline and Rise of the American Economy (New York: Harcourt Brace Jovanovich, 1982), chapter 1.

11. For a selection of articles and documents on these issues, see "Reindustrialización y política económica," *Cuadernos Semestrales* 13 (México, D.F.: Instituto de Estudios de Estados Unidos/Centro de Investigación y Docencia Económicas, 1983).

12. See Sergio Bitar, "Relaciones comerciales entre América Latina y Estados Unidos: cambios en la década de los setenta," mimeograph, 1983. The data that follow are from Bitar.

13. Sanjay Dhar, "U.S. Trade with Latin America: Consequences of Financial Constraints," *Federal Reserve Bank of New York Quarterly Review* 8, No. 3 (Autumn 1983): 14–18.

14. Jaime Ros, "Crise economica e politica de estabiliçao no Mexico," in Roberto Bouzas and C. Plastino, eds., *Argentina, Brasil e Mexico face a crise internacional dos anos 1980s* (Rio de Janeiro: Ed. Graal, forthcoming).

Part III
Political and
Social Issues in
U.S.–Latin American
Relations

10

Can Democracy Be Exported? The Quest for Democracy in U.S.–Latin American Policy

Howard J. Wiarda

Can democracy be exported? Should the United States support democracy in Latin America (and presumably elsewhere) when it has the opportunity? Which are the democratic forces in Latin America, and could they be assisted by the United States? If so, how? What are the constraints and limits on U.S. assistance to democratic regimes and movements in Latin America? Is this a period of "opening" (*apertura*) for democracy in Latin America, and how might the United States assist that development? These are the questions explored in this essay.[1]

It must be stated at the outset that it is unlikely that the United States can "bring" or "teach" democracy to Latin America. It is doubtful that U.S.-style democracy can be exported, or even that Latin America (allowing for country variations and historical swings in democracy's popularity) wants it, at least all that much. It is also uncertain that democratic forces in Latin America can be helped more than marginally by the United States. In addition, there are numerous constraints and limits on the United States' capability to assist democratic regimes and democratic movements in the region. Not only is it unlikely that U.S. efforts in this area can be very successful, but there are also strong possibilities that Latin America's development prospects might be harmed by such initiatives. Indeed, it is not clear that asking whether democracy can or should be exported is asking the right question about U.S.–Latin American relations.[2] Such strong and provocative statements demand further explanation.

The Democracy Agenda

The "realism versus idealism" debate in U.S. foreign policy—of which the current discussion of U.S. efforts to promote human rights and democracy abroad is only the most recent manifestion—has been long and arduous. Realists argue that the United States must defend not principles but national interests, or that "we have no friends, only interests."[3] Ideal-ists favor a policy that goes beyond "mere" national interest and incorpo-rates as well a concern for international morality and ethics, including democracy and human rights.[4] In this debate, both sides have sometimes caricatured the arguments of the other.

In fact, U.S. policy has been more complex, incorporating ingredients from both the "realist" and the "idealist" schools of thought—and often denying a contradiction between them. George Kennan, long identified with the "realist" or "pragmatic" school, sees the support of democracy as part of a hard-headed defense of U.S. national interest.[5] And Henry Kissinger, a leading theorist and practitioner of realpolitik, has similarly come to view the defense of human rights as part of the U.S. national interest.[6] The real question is not the either-or one of national interest versus morality, but how to combine and reconcile the two considerations so as to achieve a judicious balance.

However, the issue by now is murkier and more complicated. The United States has had considerable experience—not all of it successful—with efforts to promote U.S.-style democracy and human rights abroad. There are strong interests, vested and otherwise, at stake. The democracy and human rights agenda has also expanded (under the impact of the Cold War and other pressures) to encompass motives and objectives not contemplated in earlier discussions. Some of these agendas are apparent and/or acknowledged. Others are not. In addition, the issue has become politicized: powerful lobbies are involved, and the question has become a heated issue in domestic politics and election campaigns.

The combination of factors (some not always complementary), mo-tives, justifications, and pressures involved in the democracy debate in-cludes the following:

1. Cold War strategy: Political democracy (for example, elections) is the one dramatic, visible thing that the United States stands for that the Soviet Union and the so-called peoples' democracies do not. This may in part explain the strong U.S. commitment to elections in El Salvador and elsewhere. The promotion of democracy is thus part of a larger Cold War strategy directed primarily at the Soviet Union and its allies.[7]

2. Foreign policy considerations: The promotion of democracy is often viewed by the United States not just as an end in itself in chroni-cally unstable countries in Latin America but also as a means to secure even more basic U.S. interests, such as order and stability. In some instances, these core U.S. interests can best be served by promoting democracy; in other circumstances, however, the promotion of democ-racy may not be perceived as serving these more fundamental U.S. interests.[8] Whether the United States opts to promote democracy in a

given instance may depend on such circumstances, especially on pragmatic considerations that may or may not lead to democratic outcomes.

3. Hegemonic considerations (or "democracy as a smokescreen"): On
numerous occasions a policy of pursuing democracy has been used as a
smokescreen for other, less glorious policy goals. Under the guise of
pursuing democracy, the United States has frequently intervened in Latin
America, used it for self-serving purposes that have little or nothing to do
with democracy, imposed U.S.-preferred solutions upon it, and sometimes used "democracy" as a cover for maintaining U.S. hegemony in the
area. In this way, "democracy" has served sometimes as a major means
to increase U.S. influence in Latin America. However, Latin American
countries have not always been convinced that these policies are beneficial to them.[9]

4. Political factors: Promoting democracy abroad is often useful in
domestic politics. Both Congress and the bureaucracy favor democracy as
a foreign policy goal, and no major interest group could be opposed.
Because politicians from all parties can agree on democracy as a policy
goal (if on little else), there are no electoral costs incurred by favoring it.
The public (or at least its opinion leaders) and U.S. allies are also supportive. Thus promoting democracy abroad is almost irresistible from a domestic politics perspective—although the results may often leave much to
be desired.

5. Democracy and human rights lobbies and constituencies: These
include some research institutes, church groups, labor organizations, academic associations, and Latin American exiles. Many of these groups and
lobbies genuinely favor democracy and human rights on the basis of
principle. Some combine this interest with other agendas, including political goals, private ambitions, and power seeking. Democracy and human
rights are no longer (if they ever were) simply a matter of individual
preference and noble purpose; they have become the raison d'être of
major interest groups and professional lobbies with a considerable range
of motives, for both good and ill.

6. Ethnocentrism: U.S. notions of democracy usually reflect North
American institutional arrangements and may not always be relevant to
Latin America. For example, U.S. observers often depict the political
process in Latin America as a dichotomous, either/or "struggle" between
dictatorship and (U.S.-style) democracy. This is a biased, overly narrow,
and ethnocentric formulation that distorts our understanding, closes off
other possibilities, and blinds U.S. observers to Latin American realities.
But perceptions such as these do shape much of the political discussion
regarding Latin America in the United States.[10]

7. Latin America as an experimental laboratory: The United States

does not follow a policy of promoting democracy in the Soviet Union, China, or Saudi Arabia. Are there special reasons why it does so in Latin America? The United States' willingness to experiment politically in the region is in part related to the fact that Latin America is a low foreign policy priority. The United States generally does not perceive the region to be of crucial importance; Latin American countries cannot retaliate, and therefore it is safe to use the region as a laboratory for policy experimentation.[11]

8. The missionary tradition: United States citizens believe that democracy is good, and that it is good for all peoples—the Churchillian notion that democracy is the worst form of government, except for all others. From this perspective, the United States has an obligation to export democracy (missionary style) to less fortunate ("developing") peoples. The Carter administration's human rights campaign was heir to this manifest destiny phenomenon—the idea of spreading U.S. expertise and institutions to the rest of the world, the naive if idealistic Wilsonian view of "making the world safe for democracy."[12]

9. Soul-satisfaction: The United States also promotes democracy abroad because U.S. citizens, particularly political activists, feel good about it. To stand for democracy is soul-satisfying in a personal and collective sense. Democracy and human rights seem almost to be a new form of religiosity and "true belief" around which to rally in an age of secularity.

10. La moda: Apart from the intrinsic value of democracy, supporting democracy in its more advanced and esoteric form is often thought to be (especially in some academic, church, exile, and literary circles) chic, stylish, and "with it." Without belittling what are in many cases sincere and well-meaning intentions, the current fashion in favor of more radical forms of democracy is in part a reflection (by some U.S. and Latin American intellectuals) of the desire to be stylish. The problem is that policymakers, politicians, the general public, and the countries to which the United States might seek to export these ideas may not always be receptive to such views or to the policy prescriptions associated with them.

Of course, many people (including the author of this paper) are in favor of promoting democracy and human rights both in the United States and in Latin America. The purpose of presenting this list of motives is not to demean democracy or those struggling to achieve it. However, this examination does show that the issue is more complex than often thought; that it is not just a matter of moral good versus moral evil; and that a variety of political, Cold War, private, and other agendas and ambitions are also involved.

Is Latin America Democratic—And Does It Want to Be?

The popular image of Latin America held by many U.S. citizens is that it is a continent seething under the tyranny of seemingly endemic oligarchies and repressive military dictatorships. If only these dictatorships can be removed or overthrown, the argument runs, then the natural democratic inclinations that have been suppressed under right wing and oligarchic rule may find fruition. This view is a happy, optimistic, and poetic one, but it does not always reflect Latin American reality.

The fact that the United States' focus is on democracy and the struggle for democratic ideals does not necessarily mean that Latin Americans similarly clamor for democracy. United States observers often *assume* that this is the case, but few bother to examine the evidence. The evidence is decidedly mixed. Four measures will be used here to demonstrate this ambiguity: Latin America's constitutional and legal traditions, survey research results, voting returns, and patterns of legitimacy. The discussion must perforce be brief and somewhat incomplete.

Latin America evidences two quite distinct traditions with regard to constitutional and legal precepts. There is no single liberal and democratic tradition with majority support, as in the United States. Rather, two currents have consistently been present, existing side by side and often alternating in power. The first is liberal, democratic, and republican; it is enshrined in many articles in the laws and constitutions of the region. This tradition has been present since Latin American countries achieved their independence in the early nineteenth century and, in many cases, simply translated the U.S. constitution into Spanish. However, the precepts inscribed in these Latin American constitutions have always been viewed as ideals to strive for, not necessarily as operating realities.[13]

There is also a second tradition inscribed both in laws and constitutions and in actual practice. It is hierarchical, authoritarian, and non-democratic, and its roots antedate the liberal tradition to the period of Spanish colonial rule. This tradition is reflected in the privileged position afforded the Catholic church in Latin American society; the extraordinary powers granted to the executive, who can rule almost as a *de jure* dictator; the special status given to land and wealth; and the position of the armed forces as virtually a fourth branch of government, authorized constitutionally and by "organic laws" (or by hallowed custom) to play a major, "moderating" political role. These (and other) hierarchial-authoritarian features frequently enjoy as great a degree of legitimacy as do the liberal-democratic ones. The two traditions coexist, with neither necessarily or consistently dominant.[14]

Survey research results are a second indicator of this heterogeneous set of beliefs. If one asks Latin Americans which form of government and what kinds of institutions they prefer, the answer is, overwhelmingly, democratic ones. That is, Latin Americans prefer checks and balances, an independent legislature and judiciary, a free press, human rights, elections, an apolitical military, and so forth. These responses lend support to the thesis that democracy is not alien to Latin America and that the political arrangements Latin Americans prefer are much like those found in the United States.[15]

However, if one probes deeper the responses are less clear cut. Latin Americans also favor strong executive leadership, which may come at the expense of an independent congress or court system. There is sympathy, under crisis circumstances, for limiting freedom of the press and other basic political rights. Considerable skepticism exists in Latin America as to whether democracy works very well in the region, or at least as to whether it works in its Anglo-American forms in the face of the endemic violence, conflict, *falta de civilización*, weak civic institutions, and powerful centrifugal forces that from time to time tear Latin American nations apart. Considerable sympathy exists for authoritative if not authoritarian rule, particularly in periods of stress and so long as a mild authoritarianism does not degenerate into tyranny (as it did under Trujillo and the later Somozas).[16]

Similarly ambiguous attitudes regarding democracy have been manifest in many Latin American countries. However, the 1983 election that brought President Raúl Alfonsín to power in Argentina is particularly instructive. This election and Argentina's return to democracy have been rightly celebrated. But such sentiments should not cloud Argentina's more complex political realities. In the weeks before the election, a nationwide survey showed 86 percent of the Argentine people in favor of democracy. Nonetheless, the same survey showed that less than half the population favors democracy's necessary institutional arrangements: only 46 percent of those surveyed supported political parties, and only 40 percent held a favorable opinion of trade unions. When asked what form of democracy they preferred, 84 percent of those surveyed responded "strong government." These responses clearly reveal a double loyalty: support both for democracy and for its Bonapartist forms. These are the "forked trails" (as they were labeled by the Argentine social scientist who conducted the survey, Natalio Botana) open to the country: broad support for a democratic opening, but widespread concern and skepticism regarding what that process will unleash—and, therefore, a concurrent preference for authoritative if not authoritarian government. Argentine citizens want democracy, but in an orderly and probably organic form. If democracy proves chaotic, the authoritarian solution may reappear as what Botana called a "wicked necessity." He concluded: "There is conflict between two trends and, perhaps, two traditions. Neither has been able to assert itself definitely in Argentina."[17]

Voting returns provide a third indicator of these mixed beliefs. The analysis here must necessarily be incomplete, but several examples are relevant. In the Dominican Republic in 1966, the conservative Joaquín Balaguer easily defeated socialist Juan Bosch in the presidential election, even though it was widely assumed that the U.S. military intervention in 1965 would provoke a radical nationalist electoral response favoring Bosch. In Chile before the 1973 military coup, voting returns consistently showed an electorate almost equally divided among rightist forces, centrist parties (chiefly the Christian Democrats), and the socialist-communist popular front. The November 1982 electoral results in Brazil could be interpreted to show the country almost evenly divided between supporters of the existing authoritarian military regime and those opposed to it. Even in beleaguered El Salvador in 1981, the U.S.-favored centrist Christian Democrats could manage only 40 percent of the vote, and they lost to a coalition of conservative and rightist forces. In 1984 the Christian Democrat candidate won the presidency, but the candidate representing unabashed authoritarianism, Roberto D'Aubisson, won 46 percent of the vote in an election generally regarded as open and fair.

One should not read too much into these examples. However, electoral returns do show what U.S. citizens often find to be surprising facts—that is, the continued strength of the Latin American right, traditional caudilloism, and authoritarianism even in an era that is almost always referred to as change-oriented and "revolutionary." Labeling such rightist sentiment the result of "false consciousness" is too simple an explanation. The fact is that electorally (and in other ways, as well) many Latin American societies are deeply divided among their historical authoritarian and conservative, liberal, and more recent socialist traditions. The clashes among these traditions—which are not just differences among rival party platforms but among wholly different perspectives and worldviews—help explain present instability in the region and the existence of what the longtime Latin Americanist Kalman Silvert called a "conflict society."[18] In short, it is clear that electoral preferences in Latin America are not unambiguously liberal, democratic, or leftist. The situation is much more complex.

The fourth point to be made here concerns democratic legitimacy and the means to achieve it. In the United States elections are the only legitimate route to power. In Latin America, elections are but one route to power; other routes are also open.[19] These may include a skillfully executed coup d'état, a heroic guerrilla movement that holds out against all odds and finally seizes power, a well-planned protest movement, a general strike or street demonstration that succeeds in toppling a minister—or perhaps even a government. Actions such as these are not only widely admired, but they also have the potential to help a regime that comes to power through nonelectoral means to achieve the legitimacy it may initially lack. The "populist" regimes of Omar Torrijos in Panama or René Barrientos in Bolivia are cases in point. Democratic elections offer one route to power, but there are also other means to achieve both legitimacy and democracy, Latin American style.

These comments are not meant to imply that if Latin Americans had their choice, they would not—at least in the abstract—choose democracy. In fact, democratic sentiment is vigorous throughout the region. But it is not the only widespread sentiment, and in a number of countries it may not even be the majority sentiment. Especially as one probes beneath the surface, Latin Americans' doubts and fears concerning democracy's viability or their own nations' capacity for democratic politics become clear.[20] Thus the answer to the question "Is Latin America democratic, and does it want to be?" is ambiguous: many Latin Americans want democracy, but many do not; some Latin Americans (primarily in older generations) want a democracy structured largely in terms of U.S.-style institutional arrangements, but others (the rising younger generations) prefer their own indigenous forms ("populist" or other kinds). Any effort by the United States to export or encourage democracy in Latin America must come to grips with these differences.

The Problems and Consequences of a Foreign Policy Oriented Toward Promoting Democracy

The historical record offers little cause for optimism or enthusiasm regarding vigorous new U.S. efforts to promote democracy in Latin America. This record merits a brief review.

Commodore Cornelius Vanderbilt, his agent, William Walker, and the latter's "merry" bunch of filibusterers were no doubt sincere in believing that, by taking over Nicaragua in the 1840s and holding elections in which U.S. citizen Walker was "elected" president, they brought the benefits of democratic civilization to that poor, benighted land. Sam Houston and others were also probably genuinely convinced that depriving Mexico of half its national territory and ultimately absorbing it into the United States would be infinitely better *even for the Mexicans* than continued rule by the mercurial López de Santa Anna. The former slaveholders who sought to annex or control Cuba, Hispaniola, Puerto Rico, and other islands after the Civil War were also convinced that U.S.-style "democracy" was good for "our little brown and black brothers" throughout the Caribbean.[21]

Similarly, the Spanish-American War of 1898 was in part rationalized on the basis of the presumed superiority of U.S. democratic political arrangements to "Catholic-inquisitorial" Spanish institutions. Under the same aegis, the United States acquired Puerto Rico as a protectorate and attached the Platt Amendment to the Cuban constitution, giving the United States virtual carte blanche to intervene in Cuba at any time. When Theodore Roosevelt, William Howard Taft, and Woodrow Wilson dispatched U.S. occupation forces to Haiti, Cuba, the Dominican Republic, Nicaragua, and Panama, they also believed that these actions were part of a larger mission to make the world safe for democracy. However brief and one-sided, this background survey provides ample reason to be skeptical regarding the presumed benefits to Latin America of U.S. efforts to encourage "democracy" in the region.[22]

Setting the Parameters of Permissible Behavior: The Post-World War II Period

At the end of World War II, the United States displaced both Germany and Great Britain to achieve unquestioned hegemony in Latin America. With the war over, the United States viewed Latin America primarily as a vast preserve of untapped resources and potential markets. However, gaining access to those markets required a diminution in Latin America's system of economic statism, cartels, monopolies, and other controls. The United States therefore exerted pressures for economic liberalization (reduced state economic controls), which carried with it the need for a certain degree of political liberalization. The United States insisted on new elections in several countries, and it exerted strong pressures on a number of populist leaders to resign from office. Among those leaders forced from office or pressured into taking unwelcome actions were Vargas in Brazil, Morínigo in Paraguay, and Perón in Argentina, as well as a number of others.[23]

The immediate post-World War II period in U.S.–Latin American relations was important beyond its specific time frame because it largely determined the future parameters and range of permissible options for Latin American political behavior. Latin America was forced to choose between "dictatorship" (statism, neocorporatism, neomercantilism, and so forth)—which the United States would no longer countenance—and U.S.-style democracy, which was not entirely compatible with the region's history and traditions. Whatever the original intention, Latin America was subjected to far greater U.S. economic penetration in the name of "democracy." In addition, forcing Latin American countries to choose a form of democracy for which they were ill suited, the United States effectively ruled out both a Latin American form of democracy (for example, Vargas-style populism) and various intermediate political arrangements (for example, combined civil-military regimes). Latin American politicians have always had a genius for improvising such arrangements, which might have better enabled these nations to manage the wrenching transition to modernity that they had recently begun. By insisting on democracy (and only its U.S. variant), the United States helped precipitate wild swings of the political pendulum in Latin America, leading to the kinds of imbroglios that the United States now confronts in Central America and elsewhere.[24] This is not the only reason for Latin America's post-World War II political instability, but it was certainly a major contributing factor.

Kennedy and the Alliance for Progress

John F. Kennedy and his Alliance for Progress are widely admired for supposedly ushering in a new era in U.S.–Latin American relations. There *were* changes in terms of the personal qualities for which the president was noted in Latin America (including his youth, vigor, idealism, Catholicism, his beautiful and artistic wife, and so forth); changes in the means used to pursue basic U.S. interests (stability and anticommunism would be achieved by aid to liberal democrats rather than to dictators); and changes in personnel appointments within the U.S. Department of State.[25] But there were also important continuities. The basic elements of U.S. policy remained constant: stability, anticommunism, hegemony, and political-economic-military penetration.[26]

But it is specifically the issue of democracy that is relevant here. Once again, the record was mixed. Kennedy supported Latin America's democratic left during the first part of his presidency, but his attitude toward these groups cooled considerably toward the end of his brief tenure. Although Kennedy favored democrats, he was also reluctant to undermine or remove dictators if he could not be assured that a Castroite takeover would not occur. He showed reserve regarding wobbly democrats like Bosch in the Dominican Republic, and he eventually chose the lesser evil of military juntas there and in Honduras rather than risk weak, ineffectual democrats unable to deal with guerrilla threats.[27] The United States helped some of these democrats come to power, but it often failed to come to their assistance when they were threatened by military coups. Nor did the dramatic and highly publicized U.S. efforts in Peru in 1962 to reverse a coup and ensure democratic rule succeed. If anything, these efforts harmed U.S.-Peruvian relations in the long run and probably led directly to the confrontation between the United States and Peru that occurred in the late 1960s. In summary, one would be hard pressed to conclude that U.S. efforts to promote democracy under Kennedy and the

Alliance for Progress were very successful. In fact, a strong case could be made that these efforts were counterproductive and that they helped precipitate a wave of antidemocractic coups that swept Latin America in the early and mid-1960s (Argentina, Dominican Republic, Honduras, Peru, Brazil).

Carter and Human Rights

The Carter human rights campaign also produced decidedly mixed results. There is no doubt that, as a result of this campaign, some people were not tortured; some liberties were preserved; some people were released from jail; and some restraints were placed on military repression. These are not small accomplishments, particularly from the point of view of the individuals and groups affected.

On the other hand, the costs incurred and the damage done were also considerable. Some of the human rights activists' actions were unrefined, heavy-handed, and often counterproductive. By engaging in wholesale condemnations of entire nations, regimes, and military establishments (as in the cases of Brazil and Argentina) as human rights violators, they insulted national sensibilities and often forced public opinion—which otherwise would have been opposed to or neutral toward these regimes— to rally behind repressive governments. Such unrefined condemnations blurred the differences between the repressive forces in the Latin American militaries and more democratic elements, obliging the latter to defend the military institution as a whole. The differences between honest and well-meaning governments and their out-of-control security forces were also blurred, at the cost of antagonizing or sometimes undermining the former. The Carter human rights campaign needlessly alienated important countries such as Argentina, Brazil, and Chile, and it produced precious few changes in the behavior of these countries' governments. Nor was the policy evenhanded. Right wing dictatorships were condemned, but leftist dictatorships did not receive the same attention. Ethnocentrism was also strong. The human rights campaign in Latin America was often viewed as an extension of the civil rights struggle in the southern United States in the 1960s. Moreover, the criteria for judging human rights violations were exclusively U.S. criteria, with little interest in or comprehension of differences in Latin American values.[28]

Even the greatest success story of the Carter administration's campaign for democracy—the United States' political and diplomatic intervention in the 1978 Dominican presidential election—was not the unqualified success that the action's defenders claim. In the face of blatant military ballot tampering, the Carter administration acted to ensure an honest vote count—thereby securing victory for Antonio Guzmán. Intervention of this kind may have produced a beneficial result, but it was intervention nonetheless—and not much different from countless other U.S. intrusions into Latin American countries' internal affairs. Furthermore, because of the Carter administration's actions, Guzmán became known in the Dominican Republic as "Jimmy Carter and Cyrus Vance's boy," dependent upon them and presumably certain to fall when they left office. In the end that did not happen. But there is no doubt that U.S. actions strongly reinforced the absolute dependence of the Dominican Republic and its government on the United States. Whether that is good or bad is irrelevant here. The point is that this most recent U.S. intervention in the Dominican Republic was not quite the shining, unambiguous achievement that it is sometimes held to be.[29]

One need not exaggerate these failures, self-deceptions, hypocricies, and limited and ambiguous accomplishments in order to make the main point: past U.S. policies to promote democracy and human rights in Latin America have not been unqualified successes. For reasons to be explained in the next section, such efforts are likely to be even more problematic in the future. In fact, a close examination of the historical record would leave one skeptical that promoting democracy was *ever* a primary U.S. objective or that it is soon likely to become one. If, as most analysts would agree, the major goals of U.S. policy toward Latin America have been stability, anticommunism, and access to the region's markets and resources, promoting democracy has been chiefly a means to achieve those ends. Its greatest importance has been as an instrument to be employed under the right conditions (and only in some administrations) to help secure the higher-priority goals of stability and anticommunism.[30]

However, this argument does not rest only on the conclusion that U.S. efforts to promote democracy in Latin America have not been very successful. In some cases these initiatives were actually *harmful* in the long run. The reasons for this negative assessment can be summarized briefly as follows:[31]

1. Immense amounts of money, time, and resources have been wasted, with but very modest results. Taxpayer and congressional support for such activities has been squandered. The widespread popular notion is that in seeking to promote democracy abroad, the United States may be chasing chimeras.

2. The effort has produced a host of foreign policy setbacks, unanticipated consequences, and sheer disasters. The simple listing of these reverses in just one country—for example, the Dominican Republic—would fill more than the remainder of this essay.[32]

3. United States attempts to promote democracy abroad have helped perpetuate and reinforce condescending, superior, and patronizing attitudes toward Latin America. The notion is still widespread in both gov-

ernment circles and popular opinion that "the United States knows best" for Latin America.

4. The emphasis on democracy has also perpetuated misleading conceptual models for understanding Latin America. By focusing attention on the supposed "struggle for democracy," U.S. citizens often fail to appreciate the complexity of events in the region. The emphasis on democracy has contributed to a misunderstanding of many developing nations and of the real dynamics of change in Latin America.[33]

5. The stress on democracy also encourages U.S. interventionism and proconsularism. Although the United States generally acts with the best of intentions, it sometimes attempts to run some Latin American countries from its embassies. There is considerable reason to be suspicious of such U.S. interventionism, whether it comes from "bad" agencies such as the Central Intelligence Agency or "good" agencies such as the Department of State or the Agency for International Development.

6. The democracy that the United States espouses always seems to conform to its own notions of democracy, not to Latin America's. The United States stresses elections, political parties, apolitical trade unions, apolitical armed forces, and so forth. Latin American forms of democracy—emphasizing populism, organicism, the accommodation of new "power contenders," corporatist representation and societal pluralism, and shared power—are seldom given serious attention.[34] This represents a form of what some have called "cultural imperialism."

7. By emphasizing democracy so strongly in rhetoric and in policy pronouncements, the United States has limited Latin America's choice to a false dichotomy: democracy or dictatorship. It rules out the various intermediate solutions that Latin Americans themselves have historically demonstrated a flair for fashioning. It also means that the United States has a certain responsibility for causing political instability in Latin America, the prevention of which is one of the pillars of U.S. policy toward the region. Rather than allowing these countries to settle more or less naturally and Latin American-style on some murky middle ground, the United States has sometimes imposed two extreme options on the region, neither one of which is always appropriate or especially comfortable.

8. Finally, the United States' emphasis on democracy has undermined various traditional institutions (patronage networks, religious agencies, family and clan groups, and so forth) that might have helped Latin America make the difficult transition to modernity, while failing to create viable structures to replace them. In this way the United States has helped create the very problems and institutional vacuums that U.S. policies were ostensibly intended to prevent.[35]

On balance, U.S. efforts to promote democracy in Latin America have produced mixed results. There have been successes as well as failures. Neither outcome ought to be emphasized at the expense of the other.

Nonetheless, the troubling questions raised here are seldom considered in policy discussions in the United States. The lessons of the past are forgotten or unlearned. Policy is often based on romantic hopes and wishful thinking rather than on an examination of the historical record. Past experiences have had very little impact on U.S. perceptions of its various campaigns to export democracy to Latin America. Yet U.S. citizens are often so committed to the democracy agenda (albeit for diverse reasons and motives, as suggested earlier) that they would prefer not to deal with the more difficult questions of whether the United States should become involved in these efforts at all, or to what extent, or whether such actions are helpful or harmful. Inattention to the negative consequences of these policies is particularly poignant and troubling now, because the U.S. government is poised on the threshold of a new attempt to promote democracy abroad. Both President Reagan and prominent figures in the Democratic party have announced plans to this effect.[36] It is necessary to interject some realism into this discussion based on the historical evidence—a perspective that is woefully lacking in all the current proposals. At the same time, it is important to consider new realities in the United States, in Latin America, and in U.S.–Latin American relations.

New Realities and New Directions

The previous sections of this essay examined democracy in Latin America and U.S. efforts to promote democracy in the region in largely theoretical terms—whether such efforts are desirable, what the motivations are for pursuing this course, what the prospects are for achieving this goal, what the historical record shows, and so forth. The discussion now turns to the newer *realities* in Latin America, in the United States, and in U.S.–Latin American relations. Few of these factors augur well for U.S. efforts to promote democracy in the hemisphere.

The first issue with which the United States must come to terms is that in recent years Latin America has become increasingly independent, nationalistic, and assertive. This is less true in the smaller, more dependent countries of Central America and the Caribbean than in the larger countries of South America, but the trend is manifest throughout the region. Therefore Latin American countries are less willing to accept U.S. advice, including advice on the issue of democracy. Most Latin American countries are willing to look to western Europe for advice and/or models to emulate, but they turn less and less to the United States. Latin America (at least most of the region) seeks to reduce or modify its dependence on the United States, not increase it. This is the case regarding not just economic issues, but cultural and political questions as well. It is unrealistic to expect that this trend will be reversed, and that Latin America will suddenly (or even gradually) look again to the U.S. political system as *the* model to follow. Too much has changed in Latin America in the last twenty years (as well as in the United States) for that to be possible.[37]

A second, related new reality is the situation in the United States itself. In comparison with the prevailing situation twenty years ago, the United States is now a diminished presence in Latin America. This is not to say that the United States is unimportant or that it does not continue to have great influence in the region. But many aspects of the U.S. role have changed considerably. United States foreign assistance to Latin America has declined; there are far fewer U.S. diplomatic personnel in the field; and, except in the special case of Central America, U.S. military missions are greatly reduced. The hotels in Latin America are filled not with U.S. businessmen but with West Germans, Japanese, French, Spaniards, Italians, Scandinavians, eastern Europeans, Russians, and Chinese. These are the countries that now often win the contracts for dams, highways, port facilities, and development projects, rather than the United States. Together these changes mean a greatly reduced U.S. presence in Latin America in a wide variety of spheres, with a concomitant lessening of U.S. influence.

Moreover, this decline in U.S. hegemony and influence is unlikely to be reversed soon. Opinion polls show that the U.S. public is overwhelmingly opposed to foreign aid, a sentiment that is certain eventually to be translated into congressional votes.[38] Those who would promote a stronger U.S. role in support of democracy in Latin America must ultimately ask themselves what means will be available to implement such a strategy. Where are the foreign assistance funds comparable to those available under the Alliance for Progress to give the United States the leverage it needs to carry out a foreign policy promoting democracy? Where is the necessary commitment on the part of the public, the Congress, or the presidency? Where is the Peace Corps-like enthusiasm for this cause, the willingness to go "any distance" (as John F. Kennedy described it)? And what are the realistic possibilities of asking U.S. citizens to suffer further unemployment in order to provide Latin American products with increased access to U.S. markets? The fact is that the domestic infrastructure and support for a major new U.S. initiative to promote democracy in Latin America simply do not exist. The resources, commitment, and the public and official support for such activities are simply not present in the United States today.

A third new reality, related to the first, concerns Latin America's increasing assertion of its own, indigenous models of development and

democracy.[39] Latin American nations increasingly wish to develop au-
tonomously in the political arena as well as in the economic sphere,
independent of U.S. wishes and preferences. Thus U.S. citizens must face
the unsettling fact that democratic forces in Latin America may not want
U.S. assistance even if it is proffered. Latin American countries may wish
to fashion their own forms of democracy, but they are less and less
inclined simply to imitate the United States. Whether the United States is
capable of dealing with this new situation is uncertain.

The problem is complicated by the fact that many Latin Americans
(especially an older generation that is now fading away) still look to the
United States, including the U.S. political model, for guidance and direction. They also believe in the institutional mechanisms that characterize
U.S.-style democracy: political parties, separation of powers, competitive
elections, and so forth. Given a choice, and all other things being equal,
many of these Latin Americans would probably prefer regular elections
and U.S.-style democracy.

But all other things are not equal. First, as previously noted, there are
other legitimate routes to power in Latin America besides elections, and
democracy itself is often of tenuous legitimacy. Second, Latin Americans
have traditionally meant something different by "democracy" than U.S.
citizens do. Whereas U.S. citizens emphasize the procedural dimensions
of democracy (elections and so forth), Latin Americans are more inclined
to judge a regime "democratic"—regardless of its route to power—that
governs for, and in the name of, the common good; that is broadly
representative of society's major interests; that evidences a degree of
populism and nationalism; that promotes economic and social development; and that is not brutal or oppressive. In short, the meaning of
"democracy" may differ considerably in different parts of the hemisphere, with Latin America following a tradition that is closer to French,
Spanish, and Italian models than to the Anglo-Saxon tradition.[40]

Furthermore, the United States must (although this is so far largely
unacknowledged at the official level) come to terms with the newer and
innovative democratic forms in Latin America that have experienced notable growth in the last decade. These include community self-help groups,
consciously nonpartisan movements for political reform, neighborhood-
based and/or popular organizations, and nascent human rights and reform
groups seeking to strengthen the rule of law.[41] In all the discussion emanating from the United States concerning the need to strengthen democracy in
Latin America, almost nothing has been said about any of the newer, *Latin
American* forms of democracy that exist outside standard U.S. terms of
reference and the customary framework of U.S.-style institutions.

A fourth factor concerns the severe downward turn of the world economy beginning in 1979 and its implications for democracy in Latin Amer-

ica. This issue can be approached in terms of the U.S. economy and the United States' capacity and willingness to provide assistance to Latin America, from the perspective of worldwide economic conditions and what impact they have in Latin America, or from the perspective of the depressed Latin American economies themselves. From whatever vantage point, the prospects for democracy are hardly encouraging.

The facts are quite obvious. The global economy has been in the midst of the worst depression since the 1930s. Oil prices have fallen, at least temporarily, but the impact of earlier price increases on Latin America was (and remains) devastating. The U.S. economy has also encountered serious problems. Even a major U.S. economic recovery may be insufficient to produce renewed growth in Latin America. Protectionist sentiment in the United States is also strong, which is not propitious either for Latin American export possibilities or for necessary U.S. foreign assistance programs such as the Caribbean Basin Initiative. None of these economic conditions is encouraging to the cause of democracy in Latin America, nor do they help established democracies in the region to survive.

Economic conditions in Latin America are terribly depressed. The boom years of the 1960s and early 1970s are over. Because the economies in the area are stagnant or contracting, the traditional Latin American means (not altogether undemocratic) of responding to change—accommodating new power contenders that agree to abide by the established rules of the game—cannot work.[42] In the present prevailing economic circumstances, there are no new resources to distribute to emerging groups. Given rising expectations, competition for control of the fewer resources that do exist becomes intense, polarized, and violent. Thus it is easy to understand why political challenges to the status quo in Latin America (where economic conditions have been even more depressed than in the United States) have been so intense. Liberal-pluralist democracy is difficult to sustain under such conditions, and even more difficult to renew or create anew. The major victim of the worldwide economic downturn in Latin America may be the very democracy the United States would hope to stimulate.

Fifth, the United States must consider why some Latin American regimes have in fact chosen democracy. The motives are complex, but not all of them have to do with a strong commitment to democracy. For example, it is clear that for some regimes a new "opening" to democracy has been dictated not so much by a firm or enduring commitment to democracy per se but by a discrediting of the established bureaucratic-authoritarian model. Rather than have the blame for economic and other policy failures fall entirely on the ruling military or military-cum-civilian groups, the incumbents opted to step aside for a time and allow eager civilian groups and political parties to share responsibility. This was clearly the motivation behind the recent so-called democratic *aperturas* in Honduras, Peru, and Bolivia, where the military had been thoroughly discredited by charges of graft, inefficiency, and repression, and where continued military rule would only further embarrass and debase the armed forces. In Argentina, military mismanagement and brutality were sufficiently exposed that it was no longer advantageous for the armed forces to stay in power. In Brazil, too, the generals opted for a democratic opening only after the glory of the vaunted "economic miracle" began to fade and new challenges confronted continued military rule.[43]

Of course, these and other cases of political transition require more detailed analysis than is possible in this essay, and the factors involved are not so simple as indicated here. But in many cases the dominant motives clearly were not a strong commitment to democracy, but rather the military's fear of further discrediting of the military institution. This also implies that the commitment to democracy in these countries may not be especially strong. Indeed, it may well be reversible in Bolivia, Peru, and other countries where recently established democracies are already in trouble. It is hard to believe that the transition from authoritarianism to democracy in Latin America (the recent subject of many conferences and much wishful thinking) is really firm, unilinear, and irreversible.

A related question concerns who in these several Latin American countries initiated the democratization process. The sources are sometimes difficult to identify, but in general these processes were initiated as an elite response to changed circumstances, not as a result of much popular clamor or grass roots pressures from below. Of course, these two dimensions are often interrelated, and one could argue that elites act only when they are pushed or threatened from below. But that does not appear to be the case in this instance. Instead, there is strong evidence that change was initiated primarily "from above" rather than "from below."[44] Although this issue cannot be fully resolved here, there is room for considerable doubt regarding both the degree of elite commitment to democracy and the depth of this commitment in society at large.

Why national elites want "democratization" is also an important question. Although these groups are accomplished at voicing the slogans of representative government, many civilian politicians in military-dominated countries leave the strong impression that they have other agendas besides democracy. What often comes through most clearly in interviews with these politicians is not so much a firm commitment to a democracy that serves the public purpose, but rather a democracy that serves private well-being. Civilian politicians in these countries are united on few issues, but the one goal they do seem to have in common is a desire to reoccupy the ministry, subministry, government corporation, or autonomous agency positions—

and the opportunities that go with these positions—from which military rule has long deprived them. If this impression is well founded, it is the basis for some considerable skepticism regarding the underlying motives for some efforts at democratization.

Another aspect of democratization in Latin America also merits close examination: the political and partisan use of this process by some elements. For example, some Latin American opposition groups have used the "democratization" issue both to strengthen their position and to undermine their own government. This result may be well and good in some cases, but not necessarily in all. Why should one opposition movement become the recipient of U.S. funds and favors and not others? Does a particular opposition group really have the popular support it claims, and does it deserve the assistance that outside groups may therefore give it? Is the opposition's claim to democratic values really merited? Does the opposition's claim to democratic legitimacy necessarily outweigh that of the government it seeks to replace? These are complex questions that can only be answered in individual circumstances. But they do serve to indicate that the issues are not always clear cut and that on numerous occasions partisan priorities are served rather than broader public interests.

In an overall examination of Latin American regimes' movement toward democracy, what is striking is the degree to which these have been autonomous Latin American choices, not U.S.-inspired decisions. There may be some congruence of interests on the democracy agenda, and in some cases a push by the United States or a deftly administered aid program has been crucial in tipping the balance toward democracy. But the real story, even with these qualifications and reservations, has been one of Latin American efforts. In fact, U.S. commitment and assistance to emerging Latin American democracy (if it is emerging) has historically been quite limited. Thus some modesty is required in an assessment of U.S. influence, capacities, and accomplishments in promoting democracy in Latin America.[45]

The sixth factor to be considered here concerns U.S. domestic politics, especially the ways in which it impinges on U.S. efforts to promote democracy in Latin America. Reviewing recent U.S. efforts to export democracy does not leave one overly confident of future success in this area. United States foreign policy goals in the region have traditionally included political stability, access to markets, support for anticommunism—and occasionally democracy insofar as it serves these other goals, which have often been considered more important.[46] Democracy as a policy goal has been pursued only up to the point at which more fundamental U.S. strategic interests were affected. For example, one must wonder how interested the United States would be in democracy in Nicaragua if the Sandinista government suddenly (and unexpectedly) renounced Marxism, expelled Cuban advisers, and realigned itself with the United States.

Moreover, the democracy that the United States envisages and will accept consistently looks remarkably like the U.S. system. Ethnocentrism is still present within the U.S. government, despite protestations from some officials that this has changed and that "they [the Latin Americans] know how."[47] To the extent to which U.S. foreign policy favors democracy at all, the emphasis is on U.S.-style political institutions, such as political parties, elections, and so forth. Democracy on Latin America's own terms—involving populism and power sharing, new community-based organizations, and institutional arrangements other than those familiar to the United States—has not yet been seriously considered.[48]

Then, too, the kind of democracy that the United States can and will officially support will almost certainly be a reflection of U.S. domestic pluralism and interest group politics. Business groups will insist that the private sector be given a major role; labor groups will claim a similar privilege concerning labor relations; the Democratic and Republican parties will each want to create and assist like-minded groups abroad; church and human rights groups will exercise veto power over human rights policy; the Cuban exile community will demand veto power over U.S. relations with Cuba; and so forth. Every special interest involved will seek a role in policy formulations, and no administration will be able to resist these pressures. Observers who search for a coherent, sustained, integrated, nonfragmented definition of the kind of democracy the United States will export, as well as for some recognition of Latin America's own special needs, definitions, and preferences in these matters, are certain to be disappointed.[49]

Finally, one must recognize that any U.S. program to promote democracy abroad is certain to be partisan and to be regarded as such. The plan announced by President Reagan in early 1983 was strongly criticized because it channeled aid and contracts chiefly to groups thought to be conservative.[50] Although this program may demonstrate a certain bias, it is difficult to believe that a Democratic administration would not also— and equally lamentably—award those same contracts to *its* friends and supporters. In either case, partisan rather than public purposes will be served. Democracy in Latin America will once again be an accidental by-product of (or perhaps victimized by) such overweening domestic U.S. political considerations.

Conclusions and Implications

To the somewhat rhetorical question posed in the title of this essay, "Can democracy be exported?" the answer must be: no. It is not possible for the United States to *export* democracy to Latin America or to other areas. The United States can hardly shape (much less determine) the political preferences and institutional arrangements of other countries.

But perhaps the title asks the wrong question. Perhaps the issue is not whether democracy can be exported, but whether this is one of those periods in Latin American history when democracy could grow and develop. Is Latin America at the end of a bureaucratic-authoritarian epoch and on the threshold of a democratic one? Are the forces and currents now present in Latin America propitious for democracy? Is this democracy's historical "moment" in Latin America? If so, what should and can the United States do to assist and encourage this presumed transition to democracy? Are there elements of congruence between U.S. foreign policy and Latin America's recent movements toward democracy? Should the United States support democracy in Latin America when it has the opportunity to do so?[51] What specific actions should the United States take?

To begin, it is necessary to strike a balance between observers who are entirely cynical about democracy's future in Latin America and those who are excessively enthusiastic. There *are* new democratic trends in Latin America. With great care, empathy, prudence, and a sustained, coherent policy, these trends might be encouraged and developed. With sensitive foreign policy officials, the judicious use of assistance funds, and a sense of restraint and modesty as to what the United States can accomplish, there are things the United States can and should do to aid Latin American democracy. Some of these tasks can be accomplished unilaterally, while others require multilateral cooperation. A number of different approaches and techniques are available.

On the other hand, one should oppose a loud new official *campaign* in favor of democracy, especially if it is characterized by the missionary zeal so typical of such efforts. U.S. pressure is unlikely to work and may backfire.[52] Hopes and expectations in favor of democracy should not be raised too high. One should still be skeptical as to whether this is democracy's "moment" in Latin America, or whether that moment may not be very temporary or have already passed in at least some countries. One must caution against the belief that Latin America is clamoring for democracy (especially U.S.-style democracy) or that the Latin American countries cannot resolve their own problems in their own sometimes incompletely democratic ways. One must also recognize that U.S. domestic public opinion and the U.S. Congress are not enthusiastic about new aid programs; that worldwide economic depression augurs ill for new democratic openings; that trade protectionism is strong and will further hurt Latin America's economic prospects; that special interests will undercut or capture parts of any such democracy program; that diverse motives and ambitions are at work in this area; that much of Latin America may reject U.S. initiatives; and that the United States rarely understands and cares about Latin America sufficiently to help fashion an indigenous democracy for the region rather than a system based patronizingly and condescendingly on its own preferred political arrangements. The "new realities" in Latin America, in the United States, and in inter-American relations make a U.S.-sponsored effort to promote democracy in the hemisphere problematic at best.

In conclusion, it is important to note a series of dilemmas that must be resolved if democracy is to be promoted in Latin America. First, the issue of idealism versus realism in U.S. foreign policy is still a concern. Is the United States really trying (in El Salvador and elsewhere) to promote democracy, or is it simply protecting its own interests? Second, are the differences between U.S. and Latin American preferences for—and understandings of—democracy reconcilable? In ostensibly promoting democracy abroad, does the United States fully understand what it is doing? Third, limits and constraints on U.S. actions in this area must be recognized. The United States must appreciate what it can and cannot do in Latin America, as well as the difference between good intentions and complex realities. Fourth, there are difficult problems of consistency and double standards, of reconciling democracy and human rights concerns with strategic and other U.S. interests, and of whether to treat all countries equally in this regard (that is, whether to be as concerned with democracy in Cuba or Nicaragua as in Chile or Guatemala).

Fifth, there is yet another difficulty in achieving U.S. goals for democracy in Latin America without that implying blatant interference in the internal political affairs of other countries. Sixth, the United States must also reconcile domestic political considerations with the realities of other countries—especially the awareness that what is advantageous in the United States may not be realistic elsewhere. Latin America has often been an unfortunate laboratory for U.S. social and political experiments that frequently produce unforeseen consequences. Finally, the United States should not pursue efforts to promote democracy so zealously that it overlooks the nuances, combinations, and heterogeneous patterns that are the real world of Latin American politics.

It is doubtful that the United States can reconcile these various dilemmas and pursue a policy to promote democracy in Latin America that is rational, coherent, and sustained over a relatively long (twenty-year) period. Thus on this issue as on others, the United States must recognize severe limits on the possibilities for its policy. The United States must have modest expectations and recognize the strong constraints on what can and cannot be accomplished. The United States should pursue a policy that is realistic, prudent, enlightened, pragmatic, and based on some understanding of and empathy for Latin America—a policy that is not overzealous in any aspect, including its pursuit of democracy.[53] This would seem to be an appropriately modest agenda. But given the pressures in which U.S. foreign policy now operates, and the special conditions of U.S.–Latin American relations within that broader context, this may be all that one can reasonably hope or expect.[54]

Department of Political Science
University of Massachusetts–Amherst

Notes

Peter Bell, Margaret Crahan, Kevin J. Middlebrook, and Iêda Siqueira Wiarda offered helpful comments on an earlier version of this paper. However, the views expressed are the author's own.

1. See also Howard J. Wiarda, ed., *The Continuing Struggle for Democracy in Latin America* (Boulder, Colo: Westview, 1980), especially the editor's introduction and conclusion. On the same theme, see Frank Tannenbaum, *The Future of Democracy in Latin America* (New York: Knopf, 1974).

2. For an elaboration, see Howard J. Wiarda, ed., *Politics and Social Change in Latin America: The Distinct Tradition*, rev. ed. (Amherst: University of Massachusetts Press, 1982), and Wiarda, *Corporatism and National Development in Latin America* (Boulder, Colo: Westview, 1981).

3. The quote has been attributed to John Foster Dulles. The foremost representative of the "realist" approach is Hans J. Morgenthau, *Politics Among Nations: The Struggle for Power and Peace*, 5th ed., rev. (New York: Knopf, 1978).

4. Reinhold Niebuhr, *Moral Man and Immoral Society: A Study in Ethics and Politics* (New York: Scribner's, 1932), and Ernest Lefever, *Ethics and United States Foreign Policy* (New York: Meridian Books, 1957).

5. George F. Kennan, *The Cloud of Danger: Current Realities of American Foreign Policy* (Boston: Little, Brown, 1977).

6. Henry Kissinger, "The Realities of Security," 1981 Francis Boyer Lecture on Public Policy, in *AEI Foreign Policy and Defense Review* 3, No. 6 (1982): 11–16.

7. Theodore P. Wright, Jr., *American Support of Free Elections Abroad* (Westport, Conn: Greenwood Press, 1980).

8. James Kurth, "The United States, Latin America, and the World: The Changing International Context of U.S.–Latin American Relations," part 1 in this volume; see also the report of Susan Kaufman Purcell's remarks on this issue, in Lisa L. Condit, "Rapporteur's Report on the Inter-American Dialogue Workshop on United States–Latin American Relations in the 1980s," Woodrow Wilson International Center for Scholars, Latin American Program, Washington, D.C., 21–22 January 1983.

9. See the fascinating cable by Ambassador Spruille Braden (soon to become even better known—or infamous—through his opposition to Argentina's

Juan Perón), "Policy Respecting Dictatorships and Disreputable Governments" (Havana, 5 April 1945), Department of State, Document No. 711.00/4-545. An excellent book on this theme is Michael Grow, *The Good Neighbor Policy and Authoritarianism in Paraguay: United States Economic Expansion and Great-Power Rivalry in Latin America During World War II* (Lawrence: University of Kansas Press, 1981).

10. Wiarda, *The Continuing Struggle for Democracy*, "Conclusion."

11. These points are elaborated in testimony delivered at the time of the Falklands/Malvinas crisis in 1982: Howard J. Wiarda, "The United States and Latin America in the Aftermath of the Falklands/Malvinas Crisis," *Latin America and the United States after the Falklands/Malvinas Crisis: Hearings Before the Subcommittee on Inter-American Affairs of the Committee on Foreign Affairs, House of Representatives, Ninety-Seventh Congress, Second Session, 20 July and 5 August 1982* (Washington, D.C.: U.S. Government Printing Office, 1982): 22–42, 77–82.

12. Larman C. Wilson, "Human Rights in United States Foreign Policy: The Rhetoric and the Practice," in Don C. Piper and Ronald J. Terchek, eds., *Interaction: Foreign Policy and Public Policy* (Washington, D.C.: American Enterprise Institute for Public Policy Analysis, 1983), pp.178–208; Joshua Moravchik, *The Carter Experience and the Dilemmas of Human Rights Policy*, Ph.D. diss., Department of Government, Georgetown University, 1984.

13. James L. Busey, "Observations on Latin American Constitutionalism," *The Americas* 24, No. 1 (July 1967): 46–66.

14. Glen C. Dealy, *The Public Man: An Interpretation of Latin American and Other Catholic Countries* (Amherst: University of Massachusetts Press, 1977); Claudio Veliz, *The Centralist Tradition in Latin America* (Princeton: Princeton University Press, 1980).

15. The literature on this point is vast; particularly useful is Enrique A. Baloyra and John D. Martz, *Political Attitudes in Venezuela: Societal Cleavages and Political Opinion* (Austin: University of Texas Press, 1979).

16. Veliz, *The Centralist Tradition;* Dealy, *The Public Man;* Wiarda, *Corporatism and National Development.*

17. Natalio R. Botana, "New Trends in Argentine Politics," paper presented at the Southern Cone Seminar, Washington, D.C., 5–6 June 1983.

18. Kalman H. Silvert, *The Conflict Society: Reaction and Revolution in Latin America* (New York: American Universities Field Staff, 1966); John Mander, *The Unrevolutionary Society: The Power of Latin American Conservatism in a Changing World* (New York: Knopf, 1969).

19. For conceptual overviews, see Charles W. Anderson, "Toward a Theory of Latin American Politics," Occasional Paper No. 2, The Graduate Center for Latin American Studies, Vanderbilt University, Nashville, Tenn., February 1964.

20. For a sensitive treatment of these themes, see Richard Nuccio, "The Family as Political Metaphor in Authoritarian-Conservative Regimes: The Case of Spain," Occasional Papers Series No. 9, Program in Latin American Studies, University of Massachusetts, 1978.

21. See the two-volume study by Lester D. Langley, *Struggle for the Ameri-*

can *Mediterranean: United States-European Rivalry in the Gulf-Caribbean, 1776–1904* (Athens: University of Georgia Press, 1976) and *The United States and the Caribbean in the Twentieth Century* (Athens: University of Georgia Press, 1982).

22. See Reginald Horsman, *Race and Manifest Destiny: The Origins of American Racial Anglo-Saxonism* (Cambridge, Mass.: Harvard University Press, 1981).

23. Grow, *The Good Neighbor Policy.*

24. Howard J. Wiarda, "Corporatism and Development in the Iberic-Latin World: Persistent Strains and New Variations," *The Review of Politics* 36 (January 1974): 3–33; reprinted in Fredrick B. Pike and Thomas Stritch, eds., *The New Corporatism* (Notre Dame, Ind.: University of Notre Dame Press, 1974).

25. Based on a personal communication with former Assistant Secretary of State for American Republic Affairs Edwin M. Martin, who is writing a book on the subject; 18 January 1983.

26. For elaboration on this point, see Howard J. Wiarda, "The United States and Latin America: Change and Continuity," in Alan Adelman and Reid Reading, eds., *Confrontation in the Caribbean Basin: International Perspectives on Security, Sovereignty, and Survival* (Pittsburgh: University of Pittsburgh, Center for Latin American Studies, 1984), pp. 211–25.

27. Karl Meyer, "The Lesser Evil Doctrine," *The New Leader* 46 (14 October 1963): 8.

28. Moravchik, *The Carter Experience.* Also see Howard J. Wiarda, ed., *Human Rights and U.S. Human Rights Policy: Theoretical Approaches and Some Perspectives on Latin America* (Washington, D.C.: American Enterprise Institute for Public Policy Analysis, 1982).

29. Michael J. Kryzanek, "The 1978 Election in the Dominican Republic: Opposition Politics, Intervention and the Carter Administration," *Caribbean Studies* 19 (April–July 1979): 51–73.

30. Howard J. Wiarda, *In Search of Policy: The United States and Latin America* (Washington, D.C.: American Enterprise Institute, 1984).

31. More extended treatments are in Howard J. Wiarda, "The Ethnocentrism of the Social Sciences: Implications for Research and Policy," *Review of Politics* 43 (April 1981): 163–97 and "Toward a Non-Ethnocentric Theory of Development: Alternative Conceptions from the Third World," *Journal of Developing Areas* 17 (July 1983): 433–52.

32. John Bartlow Martin, *Overtaken by Events: The Dominican Crisis from the Fall of Trujillo to the Civil War* (New York: Doubleday, 1966); for another perspective, see Howard J. Wiarda, *Dictatorship, Development and Disintegration: Politics and Social Change in the Dominican Republic* (Ann Arbor, Mich.: Xerox University Microfilms, 1975).

33. See Howard J. Wiarda, *Politics and Social Change in Latin America,* especially "Introduction."

34. The concept is defined in Anderson, "Toward a Theory of Latin American Politics."

35. The point is elaborated in Wiarda, *Politics and Social Change in Latin America.*

36. The outlines of the program were reported in the *Washington Post,* 24 February 1983, p.1.

37. See James R. Green and Brent Skowcroft, eds., *Western Interests and U.S. Policy Options in the Caribbean Basin* (Boston: Oelgeschlager, Gunn, and Haim, 1984).

38. John E. Reilly, "The American Mood: A Foreign Policy of Self-Interest," *Foreign Policy* 34 (Spring 1979): 74–86.

39. These concepts are elaborated in several writings by the author, especially "Toward a Non-Ethnocentric Theory of Development."

40. Howard J. Wiarda, "Democracy and Human Rights in Latin America: Toward a New Conceptualization," *Orbis* 22 (Spring 1978): 137–60.

41. Margaret E. Crahan, personal communication, 9 February 1983; see also her chapter in this volume, "Human Rights and U.S. Foreign Policy: Realism Versus Stereotypes."

42. Anderson, "Toward a Theory of Latin American Politics." For an application of Anderson's model to the crisis in Central America, see Howard J. Wiarda, ed., *Rift and Revolution: The Central American Imbroglio* (Washington, D.C.: American Enterprise Institute for Public Policy Analysis, 1984), "Introduction."

43. Douglas A. Chalmers and Craig H. Robinson, "Why Power Contenders Choose Liberalization: Perspectives from Latin America," paper presented at the 1980 annual meeting of the American Political Science Association, Washington, D.C., 28–31 August 1980; Richard Sholk, "Comparative Aspects of the Transition from Authoritarian Rule," Latin American Program, Working Paper No. 114 (Washington, D.C.: Woodrow Wilson International Center for Scholars, 1982).

44. Chalmers and Robinson, "Why Power Contenders Choose Liberalization."

45. Sholk, "Comparative Aspects." These comments are also based on Ronald C. Schneider's analysis of the Brazilian *abertura,* as presented in a series of discussions at the Center for Strategic and International Studies, Georgetown University, Washington, D.C., 1982–83.

46. Langley, *Struggle for the American Mediterranean* and *The United States and the Caribbean.*

47. After the title of the volume prepared by the Inter-American Foundation, *They Know How* (Washington, D.C.: U.S. Government Printing Office, 1977).

48. See the references given in notes 24, 31, 37, and 40.

49. This paragraph was written before the establishment of the National Endowment for Democracy, the agency created to carry out the new democracy agenda. As predicted, the Endowment has a corporatist structure: business and labor are both represented, as are the two major U.S. political parties. For early congressional and other critical comments on the plan, see the *Washington Post,* 24 February 1983 and 27 February 1983. For contrasting views, see David D. Newsom, "Can Democracy Be Promoted Around the World?" *Christian Science Monitor,* 24 November 1982, and the materials prepared for the American Enterprise Institute–Department of State "Conference on Free Elections," Washington, D.C., 4–6 November 1982, at which a variety of divergent conceptions of democracy were presented. Perhaps the best statement on what one might call the

"indeterminateness" of U.S.–Latin American policy is Richard J. Bloomfield, "Who Makes American Foreign Policy? Some Latin American Case Studies," paper presented at the Center for International Affairs, Harvard University, March 1972.

50. *Washington Post,* 28 February 1983, p.C11, and 3 March 1983, pp. A3, A25.

51. Peter Bell, former president of the Inter-American Foundation, has suggested this approach.

52. See former Undersecretary of State David D. Newsom's interesting qualifications in his essay "Pressure," *Christian Science Monitor,* 23 February 1983.

53. I have presented such a "prudence model" of U.S.–Latin American relations in Wiarda, *In Search of Policy,* chapter 8.

54. For a similar statement, see Paul E. Sigmund, "Latin America: Change or Continuity," *Foreign Affairs* 60 (1981): 629–57.

In a short paper written subsequent to this essay, I have set forth an agenda of possible measures (stated in quite modest terms, in comparison with the grandiose claims often made in discussing this subject) to further democracy in Latin America. These suggestions include: a vigorous publication program to spread abroad U.S. ideas, writings, constitutional and political precepts, technological discoveries, and innovative social science concepts; an active translation program with similar goals and objectives; greatly expanded student and faculty exchanges; increased cultural and political exchanges at all levels; expanded fellowship and study-abroad programs intended to bring Latin Americans to the United States and send U.S. citizens to Latin America; a strong but tempered human rights policy; some assistance to journals, reviews, and research centers studying Latin America; some assistance (under appropriate auspices) to Latin American political groups, trade unions, and peasant associations; additional assistance to international conferences examining democracy; some nudges and pushes at key junctures to assist the transition to democracy in Latin America; and a major research project on Latin American forms of democracy and how these may differ from U.S. arrangements. This is a positive and realistic set of proposals with strong possibilities for success. As such, it is preferable to more ambitious, often wishful proposals that are likely to fail or to produce unanticipated consequences. For a discussion of this more modest agenda, see Howard J. Wiarda, "Project Democracy in Latin America: Reservations and Suggestions," paper prepared for conference on Project Democracy, United States Information Agency, Washington, D.C., 9 May 1983.

11

The United States, Latin America, Democracy: Variations on a Very Old Theme

Guillermo O'Donnell

This essay revolves around a simple argument: despite the world economic crisis and its particularly severe repercussions in Latin America, and despite the Reagan administration's regrettable orientation toward Latin America, some trends have emerged in the hemisphere that encourage the emergence and eventually the consolidation of democratic regimes. This *possibility*—and the field of opportunities that it generates for conscious prodemocratic actions—is mainly the outcome of a costly learning process that many Latin Americans experienced, either at firsthand or in neighboring countries, during the last two decades of particularly repressive and socially regressive authoritarian regimes. A wide range of political, social, and cultural forces in Latin America has rejected this authoritarianism and its innumerable effects. This critique has led to the renewed valuation of constitutional democracy per se as an important goal in and of itself.

These factors *may* become decisive.[1] But they are subtle, they must be recognized as such, and it is impossible to determine a priori how much they "weigh" against the present economic crisis and the numerous authoritarian threats that still exist. As I will argue, one corollary of this assertion is that—with the partial exceptions of Central America and the Caribbean—domestic political and social forces hold principal responsibility for success or failure in achieving democratic goals. Another corollary is that both the U.S. government (or more precisely, the various U.S. government agencies that deal with Latin America) and diverse private sector groups in the United States can make important contributions to this process—both through positive actions and by ending some of their current policies and practices. It is not a question of the United States "exporting" democracy to Latin America. Rather, the United States and Latin America must converge in a recognition of their common medium- and long-term interest in the existence of politically open and socially progressive institutions throughout the hemisphere.

The current situation in most Central American countries and the Caribbean must be carefully distinguished from that in South America. Nonetheless, what is at stake in both areas is the possibility of moving along an arduous path toward (probably varied) democratic forms of political organization. I will argue that for this to happen it is important to end the tradition of jealous paternalism toward Latin America embraced by not a few sectors in the United States. Finally, I suggest some practical criteria for action in this area, including the creation of a new institution that would embody and monitor the effectiveness of certain democratic values that I believe constitute an overall common denominator among numerous sectors in the hemisphere.

On a Logic That Is Perverse for Almost Everyone

The issue of democracy in Latin America lends itself to oscillations between expressions of melancholic pessimism and the silly expression of utopian hopes. In an attempt to avoid these extremes, I begin with several factual affirmations and then present some suggestions that may be worth discussing. No formulas or condemnations are offered here, although I have not attempted to disguise my own values and hopes.

Almost no one in Latin America today holds illusions possible twenty years ago: there are no entirely autonomous national paths to development, and dependence on the Soviet Union entails extremely heavy costs. With the exception (not so certain in many cases) of communist parties (which are weak almost everywhere in the region), there is no movement or party in Latin America that would not prefer an autonomous relationship vis-à-vis the Soviet Union. This fact must be taken seriously. Yet in the United States, numerous decisions continue to be taken with the intention of preventing precisely that which a decisive majority of political forces in Latin American countries does not want. That the Soviet Union attempts to increase its influence in the region, and that Latin American governments view the establishment of normal relations with the Soviet Union as a positive step, are inevitable facts in contemporary international relations.

The paranoia of diverse sectors in the United States, the inclination in U.S. policies (present in varying degrees, but never absent) to perceive that Latin America is riddled with powerful outside "infiltrators" (they exist, but not only from the Soviet Union), and the assumption that Latin American countries are governed by leaders so foolish as to wish to make their countries satellites of the Soviet Union are all beliefs that work to bring about precisely the kind of situation that those U.S. actors want to avoid. This is so obvious that one blushes to repeat it: given the asymmetry of power between the United States and Latin America, and given the eagerness of each Latin American government, party, or movement to survive, the more aggressive U.S. policy toward the region is, the closer the resulting force field will push these actors toward the Soviet Union. And the more aggressive that U.S. policy is, the more important it becomes for these actors to find some support in the international arena, and the more exacting the price that the Soviet Union will demand in exchange for such support—if it is forthcoming at all. Such circumstances make it more likely that Latin American countries will offer further concessions to the Soviet Union, and this in turn further aggravates the United States. This process is almost always violently aborted by combined action by the United States and the most reactionary local classes, with which the United States cannot fail to ally itself. These cycles have occurred again and again. Nothing appears to have been learned from them.

Old rancors and mistrusts thus feed on each other. They "prove" to many in the United States what their mistrust initially invented, and many Latin Americans are reconfirmed in their belief that there can be no space for coexistence and cooperation with the United States. The resulting tragedies imply the victory of Latin American sectors and classes that then unleash the most repressive and socially destructive aspects of their domination. That the United States appears to be (and is) frequently allied with governments that are detested by their own citizens is not due principally to a particular U.S. official's ineptness or "wickedness." Much more significantly, it is the result of the interpretation that some groups in the United States give to what will, nonetheless, occur time and again: the emergence in Latin America of parties and movements that, with significant popular support, postulate major changes in an untenable status quo.

The United States' claim to hegemony over all of Latin America, made during its years of triumphal expansionism in the 1950s, expresses the same perverse logic. The claim included a corresponding paternalistic desire to monopolize or jealously control any relationship between its wards and third countries—which, given the terms of the relationship, are necessarily viewed as hostile intruders. Even if this hegemonic claim and its accompanying paternalism at one time had some basis in the United States' overwhelming power vis-à-vis both Latin America and the rest of the world, such a relationship is no longer realistic.[2]

The Soviet Union, with its closed authoritarian regime, can maintain its geopolitical periphery under harsh military control. But all evidence indicates that this has involved immense costs. As for the United States, its society appears to be sufficiently healthy to pay the self-poisoning price of extending its domination by military means. However, hegemonic pretensions must lead either to severe authoritarian repression at home (which is improbable) or to what has been repeated practice: alliance with and military support for groups, parties, and governments in Latin America that are the antithesis of democracy and social progress.

The logic described above combines with one that is a crucial characteristic of authoritarian regimes: they are profoundly and intrinsically irrational systems of government, and they are more so the more closed and repressive they are.[3] Because the population is terrified, these regimes hear only the echoes of their own voices, which they confuse with the public opinion they have suppressed. Somoza's blindness to accumulated political and social pressures and the gangster-style madness of Galtieri and his fellows are only extreme examples of the constitutive irrationality of such regimes. Despite their (brutal and temporary) capacity to impose "order" and their (eventual) "efficiency" in the short-term management of certain economic variables, these regimes are unable to resolve three major challenges. First, in the medium and long term they are unable to achieve legitimation, or active consensus, regarding the government and its policies. Second, these regimes are unable to resolve the problem of presidential succession. Third, they have enormous difficulties resolving crises (problems that are aggravated by the "feudalization" of the state bureaucracy, which is provoked by rivalries among the different military services and/or the cliques that compose such regimes). Thus, quite apart from the idiosyncracies of countries and rulers, these regimes usually end abruptly and convulsively, leaving behind them a heavy heritage of suffering and hatred.[4] It often seems that some U.S. government agencies would prefer that their support for authoritarian regimes be unpublicized. However, these regimes usually seek to publicize such support, often adding embarrassing (for their protectors) declarations of support for "the western cause." This, too, is part of the perverse logic I am discussing here: the more repressive and socially exclusionary such a regime is, the more crucial it is to be able to exhibit internally (and even to exaggerate) its "excellent relations" with, and "fraternal support" from, the United States.

The final point of this logic initiates another act in these dramas without grandeur: either the U.S. government's vain search for "respectable" elements within the authoritarian regime to ally with a democratic center that the regime has made every effort to erase, or (worse still) increased emphasis on U.S. military "aid" to these regimes. The latter response may yield the desired results in the short and medium terms by maintaining a "friendly" authoritarian regime in power. But this entails resolving one crisis at the expense of generating many others not long afterward. Perhaps it is not sufficiently appreciated in the United States how viscerally the immense majority of the politically informed population in Latin America reacts to invasions and sabotage by "patriots" who are sustained by the Central Intelligence Agency, to U.S. "advisers" to armies that assassinate their own citizens, and to less obvious but no less sinister interventions such as that revealed in Chile.

What is to be done? How and what can be learned in order to avoid repeating processes that, in addition to producing immense tragedies, do not favor almost anyone's long-term interest? Any discussion of these questions involves complex sets of actors in each Latin American country, in the United States, and perhaps elsewhere. But some answers to these questions can be formulated by taking into account both political actors' intentions and the new opportunities inscribed in the scars of these last decades.

On Actors, New and Old

As I have already noted, few on the political left in Latin America (not to mention other parts of the political spectrum) want dependence on the Soviet Union—much less military dependence. But almost everyone, not only on the left, wants normal relations with the Soviet Union. This is true despite the Cold War crusaders who have again proliferated in both North and South America in recent years. I emphasize this point because it is linked to a subject that deserves close consideration.

Almost all South American countries have achieved a degree of social complexity (including domestic entrepreneurs, a labor sector, and a middle sector linked to modern industries and services, and armed forces that have clear control over the domestic means of violence) that makes the success of an insurrectional-revolutionary strategy highly improbable. After the abysmal failures of these aims more than a decade ago, this lesson is clear to practically all political actors.[5] Furthermore, the Soviet model is in disrepute, and there is more generally a profound ideological crisis of Marxism-Leninism. These affirmations reflect the discussions and opinions now prevailing within the Latin American left, although a more detailed discussion of these trends is beyond the scope of this essay. The disrepute of the Soviet model largely results from the increasingly obvious frictions in the functioning of Soviet society and its oppressive authoritarianism, as well as from the strict military and economic dependency that the Soviet Union imposes on its satellites.[6] If this evidence led some to admire China as a more authentic revolutionary model, the turns and reversals that have occurred there and the evidence of the phenomenal costs incurred during some of the stages that were once most admired have produced similar effects. Finally, the criticisms that emerged in Europe in the early 1970s of the Leninist model of revolutionary party organization, the seizure of power through insurrection, and the dictatorship of the proletariat had a major influence in Latin America, at a moment of failure of armed and/or insurrectional strategies that (in a more or less heterodoxical manner) at one time proclaimed the application of these or similar ideas.

These changes are quite recent, and they affect many actors that previously were at best ambiguous concerning political democracy. These actors converge nowadays with other sectors embodying a longstanding democratic tradition in Latin America (they exist, despite interpretations obsessed with "the Iberic, corporatist tradition") and generate a situation pregnant with new potential. Most of the political left and sectors of the right disillusioned with various authoritarian adventures have engaged in a positive, authentic revaluation of democracy. Political democracy in the strict sense of the word—linked to the liberal-constitutional model, with its guarantees of individual rights, the right of association, and truly competitive elections—is no longer disdained as being purely "formal." What some people already understood, others learned during the harsh experiences that a number of Latin American countries have endured in the last several decades, during which authoritarian regimes systematically negated all such rights. In addition, given the aforementioned critique of Leninism and the "dictatorship of the proletariat" as a transition stage to "true" democracy, many in Latin America have learned that constitutional democracy is a goal that is worthwhile achieving and defending per se. As a result, today some form of democracy—constitutional democracy—is a fundamental goal for what are by far the region's most significant political forces situated at diverse points across the ideological spectrum.[7]

Of course, the current revaluation of democracy in Latin America does not mean that authoritarian elements have entirely disappeared. It is unrealistic and profoundly ahistorical to argue that social conditions and political forces in a country that is in the process of political transition must uniformly favor democratic political arrangements. The consolidation and expansion of democratic institutions is always the result of a long process of learning and adaptation; no country was "democratic" from the outset. In the United States, it took nothing less than a civil war to suppress partially an institution—slavery—that was hardly compatible with political democracy. One should not assume that conditions present at any given time will forever remain unchanged. The choice is either to accept authoritarianism—no matter which euphemistic label one might choose to apply to it—or to mobilize progressive forces and explore opportunities for more positive outcomes. It is particularly lamentable that, precisely when changes such as these are occurring in Latin America, the Reagan administration responds to existing or potential tensions and conflicts with an "anticommunist" ideology that suspects nearly everyone and, because of the logic discussed above, leads the United States to ally itself with sectors in Latin America that can hardly be called democratic.

In this context it is useful to comment on a policy that, despite its ambiguities and the declining inclination to implement it, has been evaluated unjustly: the Carter administration's human rights policy. This policy irritated (as it could not fail to do) those regimes that consistently and repeatedly violated human rights on a scale not previously known in Latin America. In some cases these violations reached levels similar to the greatest atrocities committed in other parts of the world.[8]

Critics of this policy insisted that it only alienated loyal and tested friends of the United States. But criticisms such as this ignored at least two considerations. First, the great difficulty with assessing human rights policies is that their principal impact is negative; it is well known that it is practically impossible to measure nonevents. In other words, anyone who lived in Latin America during those years can testify that there was much that the United States' activist human rights stance *prevented* from occurring. The atrocities committed would doubtless have been more severe and greater in number but for the partial disuasion implied in informing repressive governments that they would not escape international condemnation for such actions.

Second, if there is today in Latin America a stock of good will toward the United States, and if there is a feeling that the United States can pursue policies that are not necessarily hostile to elemental interests of Latin American countries, the reasons are to be found principally in the Carter human rights policy. The great merit of this policy was that it addressed itself not only to governments but also to society. Critics of this policy, in emphasizing the extent to which it irritated repressive governments, forget what their own distinction between "totalitarian" and "authoritarian" regimes implies: the precariousness of their "friends' " rule in those regimes when opposed by numerous and significant sectors in Latin American nations. Of course, these sectors include the democratic forces in each country in the region. What, then, is more realistic—the Carter administration's "utopian" human rights policy or the "realism" of the Reagan administration?

Reinitiating and broadening the democratizing implications of human rights policy would now encounter a favorable conjuncture: the vigor with which democratic parties and movements are emerging (or reemerging) across the ideological spectrum in a number of Latin American countries, including those that must still do so under harsh authoritarian conditions. As noted above, the opportunities that can be created with a minimum of imagination and by forsaking mutual prejudices arise from the learning process through which many people in Latin America have reevaluated the meaning of constitutional democracy. The creation of such opportunities also depends on the possibility that the United States will in the future appreciate better (and in a less parochial fashion) the profound positive repercussions of policies that would clearly support efforts made, in Latin America and by Latin Americans, to establish constitutional democracy and to safeguard human rights. Despite the economic crisis that the region will continue to face, the convergence (from the Latin American side) of a firm commitment to democracy across a significant part of the political spectrum and (on the U.S. side) public policies unmistakably oriented toward the consolidation of democracy and the effectiveness of human rights in the region, would at least pose a novel prospect because such a convergence has never yet occurred. That it may be worthwhile to attempt to bring about such a convergence is indicated (even if negatively) by both North and South Americans' sad experience with the brutality, irrationality, and unpredictability of the authoritarian regimes that plagued Latin America in recent years.

Distinguishing Between Cases and Regions

The preceding comments have focused principally on South America. The situation in Central America and the Caribbean merits separate attention. In almost all of these countries, the absence (or tenuous existence) of structural conditions favorable to constitutional democracy is complicated by a history of particularly traumatic relations with the United States. This long, bitter history revealed the greatest limitations of the Carter administration's policies toward Latin America, and now under the Reagan administration it returns to traditional patterns of paternalistic interventionism.[9]

In Central America and the Caribbean, there is and there will continue to be a pattern of insurrections with strong popular support against armed forces that are hardly professionalized and whose relationship with the population is characterized by plunder—not just the corruption that characterizes a good many of their colleagues in South America. If the insurrectional path is possible due to the characteristics of these armed forces, the denial of real or fair electoral alternatives makes it practically inevitable. Moreover, these insurrections, which occur in a context of extreme social polarization marked by barely entrepreneurial oligarchies based on direct repression of the labor force, cannot but articulate the goal of dislodging the oligarchies and their henchmen. Furthermore, the history of U.S. relations with these countries has left a bitter memory that necessarily includes the definition of their national identity as, to a large extent, opposed to the United States. No country constructs its identity without reference to its own historical origins. In Central America and the Caribbean, the heavy hand of the United States has had too great an impact on the weaving of these countries' histories to be easily or rapidly erased by even the best intentions.[10]

Nonetheless, if these are probable tendencies in Central America and the Caribbean, there is still room for an enlightened policy that acknowledges different parties' interests, that is alert to the nuances and flexibilities of the other party, and that is relieved of habitual prejudices. No ineluctable and unvarying historical "necessity" drives these popular-revolutionary movements to become satellites of the Soviet Union or should force the United States to ally itself with the most reactionary and repressive sectors in these countries. These possibilities must be mutually understood.

What room for choice remains? Although the argument that such a situation would not change the United States' strategic situation merits attention, I assume that no U.S. government will tolerate any Central American or Caribbean country becoming a base for Soviet weapons aimed at its territory. But as I indicated at the outset, except for aggressive U.S. actions that make *any* alternative support desirable, there are no political forces of any significance in Latin America that are unwilling to accept the United States' strategic limit in this regard. As for popularly based political movements and governments in Central America and the Caribbean, their own nonnegotiable limit is that the United States not attempt to prevent that which most deeply defines their own existence: the dissolution or radical transformation of their armed forces and the expropriation of the local oligarchy.

But when the logic outlined at the beginning of this essay unfolds, solutions are no longer possible. The outcomes are tragedy and defeat for most domestic political and social forces, or eventually the retreat of the temporarily demoralized United States. The possibility of overcoming these very real absurdities depends on the timely "de-linking" of those questions that (even though they may be perceived to be important) are negotiable in the medium and long term from those issues on which neither party can in reality compromise. On the one hand, the United States should de-link its strategic/territorial interests from its support for particularly murderous and predatory militaries and local ruling classes that have no future other than that offered by their own armed forces and the United States. On the other hand, the leaders of popular and insurrectional movements should not derive from the history of their countries a vision of necessary and permanent antagonism with the United States.

But the problem becomes complicated because the first unequivocal signal of this separation must be given by the most powerful actor. This reflects the dynamics of power: the party with the greatest capacity to damage the other must be the first to offer unequivocal signs of its willingness to negotiate. Otherwise, the opposing party's only option is either to cede completely or to continue to offer as serious a threat as possible. If such distinctions between different parties' interests could be made, Central American and Caribbean countries could establish forms of government that more or less approximate forms of constitutional democracy, which for some time would necessarily reflect their revolutionary origins.

New Paths Toward Different Types of Democracy

The previous section raised an issue that must be considered in any discussion of democracy in Latin America: the variety of forms of democratic regime and government that—given differences in historical tradition in each country, the characteristics of its social structure, and diverse conjunctural factors—will persist or emerge in Latin American countries in the years ahead. In contrast to Central American countries, I believe that it is highly improbable (for the reasons already indicated) that the South American countries now emerging from the authoritarian regimes of the 1970s will follow an insurrectional-revolutionary course. Authoritarian rule and rulers have been deeply discredited in these countries; even many of those who originally supported these approaches have carefully distanced themselves from such regimes, and the armed forces are politically weak and divided.

These factors open the possibility of a democratizing period in South America. It may be, as a good many observers have already warned, that the present period of redemocratization is only another cycle in the pendulum of authoritarianism and democracy that much of the continent has long experienced. There are indeed powerful factors that constrain this democratizing process. First, the international economic crisis has had particularly severe repercussions in Latin America, especially in those countries that sacrificed their economies to the postulates of a dogmatic economic neoconservatism. Second, the U.S. government's current policy toward Latin America hardly helps to create a climate that is propitious to the development and consolidation of prodemocratic political forces in the region.[11] Finally, the armed forces' current (or imminent) withdrawal from various authoritarian regimes occurs (with the partial exception of Brazil) in conditions of undeniable failure that leave behind an enormous burden of rancor and unsatisfied demands. These defeats for authoritarian/military rule open up space for democratizing efforts. But these spaces can also be, as on other occasions, periods in which the armed forces and their social supporters nurse their own grudges, capitalize on real or supposed errors made by newly installed civilian governments, and prepare the conditions for their abrupt return to power.

All this is quite obvious and may produce a sense of pessimism that would actually help realize the possibility of an authoritarian regression. But what is less obvious (because to a considerable extent it depends on a learning process that in some cases has not yet surfaced because of the repressive conditions in force) is that an awareness of these cycles, an appreciation of those factors described above that are determinants of authoritarian regressions, and above all the self-criticism in which many actors have engaged concerning their own contribution to previous defeats for democratic forces all open up new possibilities for political action. The principal political, intellectual, and ethical challenge facing democratic forces in Latin America and the United States is how to realize these possibilities.[12]

The actors involved in the democratization process are conscious of the fragility of existing democracies and of those that are yet to be established, and they understand the need to nurture carefully an achievement that will require time to develop roots. Having rejected the revolutionary path, and being conscious of the extremely serious economic difficulties that future governments must face, democratic leaders of the left and center (as well as some emergent "democratized" sectors from the preceding authoritarian regime) know that they have no alternative other than negotiation and compromise if the authoritarian stage of the cycle is not to be reproduced.

Here the specific situations prevailing in each country preclude generalization. Brazil stands at one extreme. The relative success of the authoritarian regime, the not-insignificant electoral base that in part derives from such success, and a population scarcely activated politically led to a comparatively gradual and continuous transition process—though the Brazilian transition, like all others, is not exempt from risks, regressions, and dramatic situations. At the other extreme in some South American countries, democratic leaders will face more volatile situations. This is already apparent in Bolivia, Uruguay, and Argentina; and Chile, with differences resulting from a more structured political party system, will certainly present similar challenges. On the one hand, the abysmal failure of these regimes permits a rapid "leap" to constitutional democracy. But, on the other hand, the collapse of the authoritarian regime can leave both the armed forces and the powerful social actors that previously supported them without means of political representation. These actors must be taken into account, and some way will have to be found to incorporate them into normal patterns of representation in a constitutional system if they are not to become too threatening to new and fragile democracies.

The problem in this regard is not so much the intransigence of democratic political leaders, who have certainly shown great flexibility in recent transition processes. Rather, the principal difficulty is that political representation in a democratic regime is largely determined by the capacity to win votes. In Argentina, Bolivia, and Chile, conservative sectors have few possibilities of building political parties with significant weight in the electoral arena after the resounding failure of regimes with which they were so closely associated; in this regard, their experiences differ from those of conservative parties after partially successful authoritarian regimes in Spain and Brazil. Compounding this difficulty, the clearer the failure of the preceding authoritarian regime, the more urgent and numerous are popular and middle-class demands. This problem arises in a context (as in Argentina, Chile, Bolivia, Uruguay, and, although in a different way, Peru) in which levels of popular organization and political activation are significantly higher than in Brazil (as well as in the earlier cases of transition in Colombia and Venezuela).

Thus recent democratic governments have taken office in the midst of a major crisis brought about by the preceding authoritarian regime, when the constraints on economic and social policy that this situation implies collide with a surge of popular demands that the new government cannot but recognize as both urgent and legitimate. This dilemma demarcates the narrow and uncertain path that these governments will have to traverse. These governments are formed by political parties that draw their electoral support from, and whose social base is in, popular and middle sectors. These parties cannot easily ignore their bases, and the experience of a number of countries shows that to do so is one of the surest routes to a coup d'état. But at the same time, at least in the short and medium terms, these governments cannot but "disenchant" (a term coined in Spain to describe a phenomenon that will be repeated in Latin America) many of their initially most active supporters. Unless there are unexpected changes in the international economic environment, this situation will result both from the "objective" necessities of managing the balance-of-payments situation, maintaining the rate of investment, and controlling inflation, and from governments' (learned) concern with preventing degrees of "disorder" that would threaten their own survival.

This is the hard reality that newly established democratic regimes face. But even the Mexican case shows that when an authoritarian regime is confronted with unexpected or crisis situations—even though it may have achieved a relatively high degree of institutionalization, including a heritage of popular support that is lacking in the other types of authoritarianism considered here—decisions are apt to be taken spasmodically and without minimal consultation. This characteristic, inherent in any type of authoritarian regime regardless of its origin and social base, is especially pronounced in much more closed and repressive authoritarian systems; witness the abrupt shifts in public policy in contemporary Chile and, at the extreme, the international adventurism of a government (once so flattered by the Reagan administration) such as that of Galtieri in Argentina.

In contrast to authoritarian patterns of decision making, the complex systems of consultation, the overlapping decision levels, and even the delays and indecision typical of constitutional democracy (characteristics that tend to be more pronounced in democracies that can only be constructed on the basis of complex alliances among diverse social and political sectors) have important advantages that offset their lack of glamour. Furthermore, I would argue that these advantages are accentuated rather than weakened in situations of acute crisis such as those that Latin American countries will continue to confront in the future.

Within this panorama, the Latin American countries now emerging from authoritarian rule will exhibit such a varied range of public policies that it would be futile to try to predict them. But in part because of accumulated dissatisfactions and in part because of the social bases of those parties that have good chances of winning elections in these countries, some policies cannot be excluded. These include certain nationalizations and state takeovers, especially in sectors dominated by an oligarchy that is considered to be particularly parasitic or politically hostile; administrative controls on foreign exchange; expanded representation for trade unions and other popular sector organizations in the decision-making process; and tax reforms that will attempt with varying degrees of success to alleviate the extreme inequalities in income distribution with which these governments will be faced.

Measures such as these will be undertaken in a political context that at least for some time will be characterized by a high degree of middle- and popular-sector mobilization, often articulating demands whose satisfaction would exceed the limits that rulers have imposed on themselves in order to preserve the fledgling democratic regime. What is more, except in extreme cases, these governments will not want to repress violently long-delayed demands from a society that was severely chastised by their authoritarian predecessors. Thus we should expect a situation that recurrently presents some significant degree of disorder (as occurred in Spain and Portugal), which some people will contrast nostalgically with the sepulchral "order" previously imposed by the authoritarian regime.

That "disorder," together with governmental policies such as those described above, may reawaken domestic fears and the tendency of diverse groups in the United States to conclude that *communism* is once again on the verge of devouring one Latin American country or another. That this perception will occur, and that it will constitute an important factor in this situation, must be taken for granted. The problem—and the hope—concerns who will *not* fall into this old pattern and what kinds of relationships they will establish among themselves on the basis of a more intelligent interpretation of the situation.

For this more positive reaction to occur, actors and observers should focus on several elements that are especially relevant to Latin American relations with the United States: (1) as I indicated above, none of the political leaders governing today or likely to do so in the future in the new Latin American democracies is willing to bind his country to dependence on the Soviet Union; (2) in contrast to the immediate past, it is unlikely that these political leaders will encourage coups d'état when they are in opposition; (3) some of the public policies initiated by new democratic governments may, of course, adversely affect the interests of U.S. firms in certain sectors. But these measures may favor other U.S. firms, especially if one considers that (4) one of the lessons Latin Americans have learned in recent years is that it is a mistake to treat foreign capital as a monolith. Thus governments will tailor their actions to fit conditions prevailing in different sectors, rather than threaten across-the-board expropriations simply because certain firms are large and/or foreign owned; and finally, (5) as occurred in southern Europe, the often ambiguous relationship that Latin American popular or socialist parties maintained with political movements oriented toward violent social change has now been replaced by a clear rejection of that type of transformation.

None of these considerations will dissolve the irascible opposition of socially reactionary and profoundly authoritarian sectors in Latin American societies. Nor will these considerations cease to provoke peals of alarm in government agencies specializing in the most paranoid aspects of U.S. foreign policy or fail to exacerbate frictions with government agencies or sectors of Congress linked to economic interests that may feel affected by some Latin American governmental decisions. But this is also the new field of opportunity that I am attempting to delineate. On the Latin American side, I have already mentioned various aspects of a learning process that leads not only to avoiding situations of global confrontation with the United States, but also to searching for a relationship that is less dogmatic both in its confrontations with and in its "loyalties" to the United States. Such a relationship would attempt to differentiate situations and interests across diverse issues, as is normal in international relations that are not contaminated by relations of extreme dependence or generalized confrontation. This attitude is today perceived to be appropriate and necessary by a significant share of the political actors in Latin America.

That such an effort in fact be made appears probable in all the situations examined here. In the case of democracies or democratization processes characterized by the interplay among "elites," with comparatively few popular pressures and/or without strong leftist forces (Venezuela, Colombia, Brazil, Mexico, and to some extent Ecuador), there is quite ample room for flexibility in reshaping relations with the United States. In other cases where leftist and populist forces have more weight and/or higher levels of popular activation prevail than in the cases just mentioned (Argentina, Chile, Bolivia, Peru, and Uruguay), governments have attemped, or will try, to reshape such relations in the context of numerous demands presented by interlocutors that are less easy to reconcile than in a basically elitist political framework. The probability of zigzagging public policies, some conflicts with foreign interests, and fomenting fears of processes that include significant popular mobilization is obviously greater in these latter cases. But even here it is clear—and I believe that it is especially important *to make it clear*—that the medium- and long-term interests of those domestic and foreign actors that glimpse reasonably mature inter-American relations lie in the consolidation of governments that rule with some (and one hopes, increasing) degree of institutional continuity.

If this can be achieved, then perhaps a paradox will result that is not unknown in humanity's historical experience: following a particularly traumatic and destructive period, in the midst of an unprecedented crisis, and in large measure because of an interpretation of these events that appeals to what is most sound and rational, a community encounters conditions for constructive coexistence that it previously denied to itself.

This is, at least, the hope. Although I cannot base it on rigorous data, and although I cannot determine its "weight" against numerous negative factors, I see this hope in the learning process that many in Latin America have undergone as a result of the misfortunes experienced in recent years. This *possible* space for positive change must be widened through political action by a sufficient set of relevant actors. Of course, this set includes the United States, insofar as those who claim to detect (whether explicitly or obliquely) that Latin Americans share a congenital affinity for authoritarianism cease to prevail.

This argument applies to everyone. To extend it to its most polemic pole, the argument is no less valid for the popular and insurrectional parties, movements, and governments that exist and will continue to emerge in much of Central America and the Caribbean. If the perverse logic outlined at the beginning of this essay could be interrupted, it should be possible to identify bases for political and economic accommodation with most of the U.S. public and private sectors with interests in the region. The expulsion or displacement of the armed forces and archaic and predatory ruling classes in these countries will certainly jolt some U.S. economic interests. But it is not necessarily true, as extremists on both sides believe, that the principal political and economic interests of the United States are limited to, or completely identified with, these interests.

Maturing and Normalizing Relations Between Latin America and the United States

This discussion leads to a central issue in U.S.–Latin American relations: the best means by which the U.S. government could facilitate the emergence and consolidation of democratic regimes south of its border and secure its influence at reasonable cost (that is, at a cost less than that which it presently incurs) would be simply to establish, once and for all, normal relations with Latin American countries. In other words, the United States must renounce its claims to a jealous and paternalistic hegemony. If this occurs, Latin American governments should put aside the attribution of interventionist intentions in the context of what would be, under the first assumption, normal relations. Of course, the normalization of relations would not eliminate differences in power across various issues between the United States and Latin American countries. A corollary would be for Latin American governments to forsake a mendicant attitude that presupposes, and reinforces, U.S. paternalism. Given a power relationship as unequal as that which characterizes relations between Latin America and the United States, any demand for "special treatment" is nothing but the offer of a semicolonial status that may coincide with some interests in each country but which must be combated throughout the region. Almost all actors share a medium- and long-term interest in paying the short-term costs necessary to establish a more mature and constructive hemispheric relationship.

Without these more or less simultaneous achievements in the United States and in at least those Latin American countries that together have decisive influence in the region, other measures—however commendable in and of themselves—will not succeed in cutting the Gordian knot implied by the *type of relationship* that, throughout many years and avatars, has been reproduced between the United States and Latin America. Although this will certainly not be easy, to speak of *governmental* policies raises two complicated corollaries. First, the new criteria must be transmitted to diverse governmental agencies through decisions that must be coordinated, implemented, and monitored at decision-making levels with sufficient authority and continuity to ensure compliance. For example, a sound orientation in the U.S. Department of State and/or some congressional committees means little if the gears of military, security, and economic agencies continue turning in the habitual direction. Certainly, the goal is not to achieve perfect policy coordination, which is difficult in the baroque and decentralized U.S. political system. Rather, the challenge is to increase coordination sufficiently so as to prevent recurrent, serious sabotage of overall policy orientation.[13] Of course, analogous comments apply to Latin American governments.

Second, government authorities in both the United States and Latin America must be capable of placing sectoral demands that are contrary to the continuity of such policies in the context of these new goals and premises. This refers not only to the demands of certain economic interests, but also to the pressures of zealous exponents of "anticommunism" in both continents.

These points underline the enormous difficulty involved both in the United States and in Latin America in achieving the subtle but radical changes needed to establish normal relations. But if this task could be proposed and discussed throughout the hemisphere, and if the discussion could be framed in terms of the medium- and long-term interest shared by all parties, then it might be possible to incorporate key actors into the debate and create the public awareness that is impossible to achieve if these issues and possibilities are not even considered. I do not assume that U.S. interests lie only in the promotion of democracy and basic human rights in Latin America. But, in terms of its military security as well, it is difficult to imagine a more solid, stable, long-term basis for U.S. interests than the maintenance of normal relations with countriès that have political institutions that reject violent means of access to government, cataclysmic social transformations, and closed systems of governmental decision making.

Perhaps it is worth repeating that the United States and Latin American countries share an interest in accepting the costs and risks involved in the creation and consolidation of democratic regimes. This interest outweighs the short-term advantages that some may detect in authoritarian rule. Whatever the immediate advantages that they might offer from some perspectives, these regimes' inflexibility and irrationality can only jeopardize the military security interests of the United States in the medium- and long-term future. Experience shows that regimes that suppress most of the feedback information necessary to govern effectively tend to generate explosive social conditions. Their incapacity to resolve the problem of presidential succession produces recurring and always uncertain political crises. Moreover, authoritarian regimes are wont to take crucial decisions in impulsive political isolation when confronted by crisis situations. For all these reasons, one should seriously question whether these regimes are in fact reasonably satisfactory guarantees—except in the very short term—of U.S. military security interests however they are defined.

Similar considerations would apply even if U.S. policies toward Latin America were motivated simply by an unreflective continuation of pater-

nalistic assumptions, rather than by rising tides of rabid "anticommunism" or ever more comprehensive definitions of military security.[14] The
disparities that exist in the control of diverse and important power resources tend to generate differential benefits for those who control most
of these resources. This is a predictable consequence of differences in
power, and although normalized U.S.–Latin American relations might
alleviate some of the problems caused by such power disparities, normalized relations would not deny what is a "fact of life." But the fact is that
the United States must incur (as it in fact now does) increasingly heavy
costs, including the medium-term costs of imposing increasingly heavy
tolls on Latin America, to sustain a paternalistic and exclusionist relationship that until recently it imposed with relative ease and low costs. Now,
for a number of reasons discussed in different chapters in this volume, a
strong disparity between the United States and Latin America in the
control of power resources is no longer sufficient to sustain that kind of
relationship. Thus even from this perspective it would be worthwhile to
consider if the normalization of hemispheric relations would not reduce
the heavy costs involved for both sides—on the one hand, in the maintenance of an obsolete relationship and, on the other hand, in searching for
various ways of escaping from such a relationship. Although some sectors
in both the United States and Latin America must lose from such a
change, the equation of benefits (not just economic benefits) would
probably improve for both sides. Once again, the question here is
whether there will be *political* decisions and opportunities to establish
perspectives that escape the fatal embrace of the short term and its my-
opic worshippers.

What has been said up to this point does not translate into specific
recommendations, but it does suggest two themes that are important as
general guidelines. First, the U.S. government cannot sincerely declare
itself in favor of democracy while at the same time continuing through
other agencies to encourage the most delirious "anticommunism" in Latin
American armed forces—the most direct and necessary actors in authoritarian regressions. The question is not how many weapons Latin American armed forces have or have not purchased from the United States in
recent years. Rather, the crucial problem concerns the intensive training
and subsequent contacts through which Latin American militaries receive
ideological frameworks such as "national security doctrine" (or its more
or less subtle variations) that seem to be tailor-made rationalizations for
their overthrow of civilian government.[15] Furthermore, continuous, intense exchanges between U.S. and Latin American military establishments—a veritable parallel diplomacy—ensure interventionist Latin
American officers important allies in the U.S. government who share
their extremist views of Latin American societies. This raises the larger

problem of civilian control of the military. But if it is not reasonable to expect civilian control to function effectively even in the United States, very little hope is left for Latin Americans—except to survive in the midst of the convulsive reproduction of the logic discussed above.

A second problem is that agencies colonized by certain interests will exert pressure within their own governments and, when they can, on other governments as well in an effort to resist normalization of U.S.–Latin American relations. This is another fact of life; it would be utopian to expect to change this situation. But this does not preclude the possibility that government authorities with sufficient decision-making power and the capability to create public opportunities to dispute such interests could guarantee, despite the inevitable incongruities, reasonable coordination of most issues related to a policy of normalizing U.S.–Latin American relations. Note that my relative conformity regarding this topic contrasts with the radicalness of the previous proposal. This reflects the fact that the interplay and conflict of economic interests usually produces a complex vector of influences that does not wholly determine the type of political regime existing in a given Latin American country. In contrast, the reinforcement of the (very self-serving) paranoia of Latin American armed forces in terms of "anticommunist" and "antisubversive" indoctrination and support generates causal relationships that point in only one direction: toward coups d'état that have so long plagued the region.

These considerations once again underline the importance of a hardly novel but today perhaps appropriate idea: nothing more and nothing less than the need to establish relations among nation-states between the United States and Latin American countries—that is, relations among units of varying power in the international arena that respect each other as nation-states. The achievement of this type of relationship can only be the result of an intense political process in each of the respective countries and governments, one that generates sufficient domestic support for foreign policies that move toward the achievement of such a relationship. Because this process requires enlightened discussion, bargaining, and consensus-building in each country, it can only occur in a democratic context.

At this domestic political level, international or regional organizations can make only a marginal contribution. Without firm decisions by national governments, the contributions made by international organizations or different private sectors can do little to achieve or sustain a new pattern of U.S.–Latin American relations. On the other hand, when repressive rule still prevails in a given country, some of these sectors (often religious groups) and international organizations can contribute greatly to demands for respect of alternative values such as democracy and human rights.

Other Possible Steps Toward a Better U.S.–Latin American Relationship

As I have argued, any democratic government and its supporters in the United States and in Latin America share a real medium- and long-term interest in the emergence and consolidation of democratic regimes in Latin America. Political actions and enlightened discussion should make this interest be recognized as real. Furthermore, the recognition of this shared interest would carry with it an obvious corollary: an interest in respect for, in each country, the individual rights and associational guarantees of classical constitutionalism. The recognition of this shared interest does not refer only to the government of the United States; it should also be the focus for all democratic Latin American governments as a joint (and, one hopes, to a significant degree, coordinated) expression of their recognized common interest in the promotion and maintenance of constitutional democracy and the human rights that it guarantees. This, in turn, presupposes a sufficiently clear and explicit definition of political/constitutional democracy so that its meaning cannot easily be perverted, as has frequently occurred in the present "inter-American system" and in the hardly democratic "people's democracies" of the communist bloc. Such a definition can only be elaborated through extensive political and intellectual debate, which will have to be broad enough to encompass forms of democratic government and regime that may emerge in different cases.

Concern for supporting democratic values in Latin America would then become an explicit guiding orientation for *all* these governments' regional foreign policies. This concern might be given some relatively low but not insignificant degree of institutionalization. A simple declaration of intentions, however sincere it might be when first made, is unlikely to have much practical impact. Yet excessive formalization or bureaucratization would soon lead to repeating the known defects of many inter-American institutions. Perhaps a satisfactory intermediate solution would be the creation of a kind of ombudsman for analyzing and, if necessary, denouncing violations of democratic values and human rights. The organization might also propose sanctions against violators when appropriate. These would be for the most part moral sanctions, but this does not mean that such sanctions necessarily would be ineffective.

This role could be accomplished by a small, flexible institution created with this explicit mandate by a significant number of governments, representing not only western hemisphere countries but eventually other democratic countries as well. The institution would be provided with an endowment that would guarantee its economic independence for a period of no less than ten years. At that time its operations, achievements, and failures would be reviewed. This "ombudsman institution" would regularly produce studies and reports on the state of democracy in the hemisphere, obstacles to democratization, and their impact on human rights in any country in the hemisphere. It would also conduct studies and produce reports and recommendations whenever necessary on violations or serious threats to democratic values or human rights. This institution could work closely with the recently created Inter-American Institute of Human Rights in those areas in which their interests and concerns converge.

Such an ombudsman institution would have to accept the intrinsically polemic character of its opinions and recommendations, knowing that debate on these questions in itself helps to promote democratic values and practices. The institution should also be aware that its principal capital would—and should—derive from its prestige as a serious, independent custodian of such values. Furthermore, membership in this organization should be open to any government—in the Americas or elsewhere—that in the judgment of its founding members clearly respects democratic values in its own domestic context.

One important consequence of the functioning of an institution such as this would be to make clear to any government that violated or attempted to violate democratic values or human rights that an international context exists that determines that such violations are not free of costs. This international context is more than just the United States or eventually some Latin American country solitarily pronouncing some variant of the Betancourt doctrine.[16] The fact that some Latin American governments have been able to commit numerous atrocities with impunity—and even be rewarded for their pretended "defense of the West"—is one of the most disagreeable characteristics of the present "inter-American system." The costs that such governments would incur would include the diffuse but not insignificant impact of the studies, reports, and recommendations produced by the ombudsman institution and—more important over the longer term—the climate of domestic and intergovernmental opinion that this institution would sustain and (if reasonably successful) help nourish.

Finally, given the prevailing climate of opinion in Latin America and like-minded sectors in the United States that (also on the basis of the hard experience of recent years with Latin American authoritarian regimes) seek a healthy redefinition of prevailing hemispheric relations, the very process of creating such an ombudsman institution would generate a point of convergence and useful discussion that would open up new possibilities that today cannot be visualized. The institution could not substitute for contributions made by domestic political forces in each case. However, it could help sustain a context favorable both to them and to the elaboration of more mature and constructive hemispheric relations.

Conclusions

The suggestions made in the course of this essay will certainly be difficult to realize. At best, advances will occur through complex national and international processes that will require time and patience. But, on the other hand, by now it should be clear that the perpetuation of the traditional U.S.–Latin American relationship feeds a perverse logic that is convenient only for the more repressive and aggressive forces in the hemisphere. The changes suggested here seek, first, the abandonment of the United States' hegemonic and paternalistic orientations toward Latin America and, on the other hand, the abandonment of Latin American governments' prejudiced and mendicant orientation toward the United States—that is, the suggestion here is for the normalization of hemispheric relations. Normalization of relations would not cancel out asymmetries in power, but it would frame them in a context that is more constructive for all countries. Second, these changes would be based on a recognition of the common interest that all American countries have in achieving and consolidating democracy and basic human rights.

These changes, and the momentum they might acquire if pursued with adequate firmness and continuity by a sufficient number of governments, will require policies that are far from passive. The "intervention versus nonintervention" dichotomy simply has no meaning in relations between nation-states. The challenge is to define, in a given international context (which is not amenable to hegemonic pretensions, although it necessarily reflects asymmetries of power) and in a given state of political and ethical opinion on the part of the actors involved, both the scope of legitimate intervention and the limits to such action. As noted previously, some present forms of U.S. intervention in Latin America must be (urgently) terminated or drastically restricted. But this is not to postulate inertia. On the contrary, redoubled activism is required by both public and private groups and organizations throughout the Americas to protect and promote certain basic values that supposedly we all share. "Intervention" of this *type* and *orientation* is, I believe, legitimate and relevant for all that is not an obstinate authoritarian vocation and/or the most provincial nationalism. It would be a silly paradox if democratic forces throughout the hemisphere (and throughout the world, especially the increasingly active West European political presence) fail to recognize their shared interests and act together to promote them, while powerful proauthoritarian forces do so without restrictions.

For those familiar with the graveyard of wrecked and discredited ideas in Latin America, these suggestions are not very original. That they have been reformulated here indicates the persistence of a type of relationship between Latin America and the United States that for years has cried out for a perhaps subtle but nonetheless drastic redefinition. What may be original (although it is not original to have thought so) is that the present conjuncture offers a unique challenge and opportunity to produce the changes in U.S.–Latin American relations that many reasonable minds have wanted for so long.

Finally, if what has been argued in this essay makes any sense, then democratic governments throughout the hemisphere, as well as parties, movements, and diverse groups and agencies that share values that point toward democracy and respect for human rights, all have an obligation to support actively those forces that are now struggling (at times under very adverse conditions) for these same values. These forces need support and solidarity. The skein will begin to unravel when they become (as they will) democratic governments under the unfavorable domestic and international conditions that now exist. For current or future Latin American democratic governments, the cancellation of their mistrust for the content and goals of U.S. policy will have to interact closely with concrete signals from the U.S. government that it is abandoning its hegemonic and paternalistic temptations regarding Latin America. For these developments to occur, it will be essential that private and public groups throughout the hemisphere that share these goals establish communications and active links. It will also be crucial that these groups realize that the emergence and strengthening of democratic regimes is a necessary condition for the change in U.S.–Latin American relations described above. Such solidarity and awareness is never so decisive as when the struggle is still going on to end authoritarian rule, or when fragile democracies seek to consolidate their positions.

Kellogg Institute for International Studies
University of Notre Dame
and Centro Brasileiro de Analise e Planejamento (CEBRAP)
Rio de Janeiro, Brazil

Notes

1. To argue for the worth and sense of what is possible, as an area of human action oriented toward the future and inspired by values, is to render tribute to the person who has written most insistently and fruitfully on this subject and closely related issues, Albert O. Hirschman. See especially his collections of essays, *A Bias for Hope: Essays on Development and Latin America* (New Haven: Yale University Press, 1971), and *Essays in Trespassing: Economics to Politics and Beyond* (New York: Cambridge University Press, 1981).

2. See Abraham F. Lowenthal, "The United States and Latin America: End-

ing the Hegemonic Presumption," *Foreign Affairs* 55, no. 1 (October 1976): 199–213, and his forthcoming book on U.S.–Latin American relations.

3. For an examination of this phenomenon, see Wanderley Guilherme Dos Santos, "Autoritarismo e Apos: Convergencias e Divergencias entre Brasil y Chile," *Dados* 25, no. 2 (1982): 151–63.

4. The exception to this statement is Brazil. However, the high rate of economic growth achieved by the Brazilian regime has not been, and will not be, repeated in other cases. In addition, the Brazilian authoritarian regime wisely did not suppress the institutions of representative democracy. Finally, for some years the regime was indeed repressive, but it never engaged in the systematic horrors of its homologues in the Southern Cone, Bolivia, and Central America.

5. This does not prevent the sporadic appearance of guerrilla movements that disturb the functioning of a civilian government and provoke a worrisome extension of the armed forces' role, as in contemporary Peru. But it is very unlikely that such movements will be successful; they will not "heighten contradictions" in the direction they desire.

6. Large numbers of Latin Americans—not only those on the left—admire Cuba's resistance to U.S. harassment as well as the progress toward social equality it has achieved under highly adverse conditions. However, these opinions do not lead most politically aware Latin Americans to ignore considerations that discourage them from imitating Cuba. These especially include Cuba's dependence on the Soviet Union and the severe costs it imposes.

7. For a discussion of these themes, see Angel Flisfish, "Una nueva ideología democrática en el cono sur de América Latina," mimeograph, FLACSO-CHILE, Santiago, Chile, December 1982.

8. Despite the risk of reaching a point at which the "banality of evil" makes it meaningless to quantify and compare horrors, this was true of a number of Latin American countries in the 1970s—and still applies in some cases. Whether these regimes are "authoritarian" or "totalitarian" is essentially irrelevant to this point. The well-known argument on this matter (Jeane J. Kirkpatrick, "Dictatorships and Double Standards," *Commentary* (November 1979): 34–45, and "U.S. Security and Latin America," *Commentary* (January 1982): 29–40) seems more than anything to be a way of avoiding discussion of the issues involved in human rights policy. Would one have preferred to be a dissident in "authoritarian" Argentina after 1976 or in Mussolini's "totalitarian" Italy? Is the possibility of being assassinated for political dissent (or even without cause) lesser or greater in Guatemala than in Poland?

9. Among the most useful recent works that discuss this issue (with different nuances) from a perspective critical of U.S. hegemonic and paternalistic positions, I have found the following particularly useful: Walter LeFeber, *Inevitable Revolutions: The United States in Central America* (New York: W. W. Norton, 1983); Tom J. Farer, "Searching for Defeat," *Foreign Policy* 40 (Fall 1980): 155–74; Laurence Whitehead, "Explaining Washington's Central American Policies," *Journal of Latin American Studies* 15 (1983): 321–63; Eldon Kenworthy, "Central America: Beyond the Credibility Trap," *World Policy Journal* 1, no. 1 (Fall 1983): 181–200; Richard Fagen and Olga Pellicer de Brody, eds., *The Future of*

Central America: Policy Choices for the U.S. and Mexico (Stanford, Ca.: Stanford University Press, 1983); Stanford Central America Action Network, *Revolution in Central America* (Boulder, Colo.: Westview, 1983); Robert Leiken, ed., *Central America: Anatomy of Conflict* (New York: Pergamon Press, 1983); Richard E. Feinburg, ed., *Central America: International Dimensions of the Crisis* (New York: Holmes & Meier, 1982); and Martin Diskin, ed., *Trouble in Our Backyard: Central America and the United States in the Eighties* (New York: Pantheon Books, 1984).

10. See especially Edelberto Torres-Rivas, *Crisis del poder en Centroamérica* (San José, Costa Rica: EDUCA, 1981), and "Escenarios, sujetos, desenlaces (reflexiones finales sobre la crisis Centroamericana)", mimeograph, San José, Costa Rica, 1983.

11. For an examination of more permanent international factors in this process, see Laurence Whitehead, "International Aspects of Democratization," in Guillermo O'Donnell, Philippe Schmitter, and Laurence Whitehead, eds., *Prospects for Democracy: The Transition from Authoritarian Regimes* (Baltimore: Johns Hopkins University Press, 1986).

12. Here my position differs fundamentally from that taken by Howard Wiarda in his contribution to this volume. Acknowledging difficulties is the basis for posing a problem; it is not the solution to the problem or reasonable grounds for failing to consider what possibly could be achieved in this regard in both South and North America.

13. According to the evidence available, such coordination was possible in periods of highly aggressive U.S. policies (for example, toward Guatemala, Cuba, and Chile at different moments). Perhaps it would be possible to produce similar coordination where more constructive purposes are involved.

14. On this issue and related topics, see James R. Kurth's essay in this volume.

15. For discussions of this "doctrine" and its intrinsically antidemocratic orientation, see, among others, Genaro Arriagada, "National Security Doctrine in Latin America," *Peace and Change* 6, nos. 1–2 (1980): 49–60; John Child, "Strategic Concepts of Latin America: An Update," *Inter-American Economic Affairs* 34 (Summer 1980): 61–82.

16. The "Betancourt doctrine" (formulated by the former president of Venezuela, Rómulo Betancourt) calls for a state's diplomatic relations with other countries to be conditioned by whether the latter respect the principles and mechanisms of representative democracy.

12

The Human Rights Question in U.S.–Latin American Relations

Rafael Braun

This essay approaches the question of human rights in U.S.–Latin American relations from an essentially political perspective. This point of view is not the only one possible, and the subject could be enlightened and enriched through other, complementary approaches. However, it offers the widest explanatory context for understanding why a topic on which presumably there should be agreement is, in fact, a source of conflict. This perspective is also important because the proper guarantees to the full enjoyment of human rights exist only within the framework of a democratic, legitimate, and stable political regime.

Of course, not everyone thinks alike. Therefore the first section of this essay explores the sources and dimensions of ambiguity in the expression "human rights." The essay then examines the mechanisms that are most important in promoting respect for human rights, including the roles of the state, voluntary associations, multilateral institutions, and the U.S. government in bilateral relations. Finally, the conclusion analyzes the possibilities for cooperation and conflict between Latin America and the United States on human rights issues in the coming decade.

"Human Rights": An Ambiguous Expression

The dialogue between the United States and Latin America on human rights did not begin in the 1970s. The question had been analyzed long before, although from different viewpoints, in both North and South America. This is not the place to review the history of this asymmetrical progression toward consciousness of every human being's equal dignity. However, it might be useful to remind readers that before the United Nations General Assembly approved the Universal Declaration of Human Rights on December 10, 1948 (with forty-eight votes in favor and with 8 abstentions by the Soviet bloc, South Africa, and Saudi Arabia), the ninth American International Conference had approved (in Bogotá) the American Declaration of the Rights and Duties of Man. To recall these landmarks—and the decisive role that Latin America played in them—is useful in order to set the balance right and to enable both Latin America and the United States to approach the subject well aware of its extreme complexity.

It would appear that the seed sown by the Universal Declaration produced many fruits, since it was succeeded by the European Convention for the Protection of Human Rights and Basic Freedoms (1952), the International Covenant on Civil and Political Rights (1966), the International Covenant on Economic, Social, and Cultural Rights (1966), the American Convention on Human Rights (1969), and the Helsinki Conference (1975). At the declaratory level, the fullest consensus seems to exist on human rights. However, considerable distance exists between good intentions and reality, between what should be and what is.

It would be overly simple to conclude that human rights are not fully in force in the world only because, in some regions, certain perverse, cruel, and selfish individuals have taken over the state and oppressed citizens. This may be true, but one must also recognize that the scope of what is stipulated in the declarations and treaties on human rights is not evident and that the indispensable task of exegesis is dependent on general philosophical conceptions that interpret the world in radically different ways. Although people may say similar things, they do not necessarily interpret these statements in the same way. Thus it is first necessary to analyze the internal structure of international and hemispheric documents on human rights in order to determine to what extent they express a consensus.

Seeking an explanation of why the articles of these documents have a double canonical form ("Everyone has the right to . . . " and "No one shall be . . . "), John Finnis proposes this hypothesis: differences in expression are linked to the fact that all of the documents in question admit a clause that imposes limits on the free exercise of recognized rights. Finnis also warns that several of the articles of the "No one shall be . . . " form contain internal qualifications, although others do not. He suggests that only the latter "are intended to be of conclusory force"; the former "have guiding force only."[1] This hypothesis is reinforced by the fact that both the International Covenant on Civil and Political Rights and the American Convention on Human Rights recognize that—in exceptional cases—states can temporarily suspend the obligations contracted in these treaties, but that this disposition does not authorize any suspension of those articles that are restrictively listed (see Articles 4.2 and 27.2, respectively). An examination of these articles leads to the following conclusions:

1. There is no full agreement concerning which rights cannot be derogated or limited. In effect, the U.N. Universal Declaration contains four

articles of the "No one shall be . . . " type that do not contain limiting clauses. This short list is lengthened to seven when the International Covenant on Civil and Political Rights sets forth the rights that may be suspended in exceptional circumstances that place the life of the nation in jeopardy. The American Convention on Human Rights, following the trend toward lengthening this list, adds five more articles.[2] Confronted with this diversity of approach, one can follow two paths. The first alternative is to adopt this last document as valid, judging it to be the most complete result of a process of asserting human rights. The second path is to determine the lowest common denominator among these different documents. In practice, however, there is not even consensus on this point. Broad agreement exists only on the right to the physical integrity of the person.[3]

2. There is no justification for urging the promotion of civil and political rights more vigorously than economic, social, and cultural rights. The states that signed these covenants commit themselves "to respect and to ensure to all individuals" their civil and political rights (Article 2.1), while they only commit themselves to "achieving progressively the full realization" of economic, social, and cultural rights (Article 2.1). The distinction between both sets of rights, and the priority accorded in the documents to civil and political rights, do not express a consensus. Rather, they represent the liberal tradition's view on the issue.[4]

3. There is no agreement on the scope of certain basic rights such as the right to life. The International Covenant on Civil and Political Rights states in Article 6 that "no one shall be arbitrarily deprived of his life." The remaining five clauses are devoted to justifying and limiting the death sentence, which "shall not be carried out on pregnant women" (Article 6.5) as an implicit recognition of the fetus's right to life. The American Convention, in turn, states that "every person has the right to have his life respected. This right shall be protected by law and, in general, from the moment of *conception*" (Article 4.1, emphasis added). The American Convention is abolitionist in its ideology, since clause 3 says that "the death penalty shall not be reestablished in states that have abolished it." Clause 4 later specifies that "in no case shall capital punishment be inflicted for political offenses or related common crimes," thus granting greater protection to the life of the political criminal than to that of the common criminal.

4. There is no agreement concerning limitations to the exercise of these rights. Article 29 of the Universal Declaration admits that "in the exercise of his rights and freedoms, everyone shall be subject only to such limitations as are determined by law solely for the purpose of securing due recognition and respect for the rights and freedoms of others and of meeting the just requirements of morality, public order and the general welfare

in a democratic society." To make the right of the individual compatible with the rights of others is no easy task. But arriving at a consensus with regard to which demands are "just," what should be understood by "democratic society," and the meaning of expressions such as "morality," "public order," and "general welfare" is highly problematical in the academic field and an impossible task in politics.[5] The International Covenant on Civil and Political Rights contains no general restricting clause. However, it does include a similar structure in several of its articles, adding "national security" to those elements to be protected.

This analysis of major human rights documents shows to what extent the expression "human rights" is ambiguous and can legitimately be interpreted in different ways by philosophies that give priority to different values. Human rights are not absolute commodities whose relevance can be verified in isolation in any one society. The clause that states that individual rights must be made compatible with the rights of others poses the arduous problem of ranking rights, because it seems obvious that the right to life cannot be placed on the same axiological level as the right to paid holidays.

Any political community is historically organized on the basis of one culture—that is to say, a general conception of mankind, society, history, and divinity. This conception establishes a scale of values that slowly structures a concrete pattern of rights in response to the difficulties posed by the real world. These patterns are not rigid, because certain transitory circumstances lead to higher priorities being attached to particular values, without this implying a definitive choice. Different cultures, based on their own value scales, have their own responses to the challenges posed by history.

One must accept the existence of different value scales in the Western Hemisphere because even if it is true that these value scales make explicit an ideal of human development, the concrete patterns of rights express conceptions of man that are frequently antagonistic. A conception of basic human rights and their ranking that derives from a Christian anthropology differs from an analogous conception derived from a Marxist or utilitarian anthropology. Several examples are instructive here. Cuba's Marxist-Leninist regime has a conception of freedom of conscience and religion that depends on its ideology, which is considered to be the only valid science and which is in open contradiction with the Christian ideal of religious freedom.[6] In the United States, the controversy concerning abortion illustrates deep philosophical differences regarding the right to life.[7] In Nicaragua, the Sandinista government's Marxist orientation gives priority to the satisfaction of economic, social, and cultural rights over political rights. Similar positions inspired by "developmentalist" ideologies were common among South American military governments in the

1960s and 1970s. There is no reason to hide these differences by translating ethical choices into a supposedly universal language. If there is no agreement at the ethical level, these general formulas will constitute ambiguous statements intended to disguise basic disagreements.

If one adds to this plurality of ethical conceptions the diverse perspectives held by different sectors of society regarding the possibility that those human rights recognized at a normative level can be realized here and now, the sources of conflict among cultures, governments, ideological movements, and social classes multiply rapidly. From a political point of view (and politics, it is important to remember, is the art of the possible), the human rights issue is an ideological question that expresses the idea of justice that everyone constructs for himself, an idea basically inspired by values but also influenced by the interests at stake. Political communities that permit the free expression of their values and interests present a plural image that impedes the identification of one sector's opinions with those of the country as a whole. Can one say that the United States, Brazil, or El Salvador has a homogeneous conception of human rights? Certainly not, as evidenced by the different values that civilians, the military, liberals, conservatives, and Marxists attribute to individual rights and to national security, or to civil and political rights in comparison with economic, social, and cultural rights. Political communities governed by totalitarian regimes do not permit the free expression of values and interests, but the underlying diversity of opinion does not seem to fade away because of political control. To deny this would be equivalent to stating that the oppressors and the oppressed share the same idea of justice.

To note the existence of a plurality of value scales does not in any way close the debate regarding human rights. To do so would be to adopt a relativist philosophy of values that I do not share. Nor do I share a skeptical attitude concerning the possibility of affirming the essential dignity of man. For philosophical and religious reasons, I believe it is feasible to distinguish good from evil, truth from error and lies. Moreover, without these distinctions there could be no political community. It is this capacity that prevents us from looking on with indifference when human dignity is subjugated, and that commits us to the critical task of denouncing whenever necessary—first of all in one's own community, and then in the world—the failure to respect those rights that any human being has by virtue of the simple fact of being human.

This ideal of justice makes concrete an aspiration to the absolute that must be carefully maintained as a normative goal—one that may never be fully realized but that serves to measure the inevitable degree of injustice in every historical situation. Like any ethical ideal, this one must be proposed, not imposed. This does not imply that a political community can remain neutral when confronted with differing value scales. By establishing a positive juridical order, a community is forced to choose a particular conception of the good of society and of its people. Thus it is necessary to underline the essential difference between the plurality of ethical ideals that coexist within a particular national juridical system and the plurality of political and juridical systems inspired by opposing conceptions of man. The first case always involves a limited plurality because penal law (by establishing what is or is not lawful) determines what behavior is punishable. In contrast, in the international arena there is no common authority with the capacity to punish effectively; thus diversity of behavior cannot be limited except by the use of force. Therefore the crucial work of denouncing and proposing should be left not to political power but to the moral force of society—represented in a free community by religious, academic, humanitarian, and public opinion institutions—if one wants to avoid the manipulation of ideals and their subordination to particular interests.

Understanding a culture demands understanding both its historical traditions and its ethical and religious components. For example, one cannot understand the culture of the United States if one knows nothing of Puritanism and the Mayflower pilgrims or of the division between North and South on the issue of slavery. Nor can one understand Latin American cultures if one overlooks the presence of the Catholic church, the characteristics of different colonial administrations (principally Spanish and Portuguese), the process of racial mixing, and the influence of the Enlightenment—to mention only the earliest background experiences. The idea that a country's inhabitants hold regarding their rights stems from this history, and it is only gradually modified in one direction or another. This is why political voluntarism that ignores the popular conscience is irredeemably doomed to failure unless it seeks to implant a totalitarian system. A fruitful dialogue between the United States and Latin America demands a reciprocal knowledge of cultural traditions and national histories, because the behavior of the present is conditioned by both the recent and the remote past, and because possible understandings spring from the mutual recognition of the right to be different.

Finally, understanding a culture requires knowing the forms of economic organization, social life, and political relations in force in a given society. This knowledge must not stem from the cold glance of an observer who perceives reality only in terms of his own cultural experience. Rather, it must be based on a comprehension of the meaning that institutions have for those who act in them. A sociological analysis that would limit itself merely to describing reality on the basis of statistics, or that would consider events only in terms of their surface meaning, would be incapable of grasping the concealed rationality behind so many "unfair" structures and apparently "absurd" actions. Behind a social institution there are always reasons that explain its existence. One cannot reasonably say that a culture is understood unless these reasons are grasped. The desire to modify a situation (even with the best intentions) that one does not understand to begin with often produces greater social disasters than those that one sought to correct.[8]

Intercultural dialogue from this multidimensional perspective will not make disagreements disappear, but at least it will be of significant help in dissipating misunderstandings and prejudices. Distinguishing between levels of discourse will make it possible to discover partial consensus regarding certain general principles. But one must ensure that these arrangements are not based only on formal principles, thus forgetting or sacrificing substantive values. Nothing ensures that what is legal is also moral. Human rights—even before being translated into positive law and transformed into civil, political, and social rights—represent an ethical demand that is above the will of legislators or judges.

Nonetheless, this agreement on principles does not obviate the need to implement them. At the level of action, where prudence is also required, concrete options may differ. For example, the Catholic church recognizes as legitimate the fact that its members, although inspired by the same faith and the same idea of man, operate freely in the political, economic, and social fields. In the last analysis, this freedom is expressed in a legitimate plurality of options in the temporal field.[9] Catholics share the same principles, but they adopt positions that are partially divergent—even on the subject of human rights—because different appreciations of reality lead them to formulate opposing prudential judgments, as evident during the last few years in El Salvador, Chile, Argentina, and Brazil. Politics is a matter of opinion, and it is fundamentally important that it remain so. Thus it is also possible at times for groups that differ at the level of principles to reach agreement in action.

For those who believe, as I do, that man from the moment of conception has universal and inviolable rights stemming from his condition as a free and intelligent being, it is painful to see the actual disagreement that reigns on this subject in the Western Hemisphere. One must recognize frankly that Marxism-Leninism and the conservative doctrine of national security do not endorse—either in theory or practice—the minimum nucleus of rights that one would wish to exclude from all controversy, such as the right not to be deprived of life arbitrarily, or the right not to be subjected to torture or cruel, inhuman, or degrading treatment. The conflict regarding human rights is philosophical, ideological, and political. Minimizing its scope can only lead to an incorrect diagnosis of reality.

Promoting Human Rights

Recognizing the complexity of the problem should not serve as a pretext for failing to do something about it. Having discarded utopian solutions, one must seek legitimate and effective means for ensuring the protection of the rights of man wherever he may be. The object of this concern is not an abstract and universal mankind, but the individual human being of flesh and blood who suffers from injustice and who in most cases is so weak that his complaint is not even heard. This individual lives in a political community governed by authorities whose ethical goal should be to achieve the common good, but who in practice frequently act according to the logic of power accumulation described so well by Hobbes. It is they who have both the direct responsibility for the fate of society and the capacity to change it. These authorities come from ruling classes that have accumulated strength, prestige, and wealth. Focusing attention on national communities and their ruling classes is thus the first step in developing an effective strategy for promoting human rights.

The Role of the State

With great realism, the United Nations General Assembly proclaims the Universal Declaration to be "a common standard of achievement for all peoples and all nations, to the end that every individual and every organ of society, keeping this Declaration constantly in mind, shall strive by teaching and education to promote respect for these rights and freedoms and by progressive measures, national and international, to secure their universal and effective recognition and observance" (Preamble). Ethical ideals have no force if they are not imbedded in the popular conscience. Before attending to laws one must attend to people, because a fair (or less unfair) order can only be instituted and maintained by rulers imbued with the virtue of justice—that is, with the will to recognize everyone's own right.

It would be interesting to determine what portion of the time devoted to civilian and military elites' teaching and upbringing in different countries is dedicated to ethical formation of the conscience and to discussion of different conceptions and problems of justice. Many professionals have been trained in a positivist conception of science so rigorous that it regards ethical problems as irrelevant. The only rationality that interests them is that which effectively enables them to link means to ends, thus allowing them to overlook the delicate problem of ethical coherence that must exist between ends and means. When this attitude carries over into political, economic, and social fields, it generates ostensibly "realistic" behavior that pays attention only to the result (a presumed net balance of good and evil, or the "sense of history"), a result that is obtained at the cost of sacrificing those who interfere with the project. Educating politicians, businessmen, the military and police forces, professional people, those who shape public opinion, and trade union leaders in justice is an indispensable requirement in order that they see the ethical dimension of their acts and evaluate their consequences from this perspective. A policy for promoting human rights that is limited to setting up legal prohibitions restricting the actions of those who govern, and that overlooks this educational activity, would be difficult to apply and would fail to address the most serious problems facing contemporary societies. What is required is a morality of ends, not solely a morality of means. Only a general conception of justice can provide the proper theoretical framework that synthesizes (without establishing arbitrary priorities among) civil, political, economic, social, and cultural rights.

The difficulty in carrying out such educational action is that these activities would have to be implemented in societies characterized by great political instability and ideological diversity. Experience shows that the creation of a legitimate political regime is a necessary but insufficient condition for enjoying human rights. Despite the passage of time, Tocqueville's prediction continues to be valid: the legitimacy formulas that are today crystallized in collective beliefs are pluralistic and representative democracy on the one hand, and one-party Marxist democracy on the other. In the Western Hemisphere, the United States and Cuba, respectively, represent the purest examples of these two models. But whereas the U.S. political system has endured for the last two centuries, the Cuban experience has not yet been subjected to the crucial test of succession. It should also be added that whereas the United States is a pole of attraction for immigrants and refugees in search of a better life, Cuba is a permanent source of emigration, which demonstrates that the totalitarian system's degree of legitimacy is low.

Distinguishing among totalitarian, authoritarian, and democratic regimes in Latin America is useful in order to understand the nature of political processes such as military intervention. The armed forces do not propose new formulas of legitimacy. Their eruption into the national political arena is the result of very different motivations in different countries and at different times. But the authoritarian systems that they establish—although they may sometimes be of very long duration—must be considered transitory and unstable. They do not enjoy the legitimacy of origin of representative democratic regimes, nor are they characterized by the rigid, all-embracing controls imposed by totalitarian regimes. Hence the importance of remembering the old distinction between legitimacy of origin and legitimacy of exercise in order to inquire not only from what source a government comes but also where it is going and what aim it pursues.

The greater openness of authoritarian regimes in comparison with totalitarian systems is empirically verifiable, but this does not make them a desirable alternative. On the contrary, everything that directly or indirectly encourages the emergence of totalitarian or authoritarian regimes undermines respect for human rights. Nonetheless, the distinction has considerable practical importance when one analyzes the ideologies that inspire those forces opposing authoritarianism. If those who are in favor of a totalitarian model triumph, the human rights situation will be worse in the medium and long run, at least for those who do not have a materialistic conception of man and who perceive that the systems of totalitarian domination imposed until now have been irreversible.

The formation of a democratic regime is the only desirable alternative. Jeane Kirkpatrick rightly states that "democratic governments have come into being slowly, after extended prior experience with more limited forms of participation during which leaders have reluctantly grown accustomed to tolerating dissent and opposition, opponents have accepted the notion that they may defeat but not destroy incumbents, and people have become aware of government's effects on their lives and of their own possible effects on government."[10] Democracy as a form of government is a work of art that requires leaders brought up in its values and trained in its practices. Habits, customs, and behavior are not created by a decree calling for elections. But these attitudes are not learned if they are not practiced. To require a democratic regime to solve all human rights problems overnight is to create a demand that is impossible for it to fulfill. How long did it take the United States to abolish slavery and racist legislation? To be patient is not to be complacent, but to be a disciple of history.

A thorny question that will be at the center of the debate on human rights during the next decade is the relative priority that different ideological sectors will grant to civil and political rights on the one hand and to economic, social, and cultural rights on the other. For those whose thinking is reflected in existing international agreements on this issue, civil and political rights must be "ensured" and "respected" by states, whereas with economic, social, and cultural rights, states only commit themselves to "adopting means . . . for achieving progressively . . . (their) full realization." For others, the first priority is to remedy the basic needs (food, health, education, water and sanitation, shelter) of the poorer social strata without attaching any great importance to the political framework in which these reforms are carried out.

This primacy of economic and social measures over political rights has had various manifestations in Latin America. In Peru the military government of General Velasco Alvarado adopted a populist formula; in Chile, General Pinochet's government chose a free-market formula; in Nicaragua the Sandinista junta subordinated elections to the achievement of certain socialist objectives. The position favoring the primacy of civil and political rights might be accused of formalism to the extent to which it places almost exclusive emphasis on state activity with regard to civil liberties, confident that democratic processes will eventually lead by themselves to greater social justice even though this may not happen in the short and medium terms. The position favoring economic, social, and cultural rights might be accused of being elitist, because those who take power assume the right to decide when their subjects will be capable of determining for themselves what is suitable for them. In this case it is particularly important to know how governing authorities define "basic needs," because a unidimensional conception of man may lead to reductionist policies that ignore his dignity as a free being.[11]

As noted earlier, only a general conception of justice can properly synthesize these two extreme positions. As a subject (and not merely an object) of social life, the human being has the right to participate freely in determining both his political and social destinies. To accept that enlightened minorities—authoritarian or totalitarian, liberal, socialist, or populist—arbitrarily determine what people's true interests are (without their participation) is to deny the essential dignity of man that is the basis of any substantive theory of human rights. The same can be said of majorities that, recognizing no other limits than their own desires, violate the guarantees that the law grants to minorities.

A strategy that renounces "revolution from above" must organize participation, make marginal groups aware of their rights, and motivate those with influence, resources, education, and power to act in favor of the weaker members of society. This is a strategy of mobilization and conflict based not on the suppression of adversaries but on the creation of a new social conscience.[12] Of course, a strategy of this kind—directed not toward the immediate assumption of control but toward a lasting modification of a society's balance of power—will face formidable adversaries. In addition to the elitism of the left and the right, it will have to face the powerful opposition of corporate interests that are against such change, both in the United States and in Latin America. Such a strategy must also ensure that ideological schemas originating in other circumstances do not impose themselves dogmatically on realities that are completely alien to them, for it is the responsibility of each country's social forces to diagnose their own reality and to define a viable strategy that reflects possible social and political alliances.

From this perspective, the struggle for economic and social rights cannot be separated from that waged to exercise civil and political rights; Aristotle has already noted that majority government is also the government of the poor. Exercising the right to free association will demonstrate the degree of freedom that a society grants to its members, because it is through voluntary association that one transcends one's individuality and becomes a collective force. This is the only effective means of curbing arbitrary actions on the part of rulers and "big bosses" who control the resources of social and economic power.

A strategy of this kind will also help overcome the differences that exist between those who consider the state as almost the only source of abuses of civil and political rights and those who consider it the supreme remedy for social and economic injustices. The former want the state to play as small a role as possible, whereas the latter want an interventionist welfare state. As various authors have noted, rights can be properly protected only when institutions and procedures exist for preserving them.[13] In this sense, the creation of an independent judiciary and a body of suitable lawyers, the subordination of the police to judges, speed and ease of access in the administration of justice, and the existence of a prison system that respects the individual are all basic requisites of a state of law. But even when practice is in accordance with theory, the remedy would be insufficient if citizens did not respect of their own free will the norms that govern them and give them cohesion. Without such respect, the state would be overwhelmed by societal demands and would be incapable of offering protection to the innocent. This clearly demonstrates that the state may fail in its tasks because of either excesses or defects. Although rarely discussed in the literature on human rights, this is a central issue.

Indeed, it is essential to recognize that the violation of human rights stems not only from the state but also from society. In order to avoid the former, the state's actions must be limited by proscriptions based in law that prevent the abuse of power. To avoid the latter requires efficient protection for the citizen because it is more important to prevent a crime than to punish one. For example, a woman should have the right to walk the streets without running the risk of being raped or mugged. If she cannot do so, the government does not fulfill its task, because its responsibility covers both what its agents do (for example, mistreatment of prisoners in places of detention) and what they fail to do (for example, not guaranteeing personal security and integrity of the person). However, human rights analysts are concerned almost exclusively with what the state does rather than with what it fails to do.

Posing the issue of human rights protection in this way requires a careful country-by-country analysis of where threats to human rights originate. An analysis of this kind shows that the problem is everyone's, not just that of some countries. A brief consideration of the major threats to personal rights illustrates this point. (1) Common criminals acting individually. These include both those who resort to the use of violence and the so-called white collar criminals who, by taking advantage of positions of influence, commit crimes with total impunity (especially in the economic and social fields). Their main victims are the poor. (2) Organized crime, including gambling, prostitution and white slavery, pornography, and drug traffic. Organized crime holds great power for corruption. Criminals of this kind are linked to existing spheres of power and generally act with impunity in the Americas, except in Cuba. (3) Political movements that resort to the systematic use of force in order to achieve their aims and win power. They practice various forms of selective crime such as robbery, kidnaping for ransom, and assassination. They almost always have outside support, whether explicit or concealed. (4) Clandestine paramilitary or parapolice groups organized or tolerated by state intelligence or counterinsurgency services. They frequently have support from specialized organizations with similar tasks in other countries. Although they are called "security forces," they create situations of extreme insecurity for the population at large.

Listing so many potential threats to human rights should engender caution with regard to the possibility of properly guaranteeing rights by government fiat. To believe that the human rights situation in a country improves decisively because the rulers stop torturing their opponents is to forget that the country itself may have become a prison.[14] At the opposite extreme, in a situation of anarchy bordering on a Hobbesian state of nature in which everyone has a right to everything, no one really has a right to anything. Effective therapies spring from correct diagnoses, and both diagnoses and therapies improve by trial and error. The time has come to undertake a thorough reevaluation of existing diagnoses, setting aside political exigencies and emotional appeals in order to address the manifold roots of injustice. It will be necessary to alter structures, correct behavior, revise laws, and change rulers, knowing full well that even men and women moved by the same desire for justice will differ with regard to the best means of achieving it. Therefore, the essential basis for this search must be a reciprocal commitment not to impose ideas by force and to respect both the freedom of the individual and the freedom of countries to determine for themselves how they wish to live.

The Role of Voluntary Associations

If the creation of a legitimate political regime is a necessary but insufficient condition for the enjoyment of human rights, and if the only desirable alternative is a democratic regime, political parties should play an essential role in the struggle for the respect of human dignity as channels for the free participation of citizens in political life. They generate the cadres that enter government, and it is their task as political opposition to exercise control over the government's actions. In order for these activities to serve human rights, political parties must fulfill a double requirement. First, parties must be capable of articulating a nation's main social interests so that their representative capacity is demonstrated at the polls and adequately espresses the existing constellation of social powers. If the armed forces, business and trade union associations, and religious communities are not convinced that their values and interests are sufficiently well represented by political parties, they will fall back on themselves and forge praetorian alliances that destabilize democratic governments. A political party can only govern or act effectively in opposition if it mobilizes social forces. Experience shows that electoral force and the formal power that legality grants are not sufficient bases for those who hold political power to prevail over those who control social power. Without the existence of strong political power capable of commanding obedience, human rights cannot be guaranteed effectively.

The second requirement is ideological in nature. The twentieth century has witnessed notorious examples of ideologically totalitarian or authoritarian political parties that came to office democratically but maintained themselves in power for long periods of time by systematically violating the rights of their citizens. Some of the most notorious cases occurred in Latin America in the 1950s: Perón in Argentina, Rojas Pinilla in Colombia, and Pérez Jiménez in Venezuela (not to mention the more than doubtful "democracy" of the Institutional Revolutionary Party [PRI] in Mexico). The problem, then, is how to establish a state of law in a democratic political regime if a significant group of parties does not adhere with conviction to the principles and precepts of a constitutional and pluralistic system. In order to evade this issue, observers very often underestimate the difficulties faced by Latin American countries—which usually lack a democratic tradition—when they attempt to establish civilized and durable forms of political coexistence. Authoritarian traditions of a personalistic, populist, or bureaucratic type are very strong. A similar threat is posed by various Marxist ideologies that may espouse electoral politics as a tactic (depending upon the circumstances), but which do not adhere to the values that are the fundamental basis of the rights of man.

In addition to political parties, those organizations specifically devoted to defending human rights have played a significant role in shaping public opinion by denouncing abuses. Their action is nonexistent in totalitarian regimes such as Cuba, which do not permit their presence. Their activities are more effective in authoritarian regimes, where they enjoy sufficient freedom to operate but often lack the personal security to develop fully. As a result, many of their members have been killed or have suffered imprisonment or exile for their commitment to furthering justice.

A strategy for promoting human rights must be able to count on these organizations' participation, but it should not be based on them. In the space available here it is not possible to evaluate the frequently heard objection that not all human rights organizations are impartial in their judgments (which would require a detailed discussion in order to avoid unfair generalizations). However, it is possible to conclude that one cannot demand of these groups more than they can provide. Their denunciations help to publicize condemnable acts and situations, thus weakening the arbitrary use of power. But this does not mean that these organizations themselves have the capacity to remedy the evils that they reveal. Human rights organizations also engage in the legal defense of the oppressed when a more or less independent judiciary is present, but they are incapable of doing so if such institutions do not exist. Their role is to exercise a monitoring function, and their testimony will be all the more effective if it is not linked to the political interests in conflict. If public opinion perceives that the denunciations are biased, they lose credibility.

Meaningful contributions in this field can and must be made by other institutions that together constitute so-called moral power. These include churches and religious communities, especially Christian groups (which are the most numerous). Their actions to promote human rights are already well known, their testimony often having been sealed with their blood. The services that religious organizations can offer in the future include diagnosing human rights situations, educating consciences, training leaders, organizing solidarity, creating spaces for dialogue, accepting the responsibility of mutual toleration and scrupulously respecting religious freedom, and rejecting any temptation toward clericalism—of either the right or the left—that would undermine their integrity.

Universities have traditionally played a decisive role in forming elites' ideology and providing moral leadership in Latin America. It is sufficient to recall here what was said earlier regarding the importance of the ethical training of consciences, which should take place in the educational system. Finally, the mass media (television, radio, the press) can, if they enjoy freedom, constitute sounding boards for society. They can carry out educational tasks, and they can denounce and oppose human rights abuses. These functions complement and amplify the work conducted by other humanitarian institutions.

The Role of Multilateral Institutions

The principle on which the foreign policy of western hemisphere countries should be based is stated in Article 1.1 of both international covenants on rights: "All peoples have the right of self-determination. By virtue of that right they freely determine their political status and freely pursue their economic, social and cultural development." Like any statement of right, self-determination is an ideal that is threatened both by the internal action of authoritarian and totalitarian movements that resort to force in order to frustrate the expression of a people's sovereignty and by the external action of countries that openly intervene in the internal affairs of others by supporting particular parties or sectors. In the case of Latin America, states are subjected to such an intense play of external pressures that their effective capacity for self-determination sometimes disappears, and their internal conflicts often merely mimic what occurs on a global scale. Totalitarian currents work both at the level of the state and at the level of ideology, making their influence felt on kindred parties and trade unions, in the cultural field, and by offering support to revolutionary movements. The relations between the continent's armed forces have often reinforced their authoritarian tendencies. Democratic currents are also active; the role played by international socialist and Christian Democratic organizations in Latin America is well known. The dramatic situation in El Salvador, for example, cannot be understood outside this context of foreign interference.

The contemporary tendency of great powers to pursue their rivalry in developing countries has produced a number of deleterious effects, often including severe criticism of these countries' human rights records. This double violation of the principle of self-determination constitutes international hypocrisy: the governments of industrialized countries—responsible for both an unjust world economic order and a significant part of the ideological and armed conflicts waged in developing countries—act as judges of situations that they themselves have helped create in dependent states.

In order to neutralize great powers' unilateral intervention and limit the excesses of individual states, efforts have been made to give international organizations a more active role in defending human rights. States in the Western Hemisphere adopted the American Convention on Human Rights in San José, Costa Rica, in November 1969. This Convention (in force only since 1978) did not confine itself to enumerating the rights that the signatory countries must protect. Rather, it established two organs competent to investigate whether the commitments taken on by signatory states are in fact fulfilled: the Inter-American Commission on Human Rights and the Inter-American Court of Human Rights. From both juridical and moral perspectives, the creation of supranational institutions is a positive development. These steps were taken because the essential rights of man do not spring from citizenship in a particular state. They "are based on the attributes of the human personality, and . . . they therefore justify international protection in the form of a convention reinforcing or complementing the protection provided by the domestic law of the American States" (Preamble).

However, several factors lessen the potential effectiveness of these institutions. First, large countries such as Brazil and Mexico—which make up more than half of the Latin American population—have not signed the Convention. Second, there is reason to doubt some signatories' commitment to the protection of human rights. One can only wonder what the practical significance is of adhesion to the Convention by Duvalier's Haiti, Stroessner's Paraguay, Somoza's or the Sandinistas' Nicaragua, or by El Salvador, Guatemala, or Chile.

The behavior of the United States is especially striking in this regard. In 1977 the United States signed the Convention, which states in Article 4.1 that "every person has the right to have his life respected. This right shall be protected by law and, in general, from the moment of conception. No one shall be arbitrarily deprived of his life." In Article 3 it states that "every person has the right to recognition as a person before the law." But in 1973 a U.S. Supreme Court decision had allowed (without participation by elected representatives) almost total freedom to abort, denying the fetus the condition of being a person and thus the legal protection that accompanies the recognition of juridical personality.[15] This example clearly depicts the contradiction that often exists—on such a central issue as the right to life—between national legislation and what is stipulated in international conventions to which a state adheres.[16] One can only conclude that no sovereign country unwillingly models its behavior or its domestic legislation on what is prescribed in international conventions if it has sufficient power to do otherwise.[17]

The Inter-American Commission on Human Rights was created by the Convention to promote the observance and the defense of human rights. It hears "denunciations or complaints of violations of this Convention by a State Party" (Article 44). But this competence is insufficient, and it distorts the Commission's overall task. Although anyone may present such denunciations before the Commission, they necessarily involve only human rights violations by the state, not those stemming from society. This restriction politicizes the Commission's activities. By investigating only actions imputable to governments, the Commission becomes their prosecutor—but not the defender of rights injured by private individuals. In situations of widespread violence, the Commission seems to condemn one of the parties while maintaining silence about others' abuses. The election of its members is also influenced by ideological factors, not just juridical criteria. For these reasons the Commission is essentially a political organ, and it still has not managed to achieve consensus regarding its work. Moreover, its reports are presented to the General Assembly of the Organization of American States, where they are examined and approved by governments that often lack the moral authority to act as judges of other governments.

Despite these imperfections, the Commission has succeeded in making the people of the Americas aware of human rights issues, and its reports have put authoritarian governments on the defensive. But its pronouncements have not at all modified the behavior of totalitarian governments and revolutionary movements that try to achieve their aims by force.

The competence of the Inter-American Court of Human Rights is even more limited than that of the Commission: "only the States Parties and the Commission shall have the right to submit a case to the Court" (Article 61.1). Furthermore, not all states recognize its jurisdiction. Thus its actions are mainly symbolic.

It is unrealistic to expect that these multilateral institutions can play a major role in promoting human rights in the near future. The signing and ratification of the Convention by all western hemisphere states, adapting national legislation to its provisions, and expanding the competence of the Commission and the Court are all desirable steps. But these changes are unlikely to occur soon because of the zeal with which each national community strives to preserve its sovereignty and because of the legitimate prejudice felt toward new international bureaucracies that may be prompt to judge but hesitant to share the physical and economic insecurity of those struggling on the scene to establish a more fair and equitable state of affairs.

Given the relative impotence of international juridical mechanisms, there have been calls for multilateral financial institutions to punish governments that are recalcitrant with regard to human rights issues by denying them loans.[18] There are three serious disadvantages to such proposals. First, the principle of equality does not govern these institutions; decision-making power is based on the amount of capital contributed. Their supposed multilateral character is therefore nothing but a disguise for the hegemonic role of the United States. The advantages of multilateralizing the implementation of national policies are obvious from the perspective of the United States because it avoids accusations of interventionism. But for the same reason, this is an unacceptable mechanism for Latin Americans. Second, international financial institutions must necessarily act without ideological bias; they are instruments of cooperation, not domination. To place them in the service of goals that are alien to their specific aims is to destroy their raison d'être; it would oblige each government to act as judge of the others, thus destroying the indispensable sense of mutual confidence. Third, economic sanctions would affect people more than their governments. International financial institutions must be at the service of nations rather than governments, and the former have permanent interests to be safeguarded regardless of whether the behavior of some rulers merits such sanctions.

Nonetheless, multilateral financial institutions should take into account the impact that projects have on the population's basic needs. This would be a meaningful way of promoting the rights of the weakest based on criteria of social justice, instead of strengthening the position of the strong based solely on criteria of economic efficiency.

The Role of the U.S. Government in Bilateral Relations

In a lucid analysis of U.S.–Latin American military relations since World War II and their implications for human rights, Brian H. Smith demonstrates that the objective of the United States in Latin America has been to promote democratic processes and constitutional governments, limiting sales of sophisticated weapons and allocating budgetary resources to economic projects rather than defense programs. However, he also notes that "other priorities have traditionally competed with the pursuit of such goals in the past and at times have overshadowed them in U.S. security assistance decisions, e.g., containment of communism, U.S. access to raw materials in Latin America, protection of stable environments for U.S. private investments, and ongoing contact and communication with allied military leaders in the hemisphere." Smith adds: "In the past 35 years, whenever the Office of the President, the Department of Defense, the State Department, and the Congress have felt that this latter set of objectives was being threatened, concern about democratic processes, civilian government, and human rights has not been given priority in decisions about security assistance."[19]

The importance of these statements—with which many Latin Americans agree—is that they place a discussion of human rights issues on a realistic basis. Any political community (and the United States is no exception) organizes its armed forces and its diplomatic corps in order to place them at the service of the national interest and national security. Several recent studies have examined the "national security" ideology or doctrine that inspires certain military regimes in the Southern Cone.[20] But the same attention has not been devoted to the national security doctrine that inspires U.S. diplomatic and military action (expressed briefly in the four priorities identified by Smith) or to the connections that exist between both doctrines.

Established security policy for the Western Hemisphere confers on the United States responsibility for defense against external enemies, while Latin American armed forces have responsibility for the defense of their countries against enemies from within. This explains both U.S. opposition to the sale of sophisticated weapons to Latin American countries that are of no use in the fight against internal subversion and the type of training Latin American military cadres receive in mutual assistance programs. It is an essential part of a country's defense interests to place its frontiers as far as possible from its borders and if possible to make others responsible for defending its interests. In Latin America, these "others" are not governments but "allied military leaders" with whom the United States maintains ongoing communication so as to protect its broad security interests. This policy enables the United States to pursue its other national security objectives while leaving the dirty work to Latin American armed forces—criticizing them for their excesses and benefiting from the results. At times this strategy has proved insufficient, and the United States has had to commit its own combat troops (as in the Dominican Republic) or at least to advise, finance, and counsel extensively those national armed forces directly involved (as in contemporary Central America). This is the origin of the double standard in U.S. human rights policy: civilized goals are invoked when its own national security is not at stake, but other criteria prevail when a Latin American country attempts to redefine its relations with the United States. This double standard (which some might call cynicism) is politically explicable but ethically unacceptable.

It is a fact that Latin America occupies a second or third place among the United States' foreign policy priorities. According to Lars Schoultz, "The two foreign affairs subcommittees responsible for U.S.–Latin American relations are largely composed of lawmakers without substantial knowledge of Latin America," and the degree of disinterest and ignorance is such that "virtually any member of Congress has a reasonable chance of having his or her favorite topic become part of United States policy toward Latin America."[21] This combination of widespread disinterest and ignorance enables some minority political sectors to raise the flag of human rights more as an issue of domestic policy and image than as a subject of real substance. To make military and economic assistance dependent on the Department of State's Bureau of Human Rights and Humanitarian Affairs is certainly within the realm of legitimate action for a sovereign state that considers public opposition to unpopular military autocracies as part of its national interest. But no one should believe that such a policy is a humanitarian act unconditionally serving the rights of man, that the Bureau of Human Rights is an agency of the International Red Cross, or that there are no other channels for U.S. aid except public and official ones—as demonstrated by the United States' increasingly overt "undercover" action against the Sandinista government in Nicaragua.

It is therefore not surprising that U.S. foreign policy has been subject to frequent changes linked to shifts in domestic policy. Whereas the United States conducts its relations with western Europe within the stable framework of the Atlantic Alliance, its relations with Latin America oscillate between periods of "benign neglect" and interventionism, sometimes favoring democratization and sometimes favoring military coups. The question remains whether this lack of diplomatic continuity denotes simply erratic or contradictory conduct or whether it reflects the interests of those military and business sectors identified with national security interests. Although I do not wish to endorse conspiracy theories or judge actors' intentions, this second hypothesis is more convincing. In the global partition of zones of influence, Latin America is reserved for U.S. dominance. The principal goal of any hegemonic power is to prevent peoples under its sway from accumulating power and uniting against it. Its actions are therefore guided by the logic of "divide and rule." Although there are important positive elements in U.S.–Latin American relations, the combined action of the United States' diplomatic, military, economic, and cultural forces over time has in fact contributed to internal political instability, to lack of support for regional economic integration, to opposition to access to advanced nuclear technology, to the overwhelming attention given to military dimensions of social problems, and to the cooptation of cultural elites in Latin America.

The pragmatic, nonideological character of U.S. political parties makes it difficult to identify the values that inspire this policy. Whereas West European politics can draw upon the ideological dynamism of communism, social democracy, and christian democracy, political and ideological movements in the United States—both "liberal" and "conservative"—reflect a utilitarian pragmatism that does not inspire lasting loyalties. In the absence of stable political alliances formed to achieve specific objectives, only circumstantial policies are adopted to benefit a particular group's own interests. The absence of a bipartisan U.S. policy toward Latin America is then exploited by the region's military and business forces as a basis for establishing close ties to the Pentagon, ideologically conservative sectors, and business groups in the United States. Democratic political groups and intellectuals in Latin America do likewise with U.S. academic circles and liberal politicians. When the Carter administration handed over a part of the U.S. Department of State to liberal forces for domestic political reasons, allied sectors in Latin America temporarily prospered. When the Reagan administration took office, Latin American conservative elements benefited. Neither the United States' image abroad nor human rights obtain any lasting advantages from this pattern.

United States human rights activists who embrace their cause with missionary zeal are worthy of admiration and respect, but they should bear in mind that their own country also has a history of human rights problems. Latin Americans remember that history. In the last several years the United States has approached this subject with an almost religious zeal resembling the ardor of converts who have recently discovered truth. But a foreign observer might prudently remind the United States that scarcely twenty years have passed since it abolished segregation laws and that in order to combat persisting patterns of racial discrimination it has resorted to questionable legislation that institutes discrimination in favor of minorities through "affirmative action." A foreign observer might also remind the United States of its high level of private violence and of the fact that in the past century it has frequently resorted to bloody foreign wars in which respect for the enemy's human rights has sometimes been conspicuously absent (for example, Vietnam). Given this record, one would hope for more humility on the part of U.S. human rights activists in their contact with Latin Americans. They should not approach the problem as if the United States were not also concerned about this question as a domestic issue.[22]

A greater awareness of the United States' own limitations would help reformulate the human rights policy that was inaugurated by the Carter administration. Until now the discussion between U.S. liberals and conservatives has largely centered on whether Latin American governments with poor human rights records should be reproached in public or in private. Both positions share the perception that it is the United States' mission to act as the custodian of human rights throughout the world. It is in this context that the executive branch—acting at one and the same time as prosecutor and judge—informs the Congress annually on every country's human rights record. Countries are then awarded prizes or punishments, depending upon their rating.

If one admits this basic position, it is appropriate to ask at what point preoccupation becomes intervention. If, on the other hand, one rejects this position because any participation by one state in another's internal affairs violates the principle of self-determination, then the balance shifts to the importance of leading by example rather than through coercion, attracting people to a way of life rather than imposing it on others.

Latin Americans are tired of being examined by others, especially by those whose historical record is far from exemplary. After all, not Latin Americans but those who judge us created imperialism, colonialism, totalitarian systems, slavery, wars, and atomic weapons. The Latin American tradition (which has guaranteed long periods of peace in the region) stresses nonintervention in other states' domestic affairs. Latin Americans only seek a parallel attitude on the part of other countries. It would be ridiculous for a Latin American government to question the U.S. Supreme Court's decision on abortion or the Federal Bureau of Investigation's methods of detecting corruption among legislators. Latin Americans react negatively when the U.S. government questions the conduct of their domestic affairs and then pretends to impose its own preferences by means of sanctions.

It is important to note that adhering to the principle of self-determination obviates the question of who is favored and who is damaged by U.S. government intervention in support of human rights. In the same way that the armed forces' disruption of the constitutional order is wrong, regardless of whether its administrative record is bad or good, justifying "good" intervention opens the way to all kinds of arbitrary action, transforming one's own country into a battlefield and a laboratory for experimenting with strategies designed by rival political groups in the intervening state. If the United States has the right to intervene in other countries in order to impose democracy, how can one deny Nicaragua the right to promote the "liberation" of El Salvador, or Argentina the right to promote "national security" in Bolivia? It is unlikely that anyone is an unconditional apostle of intervention in favor of human rights; those who favor destabilizing military regimes in the Southern Cone are opposed to similar actions in Nicaragua or Cuba, and those who criticize but tolerate military autocracies support intervention only against totalitarian regimes. No government is impartial on this question, and judgments concerning political advantage generally prevail over purely ethical considerations. For this reason critical realism is more advisable and prudent in this area than militant idealism.

A state has the right to defend the rights and interests of its citizens wherever they may be, but it may not interfere with the policies other states adopt regarding their own citizens. This is the classic limit to state action that respects the principle of sovereignty among states. The main reason that the United States attaches such importance to human rights issues in Latin America is that in this region it has the power to make and unmake governments, reorienting their policies in the process without any great risk of their escaping from its sphere of influence. The major exception has been Cuba. Because the United States has lost virtually all leverage over Cuba, the U.S. government does not systematically gather and analyze information concerning its human rights record. An uninformed observer would conclude either that Cuba is not part of Latin America or that it has an impeccable human rights record—when in reality it is the only totalitarian regime in the Western Hemisphere.[23]

The United States can adopt a foreign policy that, without interfering in the domestic affairs of other states, gives preferential treatment to those Latin American countries that have democratic political regimes and assure respect for human rights. Self-determination is a two-way street, and the United States has every right to choose its allies and its friends. It can establish with them plans for cooperation and assistance that facilitate the emergence of conditions favorable to the enjoyment of basic human rights. To serve this purpose, U.S. foreign assistance should be used to train civilian leaders drawn from the middle and lower strata of the population, rather than wasting so many resources to form a military ruling class. Without the cooperation of civilian political and social leaders of this kind, a pluralistic society cannot function. Of course, the international economic order (through trade, the transfer of technology, and financial transactions) significantly determines national economic policies, thus influencing the effective observance of economic, social, and cultural rights. One example is especially telling: a 1 percent increase in the discount rate fixed by the U.S. Federal Reserve Board has more influence on Latin American countries than all the loans tied to a presumed respect for human rights. Nonetheless, much of what could be done is not done. Latin America is quickly sanctioned but never generously rewarded for friendship—as was the case with western Europe after World War II, Israel, and, to a lesser extent, Egypt today.

However, U.S. national security interests in Latin America are not limited to a concern for human rights. That is why the United States maintains its alliances with authoritarian regimes and why it may come into conflict with democratic governments that seek to regain control over their natural resources, reorient their foreign trade, or promote a more independent military strategy. There has been criticism within the United States directed at the negative influence that domestic pressure groups have had on recent elections by focusing voters' attention on a single issue rather than considering broader aspects of the common good. The same criticism could be directed at those who propose that all U.S. foreign policy decisions should focus on promoting human rights. Not even Carter was able to pursue a coherent policy in this area during the four years of his presidency.

There is a clear need to imbue domestic and international political life with an ethical content, but one must not confuse politics with religion. Rulers are not missionaries. They wield force, and they may be tempted to use it to impose their own values on others. Their function is to establish a peaceful and just international order, thus furthering all forms of international cooperation. It is not through embargoes, "quarantines," and covert activities that these goals can be achieved.

Prospects for the Next Decade

Exploring the future is always more risky than interpreting the past. Nevertheless, the lessons of the past do provide a basis for a cautious evaluation of future opportunities for cooperation and of possibilities of conflict in U.S.–Latin American relations on the issue of human rights.

Cooperation depends upon a double prior commitment from the two parties. First, the United States should not insist that human rights issues are an exclusively Latin American problem. The United States must recognize that its own record is far from perfect, both because human rights problems are far from resolved in U.S. society and because of the decisive role that the United States plays in shaping an inequitable international order from which human rights violations derive. For its part, Latin America must recognize that it is part of that international order. As a consequence, it must renounce isolationist attitudes or extreme nationalism in order to assume the responsibilities this implies. Second, the human rights issue must not be dealt with frivolously in pursuit of narrow party or domestic policy interests. Both the United States and Latin America should approach the question in terms of a permanent commitment to basic values that shape society and the state in ways that are worthy of man.

If these prior conditions hold, it is possible to identify four areas of possible future cooperation. First, because of its importance to people's daily life, U.S.–Latin American cooperation on economic and military matters should take priority. Cooperation in these areas will constitute practical proof of the degree of commitment to the ethical cause of human rights. If there are no substantial changes in these areas, the sincerity of measures adopted in other fields will be open to serious doubt.

Second, sustained efforts should be undertaken to create and strengthen both public and private institutions to promote human rights. As Michael Novak notes, "The real defense of human rights does not lie in words on paper, or even in moral sentiments among leaders, or in the moral sentiments of the population as a whole. The real defense of human rights— indeed, their substantive reality—is constituted by access to institutions in which the exponents of competing rights can legally and fairly contend."[24] Therefore, improving the quality of government services, organizing social solidarity through the training of trade union leaders, establishing cooperatives and political parties, and so forth, are all important means of helping those who want to help themselves. Cuba is frequently criticized for sending to allied countries civilian "assistants" who, in addition to their work as teachers or technicians, devote themselves to Marxist indoctrination. But what prevents other countries from undertaking similar actions elsewhere, with other goals, within the framework of multilateral agreements?

A third possible area of cooperation is joint repression by legal means of illicit activities that endanger basic human rights. These include illegal traffic in arms, persons (undocumented workers and the white-slave trade), and drugs, and clandestine activities by totalitarian revolutionary groups. Historical experience shows that armed combat creates conditions for the widespread violation of human rights; contemporary El Salvador, and Argentina, Vietnam, and Algeria at an earlier time, all exemplify this problem. Marxist-Leninist movements that resort to terrorist and guerrilla warfare use these methods without regard for the political formulas in force (for example, in Colombia, Peru, and Argentina), constituting a threat to democratic regimes and domestic political peace. Western hemisphere governments should not allow their territories to be used as bases of operation for groups such as these, and they should share information that would allow them to neutralize terrorist actions, as West European countries have done. Similar actions should also be taken against terrorist actions by right wing elements (for example, the assassination of Orlando Letelier in Washington, D.C., and the García Meza coup in Bolivia). Pretending that these groups do not enjoy significant support from abroad (the roles of Cuba, and now Nicaragua, as centers for promoting revolutionary activities are well known) is to ignore reality. Reaching specific agreements in these areas will be difficult because in some cases there are not only opposing interests (for example, those who produce drugs and arms and those who buy them) but also widely differing points of view concerning the degree of freedom that is desirable in a given society. Nevertheless, an effort must be made to overcome these obstacles because of the importance of what is at stake. Human dignity cannot flourish in a society corrupted by vice and violence.

Finally, large-scale programs should be organized to satisfy basic human needs. In education—which is so decisive for an individual's commitment to the ideals expressed in the Universal Declaration of Human Rights—specific efforts should be made to use unconventional means (television, satellites, radio, computers, and so forth) to combat illiteracy, offer professional training courses, and create a civic and social conscience. In housing, building programs for low-cost prefabricated housing could be developed for several countries at the same time in order to take advantage of economies of scale. Apart from the relative value that these examples may have, the important thing is to move from the stage of diagnosis and denunciation to the stage of imaginative and effective solutions, while respecting the idiosyncracies of the people to be assisted. Cooperative arrangements of this kind (as in the case of institutional innovation) can be developed even without government participation.

The most obvious possibilities for conflict between Latin America and the United States on human rights issues involve failure to comply with the necessary double prior commitment described above. If the United States and Latin America fail to renounce self-righteous indignation and irresponsible nationalism, respectively, then it is likely that conflict over human rights issues will persist. The frivolous manipulation of human rights questions for domestic political purposes will have a similar consequence. But apart from these general concerns, there are four specific areas of conflict and misunderstanding that may surface in the years ahead.

First, the United States and Latin American countries have different histories and cultures, and they play different roles in the international system. They therefore interpret world events from points of view that are at times diametrically opposed. For example, Latin Americans perceived the 1982 war in the South Atlantic for the possession of the Malvinas (Falkland) Islands as a colonial conflict in which the imperial power (Great Britain) was the party that exercised illegal force, while the U.S. government viewed the conflict as a case of illegal use of force by an authoritarian government (Argentina). This interpretation led the United States to lend military assistance to an extracontinental power that defined the conflict as a struggle between democracy and fascism. The same difference in perspective is evident regarding Central America. The Reagan administration has interpreted developments there in terms of East-West conflict, while Latin Americans (without dismissing this dimension) give greater emphasis to specific factors in each country. This leads them to emphasize political responses to the conflict rather than purely military ones. Whether a political solution or a military response is emphasized in any given conflict obviously has great significance for the human rights of the individuals and peoples involved. Civil war breeds conditions for generalized violations of human rights. Any policy that prolongs armed conflicts in Central America (or elsewhere in Latin America) is necessarily incompatible with the promotion of these rights. Much the same can be said concerning the opposing points of view that the United States and Latin America hold on the question of some Latin American countries' large external debt. The high rates of interest that Latin American countries pay on this debt make it difficult for them to satisfy their citizens' basic needs. Here, too, the disagreements and the potential for conflict between the United States and Latin America hold important implications for human rights issues.

In addition, because Latin American issues receive low priority in overall U.S. foreign policy, they are managed by a relatively small number of people There is no guarantee that these specialists represent a bipartisan consensus. Much the same could be said of many Latin American leaders' ignorance of the distribution of power and the characteristics of the decision-making process in the United States. Mutual ignorance always constitutes a potential basis for conflict.

Second, future conflicts with broad implications for human rights may also arise from different interpretations of the nature of government. It is probable that over the next decade Latin American countries will experiment with different forms of expanded state economic participation under the general label of "socialism." The national and foreign interests affected are unlikely to accept such changes silently, and they may attempt to characterize them as a first step toward communism. In western Europe, the United States has been reconciled to socialism in Spain, France, and Greece. But in Latin America the United States often tends to favor a rigid capitalism that offers "stable investment environments" for U.S. business interests. If this U.S. attitude confronts highly nationalist Latin American policies hostile to the role of foreign capital, the stage will be set for a classic conflict over sovereignty. The right to self-determination is one of the rights most highly prized by small and medium-sized developing countries struggling against neocolonialism.

Something similar might occur with democratic governments that, when harassed by subversive movements, are obliged to rely heavily on the armed forces and impose strict domestic security measures. They may be accused by Marxists of being "lackeys of the bourgeoisie" and by liberals of being motivated by national security doctrines. According priority to an effective containment of communism may in this case be an important factor in destabilizing a democratic regime, which implies losing the guarantees of law that protect human rights.

Third, Latin America will in the future present an increasingly diverse political, social, and economic setting that will require closer attention to the particular characteristics of individual countries. There already exists a tendency to exclude Cuba and perhaps Nicaragua and other countries from discussions of Latin America as if they no longer belonged to the region by virtue of the fact that they have passed into the Soviet Union's sphere of influence. Failure to accept plurality in the region may be a source of conflict because, despite the tremendous difficulty of living peacefully with those who export revolution, Latin America will probably not accept new quarantines in the region such as that which at one time isolated the island of Cuba. A commitment to protect human rights includes the willingness to tolerate diversity, including differences in interpretations of human rights.

The fourth potential source of conflict derives from the "imperial" relationship that the United States maintains vis-à-vis Latin America in economic, diplomatic, military, and cultural affairs. Schoultz is correct when he states that "many [Latin American] nations were understandably suspicious of the role of the United States in the human rights effort. One need not know much about U.S.–Latin American relations to recognize why Latin Americans might be wary of the motivations behind yet another U.S. crusade in Latin America."[25] Nationalism permeates Latin American societies and, therefore, popular political movements. If the current trend toward democratization should strengthen, it is probable that ruling civilian political parties will have an even more "anti-imperialist" bias than military governments. Under constitutional government, a country may view activism in favor of human rights (considered welcome when it opposed military autocracies) as a new pretext for intervention in its domestic affairs. The situation of blacks and Hispanics in the United States, the Pentagon's schemings, and maneuvers by multinational corporations or banks will be reasons or pretexts for Latin Americans to enliven rhetorical conflict with the United States. However, superficial conflict such as this, which provides political returns for the parties involved, may coexist with basic agreements. In politics there has always been, and always will be, a large gap between words and actions, between rhetoric and deep commitment to a cause. Unfortunately, human rights issues are no exception to this rule.

Facultad de Teología
Universidad Católica Argentina
Buenos Aires, Argentina

Notes

1. John Finnis, *Natural Law and Natural Rights* (Oxford: Clarendon Press, 1980), pp. 211 and following.

2. Universal Declaration of Human Rights, Articles 4, 5, 11.2, and 10.2. The International Covenant on Civil and Political Rights takes up the first three cases in Articles 8.7 and 15, but also adds to the list Articles 6, 11, 16, and 18. The American Convention on Human Rights adds Articles 17, 18, 19, 20, and 23.

3. The speech by former Secretary of State Cyrus Vance is quoted in Lars Schoultz, "The Carter Administration and Human Rights," in Margaret E. Crahan, ed., *Human Rights and Basic Needs in the Americas* (Washington, D.C.: Georgetown University Press, 1982), p. 309. See Howard J. Wiarda, "Democracy and Human Rights in Latin America," in Howard J. Wiarda, ed., *Human Rights and U.S. Human Rights Policy: Theoretical Approaches and Some Perspectives on Latin America* (Washington, D.C.: American Enterprise Institute for Public Policy Research, 1982), p. 50, and *The Americas at a Crossroads,* Report of the Inter-American Dialogue (Washington, D.C.: Smithsonian Institution, 1983), p. 32.

4. See John Langan, S.J., "A Revision of the Liberal Tradition," in Alfred T. Hennelly, S.J., and John Langan, S.J., eds. *Human Rights in the Americas: The Struggle for Consensus* (Washington, D.C.: Georgetown University Press, 1982), pp. 69–101.

5. For an analysis of certain difficulties in this regard, see Finnis, *Natural Law and Natural Rights,* pp. 213–21.

6. See Elias Cardoso Pinto, "La tesis sobre la religión, la Iglesia y los creyentes del Primer Congreso del Partido Comunista en Cuba," *Tierra Nueva* 6, No. 24 (1978): 41–51.

7. See, for example, Joseph F. Fletcher, *Humanhood: Essays in Biomedical Ethics* (Buffalo, N.Y.: Prometheus Books, 1979), and Germain G. Grisez, *Abor-*

tion: The Myths, the Realities, and the Arguments (New York: Corpus Books, 1970).

8. An interesting restatement of the human rights question in Latin America, based on an understanding of its culture, is Howard J. Wiarda, "Democracy and Human Rights in Latin America: Toward a New Conceptualization," in Wiarda, *Human Rights and U.S. Human Rights Policy,* pp. 30–52.

9. Paul VI, *Octogesima adveniens,* Nos. 48–50.

10. Jeane J. Kirkpatrick, "Dictatorships and Double Standards," in Wiarda, *Human Rights and U.S. Human Rights Policy,* p. 12.

11. An interesting discussion of development strategy based on "basic needs" can be found in Drew Christiansen, S.J., "Basic Needs: Criterion for the Legitimacy of Development," in Hennelly and Langan, *Human Rights in the Americas,* pp. 245–88.

12. See Rafael Braun, "La democratización del poder," *Criterio* 1657–58 (1972): 684–89.

13. Finnis, *Natural Law and Natural Rights,* p. 271; Michael Novak, "Human Rights and Whited Sepulchres," in Wiarda, *Human Rights and U.S. Human Rights Policy,* p. 80.

14. A similar opinion is: "This is not to suggest that regimes that engage in gross violations of human rights cannot endure for some time. In fact, recent years have seen the development of increasingly sophisticated means of social control by such governments that eliminate dependence on some of the more notorious violations of human rights such as torture." Margaret Crahan, "Introduction," in Crahan, *Human Rights and Basic Needs in the Americas,* p. 16. I expressed my own opinion on torture some time ago: Rafael Braun, "Contra la tortura," *Criterio* 1644 (1972): 269–70.

15. See John T. Noonan, Jr., *A Private Choice: Abortion in America in the Seventies* (New York: The Free Press, 1979).

16. A similar contradiction is found in the reestablishment of the death penalty in several states, in opposition to what Article 4.3 establishes.

17. Both international covenants and the American Convention on Human Rights have been awaiting approval by the U.S. Senate Foreign Relations Committee since February 23, 1978.

18. See Schoultz, "The Carter Administration and Human Rights," pp. 324–25.

19. Brian H. Smith, "U.S.–Latin American Military Relations Since World War II: Implications for Human Rights," in Crahan, *Human Rights and Basic Needs in the Americas,* p. 286.

20. Margaret E. Crahan, "National Security Ideology and Human Rights," in Crahan, *Human Rights and Basic Needs in the Americas,* pp. 100–27.

21. Schoultz, "The Carter Administration and Human Rights," p. 329.

22. For example, it is striking that the book edited by Margaret E. Crahan, whose title is *Human Rights and Basic Needs in the Americas,* does not even refer to U.S. domestic problems.

23. "During the 1970s the U.S. Congress and Department of State, the Inter-American Commission on Human Rights of the Organization of American States, and Amnesty International, among others, reported serious violations of human

rights in the following countries: Argentina, Bolivia, Brazil, Chile, El Salvador, Guatemala, Haiti, Nicaragua, Paraguay, and Uruguay." Margaret E. Crahan, "Introduction," in Crahan, *Human Rights and Basic Needs in the Americas,* p. 17, fn. 2. As noted, Cuba is not mentioned.

24. Novak, "Human Rights and Whited Sepulchres," p. 80.

25. Schoultz, "The Carter Administration and Human Rights," p. 321.

13

Human Rights and U.S. Foreign Policy: Realism Versus Stereotypes

Margaret E. Crahan

A major impediment to the use of human rights criteria to build a more effective U.S. foreign policy has been the prevalence of popular misconceptions in this area. Perhaps the most common of these is that a strong human rights posture is antithetical to the pursuit of national security interests. An alternative position is that these two concerns are mutually supportive, with the promotion of basic human rights being the key to long-term national and international stability. Recent developments in the Americas have highlighted the relationship between the observance or nonobservance of human rights and the security of the United States.

The United States' relationships with Mexico and Central America are illustrative. Since the 1920s Mexico has been one of the most politically stable countries in Latin America. This is in part because, although substantial economic inequalities exist in Mexico, there has been gradual improvement over time in meeting food, housing, sanitation, health care, and educational needs.[1] However, recent Mexican economic reverses produced escalating domestic social pressures and resulted in massive migration to the United States, which placed substantial burdens on the U.S. economy and legal system. This situation has been exacerbated by an increase in migration to the United States from Central America and the Caribbean resulting largely from warfare in the area and the denial of basic civil, political, social, and economic rights. Analysts of differing political orientations (such as those who participated in the National Bipartisan Commission on Central America, the Inter-American Dialogue, and Policy Alternatives for the Caribbean and Central America) have all concluded that it is imperative to promote improved rights observance in the Americas if U.S. security is to be preserved.[2]

Although the connection between human rights observance and political stability is often recognized, the use of human rights criteria in the formulation of U.S. foreign policy has been erratic. For example, during both the Carter and Reagan administrations, U.S. policy toward El Salva-

411

dor attached considerably more importance to U.S. security concerns than to human rights, although human rights issues were not totally ignored. The United States' fear of Marxist revolution in Central America led it to support several governments in El Salvador that were implicated in gross violations of human rights. The United States' identification with these governments has contributed to rising anti-U.S. sentiment in Central America and elsewhere. It has also encouraged criticism of the United States by its allies and undermined U.S. moral and political leadership in international fora. Until human rights goals and security objectives are regarded as integral parts of the same policy, it is unlikely that the United States will be able to respond adequately to the challenges posed by a world that is increasingly polarized ideologically, politically, and economically.

This essay argues that a U.S. foreign policy supportive of greater national and international human rights observance is likely to promote global political stability and, hence, U.S. interests. To accomplish this goal it is necessary to transcend popular stereotypes and incorporate human rights criteria in the formulation of U.S. foreign policy. This essay attempts to promote this process (which is already underway, albeit haltingly) by examining whether sufficient international consensus exists regarding the nature of basic human rights to support a strong U.S. foreign policy commitment to human rights. It also analyzes the consequences of rights violations for hemispheric stability, past U.S. foreign policy concerning human rights, the means developed (particularly in Latin America) to defend human rights, and whether the United States can assist in these efforts while respecting the principle of nonintervention. The essay concludes with some specific recommendations for U.S. human rights initiatives in the 1980s. These recommendations are based on past experience and offer no guarantee of utopian solutions to human rights problems. However, they may make U.S. foreign policy more effective and therefore more conducive to hemispheric stability and the national security of the United States.

Employing human rights as a foreign policy criterion is in no sense an assertion that the United States' own rights record is unblemished. However, it does reflect a belief that the observance and promotion of human rights are related to the legitimacy of the U.S. political and economic systems. The outcome of competition between world powers such as the United States and the Soviet Union will be determined in good measure by each country's success in demonstrating the superiority of its respective systems, not only in terms of material benefits, but also in terms of the values propounded. Human rights are expressions of values that have universal appeal despite obvious historical and cultural differences in the interpretation and prioritization of those rights.

Differences such as these have not impeded the growth of agreement regarding what basic human rights are. They include the right to life and the means to maintain it with dignity. The latter include respect for the physical integrity of the person, freedom from arbitrary arrest and imprisonment, the physical requirements for life (food, clothing, housing, health care), and the prerequisites for self-reliance (education and effective political and economic participation). Basic human rights are accepted by specialists in the field as priority claims on society and government that inhere in persons or groups of persons. The idea that the validity of human rights depends on legal recognition or social practice is much less commonly held.

The Growth of Consensus on Human Rights

The progressive internationalization of human rights documents and organizations, particularly since the 1940s, demonstrates increasing consensus on core human rights and a growing realization that respect for civil/political rights is directly related to the fulfillment of economic, social, and cultural rights. This process was stimulated by the post-World War II desire to reach agreement on a normative basis for peace (without ignoring the real differences that exist among cultures and political and economic systems), which led in 1948 to the drafting of the Universal Declaration of Human Rights and the American Declaration of the Rights and Duties of Man. The subsequent approval of implementing covenants and conventions affirmed the principles expressed in these documents. In 1976 the United Nations' International Covenant on Civil and Political Rights and the International Covenant on Economic, Social, and Cultural Rights came into force. As of January 1984, seventy-seven countries had ratified the former and seventy-eight had ratified the latter.[3] The American Convention on Human Rights came into force in 1978, and by late 1984 eighteen western hemisphere countries had ratified it.[4] The creation of the Inter-American Commission on Human Rights (1960), the Inter-American Court of Human Rights (1979), and the Inter-American Institute of Human Rights (1980) by the member states of the Organization of American States (OAS) further indicated the extent of consensus on human rights issues in the Western Hemisphere.[5] Their activities help promote respect for human rights, which legal scholars have increasingly accepted as an international legal obligation of states.[6]

The charge that organizations such as these are concerned only with governments' human rights abuses and ignore general threats to society is not upheld by an examination of their work. As creations of the member states of the OAS, both the Inter-American Commission on Human Rights and the Inter-American Court of Human Rights are legally bound to focus on the actions of governments. Nevertheless, the Commission has also addressed some generalized threats to society.[7] However, it does not have the legal authority to investigate either terrorism or subversion.[8] The Inter-American Institute of Human Rights (which dedicates itself to the promotion of human rights through research, education, and publishing) has examined the impact of terrorism on human rights, most notably at a September 1982 conference on this subject.

It has also been alleged that human rights organizations tend to condemn right-wing regimes for human rights violations while ignoring the abuses of left-wing governments. This charge was also leveled against the Carter administration. Neither charge has a basis in fact. The Soviet Union has been the major focus of reports concerning human rights violations by organizations such as Amnesty International and the International Commission of Jurists, as well as a variety of church groups, U.S. governmental agencies, and international bodies. In Latin America, Cuba has been the most frequent object of attention by both nongovernmental and governmental human rights agencies. Since the Sandinista government took power in 1979, Nicaragua has also been the object of close scrutiny.[9]

Recognition of the existence of human rights bridges cultures and national boundaries by virtue of shared humanity, even though there are both sharp ideological differences and systemic variations throughout the world that affect the conceptualization and enjoyment of human rights. Scholars and human rights activists note some overlap between western liberal and socialist views, as well as between views of industrialized and developing countries, on this issue. This interpretation does not gloss over differences in this regard; rather, it suggests that treaties, international documents such as human rights covenants, and international law definitely reflect a degree of consensus on human rights.[10]

Although very little survey research has been done regarding the extent of this consensus, the results of one study are illuminating. In an examination of the attitudes of working class residents in the Brazilian municipality of Nova Iguaçu, researchers found that (contrary to their expectations) there was considerable unanimity regarding concepts of basic human rights. These were the right to life and the means to support it in a dignified fashion. Respondents gave higher priority to basic needs such as food, clothing, sanitation, and access to health care and education than to the right to property. They also shared a belief that all individuals should enjoy equality of opportunity and economic security and that they should be allowed to participate in political decisions in order to influence the direction of social change.[11]

As evidence of this kind indicates, to suggest that there is a degree of consensus on human rights issues is not to assert that all countries will have the same level of human rights observance. Rather, there is agreement that a minimum level of human rights protection should be striven for. Nor do human rights specialists argue for a single measure of human rights observance for all societies, particularly given differing levels of development.[12] Nevertheless, a minimum standard of human rights would include the right to life and the means to sustain it with dignity, as well as freedom from torture, arbitrary arrest, and imprisonment. The fact that some regimes violate these rights does not prove that there is no consensus concerning the conceptualization of basic human rights; rather, it shows that rights violations occur.

Human rights violations themselves have contributed to the building of consensus in this area. An upsurge of human rights violations in the 1960s and 1970s produced a concomitant proliferation of efforts—local, national, and international—to combat them.[13] In turn, the actions undertaken by human rights activists and organizations produced broader agreement concerning what basic human rights are, what relationships exist among them, and which rights should be given priority. Again, this does not mean that there is perfect agreement on these issues; rather, it suggests that crises in countries such as Argentina, Bolivia, Brazil, Chile, El Salvador, Guatemala, Haiti, Nicaragua, Paraguay, and Uruguay— which together contain more than half of Latin America's population— forced both individuals and institutions to rethink the role of human rights in the maintenance of social concord and the promotion of political and economic development.[14] One example of this increased attention to human rights issues is the fact that no other topic received more attention from the press and publishers throughout Latin America in the 1970s.[15]

To demonstrate the degree of international consensus on human rights issues, legal scholars point out that articles concerning human rights have been incorporated in the constitutions of over 150 countries. There is admittedly some variation in the rights included and the priorities given them. Nonetheless, virtually all of these constitutions focus on the right to life with dignity.[16] Although variations in culture, values, and historical experience certainly affect interpretations of human rights, they do so primarily in terms of priorities and strategies for their fulfillment. To argue that variations of this kind, or disagreements in academic analysis or politics regarding what is just, democratic, moral, or conducive to public order and the common good, preclude the possibility of some consensus on human rights is to advocate a total cultural relativism unsupported by reality. For example, there is widespread agreement that genocide is immoral. The fact that it occurs does not mean that there is no consensus on this point; instead, it shows that basic human rights are violated. Furthermore, analyses of the concept of human rights in the world's major religions indicate that there is agreement on core rights.[17]

It is even less convincing to argue that variations in the texts of human rights documents prove there is no consensus in this area. This is using the narrow focus of textual analysis to deny that government officials representing a broad spectrum of peoples concurred sufficiently on basic principles to draft documents such as the Universal Declaration of Human Rights and the American Declaration of the Rights and Duties of Man. The drafters of these documents were generally pragmatic political leaders and diplomats deeply affected by severe human rights violations during World War II and intent upon devising means to prevent an even greater tragedy in the future.

A strong human rights posture in U.S. foreign policy encourages charges that the United States judges other countries from a position of unwarranted superiority. This problem has been recognized by U.S. policymakers, even if it has not always been addressed successfully.[18] A related charge is that the U.S. government and U.S. human rights specialists fail to recognize that the United States is part of the problem. What this view does not recognize is that the recent U.S. interest in human rights largely flows from an agonizing reappraisal of the legitimacy of U.S. foreign policy and the morality of political leadership in the United States.[19]

The roots of this recent interest in human rights are in the contemporary crisis of confidence in the U.S. political system and leadership. In the aftermath of the Vietnam war and the Watergate political scandal, there was a desire to reassert certain basic democratic values. These efforts have admittedly been flawed and occasionally counterproductive, partially because these democratic values and their relationship to governmental policies are ill defined. This has been particularly true of the role of human rights in informing U.S. foreign policy. Thus it has been relatively easy to stereotype these efforts and categorize them as utopian, arrogant, or cynical. For this reason there is a crucial need to rethink both the relationship between human rights and U.S. interests and the best means to promote these interests in a conflictual world. This essay does not pretend to be a full exploration of these topics, but rather a stimulus for such attempts.

The Consequences of Human Rights Violations for Democracy and Hemispheric Stability in the 1980s

There are three commonly recognized contexts in which human rights violations occur in Latin America.[20] Countries that have experienced ongoing political violence resulting from official repression of substantial and persistent political opposition constitute one group. Political opposition in these countries was frequently strengthened in the 1960s and 1970s by economic development, increased social mobility, and political differentiation. Examples include El Salvador, Guatemala, and Colombia. A second group is composed of personalistic dictatorships facing a relatively weak political opposition that is usually kept in check by the constant use of repression. Given the generalized internalization of fear in these societies, broad-based opposition does not normally exist. Haiti and Paraguay are examples. Because there has been less generalized human rights activity in these countries, they are not particularly illustrative of means developed to defend human rights. In order to evaluate better those strategies that have proven most effective in this regard, this essay will focus on countries in which human rights activities are more highly developed.

Examples of this third context include (or have included) several countries in South America (Argentina, Brazil, Chile, Uruguay) that historically respected human rights to an important degree. These countries underwent a process of polarization in the 1960s that originated in growing disenchantment with traditional politics, parties, and reformist/developmentalist economic models. Influential sectors of the national elite (intellectuals, for example) increasingly accepted Marxist critiques of capitalism, while others (including the military) embraced conservative alternatives emphasizing the centralization of power in the executive branch of government and the imposition of monetarist economic models. Polarization led both groups to pursue radical solutions, and progressive elements (including some church people) frequently sanctioned armed revolution. This contributed to the legitimation of guerrilla movements. The threat of armed revolution, together with the inefficacy, incompetence, and corruption of some civilian governments, convinced the armed forces that they had to "save" their countries. The strongly anti-Marxist military viewed both violent and nonviolent proponents of class conflict and revolutionary change as disloyal groups undeserving of civil/political rights. The spread of such military governments in the 1960s and 1970s thus resulted in human rights violations on an unprecedented scale.[21] Human rights groups subsequently became very active in these countries.

Military coups and human rights violations in Latin America in the 1960s and 1970s resulted in part from the prevalence of authoritarian definitions of the state. Indeed, human rights activists in the region generally believe that the most serious long-term threat to human rights is the growth of national security ideology.[22] Although elements of this ideology can be found throughout the Americas, it has reached its fullest expression in the Southern Cone. National security ideology has little to do with a country's internationally recognized right to protect itself from external or internal attack. Rather, it is a conceptualization of the state, nation, and war that gives absolute priority to national security. The state is held to be an organism with natural rights and its own needs, which take precedence over individual rights. The definition of citizens' rights is, therefore, a highly restricted one. In addition, the decisions of the ruling elite take precedence over the rule of law. Because the state, nation, and armed forces are identified as one, a challenge to one is regarded as a threat to all. Individuals who challenge the state through either violent or nonviolent dissent are labeled noncitizens with no claim to rights. Individuals whose racial or cultural identity or religious beliefs set them apart from the state's vision of a citizen are also liable to be denied rights. Criticism of the military is regarded as unpatriotic or treasonous. Loyalty to the nation is confused with support for a particular government. Moreover, the armed forces' control of the state is justified as the only means of realizing the country's economic and political destiny. The enormity of this task helps explain why the military, when it took control in Brazil (1964), Uruguay (1973), Chile (1973), and Argentina (1976), intended to retain power indefinitely (in contrast to its historical tendency to relinquish political power to civilians once order was thought to have been restored).[23]

The consolidation of national security states in these Latin American countries resulted in the suspension of constitutional guarantees through declared states of emergency and/or siege and expanded operations by security forces and clandestine paramilitary groups. Paramilitary groups and the armed forces saw themselves engaged in a total war against subversion in which no quarter was to be given. Torture, assassination, and other violations of the physical integrity of the person were sanctioned. Violations of civil rights, censorship, the dissolution of existing means of political and economic participation (for example, political parties, labor unions, urban and rural popular movements), and the suspension, reconstitution, or abolition of legislatures were frequent. Military governments often justified actions such as these on the basis of real or alleged guerrilla threats or terrorist activities, economic stagnation or decline, and the inefficiency, incompetence, and corruption of previous civilian administrations. These regimes argued that it was necessary to restrict individual rights in order to realize national potential and promote the common good—as defined by a hegemonic elite and the requirements of particular political and economic models.

These broad national development goals required a highly centralized state in which power was concentrated in the executive branch, with the elimination or subordination of the legislative and judicial branches. Traditional means of popular participation were sometimes replaced by corporatist mechanisms aimed at organizing and mobilizing the population in support of the government, rather than allowing the formation of groups representing competing interests. These actions contributed to violations of freedom of opinion and expression, the right to peaceful assembly and association, and the right to participate in government either directly or through elected representatives.[24] Furthermore, the rights of political prisoners were generally not recognized; indeed, political prisoners often were not regarded as citizens because their actions were deemed contrary to the rights of the state, which superseded those of the individual.

In sum, the concentration of political authority in the hands of a hegemonic elite redefined the rights of the state and the individual so that the former overrode the latter. The suspension of constitutional and legal guarantees permitted violations of the physical integrity of the person, creating a climate of fear that stifled dissent and discouraged the activities of established political organizations. Secrecy was used to maintain the level of fear necessary for almost total social control. This frequently was facilitated by the expansion and technological upgrading of the governmental intelligence apparatus. The inculcation of fear in the populace further contributed to the consolidation of power and the implantation of the machinery of repression. However, the exercise of the state's coercive powers in this fashion was contrary to the rule of law and thus undermined the basis for social order. As opposition to the illegal and arbitrary exercise of power mounted, it was frequently necessary to increase repression. The end result was distrust and disrespect for government authority.

This tendency was reinforced when state power was used to impose and sustain economic policies that, rather than stimulating long-term economic growth as promised, led to falling real wages, escalating unemployment, and increasing bankruptcies of businesses of all sizes. These developments markedly decreased the lower and middle classes' capacity to fulfill their basic needs. Furthermore, these policies frequently required government suppression of independent trade unions, the imprisonment or expulsion of labor leaders, and the prohibition of strikes and worker coalitions. Rights violations of this kind became a significant part of the institutionalization of social control mechanisms. Thus even after torture, disappearances, and assassinations diminished in frequency, rights violations continued and further contributed to the maintenance of fear.

Few human rights organizations existed when national security states began to emerge. Those that did exist focused more on legal recourses than on humanitarian aid. Invocation of legal protections such as habeas corpus and appeals to the courts were for the most part ineffective.[25] Nevertheless, the absence of instruments of defense or strategies other than those provided by traditional jurisprudence focused human rights activities on the courts. This was the case in Brazil, Chile, Uruguay, and

Argentina. In countries that did not have notably independent judiciaries (such as Paraguay, Haiti, El Salvador, Nicaragua, and Guatemala), the response of human rights activists and organizations to crises was publication and dissemination of data concerning rights violations in an effort to generate pressure (particularly at the international level) that would reduce governments' rights violations. Countries with a critical mass of lawyers and other individuals willing to use existing legal structures generally have had a better opportunity to galvanize and focus energies and activities in support of human rights. Over a period of time, the knowledge and experience gained through such activity can provide a basis for the development of mechanisms and strategies capable of reducing repression or ameliorating the consequences of any resurgence in human rights violations.

Authoritarian governments' attempts to use traditional values and beliefs to legitimate their actions and policies, together with actual human rights violations, frequently brought these governments into conflict with the Roman Catholic church and other religious organizations to such an extent that these groups became the most vocal critics of the state. This happened in Chile after 1975, in Brazil in the early 1970s, and in El Salvador and Nicaragua in the late 1970s.

A combination of international and national factors led religious groups to assume this role. Among the most important of these were theological and pastoral developments within the Catholic church stimulated largely by the Second Vatican Council (1962–1965) and the Medellín (Colombia) Conference of Latin American bishops in 1968. These two gatherings defined the mission of the church as the promotion of social justice, human rights, and peace. The "theology of liberation" provided the justification for this mission by emphasizing Christians' responsibility to struggle for the establishment of the Kingdom of God on earth. The church's principal responsibility was the defense of the poor and exploited. In addition, this interpretation emphasized the church as a community of believers rather than the church as an institution. These changes led the church to expand its activities among rural peasants and urban slum dwellers, which in turn helped to politicize church people. Similar trends were apparent among mainstream Protestant denominations in Latin America in the 1960s and 1970s.

Developments of this kind increased the receptivity of church people to political and economic change, including socialism. Although few subscribed to Marxist interpretations, a significant number lost their faith in capitalism. The vast majority of church people did not support violent revolution, but ideological and political polarization in Latin America caused the Catholic church to become increasingly identified with the left. As a result, it often became the object of government repression. This caused the church leadership (including conservatives) to unite in defense of church personnel and in opposition to the generalized violation of human rights. In countries in which established mechanisms of political and economic demand making were suppressed or inadequate, the church attracted many of those individuals seeking to express their opposition to authoritarian regimes. Thus alliances were formed between church people and secular activists that further involved the church in politics.

More recently, under the leadership of Pope John Paul II, progressivism within the Catholic church has been moderated, and the church hierarchy has reasserted doctrinal and political orthodoxy (including anti-Marxist interpretations). This has clearly been the case in Nicaragua, and recent leadership changes in the Archbishopric of Santiago de Chile and the Brazilian National Bishops' Conference suggest a reassertion of more traditional positions. However, this trend depends in part upon continuing improvement in these governments' human rights records. In the mid-1970s, progressive activities such as the *Cursillos de Capacitación Social* ("Courses in Social Promotion") in Guatemala and the Third World Priests Movement in Argentina were suppressed by the church hierarchy and government officials. Only recently has the Catholic church in these countries strongly criticized government human rights abuses.[26]

Church involvement in human rights activities in Latin America made more resources available, particularly from international sources. It also provided important national and international networks for the dissemination of information and the documentation of rights violations. Moreover, church involvement legitimated efforts to defend human rights, and it offered some protection to human rights activists.

After the consolidation of authoritarian national security states, as guerrilla threats and generalized public protests subsided, government repression generally became less visible. Challenges to state authority became infrequent or remained within relatively restricted bounds. The reduction in open repression made the molding and control of public opinion increasingly important. Thus authoritarian governments generally devoted more attention to the media, education, securing international support, and expressions of national strength. This change increased the importance of human rights organizations' attempts to document and publicize less obvious rights violations as well as their continued efforts to use existing structures to reassert legal protections and increase their own legitimacy as representatives of alternative visions of society. This last goal was accomplished primarily through these organizations' publications and educational efforts.

Analysts have only recently begun to examine the consequences of the internalization of repression by the general populace. Human rights organizations have an important role to play in this regard by stressing the abnormality of authoritarian and totalitarian situations. The psychological toll of repression must be measured in terms of the context it creates— not only in terms of those who are detained, tortured, imprisoned, or killed, but also in terms of its impact on the general population and ultimately on the polity. Preliminary research suggests that attempts to build democratic structures in these societies will encounter serious difficulties in mobilizing citizens to participate politically and become less passive and fearful of government.[27]

After more notorious human rights violations decline, international support for human rights organizations and activities has sometimes decreased. This is regrettable because human rights organizations at this point generally have more capacity to take advantage of government weaknesses and promote political liberalization. In the case of Brazil, human rights organizations were joined by established political parties, unions, and business and professional groups in efforts to exploit the military government's policy of *abertura* ("political opening") in order to create more space for their own activities. Their primary objective was to ensure both a role in the transition process and participation in a new civilian government.[28] The liberalization or disintegration of an authoritarian or totalitarian regime may cause individuals, groups, and institutions that had not previously been active in the defense of human rights to become more actively involved (for example, the Catholic church in Argentina). Rights violations that had previously been unreported may also become known.

For these reasons, human rights organizations continue to have important tasks. They must struggle to ensure that their experience is drawn upon in the formulation of the new government's structures and policies, particularly the creation of an independent judiciary and of policies that promote the rule of law and its even-handed application. These organizations must also see that previously unreported violations are documented and that redress is sought for those affected. Similarly, human rights groups must promote civilian control of the military through their work with both civilian officials and members of the armed forces. Finally, they must devise more effective means of popular participation in government decision making. This last task is especially appropriate for human rights organizations because they often serve as exemplars of broad-based, multiclass coalitions potentially capable of transcending the limitations of partisan, narrow-based political parties that sometimes contributed to the instability of previously elected governments.

In order to accomplish these tasks and contribute to the creation of democratic governments and stable societies, human rights organizations must remain active. It is essential that they have the resources necessary to reach those in society who, through lack of knowledge or fear, were unable to seek the help of these organizations previously. The vast majority of Latin American human rights organizations are based in capital cities, and they are limited in their ability to assist the urban and rural poor. The research and analysis that human rights organizations have initiated and encouraged must be continued if serious rights violations are to be prevented in the future. Similarly, the legal and political basis for democratic control must be strengthened in order to protect broad human rights.

Nonpartisan cooperation within and among human rights organizations should be used as a model in building coalitions to influence government. This experience can also provide alternative associational models for the general public. These tasks require the development and expansion of human rights organizations' mass-educational role. The fact that human rights organizations have the potential to undertake such tasks is the direct result of the consensus on human rights issues that has emerged in Latin America in the last two decades.

It is important to note in this context that even a return to nonauthoritarian civilian government is no guarantee of long-term respect for human rights. Indeed, the Peruvian experience after Fernando Belaúnde Terry assumed the presidency in July 1980 suggests that human rights violations will continue until a number of conditions are fulfilled. The rule of law must be firmly implanted and the judiciary must be relatively independent of other branches of government. The country's constitution must be purged of articles granting the executive branch and the armed forces extraordinary powers in all but exceptional situations. Government response to terrorist activities must fall within legal boundaries. In addition, human rights violations are likely to occur unless a substantial proportion of the population has access to the legal redress of grievances. Lawyers and ordinary citizens must be able to pursue legal recourse without fear of the government or lack of confidence in public officials. Similarly, human rights problems will persist if the security apparatus that engages in rights violations remains in place and is not placed under effective legal controls. The armed forces' attitudes regarding human rights issues must be changed and civilian control of the military must be ensured. Civilian officials must be able to enforce legal penalties against the armed forces for illegal or unconstitutional actions. Moreover, governmental bureaucracies must be purged of corruption. As long as government officials believe that they can act arbitrarily and disregard public needs with impunity, rights violations will persist. This is especially likely if other countries remain silent in the face of all but the most egregious human rights violations.

Because these conditions are not easily fulfilled, promotion of human rights requires a permanent commitment to rights protection. The mechanisms available to protect human rights must be strengthened and expanded. The essence of a successful human rights policy is, therefore, an awareness of the dimensions of the problem, a careful evaluation of the effectiveness of different means developed to promote and safeguard human rights, and a commitment to employ these means on a permanent basis.

The Means Developed to Defend Human Rights

Two principal methods have been used to defend human rights: the documentation and publicizing of rights violations in order to mobilize influential national and international actors and the general public, and recourse to the judicial system. Most of the resources available to human rights organizations are devoted to these activities, and they are generally the actions taken first in crisis situations. However, in order to be effective, both the documentation and publicizing of violations and judicial recourse must be supported by analysis, education, and training. These tasks constitute the other main aspects of human rights activities.

The Documentation and Publicizing of Violations

Most human rights organizations (local, national, and international) devote their principal efforts to the investigation and documentation of rights violations. This strategy has been used successfully by a wide variety of groups, including church-related justice and peace committees, national human rights commissions, and international organizations such as the OAS' Inter-American Commission on Human Rights, the International Commission of Jurists, and Amnesty International. Documentation has two main purposes: to provide the basis for eventual legal action and to generate public and private pressure for the cessation of rights violations. For documentation to have a substantial impact, it must meet the requirements of legal evidence and withstand the scrutiny of the public, the media, and critics.

Human rights organizations have emphasized publicizing individual cases of human rights violations, and this strategy has proven highly effective in molding public opinion. In Latin America, a significant number of churches have taken up this work. Given the churches' credibility and their position as moral arbiters in society, their involvement has had a very positive effect. The OAS' Inter-American Commission on Human Rights has also played an important role in documenting and publicizing violations, particularly after 1977 when the United States was instrumental in increasing the size of its budget and expanding other resources available to it.[29] Many human rights organizations have become quite sophisticated at focusing public and mass media attention on rights violations. They have also developed extensive networks on both national and international levels to disseminate information concerning such violations. Nevertheless, their resources for this work are limited.

Contrary to some allegations, there is no firm evidence that publicizing human rights violations results in an increase in their number, although action of this kind may precipitate reprisals against human rights organizations and individual activists. Instead, the documentation and publicizing of rights violations have been effective ways of pressuring violators to abandon such practices, especially when these pressures come from influential national actors, international organizations, and foreign countries.

Judicial Actions

Recourse to existing legal mechanisms and efforts to expand their effectiveness are also major strategies used to defend human rights. These activities focus primarily on judicial measures such as habeas corpus and providing lawyers to those accused of political crimes. Actions such as these are especially important in periods of crisis, but they continue to comprise a major portion of human rights work after repression has diminished. This has been the experience of the most effective human rights operations, including actions undertaken by the Comité de Paz and the Vicaría de la Solidaridad in Chile, the Centro de Estudios Legales y Sociales in Argentina, and the Archbishopric of São Paulo in Brazil. In countries in which the legal community is relatively homogeneous and closely identified with traditional elites (for example, El Salvador and Guatemala), it is much more difficult to involve lawyers in human rights work. In Chile and Brazil, where lawyers traditionally have represented a broader spectrum of political opinion, it has been somewhat easier to incorporate them in human rights activities.

The recent experiences of Chile and Brazil suggest that judicial measures can be effective instruments to pressure governments to reduce human rights violations. In these countries, the combination of relatively sophisticated legal training and practice and significant numbers of legal professionals increased the effectiveness of legal defenses of human rights. The presence of a politically experienced legal community also helped reduce the fear of repression.

The legal defense of human rights in Latin America in the 1960s and 1970s also provided a focal point for support groups that assisted with research, investigation, identification, and referral of specific cases. In the early stages of repression, this work provided an outlet for the nonviolent opponents of governments that had suppressed previously existing means of political action. The proliferation of legal briefs and court cases pressured governments to either justify their actions legally or abandon them. However, this approach had both positive and negative consequences. On the one hand, it brought about a reduction in some of the more egregious violations. On the other hand, it also prompted repressive governments to revise national constitutions and legal codes in order to justify state actions.

Human rights activists' legal actions raised the consciousness of lawyers, judges, and other members of the judicial community regarding human rights. One of the most effective strategies used by human rights groups to raise consciousness within the judicial community was to limit the number of full-time lawyers on their staffs and employ a larger number of part-time lawyers. This had the advantages of sensitizing and training a significant number of lawyers as well as of indicating to governments that an influential sector of society was committed to human rights.

Analysis of Human Rights Violations

Second-line means of defending human rights include the creation or expansion of institutions that analyze the causes and consequences of rights violations in order to devise more effective strategies to combat them. The impulse for these activities stems largely from the requirements of documentation and judicial defense. These efforts also contribute to the development of practices and procedures that will better protect human rights in the future. A common complaint of human rights activists is that they are unable to disengage themselves from everyday pressures in order to evaluate past experiences, identify trends, and develop and refine strategies. Activists also have little opportunity for long-term planning that is responsive to the situations in which they work. Comparing their experiences with those of other activists (particularly those who are geographically isolated) is also difficult. Thus the opportunities to take advantage of past lessons or others' experiences are often limited. In order to remedy this situation, documentation and judicial action groups with the necessary resources have developed research branches. The most active of these are the Academia de Humanismo Cristiano (Academy of Christian Humanism) in Santiago, Chile, the Archbishopric of São Paulo in Brazil, and the OAS's recently created Inter-American Institute of Human Rights in San José, Costa Rica.

All of these institutions have focused primarily on the ideological and structural causes of human rights violations. Special attention has also been devoted to understanding the mechanisms of repression in order either to use existing defenses more effectively or to devise new ones. This work requires the dissemination of results, such as the publication of monographs for human rights specialists; periodic evaluations of national political, economic, and social conditions in order to establish the current level of rights violations and future trends; and popular educational materials. General educational materials are aimed at helping individuals and groups claim their rights. Seminars, courses, scholarly conferences, and press briefings to explain and disseminate research results have also been effective.

Much of this analysis has been supported by the Catholic church and European public and private foundations.[30] Although a substantial literature has been produced, it suffers from two limitations: a lack of analytical rigor (many of the studies have been written by nonspecialists, because of a shortage of human rights scholars) and the absence of a comparative perspective (largely because of the limited resources available for research of this kind). However, a sufficient number of studies is now available to permit more sophisticated analysis in the 1980s. Comparative studies will also be possible if the necessary financial resources become available. Furthermore, the studies produced thus far make possible a considerable expansion of educational activities on human rights questions.

Educational Efforts on Human Rights Issues

Human rights educational activities range from the training of lawyers to mass popular education. Educational work of this kind has been promoted chiefly by the Catholic church, international organizations such as the United Nations Educational, Scientific, and Cultural Organization (UNESCO), private foundations, and local human rights organizations. Popular education in defense of human rights had already made some progress in Brazil and Chile prior to the upsurge of repression in those countries. Human rights groups' most immediate response to this crisis was to focus on specialized training for legal personnel. Courses were subsequently developed for other human rights activists and, more recently, for grass roots groups. These latter courses range from basic literacy training that incorporates some human rights content (such as the efforts by the Integral Corporation for Cultural and Social Development [CODECAL] in Colombia and the Peace and Justice Service [SERPAJ] in Chile) to education for factory workers in basic economics and business practices in Ecuador, Chile, and Brazil. Although educational efforts such as these are widely considered to be essential to the long-term defense of human rights, limited financial resources and the lack of trained teachers have hampered progress in this area. The UNESCO recommendation that human rights education become a part of regular school curricula could be beneficial. However, national governments must have the will to initiate educational programs of this kind.

Technical Assistance to Human Rights Organizations

In recent years human rights organizations have also provided diverse kinds of technical assistance to help individuals secure their rights. This assistance includes providing information about how to obtain additional basic services from local governments, how to form production and consumer cooperatives, and how to benefit from other workers' experiences in negotiations with management. The efforts of the Brazilian Institute of Social and Economic Analysis (IBASE) to arrange for labor negotiators from Fiat in Italy to advise their counterparts in Brazil is a particularly imaginative example of this last form of technical assistance.

Technical assistance programs operated by a number of national and international agencies have also made some progress in meeting basic needs for food, health care, and housing. These organizations include the United States Agency for International Development, the United Nations Development Program, the Inter-American Development Bank, the World Bank, and some private voluntary organizations. Voluntary organizations have had more success than the others in tailoring their efforts to local needs and in ensuring that these programs survive after the withdrawal of foreign technicians. The success of efforts in this area is dependent upon improved evaluation of past programs and the availability of more trained specialists from the target population. Although it has not been given high priority to date, technical assistance is crucial for major improvements in social and economic rights.

Appropriate Realms for U.S. Foreign Policy Concerning Human Rights

The expansion and activation of mechanisms to defend human rights in Latin America are not antithetical to U.S. interests. United States human rights policy can and should make a direct contribution to these activities. Those who charge that the United States "lost" Iran and Nicaragua as a result of efforts to promote human rights misread history. Furthermore, the contention that Carter administration officials singled out for criticism friendly authoritarian regimes such as those in Iran or Nicaragua has no foundation. So evident was the concentration of U.S. official attention on the Soviet bloc in 1977 that Soviet dissident Valery Chalidze reminded the Carter administration in print that human rights violations were not confined to communist countries.[31]

In both Iran and Nicaragua, the government's abuse of authority and its failure to respond to popular pressures brought an end to the Pahlavi and Somoza dynasties, respectively. Traditional U.S. identification with and support for these regimes contributed to the anti-U.S. character of the new governments. However, there are also reasons internal to the Khomeini and Sandinista regimes that help explain U.S. foreign policy difficulties with them.

These two cases strongly suggest a need for the United States to project an image of principled support for human rights as the basis for a foreign policy that is tailored to the specific conditions of each country. In large measure, problems tend to arise from the United States' inclination to categorize countries as friends or foes. Instead, the United States should regard other countries as sovereign states with which it should maintain mutually supportive relations whenever possible, without becoming identified with all of another government's actions. United States foreign policy should be pragmatic and diplomatic (in the original sense of the term) so that it can avoid becoming identified with the abuses of other governments. This requires maintaining some distance from dictators and authoritarian regimes that engage in human rights violations.

The United States should be willing to grant or withhold foreign assistance to promote its interests abroad. This is accepted international practice. Debate on this question has focused on how and when to use leverage of this kind, not whether it is permissible to do so. Confusing support for democracy with support for anticommunist governments, and confusing capitalism as a system with support for a particular government or an economic model that may be damaging an economy, have limited the effectiveness of U.S. efforts to promote hemispheric stability. Opinion polls suggest that the U.S. public expects the government to act in accordance with basic humanitarian values. When it does not, the government's domestic support declines.[32] A foreign policy that is not responsive to U.S. domestic opinion is not long sustainable.

It was, in fact, the breakdown of domestic consensus regarding U.S. policy toward Vietnam that served as the stimulus for renewed interest in human rights as a principal criterion in the formulation of U.S. foreign policy. Not since the end of World War II and U.S. involvement in the drafting and promulgation of the United Nations' Universal Declaration of Human Rights (1948) had human rights issues stimulated so much public and congressional debate. The first wave of U.S. human rights legislation adopted in the late 1960s focused specifically on U.S. involvement in Vietnam. The upsurge of human rights abuses in Latin America beginning in 1968, revelations regarding U.S. involvement in the overthrow of the Allende government in Chile in 1973, and subsequent gross violations of human rights in that country turned public and congressional attention to Latin America. This interest has not diminished, because as human rights violations declined in the Southern Cone, the situation worsened in Central America. Thus when President Carter declared in 1977 that human rights were to be the soul of U.S. foreign policy, this issue was already a major public concern in the United States. Moreover, much of the relevant legislation was already in place.

In a recent study, international lawyers, U.S. policymakers, and scholars affirmed that the principal factor explaining the widespread U.S. interest in human rights issues was "public disillusionment with the Nixon-Watergate revelations and, to a lesser extent, Kissinger's ultrarealistic foreign policy." In addition, "United States world leadership has been damaged by the defeat in Vietnam. Through the human rights policy the Carter administration was able to draw on a domestically acceptable source for reviving American stature in international affairs: the American tradition reflected in the Declaration of Independence and the Bill of Rights."[33] The Carter administration and the general U.S. public were also affected by increased activism on the part of national and international human rights organizations.

Thus the stimulus for increased emphasis on human rights as a criterion for U.S. foreign policy came principally from domestic factors in the context of certain international challenges.[34] There is no evidence that the United States sought to establish itself as judge of other countries in order to demonstrate its moral superiority as a nation. Indeed, the goal was substantially different: to demonstrate the moral superiority of western liberal democracy and capitalism in the face of Soviet competition.

This goal heightened tensions between those who wished to use U.S. human rights policy to undercut Marxist governments and those who felt that human rights policy should also be used to criticize anticommunist authoritarian regimes that violated human rights. The Carter administration did not succeed in resolving these differences. Nor did it succeed in defining its human rights policy in a way that resolved the apparent conflict between human rights concerns and traditional definitions of national security interests, especially those interpretations that emphasized pragmatic support for anticommunist governments despite the fact that lack of popular support due to human rights abuses made them inherently unstable over the long term. By 1979 the Carter administration's human rights policy left both the U.S. public and the U.S. Congress with the impression that human rights and national security interests were, if not antithetical, at least frequently in conflict.

This situation resulted from problems common to all recent presidential administrations that impeded the development of a U.S. foreign policy responsive to long-term needs rather than immediate demands and partisan pressures. In addition, ongoing debates concerning the relative merits of "quiet" versus "aggressive" diplomacy and whether to use bilateral economic assistance or multilateral aid to promote social and economic rights combined to make the Carter administration's human rights policy appear contradictory at times. Thus there was no true test of the proposition that a U.S. foreign policy firmly supporting humanitarian values would over the long term help the United States in competition with communism.

Instead, the United States' commitment to human rights was interpreted by Carter's critics as a sign of weakening U.S. power abroad. Pressures for change and sociopolitical conflict in Latin America were viewed as reflections of Soviet adventurism that required U.S. support for anticommunist governments—even those governments that engaged in gross violations of human rights. In pursuit of its conservative definition of U.S. security interests in Latin America, the Reagan administration rejected strong support for human rights and stressed more traditional diplomatic and foreign aid efforts to bolster anticommunist governments.[35] However, attempts to present the United States as a champion of democracy have been undercut by its identification with governments that employ state terror. This policy has contributed to further ideological polarization in Latin America, thereby decreasing the possibilities of moderate political and economic solutions.[36]

Support for repressive governments served to delegitimate the Nixon administration's foreign policy and, to a lesser extent, that of the Ford administration. The Carter administration's partial disassociation from repressive governments increased both domestic and international support for U.S. foreign policy, despite what some critics alleged. Although there is no firm evidence that Carter's human rights policy caused some military regimes to initiate liberalization processes, U.S. efforts to promote human rights reinforced tendencies in that direction, particularly in Latin America.[37] The principal benefit to the United States was that it was less identified with fundamentally illegitimate governments. In contrast, the Reagan administration's foreign policy increased U.S. identification with such governments.

The United States' foreign policy should promote international stability by supporting governments that respond to their citizens' needs, as citizens determine them. Although the United States may not (and probably should not) have much influence over this process, the legitimacy of U.S. diplomacy and foreign assistance must first be measured in terms of the well-being of the people involved rather than by whether such actions are beneficial to specific governments. In situations in which a conflict of interest develops, decisions should be made in terms of human rights priorities, with those rights related to physical survival taking precedence. This position does not deny the need on occasion for very pragmatic decisions (for example, military cooperation with governments that violate human rights if a substantial security threat to the United States exists). Instead, it underlines the need to make the overall U.S. commitment to human rights clear and to conduct diplomatic relations in such a way as to allow for bilateral cooperation without legitimating the government in question.

Furthermore, the concepts of human rights and national security need to be understood better by both the U.S. public and government officials. "National security" is defined by some as anticommunism and support for U.S. economic interests. Ironically, the growth of U.S. power in the post-World War II period has led not to a greater sense of security, but to an increased tendency to defend and advocate a particular ideology and way of life in response to a heightened perception of external threats.[38] Although the Soviet Union's ideological, political, and economic opposition to the United States should not be discounted, there is no convincing evidence that support for anticommunist, capitalist governments that violate human rights is a useful strategy to counteract Soviet expansion. Studies of U.S. military assistance to such governments do not show that U.S. security has been improved as a result.[39]

Nor is there evidence that U.S. security assistance to Latin American armed forces has made them more respectful of democracy, more receptive to civilian control, less likely to stage coups d'état, or more supportive of human rights. On the contrary, U.S. assistance has made them more confident of their managerial and technological capabilities. As a result, since the early 1960s Latin American armed forces have increasingly intervened in politics, not simply to curtail instability, but also to restructure their societies along authoritarian lines.[40] This has been a major blow to democratization in Latin America.

A similar pattern holds regarding U.S. economic aid to Latin America. There is no real indication that withholding aid directly produces reductions in rights violations. Rather, the principal consequence of this action is to reduce official U.S. identification with governments that violate the rights of their citizens. Moreover, at present levels of bilateral economic assistance to South America, there is little likelihood that U.S. leverage will increase. In Central America, the constraints on each country's economy and damages caused by war have limited the *economic* impact of congressional appropriations for efforts such as the Caribbean Basin Initiative.[41]

During the 1960s and 1970s there was some progress in linking U.S. bilateral and multilateral economic assistance to the fulfillment of human rights. This effort resulted from a growing conviction within the U.S. and international development communities that long-term progress required that aid strategies focus on the promotion of basic social and economic rights. This view took hold initially in the International Labor Organization and subsequently in the World Bank, the United Nations Development Program, the Inter-American Development Bank, and the U.S. Agency for International Development. The goal was to identify the most effective strategies to meet basic needs, especially the needs of the poorest segments of the population. Debates centered on whether to emphasize growth or redistribution. Most of the major development institutions were inclined toward the latter orientation. But with the vast numbers of poor and major structural problems in developing countries, the resources available in the form of bilateral and multilateral aid had limited impact beyond raising recipients' expectations. In addition, unless assistance programs were strongly supported by the recipient country's government, they had little chance of success.[42]

The level of U.S. bilateral assistance in recent years frequently has been too low to influence significantly developing country resource allocation. Nor have U.S. basic-needs programs been coordinated with other U.S. activities, such as trade policy. Thus these policies sometimes work at cross-purposes. In addition, declining levels of U.S. foreign aid appropriations not only constrained existing programs, but they also hindered program evaluation and the elaboration of more sophisticated strategies.[43]

When, as during the Carter administration, the U.S. Congress passed legislation, over the opposition of the president, to tie financial assistance from multilateral institutions such as the World Bank and the Inter-American Development Bank to human rights goals, the executive branch made little effort to implement it. This occurred with Public Law 95–118 (1977), which required the U.S. government to oppose loans by multilateral development banks to governments that violate human rights. Institutions such as the World Bank were themselves opposed to this legislation on the grounds that only economic criteria should be considered in making loans. This position continues to be endorsed by the World Bank, and it is a defensible one. This has also been the position of the International Monetary Fund (IMF), although in the late 1970s the IMF began to reconsider some of its policies in order to decrease the negative impact of economic stabilization programs on the basic needs of the poor.[44] Given the severity of the current debt crisis in a number of Latin American countries, the IMF's capacity to redefine further its stabilization policies is circumscribed without major concessions by lender governments.

The Reagan administration's emphasis on self-help and free enterprise as means for diminishing these tensions has not proved efficacious. The U.S. private sector frequently does not appreciate the relationship between the fulfillment of basic human needs and the development of markets and stable investment climates. However, the debt crisis of the early 1980s and decreased U.S. exports have stimulated some U.S. businesses to rethink their overseas strategies. As corporations engage in more sophisticated risk analysis, the connection between stability and human rights fulfillment has become more apparent to them. United States-based corporations have generally been relatively adaptable in their over-seas behavior. Thus there is some possibility that transnational corpora-tions will respond over time to the threat to hemispheric stability posed by widespread denial of social and economic rights.

The record of human rights initiatives in Latin America in the 1960s and 1970s suggests that U.S. efforts to promote human rights through diplomacy and foreign assistance policy had positive benefits for the United States' prestige and influence. There is no conclusive evidence that the Carter administration's foreign assistance notably improved the enjoyment of basic human rights, particularly social and economic rights.[45] These efforts were hampered by the shortage of financial and technical resources and the frequent lack of political will on the part of recipient governments. Large private capital flows to Latin America di-minished the relative impact of bilateral and multilateral aid,[46] and there was no strong consensus within the U.S. government in favor of this strategy. The decline in egregious human rights violations in Southern Cone countries in the late 1970s resulted largely from the elimination of the threat of armed revolution, the development of more sophisticated methods of social control by authoritarian regimes, and increasing domes-tic and international pressures to protect human rights. There could well be an upsurge in human rights violations in some countries as domestic political opposition to military regimes increases in the 1980s.

Although U.S. pressures in the form of diplomatic initiatives and withholding military or economic aid cannot be shown to have been the direct cause of a reduction in human rights violations, these measures nevertheless dissociated the United States from governments of question-able legitimacy. In addition, as one U.S. official noted, "Promoting ful-fillment of basic economic and social rights is not a simple matter of charity. It serves long-term U.S. self-interest by defusing tensions be-tween rich and poor and expanding access to markets and resources."[47]

United States policies in the 1970s improved human rights situations in Latin America by legitimating the work of human rights advocates and supporting initiatives by international actors such as the Inter-American Commission on Human Rights, Amnesty International, the United Na-tions, the International Commission of Jurists, and the Washington Office on Latin America. None of these groups could exercise major influence by itself. Together, however, they were highly effective in collecting and disseminating information in order to mobilize sufficient international pressure to make gross violations of human rights too costly for many governments.

Are benefits of this kind sufficient to override charges that a strong U.S. human rights posture is interventionist? Specifically, do diplomatic representations and the withholding of military and economic aid constitute "intervention" as defined by U.S. treaty obligations and international law? Article 15 of the Charter of the Organization of American States holds: "No state or group of states has the right to intervene, directly or indirectly, for any reason whatever, in the internal affairs of any other state. The foregoing principle prohibits not only armed force but also any other form of interference or attempted threat against the personality of the state or against its political, economic and cultural elements." Thus two questions arise: Have any modifications of this prohibition been accepted in inter-American practice, and have actions undertaken by the U.S. government in support of human rights violated this prohibition?

In the context of the inter-American system, most governments and legal scholars agree that interference by one government in the internal affairs of another is not intervention when it is collective, or when action of this kind is undertaken in the name of inter-American declarations, resolutions, and treaties concerning democracy, human rights, social justice, and hemispheric security.[48] The dangers involved in making the prohibition against intervention absolute were raised as early as 1928 at the Sixth International Conference of American States. The Cuban delegate to the conference held that to condemn intervention totally would result in "sanctioning all the inhuman acts committed within determined frontiers."[49] Furthermore, the United Nations Charter provides that a member state that "in any way violates the dictates of humanity and shocks the conscience of mankind to such an extent that the breach of human rights constitutes a threat to international peace" cannot claim immunity from collective intervention by the organization.[50]

International law clearly justifies intervention in some circumstances. The classic study *Non-Intervention: The Law and Its Import in the Americas* argues that intervention in the defense of human rights is not, as sometimes alleged, a threat to peace.

Historical hindsight proves that in the long run . . . peace is in more danger from tyrannical contempt for human rights than from attempts to assert, through intervention, the sanctity of human personality. It has been suggested that intervention, far from improving the position of the victims of persecution, may, by drawing upon them the wrath of their government, attain a contrary result. Contrariwise, the fury of persecution may receive an impetus not only from foreign acquiescences, but also from the hesitation and reserve of foreign intercession coupled with courteous admission that there is no right of intercession.[51]

The 1947 Inter-American Treaty of Reciprocal Assistance (the Rio Treaty) specifically noted the negative consequences of human rights violations for international peace. It argued that peace is rooted in justice and moral order, including the recognition and protection of human rights and freedom. Hence the prohibition against intervention in Article 15 of the OAS Charter was modified by Article 19, which stated that "measures adopted for the maintenance of peace and security do not constitute a violation of the principles set forth in Article 15."[52] The subsequent creation of the Inter-American Commission on Human Rights, the Inter-American Court of Human Rights, and the Inter-American Institute of Human Rights was a logical extension of the conviction that the promotion and defense of human rights are essential to the maintenance of hemispheric peace and security. Although the clear preference of OAS member states is that intervention be collective when it is necessary, unilateral intervention is considered legitimate in some cases.

There has been considerable discussion among international legal scholars concerning the criteria employed to determine legitimate intervention on behalf of human rights. A recent summary included the following criteria:

That there must be an immediate and extensive threat to fundamental human rights.
That all other remedies for the protection of those rights have been exhausted to the extent possible within the time constraints posed by the threat.
That an attempt has been made to secure the approval of appropriate authorities in the target state.
That there is a minimal effect on the extant structure of authority (e.g., that the intervention not be used to impose or preserve a preferred regime).
That the minimal requisite force be employed and/or that the intervention is not likely to cause greater injury to innocent persons and their property than would result if the threatened violation actually occurred.
That the intervention be of limited duration.
That a report of the intervention be filed immediately with the United Nations Security Council and, when relevant, regional organizations.[53]

These criteria obviously refer to far more dramatic actions than those undertaken by the U.S. government in the 1970s in support of human rights.

In international law, actions such as diplomatic protests and withholding foreign assistance do not constitute intervention. Commonly cited forms of intervention are the "manipulation of tariffs, the imposition of an embargo, and the imposition of a boycott."[54] Diplomatic representations and withholding or granting aid are considered in international law to be humanitarian intercession, *not* intervention.

Although both intervention and intercession are forms of interference in the internal affairs of other states, the important distinction between the two concepts is that intervention is dictatorial and often forceful, while intercession includes a wide range of nominally friendly acts ranging from expressions of sympathy for oppressed persons in another state to economic or political sanctions, stopping short only of the actual use of force.[55] Examples of humanitarian intercession include "correct" rather than "warm" diplomatic relations, formal diplomatic inquiries concerning the status of political prisoners, support for investigations by agencies such as the Inter-American Commission on Human Rights, sending observers to trials involving human rights questions, formal and informal protests over situations concerning human rights violations, supporting the work of the Inter-American Court of Human Rights, and granting or withholding aid. Past U.S. actions in support of international human rights have not exceeded the parameters established by these examples. Diplomatic protests and withholding aid do not threaten another nation's sovereignty, although they may cause some difficulties for a particular government.

The fact that both international law and the OAS Charter give priority to respect for human rights and the maintenance of peace over nonintervention is too often ignored. Nonintervention is certainly a vital principle in the international order. But to use nonintervention as justification for failing to protest violations of basic human rights in another state has been sharply challenged historically on the grounds that every government has a dual responsibility: not to violate the rights of its own citizens *and* not to contribute to another government's human rights violations. This second responsibility includes avoiding actions that strengthen or legitimate governments that violate human rights. Moreover, "uncertainties about when, if ever, to intervene are no excuse for failure to refrain from collaboration with deprivation, especially when an alternative to the violating government is available and the deprivations are essential, that is, inherent in an economic strategy that the incumbent government refuses to change."[56] In other words, governments have a responsibility not to collaborate in the violation of both civil/political rights and social and economic rights.

Furthermore, the assertion of an absolute principle of nonintervention raises important moral issues.

A state adhering to an absolute principle of nonintervention must tolerate injustice, such as the abuse of human rights, within another state because to interfere against it would be to violate the principle of state sovereignty; the values associated with statehood would be deemed superior to the plea for humanitarian intervention. . . . For the principle, in requiring mutual toleration by states of what happens in their domestic affairs, in so placing order between states before justice for individuals within them, allows states to avoid the responsibility of making a decision as to whether an act or institution within any of them is just or unjust. It provides the state also with a convenient legal excuse for ignoring

considerations of justice for individuals within other states. A general moral judgment, then, might be that the principle of nonintervention is an amoral rule.[57]

Thus there is no basis in international law, the inter-American system,
or morality for asserting a principle of absolute nonintervention. Nor can
claims that Latin American countries never intervene in other states'
internal affairs be supported.[58] Nevertheless, the principle of nonintervention should be respected whenever possible, and humanitarian intercession is far preferable to intervention. Intervention should be undertaken
only in extreme cases of gross violations of human rights, and whenever
possible intervention to protect human rights should be undertaken collectively rather than unilaterally. The importance of collective action in
defense of human rights also implies that the United States should cooperate with initiatives undertaken by multilateral human rights agencies.

Opportunities for Multilateral Cooperation Concerning Human Rights

Several factors will affect future U.S.–Latin American cooperation on
human rights issues. These include the current debt crisis, differing levels
of economic development in the Western Hemisphere, divergent perspectives regarding hemispheric security, and the United States' response to a
rising tide of immigration. Economic problems in both the United States
and Latin America make the satisfaction of basic human needs more
difficult, resulting in increased societal tensions. Difficult though it may
be, social and economic rights must be duly considered in efforts to
resolve the debt crisis if increased social and political conflict is to be
avoided.

Given existing economic conditions and regional warfare, there is
likely to be much heavier Latin American migration to the United States
in the 1980s. The credibility of the United States' commitment to human
rights will be measured in part by how these immigrants are treated. The
morality and constitutionality of the United States' response will affect
the U.S. government's legitimacy and its effectiveness as a world leader.
If legislation affecting immigrants and the treatment they receive does not
promote the rule of law, then the domestic stability of the United States
will be adversely affected. Greater U.S.–Latin American cooperation in
the promotion of human rights observance in Latin America is one of the
most effective means of avoiding an even more serious U.S. immigration
crisis in the years ahead.

A number of mechanisms are already in place to facilitate U.S.–Latin
American cooperation on human rights issues. The principal inter-Ameri-

can actor in this area is the Organization of American States' Inter-American Commission on Human Rights. Since 1977 the Commission has played an increasingly important role in documenting human rights violations and analyzing their causes. The Commission's heightened involvement in these activities was made possible in large part by increased U.S. financial support for its operation. The Commission's expanded involvement also resulted from the support it received from a majority of OAS member states, a substantial number of which fear the destabilizing effect of repressive governments. Because the United States is a major financial supporter of the OAS, a high level of Commission activity is contingent on continued U.S. support. Given the fact that most OAS members support the Commission's work, continued U.S. backing would demonstrate the United States' willingness to respect the will of the majority on a key issue.

The Inter-American Court of Human Rights and the Inter-American Institute of Human Rights were founded in part because of the worsening human rights situation in much of Latin America in the 1970s. Both organizations are based in Costa Rica. The Court is patterned after its West European counterpart, and although it has heard only a handful of cases, it is intended to provide individuals with an opportunity to redress grievances if national judiciaries are unable to do so. The Court's functioning is hampered because most victims of human rights violations do not have the knowledge or resources to take advantage of it and because a few countries do not accept the Court's jurisdiction.

The Inter-American Institute of Human Rights is devoted primarily to education, analysis, and promotion of human rights. Its goal is to fund activities in these areas that already exist at the national level, as well as to assist in the coordination of international human rights activities. The Institute has initiated a series of seminars and publications concerning those factors that affect the observance or nonobservance of human rights. One of its most innovative efforts is the organization of courses for government officials, human rights activists, scholars, and politicians, among others, concerning strategies for defending human rights. The Institute's priorities reflect needs that human rights specialists have long perceived but did not have the resources to address.

The upsurge in severe human rights violations in the 1960s and 1970s produced both a sharp increase in the activities of international human rights organizations and a proliferation of new human rights groups. The United Nations Commission on Human Rights, the United Nations Economic and Social Council, UNESCO, and the United Nations Conference on Trade and Development (UNCTAD) were all involved in attempts to discourage gross violations of human rights. During the Nixon and Ford administrations, the United States generally voted against resolutions by

United Nations agencies criticizing countries such as Chile, Argentina, and Brazil. This policy changed under the Carter administration. However, the United States has rarely accorded much importance to United Nations resolutions; this has been particularly true under the Reagan administration. In addition, the U.N. Commission on Human Rights has for some time played a limited role in the international defense of human rights because of its internal political divisions.

Nongovernmental groups such as Amnesty International, the International Commission of Jurists, the International League for Human Rights, and the Washington Office on Latin America, among others, have had more impact on international public opinion and U.S. policies and legislation regarding human rights than other organizations mentioned above. Working closely with members of the U.S. Congress and (during the Ford and Carter administrations) with the U.S. Department of State, these organizations played a vital role in providing data, devising strategies, and even drafting legislation. They also helped channel resources to Latin America-based human rights groups. These groups facilitated the formation of human rights networks, and they arranged contacts for Latin American human rights activists with U.S. government officials and opinion molders. They also worked closely with churches, whose resources and membership networks greatly expanded their capabilities. The international character of many religious denominations and their grass roots presence were perhaps the principal reasons that human rights became a major issue in the United States in the 1970s. The international human rights network continued to expand in the early 1980s, as did support facilities such as the Washington-based Human Rights Internet (a clearinghouse for information from all over the world concerning human rights issues).

Attacks on the credibility of some human rights organizations by the U.S. Department of State's Office of Human Rights and Humanitarian Affairs under the direction of Assistant Secretary of State Elliott Abrams are an important recent development.[59] In addition, U.S. embassy personnel in some Latin American countries have often questioned statistics on rights violations gathered by human rights organizations. This was the case in El Salvador, where the number of civilian deaths and disappearances reported by Judicial Assistance (Socorro Jurídico) has frequently been challenged by U.S. officials. Yet in his memorable luncheon address to the San Salvador Chamber of Commerce in late 1982, then-Ambassador Dean Hinton referred to a total as high as that cited by Judicial Assistance (thirty thousand). Moreover, Hinton agreed that most of these deaths could be attributed to the army and security forces. Human rights organizations are not infallible. However, attacks on these groups by U.S. government officials and agencies are inappropriate. These attacks raise questions concerning both the critics' motives and the U.S. government's commitment to the promotion of human rights. If "quiet diplomacy" is to be the U.S. government's strategy for responding to governments that violate human rights, then it is appropriate to employ the same approach in contacts with those groups that promote human rights.

Conclusion

The 1960s and 1970s witnessed increasing polarization in Latin America, primarily between groups whose basic needs were more than adequately met and strata whose basic needs went unfulfilled. Economic models that emphasized growth at high social cost required the repression of civil and political rights. Government repression further polarized many Latin American societies, and it increased the potential for internal conflict and instability. In the 1970s U.S. congressional and administrative initiatives that opposed the worst of these rights abuses (especially violations of the physical integrity of the person) through diplomatic representations and withholding military and economic aid did not destabilize governments. The principal effects of these actions were to disassociate the United States from repressive regimes and hearten Latin Americans working for a return to more democratic political arrangements.

Over the long term, conditions in Latin America require a stronger U.S. commitment to human rights if there is to be stability in the region. The U.S. government, regardless of changes in administration, should make clear that the promotion of human rights is an essential element of its foreign policy. If the United States is to be true to the democratic principles that it propounds, it must recognize that legitimate governments are those that respond to citizens' needs. Diplomacy is the instrument that allows the United States to maintain relations with governments of varying degrees of legitimacy. It should be employed as part of a foreign policy that has as its overall objective the encouragement of governments whose stability rests on the will of the people, rather than on force. Governments whose rule is based on force are frequently tenable only in the short term, as recent events in Argentina and Uruguay have amply shown. In the 1980s the United States should focus on assisting democratic forces in the arduous task of constructing societies in which human rights are more fully enjoyed. As access to rights is expanded, hemispheric stability will be increased.

To accomplish this goal, U.S. policymakers should abandon the notion that support for human rights and the pursuit of security interests are antithetical. The cases adduced (primarily Iran and Nicaragua) do not demonstrate that the Carter administration's human rights policies brought anti-

U.S. regimes to power, for there is no firm evidence that either the shah or Somoza could have been saved except by direct U.S. military intervention. As one analyst noted, "Any government which has to resort to torture or assassination to maintain itself in power is already terminally ill."[60]

A reconceptualization of the roles of human rights and national security in U.S. foreign policy is necessary in order to clarify their relationship. The denial of basic civil and political rights—as well as of social, economic, and cultural rights—has had a destabilizing effect on developing countries. Because many of these countries are capitalist, Marxists have been able to exploit the alienation of substantial sectors of the population. If it is the intention of the United States to counter "Marxist inroads" in developing countries, then strategies must be devised to identify capitalism with the greater observance of human rights. Support for repressive capitalist regimes identifies the United States with governments whose long-term survival is questionable. Thus a conception of U.S. national security that is relatively inflexible toward sociopolitical and economic change in Latin America (including socialist change) will not reinforce hemispheric security. An analysis of U.S. foreign policy in the twentieth century shows that diplomacy and negotiations are more cost effective and stabilizing than military strategies.

The longer basic human rights are denied on a broad scale, the more likely it is that the eventual eruption of discontent will be violent and will lead to a radical rejection of established governments and political and economic systems. If the United States wishes to defend capitalism, then it must demonstrate that capitalism is an economic system capable of providing benefits to the majority of Latin America's population. If the United States wishes to preserve its political system, then it must promote the humanitarian values it claims to defend.

In addition, diplomatic relations should transcend categories such as "friends" and "enemies." This would permit the maintenance of diplomatic ties without associating the United States with the noxious actions of some governments. West European countries are more successful at maintaining useful relations with other states without becoming identified with a particular government. This approach is possible in part because West European states accept the idea that pressures for sociopolitical change are frequently rooted in domestic socioeconomic conditions rather than international subversion. European diplomats also receive training that prepares them to respond to diverse national realities.

The United States should use all means at its command—diplomatic, economic, and the denial of military aid—to promote human rights in proportion to the severity of the situation, without violating another country's sovereignty. In order to respond proportionately, the United States should improve its capacity to analyze Latin American realities, and it should focus more intensively on long-term consequences and planning. Greater coordination within the U.S. government and improved training for U.S. diplomatic personnel are important means for accomplishing these goals.

A number of specific changes should be adopted in this regard. First, a U.S. government interagency committee should be charged with both the resolution of disputes concerning the implementation of human rights legislation (as was the case with the Christopher Committee) and the coordination of human rights policy with other U.S. policies (for example, trade, military affairs, and immigration).[61] The Foreign Service Institute should provide longer and more advanced training for U.S. diplomatic personnel in order to promote more sophisticated analysis of local conditions. Ongoing seminars devoted to long-range projections for U.S. foreign policy should be organized. Training of this kind might impart greater coherence to U.S. human rights policy from one administration to the next, and it could increase the possibility of successful implementation of human rights policy. In addition, more efforts should be made to familiarize embassy staff personnel with the dominant modes of political, economic, and social analysis in their host country.

Greater coordination between the Department of State's Office of Human Rights and Humanitarian Affairs and the Office for the American Republics Area could also help clarify the role of human rights in U.S. foreign policy toward Latin America. These offices should undertake a careful analysis of the efficacy of past initiatives, actions, and strategies regarding human rights, and they should examine closely the impact of these policies on U.S. security interests. Studies already completed on this question suggest that an analysis of this kind could very well discredit some stereotypes and indicate new directions for U.S. foreign policy.

In addition, the U.S. Congress should support the study and drafting of international conventions concerning states of siege, states of emergency, and other such grants of extraordinary powers to government authorities, in order to help reduce abuses in this area. Similarly, the U.S. government should promote the drafting of international codes of conduct for those authorities dealing with prisoners, detainees, and demonstrators (for example, police, security forces, soldiers, jailers, judges, doctors, and other medical personnel). Both the executive and legislative branches of the U.S. government should redouble their efforts to secure international guarantees for the protection of individuals and organizations engaged in human rights work. Because greater public understanding of human rights issues is a necessary basis for the success of these recommendations, the United States should support UNESCO and the Inter-American Institute of Human Rights in their educational and research work.

Both bilateral and multilateral economic assistance programs should be reviewed in an effort to make them more effective in satisfying basic human needs. Market and nonmarket mechanisms should be incorporated in the production and distribution of goods and services that are deemed essential to fulfill basic needs. Specifically, U.S. bilateral economic aid to improve the fulfillment of basic needs should be increased, together with appropriations to evaluate the efficacy of past programs and strategies. Both bilateral and multilateral aid must also be coordinated with other aspects of U.S. economic policy (for example, trade policy) in order to ensure the realization of aid objectives. Initiatives such as these could be strengthened if the U.S. government encouraged the private sector to increase exports of basic commodities on terms favorable to Latin America.

Given the current heavy involvement of the United States and the IMF in the Latin American debt crisis, amendments to the U.S. foreign appropriations bill should require the IMF to weigh the effects of its loan conditions on employment, investment, income distribution, and basic human needs. In addition, the IMF and the World Bank should be encouraged to cooperate more closely if the IMF is not to undermine World Bank basic-needs strategies. This would require the IMF to give greater emphasis to human capital formation and to accept a more active public sector role in satisfying basic needs.

The U.S. government should not use military assistance (particularly renewed security assistance) to reward Latin American military governments merely for less frequent use of torture or a decline in the number of disappearances of political dissidents. More significant structural changes must first occur in the state's repressive apparatus and in the economy before U.S. military assistance is warranted. These changes would include setting a definite timetable for a full return to civilian government, reestablishing civilian control over the military, restoring guarantees for the exercise of civil liberties and the jurisdiction of the civilian courts, eliminating illegal paramilitary forces, and protecting the rights of labor (including the right to organize and engage in effective collective bargaining). Loopholes in current U.S. legislation that permit the sale to Latin American security forces of equipment that can be used for repression should be closed. Licensing limits on export sales are necessary to prevent U.S. companies from selling items such as "shock batons," thumbscrews, and leg irons to Latin American governments. Explicit limitations on the International Narcotics Control Program are also necessary in order to prevent the police and security force personnel they train from being used against civilian dissidents.

There should also be stricter congressional monitoring of U.S. security assistance programs to ensure that the provisions of the Foreign

Assistance Act are fully observed. Article 502B denies military assistance to governments that engage in gross human rights violations unless extraordinary circumstances dictate that this assistance is in the U.S. national interest. The current situation in El Salvador has focused attention on both the difficulties of applying this legislation and the need to do so.

These specific recommendations are neither easily accomplished nor exhaustively inclusive. Instead, they are pragmatic steps in the continuing process of integrating human rights concerns more firmly into U.S. foreign policymaking. As arduous and conflictual as this process may be, it is the most realistic means to achieve hemispheric stability. The validity of the belief expressed by governmental representatives meeting in 1948 to draft the Universal Declaration of Human Rights—that long-term peace could only be achieved through a firm commitment to human rights—has been amply demonstrated in the years since then. Peace in the 1980s might not be so elusive if the commitment expressed in the Universal Declaration informed U.S. foreign policy more directly.

Henry R. Luce Professor of Religion, Power and the Political Process
Occidental College

Notes

1. A comparative analysis of the fulfillment of basic needs in six Latin American countries (Brazil, Chile, Mexico, Nicaragua, Peru, and Venezuela) indicated that Mexico had achieved greater overall progress with slower growth rates than Brazil and lower per capita income than Venezuela. This situation reflects the greater attention that governing elites in Mexico devote to basic needs, and it suggests a positive relationship between fulfilling basic needs and political stability. Elizabeth W. Dore and John F. Weeks, "Economic Performance and Basic Needs: The Examples of Brazil, Chile, Mexico, Nicaragua, Peru, and Venezuela," in Margaret E. Crahan, ed., *Human Rights and Basic Needs in the Americas* (Washington, D.C.: Georgetown University Press, 1982), pp. 150–87.

2. The term "Americas" is used consciously in this essay to indicate that the problem of human rights observance is a hemispheric concern and to suggest that the United States shares responsibility in this area.

3. Natalie Kaufman Hevener, ed., *The Dynamics of Human Rights in U.S. Foreign Policy* (New Brunswick, N.J.: Transaction Books, 1981), pp. 356–58, and personal communication with the United Nations, 8 November 1984.

4. These include Argentina, Barbados, Bolivia, Chile, Costa Rica, Colombia, Dominican Republic, Ecuador, Grenada, Haiti, Honduras, Jamaica, Mexico, Panama, Peru, United States, Uruguay, and Venezuela. Although some countries (particularly the newer island nations of the Caribbean) have not yet affirmed the Convention, it should be noted that they have indicated their interest in doing so.

Other countries (such as Brazil) have delayed affirming the Convention because of concern regarding the impact of accession to the Convention on their domestic judicial systems. Nevertheless, all these countries' constitutions include guarantees of rights akin to those in the Convention. Personal communication with the staff of the Inter-American Commission on Human Rights, Organization of American States, Washington, D.C., 8 November 1984.

5. On the purposes of the Commission and Court, see Comisión Interamericana de Derechos Humanos, *Diez Años de Actividades, 1971–1981* (Washington, D.C.: Organization of American States, 1981), pp. 5–7, 12–14. For the Inter-American Institute of Human Rights, see *El Instituto Interamericano de Derechos Humanos* (San José, Costa Rica: IIDH, 1981).

6. Hugo E. Frühling, "Derechos humanos: Naturaleza, vigencia y futuro," paper presented to the Seminario Sobre Ciencia Política y Derechos Humanos, UNESCO and the Instituto Interamericano de Derechos Humanos, San José, Costa Rica, 1982, p. 1, and Louis Henkin, "International Human Rights as 'Rights,' " in J. Roland Pennock and John W. Chapman, eds., *Human Rights* (New York: New York University Press, 1981), p. 259

7. Comisión Interamericana de Derechos Humanos, *Diez Años*, pp. 313–39.

8. Ibid, pp. 335–36.

9. For example, the Inter-American Commission on Human Rights recently published its seventh report on Cuba since the early 1960s. The Commission has conducted a half dozen on-site investigations in Nicaragua since 1980, and its resulting reports have included extensive discussions of the rights situation of the Miskito Indian population in Nicaragua. See Comisión Interamericana de Derechos Humanos, *La situación de los derechos humanos en Cuba: séptimo informe* (Washington, D.C.: Organization of American States, 1983); Inter-American Commission on Human Rights, *Report on the Situation of Human Rights of a Segment of the Nicaraguan Population of Miskito Origin* (Washington, D.C.: Organization of American States, 1984).

10. George W. Shepherd, Jr., "Transnational Development of Human Rights: The Third World Crucible," in Ved P. Nanda, James R. Scarritt, George W. Shepherd, Jr., eds., *Global Human Rights: Public Policies, Comparative Measures, and NGO Strategies* (Boulder, Colo.: Westview, 1981), pp. 214–15. Studies that focus on differences in perceptions regarding human rights issues include Abdul Aziz Said, *Human Rights and World Order* (New Brunswick, N.J.: Transaction Books, 1978); Adamantia Pollis and Peter Schwab, eds., *Human Rights: Cultural and Ideological Perspectives* (New York: Praeger, 1979). For an analysis of the impact of the western liberal, Marxist, and Judeo-Christian heritages on the concept of human rights in the Americas, see Alfred T. Hennelly, S.J., and John Langan, S.J., *Human Rights in the Americas: The Struggle for Consensus* (Washington, D.C.: Georgetown University Press, 1982).

11. Yves do Amaral Lesbaupin, "Direitos Humanos e Classes Populares do Municipio do Nova Iguaçu," MA thesis, Instituto Universitario do Pesquisas do Rio de Janeiro, Rio de Janeiro, 1982, pp. 11, 203–08. Fifty-seven persons were interviewed in this study, almost all of whom were married. The majority were between thirty and fifty years of age. Sixty-seven percent of the respondents

received between one and three times the official minimum wage, while twenty-two percent received three to four times the minimum wage.

12. The difficulty of devising such a measure of human rights observance is clearly evident in the attempt made by Jorge I. Domínguez, "Assessing Human Rights Conditions," in Jorge I. Domínguez et al., *Enhancing Global Human Rights* (New York: McGraw-Hill, 1979), pp. 21–104.

13. The private, Washington-based Human Rights Internet lists several thousand such groups in its *North American Human Rights Directory* (Washington, D.C.: Human Rights Internet, 1980), *Human Rights Directory: Latin America, Africa, Asia* (Washington, D.C.: Human Rights Internet, 1981), and *Human Rights Directory: Western Europe* (Washington, D.C.: Human Rights Internet, 1982).

14. For the nature and extent of human rights violations in Latin America, see the U.S. Department of State's *Country Reports on Human Rights Practices* from 1977 to 1985, and the OAS Inter-American Commission on Human Rights' *Annual Reports* and *Informes* on the situation in particular countries. The latter are summarized in Comisión Interamericana de Derechos Humanos, *Diez Años,* pp. 249–309. See also the reports of Amnesty International, International Commission of Jurists, and International League for Human Rights, among others.

15. A bibliography on human rights in Latin America prepared by the Hispanic Division of the Library of Congress contains over 4,000 items. See Library of Congress, *Human Rights in Latin America, 1964–1980: A Selective Annotated Bibliography Compiled and Edited by the Hispanic Division* (Washington, D.C.: Library of Congress, 1983). Also see Center for the Study of Human Rights, Columbia University, *Human Rights: A Topical Bibliography* (Boulder, Colo.: Westview, 1983).

16. Louis Henkin, *The Rights of Man Today* (Boulder, Colo.: Westview, 1978), pp. 31–88. Henkin divides his survey of constitutions into three categories: democratic-libertarian, socialist-communist, and Third World. He concludes that "all systems and all societies now recognize some individual rights" (p. 86). He fully admits, however, that the actual enjoyment of rights is dependent on a wide variety of societal conditions and attitudes. Henkin's position is a common one among international law specialists. For other examples, see Richard B. Lillich and Frank C. Newman, *International Human Rights: Problems of Law and Policy* (Boston: Little, Brown, 1979); Louis B. Sohn and Thomas Buergenthal, *International Protection of Human Rights* (Indianapolis: Bobbs-Merrill, 1973); H. Gros Espiell, "The Evolving Concept of Human Rights: Western, Socialist and Third World Approaches," in B. G. Ramcharan, ed., *Human Rights: Thirty Years After the Universal Declaration* (The Hague: Martinus Nijhoff, 1979), pp. 41–65.

17. Arlene Swidler, ed., *Human Rights in Religious Traditions* (New York: The Pilgrim Press, 1982). This was also a conclusion of the conference "Religion and Human Rights: Historical and Comparative Perspectives," sponsored by the Committee on General Education of Columbia University and the Jacob Blaustein Institute for the Advancement of Human Rights, 14–17 October 1982, Seven Springs Center, Mount Kisco, New York.

18. As Cyrus Vance stated in his University of Georgia Law School address

on 30 April 1977, "In pursuing a human rights policy, we must always keep in mind the limits of our power and of our wisdom. A sure formula for defeat of our goals would be a rigid, hubristic attempt to impose our values on others. A doctrinaire plan of action would be as damaging as indifference." Cyrus R. Vance, "Law Day Address on Human Rights Policy," in Donald P. Kommers and Gilbert D. Loescher, eds., *Human Rights and American Foreign Policy* (Notre Dame, Ind.: University of Notre Dame Press, 1979), p. 311. Additional evidence will be offered later in this essay to show that the increased U.S. interest in human rights in the 1960s and 1970s was largely due to U.S. domestic developments rather than to any U.S. intention to judge other countries.

19. A recent national opinion survey indicated that the "moral dimension" was the main criterion in public evaluation of U.S. political leadership. In addition, 76 percent of the general public felt that government runs best when it listens to public opinion on major issues. Only 15 percent disagreed. Research and Forecasts, Inc., *The Connecticut Mutual Life Report on American Values in the '80s: The Impact of Belief* (Hartford: Connecticut Mutual Life Insurance Company, 1981), pp. 193, 238.

20. This categorization follows that of John Samuel Fitch in "A Human Rights Policy for Latin America in the 1980s," Discussion Paper No. 3, Center for Public Policy Research, University of Colorado at Boulder, 15 June 1982, p. 5.

21. The armed forces seized power in Brazil in 1964, in Chile and Uruguay in 1973, and in Argentina in 1976 and indicated their intention to retain control over the long term. In late 1983 the military in Argentina was replaced by a civilian government headed by Raúl Alfonsín, a human rights advocate. The Brazilian military government allowed elections to choose a civilian president in early 1985 and Uruguay inaugurated a civilian president on 1 March 1985. There has been less change in Chile, despite mounting opposition to the military government headed by General Augusto Pinochet.

22. This is an opinion shared by the Roman Catholic hierarchy in Latin America; see *Latin American Bishops Discuss Human Rights*, LADOC "Keyhole" Series 15 (Washington, D.C.: United States Catholic Conference, nd).

23. The political, economic, and ideological origins of national security ideology are analyzed in Margaret E. Crahan, "National Security Ideology and Human Rights," in Crahan, ed., *Human Rights and Basic Needs in the Americas*, pp. 100–19. See also David Collier, ed., *The New Authoritarianism in Latin America* (Princeton, N.J.: Princeton University Press, 1979), and Genaro Arriagada et al., *Las fuerzas armadas en la sociedad civil: Alemania, USA, URSS y América Latina* (Santiago de Chile: Centro de Investigaciones Socioeconómicas, 1978).

24. For example, Article 24 of the 1980 Chilean constitution permits the imprisonment or internal or external exile of individuals accused of ignoring government authority "to the point of open dissent." Margaret E. Crahan, "The Evolution of the Military in Brazil, Chile, Peru, Venezuela, and Mexico: Implications for Human Rights," in Crahan, ed., *Human Rights and Basic Needs in the Americas*, pp. 54–55.

25. Only two of several thousand writs of habeas corpus were granted by the Argentine courts between 1976 and 1982, and these were not granted until 1982—

after the military government had been discredited by the Falkland/Malvinas Islands debacle and economic mismanagement. This development reflected the slow reassertion of some independence by the Argentine judiciary, which was increasingly preoccupied with disassociating itself from the excesses of an executive branch of government controlled by the armed forces.

26. The literature on this topic is vast. For succinct summaries, see Margaret E. Crahan, "International Aspects of the Role of the Catholic Church in Central America," in Richard E. Feinberg, ed., *Central America: International Dimensions of the Crisis* (New York: Holmes & Meier, 1982), pp. 213–35, and Brian H. Smith, "Churches and Human Rights in Latin America: Recent Trends on the Subcontinent," in Daniel H. Levine, ed., *Churches and Politics in Latin America* (Beverly Hills, Ca.: Sage Publications, 1980), pp. 155–93.

27. Some research concerning this issue has been undertaken by the Social Science Research Council's Seminar on the Culture of Fear, directed by Juan Corradi and Patricia Weiss Fagen. Other work on this topic is being conducted by the Fundación de Ayuda Social de las Iglesias Cristianas (FASIC), located in Santiago, Chile.

28. Maria Helena Moreira Alves, *Estado e oposição no Brasil (1964–1984)* (Petropolis, Brazil: Vozes, 1984).

29. Bryce Wood, "Human Rights Issues in Latin America," in Jorge I. Domínguez et al., *Enhancing Global Human Rights,* pp. 178–79, 191.

30. Information concerning the size of foreign financial flows is not readily available. Some information can be found in Smith, "Churches and Human Rights," pp. 159–60.

31. Alan Tonelson, "Human Rights: The Bias We Need," *Foreign Policy* 49 (Winter 1982–1983): 54.

32. Research and Forecasts, Inc., *Report on American Values,* pp. 186, 193, 238. Some data indicate that the U.S. public generally opposes favorable treatment for prowestern authoritarian governments; Tonelson, "Human Rights," pp. 54, 70. A former U.S. policymaker has concluded that "indifference to expressed American values (i.e., human rights) does violence to Americans' view of themselves and saps domestic support for U.S. foreign policy." Sandy Vogelgesang, *American Dream, Global Nightmare: The Dilemma of U.S. Human Rights Policy* (New York: W. W. Norton, 1980), p. 253.

33. Hevener, *The Dynamics of Human Rights in U.S. Foreign Policy,* pp. 1–2.

34. This conclusion is supported by Kommers and Loescher, *Human Rights and American Foreign Policy;* Lars Schoultz, *Human Rights and United States Policy Toward Latin America* (Princeton, N.J.: Princeton University Press, 1981); Vogelgesang, *American Dream, Global Nightmare.*

35. Susan Kaufman Purcell, "War and Debt in South America," *Foreign Affairs* 61, No. 3 (1983): 660.

36. Fitch, "Human Rights Policy," pp. 26–27.

37. Schoultz, *Human Rights,* pp. 355–56.

38. Henry Shue, *Basic Rights: Subsistence, Affluence, and U.S. Foreign Policy* (Princeton, N.J.: Princeton University Press, 1980), pp. 168–69.

39. John Samuel Fitch, "Human Rights and U.S. Military Training Pro-

grams: Alternatives for Latin America," *Human Rights Quarterly* (Winter 1981): 65–80; Schoultz, *Human Rights,* pp. 211–66; Brian H. Smith, "U.S.–Latin American Military Relations Since World War II: Implications for Human Rights," in Crahan, ed., *Human Rights and Basic Needs in the Americas,* pp. 260–300.

40. David Scott Palmer, *Peru: The Authoritarian Tradition* (New York: Praeger, 1980).

41. Constantine Michalopoulos, "Basic Needs Strategy: Some Policy Implementation Issues of the U.S. Bilateral Assistance Program," in Crahan, ed., *Human Rights and Basic Needs in the Americas,* pp. 256–58. On the Caribbean Basin Initiative, see Otto Reich, "Aid to Our Southern Neighbors," *Washington Post,* 25 June 1983, p. A18; Joanne Omang, "As Economy Improves, Congress Hears New Distress Signals," *Washington Post,* 11 July 1983, pp. A1, A8; Jonathan Fuerbringer, "House Votes Trade Part of Caribbean Basin Plan," *New York Times,* 15 July 1983, p. 41; Paul Houston, "Caribbean Basin Plan Wins House Approval," *Los Angeles Times,* 15 July 1983, pp. I-1, 24; Douglas H. Graham, "The Economic Dimensions of Instability and Decline in Central America and the Caribbean," in *Revolution and Counterrevolution in Central America and the Caribbean,* ed. D. E. Schulz and D. H. Graham (Boulder, Colo.: Westview, 1984), pp. 181–82.

42. John F. Weeks and Elizabeth W. Dore, "Basic Needs: Journey of a Concept," in Crahan, ed., *Human Rights and Basic Needs in the Americas,* pp. 131–49.

43. Michalopoulos, "Basic Needs Strategy," pp. 256–58.

44. Richard E. Feinberg, "The International Monetary Fund and Basic Needs: The Impact of Stand-by Arrangements," in Crahan, ed., *Human Rights and Basic Needs in the Americas,* pp. 228–31.

45. Lars Schoultz, "The Carter Administration and Human Rights in Latin America," in Crahan, ed., *Human Rights and Basic Needs in the Americas,* pp. 326-27.

46. John A. Willoughby, "International Capital Flows, Economic Growth and Basic Needs," in Crahan, ed., *Human Rights and Basic Needs in the Americas,* pp. 188–214.

47. Vogelgesang, *American Dream, Global Nightmare,* p. 248.

48. C. Neale Ronning, ed., *Intervention in Latin America* (New York: Knopf, 1970), p. 23.

49. Ibid, p. 13.

50. Ann Van Wynen Thomas and A. J. Thomas, Jr., *Non-Intervention: The Law and Its Import in the Americas* (Dallas: Southern Methodist University Press, 1956), pp. 376–77.

51. Ibid, p. 374. In law, a distinction is made between intervention and intercession. The latter is defined as "interference consisting in friendly advice given or friendly offers made with regard to the domestic affairs of another state." L. Openheim, *International Law,* vol. 1 (New York: Longrenaus Green, 1905), p. 181.

52. Thomas and Thomas, *Non-Intervention,* pp. 386-87.

53. Richard B. Lillich, "A United States Policy of Humanitarian Intervention

and Intercession," in Kommers and Loescher, eds., *Human Rights and American Foreign Policy*, p. 290. These criteria incorporate elements from Ved Nanda, "The United States' Action in the 1965 Dominican Crisis: Impact on World Order, Part I," *Denver Law Journal* 43 (Fall 1966): 439, 474–79; Richard B. Lillich, "Forcible Self-Help by States to Protect Human Rights," *Iowa Law Review* 53 (1967): 325; Richard B. Lillich, ed., *Humanitarian Intervention and the United Nations* (Charlottesville: University Press of Virginia, 1973); J. Moore, "The Control of Foreign Intervention in Internal Conflict," *Virginia Journal of International Law* 9 (May 1969): 205, 261–64; Louis Henkin, "Human Rights and 'Domestic Jurisdiction,' " in Thomas Buergenthal, ed., *Human Rights, International Law, and the Helsinki Accord* (Montclair, N.J.: Allanheld, Osmun, 1977), pp. 21–40; Thomas Buergenthal, "Domestic Jurisdiction, Intervention and Human Rights: The International Law Perspective," in Peter G. Brown and Douglas MacLean, eds., *Human Rights and U.S. Foreign Policy: Principles and Applications* (Lexington, Mass.: Lexington Books, 1979), pp. 111–20. For a critique of these criteria, see Thomas Farer, "The Regulation of Foreign Intervention in Civil Armed Conflict," *Recuell des Cours* 2 (1974): 394.

54. Thomas and Thomas, *Non-Intervention*, pp. 402, 410.

55. Lillich, "A United States Policy," p. 279.

56. Shue, *Basic Rights*, p. 165.

58. This is clearly established in Gregory Treverton's discussion of interstate relations in "Interstate Conflict in Latin America" 344.

58. This is clearly established in Gregory Treverton's discussion of interstate relations in "Interstate Conflict in Latin America" in this volume.

59. In mid-1982 the U.S. Department of State prepared a critique of reports of human rights violations by Amnesty International, the Washington Office on Latin America, the Guatemalan Human Rights Commission, and the Network in Solidarity with Guatemala, which it stated was intended for internal use only. (U.S. Department of State, "Guatemala: Human Rights Analysis," mimeograph, nd, 4 pp.). It was, however, released to Guatemalan government officials, who saw that it was published. This was one of a series of efforts aimed at discrediting human rights organizations.

60. Fitch, "A Human Rights Policy for Latin America in the 1980s," p. 36.

61. The Christopher Committee (named after its chair, Assistant Secretary of State Warren Christopher, and officially entitled the Interagency Committee on Human Rights and Foreign Assistance) was responsible for evaluating foreign economic assistance policy to ensure that it was consonant with executive branch objectives and existing human rights legislation. It served to mediate policy disagreements on this issue within the U.S. Department of State, particularly between the Office of Human Rights and Humanitarian Affairs and the offices concerned with specific geographic regions.

14

COMMENT: Democracy, Human Rights, and the U.S. Role in Latin America

Giuseppe Di Palma

Perhaps the only point on which the four essays in this section may seem to agree is that, strictly speaking, democracy and human rights are not for export. But different factual and value premises, as well as different meanings of "exporting," belie the authors' common position on this question.

Rafael Braun starts from two premises: that the definition and priority ordering of human rights are imbedded in a country's history, specific to its culture, irreducible to a universal principle; and that the defense of human rights in a country is as much the task of its society—represented in its political, religious, academic, humanitarian, and other public institutions—as it is of that country's government. Not even a new democratic government is in a position to redefine and improve alone, abruptly, and by political fiat a country's human rights. It follows that a foreign power (in this case, the United States) can do even less. It lacks both the necessary international authority and an understanding of specific cultures and histories. For these reasons, actions by foreign countries in support of human rights can sometimes be counterproductive.

Howard Wiarda builds much of his essay around Braun's last point. He discusses at length how the United States after World War II insisted on exporting "U.S.-style" democracy to Latin America—a region with its own special conception of democracy and political authority—and why this produced a lasting backlash in almost all cases. In fact, Wiarda goes so far as to present U.S. insistence on exporting democracy as one of the most important causes of Latin American instability and abrupt changes in political regimes over the last several decades. Wiarda also argues that the United States has been losing progressively its semihegemonic position in the region because of what he calls "new realities" in Latin America. Thus, if exporting democracy was problematic in the past, there are numerous factors that make it even more problematic today: the growing nationalism and independence of the region; Latin America's increasing assertion of its own models of development and politics; the global economic crisis; as well as the diminished presence of the United States in Latin America and U.S. domestic dissent concerning the meaning of that presence.

However, neither Margaret Crahan nor Guillermo O'Donnell shares Braun and Wiarda's cultural relativism concerning democracy and human rights, the political conservatism that underlies it, and the fear of a Latin American backlash. On the contrary, both authors explicitly state their beliefs that Latin America is ready for developments favoring human rights and democratization and that the United States stands only to benefit from them. Indeed, Crahan emphasizes how Washington's wavering attitude on this issue, and the support of repressive regimes by some U.S. administrations, has instead done nothing to correct the region's present instability. These two authors' position is not that Washington *cannot* and *should not* export democracy and human rights; it is simply (and in my view quite differently) that there is no such thing as exporting democracy, whatever such a loaded term may mean. If and when the United States has been or is serious about human rights and democracy in the Western Hemisphere, what it does is only to recognize and assist positive regional developments that are factually independent of Washington's will and desires.

Accordingly, neither O'Donnell nor Crahan is trapped by what the other authors construe as the moral and practical ambiguities of "exporting" democracy and human rights. O'Donnell (who is the most articulate in exploring what he sees as the real possibilities of democratic development in the region) limits himself to asserting what needs no demonstration: that given the complexity and modernity of most Latin American societies, domestic forces have in any case the main role and responsibility for success in achieving democratic goals. He allows only a partial factual and normative exception to this in the case of Central America and the Caribbean—two regions where the overwhelming repressive role traditionally played by the United States admits and requires just as overwhelming a role reversal.

Crahan does not even mention exporting roles, and when she is called to comment on U.S. intervention in response to human rights violations, she presents a forceful legal and ethical case on behalf of some forms of intervention. Like O'Donnell's contribution, her essay reflects the belief that, given the complexities of Latin American societies, U.S. human rights policies can have only an indirect impact. The importance of these policies is not in what they single-handedly accomplish for Latin America that Latin Americans cannot do on their own; rather, their importance is in what they accomplish for the international image, national security, and domestic political cohesiveness of the United States. Crahan works from the premise that human rights are susceptible of universal definition and enjoy a consensus with international legal backing, that human rights violations in Latin America are just that (and not a matter of cultural relativism), and that the region expects their preservation and enhancement. It is her view, therefore, that regional and international laws and covenants give ample and justified space to international—even unilateral—action for the purpose of discouraging serious violations of human rights. This argument (a clear rebuttal of Braun's view of the limited authority and competence of international agents) implies a narrower and less stifling definition of what it means to "export" political models and to exercise undue foreign intervention.

In sum, although all four authors appear at first to agree in their views on the "exportation" of human rights, a closer examination shows that they are in fact at considerable variance with each other on a whole series of points concerning human rights, democratization, the regional cycle of revolution and reaction, hemispheric security, and the United States' role in these matters. Nor are the axes of disagreement confined to the conservative pessimism of Wiarda and Braun versus the liberal optimism of Crahan and O'Donnell. Other, equally significant axes set each author apart, thus providing a range of analyses fairly representative (with the exclusion of the extreme fringes) of the ongoing hemispheric debate on these questions.

In order to describe and explain the diversity of these analyses, highlight their respective contributions and shortcomings, and supply new perspectives when helpful, the remainder of this comment is divided into two parts, covering the double core of the Latin American predicament. First, in the authors' views, are domestic Latin American conditions conducive to human rights and democratic development? Second, what is the United States' role in these areas? Each of these sections considers those definitional, factual, analytical, and normative issues that are appropriate to a discussion of these questions.

Is Latin America Ripe for Human Rights and Democratic Development?

Given the relative assignments of the four authors, only Wiarda and O'Donnell consider explicitly and extensively the question of "ripeness," and they offer quite contrasting assessments. Braun, aside from a series of closing invectives against the United States' uninformed and self-serving condescension toward Latin America, appears to be much more interested in presenting a pluralist model (in the Catholic corporatist meaning of the term) of the kind of state-society mix that can best protect human rights against threats by public authority *and* by society itself.[1] Briefly, the model assumes that democratic government is the necessary legal-institutional guarantor of human rights, but it supplements government's insufficient action through the indispensable popular participation of freely constituted functional and sociopolitical bodies. How easy or difficult it may be to achieve this state-society mix in Latin America is not, however, Braun's first concern. My own view is that Braun's cultural relativism on human rights, his skepticism about "political voluntarism," his belief that democratic habits and attitudes are not created by decrees calling for democracy but by time and practice, all suggest to him (as to Wiarda) that the way to democracy in the region remains long and perilous and allows no shortcuts.

In contrast, Crahan's view of human rights suggests that, whether or not the moment for radical transformation in Latin America is ripe, the space for concerted and self-reinforcing human rights action is often greater than many policymakers and analysts are willing to acknowledge. Her position stems from several considerations. More than the other authors, Crahan is convinced both of the universality of human rights ("violations are only that") and of their moral and political potential. She assigns a potential and growing role to multilateral agents, international law, and foreign actors. And she seems at least as impressed by the role that action in defense of human rights can play in promoting democratic transformation as she is by the inverse process. In fact, on all these points Crahan takes an approach opposite to that of Braun. Her more activist stance is in part due to her belief that the pursuit of human rights can do as much for the United States as for Latin America. Finally, Crahan's assignment to analyze human rights and the effects of their constant violation on the regimes where violations occur leads her almost unavoidably to point to factors of regime crisis and instability that originate from the ground up. Accordingly, she focuses on popular vigilance and participation, the importance of popular legitimacy, and the "inherent" instability of regimes that—by violating human rights—alienate popular support.

The question that needs exploration, and which goes beyond Crahan's assignment, is how small or big the step is between "inherent" instability and regime demise. Unfortunately, the concept of inherent instability is a treacherous one, only proven if regimes topple—which they sometimes do and sometimes do not. The matter is not only of epistemological importance. Misconceptions as to whether and under what conditions actions intended to take advantage of instability produce the desired result, or produce the wrong change, or trigger a backlash, can have devastating political consequences. These are exactly some of the issues that O'Donnell addresses in his assessment of regime instability. It is an assessment that, by focusing on the Latin American context and on the region's present conjuncture, appears to rule out the notion that instability is "inherent." Because my own position corresponds most closely to this view, I will return to it after examining Wiarda's position on these matters.

As far apart as Wiarda and O'Donnell are, Wiarda's analysis of democratic change has one element in common with O'Donnell's, and O'Donnell's alone. This is the special emphasis that both authors place on the role of elites, strategies, and political choice. In his discussion of the "new reality" of Latin America and of why some regimes (Honduras, Peru, Bolivia, Argentina, Brazil) recently have moved toward democracy or are in the process of doing so, Wiarda asserts that these developments represent "changes from above," elite responses to changed circumstances—not the result of much popular clamor or grass roots "challenge from below." But Wiarda's privileged treatment of elites, resting as it does on the added claim that little of significance has really changed in the ingrained political values of elites and mass alike, is part and parcel of the author's *"plus ça change . . ."* perspective on Latin America. It combines a historicist justification of what has been and an ahistorical view of events. History as events molding events—and deflecting history—is obviously not part of Wiarda's metatheory, at least with regard to Latin America. Instead, in Wiarda's view (as stated in his present essay, and more explicitly in other publications) the region has an old and deepseated natural affinity toward a corporatist-Catholic-authoritarian model of political authority.[2] It is a model that cosmetics do not hide, that ephemeral and possibly self-serving deviations do not belie, that outside interference cannot uproot—and toward which Latin America tends to revert naturally when left to its own "genius." It is true that because the model accommodates elements of *personalismo, caudillismo, paternalismo, clientelismo, populismo,* and even *machismo,* it admits of extensive elite manipulations, recombinations, and retreats. But it bears repeating that these are still contained within the model.

This metatheory has self-evident implications for the question of whether Latin America in the present conjuncture is ripe for democracy. In Wiarda's culture-bound view of development (a view that is reminiscent of Braun's cultural relativism), even to raise such a question is to mistake Latin America's indigenous—and, indeed, unique—logic of development for a logic that is strictly Anglo-Saxon and foreign. Instead, the present conjuncture points specifically to a series of calculated retreats by military and authoritarian elites that are aimed at rescuing them from the policy failures of the old bureaucratic-authoritarian regimes. It is hard to see in these actions a desire for or commitment to democracy, and therefore it is difficult to believe that such transitions to democracy are really firm, unilinear, and irreversible. Wiarda concludes that if these considerations are linked to other aspects of the "new reality" in Latin America, the prospects for "U.S.-style" democracy are even less promising.

It is not Wiarda's factual analysis that is unconvincing. Indeed, his insights into many disparate facts are often persuasive, and his skepticism about actors' motivations and the twists of events are often salutary. Rather, Wiarda's ultimate inferences from his factual analysis and the theoretical orientation that justifies them are what is unpersuasive. Tied to Wiarda's cultural relativism is a theoretical orientation toward democratic transitions that predicates their success on the existence of a consensual democratic culture. But the historical record does not support Wiarda. If a consensual democratic culture does not exist in Latin America, neither did it exist in the United States at the time of independence, or for that matter among British elites in the nineteenth century. The record shows that democracy has often been brought about by ruling oligarchies whose rule had little in common with it. No democracy was ever born without opposition, doubletalk, and self-interested calculations.

O'Donnell's contribution to these points is double. He offers an alternative theoretical perspective on democratic transitions in general, as well as an alternative view of Latin America's present crisis conjuncture and the instability of its dictatorships. Without disregarding Wiarda's concerns (which he often explicitly shares), O'Donnell refuses to confine himself to the notion—theoretically unproductive, although sometimes factually indisputable—that there are lasting enemies as well as lasting friends of democracy. A new democracy may still come into being as only a second-best choice: a minimum common-denominator agreed upon by democrats and foes of democracy who nevertheless find alternative regimes increasingly unattainable, unviable, or potentially even dispensable. And such choices can become lasting and progressively irreversible once implemented and lived out. In O'Donnell's perspective, calculus, accommodations, and conjuncture replace cultural affinities, functional prerequisites, and stages of development.

Is, however, the present Latin American conjuncture a favorable one in O'Donnell's sense? Is the time now ripe for democratization, or are we witnessing still another swing in the eternal pendulum of Latin American politics? From O'Donnell's perspective, the answer to this question depends on what Latin American elites competing for regime positions believe and perceive about the nature of the situation and about each other, as well as on their capacity to learn from past episodes of elite interaction. In the past, swings back to authoritarianism often reflected a self-fulfilling prophecy. By resisting accommodations (either for fear of aiding a recovery by the authoritarian right or because of excessive optimism about the extent of its crisis) democrats and radicals contributed to the reconstitution of the dissolved authoritarian coalition and to a backlash against democratic forces. However, Latin American democrats today show much greater awareness of the damage that nonaccommodating attitudes have done to the democratic cause. Similarly, radicals understand better the extent to which the growing complexity of Latin American societies increasingly narrows the space for revolutionary outcomes. This change in attitude has helped social formations formerly allied with dictatorship appreciate the extent to which, as O'Donnell puts it, dictatorships are constitutionally incapable of either reacting to or anticipating crises in a way that is not uninformed, convulsive, inflexible, repressive— and thus damaging to the interests of those same formations. The change has also helped those formations to come to terms with the relative *desencanto* of democracy's unpredictability, uncertainty, delays, and lack of glamour.

One might ask why Latin America should now be ripe for such a significant reorientation of attitudes and strategies rather than at some previous time. Although O'Donnell does not explicitly examine this question, I am confident he (as well as Crahan) would agree that the duration of authoritarian regimes is one important factor. Given their constitutional incapacities, time reveals and cumulates weaknesses, discloses the rigidities and obsolescence of founding ideologies and purposes, builds cynicism and apathy, and in sum undermines rather than assists legitimacy. In particular, time is revealing the failure of Latin America's bureaucratic-authoritarian model. Because this is historically the last model of authoritarianism to be theorized and legitimized in the name of national development and security, because international fascism has long lost its intellectual appeal, and because the United States—the international power that traditionally has lent support to hemispheric dictators— is actually a democracy, Latin American authoritarianism has no legitimizing creed on which to rely.

In sum, although authoritarianism may not be *inherently* unstable, and times may not always be ripe for democratization, authoritarian regimes may have a tendency toward entropy over time that—*if appropriately exploited*—may channel regime crises in a democratic direction. As the case of post-Franco Spain suggests, the initiation and the leadership of a democratic transition may even come, smoothly and with some distinctive advantages, from inside the authoritarian regime itself.

The next question concerns the role of the United States in this process.

What is the United States' Role in Latin America?

Is "knowing" what the Latin American predicament is all about sufficient to conclude what the United States should *and* can do in the hemisphere? Equally, is having a perspective on human rights, democracy and its development, and the role of international actors in these areas a sufficient basis on which to determine what policies are beneficial *and* possible? As the first section of this comment suggests, our authors assume so. Not surprisingly, the policies they suggest for the United States correspond to their views of democracy and human rights in the Latin and inter-American perspective; in turn, what *can* be done turns out to be in keeping with what *should* be done. Thus their policy suggestions generally show the same strengths and weaknesses as their overall perspectives on these matters. In point of fact, because I have already indicated my sympathy for one perspective on regime change, I myself presumably have no difficulty in justifying the correctness and "can-do" quality of the policies that stem from it.

But this is not sufficient. What the United States should do in the hemisphere is not necessarily the same as what is possible, nor is what is possible the same thing as what is likely. These are separate issues. In particular, none of the authors is explicitly concerned with the distinct importance of the last issue—despite the obvious fact that what the United States has recently been doing in the area of democracy and human rights does not follow the advice of any of them. The United States has not gone out of its way to support liberalization and human rights, but neither has it acted with resolve to arrest destabilization. It has not decided to stay out of hemispheric affairs, but to the extent to which it is involved, U.S. actions have been both wavering and something less than weighty one way or another. Yet with the partial exception of Wiarda (understandable in view of his advice against "exporting" democracy), and despite their criticism of current U.S. policies, our authors miss (or possibly only leave out) the ultimate reason why the United States may be incapable of immersing itself in and attuning itself to the realities of Latin America (however scholars define them). Are there other realities, stimuli, or agendas that shape U.S. policies in this area?

Before examining these issues in more detail in the concluding section, it is worthwhile to consider each author's policy suggestions. Braun and Wiarda are very guarded in this regard, tending to discourage U.S. (and multilateral) activism. Braun's central interest is not in strategies and policies of democratic transitions, nor in whether and how present realities can be exploited to accelerate such transitions, nor in specific policies to alter efficiently and for the better the human rights situation. Although Braun views democratic institutions as necessary for the protection of human rights, he also emphasizes that the achievement of democracy is not the end point but only the beginning of a long process of liberalization and human rights development, requiring practice and attitudinal change more than concrete policies. His principal interest is in the slow transformation of Latin American societies from within, with particular attention to the region's diversity and the specificity of each society. It is a perspective that emphasizes autonomy and independence, self-help, education and information, and that confines the role of multilateral actors to assisting in these tasks. It is also a perspective that, at times in a very strident fashion, accuses great power interference in the region—as well as the exportation of armed violence by the left or right across Latin American societies—of being principal factors in the region's predicament.

Braun's suggested policies for U.S.–Latin American cooperation can thus be interpreted as steps intended only to remove internal and external obstacles to domestic, self-initiated development. Some of these policies are quite plausible. Some suggestions are not even policies, but demands for changes in attitudes: greater respect for the diversity of political solutions that individual Latin American countries may achieve, noninterference with prospective socialist democratic governments, and acceptance of greater nationalism. Other recommendations (on education for democracy and human rights and on economic assistance) are in the realm of international cooperation. They require a recognition of Latin American countries as equal in national political worth, if not in resources. Still others, however, sound troublesome and contradictory. United States or multilateral assistance in "legally" controlling subversion across national borders obviously raises delicate questions, at least of definition, feasibility, and limits. And asking the United States, whose asserted political and cultural imperialism Braun instinctively abhors and consistently mistrusts, to step into the fray is internally inconsistent with his premises and perspectives.

There are no such inconsistencies in Wiarda's suggestions. As previously noted, he shares with Braun a conservative view of Latin American democratization. This perspective is based not only on an assessment of present regime realities but also (more explicitly than Braun's) on a metatheory of political development and change. In addition, Wiarda is much more concerned with how hemispheric policies reflect on the United States itself, and he devotes much greater and more detailed attention to the intricate yet loose web of U.S. domestic policies. Each aspect of Wiarda's analysis leads to one almost inexorable conclusion: the need for a benevolent withdrawal from the hemisphere.

Although Wiarda's conclusion has at least the scholarly virtue of internal consistency, it is presented in so stark a fashion (for example, there are no recommendations for a carefully phased withdrawal) that it leaves many questions unanswered—including whether Wiarda is ready to subscribe to some of the obvious implications of his recipe. For example, one may wonder what genius for solving its domestic problems "the Latin American way" El Salvador would reveal once left to its own devices.

Would the chance for victory that the insurgents may have at present levels of limited U.S. support suddenly diminish, and at what price to Salvadoran society? Or would the incumbent government and insurgents find their own way to an accommodation? Would the loss of El Salvador following the United States' withdrawal leave U.S. interests intact? Some analysts may so argue, but despite Wiarda's denunciation of the pro-democratic missionary zeal of both Republican and Democratic administrations, I hesitate to include him among those analysts. In view of the complexity of South and Central America about which Wiarda writes at length—the diversity of regime types, the diversity of their crises, the degrees of U.S. involvement—it is difficult to accept Wiarda's recipe of benevolent withdrawal at face value.

Internally consistent as Wiarda's analysis may be (too consistent for its own good?), there is the further question of whether it is excessively conservative. Should and can the United States do more on behalf of human rights and democratization than Wiarda (and Braun) recommend? Based on their own perspectives on Latin American realities and opportunities, as well as on U.S. regional and global interests, both Crahan and O'Donnell so argue. For them, Latin American realities are no obstacle to activist U.S. policies in these areas; quite to the contrary, they offer serious opportunities for democratization. And democratic regimes would better serve U.S. security and political interests in the region than authoritarian ones.

Personally, I have no difficulty in agreeing with the broad contours of these authors' perspectives. O'Donnell and Crahan are convincing in their argument that the United States would live better with unstable and turbulent democracies (as many would be in Latin America) than with the convulsive inflexibility of crisis-ridden authoritarian regimes. This is especially so if U.S. politicians and analysts would become convinced that instability (an unfortunately value-loaded word) does not at all imply an inherent incapacity to survive. Forty years of unstable Italian democracy speak to the point. However, agreeing with Crahan and O'Donnell on these points is not agreeing on very much. Although the potentials and opportunities to be exploited in Latin America may be greater than Braun and Wiarda admit, the crucial points are how exactly to bring about the desired end-state, how extensively the United States should and can exploit these opportunities, and what concrete policies it should pursue regarding democracy and human rights.

In fact, unless I am reading backward into their premises, there appear to be some substantial differences between Crahan and O'Donnell on these points. Crahan, it will be recalled, starts from a strong belief in the liberating power of assertive human rights policies. She argues for their universality; she points to their capacity to embarrass and constrain authoritarian regimes; she denies that they have long-term, substantial counterproductive and backlash effects; she spells out their central importance in bringing about and consolidating a successful transition to democracy. It will also be recalled that she combines these beliefs with the view that the inherently destabilizing and alienating nature of authoritarianism's repressive policies is one factor contributing to the demise of authoritarian regimes. Accordingly, Crahan's suggestions for U.S. (and multilateral) policies on human rights and democratization are quite unambiguous, forceful, and articulate. They amount to a request that the United States use all its resources, moral and material (economic and military aid), to withdraw legitimizing assistance from authoritarian regimes. Instead, Crahan argues, moral and material assistance should only go to regimes well on the way to certain liberalization and democratization (if not already there). Crahan does admit the possibility of military aid to human rights violators when a substantial security threat to the United States exists. But then she also states forcefully her view that support for human rights and the pursuit of security interests are in no way antithetical.

Compared with Crahan, O'Donnell is somewhat more restrained and vague in making specific policy recommendations, especially those of a punitive-depriving nature. It is true that he is firm on one point: that the United States withdraw its support from the local military. But his recommendation is made in the special context of his analysis of Central America—an area in which the primitive, predatory nature of the military and local oligarchies, plus the historically heavy presence of the United States, continue to feed yet undefeated revolutionary options and narrow the spaces for democratic *salidas*. Precisely because of this, Central America is a region in which the United States (and perhaps the United States alone) has the capacity to open new political options by drastically curtailing the option of violence.[3]

However, when O'Donnell focuses on South America, he is more concerned that the United States understand, accept, and coexist with prospective democratic governments than with what the United States should and can do directly to foster democracy. He gives even less attention to what the United States might do directly to undermine authoritarian governments, groups, and interests. These distinctions may be subtle, but they are not inconsequential. It is striking that O'Donnell makes no recommendations concerning how the United States should rethink its policies in the human rights and economic assistance fields, whether it should make a concerted effort to campaign openly for reforms, and so forth. This does not mean that O'Donnell does not have instinctive and ultimate preferences in this regard; however, he does not discuss them. Instead, his attention is directed to a promising and unprecedented conjuncture of democratization in South America. The United States may help this transition process in some unmeasurable way, but it remains both indigenous and delicate. It is a process that the United States is called upon to help by empathy, a change of attitude, and a redirection of thinking more than through concerted campaigns and material instrumental steps. In sum, O'Donnell's recommendations amount to a call for (mutual) good will and understanding.

What explains O'Donnell's relative policy restraint, given the liberal perspective from which he works? In large part it appears to be the result of O'Donnell's theoretical orientation on regime transitions and its indications regarding how to channel authoritarian crises in Latin America in a democratic direction. In order to avoid radical-revolutionary adventurism and the more likely *revanche* of temporarily disarrayed but never really defeated authoritarian forces, this theoretical orientation requires negotiation and compromise between democratic leaders and the "democratized" sectors of the preceding authoritarian regime. It also requires a special effort by the first democratic governments to take into account those constituencies previously tied to the authoritarian regime, which may be suddenly left without tangible avenues of political representation and which are otherwise likely to personalize and overreact to the threats posed by the instant mobilization, escalating demands, and "natural disorder" of new democracies. All of these considerations require carefully calculated and executed choices by democratic governments, precise but adaptive knowledge of the kinds of local differences within Latin America that O'Donnell discusses at length, and limited external interference. Thus the United States can better serve indigenous democratic developments by showing an understanding of and confidence in local democratic governments than by direct policy steps taken without much knowledge and with the risk of unanticipated consequences.

If this seems to parallel Wiarda's position, it is important to stress once again that despite their radical differences, O'Donnell shares with Wiarda an acute awareness of local complexities and the weight of calculations and choices. In my opinion, it would be inappropriate for the United States to make choices among the various forces involved in shaping and restructuring democratic coalitions in the periods of transition and initial consolidation. Precisely because these forces may include authoritarian or radical-revolutionary elements caught in a difficult process of realignment, foreign recognition or withdrawal of democratic credentials—especially selective material assistance or punishment—may disrupt or set back the process. Actions such as these may undercut the political space of these forces, perhaps not defeating them but causing them to curtail or reconsider their search for a prospective commitment to a democratic compromise. Much more important and fundamental (and obviously preliminary to informed choices) is the ability of the United States to empathize with fledgling democratic regimes, lend them broad and unquestioned legitimacy, trust their actions, and come to understand why (as O'Donnell argues) their apparent instability, shifting policies, and possible anti-U.S. rhetoric would still make them the best and most stable regimes the United States could want in the region.

Conclusion

But is the United States likely to achieve this level of understanding? The policies implicit in O'Donnell's recommendations would require both a careful reconceptualization of democratic resilience in the midst of turmoil and renewed U.S. acceptance of such turmoil. Because these policies would not be very glamorous, they would be difficult to explain to public opinion (left or right) and difficult to mold public opinion with. This would be especially the case because the policies advocated by O'Donnell should be generally limited to situations in which (although turmoil may suggest otherwise) democratic coalition-mongering is well underway. In contrast, a more active U.S. presence in support of democracy should not be ruled out in situations that are both predemocratic and more open to a positive U.S. role. O'Donnell has already noted the importance of the United States in removing the option of violence in Central America. Finally, one can envision yet another set of situations in which the United States should instead take distance from or retard processes of liberalization because, far from succeeding, they are tragically leading to authoritarian backlashes or to equally repressive and more durable revolutionary regimes. The problem for the United States in the three situations described here is to assess the proper nature of the conjuncture, to understand when conjunctures change (for example, from backfiring liberalization to democratic coalition-mongering), and to adjust its policies accordingly.

The patchwork of policies that would result would not be easy for U.S. public opinion to grasp. Nor would this set of policies be easy to assemble, since it would require a mode of policy analysis (and an underlying mode of analysis of regime change) much more centered on the calculation of contingencies than, for example, the analysis presented in these four papers or in this comment. Would blanket policies (for example, an all-out human rights campaign, full military assistance, or even total withdrawal) be comparatively easier to understand and assemble? They would have a clear normative-political justification and clear objectives (whether or not they could be achieved); they would need no special knowledge or theory of the Latin American situation; and they would be of simple and reliable execution. However, regardless of the particular policy approach, the U.S. record appears ready to disappoint us. Policies have been both stubborn (rather than determined and reliable) and wavering (rather than pliable). Why? And what, then, is the United States likely to do?

Laurence Whitehead has an interesting but disturbing answer to this question.[4] It implies a critique of these four authors' excessive concentration on Latin America, their limited attention (Wiarda is a partial exception) to the intricate ways and concerns of U.S. domestic politics, and therefore their lack of attention to what the United States *is likely* to do. Writing on U.S. policies in Central America, Whitehead argues that what counts in shaping those policies is not so much the complexities of the local situation, but the extremely selective way in which these complexities are perceived and presented among U.S. decisionmakers. In other words, the U.S. policy-making process operates by a bounded rationality that excludes a priori many ways of thinking about a problem. In the case of Latin America (to extend Whitehead's analysis to the hemisphere), this bounded rationality reflects four conflicting elements: (1) unfamiliarity with and lack of U.S. interest in the region, especially the smaller countries; (2) the politico-strategic marginality yet geographical proximity of the area, which (as Wiarda also notes) makes the region a suitable object of political experimentation and one that is unable to retaliate; (3) the U.S. tendency to package complex foreign events (especially crises in unfamiliar countries) into familiar, capsulelike domestic categories; and (4) the presence of unresolved ideological disputes about the nature of U.S. society and the purpose of U.S. power—disputes that, given Latin America's strategic marginality, the United States tends to reenact in the region.

Thus the unsettled nature of U.S. policies in Latin America does not stem from the complexities of the region (which the United States can and does disregard), nor from ignorance and lack of interest alone, nor from the complexities of U.S. plural institutions. Rather, such policies result from the unfortunate conjunction of these factors with the ongoing crisis of U.S. national purpose. It follows that in its bounded rationality, the United States adopts policies toward Latin America that reflect reactions to events occurring elsewhere in the world. The United States' concern—in the incumbent administration or in the opposition—is not so much with the improvement of Latin America as with U.S. identity and national purpose.

"It happens," Whitehead writes, "that Washington has turned to Central America as the location for a prospective victory, but the location is almost accidental."[5] And so, perhaps, are the policy choices. If White-head is essentially correct, and if his argument can be extended to the region as a whole, then much of the debate on the role of the United States in the promotion of democracy and human rights must go beyond where the essays in this section and this comment have taken it. The justifications that these four essays offer for their policy recommenda-tions, whatever those recommendations may be, are somewhat beside Washington's point. They may not cause the United States to behave differently in practice.

Department of Political Science
University of California, Berkeley

Notes

1. Unfortunately, Braun is the only author who treats extensively the viola-tion of human rights by forces (in particular by armed movements, guerrillas, and terrorists) other than governments. The other authors' focus (even when, as in Crahan, allegations of international double standards are analyzed) is almost exclusively on right wing authoritarian regimes and their likely future.

2. Wiarda also refers to the model as a "murky middle" between democracy and dictatorship. Granted that some dictatorships are more benign than others (Mussolini's was certainly more benign than most Latin American dictatorships, despite its totalitarian features), a *tertium genus* between dictatorship and democ-racy is still conceptually impossible.

3. One reason for the difference between O'Donnell and Crahan may be precisely that, given their special interests, the former is more concerned with South America, while the latter is concerned with Central America as well. Dras-tically curtailing the option of violence, and therefore producing a dramatic change in U.S. policies in Central America, may in fact be the only way in which a peculiarly Central American obstacle to democratization can be removed. Here I refer to the extremely weak institutionalization of the state apparatus (particu-larly the armed forces) in Central American countries. An impersonal profes-sional army is in principle capable of opting for or serving under democracy; an army that makes the state and society objects of patrimonial appropriation is not.

4. Laurence Whitehead, "Explaining Washington's Central American Poli-tics," *Journal of Latin American Studies* 15 (1983): 321–63.

5. Ibid., p. 359.

15

COMMENT: Constraints on Policies Regarding Human Rights and Democracy

Edelberto Torres-Rivas

Human Rights in Contemporary U.S.–Latin American Relations: Contradictions and Paradoxes

If the reasoning and prognoses set forth by Samuel P. Huntington's *American Politics: The Promise of Disharmony* are valid, U.S. domestic politics has for some time been governed by somber cynicism. The perceived gap between ideals proclaimed by "the American creed" and the demands of unpredictable practical politics has been accepted as inevitable; thus the United States is in a period of either complacency or cynicism.[1] Consequently, this same mood may have affected the substance of U.S. foreign policy. From this perspective, it is necessary to act pragmatically. Results are important, not the means used to achieve them.

The originality of this interpretation is not equaled by its real explanatory power. However, this formulation does not have the merit of recognizing the structural linkage between the United States' domestic politics and its international actions. What ultimately counts in the United States is the former: domestic institutions and internal practices, respect for public opinion and, above all, those interests that are most important in shaping public perceptions.

This is an appropriate point of departure—perhaps obvious, but for this reason too often forgotten—for a discussion of human rights and democracy in U.S.–Latin American relations. In relations between the United States and Latin America, U.S. interests are more important. It was the same classical fable: the lion took the first portion because it was the lion, and the second share because it was strongest. The way in which U.S. domestic interests interact at different times to define foreign policies with distinct goals and content is an important subject for academic investigation.[2] Of course, this subject is also a matter for ethical and practical concern because changing domestic conditions and priorities in the United States often have a major impact on Latin America.

469

The perspective outlined here also provides a basis for understanding why the periods of most dramatic human rights violations in Latin America do not correspond to those periods in which the defense of basic human rights is a public issue in the United States, the subject of denunciations by humanitarian organizations, and even a U.S. foreign policy concern. At least there is no clear relationship between the increase in repressive acts by authoritarian regimes in Latin America and concern in the United States with denouncing these violations as part of a consciously prohuman rights policy.

This line of reasoning immediately suggests a first comment regarding a central topic in the essays on human rights under discussion here: the need to examine more closely the origins of recent U.S. policies concerning human rights in Latin America and the contradictions they embody. This comment refers less to the chronological moment at which human dignity became the subject of public concern than to how this preoccupation came to form part of U.S. foreign policy. We know that considerations regarding human rights began to play a central role in U.S. diplomacy toward Latin America in the 1970s, and that given the United States' great influence in inter-American relations, its concern with the brutal violations of human rights by numerous governments in the region became the focus of controversy and tension. This tension was manifested both in the domestic politics of those Latin American countries involved and in their diplomatic interactions with the United States.

The essays by Braun and Crahan offer a representative description of the different perspectives from which human rights issues have been addressed. They examine: consequences of human rights violations in Latin America in the last decade; means of protecting and promoting basic human rights; the public and private institutions active in this area; the appropriate role of bilateral diplomacy in protecting human rights; and so forth. Braun and Crahan also carefully analyze the realistic opportunities for protecting human rights in Latin America under difficult existing conditions, and especially what can be done in this area in the future.

We also note that analyses concerning U.S. foreign policy and human rights take one of two approaches: either they adopt a somewhat ambiguous perspective on this relationship or they consciously acknowledge a contradiction in terms. One need not pursue a criticism of these positions far to observe that the humanitarian imperative structures and influences wills, not only in private assocations (which are today the most important in the United States) but also among liberal political leaders, journalists, academicians, and other individuals linked in various fashions to official decision-making processes. Nonetheless, despite the presence of such positive will, the political exigencies of a superpower strategy create different—and at times contradictory—pressures. The reference here is not to internal contradictions among functionaries of different levels or among leaders of rival factions, but to governmental actions that vary sharply within a short period of time.

The major question facing Latin Americans concerned with these issues (as Braun clearly notes) is how to explain the lack of continuity in U.S. diplomacy regarding human rights. Either U.S. official conduct is essentially erratic and contradictory, or U.S. policy pursues a logic shaped by a permanent interest in supporting the military and big business in Latin America (both of which are sometimes identified with "national security" interests). Latin Americans are necessarily divided regarding this question, not because some are committed to the first explanation or because others more easily accept a "conspiracy theory," but because realism is a question of degree and oscillates between perceptions of what is necessary and what is possible. To carry this reasoning to the extreme, one perception of realism is to argue that in the global partition of zones of influence, Latin America is reserved for U.S. control. Thus erratic U.S. policies are within its prerogative. In contrast, other Latin Americans demand different behavior by the United States precisely because of this geographical proximity, and because nations within the Western Hemisphere share a destiny imposed by their position as neighbors. But, again, how does one explain the translation of public concern regarding human rights violations into an activist foreign policy stance—especially during a period in which the U.S. domestic mood was supposedly characterized by complacency or cynicism?

The answer to this question may lie in the general development of an international consensus on the importance of human rights issues. As Margaret Crahan notes, for a considerable period of time discussions concerning human rights were limited to general declarations of the rights and responsibilites of states. The condition of international public opinion in 1948—following World War II and the defeat of fascism (the tragic expression of the most brutal violations of human dignity)—made possible the drafting of the Universal Declaration of Human Rights and the American Declaration of the Rights and Duties of Man. From then until the 1970s, international public opinion increased its comprehension and consensus regarding these issues, but national circumstances favorable to the respect of civil and political rights improved at a decidedly slower rate in almost all Latin American countries.

The written systematization of those rights inherent to the human person—including not only political rights, but also the right to employment, the right to education, the right to housing and a better future, and so forth—also favored the gradual development of this international consensus. The publicity associated with these efforts at codification and direct information concerning human rights conditions throughout the world have created an active interest in rights conditions. This is embodied in highly responsive international public opinion, actively involved private groups, and a general inclination to denounce human rights violations when they occur. The fact that acts recognized as a violation of civil rights increase in some periods (especially the most brutal forms of police-state repression, such as arbitrary imprisonment, the use of special-jurisdiction tribunals, torture, kidnappings, murder, and so forth) has only strengthened this public consensus. But, at the same time, it is important to note that this consensus is damaged when political leaders and/or the state tolerate or disguise human rights abuses (as has sometimes occurred in U.S. foreign policy).

Moreover, the specific issues concerning human rights are now better understood—partly because of the recognition that material and spiritual contexts contribute to the realization of human dignity, and partly because of the recognition that respect for human rights is acquired by exposure to and internalization of the rights and responsibilities derived from social coexistence and historically conditioned factors. Hence, although there is broad international consensus on the importance of human rights issues, the concrete appreciation of human rights can only be defined and understood in cultural terms.

The historicity and relativity of the human rights concept does not diminish the defining capacity it may have in any culture. Any attempt to interpret human rights is necessarily relative in time and space. But the point requires further clarification because—despite the western, Christian, humanist orientation of the concept—political, ideological, and national differences do not prevent "human rights" from being defined in almost unanimous fashion. Nor is the concept of human rights unique in this regard. For example, with the development of a capitalist domestic market and an ascetic vision of life, work became a fundamental duty. But given the socioeconomic divisions produced by the labor market in developing countries, work has come to be considered a right. Thus over the long term, the cultural basis for the interpretation of rights is decisive.[3]

To complicate matters further, the demands of international politics are shaped not only by a general commitment to some principles or by geopolitical factors but also by the evolution of local contradictions, in which the issue of human rights is sometimes brushed aside in the short run. The experiences of Iran and Nicaragua illustrate this point well. Ending U.S. support for friendly governments in these countries paradoxically *contributed* to the triumph of openly anti-U.S. political forces. The shah and Somoza were for many years proven friends of U.S. foreign policy in their respective geographical areas. Both also embodied regimes based on the assassination of political enemies. They violated human dignity repeatedly, and they practiced corruption even more extensively.

At the same time, these regimes received military, technical, and economic assistance from the United States. Ending these ties unraveled the knot. These regimes did not fail because of the lack of foreign support but because of popular will put to the test. These were extreme cases that have no alternative explanation. The contrasting cases of Haiti and Paraguay confirm that popular will is ultimately most important in producing dramatic changes in regime.

Human Rights and Democracy vs. Stability and Security

Widespread attention to human rights issues in the 1970s strengthened private faith in the existence of common values that are based on human existence and fundamental rights. These fundamental rights were initially expressed in formal juridical terms, and their declarative value is recognized as a constitutional principle in the laws of *all* Latin American states. However, the fact is that human rights assume real meaning only in the context of electoral democracy, when consensus is achieved through participatory mechanisms. That a superpower should attempt to incorporate these values in its diplomatic initiatives abroad is an act that should be positively perceived. But here again there is a problem of realism at diverse levels. Who defines what is a friendly or hostile nation, and how? What degree of tolerance does the United States have toward *autonomous* social change in the context of national security considerations?

None of the previous questions can be answered unless understood in terms of a central underlying premise: the United States is the most powerful nation in contemporary history. The United States was not born with all of its current characteristics. Rather, they were acquired through a relatively rapid historical process in which a favorable combination of internal and external factors contributed to the country's emergence as a major power. The United States first took a decisive role in the Caribbean area, then vis-à-vis Europe, and finally at the international level. Since World War II, the United States has faced a wide range of tasks associated with its status as a global power.

This is a basic point that underlies the subject of U.S. security, whether the question is posed in terms of national security or, more rhetorically, continental or hemispheric security. The theme is repeatedly raised in *all* kinds of literature on human rights issues, and it appears in the essays by Braun and Crahan. For the purposes of this comment, it may be useful to link the contemporary issue of U.S. national security with past concerns regarding the United States' territorial expansion, when the expansion phase formed a necessary part of its national affirmation. What is most impressive, then and now, is the range of ideas and moral doctrines proposed as justifications for such orientations. One might say that these ideas and doctrines were formulated by different thinkers and strategists but for the same purpose: to justify the expansion of national control.[4]

It is not possible in the brief space available here to comment on the topic of security except as it relates to the problems of human rights and democracy—particularly its connection to the stability of political regimes in Latin America. Is there a necessary relationship? A conceptualization of security in vogue since the era of Theodore Roosevelt holds that the stability of Latin American regimes reinforces U.S. national security. Although with differing degrees of emphasis, the authors in this section agree with this proposition. For example, Crahan (who is intensely interested in improving U.S.–Latin American relations) takes as her central hypothesis the proposition that the defense of basic human rights promotes political stability, and thus the promotion of human rights and national security objectives are held to be complementary. Crahan also argues that the concept of national security should be applied more flexibly so as not to be identified merely with the permanence in power of certain U.S. allies in the region.

Braun correctly affirms that neither regime stabililty nor regime change in itself guarantees protection for human rights. In any event, U.S. national security interests are not limited to the permanence of allied or friendly Latin American regimes. Wiarda's skeptical view of these issues repeatedly states that U.S. insistence on issues such as democracy or human rights in its dealings with Latin America is not functional to the search for stability; therefore, it undercuts an essential aspect of security. However, Wiarda does recognize that in the Kennedy presidency, when a variety of reforms were initiated under the so-called Alliance for Progress, there was essential continuity in the basic elements of U.S. policy toward Latin America: stability, anticommunism, hegemony, and political-economic-military penetration. Thus what is important is continuity in certain principles underlying U.S. foreign policy, even though economic and political change occurs in Latin America.

However, the continuity ended in the 1970s with the emergence of authoritarian regimes in some South American countries and the beginning of the Central American crisis. The stability of authoritarian regimes is usually short lived, and it is doubtful that their longevity would contribute to U.S. national security. Nor do human rights and democracy fare well in such circumstances. In reality, experience shows that whether or not U.S. foreign policy toward Latin America is successful, its essential motivations and goals remain independent of the failure or success of democracy and respect for human rights.

Democracy as the Central Issue

The question of democracy touches on all the subjects discussed so far, because respect for human dignity, broad-based stability, and development are only possible in the context of open, participatory political structures. Some (strictly political) rights give meaning to democratic life *strictu sensu*. But there are other rights that transcend political life and concern the essential functioning of a society. These social rights complete and perfect a political democracy.

For this reason, it is necessary to emphasize one crucial point: no unidimensional conceptualization of democracy exists, nor is it possible to formulate one. The lack of conceptual precision in this regard often results in truly fruitless exchanges. A better understanding of the two historic directions in which popular struggles for democracy in Latin America are now moving may help clarify this issue. The crisis of authoritarian regimes in Chile, Argentina, Uruguay, and (to a lesser degree) Brazil has focused discussion on the construction of a *renewed* democratic order— that is, not merely a return to previously established democratic arrangements, but an effort to use past experiences to reconstruct a political life that is cleansed of past faults and that assures the integration of those sectors least capable of defending their interests under authoritarian rule. This is an effort to "appropriate" past history in order to surpass it. Democracy thus finds its roots in society itself.

The crises of military regimes in Nicaragua (before June 1979), El Salvador, and Guatemala also raise the issue of democratic life as a real alternative. But in these cases, it is a question of a historical project without previous referents. Democracy is constructed more as programmatic discourse given meaning by social forces that dictatorship created as its inevitable negation. Democracy has never existed in these countries; the only deeply rooted traditions are authoritarian. This explains the different flavor that contemporary political struggles have in these Central American nations, in contrast with efforts to reestablish democratic life in the Southern Cone. This is the central argument in O'Donnell's essay and the sense of his statements concerning the prodemocratic consciousness that has emerged as the result of lengthy experiences with politically repressive and socially regressive regimes.[5]

These examples are useful because they allow us to identify certain aspects of the problem that are directly related to a central issue: can democracy be the object of international negotiation? To what extent can democracy form part of diplomacy in relations between states?

The first point to emphasize here is that democracy forms part of a process of historical composition; democracy is the result of social struggles actively seeking to establish it. Democratic order is not an inherent structural characteristic of liberal capitalism, nor is it the merit of any particular social class. The formal equality on which a democratic system is based (and which constitutions recognize in technical juridical terms) only ceases to be formal when social struggles give it substantive content, when formal equality becomes real equality. Democratic structures or democratic liberties depend, then, on the political capacity of diverse, contradictory social forces that under certain conditions succeed in winning the active participation of previously marginalized groups.

In other words, if democracy is a form of organizing consensus, it is also a means of transaction among social groups with counterposed interests. This can only be achieved over a relatively long period of time. The construction of democratic practices is the building of a democratic tradition. What manner of theoretical perspective or vision of history do those observers have who irresponsibly state that a democratic structure—practices, tradition, culture—can be implanted in a country? This is not even a question of constructing what one might call a *real* democracy. The distinction is well understood. Agnes Heller has indicated that formal democracy is the existence of norms that regulate political relations among individuals and social groups, based on political pluralism, individual liberties, and the delegation and representation of power.[6]

The metamorphosis of constitutional legality into real democracy constitutes the essence of the problem. Here "real" (as Hegel would say) is "rational": to take part in free elections; accept political opposition and dissent by diverse ideological tendencies; tolerate an independent press and professional/occupational organizations; and permit effective action in diverse forms by popular sectors such as workers, peasants, and the lower-middle class to achieve their interests conveniently expressed. ("Diverse forms" refers to the fact that popular participation in a multitude of forms and at widely divergent levels is the antecedent to these groups' full integration into those mechanisms that form consensus.)

In the history of Latin America, real democracy has diverse *degrees* and *moments* of realization. This is not the place to review these processes or to chronicle their repeated failures. But it is important to note that, with exceptions such as the 1980 Chilean constitution and the Haitian constitution under Duvalier, all Latin American legal doctrines establish and recognize the fundamental principles of liberal democracy.[7] The problem is being able to build real (in comparative historical terms) democracy, which cannot be done through symbolic elections that invent a nonexistent consensus. Instead, success in this effort requires a political and cultural tradition that derives from a complex structure of social, economic, and ideological relations. Rather than deny the democratic possibilities of any particular Latin American society, these statements suggest the difficulties of this transition process and the importance of knowing how to accept risks and costs. Latin American citizens have never ceased fighting for the construction of a democratic order.

For this reason, Wiarda's suggestion that Latin Americans do not really want democracy must be questioned for both its explicative purpose and the factual confusion that surrounds this part of his argument. In distinct contrast to an interpretation of this kind, one might conceivably argue that those responsible for terror, repression, and the absence of democratic tolerance in Latin America are the military and right wing political groups that are partners and friends of dominant sectors in the United States. Such banality is just as partially correct as the pessimistic judgments on which Wiarda bases his argument.

Both Wiarda and O'Donnell are correct—although from distinct perspectives and with opposite results—in recognizing a long-standing authoritarian tradition in Latin America. It is not necessary to cite authors or facts in this regard because the historical record is manifestly clear. But Wiarda's perceived dilemmas on this point do not justify his negative realism because (like the U.S. policies he criticizes) they are based on a misunderstanding of Latin American reality. And, in any event, the weaknesses of democracy in the region cannot be blamed primarily on irregularities or lack of firmness in actions undertaken by the United States to establish democracy among its neighbors. The obstacles to the survival of democracy in Latin America are internal to these societies; only Latin Americans can be responsible for successes or failures in this area.

Nonetheless, the historical record also clearly shows that U.S. actions have had a significant impact on democracy in the region. Not only have U.S. policies not *helped* promote democratic changes, but they have also pursued two pernicious lines: (1) support for authoritarian regimes for strategic reasons, economic advantages, or ideological affinity; and (2) disinterest in or active opposition to newly initiated democratic experiences. One need only recall the role played by U.S. ambassador Peurifoy (whose actions brutally departed from accepted diplomatic behavior) and the successful covert actions of the Central Intelligence Agency in Guatemala in 1954, or the activities of the International Telephone and Telegraph Corporation and the U.S. Department of State in Chile in 1973.

These outcomes are due to what O'Donnell calls the "perverse logic" of progressive change in Latin America, especially as it is affected by the Manichaean reactions of U.S. foreign policy in its global confrontation with the Soviet Union. The building and perfection of democracy in Latin America should not be presented as an alternative to Soviet-style communism, nor should it be inspired in the U.S. tradition of political monism. The cultural tradition of the United States is foreign to Latin

American sensibilities, and the imitation of another nation's political institutions can be as disorienting as U.S. efforts to establish them abroad.

It is true that some leftist forces in Latin America have disparaged formal democracy. Their experience with fraudulent elections caused them to discount the value of the electoral process; the existence of monosyllabic legislatures caused them to decry party-based representation; and so forth. In Central America this experience has been overcome only with considerable difficulty, because democratic forces acting in the name of "real democracy" (which, with the exception of Costa Rica, has never existed in the region) refused to defend formal democracy or participate in the democratic struggle.

Nonetheless, the most fruitful perspective on this issue is Crahan, Braun, and O'Donnell's prudent optimism concerning the possibilities for democracy in Latin America. With the support of recent historical experiences and, obviously, without forgetting the tragic lessons of the past, it should be possible to rely more on local capabilities and indigenous pro-democratic forces now vigorously emerging in the region in efforts to construct democracy. Social and economic development, the installation of a participatory democracy, and the creation of conditions sufficient for life with at least a minimum of spiritual and material dignity are clearly major internal challenges that we Latin Americans must resolve. The rancor that sooner or later surfaces in any Latin American democrat is not caused by the United States not having helped us to achieve these goals. Rather, it is the result of the United States having again and again explicitly impeded progress toward them.

Pragmatism, Moral and Political

What, if anything, can the United States do to promote democracy in Latin America? As a summary of his doubts and perceived dilemmas on this point, Wiarda proposes a U.S. policy toward democratization that would be realistic, prudent, enlightened, pragmatic, and based on comprehension and empathy toward Latin America. Of course, if democracy resulted from such a policy, everyone would be satisfied. But in fact, Crahan's realism is more helpful: if the United States wants to defend capitalism, it should expand the benefits of the system to the majority of Latin Americans; if the United States wants to hold up its own political system as a model for others, it should promote the humanitarian values that it proclaims. Unfortunately, the specific measures that Crahan proposes to realize these goals are inspired more by sympathy than by realism. Tasks such as these will be extremely difficult in a troubled decade in which economics and politics both conspire against good intentions.

O'Donnell's essay reflects a sound political judgment: accept things as they are, avoid judgments before or after the fact, and inaugurate a new era in hemispheric relations from which all parties will benefit. This would require coordinated, simultaneous efforts by the United States and Latin America to untie the Gordian knot that has resulted from, respectively, anti-Soviet and anti-imperialist paranoia. The 1984 Kissinger Commission report on Central America added another loop to this knot.[8] The logic of violence continues to impede U.S. vision in Central America . . . for now.

Braun is correct in emphasizing the need to imbue national and international political life with ethical content. As others have noted, intellectual arguments are always islands in the sea of praxis, and they always seek some kind of moral justification. Public policies, inspired by the contingencies of immediate interests, seek a more general justification through ethical arguments. From time to time U.S. diplomacy also seeks an ethical basis and a higher moral justification, but there is an unbridgeable distance between such a justification and the goal sought. That end eventually becomes the justification for the means employed. Stated in this way, the problem of foreign policy is less a moral issue than a tactical matter. Justification can (as Socrates would put it) precede action, but Nietzsche's morality became the basis for self-justification and impunity—the reign of violence.

Dialogue between the United States and Latin America—between governments—has almost always been attempted from positions of strength, in which contrasting tendencies are locked in the logic of relentless struggle between opposing systems. This logic merely results in a monologue. A common language can be created only on the basis of artful efforts by the *peoples* of the hemisphere. This limits the role of citizens to that of the imaginative little girl in Andersen's fairy tale: to say out loud that the emperor has no clothes.

Facultad Latinoamericana de Ciencias Sociales
San José, Costa Rica

Notes

1. Samuel P. Huntington, *American Politics: The Promise of Disharmony* (Cambridge, Mass.: Harvard University Press, 1981). For a discussion of these two possible reactions, see chapter 4.

2. The writing on this topic is extensive and increases with time. See, for example, Lars Schoultz, *Human Rights and United States Policy Toward Latin America* (Princeton, N.J.: Princeton University Press, 1981); Jorge I. Domínguez et al., *Enhancing Global Human Rights* (New York: McGraw-Hill, 1979).

3. For example, the right to life is more universally valued than the right to vote. For the millions of human beings who live in abject poverty, the right to work and the right to a decent income are more important than those liberal values that are less directly associated with physical survival, such as the right to freedom of conscience and the right to dissent.

4. "This powerful pressure exercised by a people that constantly moves toward new frontiers, in search of new territories, greater power, the complete liberty of a new world, has governed our course and, like destiny, has shaped our politics." Woodrow Wilson, "The Ideals of America," *Atlantic Monthly* 90 (1902), quoted in Albert K. Weinberg, *Manifest Destiny: A Study of National Expansionism in American History* (1935; rpt. Baltimore: Johns Hopkins University Press, 1963), p. 8.

5. O'Donnell's hypothesis concerning a revaluation of democracy also appears in recent writings by Chilean and Brazilian authors, among others. A similar line of argument has not appeared in Central America, where authoritarianism is not a malignant feature of political life so much as a structural attribute of the entire system. Thus the current crisis in Central America poses the alternative of a new kind of democracy.

6. Agnes Heller, "Democracia formal y democracia socialista," *Chile-América* 68/69 (Rome) (February–March 1981): 50.

7. Among other works, see Ernesto de la Torre Villar and Jorge Mário García Laguardia, *Desarrollo histórico del constitucionalismo hispanoamericano* (Mexico, D.F.: Instituto de Investigaciones Jurídicas, Universidad Nacional Autónoma de México, 1976). As its title indicates, this work deals extensively with the development of constitutional liberalism and democratic norms in Latin America.

8. See *The Report of the President's National Bipartisan Commission on Central America* (New York: Macmillan, 1984). The commission, chaired by former Secretary of State Henry A. Kissinger, was known informally as "the Kissinger Commission."

16

Migration and U.S.–Latin American Relations in the 1980s

Michael S. Teitelbaum

The importance of international migration for U.S.–Latin American relations has become increasingly apparent over the past decade. In part this is because of the substantial growth in the size of such migration streams, much of which is outside both international and national codes of law. In addition, the same period has seen two classic "crystallizing crises," which from the U.S. perspective served to highlight the connections between foreign affairs and migration—the mass movement of over 125,000 Cubans from Mariel Harbor to Florida within a few months in 1980, and the influx of 30,000 to 40,000 Haitian migrants by boat, both movements in violation of U.S. immigration laws.

The domestic significance of international migration to the United States has also increased in both reality and perception. The reality is that total immigration numbers (legal, illegal, refugees, asylum-claimants) increased dramatically during the same period that domestic demographic patterns experienced the equally dramatic fertility decline now known as the "baby bust." As a result of these two countervailing trends, international immigration (all types combined) has become a major factor in U.S. demographic change, accounting for at least 30 to 40 percent of U.S. demographic increase (versus perhaps 15 percent in the 1960s).[1] At the same time, it is only fair to note that the gross annual number of immigrants is probably not larger than that around the turn of the twentieth century (before U.S. immigration was first numerically restricted), and that since the U.S. population was much smaller then, these earlier movements accounted for a substantially larger ratio of immigrants to residents.[2] (For a summary of available data on U.S. immigration [legal only] since the early nineteenth century, see table 1.)

Superimposed upon such realities is the perception that immigration to the United States is "out of control"—a characterization widely used by persons at all points of the U.S. political spectrum. The growth of illegal immigration at a time of high unemployment, the "boat people"

TABLE 1
LEGAL IMMIGRATION TO THE UNITED
STATES 1820–1980[a]

Year	Number of Persons	% of Total[b]
1820	8,385	0.0
1821–1830	143,439	0.3
1831–1840	599,125	1.2
1841–1850	1,713,251	3.5
1851–1860	2,598,214	5.2
1861–1870	2,314,824	4.7
1871–1880	2,812,191	5.7
1881–1890	5,246,613	10.6
1891–1900	3,687,564	7.4
1901–1910	8,795,386	17.7
1911–1920	5,735,811	11.6
1921–1930	4,107,209	8.3
1931–1940	528,431	1.1
1941–1950	1,035,039	2.1
1951–1960	2,515,479	5.1
1961–1970	3,321,677	6.7
1971–1980	4,493,314	9.0
Total	49,655,952	

Source: Adapted from U.S. Immigration and Naturalization Service, *1980 Statistical Yearbook* (Washington, D.C., nd), table 1.

a. From 1820 to 1867, figures represent alien pas-
sengers arrived; from 1868 through 1891 and 1895
though 1897, immigrant aliens arrived; from 1892
through 1894 and 1898 to the present time, immigrant
aliens admitted.

b. Percentages do not add to 100.0 because of
rounding.

crisis in Southeast Asia in 1978–1979, and the traumatic experiences surrounding the 1980 Cuban boatlift all have contributed to this perception.

The centrality of Latin America and the Caribbean for these realities
and perceptions is easy to explain. During the 1960s and 1970s, some 40
percent of *legal* immigrants to the United States originated in this one
region (see table 2). The most important regional source countries for
legal immigration were: Mexico (which in the 1970s accounted for nearly
as many legal immigrants as did the whole of Europe); Cuba; the Dominican Republic; Jamaica; Colombia; and several others, such as Haiti,
Trinidad and Tobago, El Salvador, Ecuador, and Guyana.[3]

For obvious reasons, official data are available only for legal immigrants, as described above. But many countries in Latin America and the

TABLE 2

PERCENTAGE OF LEGAL IMMIGRATION TO THE UNITED STATES BY REGION AND COUNTRY, 1881–1980

Region or Country	1881–1890	1891–1900	1901–1910	1911–1920	1921–1930	1931–1940	1941–1950	1951–1960	1961–1970	1971–1980	1971–1975	1976–1980
Latin America and Caribbean	0.6	1.0	2.1	7.0	14.4	9.7	17.7	24.6	39.2	40.3	41.2	39.7
Mexico	0.0	0.0	0.6	3.8	11.2	4.2	5.9	11.9	13.7	14.2	16.5	12.6
Caribbean	0.6	0.9	1.2	2.2	1.8	2.9	4.8	4.9	14.2	16.5	16.4	16.5
Central America	0.0	0.0	0.1	0.3	0.4	1.1	2.1	1.8	3.1	3.0	2.4	3.5
South America	0.0	0.0	0.2	0.7	1.0	1.5	2.1	3.6	7.8	6.6	5.9	7.1
Other America	0.0	0.0	0.0	0.0	0.0	0.0	2.8	2.4	0.6	0.0	0.0	0.0
Europe	90.3	96.4	91.6	75.3	60.0	65.8	60.0	52.7	33.8	17.8	21.8	14.8
Asia	1.3	2.0	3.7	4.3	2.7	3.0	3.1	6.0	12.9	35.3	30.5	39.0
Africa	0.0	0.0	0.1	0.1	0.2	0.3	0.7	0.6	0.9	1.8	1.4	2.1
Canada/ Newfoundland	7.5	0.1	2.0	12.9	22.5	20.5	16.6	15.0	12.4	3.8	4.1	3.5
Australia/ New Zealand	0.1	0.1	0.1	0.2	0.2	0.4	1.3	0.5	0.6	0.5	0.6	0.5
Pacific Islands (U.S.)	0.1	0.0	0.0	0.0	0.0	0.1	0.5	0.2	0.1	0.0	0.0	0.0
Not Specified	0.0	0.4	0.4	0.0	0.0	0.0	0.0	0.5	0.1	0.4	0.3	0.4
Total	100.0	100.0	100.0	100.0	100.0	100.0	100.0	100.0	100.0	100.0	100.0	100.0
Total Legal Immigration	5,246,613	3,687,564	8,795,386	5,735,811	4,107,209	528,431	1,035,039	2,515,479	3,321,677	4,493,314	1,936,281	2,557,033

Source: Calculated from U.S. Immigration and Naturalization Service, 1980 Statistical Yearbook (Washington, D.C., nd), table 2.

Caribbean, including some of those listed above as important source countries for legal immigrants, are also prominent sources of illegal or undocumented immigrants. A listing of such countries normally would include: Mexico, the Dominican Republic, Jamaica, Colombia, Haiti, El Salvador, and perhaps a few others.

If conservative assumptions are made about the overall size and origins of illegal immigration, the percentage of total immigration coming from Latin America and the Caribbean would rise from the 40 percent accounted for by legal immigration to 50 percent or more. Hence Latin America, comprising about 8 percent of the world's population, accounts for 50 percent or more of U.S. immigrants.[4] Moreover, the U.S. perception of "lack of control" is focused on flows from Latin America and the Caribbean, although in reality there is very substantial illegal immigration from many other parts of the world.

The phenomenon of large-scale hemispheric migration is by no means restricted to flows to the United States. Immigration of comparable, and in some cases greater, proportional magnitude has been experienced by Venezuela (where some experts estimate that 2 to 4 million of the 19 million inhabitants are international immigrants), the Bahamas (where the number of undocumented Haitians is large relative to the national population), Panama, the Dominican Republic, Honduras before the 1969 "Soccer War" with El Salvador, and other countries in Latin America and the Caribbean.

Major Contending Perspectives on the Causes of Migration

As one might expect, facts and perceptions such as these are interpreted quite differently, depending upon the perspective of the observer. Although perspectives on the signficance of international migration are almost as numerous as the perceivers, these perspectives fall into two broad categories: theoretical views of the process of international migration and political perspectives on the significance of this process.

Theoretical Perspectives

At the risk of some oversimplification, theoretical perspectives on international migration may be divided into two broad categories: (1) the so-called structuralist theoretical perspective widely held in Latin America, and (2) the so-called push-pull theoretical perspective more widely held in the United States. The structuralist perspective on international migration is in effect a subset of generalized dependency theory, in which the system of core (western industrialized nations), periphery, and semi-periphery countries (categories embracing developing nations) implies that wages are highest in the core and lowest in the periphery.[5] The periphery has a labor surplus relative to its depleted capital base, and the core has a capital surplus relative to its own labor supply. Moreover, there is a natural tendency for labor to migrate to the highest wage areas, where it is exploited to the benefit of the core countries. Thus international migration is attributed to the world capitalist system, in which it contributes to the enrichment of the core nations. The countries of origin are seen as powerless to contain it, bear no responsibility for its consequences, and should be entitled to compensation for the loss of human capital.

Both dependency theory and the structuralist migration subtheory derive from the long theoretical tradition of Marxian or quasi-Marxian analysis of international economic relations. Their answer to the problems posed by underdevelopment in the periphery and by international migration is the transformation of the world economic system through the transfer of power and resources from the core to the periphery, or to a system closer to that of a socialist model, or both.

The second major theoretical construct concerning international migration is the so-called push-pull theory. In this construct, international migration is stimulated both by "push" factors in the sending countries and by "pull" factors in the receiving countries. In a sense, international migration is analogous to the flow of electricity between two poles of differing potentials, or to the flow of water from a higher to a lower point. Both "push" and "pull" are needed for the flows to occur.

The principal "push" factors are those of unemployment, limited economic opportunity, low wages, and political instability and violence in the sending countries. The principal "pull" factors are, in turn, those of lower unemployment rates, higher economic opportunities, higher wages, and more attractive political and social circumstances in the receiving countries. Migration in response to "push" and "pull" factors is facilitated both by direct labor recruitment in the earlier stages and by the subsequent formation of so-called social networks—ties of extended family, village, or larger social groups through which information about opportunities in the "pull" countries is communicated. Other intermediary networks include those of international communications (including television, radio, telephone, and mail), international transportation facilities, and service-providers such as travel agents, immigration lawyers, and smugglers.

In effect, the "push-pull" theory of international migration is less a theory and more an empirical generalization that seeks to describe the forces furthering international migration without attributing blame to either "push" or "pull" factors.[6]

In addition to these two broad conceptual views, other perspectives on international migration are derived from concerns about human rights. Here international migration by individuals is viewed as a basic human right, on the basis of theological and philosophical ideas often derived from axioms or first principles. As such, the right to migrate is necessarily of higher importance than the right of the nation-state to control entry. From this perspective, freedom of international movement may be comprehensively defined to include any movement that any individual wishes to make, or it may be circumscribed by provisions that limit this right to those seeking to escape political repression and/or desperate poverty.

Political Perspectives

Although these different conceptions inform many political perspectives on international migration, they do not fully explain or characterize such political responses. Political perceptions are necessarily value-laden, while in some respects both the structuralist and the push-pull theoretical constructs are (or at least claim to be) scientific and value-free. A categorization of political perspectives on international migration would include at least the following:

1. Laissez faire: Migration is a positive force and should not be limited. Alternative rationales include: (a) Migration is a symptom of an inequitable economic system; the solution lies in resolving the inequities, not in restricting the flow; (b) Labor is a factor of production, and the "invisible hand" of the market should determine the size and direction of its international movement; (c) International migration benefits both sending and receiving countries; (d) International migration serves as an important "safety valve" by relieving unemployment pressures in sending countries, and it contributes to their development through remittances sent home and job skills learned abroad; (e) The right to move internationally is a basic human right that cannot morally be infringed upon by nation-states, especially when the movement is caused by desperate poverty or political repression.

2. Positive but limited: International migration is a positively valued force, but only if it is limited and regulated to ensure that it causes only minor negative consequences. (a) Immigration furthers creativity, pluralism, and/or family unity in the receiving economy, but it must not be allowed to affect negatively the receiving country's labor markets (a view typically held by labor unions) or to exceed its "absorptive capacity" in terms of social cohesion. (b) Emigration provides a productive outlet for ambitious people unable to find opportunity at home, but it must not be allowed to siphon off the most energetic and/or best-trained manpower from the sending countries (the "brain drain" perspective).

3. Negative: International migration of any significant size is a nega-

tive factor for national cohesiveness and development, and it should be reduced or halted. (a) Substantial immigration inevitably damages the lower-paid sectors of the domestic labor force, and it weakens organized labor in the receiving country. Such migration also distorts the economies of both sending and receiving countries. (b) Immigration leads to serious social and political divisions along ethnic, racial, linguistic, religious, or nationality lines.

Quite clearly, several of these political perspectives could draw upon either the structuralist or the push-pull theoretical view for support, and some often invoke human rights arguments as well.

Causes and Consequences of International Migration

What is now known, with reasonable objectivity, about the causes and consequences of recent patterns in the international movement of peoples?

It should be noted from the outset that there is a sharp distinction, in both international and national codes of law, between international movements of temporary or permanent migrants and movements of refugees. Refugees hold a special place in international law. They fall under the protection of the United Nations Convention on the Status of Refugees and its associated Protocol, to which some ninety-two nations have now acceded. Some important Latin American countries (such as Mexico, Honduras, Haiti, Cuba, and Uruguay) are not among this group, although several of these countries have a long and generous tradition of granting asylum to small numbers of political exiles.

In the United States, the Refugee Act of 1980 transformed the definition of "refugee" from Cold War concepts of the 1952 Immigration and Nationality Act (in which a refugee was defined as a person fleeing "from a Communist-dominated country or area, or from any country within the general area of the Middle East"[7]) to one that is based almost verbatim upon the U.N. Protocol. A refugee is defined as "any person who is outside any country of such person's nationality . . . . and who is unable or unwilling to return to, and is unable or unwilling to avail himself or herself of the protection of, that country because of persecution or a well-founded fear of persecution on account of race, religion, nationality, membership in a particular social group, or political opinion."[8]

Thus both international and U.S. law now seek to distinguish clearly between those people driven from their homelands by "persecution" and those emigrating for reasons of better economic opportunity, family ties, and so forth. In practice, of course, it is increasingly difficult to draw such sharp distinctions with assurance, especially in cases in which countries of origin are both poor and authoritarian. This combination characterizes many developing countries today; examples in Latin America would include Paraguay, Cuba, Haiti, Nicaragua, El Salvador, and Guatemala. In addition, since refugee status confers substantial advantages on prospective migrants in terms of legal and economic rights, it appears that this status is increasingly claimed in marginal and dubious cases.

With regard to the causes and consequences of recent migration patterns of all types, *none* of the theoretical or political perspectives described above provides an adequate analysis that draws upon all available empirical evidence. Available evidence tends to support a given theoretical or political perspective in some respects, while in other respects contradicting it. Hence an adequate response requires an eclectic analytical approach that may be viewed as "untidy" or esthetically unsatisfactory by observers with sharply defined worldviews. Unhappily for them, the facts concerning international migration are notoriously untidy.

Causes of Recent Migration

At its most general level, the acceleration of immigration from developing countries to industrialized countries may be understood as a rational response by intelligent human beings to the large and often increasing differentials in economic and political circumstances. Sometimes the perception of these differentials exceeds their reality, as in the "streets are paved with gold" fantasy. However, it is no fantasy that the real costs of international migration have declined, while access to the option has grown. In economic terms, the "value" (real and perceived) of international migration is going up, while the "real price" is going down and the availability is becoming more widespread.

The *value* of international migration is increasing because of worsening levels of unemployment and underemployment in many developing countries, the large and frequently increasing differentials in prevailing wages between sending and receiving countries, and the growing political instability of many sending countries. Although unemployment rates in industrialized countries recently have been at record post-World War II levels, averaging fully 9 percent in late 1982, these high levels are dwarfed by the 20 to 40 percent (and sometimes higher) levels of unemployment in many developing countries.[9] Similarly, although real wages have not increased rapidly in many industrialized countries over the past decade, they have often declined in developing countries, and the differential between sending and receiving countries is frequently very large and often increasing.

To take an obvious example, Mexico's estimated unemployment and underemployment rates have generally exceeded those of the United States by a substantial margin. After the onset of a severe economic crisis in 1982, Mexico's unemployment rate rose still higher, while government subsidies for food and other essentials simultaneously were reduced. Real wages declined by an estimated 30 percent from 1983 through 1984.[10] Moreover, prevailing wages for comparable jobs in the United States have long been between five and ten times as high as those in Mexico. Despite some substantial wage increases in Mexico, the peso's loss of nearly 90 percent of its value vis-à-vis the dollar (from 24 pesos to the dollar in early 1982 to well over 300 to the dollar in mid-1985) means that the already high wage differential must have increased substantially.

A related problem often tied to economic difficulties resulting from world recession is the increased level of political instability in many sending countries. This has encouraged both capital flight (thereby exacerbating existing economic problems) and the departure of those often skilled people who have the option to emigrate.

The *"real price"* of international migration has declined over the same period. There has been a broad expansion of international transport via jet aircraft, with regular flights now reaching into the hinterlands as well as the capitals of most developing countries. The information and contacts necessary to organize international migration have similarly improved with the wide diffusion of telephones, television, radio, and other means of international communication. The rapid urbanization process so characteristic of developing countries in recent decades has also facilitated international migration by bringing potential migrants into closer contact with these means of transportation and communication. Moreover, the capabilities of some receiving nations' immigration authorities (and particularly those of the United States) have deteriorated over the same period (see below).

The *availability* of the migration option has become more widespread, in part because of the aforementioned increase in knowledge and access and the parallel decline in the real cost of such movement. In addition, capital accumulation and the growth of formal and informal money-lending institutions (banks, private moneylenders, savings by the extended family) in many developing countries have facilitated the access of quite low-income persons to the capital required to finance migration. Such borrowing has been facilitated by high appreciation of land values, which in some settings now provides even small landholders with substantial loan collateral. These loans, even at high interest rates, can be expected to be readily repayable out of the incremental earnings expected from higher wages in the country to which the international migrant plans to move.

Finally, during the last decade there has been substantial growth of what might be termed "intermediaries" that facilitate international migration (either legal or illegal). These include the profession of immigration law, the appearance of so-called immigration consultants, increases in international migration services provided by various travel agencies, the

proliferation of labor recruiters, and the development of significant networks of smugglers and other individuals engaged in the illicit movement
of people across national borders. Intermediary networks are now quite
prominent in facilitating Colombian migration to Venezuela and the
United States, Mexican and Asian migration to the United States, and
Caribbean migration to other Caribbean nations and beyond.[11]

On the demand or "pull" side, there are several economies in the
Western Hemisphere that recently have encouraged or otherwise facilitated international migration in order to staff positions that cannot easily
be filled with indigenous workers. The most obvious hemispheric examples
are Venezuela's oil-boom economy between 1974 and 1981 and certain
sectors of the U.S. economy (especially agriculture and construction in the
Southwest, the restaurant and hotel industries in some regions, and the
garment industry). Employers in such settings have a strong economic
incentive to recruit workers willing to work under conditions that do not
require capital investment, job restructuring, or substantial increases in
wages and benefits. There is only limited empirical evidence that such
employers have directly solicited the migration of potential workers from
sending countries, but they do appear to recruit actively from the labor
pool provided by such immigration. It is important to note that in the
United States, it is quite legal for employers to employ persons they know
to be in the country illegally. In Venezuela it is said that "work permits can
be obtained relatively easily and quickly . . . . for a fee."[12]

Another factor encouraging increases in international migration has
been the effective immobilization of immigration controls in some of the
major receiving countries. The most obvious case is that of the United
States, which has experienced growing problems in enforcing its own
rather arcane immigration laws. The reasons for this include: (1) an endemic ambivalence concerning immigration controls, given the persistent
image of the United States as a "nation of immigrants"; (2) a national
sensitivity to accusations of "racism" (whether justified or not), growing
out of recognition of past racist patterns in the United States; (3) a
general trend toward special interest politics, in which a small minority
with strong interest in an issue often is able to prevail over a large majority with more limited interest in the subject. Such special interests in
immigration policy include employers of undocumented workers, ethnic
activists, and proponents of a variety of political or theological value
systems; (4) a national tendency toward litigiousness, encouraged generally by very large numbers of lawyers and financed in the case of immigration issues by philanthropic and government funds or the availability
of contingency fees (not allowed in many other western countries). Together these factors have led to lengthy court battles that have immobilized or weakened immigration law enforcement; (5) accidents of history;

for example, the chairmanship of the U.S. Senate Judiciary Committee in the early 1970s was held by Senator James Eastland, a conservative southern Democrat with personal agricultural interests, who blocked passage of "employer sanctions" twice passed by the House of Representatives. This pattern of waning enforcement efforts was true until 1980. There was a sharp reversal of the trend after the chaotic experience of the 1980 Mariel boatlift (in which 125,000 Cubans migrated to southern Florida outside of U.S. immigration laws) and following the electoral defeat of President Jimmy Carter.

Another important factor contributing to the growth of international migration is past international migration. These migrations, stimulated in part by past labor importation policies such as the United States and Mexico's so-called *bracero* program (1942–1964), have generated family, kin, and village networks that serve as sources of information and financing for subsequent international migration. Past migrations have also led to the separation of nuclear and extended families, which are sometimes "reunited" subsequently via further international migration.

Finally, the domestic and foreign policies of a number of hemispheric nations contribute substantially to international migration flows. An obvious example is the emigration of nearly 10 percent of Cuba's population (mostly to the United States) since Fidel Castro's rise to power in 1959 and the increase in foreign policy tensions between the two countries. Another example is the substantial number of refugees generated by internal strife in several Central American countries, strife that has been exacerbated by the foreign policies of other states. A third, less numerically significant example is the provision of political asylum within the region to 20,000 to 30,000 exiles from Chile after the military's overthrow of President Salvador Allende in 1973. Finally, there is the rather fascinating example of the migration of about 300,000 Brazilian nationals into Paraguay's eastern border region surrounding the massive Itaipu hydroelectric project. This mass migration, which now dominates about one-third of Paraguay's territory, began in the mid-1960s, accelerated after the signing of the Brazil-Paraguay treaty regarding Itaipu in 1972, and apparently has received at least implicit encouragement from the governments of both countries.

Consequences of Labor Migration

An assessment of the consequences of international migration must be as eclectic as an analysis of its causes. It is important to emphasize that the consequences of migration must be viewed in a time-bound perspective: the effects of migration at one time may be quite different from the effects of a similar migration at another time. For example, the movement of large numbers of Colombians into Venezuela may have had positive economic effects during the heyday of the oil boom in Venezuela, but negative effects after the onset of recession in the early 1980s.

There is also a distinction to be made between the short- to medium-term effects of international migration and its long-term effects. For example, in the short term, migration from Colombia to fill labor shortages in the Venezuelan construction industry may have produced a net positive contribution to Venezuela's economic development. But in the long term, there are important issues raised by the continuing presence of an immigrant population numbering perhaps 2 to 4 million in Venezuela's total resident population of 19 million people. This is especially problematic given that a substantial proportion of the immigrant population is resident without benefit of legal status.[13]

With these caveats, one assessment of the consequences of large-scale immigration to the United States would be as follows: throughout the early frontier and industrial history of the United States, immigrants supplied unskilled labor to what was the classic resource-rich and labor-poor developing country of the nineteenth century. Immigrants also provided important infusions of technical and entrepreneurial skills. However, the United States in 1985 is no longer resource rich and labor poor. Over the past decade unemployment has been at uncomfortably high levels. It is particularly high among the unskilled labor force, and among minority youth unemployment rates have ranged as high as 50 percent.

Despite high unemployment at the lower levels of the U.S. domestic labor force, unskilled immigrant workers usually find jobs. In part, their relative success is due to their willingness to hold jobs that—by U.S. standards—provide very low pay and benefits or present other unattractive conditions. Given the aforementioned differentials between sending and receiving countries, these jobs may seem very attractive to the immigrant. As they are presently structured, such jobs do not attract great interest from the domestic labor force even during times of high unemployment, because many unemployed workers have alternative sources of income that exceed the financial rewards offered by such employment. (For example, a domestic maid in El Paso is said to earn about forty dollars per week with no social security or other benefits and no limit on the number of hours that can be worked.)

As long as a labor pool is available and willing to work for this level of remuneration, employers have no economic incentive to upgrade conditions and terms of employment or to invest in labor-saving technologies that become economical only under conditions of higher labor costs. Thus one long-term effect of continuing inflows of low-skill labor may be to retard capital investment and restrain growth in the productivity of labor (or output per man-hour)—another economic indicator whose slow improvement causes great concern among U.S. policymakers when it is compared to productivity growth in Japan and other competitive economies.

On the other hand, some analysts in the United States and elsewhere believe that the immigration of low-skill labor maintains the economic competitiveness of certain U.S. economic activities (such as the garment industry). Such immigration provides cheap and willing labor to compete with that of low-wage countries such as Hong Kong and Taiwan, thereby keeping U.S. firms from exporting production. From this perspective, immigration has restrained unemployment, because marginal firms that are kept in business employ U.S. citizens as well as immigrants.

An assessment of arguments such as these depends essentially upon one's worldview. If the goal is to sustain labor-intensive, low-productivity industries that must compete in a world market with imports from low-wage nations, then the importation of cheap labor surely contributes to such a goal, as does the imposition of tariffs or quotas on such products. If, on the other hand, the goal is gradually to redirect resources toward higher-productivity industries requiring a skilled labor force, there is less concern about allowing imports from low-wage countries to prevail in sectors such as the garment industry.

Apart from such special cases, it is very difficult to argue convincingly that a highly advanced economy such as that of the United States in 1985 requires a continuing large-scale flow of low-skilled labor, although certain employers or economic subsectors surely benefit from such flows. To the contrary, the high unemployment rates in the low-skill sector suggest that domestic low-skilled labor is in considerable surplus, and that relatively high education and work skills are virtual necessities for employment in high-productivity occupations. Of course, shortages of unskilled and semiskilled labor *could* arise in such an economy during a sustained economic boom of large magnitude, such as that which led to the *gastarbeiter* ("guest worker") programs in western Europe from the 1950s to the early 1970s. But our capacity to anticipate such long-term economic trends is poorly developed.

Given the characteristics of current migration flows to the United States, it is likely that their major economic impacts are *distributional* in form. The beneficiaries of large-scale immigration are the immigrants themselves and those employers and middle-class consumers who benefit from the availability of cheap labor in the industrial, agricultural, and service sectors. The losers are the relatively disadvantaged U.S. citizens and recent immigrants who find themselves in the same labor markets that attract the newer immigrants. These U.S. workers are at a disadvantage in such markets because the economic expectations of an immigrant from a low-wage country are likely to be far lower than those of a U.S. resident. Although some direct displacement of U.S. workers certainly results, this may be small. The more important effects are likely to be indirect—the availability of an immigrant labor force willing to work under poor employment conditions tends to distort downward the conditions at the lower end of the labor force. This produces a self-fulfilling prophecy: these jobs will not be attractive to U.S. workers, and therefore they "require" the continued importation of foreign labor with lower expectations.

The impact of large-scale out-migration on sending countries is equally complex, often with variable effects in different sectors. The migrant can be assumed to benefit, or at least to expect to do so; otherwise emigration would have to be considered irrational. Such benefits may accrue to the migrant even if he is subjected to "exploitation" or other mistreatment by the standards of the host country. For example, a migrant who is paid exploitatively low wages in a highly industrialized country may still be earning far more than he could expect in his country of origin, because of large differentials between the two countries in employment opportunities and prevailing wage rates. (Indeed, such a phenomenon underlies the negative effects such migrants are posited to have on the lower echelons of the receiving country's labor force, discussed above.)

From the perspective of the government of the sending country, the effects of migration are usually perceived as mixed. If migrants are mainly low-skilled workers moving out of a high-unemployment sector of the economy, emigration is usually viewed as positive in economic and political terms. In such settings, emigration reduces unemployment, underemployment, and the political problems they often generate. Emigration also relieves the government of providing services and infrastructure for these workers, while stimulating hard-currency remittances of foreign earnings.

At the same time, sending governments are often embarrassed by the apparent desire of so many of their nationals to move abroad. They are also offended by the frequent mistreatment and exploitation to which their citizens are subjected in the host country—especially if the migration is extralegal (as in much Mexico–United States and Colombia–Venezuela migration) or "temporary" (as in Turkey–Federal Republic of Germany migration).

Finally, there is concern in many sending countries regarding the long-term effects of out-migration on their economic development. These concerns are related primarily to the loss of skilled manpower to higher-wage positions abroad, even though such workers often experience downward social mobility and may be unable to employ their skills fully in the host country. The departure of such skilled personnel can lead to development bottlenecks at home, as have occurred recently in sending countries such as Egypt, Sudan, Jamaica, and Mexico. These concerns give rise to debates concerning the so-called brain drain and whether the receiving countries should be required to compensate the country of origin for providing the migrant with the necessary education and skills training. International fora such as the International Labor Organization's (ILO) 1976 world employment conference and the U.N. General Assembly have urged the adoption of international conventions of this kind.[14]

Future Prospects for International Migration

In some respects, future prospects for international migration from Latin America to the United States are relatively predictable. However, many dimensions of the phenomenon cannot be forecast reliably. The relatively predictable elements derive from demographic projections of future changes in the labor force in Latin American countries. These projections are quite robust for the remainder of this century, primarily because most of the labor force in the year 2000 has already been born. The main uncertainties concern possible changes in labor force participation rates, but the size and age-sex composition of the *potential* labor force is relatively predictable, short of unexpected upward or downward changes in mortality.

Two useful series of labor force projections for Latin America have been produced by respected international agencies. The first was published in 1977 by the ILO and the second in 1979 by the Latin American Demographic Center (CELADE, a component of the United Nations Economic Commission for Latin America). These two series were combined in a technical document produced by the Inter-American Development Bank.[15]

In brief summary, the projections show that for much of Latin America (excluding the Southern Cone and a few other small countries), the rapid demographic increase experienced in the 1960s and 1970s will engender very substantial labor force growth in the 1980s and 1990s. The Inter-American Development Bank states that the "predominant pattern of labor force increases in the region . . . . is seen as a steady pace of gain on the order of 15–19 percent per quinquennium in the 1980–2000 interval. This is the case in such major countries as Brazil, Colombia, Mexico and all Category III (high mortality) countries (except Haiti). In all, countries where this pattern holds contain 80 percent of Latin America's labor force."[16] Once again excluding the Southern Cone, all Latin American countries are projected to experience labor force increases of from 50 percent (Trinidad and Tobago) to over 100 percent (Mexico, Honduras, Nicaragua, El Salvador) by the year 2000. For most Latin American countries, the projected 1980–2000 labor force increases exceed those in the 1960–1980 period. This is notably the case for Mexico (a 103 percent increase projected for 1980–2000), Honduras (109 percent increase), and most Central American countries other than Costa Rica.

There can be no reasonable doubt, then, that much of Latin America must expect exceptionally large labor force increases during the remainder of this century. Although many of the countries in question are seeking or experiencing important declines in fertility, such declines can have little effect upon labor force growth during this period, since most of the labor force that will be present in the year 2000 has already been born. As previously noted, some uncertainties exist concerning the course of labor force participation rates, but the basic trends are reasonably clear.

The ability of projected U.S. labor force growth to meet the future needs of the economy is much less predictable. Due to fertility declines since the mid-1960s, those groups of labor force entering age will not grow as rapidly in the 1980s and 1990s as in the early 1970s, when the "baby boom" generation born in the period from 1947 to 1965 reached working age. This fact has led some analysts to predict physical shortages of U.S. labor in the 1990s and, based on these estimates, to recommend a policy of large-scale immigration.[17]

The most recent labor force projections for the United States were published in 1983 by the Bureau of Labor Statistics (BLS); they are abstracted in table 3. The civilian labor force is projected to increase from about 107 million in 1980 to a range of 130 to 150 million in 2000. The rate of labor force growth projected for the 1990s is substantial, ranging from 0.8 to 1.4 percent and 1 to 1.9 million annually. Earlier projections (such as those by the ILO, also summarized in table 3) showed trends of similar magnitudes, though it should be noted that the most recent BLS projections indicate a considerably larger labor force for the 1990s than do projections prepared in the 1970s, upon which some of the predictions of future labor shortages were based. For example, if the 1983 BLS projections are compared to the 1978 BLS projections employed by Reynolds,[18] it is clear that the passage of only five years resulted in labor force projections for the year 2000 that are higher by 10 to 15 million, or about 10 percent.

In fact, all projections must be seen as quantitative speculations that become less plausible as they move further into the future. In practice, most U.S. labor force projections produced in the 1970s proved to be poor predictors because of underestimation of the growth of female labor force participation and immigration. Current projections may also underestimate these elements, as well as the future labor force participation rates of persons in their 60s (especially given recent legislation that bars

TABLE 3
LABOR FORCE PROJECTIONS FOR THE UNITED STATES TO THE YEAR 2000

	Bureau of Labor Statistics, 1983						International Labor Organization, 1977					
	High Demographic Variant			Low Demographic Variant			High Demographic Variant			Low Demographic Variant		
		Average Annual Growth in Preceding Period			Average Annual Growth in Preceding Period			Average Annual Growth in Preceding Period			Average Annual Growth in Preceding Period	
	Numbers (millions)	(millions)	%	Numbers (millions)	(millions)	%	Numbers (millions)	(millions)	%	Numbers (millions)	(millions)	%
1980[a]	106.9	2.4	2.6	106.9	2.4	2.6	102.0	1.5	1.52	102.0	1.5	1.52
1985	119.5	2.5	2.2	114.3	1.5	1.3	108.2	1.2	1.18	108.2	1.2	1.17
1990	131.3	2.4	1.9	120.3	1.2	1.0	114.1	1.2	1.06	113.1	1.0	.90
1995	141.0	1.9	1.4	125.1	1.0	.8	121.9	1.6	1.34	118.0	1.0	.84
2000	150.0	1.8	1.2	130.1	1.0	.8	132.5	2.1	1.67	123.2	1.0	.88

Sources: Bureau of Labor Statistics: Howard N. Fullerton, Jr., and John Tschetter, "The 1995 Labor Force: A Second Look," *Monthly Labor Review*, 106 (November 1983): 3–11; International Labor Office, *Labour Force Estimates and Projections, 1950–2000*, 2d ed., (Geneva, 1977), vol. 5, table 6.

a. 1980 ILO figure is projected from 1975 and is lower than actual labor force as estimated by BLS.

compulsory retirement before age seventy and raises the age of retirement for social security pension purposes). Moreover, it is almost impossible to predict accurately future labor force demand, given the rapid technological change now underway and the uncertainty about the path of future economic growth. In addition, there is the conceptual problem that a gradual tightening of labor markets would be expected to raise relative wages, and thereby stimulate labor-saving innovation.

Economic and political trends in the sending countries are also difficult to predict. It is not at all clear that the probable increases in Latin American labor forces will find productive employment in their own countries over the next fifteen years. This obviously depends upon the future of economic development in these countries—not only the size of aggregate increases of gross national product, but also the kind of development path (labor intensive versus capital intensive, rural versus urban) that is followed.

If employment growth in sending countries is as exceptionally rapid as projected labor force growth, unemployment will not rise. But if job creation of this magnitude does not occur, the employment prospects for those entering the labor force can be expected to decline. This situation would generate additional incentives for emigration in search of work, and it would further tempt governments to encourage such emigration to reduce domestic economic and political pressures.

It is even harder to predict the political events that affect migration, such as the likelihood of political stability, growth or decline in repressive governments in Latin America, or even the possibility of international conflict. It is self-evident that very large flows of international migrants can be produced by a combination of economic hardship, political instability, repression, and/or international tension or strife. For example, it is estimated that fully 10 percent of the populations of Haiti, El Salvador, and Cuba have left those countries for residence abroad, mostly in the United States. In all three cases, much of this migration has been motivated primarily by a desire for better economic opportunities, and therefore many of the migrants do not qualify under the internationally agreed-upon definition of a refugee. Nonetheless, it is clear that poverty and political pressure are a powerful combination inducing departure from one's homeland.

Opportunities for Cooperation and Conflict

International migration presents substantial opportunities for both international cooperation and conflict. After all, the movement of people between countries is an established means of furthering international understanding—as evidenced by the numerous international exchange programs encouraged by both governments and private organizations. Moreover, a history of substantial migration has frequently resulted in closer relations between the sending and receiving countries, as in the case of Italy and Argentina.

However, the effects of migration can also be negative. Vigorous nationalist emotions are frequently raised by real or perceived abuses surrounding international migration. Persistent international tensions can also be generated by the emigration of political opponents to exile abroad. For example, relations between Cuba and the United States have been greatly complicated by the residence in the United States of hundreds of thousands of implacable opponents of the Castro regime. In the last analysis, the contribution of migration to furthering international comity, or to exacerbating international tensions, will depend greatly upon the nature of international migrations and on the way in which they are handled by national governments, the media, and other opinion leaders.

The prospects for maximizing the positive and minimizing the negative effects of migration over the coming decades are complicated by the fact that some sending countries now have a policy (explicit or implicit) of favoring international migration, even if outside the law. Moreover, in many such cases there is also considerable national ambivalence concerning the policy of exporting countrymen abroad, often expressed in righteous indignation at the civil liberties violations and other abuses thought to be experienced by them in the receiving countries.

Most policies favoring emigration of citizens are benign in intent, and they should not be viewed as malevolent or threatening by the receiving countries. These policies are pursued for the same basic reason that other governmental policies are adopted—that is, they are perceived by government officials to be in the national interest of the sending country. Indeed, sending countries now appear to have more control over out-migration than previously thought, and they may actually view migration of this kind as a "national resource" to be managed like any other.[19] Even the United Nations Secretariat, which must confine itself to the official policies or pronouncements of its member states, reports that countries such as El Salvador and Barbados have explicitly encouraged such out-migration. Indeed, in the late 1970s El Salvador explored possible bilateral accords with countries such as Bolivia and Saudi Arabia aimed at facilitating Salvadoran emigration. The United Nations also reports that although the government of Haiti denies encouraging Haitian emigration, it officially acknowledges substantial benefits accruing to Haiti from such movements. Other such unofficial or implicit policies favoring out-migration, such as those of Mexico, are not discussed by the United Nations.[20]

The governments of sending countries may pursue such policies for several reasons. First, remittances sent home by those working abroad may comprise an important share of total foreign currency inflows for some countries. Egypt, India, Turkey, and Mexico are major contemporary examples of this phenomenon. The sums involved in these and other cases are by no means trivial. For example, remittances may exceed foreign currency earnings from raw material exports or tourism. They may make the difference between balance-of-payment surplus or deficit, thereby allowing a continuation of expansionary economic policies at home. The economic significance of remittances has been greatly increased by the foreign currency drain and economic dislocations caused by high oil prices since 1974. Indeed, one economist has estimated that for most developing countries that are not energy exporters, remittances were the only foreign exchange source that increased during the latter half of the 1970s.[21]

Second, the encouragement of out-migration may be used as an instrument of governmental policy to improve or stabilize domestic economic or political conditions. If unemployment and underemployment rates are high, such departures may reduce the need for labor-intensive investments or for unemployment benefits or other income-transfer payments. If land is scarce, the rate of increase in demand may be moderated by the departure of potential landowners. If governmental expenditures on education, health, or other social services are growing so rapidly as to strain available budgetary resources, these too can be moderated by out-migration. Effects of this kind can reduce domestic political ferment favoring the redistribution of resources toward the dispossessed, thereby constituting an emigration "safety valve" in countries such as Mexico.

Third, many developing countries regulate departures via exit visas or other control instruments, and when emigration is highly valued the issuance of such permits may be used as scarce goods, subject to official allocation. Exit visas then may be viewed much in the same way as government employment, housing, private cars, rations, or other regulated goods. Allocations of these goods may be made for a variety of reasons, including: to reward political supporters (as in some eastern European countries); to remove political dissidents (as in Cuba, Vietnam, or Haiti); or as a means of obtaining emigrants' assets, in the form of land, housing, gold, or hard currency (as in Vietnam, Haiti, Uganda, and possibly Cuba).

Fourth, some countries see emigration as an affirmative policy aimed at solidifying political relations and increasing political influence with the countries to which the migrants move. This seems to be part of the basis for Pakistan and India's policy of supplying large numbers of temporary workers to the oil-rich but labor-poor countries of the Persian Gulf, and it may also be a consideration for some Latin American political leaders.

Fifth, perhaps the most time-honored reason for encouraging out-migration is to use it as a means of establishing effective control or outright sovereignty over land outside a country's borders. This was a central component of European colonialism, and during the nineteenth century it played a role in the history of the area now comprising Texas. In recent years, out-migration of this kind has been encouraged by Brazil (to the part of Paraguay surrounding the Itaipu Dam), Israel (the settlements on the West Bank), and Morocco (to the northern part of the former Spanish Sahara claimed by Morocco).

Finally, and most malevolently, there is the tradition of governments "encouraging"—through subtle pressure or outright coercion—the departure of a despised ethnic or religious minority or of a social group or class deemed politically undesirable. Such motives underlay, at least in part, the departure of hundreds of thousands of Cubans in the 1960s and 1970s, the coerced departure of 74,000 Asians from Uganda under Idi Amin, and the flight (after payment of departure fees amounting to several thousand dollars per person) of hundreds of thousands of ethnic Chinese from Vietnam in 1978 and 1979. Similar factors may currently be at work in Central America with respect to the Miskito Indians in Nicaragua and other Indian groups in Guatemala.

If these propositions have any validity, the implication is that countries favoring out-migration can be expected to oppose efforts by the countries of destination to restrict entry of their nationals. However they may characterize their concern in diplomatic terms, it ultimately reflects the sending countries' assessment that their national interest is best served by the continued out-migration of their citizens.

Nonetheless, there are still areas that provide opportunities for important efforts at international cooperation. These fall within four broad categories: (1) measures to reduce the pressures for international migration; (2) agreements to share the burdens produced by refugee movements; (3) agreements concerning the control of undocumented immigration and the rights of such migrants; and (4) measures to compensate sending countries for the "brain drain."

Reducing future pressures for international migration above all requires the generation of sufficient employment opportunities to match the extraordinarily large labor force increases projected for many sending countries. Although the prospects for such employment-generation depend primarily upon the domestic policies of these sovereign states, the effects of international trade, investment, and concessionary assistance should not be minimized. The large size and importance of the U.S.

economy for Latin America are well-known considerations. Thus there is an important role to be played by the United States in providing fair access to its markets for goods produced in Latin America, in facilitating and regulating overseas investment where it is welcome (and especially where it is likely to generate large numbers of jobs), in offering adequate assistance on concessionary terms where circumstances warrant, and in adopting domestic economic policies that do not result in inflated real interest rates and dollar exchange values (which in turn have a negative impact on Latin American debt service problems).

In addition to such affirmative international efforts to generate large numbers of jobs, "tension-management" functions may also be important. Briefly stated, such efforts would seek to restrain internal and/or international tensions that might eventually encourage large numbers of people to leave their homelands, whether or not they qualify under the internationally agreed-on definition of a refugee.

This leads to a second potential area for international cooperation, that of burden-sharing in refugee assistance. The influx of large numbers of refugees presents serious challenges and stresses for all nations, especially for those with limited economic resources. Hence it is essential that refugee movements in the Western Hemisphere be viewed as hemispheric responsibilities to be shared by all nations whether or not they themselves experience the influx. Substantial success along these lines was achieved in the late 1970s during the mass outflow of Vietnamese, with a large number of countries offering temporary asylum, emergency assistance, or permanent resettlement. Given the long-standing commitment in Latin America to the principles of political asylum, similar successes should be possible with regard to the growing numbers of refugees or others fleeing civil strife in Central America.

International cooperation to restrain illegal immigration and smuggling activities will be more difficult, especially when sending countries have implicit policies favoring such departures, as discussed above. Nonetheless, it is worth making efforts in this direction, especially in cases in which cordial bilateral relations are threatened by continuing undocumented migration flows. However, it should be acknowledged that most sending countries in the hemisphere have limited resources to employ for such migration controls, which are primarily the responsibility of the receiving country. That success in this area is possible is amply demonstrated by the cooperation the United States government reportedly has obtained from the Bahamian government concerning the transit of Colombian nationals through the Bahamas on the smuggling route known as the "Sandoval Pipeline"; from the Haitian government regarding the interdiction of Haitian smugglers' boats; and from the Mexican government regarding the control of Mexican-based smuggling rings.[22]

The rights accorded by receiving countries to undocumented immigrants should be part of these discussions. However, sending countries that encourage or tacitly accept the undocumented migration of their citizens have only a limited basis for nationalistic anger when these people experience abuse and discrimination abroad. If it is the obligation of nation-states to protect the rights of their citizens when abroad, one important way to do so is to make all appropriate efforts to ensure that such citizens have a legal status in the countries to which they have moved.

Similarly, countries receiving large numbers of undocumented immigrants, in substantial part because of their own failure to legislate and enforce effective immigration laws, have little basis for complaint when these immigrants claim access to free education, medical care, welfare, and other benefits available to other residents. The case of the state of Texas is particularly instructive here. Under current U.S. law, it is quite legal for an employer to hire a person whom he knows is illegally in the country. In substantial measure this is because of pressures during the 1950s from economic interests in Texas that became dependent upon temporary imported labor during the 1942–1964 *bracero* program (indeed, one relevant section of current federal law is known as the Texas Proviso). Nonetheless, the Texas legislature passed a law requiring the parents of illegal immigrant children to pay fees for public education. This represented an obvious attempt by the Texas political establishment to allow illegal immigration to continue to serve its vested interests, while simultaneously denying immigrants access to services provided at state or local government expense. The U.S. Supreme Court ruled (by a close five to four decision) that such a limit on access to free education was unconstitutional. Issues such as this surely warrant bilateral and multilateral discussion between sending and receiving countries.

Finally, there is the issue of the "brain drain" and proposed multilateral agreements to compensate sending countries for their human capital investment in the migrants. Provisions such as these have been promoted by several nations and by staff members of the ILO.[23] There is obvious merit in the general proposition that nations that explicitly recruit manpower internationally, and thereby receive the benefits of other countries' investments in scarce skills, should be expected to pay some form of compensation. These provisions would apply most appropriately in cases of bilateral treaties governing official temporary worker programs, such as those in the Persian Gulf, in western Europe, and the so-called H-2 program (a temporary worker program used to import Caribbean agricultural workers to the Northeast) in the United States. Indeed, several bilateral and multilateral agreements applying to these programs already exist.[24]

The issue becomes more complicated when the exported skills are in excess supply in the sending country, as evidenced by limited prospects for full employment. This would include unskilled workers in most developing countries and some quite highly skilled workers such as nurses in the Philippines or doctors and engineers in India. The issue becomes intractable when the migrants' skills are in excess supply *and* when the migration is illegal and (implicitly or explicitly) encouraged by the sending country. Under such circumstances it is difficult to see how receiving countries could be convinced of an obligation to compensate sending countries that welcome the unlawful international migration of their nationals.

In general, then, many of the contentious problems surrounding international migration derive from nation-states' differing perceptions of their national interests. In this regard, international migration as an international issue is no different from any other issue, such as security concerns, trade policies, or the law of the sea. Unlike most other issues debated internationally, however, migration uniquely involves human beings. Thus it stimulates passions and concerns that do not arise concerning tariffs on inanimate objects. Notwithstanding such problems, there remains ample scope for international cooperation and agreement about most of the issues posed by international migration.

Alfred P. Sloan Foundation
New York

Notes

This essay was initially written while the author was a Senior Associate of the Carnegie Endowment for International Peace.

1. This "percentage of population growth" calculation can be misleading if growth is near zero. However, even the lowest projections of U.S. population increases show very substantial growth well into the twenty-first century. See United Nations, *Demographic Indicators of Countries* (New York: United Nations, 1982), p. 250.

2. Michael S. Teitelbaum, "Right Versus Right: Immigration and Refugee Policy in the United States," *Foreign Affairs* 59 (Fall 1980): 24–25.

3. See Immigration and Naturalization Service, *1980 Statistical Yearbook* (Washington, D.C., nd), table 13.

4. According to United Nations estimates, the 1984 midyear population in Latin America and the Caribbean was 400.2 million, versus a world estimate of 4.745 billion. In other words, about 8 percent of the world's population lives in Latin America. United Nations, *Demographic Indicators,* pp. 58, 176.

5. See, for example, Alejandro Portes, "Toward a Structural Analysis of Illegal (Undocumented) Immigration," *International Migration Review* 12, No. 4 (Winter 1978): 469–84.

6. For an extended discussion of such theoretical perspectives by a leading

structuralist theorist, see Alejandro Portes, *Latin Journey: Cuban and Mexican Immigrants in the United States* (Berkeley and Los Angeles: University of California Press, 1985).

7. Immigration and Nationality Act, section 203(a)(7), repealed.

8. 94. Stat. 102, Public Law 96–212, "Refugee Act of 1980," Section 201(42).

9. Organization for Economic Cooperation and Development, *OECD Economic Outlook,* No. 32, December 1982.

10. *New York Times,* 26 February 1985, p. 13.

11. See, for example, the series of investigative reports in the *Miami Herald,* 5–8 December 1982, entitled "The People Smugglers."

12. Mary M. Kritz, "International Migration Patterns in the Caribbean Basin: An Overview," in Mary M. Kritz, Charles B. Keely, and Silvano M. Tomasi, eds., *Global Trends in Migration: Theory and Research on International Population Movements* (Staten Island, N.Y.: Center for Migration Studies, 1981), p. 226.

13. Ibid. See also Centro de Estudios de Pastoral y Assistencia Migratoria (CEPAM), *Acontecer migratorio,* 2, No. 13 (November/December 1979): 26.

14. W. R. Böhning, "International Migration and the International Economic Order," *Journal of International Affairs* 33, No. 2 (Fall/Winter 1979): 194.

15. Inter-American Development Bank, "Population, Labor Force, and Employment," internal technical paper, ca. 1979.

16. Ibid.

17. Clark Reynolds, "Labor Market Projections for the United States and Mexico and Their Relevance to Current Migration Controversies," paper presented to the American Assembly on U.S.–Mexico Relations, 1979; also "Labor Market Projections for the United States and Mexico and Current Migration Controversies," *Food Research Institute Studies* 17, No. 2 (1979): 121–56.

18. Ibid.

19. Myron Weiner, "Migration and Development in the Gulf," *Population and Development Review* 8, No. 1 (March 1982): 1–36.

20. United Nations, *International Migration Policies and Programmes: A World Survey* (New York: United Nations, 1982), p. 17.

21. Philip L. Martin, "Emigration and Development: Some Background and Issues," *Migration Today* (forthcoming, 1985).

22. These comments are based on the author's personal communications with various U.S. government officials.

23. Böhning, "International Migration and the International Economic Order."

24. See Mark J. Miller and Philip L. Martin, *Administering Foreign-Worker Programs: Lessons from Europe* (Lexington, Mass.: Lexington Books, 1982), chapter 4 and Appendices B–J.

17

COMMENT: The International Migration of Labor and Its Influence on U.S.–Latin American Relations

Gabriel Murillo Castaño

The impact of international labor migration on political, economic, and sociodemographic change in both host countries and sending countries and the magnitude of contemporary international population movements in the Americas make this issue a vital part of U.S.–Latin American relations. The influence of labor migration on international relations at bilateral and/or multilateral levels is increasingly important because of the domestic political significance that it has for the countries involved. A better understanding of the causes and consequences of labor migration can enhance the quality of policy decisions, and it can thus improve relations between the United States and Latin America at a time when they have been significantly altered by events such as the 1982 Malvinas (Falklands) conflict and political instability in Central America.

Theoretical Frameworks for the Study of Labor Migration

Given the limited space available in a comment such as this, it may appear unwise to attempt a brief overview of the main theoretical frameworks used in the social sciences to study international labor migration. However, it is important to emphasize that there are only two major paradigms or theoretical frameworks from which different contemporary analytical approaches stem: historical materialism and structural functionalism. For the most part, derivative approaches are orthodox; they apply the concepts that derive from the paradigms that shelter them. Other approaches tend toward eclecticism, incorporating different elements from these two opposed major theoretical frameworks. Orthodox approaches often sacrifice explanatory power in an effort to observe the limits imposed by their particular overarching paradigm, making it difficult for theory to fit reality. Eclectic approaches are somewhat more fortunate in this regard because they readily embrace a range of theories and concepts that are more easily operationalized and that more closely approximate a complex changing reality.

Among the orthodox approaches, a Marxist perspective informs the work of Castells, Castles and Kosack, Fernández, and others.[1] This historical materialist approach starts from the assumption that the presence of a national border and/or physical distance between two countries affected by migratory flows are not sufficient elements for differentiating international from internal (intranational) migration. From this perspective, both internal and international labor migrations are caused by only two basic factors: the labor force's ties to the spatial location of means of production and the unequal development that exists between different geographical areas. This approach emphasizes a historical perspective on the emergence and evolution of those economic, social, and political contradictions that engender conflict and crisis in the capitalist system. Nevertheless, the perspective's theoretical rigidity risks overlooking those differences that result from the particular characteristics of local or regional processes, and the impact of the capitalist world system's complex, interdependent dynamics on these local or regional realities. Thus this perspective on international migratory flows necessarily employs generalizations and analogies that sacrifice some objective knowledge of the phenomenon.

In contrast, the structural-functionalist perspective posits a linear causal relationship in which both internal and international migratorys result from "push" factors in the place of origin and "pull" factors from the place of destination. This approach informs work ranging from Ravenstein's classic study (1885) to the widely known Harris-Todaro model (1970).[2] Neoclassical analysts still work from this perspective. However, despite their sophisticated methodology, the most important examples of this approach have been ahistorical, descriptive, and empirical. The migratory phenomenon has been explained by models that fail to link successfully empirical techniques with analytical explanations of structural and conjunctural factors. Such factors account for *differences* in international migratory flows. They are incompatible with the limited, but generalized, conclusions that the structural-functionalist approach offers.

These two contrasting paradigms have been diluted and surpassed in recent years by eclectic approaches that have descriptively and analytically enriched the study of labor migration. It is precisely their number and diversity that make it extremely difficult to develop a classification that embraces the whole range of recent work. However, it is important to note that Michael Teitelbaum's essay is imprecise in its classification of the dominant theoretical frameworks for the study of labor migration. Teitelbaum offers no evidence to show why he chooses one classification rather than another. And when he considers eclectic approaches and their virtues, he fails to acknowledge the analytical advances contained in a series of recent studies.[3]

Recent research on migration emphasizes the value of microlevel analysis of the problem. This approach largely corrects the tendency toward simple generalizations that characterized early descriptive and ahistorical work in this field. Recent studies attempt to advance our understanding of migration by considering the peculiarities of different areas that are affected socioeconomically and politically (either positively or negatively) by migration. They have moved from an examination of aggregate data to a detailed analysis of individuals, family units, the workplace, and grassroots organizations—considering these as differentiated units of analysis that require consideration appropriate to their respective importance and complexity. The methodological innovations developed by these studies have made it possible to do more thorough field research. This, in turn, has produced a more scientific understanding of a phenomenon that is much more complex than is generally believed. The impact of migration on the development of both "push" and "pull" countries, and the relationships among these countries, is highly significant and demands better understanding if more adequate policy responses are to be developed. Although Teitelbaum is correct to stress the advantages of eclecticism, he should consider more carefully this approach's potential for expanding our understanding of the causes and consequences of international labor migration, as well as the possible importance of this approach in improving future U.S.–Latin American relations.

Finally, it is important to note that even though existing theoretical frameworks are not sufficiently comprehensive in themselves (which is why the study of migration requires more integrated and realistic approaches), they do articulate certain values and have direct or indirect ideological-political content. Thus it is inappropriate to state, as Teitelbaum does, that there is an easy distinction between "value-free" structuralist and push-pull theoretical frameworks and their political implications. The debate regarding impartial and uncommitted science has not been very productive, and few people are now concerned with this sterile discussion.

Causes and Consequences of Labor Migration

Knowledge of the factors causing migration has expanded considerably in recent years. Teitelbaum recognizes this when he refers to eclectic studies as propitious vehicles for research advances. But this is not enough. It is also necessary to indicate those causal factors that have been elucidated by this approach.

Recent research has shown conclusively that the causes of labor migration from Latin America to the United States cannot be considered generically. Nor can the characteristics of migration from Mexico to the United States be generalized to the regional level. Similarly, it has been shown that within Mexico itself the causes of migration are quite diverse, varying according to chronological, political, geographical, and ethnic differences.

In addition, recent studies have demonstrated that the considerations that affect the spatial localization and settlement of individuals and their family units change significantly when wage incomes fail to provide them with the basic necessities required for a household to reproduce itself biologically and socially. According to this new literature, under these circumstances the individual is forced to seek economic alternatives that enable him to compensate for insufficient wages. These alternatives naturally include the possibility of emigrating to another country in order to better his condition.

Although income insufficiency is a widespread and generalized cause of migration in Latin America, it is important to note that it does not always produce the same consequences. Research on labor migration must also explain differential outcomes within the region. Specifically, future analyses must consider the impact of the present world economic recession on the factors that cause migration. Until recently, migratory flows among different Latin American countries were quite numerous. These flows and the significance of economic causal factors varied substantially between Latin America and the Caribbean. Thus migration from Colombia to Venezuela and from Colombia to Ecuador could be clearly distinguished from migratory flows from Bolivia to Argentina and from Paraguay to Argentina, or from the Dominican Republic to Puerto Rico and from Guatemala and El Salvador to Mexico.

Migratory flows from Colombia have been highly heterogeneous in terms of social characteristics and labor force composition. Both Venezuela and Ecuador have received mixed migratory flows from rural and urban areas, which then participated in a variety of industrial, agricultural, and service activities in the host economy. In contrast, Bolivian and Paraguayan immigrants to Argentina have been quite homogeneous in terms of their rural origins and low skill levels. They have generally engaged in traditional agricultural activities in Argentina. Dominican immigrants to Puerto Rico have taken advantage of the host country's cultural and ethnic similarities, and some of these immigrants subsequently have found that Puerto Rico's special relationship with the United States allows them to proceed there. Dominican immigrants to the United States generally have settled in the greater New York City area, where they work predominantly in the service sector. Finally, migration from El

Salvador and Guatemala to Mexico has had a distinctly political character, as largely rural workers flee both economic hardship and increasingly severe armed conflict in Central America.

However, under the impact of Latin America's present economic crisis, the causal role of intraregional economic differences has been drastically reduced. Countries that normally attract migration (such as Venezuela and Argentina) have suffered such severe economic declines that they no longer exercise the same "pull" effect on their neighbors. These countries' large foreign debt limits their capacity for domestic investment and reduces the scope of national development plans. Their currency has either been substantially devalued (such as the Argentine *peso*) or seriously weakened (such as the Ecuadoran *sucre* and the Venezuelan *bolívar*).

At the same time, the "push" countries' possibilities for exporting labor have been constrained. These countries have unexpectedly had to face the social and economic burden of returning migrants who necessarily enter into competition with other workers, many of whom had attempted to cope with insufficient wages and increasing unemployment by developing informal, microlevel economic activities rather than by emigrating. This is the situation that Colombia now faces as a result of currency devaluations in Ecuador and Venezuela.

It is, of course, important to recognize the impact of political factors that increase the magnitude of international labor migration. However, these causes should not be given the same explanatory weight as economic conditions. Political motivations for migration are the result of either tensions between repressive governments and specific sectors of the population (for example, in Cuba, Haiti, and Chile at the beginning of the Pinochet dictatorship), confrontations between powerful economic groups and popular opposition movements (such as in El Salvador and Guatemala), or administrative incapacity and governmental corruption that produce frustration and the desire to emigrate in search of greater security and equitable treatment (such as in Mexico, Colombia, and the Dominican Republic). Thus political factors increase the importance of economic causes of migration, and they accentuate even more the differences between the United States and Latin America and the Caribbean. That is, political instability in Latin America and the Caribbean will continue to contribute to migratory flows to the United States.

With regard to the consequences of labor migration, Teitelbaum draws up a balance sheet that suggests an overall negative impact for the United States as a receiving country, and a positive balance for sending countries in Latin America and the Caribbean. However, attempts to measure the consequences of migration are the most polemic aspects of this issue. One widespread stereotype holds that Hispanic immigrants have had a serious, damaging impact on economic development, social stability, and the quality of life in the United States. But if one considers the contributions that immigration from Latin America has made, the image is quite different. Because migration tends to be selective, and because better-educated and more highly motivated individuals are those most likely to migrate, the receiving country is likely to benefit from immigration.

It is risky to equate the "brain drain" in developing countries with the migration of higher socioeconomic status individuals to the United States, as Teitelbaum does. By doing so, Teitelbaum underestimates the contributions that selective migration makes to U.S. economic development. Teitelbaum recognizes that immigrant workers participate more actively in the U.S. production process than low-income native citizens, who frequently prefer social welfare support to unattractive and badly paid jobs. Do such employment positions permit no economic improvement at all? Are the individuals who hold these positions condemned to socioeconomic inertia? How can such questions be evaluated in the context of broader socioeconomic mobility opportunities in the United States, the "land of opportunity"?

Teitelbaum also underestimates the economic damage and opportunity costs incurred by sending countries in Latin America and the Caribbean due to the loss of their best human resources. Whether this is the result of a "brain drain" or of the massive emigration of less-qualified lower-income workers who are willing to overcome major structural obstacles or international barriers, this economic cost can be substantial. In contrast, the recent economic boom in the southwestern United States has in part stemmed from the contribution that recent Hispanic migrants to the area have made to production and consumption.

Teitelbaum suggests that the presence of an important number of immigrant workers willing to receive low pay (by U.S. standards) has contributed to the slow rise in firm productivity and to the decline in investment in automated industrial technology. Although the large-scale use of low-wage immigrants may slow growth in productivity (in the technical sense of output per man-hour worked), it is also clear that if a firm is rational in its substitution of labor for capital, its new factor combination must produce at least as efficiently as any other alternative. Thus firms employing a higher proportion of low-wage immigrant labor may actually have a greater capacity for competition with those countries that export more labor-intensive goods.

Finally, one additional consequence of labor migration from Latin America and the Caribbean to the United States is the expansion of the so-called informal sector in the U.S. economy. These activities include personal services and the handicraft production of goods and materials in small firms in the subcontracting industry. This socioeconomic phenome-non can no longer be viewed as the exclusive property of developing countries, since it is increasingly common in industrialized countries such as the United States. To some extent it has become a means of absorbing high levels of open unemployment and other labor force problems in the United States.

In conclusion, it is important to note the increasing severity of eco-nomic problems caused by the present world recession. The recession's impact on countries throughout the hemisphere (whether they send or receive migration) and worsening political problems in some areas have produced new causes for, and consequences of, international labor migra-tion. Future research must pay more attention to the conjunctural dimen-sions of migration if it is to arrive at a more thorough understanding of this complex phenomenon. Analysis of this kind is required to derive realistic policy measures capable of responding to the changing character of migration.

Future Prospects for International Migration

Having suggested that international labor migration from Latin Amer-ica and the Caribbean to the United States is likely to increase in the future, because economic differences among sending countries in the re-gion are diminishing, it is important to indicate what characteristics these migratory flows will assume and what their implications will be for U.S.–Latin American relations.

The severity of the region's present economic problems and their international implications no longer permit the illusion that labor migra-tion is a feasible solution to sending countries' domestic economic and political problems. Despite the fact that migratory flows will continue to increase, the net benefit derived from them will fall. Sending areas will continue to suffer from the absence of their most qualified and highly motivated residents. Emigration will become more costly and will entail greater sacrifices. Immigrants' integration into the social and working life of host countries will be more difficult and more expensive. Migrants' opportunities to accumulate savings—either to send capital back to the family home in the country of origin or to permit the family to migrate as well—will shrink. Even the impact of earnings repatriated to the country of origin by migrant workers will decline.

These conclusions are based on a series of specific considerations. First, recent research has shown that in the last five years, international labor migration has assumed a markedly seasonal and recurrent char-acter. Unlike earlier flows, in which migrants intended to settle in the host country on a long-term or permanent basis, recent migration has increasingly been of short- or medium-term duration. Much of the current migration from Mexico to the United States, from Colombia to Venezuela, and even from Ecuador to Colombia is of this kind. Second, because of obstacles posed by border controls, migrant workers travel as individuals or in groups of neighbors or workmates rather than as a family unit. The cost and risk involved in crossing national borders illegally make it difficult to move the entire family.

Declining economic differences between sending and receiving countries and currency devaluations in the major Latin American host countries (especially Venezuela, Argentina, and Brazil) mean that capital sent back home by migrant workers hardly satisfies basic family needs. Moreover, the possibility that surplus funds will be available for individual workers' development of informal-sector businesses is substantially reduced. The geographic selectivity of labor migration also makes it unlikely that capital repatriated by migrant workers can serve as significant assistance to the most depressed areas of sending countries. For example, research on migration in Colombia clearly shows that the urban centers that account for most emigration are the capital cities of departments as rich and important as Antioquia and Valle (Medellín and Cali, respectively).

Economic studies designed to measure the volume of capital sent back home by migrants have not been very successful. Although capital repatriation of this kind is undeniably important in the case of Mexico, there is no sound basis on which to conclude that such flows constitute a serious resource drain that negatively affects the host economy. This belief is corroborated by the highly asymmetrical relationship that exists between the benefits derived by employers and the low salaries received by migrant workers, especially illegal ones.

Finally, the migration of undocumented workers from Latin America and the Caribbean is far higher than legal migration, either between these countries or from them to the United States. This is the result of official policies that have substantially reduced the legal entry of immigrants, despite the inadequacy of means and resources for controlling the entry of undocumented workers across land and coastal borders. This phenomenon is apparent daily at major crossing points on the U.S.–Mexican border. Until very recently a similar situation existed on the Colombian–Venezuelan border, and it continues to characterize undocumented migration from Ecuador to Colombia.

Socioeconomic status does not appear to be a significant variable for distinguishing among different migratory flows within Latin America. This migration consists for the most part of undocumented low-income workers with little education or job training, who at home live in conditions of extreme poverty. However, in the case of immigration to the

United States, socioeconomic differences polarize migratory flows and dramatically shape immigrants' working life and their overall social behavior. The lower socioeconomic strata migrate illegally with considerable risks and sacrifices, while higher strata migrate legally in fewer—but not insignificant—numbers.

Lower socioeconomic-status individuals migrate (and will continue to do so) because of their poverty and because they are attracted by the difference in purchasing power between the U.S. dollar and Latin American and Caribbean currencies. They come from Mexico in larger numbers than from other countries in the region, and because distance is not such an obstacle, Mexican immigrants are willing to face higher risks than those who migrate from more distant countries. Migrants from more distant places of origin depend to a great extent on migratory networks and enclaves that facilitate their entry and integration into the United States. Thus family, ethnic, and cultural ties are undeniably important in facilitating future migration. However, the increasing difficulties faced by established immigrant communities will handicap recent arrivals, who are viewed as dangerous competitors for currently limited employment opportunities. More well-to-do migrants are especially motivated by increasing political violence and social insecurity (for example, in Colombia and Central America).

However, changing conditions for immigrants resident in the United States mark a new pattern in migratory behavior. Regardless of the immigrant's socioeconomic status, it is becoming more difficult to live permanently in the United States. Policies for controlling immigration carried out by the Immigration and Naturalization Service and the pressures accompanying adjustment to social and working life in the United States will make it more difficult for lower-status immigrants to establish permanent residence. At the same time, the difficulties that new legal requirements and government policies pose to starting a business or some other productive activity will discourage those who migrate because of insecurity or fear of political persecution from remaining in the United States permanently. Many Salvadoran businessmen who immigrated to the United States are apparently considering leaving. A similar reaction appears to be emerging among Colombians who immigrated to the United States out of a fear of being kidnapped in the late 1970s and early 1980s. This reaction is understandable when one compares the relatively low short-term profit rates in those investment areas readily open to such immigrants in the United States (real estate, the manufacture of luxury goods, and so forth) with the very high profits they had realized in their country of origin. These immigrants' only remaining economic incentive for continued residence in the United States is the value of the U.S. dollar vis-à-vis their devalued domestic currency, which is a secondary consideration for active businessmen who are unwilling to watch idly from afar as their unprotected investments in their places of origin deteriorate.

Without dismissing the importance of those demographic factors that Teitelbaum identifies as a future cause of labor migration, it is important to underline the significance of the world economic crisis as a factor that stimulates increased migration from Latin America and the Caribbean to the United States. As previously noted, the spread of severe economic problems throughout the region has reduced the salience of intraregional economic differences, thereby slowing migratory flows among Latin American countries. Economic recovery in the region is likely to be slow. Thus in evaluating the future prospects for international labor migration, a search for real solutions to the problem should not be impaired by the belief that various alternative flows within Latin America can balance access to the region's scarce resources. Migratory patterns that were well established in the 1970s are no longer significant. Although some limited flows persist (from Colombia to Venezuela, and—reversing the earlier pattern—from Ecuador to Colombia), it is unlikely that immigration to neighboring countries will offer potential migrants much opportunity for economic improvement in the near future. If they persist in their desire to immigrate to another country in search of a higher income, they will do so in response to an extremely critical situation, fully aware that opportunities are now fewer than they were before. For all of these reasons, a comparative analysis of different migratory flows in the hemisphere is not justified. What is more pertinent is a careful examination of a problem that is no longer subregional but hemispheric: the increasing polarization between the advanced capitalism of the United States and the impoverished and growing indebtedness of Latin America and the Caribbean.

Government policies aimed at addressing the problem of international labor migration show considerable variation. In contrast to the United States, policies toward international migration in countries such as Mexico, Venezuela, and Colombia are weak and disjointed.[4] In these countries—and this characterization would also apply to the rest of the region—rhetoric has impeded action. All these countries have contemplated plans for retaining their population, rechanneling migrant flows, assisting immigrants, and so forth. But such goals have not been considered a priority in national development plans. In large part, these policies have resulted from projects promoted at the regional level by entities such as the International Labor Organization. Host countries (especially Venezuela) have designed some policies based on the U.S. experience. However, in Venezuela the focus of these policies has been limited to border control and the counting and pursuit of undocumented workers (for example, through the implementation of a General Identity

Card for Undocumented Persons, which offered gradual amnesty to those who registered under the provisions of the new law).

At the regional level, the Andean countries have drafted a Migrant Worker Statute to facilitate the exchange of human resources required by regional economic integration. Nevertheless, this measure has not been implemented, because of failure to achieve the Andean Pact's overall goals. Thus neither the tenuous policies for population retention applied indirectly by sending countries nor the equally tenuous restrictive policies applied by receiving countries have been effective in resolving the migration problems within Latin America and the Caribbean. The viability of these policies has been further eroded as governments' resources have been diverted by the current economic crisis.

In the United States, restrictive policies have failed to slow or curb immigration. Nor have they resolved the internal problems and debate caused by this phenomenon. The central elements in existing policies and those currently under discussion remain the same: additional resources for border and coastal patrol; increased sanctions against employers who knowingly hire undocumented workers; changes in quotas for "guest" workers; and modifications in the terms of amnesty to be offered to those already living and working in the United States.

Whatever final form these policies take, the United States must recognize that in the short- and medium-term future, levels of international labor migration will rise. This will occur in spite of the risks migrants face and in spite of policies intended to discourage immigration. Similarly, the United States should be aware that as long as migration policies fail to incorporate measures to attenuate increasing socioeconomic polarization within the Americas, the debate prompted by the Simpson-Mazzoli bill will continue to occupy public attention and divert focus from efforts to achieve a solution to the problem. None of the recent modifications in the Simpson-Mazzoli project have lessened its repressive and remedial character.

Measures to solve the migration problem should be taken on a multilateral basis, with benefits directed to both sending and receiving countries. Such measures should include expanded export opportunities for Latin American and Caribbean countries' basic products, thus creating additional employment opportunities and increasing incentives for potential migrants to remain at home. Similarly, international financial credits should be increased and reoriented so as to permit borrowing countries to expand public spending programs with a redistributive focus. Foreign capital should be directed to duty-free zones and industrial parks that encourage the intensive use of Latin American labor in the production of high-quality goods for export and domestic consumption. In addition, there should be economic and technological incentives for smaller firms as a means of strengthening, supporting, and integrating the enormous informal sector.

In the United States, these policies should encourage public recognition of the contribution that Latin American and Caribbean migrants make to the U.S. economy, especially in the production of low-cost goods and services. They should discourage the xenophobic campaigns that some domestic groups have promoted against immigrants. Moreover, these policies should support international efforts to gather and disseminate information on the difficulties of finding a job in another country and the costs and risks of doing so. Efforts should also be made to facilitate the repatriation of capital saved by migrants abroad and to direct it toward efficient uses through the allocation of complementary credits. These policies should also link different national systems for issuing passports and immigration documentation by establishing international information networks that permit the identification of travelers without jeopardizing their rights to spatial and physical mobility.

Finally, future policies concerning migration should include an emphasis on research programs and border development programs. These programs should be physically located in those places in which major migratory flows require the constant availability of resources to study and explain the changing characteristics of flows of human resources, capital, and consumer goods. Only then will it be possible to devise appropriate policies to address these issues before they produce crisis situations.

Departamento de Ciencia Política
Universidad de los Andes
Bogotá, Colombia

Notes

1. See Manuel Castells, "Migrant Workers and Class Struggles in Advanced Capitalism: The Western European Experience," in *Politics and Society* 5, No. 1 (1975): 33–66; Stephen Castles and Godula Kosack, *Immigrant Workers and Class Structure in Western Europe* (London: Oxford University Press, 1973); Raúl A. Fernández *The United States–Mexico Border: A Politico-Economic Profile* (Notre Dame, Ind.: University of Notre Dame Press, 1977).

2. E. G. Ravenstein, "The Laws of Migration," *Journal of the Royal Statistical Society* 48, No. 2 (1885); John R. Harris and Michael P. Todaro, "Migration, Unemployment, and Development: A Two Sector Analysis," *American Economic Review* 60, No. 1 (March 1970): 126–42.

3. See Lourdes Arizpe, "The Rural Exodus in Mexico and Mexican Migration to the United States," in Peter G. Brown and Henry Shue, eds., *The Border That Joins: Mexican Migrants and U.S. Responsibility* (Totowa, N.J.: Rowman and Littlefield, 1983), pp. 162–83; Wayne A. Cornelius, "Mexican Migration to the

United States," in Susan Kaufman Purcell, ed., *Mexico–United States Relations* (New York: Academy of Political Science, 1981), pp. 67–77; Cornelius, "Mexican Migration to the United States: Causes, Consequences, and U.S. Responses," (Cambridge, Mass.: Massachusetts Institute of Technology, Center for International Studies, 1978); Ina R. Dinerman, "Migrants and Stay-at-Homes: A Comparative Study of Rural Migration from Michoacán, Mexico," *Monograph Series* No. 5 (Center for U.S.–Mexican Studies, University of California–San Diego, 1982); María Patricia Fernández-Kelly, "Feminization, Mexican Border Industrialization, and Migration," paper presented at the conference "New Directions in Theory and Methods of Immigration and Ethnicity Research," Duke University, 1981; S. Grasmuck, "Enclave Development and Relative Labor Surplus: Haitian Labor in the Dominican Republic," paper presented at the conference "New Directions in Theory and Methods of Immigration and Ethnicity Research," Duke University, 1981; Richard Mines, "Las Animas, California: A Case Study of International Village Network Migration," mimeograph (Center for U.S.–Mexican Studies, University of California–San Diego, 1980); Gabriel Murillo, "La migración de trabajadores colombianos a Venezuela: La relación ingreso-consumo como uno de los factores de expulsión," final report presented to Proyecto UNDP, International Labor Organization (COL/72/027, 1979); Gabriel Murillo, "La migración laboral internacional en la periferia: Su incidencia en la alteración de los mercados de trabajo y en la expansión del sector informal urbano de Colombia," manuscript (Bogotá, Colombia: Universidad de los Andes, forthcoming); Patricia Pessar, "The Role of Households in International Migration," paper presented at the conference "New Directions in Theory and Methods of Immigration and Ethnicity Research," Duke University, 1981; Alejandro Portes, "Illegal Immigration and the International System: Lessons from Recent Legal Mexican Immigrants to the United States," *Social Problems* 26, No. 4 (April 1979): 425–38; Saskia Sassen-Koob, "Economic Growth and Immigration in Venezuela," in Mary M. Kritz and Douglas T. Gurak, eds., *International Migration in Latin America* (Special issue of *International Migration Review*) 13, No. 3 (1979): 455–74.

4. See Gabriel Murillo, *Migrant Workers in the Americas: A Comparative Study of Migration Between Colombia and Venezuela and Between Mexico and the United States*, Research Monograph 13 (Center for U.S.–Mexican Studies, University of California–San Diego, 1984).

Part IV
Security Issues in
U.S.–Latin American
Relations

18

Security: The Extracontinental Dimension

Cole Blasier

On many occasions in this century, the U.S. government and Latin American governments have been locked in crises in which both perceived that their security was threatened. In order to deal with these crises effectively, governments need a clear understanding of both their own security interests and those of their adversaries. This essay begins by attempting to define the security interests of the United States and of Latin American countries.

Most U.S.–Latin American security crises since 1945 have been linked to perceived international communist threats arising from social revolutions. (An important exception occurred in 1962 when the Soviet Union attempted unsuccessfully to install missile bases in Cuba.) In addition, the Soviet Union often has resorted to legal and illegal measures to influence political outcomes in the region through Communist parties located in virtually every country.

Three sets of actors have been in competition in these various revolutionary situations: the governments of Latin American countries, the United States, and the Soviet Union. This essay examines their roles in four cases (Guatemala, Cuba, Chile, and the Dominican Republic), and it describes and contrasts the national security strategies of each of these actors. This discussion also includes an analysis of recent U.S. official behavior in Nicaragua, Grenada, and El Salvador. Finally, lessons learned in all these cases provide a basis for recommendations intended to protect U.S. security interests in the Western Hemisphere.

In these complicated relations among conflicting states, security as a concept has acquired so many meanings, misuses, and controversial associations that the term itself has become a problem in U.S.–Latin American relations. The public often associates the term "security" with military security—that is, the protection of territory and inhabitants from external physical threats by the armed forces of another country. Yet many conflicts do not involve external threats at all. Most leaders devote much of their time to protecting their country through nonmilitary means, such as treaties of friendship, trade agreements, multilateral treaties, and so forth.

Confusion about what security means has often complicated the resolution of public problems. United States government officials have sometimes characterized the threat to a friendly government by hostile internal forces as a U.S. security problem. The U.S. public has then mistakenly associated that situation with a physical threat to the United States itself. In fact, the episode may have involved only a conflict between opposing political forces in a remote country, and it may not have posed any direct military threat to the United States. The issue, more accurately, was one of domestic political competition in a foreign country.

Congressional appropriations are often justified and defended on security grounds—namely, that they help protect the United States from the Soviet Union and international communism. This has been the justification for much foreign military assistance. Yet, except for the 1962 Cuban missile crisis, most U.S. and Latin American government officials have considered the prospect of a Soviet attack on the hemisphere to be remote. Most of the funds appropriated and transferred to protect Latin American countries from external enemies have actually been used for internal security purposes—that is, to maintain order or suppress internal opposition, most of which has been noncommunist.

No Latin American country is capable by itself of seriously threatening the military security of the United States. In fact, barring some small country's use of nuclear weapons, the Soviet Union is now the only country likely to threaten the military security of the United States in Latin America—and then only with the cooperation of some Latin American country such as Cuba. None of the post-1945 security crises in Latin America (except the 1962 missile crisis) threatened the United States' territory or its citizens. Nor has the Soviet military threat been a major preoccupation of Latin Americans; their security concerns have focused primarily on internal matters or perceived threats from hostile neighbors.

Official U.S. behavior toward Latin America since 1945 may be explained by two dominant themes, one explicit and familiar and the other implicit and often conveniently overlooked. United States actions regarding security consistently have been shaped by perceptions of possible Soviet military threats to the hemisphere and by perceptions of political threats through Soviet ties with Latin American governments. Since the Cuban missile crisis, the Soviet military threat in the region has been only potential.

United States perceptions have often been shaped by domestic politics. Presidents have feared that failure to take decisive action against perceived security threats would be punished at the next election. President Kennedy's decisions regarding the Bay of Pigs and President Johnson's decisions regarding the Dominican Republic are cases in point. Kennedy did not want to be accused of "losing" Cuba, nor did Johnson wish to be accused of permitting "another Cuba."

United States analysts, and U.S. citizens generally, have been reluctant to recognize the other dominant theme explaining the United States' behavior—namely, its hegemonic role in the hemisphere. Hegemonic systems are not new. They appeared before the age of Rome, and they will very likely continue after the United States' global prominence is a dim memory. China, Spain, Great Britain, France, Russia, Germany, and the Soviet Union have all acted or act like hegemons in different areas at different times. The United States might prefer to be an exception in history, but it is not. Thus when revolutionary movements or governments attempt to change the status quo in particular countries within the U.S. sphere of influence or to change their relationship with the United States, U.S. leaders (subject to all the domestic and foreign pressures involved) resist change.

But U.S. officials find that justifying their policies primarily as a means of maintaining dominance—economic or political—is not very convincing. A more effective defense for such policies is to claim that there is some external threat to legitimate U.S. interests. Sometimes leaders may not be fully aware that their actions are mainly a means of protecting a hegemonic position. Or even if they are, it would be unrealistic to expect them to lay the realities bare. For example, U.S. responses to the Allende government in Chile may ultimately be best understood as an attempt to reestablish an old order more responsive to U.S. public and private interests.

Definitions of Security Interests

It is essential to recognize the divergent and sometimes contradictory security interests of the United States and Latin American countries in order to understand the relationship between them. Radicals at one end of the political spectrum insist that these interests are irreconcilable. At the other extreme, many reactionaries press their governments to act as if these interests were identical. An important step toward constructive relations is to identify and understand these differences in security interests.

The United States

1. Military Threats. The classic U.S. interest in Latin America, most authoritatively symbolized by the Monroe Doctrine, has been to prevent any rival great power from establishing a military presence in the Western

Hemisphere. In 1962 the Soviet Union attempted to violate this interest by installing nuclear missiles in Cuba. The United States forced the removal of the missiles, and the Soviet Union agreed not to return them to the island. When U.S. authorities became concerned in 1970 about evidence that the Soviet Union was building a submarine base in Cienfuegos, Cuba, Soviet leaders reassured the United States that no such base would be built. Subsequently, the Soviet Union signed Protocol II of the Treaty for the Prohibition of Nuclear Weapons in Latin America (the Treaty of Tlatelolco), thereby reinforcing and broadening its commitment not to introduce nuclear weapons into the Western Hemisphere.

For many years concern has been expressed in the United States about Soviet deployments of conventional forces in and around Cuba. Large numbers of Soviet military advisors and instructors are assigned to the Cuban armed forces, and a Soviet contingent (sometimes referred to as a brigade, and numbering between two thousand and three thousand men) has been stationed in Cuba. Soviet naval deployments (usually two or three warships, and often including a submarine and one or more supply ships) visited Cuba about twice a year between 1969 and 1979. Pairs of Bear D reconnaissance aircraft have been flying to Cuba or stopping over in Cuba since 1970; in 1978 there were eleven such visits.[1] Deployments of this kind continue.

As a result, the Soviet Union now has limited naval and air capabilities in the Western Hemisphere. Warships and airplanes refuel and operate from Cuba. Operations such as these (at least naval operations) would be possible from Soviet bases outside the hemisphere, but in far fewer numbers and with greater difficulty without Cuba. These Soviet ships could, of course, operate against U.S. shipping en route to Europe or the Pacific from Gulf of Mexico ports.

The major questions are not whether the Soviet Union has a new military capability—which it does—but what the significance of that capability is and what should be done about it. So long as they move in international waters and airspace, Soviet ships and planes cannot be forced out of the hemisphere peacefully. The United States' naval and air forces are far stronger and operate from permanent bases on or near national territory, while Soviet ships and aircraft operate at great distances from home bases and are isolated and vulnerable. If the Soviet Union anticipated or were to become involved in a conventional war elsewhere, Soviet strategists would have to decide whether forces at grave risk in the Caribbean were more useful there or nearer home. It seems unlikely that Soviet leaders would initiate a conventional war in the Caribbean where the odds are strongly against them. Moreover, the risk that a conventional war between the United States and the Soviet Union would escalate rapidly into a nuclear conflict is recognized on both sides.

Clearly, all Soviet military deployments in the Caribbean need to be closely watched. No doubt there also should be certain military counter-measures taken in the area. However, the heavy emphasis on the military aspects of the U.S.-Soviet confrontation in Latin America is dangerous insofar as it implies that the solutions for the United States are more military than political. The Caribbean is a minor military theater for the Soviet Union. Its primary interest in Latin America is in strengthening its political ties with governments in the larger and more powerful countries: Mexico, Argentina, Brazil, and Venezuela. Of course, the Soviet Union also has a strong interest in revolutionary movements that lead to pro-Soviet socialist governments, such as Cuba's. United States military action against several dozen Soviet ships and aircraft on visits to the Caribbean will not meet that challenge.

2. *Access to Strategic Raw Materials.* Access to strategic raw materials is closely associated with military security. A Congressional Research Service study indicates that six of nine important raw materials imported by the United States come from Latin America. Brazil supplies 30 percent of all U.S. imports of manganese ore. Similarly, the following Latin American countries supply important shares of U.S. strategic raw material imports: tin (6 percent) and tungsten (15 percent) from Bolivia; copper from Chile (24 percent) and Peru (12 percent); bauxite from Jamaica (42 percent) and Suriname (17 percent). Although the United States must keep the availability of these materials under review, U.S. dependence on Latin America for strategic raw materials is limited.[2]

According to the Central Intelligence Agency, the United States imported about 37 percent of the crude oil it consumed in 1981, nearly 6 million barrels per day (bpd). About 1.2 million bpd were imported from the main Latin American suppliers, Venezuela, Mexico, and Ecuador—that is, 20 percent of imports and about 13 percent of total U.S. consumption.[3] Access to this oil is important to the United States, and it may become more so in the future. Submarines of a hostile power could threaten supplies, especially from Ecuador and Venezuela. However, it is unlikely that such attacks would occur except in a major military confrontation between the two superpowers.

To summarize, U.S. military security interests in Latin America are: to enforce understandings prohibiting Soviet military bases and nuclear weapons in the hemisphere; to monitor Soviet military deployments; and to maintain access to oil and a few strategic raw materials, especially in Mexico and Brazil.

In terms of security in its broader, political sense, the United States has an interest in maintaining collaborative relations with as many governments in the region as possible. Such an objective means fostering cooperation, not conflict. The diplomatic challenge is how to structure relations so that governments find it in their interests to be responsive to U.S. influence.

Most centrist and right-wing governments in Latin America cooperate openly with the United States, or at least do not challenge U.S. interests or make common cause with the Soviet Union. It is revolutionary regimes that constitute a potential threat in this regard, and U.S.-Soviet political competition generally centers on these regimes. Hostile U.S. policies (especially armed interference) toward revolutionary regimes such as Nicaragua constitute a withdrawal from political competition with the Soviet Union. Military strategies of this kind can succeed only through the overthrow of the revolutionary leadership. Even if the strategy succeeds, the United States' espoused goals of freedom from communism, stability, and democracy may not be achieved. If the strategy does not succeed (as is the case so far in Cuba and Nicaragua), the failure of U.S. policy and the damage to U.S. interests are manifest.

Latin America

Whereas the United States can be seriously threatened by only one power (the Soviet Union), Latin American countries have two powers to fear, the United States and the Soviet Union. The United States has a long history of military actions against Latin America. In the nineteenth and early twentieth centuries, these episodes included war with Mexico (1846–1848) and military occupations lasting many years in Cuba, Panama, Nicaragua, Haiti, the Dominican Republic, and Mexico. United States military forces invaded and occupied the Dominican Republic in 1965 and Grenada in 1983. The only comparably dramatic Soviet military action was the installation of missiles in Cuba, and this was directed primarily against the United States. United States military actions against Latin America have been real, Soviet military actions mostly hypothetical. The Soviet Union's military actions have been directed mainly against its own small neighbors.

However, most Latin American governments do not now fear U.S. military action. Those that do are the revolutionary governments of Cuba and Nicaragua. The other governments in the region, although watchful for signs of intervention and interference elsewhere, do not have serious apprehensions about U.S. intervention on their own soil. Nor do most Latin American governments believe that the Soviet Union intends or is able to launch a successful conventional attack on the hemisphere. More serious for some countries is the possibility of armed attacks from neighboring countries: for example, against Nicaragua from Honduras, against Guyana from Venezuela, against Ecuador from Peru, or against Chile from Argentina. Most of these cases represent long-standing rivalries.

With some exceptions, the greatest threat to the security of Latin American governments is internal. Domestic enemies, whether of the right or the left, generally pose a greater threat than foreign rivals. The Pinochet government in Chile and recent military governments in Argentina have been most threatened from within. In order to mobilize support, incumbent governments often exaggerate external interference. Security for Latin American governments is close to political autonomy. Their first line of defense is against internal revolt.

Security Crises (1954–1973)

More knowledge of past security crises—who participated and why, and how governments coped with them—may help deal with crises in the future. Most of the major security crises in Latin America since the end of World War II have involved the Soviet Union in some way and the United States. The 1962 missile crisis was the most important of these cases, but that episode has been examined so exhaustively elsewhere that there is no need to consider it in detail here. Foreign powers other than the United States and the Soviet Union were seldom involved in an important way in these post-1945 crises. One obvious exception was Great Britain in the 1982 Falkland/Malvinas Islands crisis, discussed elsewhere in this volume.

Four cases have been selected for study: Guatemala (1954), Cuba (1960–1961), the Dominican Republic (1965), and Chile (1970–1973). United States government officials left the impression in three cases (Guatemala, Cuba, and the Dominican Republic) that U.S. military security was threatened. How else could U.S. paramilitary and military responses be justified? The crisis in Chile occurred during the period of high détente in U.S.-Soviet relations, a less threatening international context. Nonetheless, the United States applied extraordinary financial and covert sanctions against Allende.

The cases will be examined in terms of the behavior of three categories of participants: Latin American governments, the Soviet Union, and the United States. The cases of Nicaragua (1979–), El Salvador (1980–), and Grenada (1983) are discussed in the concluding section. The purpose of this analysis is to identify the U.S. interests threatened, the actors who threatened these interests and why, and the responses of U.S. governmental authorities. An effort will also be made to determine the extent of communist and Soviet participation in each crisis.

Revolts and Revolutions

These four security crises originated in the efforts of revolutionary elites to seize power from incumbent elites in order to introduce revolutionary changes in the structures of local societies and in the structures of the countries' foreign relations. The revolutionaries sought to remove old elites permanently from power, establish state control over many of the country's resources, and redistribute wealth and income.

Because the United States was deeply involved in all the countries under consideration, the changes undertaken by revolutionary groups affected adversely many different U.S. interests. The leaders of these revolutionary movements believed that U.S. influence—both public and private—inside their countries was excessive, and sometimes illegitimately acquired. Most particularly, they objected to foreign control over their economies and foreign interference in their political affairs. Many sought to reduce or eliminate the foreign presence. Newly installed revolutionary governments expropriated private U.S. land in Guatemala and Cuba; nickel and copper properties in Cuba and Chile, respectively; certain public utilities in Guatemala, Cuba, and Chile; and other U.S.-based businesses in these countries. Given these revolutionary leaders' critical attitudes toward the private sector in general, foreign business was put on the defensive along with nationally controlled firms, some of which were allied to foreign companies. Because all these governments lacked the necessary resources to pay for the properties expropriated, the U.S. owners were despoiled of their properties.

Revolutionary changes in these societies also affected U.S. foreign policy interests. The new revolutionary governments took a much more critical view of U.S. policies toward their country, as well as U.S. foreign policies in general. The United States could no longer count more or less automatically on their cooperation concerning either bilateral or global issues. For example, Arbenz in Guatemala refused to accept the U.S. interpretation of the Korean War, and Allende in Chile criticized the U.S. position on the Vietnam war. All three of these governments—and most particularly Castro's—conducted a stubbornly independent foreign policy.

The Dominican rebels did not have the opportunity of the Guatemalan, Cuban, and Chilean revolutionaries to implement their policies, because they did not gain power. The leaders of the Dominican revolt espoused nationalistic policies with anti-imperialist overtones, and they sought broader social change than had previously occurred. As a result, many of the reasons for U.S. opposition to the rebels were similar to those in the other three cases discussed here.

Almost all the revolutionary leaders in these four countries were of middle class origins, and most came from comfortable families. Many were doctors, lawyers, businessmen, teachers, and so forth. Some had been influenced by Marxism, but few could be called orthodox Marxists. Castro, who eventually moved further to the left than any of the other principal revolutionary leaders, was the son of a well-to-do sugar planter; the platform on which he won the revolution against Batista was based on the Cuban constitution of 1940, a mild reformist document. Castro's sharp turn to the left came after he had been in office for about a year and a half. Similarly, the leaders of the Guatemalan revolution were mainly reformists, as were the members of the Dominican Revolutionary Party—at least until the U.S. intervention. Allende's Socialist Party included members of many Marxist orientations, and there were more Marxists (some seeking rapid and radical change) in his government than in those of other countries considered here. However, members of pre-revolutionary pro-Soviet Communist parties did not play the leading role in the seizure of power or in controlling governments thereafter. The various patterns of communist participation are described below.

Soviet Involvement

The perceived involvement of the Soviet Union is what made these "security" crises. From the U.S. perspective, the seizures of power by the four revolutionary movements identified here probably constituted the four most important security crises in Latin America until 1979, except for the more dangerous Cuban missile crisis. In any event, the first three crises were handled as if U.S. military security was at stake. If that was the case, then some power other than the Latin American countries involved must have threatened the United States. Chile, the largest of the four countries, had only about 10 million inhabitants; the other countries all had less. The populations involved did not exceed by much the population of greater New York City. Nor were they rich countries. What caused the furor in the United States was the alleged Soviet tie to these revolutions. Without such a connection, these little countries could pose no significant threat to the United States.

The Soviet Union had ties with these countries through two channels: the Soviet government and/or national Communist parties. The Soviet Union did not maintain diplomatic or other governmental relations with any of the three Caribbean Basin countries. Guatemala had recognized the Soviet Union in 1944, but diplomatic relations had never been established. Batista had purchased sugar from the Soviet Union, but there were no official diplomatic ties before Castro. Trujillo sought relations with the Soviet Union after the Eisenhower administration rebuffed him in the late 1950s, but the Soviets turned down his advances and little is known to have happened since.[4]

There is no historical record of any significant contact between the rebel movements in Guatemala, Cuba, and the Dominican Republic and the Soviet government, not even in the early months of the Guatemalan and Cuban revolutionary governments.[5] For example, Secretary of State John Foster Dulles made much of a large shipment of Czech arms from a Baltic port to the Arbenz government in Guatemala, which desperately needed the weapons because it faced an armed opposition on its own soil. United States protests that the Guatemalans were turning to a socialist country for arms seemed bizarre given that U.S. authorities were enforcing an embargo on arms sales to the Arbenz government while simultaneously providing arms to the anti-Arbenz rebels. Guatemalan and Soviet representatives were in brief contact at the United Nations during the crisis, but this produced few results.

An early (perhaps the first) substantive contact between the Cuban and Soviet governments after Castro took power occurred with the arrival of a Tass (the Soviet press agency) correspondent in Havana in December 1959. More important was a visit by Soviet Deputy Premier Anastas Mikoyan in February 1960. Mikoyan arranged for the Soviet purchase of 425,000 tons of Cuban sugar in the first year and a million tons in each of the following five years. Batista had sold the Soviet Union substantial but smaller amounts of sugar earlier. Arrangements for the exchange of diplomatic representatives came in May 1960. At the urgent request of Castro and his close associates, who were smarting under heavy U.S. economic sanctions and fearful of U.S.-sponsored armed intervention, the Soviet Union began its active and far-reaching support for the Cuban economy and armed forces in July and August 1960.

Chile opened diplomatic relations with the Soviet Union in 1964, long before Allende came to power. The latter's predecessor, Eduardo Frei, called for relations with socialist countries during his presidential election campaign in order to attract more votes from the left and to diversify Chile's foreign relations. The Soviet Union maintained an ambassador in Chile during most of the next decade, but there is no evidence that he became significantly involved in domestic politics. To have done so openly would have jeopardized the future electoral chances of the Communist party and its allies.

The Soviet Union exerts influence in Latin America not only through the official channels described above, but also through pro-Soviet Communist parties in the region. This discussion focuses on these parties because they have a direct link to Soviet military and political power, long the principal U.S. concern. There is a wide range of political parties on the Latin American left—from Christian Democrats and Social Democrats to other Socialists, Marxists, Anarchists, Trotskyists, Maoists, and so forth. This analysis distinguishes sharply between pro-Soviet communists (that is, the orthodox communists linked to Moscow) and other leftist parties. The latter parties, or almost any party of the center or right, theoretically could raise security issues for the United States. However, U.S. concern usually arises over leftist movements such as the Sandinistas in Nicaragua—the most visible noncommunist leftist government in the hemisphere. Cuba and the Soviet Union both seek to influence leftist movements. Since right and center governments tend to stay in the western camp, the main U.S.-Soviet rivalry in Latin America tends to be over socialist or other leftist forces.

There were Communist parties in all four countries under consideration here, but the only two with a history of achievement were in Cuba and Chile—possibly then the two strongest Communist parties in Latin America. Both had been active and influential in their respective organized labor movements, controlling important national labor confederations. Both were also active in electorally successful political coalitions in the late 1930s and the early 1940s. The Communists were the third member of the Popular Front in Chile in the 1930s. In Cuba, they were the first to nominate Fulgencio Batista for the presidency, and Communist Party members served without portfolios in the cabinet in the 1940–1944 period. When subsequent governments turned sharply against Communist-controlled sectors of the labor movement and the parties themselves in the early years of the Cold War, the Communists suffered major setbacks, but the parties held together.

The Guatemalan Communists were decimated by the Ubico dictatorship in the 1930s. In part for this reason the party did not play a major role in the revolution of 1944. In the early 1950s it first began to play a prominent role in the land reform institute, in the media, and in the president's own office. Nonetheless, the cabinet, the legislature, and the armed forces were overwhelmingly noncommunist. Arbenz' political opposition—foreign property interests threatened by his government and hostile foreign governments—labeled him a Communist in order to discredit him. The weakness of the Arbenz government was shown by its sudden collapse once faced with the army's opposition.

In Cuba, the Communists had not yet regained their former influence when Fidel Castro launched his guerrilla campaign against Batista from the Sierra Maestra. Castro himself came from the orthodox wing of the Cuban Revolutionary Party, long the Communists' major rival. His attack on the Moncada Barracks in 1952 and his landing from Mexico in 1956 were accomplished on his own. Many of the Communists considered Castro's strategy putschist, ultraleftist, or infantile. Criticisms such as these continued until the eve of his victory. However, some Communists (led by Carlos Rafael Rodríguez) joined Castro in his mountain hideout. Their initiative prevented the Communists from being totally disassociated from his victory. When Castro came to power, his own lieutenants—not the Communists—were appointed to the principal government positions. Eventually Castro and these lieutenants took over the Cuban

Communist Party, not the reverse. The old-line Communists have had only a small percentage of the leading government positions, usually about 20 percent.[6] In 1980, for example, three of the sixteen members of the party's Politburo were old-line Communists.

In the Dominican Republic, the pro-Soviet Communists were among many small political parties on the left. They did not play an important part in Dominican politics before or during the 1965 revolt. The leaders and most of the participants in the revolt were anticommunist or noncommunist. Several dozen Communists (some trained in Cuba) did participate in the revolt, sometimes as leaders of armed units. José Moreno, an eyewitness, calculates that perhaps as many as one in twelve participants in the revolt served under Communist leadership.[7] Participants in the Constitutionalist cabinet and the Constitutionalist military leaders were noncommunists.

In Chile, the Communists were a major ally of the Socialists and helped make possible Allende's 1970 electoral victory. Allende's total popular vote was a plurality (36 percent). The Communists had a reasonably secure but small political base, accounting for about 17 percent of the electorate in the municipal and congressional elections of 1971 and 1973, respectively. As a member of the government coalition, the Communists played a moderating role—attempting to check the radicalism and extremism of the left socialists and other leftists (such as the Movement of the Revolutionary Left, MIR) who used violence. The Communists feared that these extremist elements would push Allende too far too fast and provoke a military coup. The Communists' predictions and their counsels for measured change proved correct but ineffectual.

During the Allende government, the Soviet Union provided Chile with a generous line of credit, much of it tied to purchases from the Soviet Union. This assistance was not of much use to Allende, particularly during his last year in office when he needed hard currency to meet payments to western creditors. The Soviet Union also gave Allende strong moral support, but it avoided close financial or military involvements. The reason probably was that the Soviet government sought to avoid heavy subsidies such as those granted to Cuba, had doubts about the viability of Allende's government, and considered Soviet capabilities insufficient to assist effectively in a crisis. Allende was also cautious about Soviet ties in order to avoid criticisms in the West.

U.S. Responses

The revolutionary changes that all these leftist governments introduced (and in the Dominican case, would like to have introduced) also had a revolutionary impact on relations with the United States. Important private and public U.S. interests were affected in each case. The revolutionary leaders gave the United States genuine cause for concern. United States-owned companies had large investments in all these countries, investments that were explicitly threatened by the announced policies of the new governments. United States government estimates place U.S. investment in Guatemala in 1953 at $107 million, in Cuba in 1958 at $861 million, and in Chile in 1970 at $748 million.[8] Although the Latin American revolutionary forces' interest in gaining national control over their own natural resources and infrastructure was understandable, it was also clear why U.S. interests viewed the new arrangements with alarm. Many associated businesses in trade, commerce, and banking felt their interests threatened, too. All these groups had influential ties in the United States, up to and including the White House.

The U.S. diplomatic and military establishment had been accustomed to receiving exemplary cooperation from Ubico, Batista, Trujillo (until the late 1950s), and earlier presidents of Chile. The new revolutionary leaders made a point of taking independent stands on various foreign policy questions—positions more independent, for example, than those of Goulart in Brazil or Frei in Chile. Moreover, the revolutionary governments could not be counted on to fall promptly in line behind military arrangements in the hemisphere. These governments seemed likely to strengthen their ties with neutralist and socialist countries.

In light of these different developments, it is not surprising that various U.S. administrations took defensive steps. Secretary of State Dulles was angered by the domestic and foreign policies of the Arbenz government in Guatemala, its adverse impact on U.S. economic and political interests, and its independent positions generally. It seems likely that he may have already begun planning to overthrow Arbenz in 1953. In any event, Dulles prepared the ground for such an action at the Inter-American Conference in Caracas in early 1954 by charging that communists had established a beachhead in the Americas. His brother (Allen Dulles, Director of the Central Intelligence Agency, CIA) subsequently organized armed émigré forces to invade eastern Guatemala and sent planes over Guatemala City. When Guatemalan military forces launched a coup d'état, Arbenz fled the country. The U.S. ambassador acted as mediator in the rivalry for the presidency. The officer whom he sponsored (who eventually won) was the head of the CIA-sponsored émigré forces.

As the Eisenhower team's chief foreign policy spokesman, John Foster Dulles had taken office decrying the reactive nature of the Truman and Acheson policies and calling for the eventual liberation of eastern Europe.[9] Once in office he had to make good on these claims, yet he backed away—quite wisely—from liberating eastern Europe. Nor was it necessary to take such risks when a country nearer home needed "liberating." After the CIA operation and the overthrow of Arbenz, Dulles could point to a great "victory" in Latin America, to which he and President Eisenhower made frequent references in the 1954 and 1956 election campaigns.

Following the Guatemalan pattern, in March 1960 Eisenhower (who was angered by what he considered to be Castro's insolence and disturbed by Mikoyan's visit to Havana) authorized a series of steps—including the organization of émigré forces—to unseat Castro.[10] Eisenhower initially thought that economic pressures would accomplish this goal, and he did not expect to call on the émigré forces. President Kennedy inherited the émigré units and had to reach a decision regarding their use before he had time to gain full control of his administration. Concerned about the adverse political effects of failing to act, disbanding a disgruntled Cuban émigré force in the United States, and accepting Soviet-Cuban ties, Kennedy ordered the Cubans onto the beaches of the Bay of Pigs. Domestic political considerations and concerns about U.S.-Soviet relations appear to have dominated his thinking.

President Johnson was panicked by the armed attempt to restore Juan Bosch to the presidency of the Dominican Republic in 1965. He at first explained the U.S. military occupation of Santo Domingo as necessary to protect U.S. lives and property. He later explained the action more convincingly as necessary to prevent "another Cuba." Early on Johnson claimed that communists controlled the revolutionary movement; later he dropped the charge. The most convincing explanation of his action is that he sought to protect his presidential prospects in the 1968 elections. His hopes of reelection were finally dashed three years later as the result of his Vietnam war record.

In 1970 as in 1964, the CIA maneuvered covertly to prevent Allende from being elected president of Chile, and it later took other clandestine actions to promote his fall from power. Much of this CIA plotting appears to have come to naught, and the actions that did take place were not very effective. What probably hurt Allende more than CIA operations were the various economic and financial sanctions that the United States levied against him.

During these years President Nixon and Henry Kissinger met frequently with General Secretary Brezhnev and his associates. Frequent collaborative contact with Soviet leaders on global issues made it less likely that the United States would exaggerate the Soviet role in Chile. The Nixon administration also had greater confidence in U.S. intelligence appraisals of the Chilean Communist Party. In short, it was not so much Soviet interference as Allende's challenge to U.S. hemispheric leadership that U.S. officials could not tolerate. Nixon and Kissinger wanted a non-

Marxist government in Chile that would be more amenable to close ties with the United States.

In reality, all these conflicts were essentially political, with their economic and military dimensions tending to reinforce political considerations. The expropriation of U.S. private property was not in itself sufficient to cause U.S. military intervention or covert interference. Nor were fears of direct Soviet military action dominant in U.S. government decisions. Rather, U.S. leaders wanted to prevent any Latin American government from falling under communist or Soviet influence.

Many of these officials' decisions were the results of perceptions of U.S. public attitudes and the operations of the U.S. political system. Secretary Dulles sought to capitalize on these attitudes politically in the case of Guatemala. Presidents Kennedy and Johnson acted to protect themselves politically, and President Nixon was not to be outmaneuvered regarding Chile. As long as the U.S. public feels threatened by leftist or pro-Soviet governments in Latin America, it will be difficult (especially in the Caribbean Basin) for presidents not to make a "security" issue of them, an issue that could lead to the use of force.

In the cases of Cuba, Guatemala, and the Dominican Republic, U.S. leaders responded to these episodes as "security" crises implying actual or potential physical threats to the United States. In many ways these U.S. responses were more a product of East-West rivalry and of U.S. domestic politics than of bilateral relations with the particular country concerned. Although U.S. responses had multiple origins, they are probably best understood as the misguided efforts of a series of presidents to maintain U.S. influence and political preeminence in the Western Hemisphere.

Several conclusions relevant to U.S. security policy may be drawn from these four cases. First, noncommunist nationalists (some reformist, some radical) led the revolutionary forces that sought to seize power in these countries. Communists did not play a significant role in any of these cases; in Chile, for example, the Communists attracted about 17 percent of the popular vote—an essential, but not the leading, component in Allende's electoral victory. Nor did the prerevolutionary Communists dominate any of the other leftist governments. In Cuba, Castro's movement took over the Communists; in Chile, leftist extremists defeated Communist appeals for more moderate change.

Second, the Soviet government had nothing to do with the accession to power of revolutionary movements in Guatemala and Cuba or the armed revolt in the Dominican Republic. United States intervention in these cases could not be justified by an existing Soviet military threat. However, Soviet aid had everything to do with sustaining Castro in power after U.S. plans to overthrow him were widely known. The Soviet Union provided Allende with strong moral support, but it avoided close economic and military relations in order to protect its own economic and political interests.

Third, the United States moved to crush the three revolutionary movements by paramilitary or military means and to bring down Allende by economic sanctions and covert political action. The president's decisions in these cases seemed to be motivated mainly by domestic political considerations, the desire to maintain U.S. political preeminence in the country concerned, and U.S.-Soviet political rivalry. The 1962 Cuban missile crisis was an exception in that it constituted a challenge to U.S. military security. Otherwise, U.S. responses are better understood in terms of political security—that is, efforts to maintain U.S. influence and preeminence in the Latin American countries concerned.

National Security Strategies

Effective U.S. security policies regarding Latin America must take into account the security strategies of more than two dozen Latin American governments and the Soviet government. The Latin American governments range from the Marxist-Leninist regime in Cuba to the nineteenth-century style dictatorship in Paraguay. Soviet policy must be understood in its many facets, including the application of its different dimensions to individual countries. In order to cope with this bewildering array of forces, U.S. security strategies need to identify and respond to the most urgent bilateral security problems, while at the same time providing a hemispheric framework that will accommodate a wide range of bilateral relations in the long term.

Latin America

Whereas the United States has been primarily concerned with external security, Latin American countries have generally followed an opposite pattern. Most are primarily concerned with *internal* security. Different categories of governments have different security policies, and external security orientations are often shaped by internal security considerations. Latin American governments are too numerous to examine individually, but security considerations in the region can be made more intelligible by discussing the subject in terms of three groups of governments.

Most governments in the region may be categorized according to their political systems and related strategies. Political upheavals in countries such as Chile and Nicaragua move a country from one group to another. Group I includes those governments of the right that eschew free elections and hold power by force. In the early 1980s examples included Guatemala and Chile. Group II includes governments of the right and center that permit some legitimate political competition and whose control is not currently threatened. Examples include Brazil, Mexico, and Venezuela. Group III includes governments of the left, which so far have eschewed national elections and maintain power by force. Examples include Cuba and, until the 1984 elections, Nicaragua. This categorization of Latin American governments is intended solely for the purpose of this analysis.

Group I governments such as Guatemala must devote major effort to staying in power. Well-organized, often armed, opposition groups are determined to overthrow them. If these governments fear external threats to their security, these fears usually are aroused by neighboring states that host opposition forces. Typically, Group I governments seek to draw U.S. authorities into the domestic conflict in order to bolster their political influence and gain support for their repression of opposition forces. Partly in order to attract U.S. economic and military assistance, they voice concern regarding Soviet interference and communist subversion. Communists are almost always present there, as they are elsewhere in the world; the question is whether their presence has political significance. In the past, the communist presence was usually not very powerful; charges of subversion were often an exaggeration employed by incumbents to defend their vested political interests. Governments such as these may endorse U.S. armed intervention as a means of preventing their own collapse.

The rightist or centrist governments of Group II often have a firm grip on power, and although they are not seriously and immediately concerned about external threats to their security, they perceive that such possibilities exist. These governments are aware that, just as Russia and the Soviet Union have played a hegemonic role in Eurasia, the United States has played a hegemonic role in the Americas in the twentieth century. They do not expect U.S. intervention in the foreseeable future, but they are concerned about protecting their political autonomy and they generally oppose U.S. intervention in neighboring countries. Most of these governments would probably prefer to have the United States as a neighbor rather than the Soviet Union. Nonetheless, they seek to diversify and strengthen their international position by maintaining beneficial economic and political relations with the Soviet Union. Soviet ties constitute a counterbalance to their more useful and comprehensive relations with the United States.

The prosocialist governments in Group III have become, through their own actions or those of the United States, the target of official U.S. hostility. Depending upon their particular situation, these governments have become dependent to a greater (Cuba) or lesser (Nicaragua) degree on the Soviet Union for their own welfare and for protection against existing or threatened U.S. sanctions. Fearful of becoming the victim of U.S. intervention, Castro has supported Soviet armed intervention to prop up pro-Soviet governments in Czechoslovakia and Afghanistan.

Group I governments, such as Guatemala, do not want and will not have relations with the Soviet Union. The feelings are mutual. Since the Nicaraguan revolution of 1979, the Soviet Union backs armed revolt boldly in some of these countries. In Group II countries such as Mexico and Brazil, the Soviet Union will seek to expand its political and economic relations, but Communist parties in these countries are less likely to use revolutionary violence. The Soviet Union wants very much to maintain positive relations with these countries, and it will go to great lengths to make the relationship attractive. Nonetheless, the relative weakness of the Soviet economy, the nature of the Soviet and international communist systems, and the inherent contradictions between socialist and capitalist societies constitute limits to these ties. Soviet bilateral relations with Group II countries will probably grow, but they will not be very extensive compared to relations between these Latin American countries and the United States and western Europe.

Cuba represents the upper limit for Soviet ties with Group III countries. Nicaragua clearly prefers more ties with the West and less dependence on the Soviet Union than Cuba, and the Soviet Union would no doubt wish to give up some political influence in Cuba in order to reduce its economic burdens there.

Some of the most destabilizing changes in international relations in the Western Hemisphere will come not from governments, whatever their political complexion, but from revolutionary movements seeking to transform their own countries and their relations with foreign powers. Movements such as these are not historical aberrations; rather, they are recurring phenomena in history. Social structures adapt to the churning social forces beneath them as frequently by revolution as by peaceful change. The United States is rare in having adapted peacefully to social change, yet even it experienced the War of Independence from Great Britain and the Civil War.

Revolutions are directed mainly against tyrannical leaders or oligarchies. Their hostility to foreign powers—usually the United States in Latin America—is a by-product of the more important domestic struggle for power between competing elites, between "ins" and "outs." Yet nations are so internally interdependent (including nations in revolution) that far-reaching changes *inside* a country invariably disturb its external relations as well. This is especially true in Latin America because most of the economies depend heavily on foreign trade for the industrial products and technology needed for national development. United States corporations are necessarily tied to incumbent elites—the only groups with which they could do business in the past. When revolutions occur, U.S. private property becomes hostage to the new leadership. Violent upheaval batters external as well as internal structures.

The revolutionary movement in El Salvador has already produced one of the major security crises faced by the Reagan administration. The civil war in Guatemala seems likely to become an even more serious crisis over time. Chile and Paraguay are also candidates for future domestic political upheaval. Contemporary Brazil is under control, but should that country ever experience revolution, the consequences would surely be dramatic. Although the location of revolutionary conflict cannot always be anticipated, new revolutionary outbreaks should come as no surprise in the future.

The Soviet Union

The Soviet Union has pursued flexible and pragmatic strategies regarding Latin America ever since Castro came to power in 1959. Soviet policy toward Cuba has been tolerant and farsighted, and its huge economic costs have paid important political dividends. Soviet policies toward other Latin American countries have also been adaptive and pragmatic, although less costly and less beneficial. In general they have positioned the Soviet Union well with respect to both the most powerful Latin American governments and revolutionary movements in the more politically unstable countries. Soviet influence in Latin America outside Cuba is not great compared with that of the United States or other powers, but it merits respect considering the weakness of the Soviet economy, the limited influence of Communist parties, and the low priority given Latin America in Soviet foreign policy. That is why the Soviet Union is a "threat." It would be imprudent not to recognize that the Soviet Union at little cost (except for Cuba) and with few risks (except for the missiles sent to Cuba in 1962) has achieved a good deal. That is why the United States should husband its own economic and political resources and respond more effectively to security problems in Latin America.

The centerpiece of Soviet policy in the Western Hemisphere is still Cuba. The Soviet leadership, which enforces such tight domestic political discipline, has done remarkably well for over two decades in dealing with an unpredictable, fractious, and temperamental Fidel Castro. Castro's political virtuosity has been equaled only by the Soviet Politburo's patience and adaptability. The Soviet Union has recently subsidized Cuba at the rate of several billion dollars a year—a large sum for the Soviet Union to give to any country, much less a small country on the other side of the world. However, Soviet economic burdens in Poland, Afghanistan, and Vietnam are heavy, and it now appears that the Soviet Union seeks to reduce the burden of its aid to Cuba. Nonetheless, a tougher Soviet line on aid will not be effective unless the performance of the Cuban economy and the price of sugar improve substantially—an outcome not to be expected on the basis of current performance. This may be one reason why Soviet policies encourage the expansion and diversification of Cuba's economic relations (including relations with the United States) as one promising means of strengthening the Cuban economy.

Soviet military policy toward Cuba is another major element in the Soviet Union's Latin American policy. No doubt Soviet and Cuban leaders both would like Cuban troops to return from Angola and Ethiopia, two costly operations now in overtime. However, it is likely that events in Africa—not in Moscow or Havana—will decide this issue. Both powers are so heavily committed to the integrity of pro-Soviet and prosocialist regimes in Angola and Ethiopia that Cuban troops are likely to remain there as long as they are really needed. In the meantime, social and economic pressure is building in Cuba to bring the troops home.

The Soviet Union has literally made a gift to Castro of the Cuban armed forces' military hardware. After the Bay of Pigs, the most pressing need was to build up those forces so as to make another U.S.-sponsored attack on Cuba so costly that it would deter the United States. Although the United States should be able to defeat Castro's forces in a direct confrontation, the monetary and human costs of such an effort would be great—not to mention the resulting adverse political consequences and the incalculable risk of Soviet military involvement. The Cuban armed forces have not generally been structured for offensive off-island operations, but they did manage to place a surprisingly large number of Cuban troops in Angola before the Soviet Union shouldered much of the logistical burden. Castro carries the historical stigma of having mounted unsuccessful armed landings against Caribbean governments in 1959 and ineffectual covert arms deliveries in the 1960s. Although he has recently transferred Soviet tanks and possibly other arms to Nicaragua, he does not appear to be inclined to initiate offensive military operations in the Caribbean Basin. One should not necessarily rely on Castro's restraint in this regard in the future, but the Soviet Union will be cautious about staking Castro to offensive military capabilities that it cannot control. In the meantime, given its already huge military investment on the island, the Soviet Union can be counted on to keep Castro's armed forces technologically up-to-date.

The Soviet Union applauded Somoza's fall in Nicaragua, and it has given political and economic support to the Sandinistas since then. This aid includes arms delivered either directly or through Cuba. The Soviets have received several high-level Nicaraguan delegations, and they have maintained diplomatic relations with the Sandinista government since early 1980. Nicaragua's revolutionary government has a handsome new embassy a few hundred yards from the Cuban embassy in Moscow. By 1983 the Soviet Union had provided Nicaragua with about $150 million in grant aid for necessary raw materials and semimanufactured items, and it has extended the equivalent of open-ended credits on standard terms for the purchase of Soviet machinery and equipment.[11] There are also parallel relations between the Communist Party of the Soviet Union and the Sandinistas.

Although the Soviet Union might develop relations with Nicaragua similar to those it has with Cuba, this appears unlikely for two reasons. First, the Sandinistas much prefer to retain extensive economic ties with both the United States and other western countries; they are cautious about becoming as dependent economically on the Soviet Union as Cuba is. Nicaragua's overland connections with other Central American countries mean that it does not enjoy the advantages and disadvantages that Cuba's island position offers. Then too, its economy is more diversified.

Second, the Soviet Union prefers not to develop in Nicaragua a client as financially costly as Cuba. Nevertheless, Soviet-Nicaraguan economic and military relations could become much closer—and more useful to the Soviet Union—without duplicating the Cuban pattern. This could become a reality especially if the Nicaraguan economy continues to deteriorate and if U.S. economic sanctions and hostile covert activities continue.

Soviet policy toward the rest of Latin America shows the same cautious, steady, and flexible qualities that it has demonstrated toward Cuba and Nicaragua, but the roles of wooer and wooed are reversed. Cuba has to "buy" most of its goods from the Soviet Union and other socialist countries, and the Soviet Union must trade with and aid Cuba. In contrast, other Latin American countries need to buy little from the Soviet Union, and they require cash payment in hard currencies for what they sell. The Soviet Union, in turn, needs many products from these countries and exports little to the region. Soviet traders have bought substantial quantities of manufactured goods, agricultural products, and nonferrous minerals from Latin America for years—substantial at least when compared with what Latin America buys from the Soviet Union. Soviet needs for grain and meat have increased substantially in recent years, but Latin American purchases have been and continue to be small.

Nonetheless, Soviet export agencies doggedly continue their promotion efforts in the region despite the superior products and marketing organizations of European, Japanese, and U.S. competitors. These agencies seek to turn Soviet economic weaknesses (that is, shortages of grain, meat, and other products) into a means of bolstering their own exports; the Soviets' argument that their extensive purchases from countries such as Argentina and Brazil should generate reciprocally increased imports from the Soviet Union will doubtless have some positive effect on future Soviet exports to Latin America. For example, Argentina is now the target of Soviet export-promotion efforts seeking contracts for demonstration projects for water control, thermal and electric power, and transportation, which over the long run are likely to attract other business for the Soviet Union in the hemisphere. Soviet determination in this area is based partly on the conviction that several generations of Soviet experience in huge development projects on the Eurasian landmass have value for a continent in which low- and medium-level (and thus lower-cost) technologies are suitable. Although lackluster so far, Soviet trade promotion efforts merit close observation because of their possible economic repercussions; although Soviet trade with Latin America is still not large, it has been expanding rapidly. Soviet purchases have become sufficiently important for some Latin American countries (especially on the eastern coast of South America) that the impact of trade on political relations with the Soviet Union is increasing.

Argentina is the main case in point. The Soviet Union is Argentina's principal foreign customer, receiving about a third of its exports. Although the two countries are at opposite ends of the political spectrum, their shared economic interests have resulted in (often tacit) political collaboration. For example, Argentina's 1976–1983 military government discriminated in favor of the Argentine Communist Party's political operations, and the Communists supported what they considered to be positive aspects of the government's policies. Similarly, the Soviet Union avoided criticizing the military government's violations of human rights, and Argentina softened its criticism of certain aspects of Soviet foreign policy. Although not wishing to be associated with Argentina's forceful seizure of the Falkland/Malvinas Islands in 1982, the Soviet Union sided with Argentina against Great Britain thereafter—as it did earlier in Argentina's dispute with Chile over the Beagle Channel. The Soviet Union has also provided Argentina with heavy water and enriched uranium for its nuclear energy program.[12]

One of the most interesting aspects of Soviet-Argentine cooperation concerns military affairs. For some years now the armed forces of both countries have exchanged visits by military officers. It is unlikely that Argentina will purchase Soviet arms under the Alfonsín government. However, Argentine military leaders welcome ties with armed forces independent of the United States and other North Atlantic Treaty Organization (NATO) countries. In part, they view contacts such as these as a means of demonstrating their prowess as global strategists.

Like Argentina, Brazil has long been a target for Soviet economic and political initiatives. However, efforts there have focused on formal government-to-government relations rather than on ties with the Brazilian Communist Party. The Soviet Union wants positive, active relations with Brazil because it is the most populous and powerful state in Latin America. The bilateral relationship is similar to that with Argentina in that leading groups in both these countries are ideologically and politically anticommunist (and to some extent anti-Soviet), yet they welcome the benefits of economic and political diversification that come from their Soviet ties. The Soviet Union will continue to expand its official relations with Brazil while attempting to minimize any negative impact that the local Communists may have on bilateral relations.

Mexico has always occupied (and will continue to occupy) a priority position in the Soviet Union's Latin American policy because of its size and, most particularly, because it is the United States' closest Latin American neighbor. The Soviet Union will push for bilateral collaboration on a wide front. Although prospects for increased trade between the two countries appeared to be slight before Mexico's 1982 financial crisis, it will be interesting to see if Soviet credits (however small in the overall economic picture) now become more attractive. In any case, both governments are likely to take advantage promptly of mutually useful political opportunities.

Similarly, the Soviet Union will continue to develop its relations with democratic countries in Latin America such as Venezuela, Colombia, and Costa Rica. In these cases, as with Argentina, Brazil, and Mexico, the Latin American section of the Communist Party of the Soviet Union's Central Committee will probably attempt to check the revolutionary proclivities of local Communist parties, encourage them to remain on civil terms with established governments, and thereby minimize friction in government-to-government relations with the Soviet Union. Until Brezhnev gained control in the Soviet Union, local applications of the party line tended to be fairly uniform. But in recent years it has become more differentiated, and it will continue to become so.

Armed revolt will receive Soviet moral and possibly material support in countries in which the *ancien régime* is fragile. For the immediate future this includes El Salvador and Guatemala. Farther down the same road are Chile and Paraguay, where dictators and exploitative systems must eventually exhibit the infirmities of age. Soviet leaders appear prudent enough to know that Soviet help will probably not be decisive in any of these cases; that is, these revolutions will be won or lost depending upon the strength of the established regime and the strategies of the armed opposition. The old order in several of these countries is so repressive, backward, and antidemocratic that Soviet leaders are confident of eventually being identified with the winning side. By waging a continuing media campaign against these established regimes, Soviet authorities leave themselves in a favorable position to conduct relations with the revolutionary victors.

The Soviet Union will also be tempted to sell arms to Latin America, not only to leftist governments such as the Sandinistas in Nicaragua but also to countries such as Argentina. Arms deliveries to guerrillas are a more delicate matter, but the Soviet Union surely would not rule out all covert deliveries. However, it is more likely that the Soviet Union will rely upon third parties such as Cuba to provide arms to Latin American allies, knowing that ultimately the guerrillas themselves can procure the minimum necessary arms through local capture, bribery, or purchases from traditional commercial sources.

Because they believe that the victory of revolution and socialism in Latin America is inevitable, the Soviet Communists are in no hurry to achieve that end, especially when haste could damage formal Soviet bilateral relations and cripple local Communist parties. Instead, the Soviet Union will pursue classic state interests with the large Latin American countries, maintain correct relations with the middle powers, and back armed revolt in small and politically vulnerable countries.

The United States: Lessons from the Past

In mapping policy for the future, U.S. leaders should attempt to benefit from the country's past experiences. Fortunately, these experiences have not been all bad. The United States' most dangerous crisis in Latin America since 1945 was the Cuban missile crisis of 1962. President Kennedy and his associates managed that crisis masterfully. Despite continuing disagreements, the United States and Mexico have reached one important accommodation after another since 1917, and there are many lessons to be learned from U.S. accommodation to the Mexican revolution. Similarly, the Eisenhower administration responded effectively to the Bolivian revolution of 1952.

Regrettably, however, U.S. authorities have not dealt very effectively with most post-1945 security crises in terms of stated long-term U.S. objectives. Short-term objectives have included the overthrow of particular governments, but events such as these should be compatible with longer term objectives as well. Ordinarily these objectives have been expressed in terms of defending or promoting stability and democracy in particular countries and preventing Soviet interference in the region. The two top priorities are stability (defined as continuity in power for a government collaborating closely with the United States) and the exclusion of Soviet influence from the hemisphere. Judging from the performance of most post-World War II U.S. administrations, democracy has been farther down the list of priorities in Latin America. However, most of the Latin American countries in which the United States has interfered did not become stable (Guatemala, Chile, Nicaragua) or democratic (Guatemala, Chile, Nicaragua, Cuba), and in some cases Soviet influence is greater than it was previously.

Proponents of U.S. intervention might argue that punitive responses to security crises in Guatemala, the Dominican Republic, and Chile succeeded in the sense that the Soviet Union did not gain a foothold in these three countries. To be persuasive, however, this argument would need to show that U.S. policy prevented the Soviet Union from establishing such a presence. But there is no convincing evidence that the Soviet Union was about to make important gains in either Guatemala or the Dominican Republic. In Chile, despite the fact that the Communists were the second party in Allende's governing coalition, Soviet trade, economic, and political ties were not substantial. To justify U.S. policy it would also be necessary to show that U.S. intervention achieved stability or democracy.

In Guatemala, where Arbenz was overthrown by the armed forces after the U.S.-sponsored paramilitary invasion, the most authoritative retrospective accounts argue that the threat of a communist victory was exaggerated.[13] Arbenz's overthrow did mark the achievement of a short-term objective, but since then Guatemala has been one of the most unstable and strife-torn countries in the hemisphere. It has been in a state of virtual civil war for years, with appalling executions, torture, and so forth. Neither stability, a capacity to resist foreign intervention, nor democracy was achieved.

The U.S. paramilitary intervention in Cuba at the Bay of Pigs failed to achieve both its short- and long-term objectives. Castro's government has established virtually total control over national economic and political life. The 1961 Bay of Pigs crisis led to the brief installation of Soviet missiles in Cuba. United States citizens lost all their property, and Cuba became a leading political and military collaborator of the Soviet Union. United States policy was a total failure.

Although U.S. economic sanctions and covert actions against the Allende government contributed to its overthrow, many analysts do not regard these efforts as especially important in bringing about Allende's political demise. A strong case can be made that the Allende government fell because it lost the support of the Chilean middle class, which placed the Chilean military in a strong position to launch the 1973 coup.[14] Many analysts believe that Allende would have had a difficult time completing his term with or without U.S. covert opposition. In any event, the post-1973 military government has been the antithesis of democracy, and the prospects for political instability have recently increased—particularly because of a severe national economic crisis.

The U.S. military occupation of Santo Domingo in 1965 achieved its short-term objective by preventing the return to office of constitutional president Juan Bosch. However, Johnson and subsequent U.S. administrations never proved the early charges (which were later dropped) that communists controlled the Constitutionalists' revolt. Unlike other countries in which U.S. intervention occurred, the Dominican Republic enjoyed relative prosperity and order for many years thereafter. This was partly because U.S. authorities played a conciliatory role vis-à-vis various opposing forces during the intervention. Nevertheless, in a longer-term perspective the Dominican Republic is still one of the Latin American countries most dependent on the United States economically and politically. Dominican trade with and investment from the United States have intensified, and U.S. governmental authorities played an important role in effecting a successful democratic political transition in 1978. In the past, the United States' worst political crises in the hemisphere have occurred in countries with which it had the closest relationship (such as the Dominican Republic). Because U.S. influence in these countries has been so great, the nationalist backlash is often particularly strong. Other examples include Mexico before the 1910–1917 revolution, Nicaragua, Cuba, and Panama.

Finally, evaluating U.S. policy toward Latin American countries principally in terms of their relationship to possible Soviet influence is too narrow a focus. Evaluations should also take into account the political benefits and costs and other consequences of the policies actually implemented, including their impact on U.S. relations with other Latin American states and with developing countries more generally.

The United States: Contemporary Security Challenges

From the time the Reagan administration took office in January 1981, it was deeply absorbed in responding to revolutionary movements in Central America and the Caribbean. Reagan engaged in more armed intervention and political interference in the region than any U.S. president since Woodrow Wilson. The Sandinistas' relations with the United States had significantly worsened by the end of the Carter administration, but the Reagan administration conducted openly hostile and punitive policies against Nicaragua, including CIA sponsorship of a counterrevolutionary émigré force (the contras). CIA operations included sabotage (most notably of Nicaragua's limited oil supplies), and the Sandinistas felt threatened by unprecedented U.S. military maneuvers near Nicaragua's borders and coastal waters. United States-sponsored economic sanctions also harmed the Nicaraguan economy. However, short of direct U.S. military intervention, these policies appeared unlikely in mid-1985 to achieve their apparent purpose—the overthrow of the Sandinista government. Indeed, U.S. sanctions resulted in closer Sandinista ties with, and dependence on, the Soviet Union, Cuba, and other socialist countries as Nicaragua increasingly turned to these sources for financial, technical, and military assistance. The Nicaraguan government also offered political and material support to armed revolutionaries in El Salvador.

Grenada's 1979 revolution was characterized by the development of one-party rule based partly on the Soviet model and close party ties with Cuba and the Soviet Union. As documents captured after the 1983 U.S. invasion of Grenada show, beginning in 1980 Cuba and the Soviet Union also supplied the Grenadian leaders with arms under secret agreements.[15] An internal struggle for political control between Maurice Bishop and Bernard Coard in late 1983 set the stage for U.S. military intervention. Bishop's execution and the imposition of harsh military rule by his successors provided other eastern Caribbean states and the United States with a justification for intervention. The U.S. invasion force landed on October 25, 1983, and took control of the island in a few days.

President Reagan initially characterized the invasion of Grenada as a mission to rescue U.S. citizens (mainly students at a local medical school) caught in growing political violence. Later he emphasized the Marxist, pro-Soviet character of the regime and the threat it ostensibly posed to hemispheric security. Grenada, with Canadian supervision and Cuban labor, was well advanced in the construction of a runway long enough to accommodate either large jet aircraft for tourism or military planes. Several neighboring states (including Jamaica) sought U.S. military intervention under the terms of a recent security agreement among eastern Caribbean states.

President Reagan was jubilant over the success of the military action, and there appeared to be considerable popular support for it in the United States. However, like other political-military operations, the invasion of Grenada can only be properly evaluated in terms of a cost-benefit analysis. The U.S. intervention removed a pro-Soviet, intermittently anti-U.S. regime and any chance (however remote) that it might soon engage in subversive activities among its Caribbean neighbors or lend its territory to Soviet stratagems. The safety of U.S. citizens was ensured. However, it is impossible to know how U.S. security would have been affected had the invasion not taken place. Just before the invasion, the Grenadian government—fearing U.S. sanctions—publicly guaranteed the safety of U.S. citizens; indeed, U.S. citizens on the island first came into physical danger during the U.S. military landing. The Soviet Union had supplied Grenada with large stocks of small arms to defend the established government from internal and external attack, but it is not clear that tiny Grenada could have been an effective subversive force in the region in the face of U.S. and neighboring countries' opposition. It is also unclear whether the airstrip would have eventually been used for military purposes. The United States, apparently no longer fearing the airstrip's military potential, subsequently encouraged Grenada to complete it so as to facilitate much-needed tourism to the island.

Supporters of the Grenada invasion have devoted little attention to assessing its political, human, and financial costs. The action was vigorously condemned by major U.S. allies, including Great Britain, France, Mexico, and Brazil.[16] The United States was completely isolated in the United Nations Security Council on the issue, and it was the only country to vote against a Security Council resolution critical of the invasion.[17] Indeed, the invasion was a violation of the Charter of the Organization of American States (Article 15) and the Charter of the United Nations (Article 2). The United States has a vested interest in the defense of the status quo, but it can hardly call on other states to observe the rule of law if it refuses to do so itself. Although the specific political costs are difficult to measure, it is indisputable that actions such as the Grenada invasion harm the United States' international reputation.

The invasion was strongly opposed by the armed Cuban construction workers on the island, and U.S. casualties totaled 18 killed and 116 wounded. If the primary purpose of the action was to protect the lives of U.S. citizens, it is not clear that more lives were saved by the use of force than by negotiating the protection or removal of U.S. citizens then in Grenada. Some 45 Grenadians were killed and 337 wounded. Cuban casualties totaled 24 dead and 59 wounded. Thus there were just under 600 total casualties.[18]

The United States' land, sea, and air attacks during the invasion also incurred substantial financial costs (approximately $75 million). United States funds subsequently allocated for reconstruction and development in Grenada and additional assistance for other eastern Caribbean states totaled approximately $70 million.[19] The United States also stationed several hundred troops on the island to perform police responsibilities.

The ultimate costs of the use of military force in this case can be evaluated only when subsequent developments in Grenada and their relationship to the United States are fully understood. However, President Reagan's decision to intervene in Grenada cannot be understood only in terms of Latin American affairs. Domestic political considerations and East-West factors were apparently the decisive motivations in reaching this decision.

Whereas the Reagan administration used force against established regimes in Nicaragua and Grenada in the early 1980s, the United States at the same time sought to use its economic and military might (short of direct U.S. military intervention) to sustain a pro-U.S. government in power in El Salvador. The United States officials attempted to prevent either rightist political forces (closely linked to human rights violations) or leftist guerrilla forces (favoring radical social transformations) from gaining control. The Reagan administration regarded the 1984 electoral victory of the centrist Christian Democrat candidate, José Napoleón Duarte, as an important step toward stabilizing the shaky regime. However, U.S. objectives continued to be threatened by the political right's de facto military and police powers and by the continuing strength of the revolutionary forces. The guerrillas undoubtedly enjoyed the political support of the Sandinista government in Nicaragua, Cuba, and the Soviet Union, but the source and significance of the guerrillas' external material support remained a controversial issue.

In the United States, political leaders in both the Democratic and Republican parties and much of the U.S. public continued to fear Soviet involvement (either directly or through Cuba) in these revolutionary situations in Central America and the Caribbean. However, the domestic political debate in the United States was not primarily over Soviet objectives in the Caribbean Basin. The Reagan administration and its critics largely agreed on this issue; for example, most participants in the debate agreed that the Soviet Union has long favored the establishment of pro-Soviet socialist regimes in Central America and the Caribbean. The Soviet position on this point was also well established: revolutions would eventually transform these societies (preferably through peaceful means, but by force if necessary), and the resulting regimes would be modeled on the Soviet example, with such variations as proved politically necessary and suited to local conditions. The anti-U.S. dimensions of these Soviet objectives in a regional and global context were clear. The realization of these Soviet objectives would constitute a political and, ultimately, a military threat to U.S. interests.

As previously noted, the domestic political debate in the United States did not concern these Soviet objectives. Rather, it focused on what the Soviet Union had done in Central America and the Caribbean to attain these goals, the Soviet capacity to manipulate developments in the area, and what the United States should do to protect its interests. The Reagan administration, despite its formal acknowledgment of the importance of the domestic origins of these conflicts, viewed revolutions primarily as part of the international communist movement headed by the Soviet Union. In contrast, critics of Reagan administration policy viewed revolutionary situations as primarily domestic upheavals from which the Soviet Union sought to benefit. The Reagan administration apparently considered the Soviet Union capable of engineering, manipulating, leading, and ultimately controlling the local revolutionary leadership. Critics of this interpretation viewed the strength and reach of Soviet influence much more skeptically.

Finally, the Reagan administration and most of its Democratic critics advocated contrasting policies to respond to revolutionary situations and the Soviet Union's relation to them. The Reagan administration's policies employed force in an effort to impose governments more amenable to the United States. The U.S. military invasion of Grenada succeeded in overthrowing the incumbent revolutionary government in part because the island is so small. The Sandinista government in Nicaragua was able to resist U.S.-supported subversion because of the strength and size of its armed forces and the support it received from socialist countries and some western governments. In El Salvador, the Reagan administration formally supported negotiations between the incumbent government and the revolutionary opposition, but as of mid-1985 it had not (as its critics urged) made significant progress toward a negotiated solution to the conflict.

The Reagan administration defended covert action against the Sandinista government on the grounds that it provided the United States with bargaining leverage that would ultimately ensure Nicaraguan cooperation in a compromise settlement. The 1984 National Bipartisan Commission on Central America, chaired by former Secretary of State Henry A. Kissinger, used this argument to justify its decision not to evaluate U.S. covert action in the area on its merits. However, actual experience with such activity offered little encouragement that U.S. covert participation in the Nicaraguan conflict was aimed at promoting a negotiated settlement. Instead, this policy appeared to seek the demise of the Sandinista regime. Whatever official U.S. motives were, the claim that hostile actions such as these were intended to promote compromise with the Sandinista government could be credible only if genuine progress in negotiations were achieved.

It is important to note in this context that most of the Reagan administration's reactions to contemporary revolutionary movements echoed earlier U.S. interventions in Latin America. United States-sponsored subversive actions against the Sandinista government were reminiscent of CIA-supported forces in Guatemala in 1954 and CIA-supported émigré forces at the Bay of Pigs in 1961. The invasion of Grenada was in some ways similar to the U.S. invasion of the Dominican Republic in 1965. The United States' support for the incumbent government in El Salvador had precedents in U.S. military and counterinsurgency programs in Latin America in the 1960s. In justifying the U.S. response to these revolutionary situations, President Reagan quoted liberally from Presidents Truman, Kennedy, and Johnson.

With these historical precedents as models, the Reagan administration developed an elaborate series of arguments to justify its use of force in Latin America and its open interference in the politics of Latin American countries. These arguments were generally labeled "the credibility gap," "the Munich syndrome," "the domino theory," and "preventive interference." It is worthwhile examining each of these four arguments in more detail.

1. "The Credibility Gap." In a 1983 address to a Joint Session of Congress, President Reagan said, "If the United States cannot respond to a threat near our own borders, why should Europeans or Asians believe we are seriously concerned about threats to them? If we cannot defend ourselves there, we cannot expect to prevail elsewhere. Our credibility would collapse, our alliances would crumble, and the safety of our homeland would be in jeopardy."[20] President Reagan was correct that U.S. policies in Central America have an impact on the country's credibility elsewhere in the world. However, the impact was often opposite to that he sought; U.S. policies in Central America were criticized widely in Europe and in Latin America not for what the United States failed to do, but for what it did. The "credibility gap" argument did identify the need for U.S. action, but it did not specify what that action should be; it advocated some form of urgent action, but it did not define a broader policy.

2. "The Munich Syndrome." In explaining his policies concerning Central America, President Reagan frequently referred to the Nazi threat in Europe in the 1930s and the need to oppose Soviet aggression before it was too late.[21] In a May 1984 television address, he said, "If we come to our senses too late, when our vital interests are even more directly threatened, and after a lack of American support causes our friends to lose the ability to defend themselves, then the risks to our security and our way of life will be infinitely greater."[22] Similarly, Reagan also recalled Truman's actions to support Greece in the late 1940s and discourage further Soviet aggression. Of course, there is some question whether the Soviet Union in the late 1940s and early 1980s was similar to Nazi Germany in the 1930s. But even if the two cases were analogous, "the Munich syndrome" argument simply called for defensive or preventive action (rather than appeasement); it did not specify *what* action was appropriate. The argument would certainly not advocate policies that only strengthened Soviet influence—as Reagan administration policies in Central America arguably have done.

3. "The Domino Theory." In his public appeals concerning Central America, President Reagan raised the fear that if one country in the area were taken over by communism, neighboring countries would follow one after another—like falling dominoes. In a March 1983 address to the National Association of Manufacturers, Reagan asserted that "if guerrilla violence succeeds in El Salvador, El Salvador will join Cuba and Nicaragua as a base for spreading fresh violence to Guatemala, Honduras, Costa Rica. . . . The killing will increase and so will the threat to Panama, the canal, and ultimately Mexico."[23] In an address to Congress six weeks later, he queried, "Must we accept the destabilization of an entire region from the Panama Canal to Mexico on our southern border?"[24]

The domino theory as applied to Central America is based on two doubtful assumptions. The first is that the decisive elements in these revolutionary situations are primarily external and that the mere presence of a revolutionary regime in the area fatally infects neighboring countries. Revolutionary forces operating in a country with a sympathetic government on its borders do have certain tactical advantages. But the history of revolutions shows that the victory of revolutionary forces depends primarily on their ability to mobilize greater strength than the incumbent regime. Some revolutionary movements in Central America may succeed; others will fail. The decisive element will be the comparative strength of the opposing domestic forces, not the political orientation of neighboring countries. Second, it is doubtful that the region from Panama to Mexico is about to "collapse." The Sandinistas are firmly entrenched in Nicaragua, and the governments in El Salvador and (to a lesser extent) Guatemala are alarmingly unstable. But Costa Rica, Panama, Mexico, and perhaps even Honduras are likely to remain relatively stable in the near- and medium-terms.

The credibility gap, the Munich syndrome, and the domino theory are essentially rhetorical devices. They rely on predictions of events that have not yet happened, and they create a climate of fear in which proponents of these arguments hope to achieve certain policy objectives. The three arguments advocate urgent action without justifying any particular policy. In the early 1980s the issue was not *whether* to respond to growing Soviet influence in Central America and the Caribbean, but *how* to respond. The Reagan administration did not demonstrate why military actions (whether "covert" as in Nicaragua or overt as in Grenada) were more likely than negotiations to further U.S. interests in the area.

4. Preventive Interference. Perhaps the Reagan administration's strongest argument in support of U.S. interference in Central America was that failure to act in this way would permit the Soviet Union to expand dramatically its presence in the area. In May 1984 President Reagan argued that Central America had "become the stage for a bold attempt by the Soviet Union, Cuba, and Nicaragua to install communism by force throughout the hemisphere."[25] The underlying argument was that U.S. interference was necessary to counter Soviet meddling and protect vital U.S. interests. Because of the obvious conflicts of interest between the United States and the Soviet Union, this was a serious argument.

However, applying this argument to particular cases has been difficult in the past. It is not easy to determine the nature and extent of Soviet involvement in a specific situation. For example, the United States made a similar argument in Guatemala in 1954 and in the Dominican Republic in 1965. The Soviet Union provided Nicaragua with economic assistance and military aid (this latter support channeled mainly through Cuba), and it encouraged other socialist countries to provide similar support. There was also a large pro-Soviet Cuban presence in Nicaragua in the early 1980s. The Soviet Union clearly wanted to help the Sandinistas defend their autonomy against U.S.-supported counterrevolutionaries and the United States itself. Indeed, Soviet assistance to Nicaragua grew as U.S. pressures against the Sandinista regime increased—making U.S. official prophecies self-fulfilling. Although the Soviet Union has ties with revolutionary groups in other Central American countries, it is even more difficult to measure Soviet influence there. Moreover, Soviet influence is not necessarily equivalent to Soviet control.

There are also more general limitations to the preventive interference approach. It is a reactive policy that yields the initiative to the Soviet Union. If the United States must support the groups that the Soviet Union opposes, then the Soviet Union is in a position to choose allies for the United States. United States diplomacy should remain flexible and capable of taking advantage of developing opportunities.

The argument that the United States should interfere in revolutionary situations simply because the Soviet Union is also involved is based on two false assumptions: that the Soviet Union can create and control revolutions and that the United States has the power and expertise to prevent them.[26] The historical record does not support either assumption as a sound basis for policy. For example, revolutions did not make most of eastern Europe socialist and "pro-Soviet"; rather, Soviet military occupation forced many eastern European countries into the Soviet sphere of influence. The two most important socialist revolutions other than the Russian revolution were the Chinese and Yugoslav revolutions—both of which were pointedly independent of the Soviet Union. On the other hand, the United States was unable to prevent the Mexican and Cuban revolutions—the two most important revolutionary transformations in Latin America.

It has been easy and fashionable to hold both President Reagan and his predecessors responsible for U.S. responses to revolutionary change in Latin America. However, the U.S. public also shares responsibility for these actions. The most pernicious and widespread public belief is that the

U.S. government knows what is best for Latin American countries (for example, that Arbenz, Castro, Bosch, and Allende were not suitable presidents for their countries). United States citizens disagree with and criticize West European leaders, but it ordinarily does not occur to them that those leaders should be displaced because they are not in favor in the United States. A second and more damaging belief is that the United States has ultimate responsibility to replace Latin American leaders perceived to endanger U.S. interests. In the security crises involving Guatemala, Cuba, Chile, and the Dominican Republic, U.S. governmental authorities tried to manipulate Latin American political leaders. They succeeded in all but Cuba, with damaging long-term consequences for U.S. interests in these countries and in the region as a whole.

The consequence of these two popular beliefs is that U.S. presidents fear (not unreasonably) that if they fail to act against troublesome revolutionary movements, and if the revolutionaries win, the U.S. electorate will take its revenge at the first opportunity. United States presidents feared "losing" Guatemala, Chile, Cuba, and the Dominican Republic for this reason. Opportunistic political opponents are poised to mobilize ill-informed public opinion against any president who can plausibly be charged with being "soft" on communism. The tragic lessons of Vietnam may have modified this dangerous public view, but too many U.S. citizens still fail to realize that U.S. interference abroad can be costly in lives, economic resources, and power. It can also actually facilitate increased Soviet influence.

If models for what not to do abound, knowing what *to do* is another matter. Public opinion and public policy should base U.S. strength on a free and prosperous United States—the physical and political base of national power. United States foreign and military policy should not determine national priorities, but rather vice versa.

The U.S. public also needs to develop more genuine respect for Latin Americans and how they rule themselves. Stated bluntly, the United States should stay out of Latin American countries' internal affairs. The stereotypical form of U.S. meddling has been the provision of economic and military assistance to keep a favored leader in power. Too many U.S. ambassadors have been unable to resist participating in their host country's local politics. Notorious past examples include Henry Lane Wilson in Mexico, Spruille Braden in Argentina, and Richard C. Patterson, Jr., in Guatemala. Some recent U.S. ambassadors to Latin America also qualify. Sensationalistic speeches about "projecting" U.S. power into developing countries, calling in the fleet, deploying counterinsurgency forces to extinguish "brush fires," and brandishing missiles at rivals have more to do with political posturing than genuine diplomatic achievement.

Revolutions in Latin America will not disappear in the future. They have occurred intermittently throughout the twentieth century. The most realistic response for foreign powers is not to attempt to initiate or prevent revolutions but to protect and advance national interests as revolutions occur. Despite failure after failure, the United States continues to seek to stem revolutionary tides—most recently in El Salvador. Soviet leaders, chastened by many policy errors of their own, have developed a healthy skepticism concerning their capacity for influencing revolutions. As a result, they devote most of their effort to maneuvering to capitalize on various possible outcomes. The United States also has an interest in protecting itself, whoever wins.

Policy Recommendations

In order to protect its security interests and other concerns in Latin America, the United States should take two sets of foreign policy actions. The first actions should seek to reduce immediately international tensions in specific countries in Central America and the Caribbean, positioning the United States to deal with a variety of possible political outcomes to ongoing conflicts in the area.

The present U.S. policy toward Nicaragua is sterile and dangerous. The Reagan administration has repeatedly denied any intention of overthrowing the Sandinista government, and the present level of pressure appears unlikely to effect such a result. However, economic sanctions and covert actions are forcing the Sandinistas to seek protection from U.S. pressures in a closer relationship with the Soviet Union. There is now reason to believe that the Soviet Union might expand bilateral relations more than originally expected, even if they remain less extensive than those with Cuba.[27] The United States should cease its covert activities against the Sandinistas and arrange for countries that share broad U.S. interests, such as the Contadora Group (Colombia, Mexico, Panama, and Venezuela) and France, to reassure the Nicaraguans that the United States will not sponsor armed attacks against them. If the Sandinistas are permitted to retain strong ties with the United States and the West, the incentive structure imbedded in these ties will encourage them to forego policies hostile to U.S. interests.

Similarly, the United States should gradually disengage from its entanglement in El Salvador and encourage other powers (such as Mexico and France) to broaden their support for the established government. The volatile political situation in El Salvador is beyond U.S. control, and more diversified international support for the elected government would be an important element in reestablishing national political stability. United States policy should specifically encourage the Contadora Group to assume greater responsibility for a negotiated settlement of the conflict. In addition, the United States should also gradually disassociate itself from the civil war in Guatemala. It is dangerous for the United States to take sides in violent conflicts such as this, whose outcome it cannot control. The United States should retain its ability to conduct relations with whatever government emerges from this prolonged political and military struggle. It should pursue a similar policy in other such cases.

Cuba is still the key to U.S. security in northern Latin America. The United States has failed in its efforts to overthrow Castro. The present relationship of tension and hostility endangers U.S. interests throughout the Caribbean and strengthens the Soviet position globally. The United States has no satisfactory alternative to seeking a negotiated settlement of the major points at issue between the two countries at the first suitable opportunity. Castro badly wants trade with the United States and access to U.S. technology, in addition to security against a U.S. attack and recovery of the Guantánamo Bay naval base. The United States needs to lessen Cuba's hostility, making it more responsive to U.S. interests and less dependent economically and militarily upon the Soviet Union. Negotiations will not turn Castro away from socialism, break his ties with the Soviet Union, or end his championship of the poor countries against rich states. Yet a negotiated settlement would improve the chances for peace in the Caribbean, and perhaps eventually lessen Soviet influence in the area.

The second set of recommendations serves as a framework for long-term U.S. policies toward the Latin American region as a whole. This framework would rule out Soviet military bases and nuclear weapons, U.S. armed intervention, and U.S. political interference in Latin American countries' internal affairs.

The United States should be prepared to take whatever action may be deemed necessary to prevent the Soviet Union from establishing a military base or stationing nuclear weapons in the Western Hemisphere. Because any U.S. armed action would risk Soviet retaliation in some other part of the world, every effort should be made to prevent Soviet nuclear weapons or bases from being established in the hemisphere in the first place. If such efforts are ineffective, the United States should proceed under the Inter-American Treaty of Reciprocal Assistance (the Rio Treaty) or, failing that, by the exercise of the inherent right of self-defense. As in the 1962 missile crisis, action of this kind should not be directed against Latin American forces but against the forces of any hostile extrahemispheric power. Nor should this action be a vehicle for U.S. military occupation or the overthrow of an established Latin American government.

The principal argument against the United States' use of armed force is that it ensures the hostility of the target and increases its susceptibility to Soviet overtures. It is precisely the cooperation (or at least the neutrality) of Latin American governments that the United States needs to guarantee its national security. Latin American countries cannot threaten the United States by themselves; they could do so only in cooperation with the Soviet Union. The United States has much more to offer these countries than the Soviet Union in terms of trade, investment, finance, technology, and arms, and it is in a far better position to compete politically and diplomatically in Latin America than is the Soviet Union. It is those Latin American countries subject to U.S. punitive sanctions—Cuba, Chile under Allende, Nicaragua, and Grenada between 1979 and 1983—that have turned to the Soviet Union for assistance. The best means of protecting U.S. security interests is to structure relations with revolutionary governments in such a way that they will respond to U.S. influence and not turn toward the Soviet Union. A strategy of this kind requires carrots as well as sticks. United States intervention only ensures that Latin American revolutionaries will warmly welcome Soviet assistance.

In addition, the United States should take the first convenient opportunity to reaffirm the principle of nonintervention—that it will not initiate armed action against its neighbors in Latin America. Apparently oblivious to U.S. treaty obligations, former Secretary of State Alexander Haig (1981–1982) seemed to take satisfaction in leaving open the option of U.S. armed intervention in Central America and against Cuba. Perhaps he thought, as President Eisenhower did in 1960, that options such as this are not dangerous until implemented. This is not the case. When Castro learned of Eisenhower's plans in May 1960, he began a rapid buildup of the Cuban armed forces with Soviet equipment—the forces that crushed U.S.-backed émigré invaders at the Bay of Pigs. Similarly, given the Reagan administration's threatening postures, the Soviet Union supported a rapid buildup of Cuban military forces in the early 1980s. The Soviet Union and Cuba also assisted in the expansion of Nicaragua's armed forces. The United States has expressed concern regarding these developments, but little else could have been reasonably expected given its stated hostility toward these regimes.

Furthermore, the United States should solemnly reaffirm the principle of noninterference in the internal affairs of Latin American states. Most North Americans and Latin Americans have grown so used to U.S. meddling over the years that ruling out political interference appears unrealistic. "Political interference" is used here to describe attempts to shape the outcomes of leadership struggles in Latin American countries.

As suggested earlier, the United States has long persisted in interfering in these struggles in the region. United States officials in Washington or in embassies in Latin America sometimes wield great power, and too

often they cannot resist using their influence to seek various short- and
longer-term local objectives. Meddling of this kind endangers U.S. interests in unfamiliar, unpredictable, and uncontrollable situations. United
States leaders lack the knowledge, experience, and expertise to shape the
politics of Latin American countries in the U.S. interest. The U.S. government is singularly unsuited for such a role. Presidents seldom average
much more than four years in office, and they frequently require one or
two years to establish their priorities. They often reverse the policies of
their predecessors on particular issues. Rarely do presidents and secre-
taries of state know anything about Latin America in general, much less
the politics of a particular country. The United States simply lacks the
capacity for deciding internal questions in the several dozen countries of
Latin America. United States interference in their internal affairs usually
produces unintended negative consequences.

Some may find the prohibition of Soviet military bases in the hemisphere inconsistent with the injunction against U.S. intervention and interference in Latin America. This would be the case if the United States
used military action against Soviet bases as a pretext for manipulating
Latin American countries. The United States has, of course, done this in
the past. However, the United States should limit enforcement of this
policy to actions against Soviet ships or offending aircraft, not against a
Latin American country. Timely action of this kind would also minimize
complications later. In the 1962 missile crisis, President Kennedy showed
that effective measures against Soviet offensive missiles in Cuba could be
taken without directly intervening in Cuba itself.

These security policy recommendations also have implications for future U.S. foreign assistance programs. In the past, U.S. economic and
military assistance has been justified mainly on security grounds. Aid is
often granted to sustain shaky governments or, in effect, to ensure that a
particular leader or group maintains control despite internal opposition.
Foreign assistance of this kind has become a way of life in U.S. diplomacy,
and U.S. officials count on it as a working tool not to be forfeited easily.
When some country is deprived of aid, its government may complain of
discrimination as if U.S. assistance were its right. Sometimes U.S. aid is
justified as essential to counter communist or Soviet intervention. These
claims are frequently exaggerated, distorted, or false. For example, although economic and military aid has often been granted in order to protect the Western Hemisphere from external enemies, there has never been
any reasonable prospect of either a Soviet conventional attack on the
hemisphere or a Cuban attack with which U.S. forces could not cope. In
practice, almost all U.S. military aid to Latin American countries has been
used not to preserve their "external security" but to maintain their "internal security" (and occasionally to help dictators repress a restive popula-

tion). Economic and military assistance has also frequently been convenient for specific, short-term U.S. political purposes.

Official U.S. foreign aid figures confirm that economic and military assistance has been a favored instrument of U.S. security policy. Between 1946 and 1982 the U.S. government extended to Latin America (less repayments and interest) $7.2 billion in grants and $5.1 billion in loans; $10.7 billion of this amount was for economic assistance and $1.5 billion was for military assistance (most of the latter in grants). Among the largest aid recipients were Brazil ($2.1 billion), Colombia ($1.1 billion), and Chile ($850 million).[28] What did the United States achieve in these three countries that was worth over $4 billion? Or, to take another group of countries, the United States provided substantial aid over the same period to Guatemala ($457 million), El Salvador ($646 million), and Nicaragua ($386 million). Foreign aid to these countries did not achieve its political purposes, as the current revolutionary turmoil in each country shows.

Official U.S. assistance to Latin America has been small in comparative terms, but similar conclusions can be drawn concerning countries that received large amounts of economic and military assistance, such as Vietnam ($22.9 billion), Israel ($18.7 billion), and Iran ($1.3 billion). Does the present state of U.S. relations with any of these countries attest to the efficacy of U.S. economic and military assistance policies? Even if supporters of U.S. foreign aid programs can identify occasional successes, such cases hardly offset an otherwise dismal record of foreign assistance as a *political* instrument. The United States might be better advised to save the money, avoid entanglements, and forego some transient benefits. Latin American governments will collaborate with the United States when it is in their interest to do so. When it is not, paid collaboration is unreliable.

Proponents of U.S. foreign assistance for the purpose of shaping internal developments in Latin American countries so as to prevent Soviet interference miss the main point. These countries will be able to resist foreign interference only when they can independently make important political decisions by themselves. Foreign meddling prevents this. Latin Americans will be vulnerable to Soviet interference as long as they are vulnerable to U.S. interference. The United States must avoid interference in order to permit Latin American states to stand strong and independent.

The United States should continue its disaster relief programs and low profile economic and technical assistance. Because the growth of Latin American economies is essential to U.S. economic well-being, the United States should sharply increase its contributions to the most cost effective international organizations promoting economic development in the region.

Although sometimes flouted in practice, the security recommendations made here are actually long and legally established declaratory policy. All presidents since John F. Kennedy have been committed to the prohibition of Soviet nuclear arms in the hemisphere. The principles of nonintervention and noninterference were articulated in Franklin D. Roosevelt's Good Neighbor Policy, approved by the Congress, and reaffirmed by the executive and legislative branches on many occasions since then. The urgent need now is to implement these policies, recognizing that U.S. interests will be better served by negotiations than by armed conflict with Latin American governments. With its immense bargaining power, the United States does not need to use force against these countries. Military operations are costly in human, economic, and political terms. They also create unpredictable dangers, and they facilitate extrahemispheric interference.[29]

Center for Latin American Studies
University of Pittsburgh

Notes

1. Cole Blasier, "The Soviet Union in the Cuban-American Conflict," in Cole Blasier and Carmelo Mesa-Lago, eds., *Cuba in the World* (Pittsburgh: University of Pittsburgh Press, 1979), pp. 46–47.

2. For a discussion of U.S. dependence on and vulnerability to foreign sources of raw materials, see Amos A. Jordan and Robert A. Kilmarx, *Strategic Mineral Dependence: The Stockpile Dilemma* (Washington, D.C.: Center for International Studies, 1979), pp. 15–28; James E. Mielke, *Strategic and Critical Minerals: U.S. Import Reliance, Stockpile Strategy and Feasibility of Cartels* (Washington, D.C.: Congressional Research Service, 22 September 1980).

3. Central Intelligence Agency, *CIA Handbook of Economic Statistics, 1982*, p. 124.

4. See Robert C. Crassweller, *Trujillo: The Life and Times of a Caribbean Dictator* (New York: Macmillan, 1966), pp. 424–25.

5. For a discussion of the Soviet relationship with the Arévalo and Arbenz governments, see Ronald M. Schneider, *Communism in Guatemala, 1944–1954* (New York, 1958), p. 294. Concerning Castro's early relationship with the Soviet Union, see Cole Blasier, *The Hovering Giant: U.S. Responses to Revolutionary Change in Latin America* (Pittsburgh: University of Pittsburgh Press, 1976), p. 203; for a critique of Castro in a Soviet journal, see *Partinaia zhizn* 20 (1958): 51. Concerning the Dominican revolutionaries, see Blasier, *Hovering Giant*, p. 247.

6. Jorge I. Domínguez, "Revolutionary Politics: The New Demands for Orderliness," in Jorge I. Domínguez, ed., *Cuba: Internal and International Affairs* (Beverly Hills, Ca.: Sage Publications, 1982), pp. 29–31.

7. José Moreno, *Barrios in Arms* (Pittsburgh: University of Pittsburgh Press, 1970), pp. 210–11. See also Blasier, *Hovering Giant*, p. 247.

8. U.S. Department of Commerce, *Survey of Current Business* (August 1956): 18; (August 1959): 30; (October 1971): 32.

9. John Foster Dulles, "The Republican Perspective," *Foreign Policy Bulletin* 32, No. 1 (15 September 1952): 4; see also *New York Times,* 28 August 1952, p. 12; 4 September 1952, pp. 1, 20; 11 October 1952, p. 14.

10. Dwight D. Eisenhower, *The White House Years: Waging Peace, 1956–1961* (New York: Doubleday, 1965), p. 533. Richard M. Bissell, Jr., former deputy director of the CIA (1959–1962), wrote the author on 14 May 1973 that he believes that the success of the Guatemala operation contributed to the Bay of Pigs decision.

11. Cole Blasier and Richard Newfarmer, "Nicaragua: Negotiations Are the Way to Go," *Los Angeles Times,* Part II, 16 December 1982, p. 7.

12. See Aldo Vacs, *Discreet Partners: Argentina and the USSR Since 1917* (Pittsburgh: University of Pittsburgh Press, 1984); *Washington Post,* 13 January 1981.

13. For example, see Richard H. Immerman, *The CIA in Guatemala* (Austin: University of Texas Press, 1982), pp. 182–86; Stephen Schlesinger and Stephen Kinzer, *Bitter Fruit* (New York: Anchor Books, 1983), p. 107.

14. Paul E. Sigmund, *The Overthrow of Allende and the Politics of Chile, 1964–1976* (Pittsburgh: University of Pittsburgh Press, 1977), p. 214. *New York Times,* 29 October 1971, p. 6; 27 September 1973, p. 3; 23 October 1973, p. 3.

15. Jiri Valenta and Virginia Valenta, "Leninism in Grenada," *Problems of Communism* 33 (July–August 1984): 11–14.

16. *New York Times,* 26 October 1983, pp. 1, 17–18; 16 November 1983, p. 3.

17. The final Security Council vote on the resolution was eleven in favor, one against, three abstentions. *New York Times,* 29 October 1983, p. 1.

18. For casualty figures, see U.S. Departments of State and Defense, *Grenada: A Preliminary Report* (Washington, D.C., 1983), p. 1.

19. *New York Times,* 15 April 1984, p. 7.

20. "Central America: Defending our Vital Interests," address by President Ronald Reagan to Joint Session of Congress, Washington, D.C., 27 April 1983, in U.S. Department of State, *Realism, Strength, Negotiations: Key Foreign Policy Statements of the Reagan Administration* (May 1984), p. 130.

21. *New York Times,* 4 March 1984, p. A22.

22. "U.S. Interests in Central America," President Ronald Reagan's Televised Address to the Nation, Washington, D.C., 9 May 1984, in *Realism, Strength, Negotiations,* p. 134.

23. "Strategic Importance of El Salvador and Central America," address by President Ronald Reagan before the National Association of Manufacturers, Washington, D.C., 10 March 1983, in U.S. Department of State, *Current Policy,* No. 464.

24. "Central America: Defending Our Vital Interests," p. 150.

25. Ibid., p. 134.

26. Cole Blasier, *The Giant's Rival: The USSR and Latin America* (Pittsburgh: University of Pittsburgh Press, 1983), p. 162.

27. Blasier and Newfarmer, "Nicaragua," p. 7.

28. *U.S. Overseas Loans and Grants, 1982* (Washington, D. C.: Agency for International Development, 1982), p. 33 (general Latin America); p. 40, (Brazil); p. 42 (Colombia); p. 41 (Chile); p. 48 (Guatemala); p. 47 (El Salvador); p. 54 (Nicaragua).

29. Margaret Daly Hayes's criticism of an earlier draft has helped me clarify several issues in this section.

19

Interstate Conflict in Latin America

Gregory F. Treverton

Many North American stereotypes of Latin America are wrong. Before the latest round of violence in Central America, the region had not been violent or prone to conflict in the middle decades of the twentieth century. Prior to the South Atlantic war of 1982, the last major interstate war in the region had been the Chaco War of 1932–1935. Between the Peru-Ecuador conflict of 1941 and the 1969 clash between Honduras and El Salvador, there was no sustained outbreak of interstate violence in the region. Nor is Latin America heavily armed in comparison with other areas of the world. During 1976–1978 military expenditures consumed only 1.6 percent of the region's gross national product (GNP) and only 10.2 percent of central government budgets compared with about 5 and 20 percent, respectively, for the developing world as a whole.[1] Arms imports by Latin American countries constituted only about 7 percent of all arms imports by the developing countries during 1976–1978.

Of course, this is not to say that the region has been tranquil or its military establishments inactive. There have continued to be changes of government by other than legally prescribed means. In South America, however, these coups d'état have been accompanied by less and less bloodshed. By the late 1970s most of the guerrilla insurgencies (both rural and urban) of the previous two decades had waned, whether because adaptations within domestic politics rendered them unnecessary or because increased sophistication of national means of repression made them unfruitful. Central America has been different: the revolution in Nicaragua ranked among the bloodiest events in the post-World War II period, leaving some fifty thousand dead. The civil war in El Salvador continues, and insurgencies have begun again even in South American countries. It is easy to imagine combinations of political and economic circumstances that would make them still more probable.

Defining the Study

This essay examines one set of security issues underscored by recent events, particularly the South Atlantic war between Argentina and Great

565

Britain over the Falkland/Malvinas Islands and the 1981 armed border conflict between Peru and Ecuador. Are interstate conflicts such as these aberrations? Or do they suggest that "traditional" conflict—even armed conflict—*between states* (over territory, resources, colonial legacies, political rivalries, or some combination of these issues) will be more likely in the future than in the past? If so, why? What implications would this development have for the policies of Latin American governments and for U.S.–Latin American relations? It is not necessarily disparaging to observe that Latin American militaries have dressed better than they have fought because, happily, they have fought (each other) so seldom. Nor is it disparaging to note that these militaries have been more likely to be preoccupied with governing than with responding to external threats. However, will this continue to be the case? Or will Latin American states begin to feel that they must prepare for war even if they do not seek it, thereby fueling arms races and raising the likelihood of armed conflict by miscalculation? Will temptations to prepare nuclear options increase?

This analysis does not presume that interstate conflict is a more important topic than other issues in Latin America or in U.S.–Latin American relations. However, conflict of this kind may well have a place on the future agenda of hemispheric affairs. A wave of major wars is unlikely in the extreme, but interstate tension to the point of armed conflict is not. The implications of such conflicts (even if shooting does not occur) are serious—for governments of the hemisphere and for existing "security" arrangements in which they participate.

The term "interstate conflict" refers here to conflicts between Latin American states, or between them and nonhemispheric powers, that could lead to the use of armed force. This could occur because the use of armed force is explicitly planned by one or both sides or, more likely, because military action for political purposes is prepared for by one or both parties, thus raising the possibility that fighting might occur even if it was not explicitly intended. This essay does not examine conflict between Latin American states and the United States.

The focus on interstate conflict is less sharp than it might appear because the line separating interstate from intrastate conflict is sometimes blurred. Hostile governments may support domestic insurgencies within opponent states. Even if neighboring governments do not openly support them, insurgencies in one country may depend on assistance from or through (or on sanctuaries in) neighboring countries—thus raising policy issues that those neighbors may wish to avoid. Similarly, a country's domestic policies may provoke a response by its neighbor, thus initiating interstate conflict. The "soccer war" between El Salvador and Honduras in 1969 began when the latter initiated a land reform that might have meant the eviction of thousands of Salvadoran migrants to Honduras.

The broader ramifications of internal violence are even more difficult for Latin American countries and hemispheric institutions to come to grips with than interstate conflicts. This is because they involve delicate questions of national sovereignty and of what constitutes "aggression."

The Historical Record

Any conclusions based on the history of interstate conflict in Latin America since World War II must be treated with considerable caution. Small numbers of cases do not permit strong generalizations. This reservation is especially appropriate in this context because the more interesting conclusions turn on definitions that are inherently subjective. For example, are "weak" states more likely to initiate conflict? Are politically weak leaders more likely to conjure external threats? Nevertheless, the historical record permits a series of tentative conclusions that at least serve as a baseline for inquiring about the future. The first conclusions presented here apply to Latin America generally; the others underscore the extent of differences within the region.

First, conflict with neighbors seldom has dominated the foreign policy agenda of any Latin American state. Most conflicts have been contained short of war or even shooting, and many incidents between states have not become lasting conflicts.[2] Explaining what has not occurred is even more difficult than explaining what did. However, attention to this question raises the important issue of which conditions have changed in the region and which have remained relatively constant.

One factor muting interstate conflict in Latin America may have been the shared history and *relative* similarity of governing elites, in contrast with the major variations in colonial patterns and the ethnic and racial cleavages that exist in neighboring states in other parts of the developing world. Until recently, the preponderance of many Latin American states' external economic and even political interactions was directed outside the region, toward Europe or the United States rather than neighboring countries. Hence there usually was little to fight over (or gain). And, again until recently, many disputed boundaries were real frontiers, physically distant from national centers of political and economic activity. Thus there was little urgency to boundary disputes.

Two other explanations are even more difficult to evaluate. One is the frequent assertion that U.S. influence (often grandly labeled "hegemony")[3] muted interstate conflict in the region.[3] Because the United States was preoccupied with East-West conflict, it supposedly promoted solidarity rather than conflict among Latin American states. Because it was so preponderant in the region, the United States ostensibly could prevent or contain interstate conflict. Earlier much more than later, the United States could direct the activities of the Organization of American States (OAS) to its own purposes (maintaining a relatively tranquil status quo) rather than those of the Latin American members (for example, pressuring the United States on economic questions).[4] Although this argument is convincing in certain aspects, it is generally hard to test and difficult to disentangle from other factors. For instance, conflict has been no less frequent in the area of greatest U.S. influence, Central America, than elsewhere in Latin America.

A more specific form of the argument holds that U.S. influence with regional military establishments has contributed to diminishing conflict by prodding militaries toward other roles.[5] In the 1950s Latin American militaries (and governments) generally accepted the United States' position that the principal security threat to the Western Hemisphere was external, the East-West conflict. In the late 1960s, when Latin American militaries increasingly took governmental power, they generally did so under the banner of "national integration." Their preoccupation thus was internal: maintaining stability through some combination of suppressing insurgencies and altering the domestic circumstances that bred them. Again, it is difficult to know how important U.S. influence was in this regard; Latin American militaries may simply have reached conclusions about their domestic mission on their own.

Second (and surprisingly), most internal characteristics of Latin American states and their governments have been only weakly associated with conflict and its outcome. Of course, this conclusion must be interpreted with special caution because of the subjectivity of judgments about internal regime characteristics. Nevertheless, "weak" rulers do not appear to have been more likely to initiate conflicts (with one important exception—that of conflicts between Latin American states and Great Britain) than politically secure ones. Shaky governments have not seemed especially prone to conjure external enemies to distract attention from internal problems, a conclusion contrary to common images of Latin America.

Similarly, military governments do not appear to have been especially prone to conflict. In fact, neither the character of the regime—civilian or military—nor the ideological distance between regimes explains much of the pattern of conflict. Civilian regimes have been about as likely to initiate conflict with fellow civilian regimes (even ideologically close ones) as with military governments, and vice versa. Civilian regimes find it neither easier nor harder to settle conflicts with civilian counterparts than with military governments. Indeed, at least until recent events in Central America, the ideological distance between regimes seemed to be even less important in the post-World War II period than earlier. Most (although not all) of the democracy-versus-dictatorship or capitalism-versus-socialism conflicts occurred before 1965 (and most of these involved the United States).[6] These conclusions also contradict customary images.

There is no obvious explanation for these tendencies, but they at least suggest a certain rationality in national calculations. Weak governments may be deterred from reckless behavior because they recognize that any upsurge in popular support produced by external adventures will be short lived, and the public reaction may be negative if the adventure fails. As the Argentine military junta discovered in 1982, crowds cheer when the adventure succeeds, but their retribution is severe when it fails. By the same token, military governments may be particularly sensitive to the fact that it will be their task if a bluff is called and reckless action leads to fighting.

Third, nongovernmental relations—mostly trade and investment—between potential adversaries generally have had more beneficial than harmful effects. When these links have been significant and not directly connected to the source of dispute, they have helped to contain conflict. It seems reasonable that when states have more to lose by active conflict, they are less likely to engage in it. However, when economic issues have been bound up with territorial or boundary disputes (when, for example, governments have given private companies natural resource concessions in disputed areas, or when new resources have been discovered in those areas), conflict has been exacerbated. Of course, there are exceptions on both counts: Brazil made concessions in 1976 concerning the Itaipu hydroelectric project in part because private financial institutions financing the project were unwilling to do so over Argentine opposition. Similarly, in 1970 Venezuela agreed not to press its boundary claims on Guyana for a dozen years despite the absence of significant economic links (and the presence of a cultural abyss) between them.

However, some specific economic issues—resources, fishing rights, and so forth—have become more important sources of conflict. Resource questions in particular have become bound up with many conflicts over territories and boundaries. Long-standing claims that had lain dormant or old grievances that seemed tolerable have been revived when governments have thought that disputed areas contain valuable resources.

The extension of coastal economic zones to two hundred miles created new conflicts and made preexisting territorial disputes less tractable. Greatly increased oil prices made energy resources into a life and death matter for Latin American states, while new technology meant that energy sources formerly unreachable (and thus irrelevant) became exploitable. Now even the hint that contested territory may contain oil is enough to prevent a resolution of the dispute. Peru and Ecuador contested only distant jungle until oil was discovered in the area. The Beagle Channel dispute between Argentina and Chile ostensibly concerned sovereignty over several islands, but to the disputants it was charged with the possibility that oil and krill might be found within a two-hundred-mile zone around the islands, or that the disposition of the islands might one day affect competing claims to Antarctica.

Fourth, even if conflicts mostly have been contained short of fighting, they seldom have been resolved. Interstate conflicts have been only frozen, or they have receded from attention. Definitive resolutions are the exception, not the rule. Less than a quarter of Latin American boundary disputes have been resolved. The 1984 agreement between Argentina and Chile over the Beagle Channel is an exception to this conclusion, but it is too early to tell whether it will prove a definitive conclusion to all their bilateral boundary disputes—for instance, over Antarctic claims.

Similarly, mediation has been neither the rule nor especially successful in interstate conflicts. Various mediating efforts have helped on balance in Central American conflicts, but they have had a mixed record in South America and have been more often hurtful than helpful in conflicts between Latin American and European states. The record of United Nations institutions has been the worst, while mediation by individual states or small groups of states generally has had positive results. The record of inter-American institutions has been mixed: largely positive in Central America (at least concerning boundary and territorial disputes), but probably more negative than positive in South America. The signal success of the OAS was its mediation of the 1969 El Salvador-Honduras war. Not surprisingly, inter-American institutions have not played an effective role in the more recent cases combining internal and interstate conflicts—particularly Nicaragua and El Salvador. Domestic actors are likely to believe that these institutions have little legitimacy in dealing with conflicts in which the structure of national society is at stake. Moreover, recent conflicts have involved the United States and countries outside the inter-American system (such as Cuba and the Soviet Union), over which inter-American institutions have little leverage.

There has been some pattern regarding who has been asked to mediate particular conflicts and why. Central American states have been more likely to resort to inter-American institutions. This is not surprising given the United States' preeminence in inter-American institutions and the fact that U.S. influence is greater in Central America than elsewhere in Latin America. In contrast, given different traditions and relationships to the United States, South American states have been less likely to look to inter-American institutions to resolve conflicts. Instead they have preferred mediation by individual countries or small groups of states. Latin American states have used U.N. institutions less as forums for conflict resolution than as audiences for continued conflict. Again, that is probably not surprising given the nature of the United Nations and its historically limited role in peacekeeping or mediation in Latin America.

Fifth, the pattern of interstate conflict has varied a great deal—from Central America to South America to conflicts between Latin American and European states. To speak of "Latin America" is easy but all too misleading. The record of conflict across the region has been different.

1. Central America

The historical record of interstate conflict provides at least limited support for the conclusion that there has been more conflict in Central than in South America.[7] At least it is clear that interstate and internal conflicts have been much more intertwined in Central America. This is understandable given the history of close ties among the societies, economies, and ideologies of the region. Thus any Central American definition of "security" must recognize the high permeability of national borders to the flow of people, goods, and ideas. In contrast, interstate conflict in South America more closely fits traditional European concepts of conflict between states.

The typical pattern of conflict in Central America has reflected the permeability of national borders. Conflict has often begun with an "internal" action by one state (in the case of the 1969 war, the Honduran land reform). The "stronger" neighbor has then responded by taking an action or making a demand across its borders. The stronger state has been more likely to "win," which means achieving an outcome closer to its initial preferences than to those of the other state. In contrast, "weaker" states in South America (as measured by GNP, size of armed forces, and size of military budget) have been more likely to take the first action or make the first demand across their borders, and thereby to "win."

This pattern suggests that war may be more thinkable in Central than in South America.[8] At a minimum, both national political leaderships and their command and control of armed forces are relatively more fragile in Central America, so that national leaders know steps toward war may be self-fulfilling even if armed conflict is not the original intention. Hence strong Central American states are more likely than weak ones to embark on what may be a slippery slope to war. Because both strong and weak states know that war may actually ensue, the actions of the strong are successful in achieving outcomes they desire. In contrast, because war has been less credible in South America (military movements to buttress political claims run less risk of provoking armed conflict), weaker states have been more prepared to take actions that would seem to threaten armed conflict.

This pattern also suggests that stronger, more cohesive and self-assured

South American states have been more able to act in pursuit of broader political and economic objectives, even at the price of acquiescing to specific demands made by weaker states. Thus there may be less chance that actions by weaker states will provoke nationalistic reactions in their stronger neighbors that preclude sober calculations of real national interests. This seems to have been particularly true for Brazil, which has been remarkably adept at muting conflicts with neighbors while it emerged as South America's preeminent state. For example, in the case of the Itaipu project, Brazil was prepared to make concessions in both political symbols and long-term economic benefits in order to secure tangible economic interests and amicable political relations with its neighbors.

2. South America

The armed battle between Peru and Ecuador in 1981 was exceptional in that fighting occurred, but the conflict otherwise conformed to most of the observations noted above. Moreover, it illustrated many of the features that have seemed particular to interstate conflict in South America. An unresolved border conflict was compounded by (or became salient because of) natural resources discovered in the disputed territory. At the time fighting broke out, Peru produced thirteen thousand barrels of oil per day in that area. The origins of the 1981 conflict are murky, but the weaker state (Ecuador) appears to have taken the first action. The fact that democratic forms of government had recently been restored in both countries appears neither to have increased nor dampened the potential for conflict. Similarly, in keeping with South American practice, the parties did not break diplomatic relations even as they fought. The OAS was only moderately effective in mediating the conflict; indeed, the two parties initially disagreed over the desirability of an OAS role. The principal means of arranging a cease-fire was a smaller group, the four countries that were guarantors of the 1942 border agreement between Peru and Ecuador—Argentina, Brazil, Chile, and the United States. Finally, just as the 1942 agreement (denounced by Ecuador in 1960) failed to resolve the conflict, so the 1981 fighting ended only with an agreement to disengage forces.[9]

3. Latin American–European Cases

These conflicts have been exceptional in almost every way. Indeed, they have been exceptional in the strictest sense of the term because there have been so few of them—a half dozen or fewer in the entire post-World War II period, depending on whether long-standing conflicts are subdivided into particularly intense episodes. These conflicts have had a postcolonial flavor, and in all cases the European power was Great Britain.

In all these cases the weaker (Latin American) state initiated actions or demands across its borders. As in conflicts between South American states, war seemed sufficiently improbable and the chances of "winning" without war sufficiently good to tempt Latin American states to do so. At least this was the case before the 1982 South Atlantic war. But unlike the South American cases, the weaker (Latin American) state was not particularly likely to win by taking the first action. Before 1982 there was no clear pattern in this regard.

In contrast to other conflicts, politically vulnerable Latin American leaders have been especially likely to initiate action with European powers. This was most striking in 1982, but the same pattern was also apparent in earlier Latin American-European conflicts. (Interestingly, if politically vulnerable leaders strengthened their position during the course of the conflict, their countries were more likely to achieve outcomes that approximated their initial goals. The British government thus appeared more inclined to make concessions if it believed that the Latin American leader was not using the dispute primarily to build internal support.) Latin American leaders probably perceived little risk of war in taking an initial action. Even if Great Britain responded with a military move of some kind, actual fighting still was hard to imagine. Taking an initial action was all the more attractive because, given the colonial flavor of the Latin American-European conflicts, Latin American leaders could be sure of rhetorical backing from both fellow Latin American states and most other developing countries. The existence of a "colonial" enemy and the certainty of international support meant that the action was popular across the political spectrum. The Falklands/Malvinas case was intriguing because this favorable national sentiment was overriding even though nongovernmental ties between Argentina and Great Britain have been important—considerable trade, cultural affinity, and a visible Anglo-Argentine community in Argentina.

The 1982 South Atlantic war fits the (exceptional) pattern of previous conflicts between Latin American states and Great Britain but for the sad fact that war actually occurred. Argentina took the first action, whether by calculation, inadequate command and control, or sheer happenstance. Certainly Argentina's willingness to take risks owed much to the government's desperate search for some internal legitimacy. Argentina received broad international support for its position, although less than it must have hoped. It failed to secure crucial active support from African, Asian, and East European states at the United Nations, and even its Latin American support was qualified in the sense that its most ardent supporters were those countries (such as Venezuela) that had irredentist claims of their own to press.[10]

The British disinclination to make concessions was reinforced by the

Argentine regime's unpopularity both at home and abroad. Both sides used the United Nations as an audience for conflict, and the OAS was an ineffective mediator, first because of divisions among its Latin American members and later because the United States sided with Great Britain. Mediation by third parties, especially the United States, fared better but also failed in the end.

As an important sidelight, the fact that Great Britain had nuclear weapons made no impact on the conduct of the war, and Argentina's possession of crude nuclear weapons would not have changed the outcome. Argentina would have been hard pressed to make credible nuclear threats. Threats against the islands would not have been credible given Argentina's claim of sovereignty over them. Nuclear threats against British troops on the islands or at sea would have been more credible, but delivering one or several crude weapons to strike an overwhelming military blow against mobile enemy forces would have been very difficult. Moreover, it is not clear that even a desperate government would have risked international opprobrium by using nuclear weapons first under such circumstances.[11]

What Has Changed

Vivid events in the recent past often encourage overly dramatic predictions concerning the future. So it may be with the outbreaks of armed interstate conflict in Latin America in the early 1980s. After all, what the South Atlantic war and the fighting between Peru and Ecuador have in common is that shots actually were fired in anger. In most other respects these conflicts differed considerably, and the preceding analysis has shown how exceptional the Falklands/Malvinas case was in almost every way. Nevertheless, there are reasons to believe that these armed conflicts were not simply aberrations, and there is a basis for concern that conflict between Latin American states will be more of an issue in the future than it has been in the past.

First, military conflict may be more thinkable in the future. Recent conflicts may change old assumptions, especially in South America. The firebreak between mobilizing troops and using them in anger may itself break down. There is a real danger of self-fulfilling prophecies. If disputants in past conflicts did not believe that their adversaries' mobilization was a signal that war was imminent, they had little reason to react dramatically with military moves of their own. Hence Ecuador did not reinforce its border posts in January 1981 even though it had acted first and despite the fact that it had declared a state of emergency. Meanwhile, Peru mobilized effectively within forty-eight hours. Similarly, even though Argentina had taken the Falkland/Malvinas Islands by force of arms and despite the fact that it had weeks to prepare, its troops were woefully unprepared when the British attacked. Different assumptions about the link between mobilization and war could induce Latin American states to react sharply to moves by a would-be adversary, reducing the time for crisis management and raising the risks of rapid escalation.

Recent events may also underscore for Latin American states the lesson that seems to be offered by events as distant as the Soviet invasion of Afghanistan or the Israeli incursion into Lebanon: military force works. If war is thinkable, then military balances cease to be esoterica to be studied only by hobbyists in London. The acquisition of military weapons ceases to be merely a means of placating armed forces or of maintaining a balance among them. Great Britain was both skillful and lucky in the South Atlantic war. But if Argentina's air force had possessed longer-range aircraft and more time to improvise, or if the Argentine navy had not been at least as concerned about its domestic position vis-à-vis the army as it was about the British naval task force . . . The list of "ifs" is long, and the lesson may not be lost on other Latin American states. Only time will tell.

Second, there will be more to fight over in the future, and there may be less incentive not to fight over the objects of dispute. As noted earlier, new technologies and international developments have made hitherto unattainable natural resources available for exploitation. This has created new objects of conflict, particularly by giving new economic salience to old territorial disputes. Because all Latin American countries face prolonged periods of low economic growth, all of them seek to increase oil supplies or raw material exports—thus adding more urgency to the quest for resources. Latin America's economic difficulties may also increase the likelihood of interstate conflict in another way. In principle, increased trade and other economic contacts between potential adversaries may either increase the possibility of conflict (if those contacts themselves become an object of dispute) or decrease it (if both parties stand to lose more should conflict occur). Yet the historical record suggests that economic issues are most likely to be sources of conflict when access to resources is at stake. Although additional economic ties between potential adversaries have generally muted interstate conflict in Latin America, economic difficulties (either the depressed state of the global economy or the special problems of particular countries) may diminish these nongovernmental links. For example, Brazil's trade with Argentina collapsed in 1982, with exports to that country dropping by one-third. Diminished trade may reduce incentives to avoid conflict because there is less at stake economically. Even if this effect is not important, the stronger Latin American states (notably Brazil) will have fewer resources—and less domestic support for spending the resources they do control—to engage in creative diplomacy vis-à-vis neighbors. Several years ago Brazil would have been likely to use economic aid in an effort to mute radical tendencies in Suriname, but given Brazil's own economic difficulties, there is no longer money or domestic support for such initiatives.

Third, Latin American states have more and more military wherewithal for armed conflict. Although the military establishments of most Latin American countries started from a small base, many of them nevertheless have grown rapidly. The overall size of Latin American armies has increased apace with population over the last two decades, although imports of major weapons systems have grown faster than imports generally. This growth is symbolized by recent imports of sophisticated weapons: U.S.-made F-5 and F-16 aircraft by Mexico and Venezuela, respectively, and Soviet MIG-23s by Cuba. All Latin American countries except Cuba have relatively limited capability to project military power far from their borders and to sustain it for long (and even Cuba's African involvements clearly would be impossible without massive Soviet assistance). But recent acquisitions by the major Latin American states have increased their ability to project power—longer-range aircraft, troop transports and, to a lesser extent, elements of deep ocean navies.

Yet there are grounds for skepticism concerning the role of arms races as independent sources of tension. At the very least, the relationship between weapons and tension is complicated. Increases in armaments more often follow than precede serious interstate tension, and too few arms may sometimes be as destabilizing as too many. For example, during the periods of sharpest tension over the Beagle Channel in the 1970s, Argentina might well have attacked Chile or taken the islands but for the knowledge that victory would not be easy or swift. Nevertheless, sharp increases in armaments (whatever their motivation) can increase tensions. For example, Nicaragua's revival of territorial claims against Colombia is bound to be viewed as more ominous in the context of Nicaragua's emergence as the strongest military force in Central American history.

Arms buildups are expensive, and they make war (if not more likely) more serious if it occurs. For example, Argentina and Chile rapidly increased their arms expenditures during moments of sharp tension in the Beagle Channel conflict. Argentina nearly doubled its expenditures (in constant value) between 1974 and 1976, while Chile doubled its outlays between 1976 and 1979. The Argentine and Chilean governments perceived that the military balance mattered, and they were prepared to spend more money on their militaries even during difficult economic times. In contrast, Brazil evidently felt secure enough domestically and externally to let its defense effort slide. Its spending in real terms and as a percentage of GNP declined after 1976; in 1974 Brazil spent about one-fifth more on defense than Argentina, but by 1981 Argentina spent almost twice as much as Brazil.[12]

Even serious economic problems may not brake arms acquisitions. For example, Latin America's regional per capita GNP fell 2.7 percent in 1981, the worst performance in the developing world. Nonetheless, with military budgets consuming only a few percent of GNP, many countries in the region could manage continuing arms buildups. The evidence from Argentina in the early 1980s is suggestive: even before the South Atlantic war, Argentina continued to give priority to military expenditures despite national economic chaos. Because military establishments in the region remain comparatively small, fairly modest increases in expenditures can produce significant changes in the local military balance.

Two aspects of the recent expansion in Latin America military establishments merit special attention. First, the sophisticated armaments that many countries in the region now possess come close to making them a military match even for their industrialized country suppliers. This was graphically illustrated during the South Atlantic war when Argentina sank the British destroyer *Sheffield* with French-supplied Exocet missiles. In the same conflict, Argentina was armed with Type 42 destroyers made both in Great Britain and in Argentina under British licenses, French-built Mirages and corvettes, and so forth.

Second, and more important, several Latin American countries (especially Brazil and Argentina) now produce considerable numbers of weapons domestically, including sophisticated aircraft. For example, Brazil produces a wide variety of ships and submarines, armored vehicles, and military aircraft.[13] In 1981 Brazil sold missiles to Iraq and contracted with Malaysia to supply as many as seven hundred armored vehicles. France and Belgium have imported the Brazilian training aircraft, the EMB-121 Xingu, and the Soviet Union has purchased armored vehicles of the EE-9 Cascavel type. Major developing country purchasers of Brazilian weapons have included Libya, Iraq, Uruguay, Chile, Gabon, Togo, and Tunisia.

Argentina's arms industry (which ranks seventh in the developing world) is smaller than Brazil's, but it still produces a wide range of weapons. These include the IA-58 Pucara, a multipurpose attack aircraft; the TAM, the first medium tank produced by a developing nation; and a broad range of small arms, more diverse than Brazil's. Argentina has been a smaller exporter of arms than Brazil, but it has sold aircraft to Bolivia, Chile, the Dominican Republic, Iraq, Paraguay, Uruguay, and Venezuela, and armored vehicles to China, Pakistan, and Peru.

These indigenous arms industries have several implications for interstate conflict in the region. They increase the number of potential arms suppliers, thus making many Latin American countries less vulnerable to the decisions of any given foreign supplier. Given the preponderant U.S.

position in the Latin American arms trade in the 1960s, it was at least possible for the United States to attempt unilaterally to prevent the inclusion of supersonic aircraft in the region's arsenals. That effort collapsed when first the French and later the Soviets filled the gap. With more and more arms being produced *in* Latin America, similar attempts by *any* supplier will become more difficult. As a result, the number of parties necessary to reach an arms restraint agreement will grow.

Domestic arms production within the region also means that producers (notably Brazil and Argentina) will have additional military instruments with which to build influence in other Latin American states. Both Brazil and Argentina have in the past transferred arms on concessional terms to Bolivia and Paraguay, but those have been obsolescent weapons originally acquired from industrialized countries. Whether these two countries will compete in the future to sell domestically produced weapons in the region, and whether this will fuel regional arms races, is difficult to tell at present. The answer is likely to depend on whether other Latin American states perceive security threats that require additional arms.

The fourth reason for a possible increase in conflicts between Latin American states is that there will be continuing turmoil in Central America. Whatever else may be said about the violence in Central America, it is not about to end. Most of the turmoil there will continue to be internal, but conflict will also spill across national boundaries. Opposition movements (sometimes armed) from one country will continue to seek sanctuary or support in neighboring states. Actions taken by one state for one purpose will cause concern in other countries. Nicaraguan leaders may regard their military buildup as a defensive measure aimed at counterrevolutionaries and their supporters, but it is bound to make neighboring states edgy regarding Nicaraguan intentions.

The East-West conflict will continue to affect developments in Central America, and ideology (sometimes compounded by political leaders' personal animosities) may again become a source of conflict. Nicaragua and Honduras are contemporary examples of this phenomenon. Cuban actions will also cast a long shadow over the region. After the 1960s, specific forms of Cuban foreign activity that other Latin American states found threatening waned, and even the smaller states of the region did not generally perceive Cuba to be a threat. Most Latin American countries were preoccupied with internal development, and therefore they were unlikely either to fear ideological deviance in neighboring states or to want to convert them. Cuba's present role is unclear and its future actions are difficult to predict, but it appeared to resume more active support for revolutionary movements in the last phases of the Nicaraguan civil war. At a minimum, Cuba's miltary might and well-trained expeditionary forces are factors with which states in the region will have to reckon.[14]

Declining U.S. influence in hemispheric affairs may increase the potential for conflict in Central America more than in South America, given the United States' traditionally greater influence in Central America and the tendency of these states to look to Washington for leadership. Although the United States will continue to loom large in Central American affairs, the growing ideological diversity and increasing external contacts of states and forces in the area will reduce somewhat the United States' leverage. This in turn will diminish the ability of the United States to prevent or mediate conflict, and it is also likely to reduce the effectiveness of the OAS and other inter-American institutions in conflict mediation.

Fifth, military regimes' "national security ethos" may be a source of future conflict. This argument is often made in South America particularly, and it reflects how different the experiences of different parts of Latin America have been. It has been argued that military regimes took power in the 1960s because of national security doctrines tinged with geopolitical considerations.[15] Those doctrines emphasized the external dimensions of internal tensions. As suggested above, for much of the last two decades South American militaries-as-governments concentrated on internal stabilization and national integration, rooting out insurgents and altering the conditions that produced them. Now, however, these military establishments have become more sensitive to the external dimensions of security. At the same time, both the military capabilities acquired during the phase of internal stabilization and the increased degree of internal integration that resulted from it give these states more room to press their external interests.

Although this argument seems plausible enough, it is striking that the country to which it applys best—Brazil—is the Latin American state that has been perhaps most active in regional diplomacy and little prone to conflict. To the contrary, Brazilian diplomacy has been characterized by a willingness to make concessions in specific disputes in the interest of building broader political and economic influence. Thus greater national integration may also mean more self-confidence, a clearer articulation of national interests, and therefore a willingness to sacrifice more symbolic issues to secure broader goals.

Nor is it clear what national security doctrines will mean as military governments are replaced by civilian regimes in South America. The consequences will surely vary in different cases. For example, recently established (and still shaky) civilian governments' continuing concern regarding the armed forces may make them more intransigent on territorial questions that seem closely linked to national sovereignty, of which the military is custodian. Something similar to this apparently occurred in

1980 in the dispute between Colombia and Venezuela over the Gulf of Venezuela, when the Venezuelan armed forces blocked a settlement—even though the governments of both countries had long been civilian.

There was a danger of something similar occurring in Argentina with respect to the Beagle Channel. Notwithstanding broad support among civilian elites for settling the dispute on terms close to those suggested by the 1980 papal mediation, Argentina's civilian government had reason to fear a military backlash on an issue that successive military governments focused public attention on and became identified with, and which in turn became linked to national sovereignty considerations. In the end the Alfonsín government resorted to a nonbinding referendum on the agreement (which 80 percent of those voting in 1984 approved) in large part to protect itself politically.

Sixth, the nuclear issue may well become involved in interstate conflict in the future. The dire predictions of the last decade indicating that nuclear weapons would emerge from the (one-sided) rivalry between Brazil and Argentina have not come true.[16] Indeed, in most respects these two countries' relations (including their contacts on the nuclear question after the May 1980 nuclear cooperation agreement) are better than ever. Who would have imagined a decade ago that Brazil would represent Argentine interests in Great Britain after the South Atlantic war?

The basic facts of the Latin American nuclear situation are clear. Many countries in the region have some aspirations to, and some cooperative programs in, nuclear energy. Yet only three—Argentina, Brazil, and Mexico—have significant nuclear programs.[17] Mexico's ambitious plans have been sharply scaled back because of the precariousness of the country's general economic situation and the higher cost of nuclear power compared with that from conventionally fired power plants, especially in a petroleum-rich country. Thus attention continues to center on Brazil and Argentina. Neither country is a full party to the regional nuclear-free-zone agreement (the 1967 Treaty of Tlatelolco); both have most of their nuclear facilities under international safeguards; and both have reserved the right to conduct "peaceful" nuclear explosions.

In 1975 Brazil and the Federal Republic of Germany signed a massive (and controversial) nuclear cooperation agreement. Under the terms of this agreement, Brazil was to receive assistance across the full range of the nuclear fuel cycle, including construction of up to eight light-water power reactors, a uranium-enrichment facility, and a plutonium-reprocessing unit. The last two items aroused the most concern because the uranium-enrichment technology could be used to produce weapons-grade uranium, and the reprocessing facility could extract low-grade weapons plutonium from spent fuel. Both facilities were to be operated under international safeguards, but the safeguards would apply only to the materials supplied by the Federal Republic of Germany—not to any subsequent national adaptations of the technology.

The agreement was also controversial from the outset (even within Brazil) on scientific, economic, and political grounds. In particular, the project was based on enriched uranium rather than natural uranium (the basis of the Argentine program), which meant Brazil's continuing dependence on foreign sources of enriched uranium. However, economic factors ultimately proved the most telling. The costs of the program envisaged in 1975 have doubled, and the Brazilian government decided in March 1982 not to build more than the two nuclear power reactors then under construction. A pilot enrichment facility has been installed, but a commercial-scale plant could not be operational before the late 1980s. Similarly, plans for the reprocessing facility were completed in 1979, but construction has been postponed. Although Brazil might somehow be able to acquire enough fissionable material to build one or several crude bombs, its current program leaves it far short of a nuclear arsenal.

Argentina long has been regarded as Latin America's leader in nuclear technology. Its program has been generally insulated from the country's political and economic turmoil; for example, although Argentina has had sixteen presidents since 1950, the Argentine National Atomic Energy Commission (CNEA) has had only four directors. Argentina's first power reactor, Atucha I (350 megawatt capacity), began operating in 1974 and was the first in Latin America. A second is nearing completion, and a third (involving cooperation with both the Federal Republic of Germany and Brazil) is under construction. Argentina's program is less dependent on foreign suppliers than Brazil's; for example, in 1981 Argentina inaugurated a plant to fabricate fuel rods for its power reactors, and it has proven reserves of natural uranium of about twenty-nine thousand tons (enough to operate one one-thousand megawatt reactor for about two hundred years).

The focus of recent concern has been Argentina's operational pilot reprocessing plant, which Argentina argues was built without foreign assistance and is thus not subject to international safeguards. The spent fuel rods from Atucha I probably contain enough plutonium, if reprocessed, to make several dozen small nuclear bombs. These rods are subject to international safeguards, but there have been reports of a plan to build a small research reactor whose fuel would not be safeguarded. Estimates of how long Argentina would require to build a nuclear bomb range from three to five years if it made a dedicated effort.

What are Argentina and Brazil's intentions concerning nuclear weapons? Why would either country build a bomb? The most likely prospect is that neither country will, but their advancing nuclear programs will give both Argentina and Brazil a plausible capability to do so—and, over time, to do so quickly. Eventually both countries could resemble Israel and South Africa, which are presumed to have bombs or the capability to build them at will. Thus any major conflict between Argentina and Brazil would be charged with nuclear possibilities. This would be the case even if neither had exploded a bomb and even if strategic analysis suggested that both would lose from any nuclear exchange. In a war, each country could be tempted to attack preemptively the other's nuclear facilities, lest the other win the race to "go nuclear."

A less likely but starker possibility would be a decision by either Argentina or Brazil to create a nuclear weapons option. In the near term this is more feasible for Argentina, even if it is not very probable. The development of this option would not have to be especially explicit. For example, an Argentina humbled by the recent South Atlantic war and frustrated by continuing domestic travails could simply become more ambiguous in describing its nuclear plans and more secretive in implementing them. For Argentina this might be merely an attempt to salvage some prestige from the area of its remaining advantage. Argentine sources close to the nuclear energy program have in recent years conveyed an undertone of interest in such an approach—not necessarily in building a bomb but in retaining a lead over Brazil in nuclear technology, even technology with military applications. This may account for some of the off-handed comments in Argentina in the wake of the South Atlantic war concerning the possibility of building a nuclear-powered submarine, a feat much more difficult than constructing a nuclear bomb. Yet Brazil could hardly permit Argentina to open a wider lead in this area even if Brazil had no real interest in a nuclear weapons option. And Chile surely would regard an Argentine nuclear option as an effort at intimidation.

Future Conflict and Implications

There are significant reasons to expect more conflict of various kinds between Latin American states rather than less.[18] Although precise predictions are bound to be wrong, even a brief review of the history of interstate conflict in the region would have suggested before the fact that serious conflict over the Falkland/Malvinas Islands was more likely than other possible outcomes, especially because a failing Argentine government would be tempted to clutch at some shred of domestic support. The analysis presented here suggests that three kinds of interstate conflict are more probable than others, in the following order.

The most serious threat is the interstate spillover from turmoil in individual Central American states. This is likely to occur in the future (as it has in the past) in at least three ways. Even if the conflict is primarily internal to a particular country, other states in the region (and beyond) may perceive an interest in the outcome and thus may provide support in various ways. As suggested above, Cuba's military might makes its possible actions a special source of uncertainty. Or, even if other states seek to remain uninvolved, various parties to internal conflicts may attempt to draw them in. Using a neighboring country's territory as a sanctuary is one obvious way in which this could happen. Finally, the outcome of a particular domestic conflict may generate losers who continue the armed struggle at a less intense level from a neighboring country. Outcomes may also produce (or deepen) ideological hostility to the point that neighboring states are willing to harbor armed dissidents. They may activate latent disputes over territory, and arms races may result as one state (feeling threatened) takes actions that themselves become threats to neighbors.

A second type of conflict of particular concern is that between Latin American and European states. This set of possible conflicts probably is now reduced to one—that inspired by the Falkland/Malvinas Islands—but is little less worrisome for that fact. New conflicts of this kind might arise as France's American departments move to independence. And there remain "colonial" overtones to other existing conflicts—for example, over Belize if a leftist government should take power in Guatemala and confront a Belize that was clearly identified with the United States and protected by British troops.

In the case of the Falkland/Malvinas Islands, all the elements for conflict remain: a clear issue, unanimously supported by Argentine citizens of all political orientations; the certainty of broad support from fellow Latin Americans and from developing countries generally, which will increase any temptations an Argentine government feels to act; an understandable but regrettable British disinclination to negotiate; and, in this context, the absence of any effort at mediation. What prevents armed conflict is deterrence—the heightened British military presence in the islands. But that presence itself deepens Argentina's sense of humiliation. Argentina is bound to contemplate using force again, not now or next year but eventually, when Great Britain again forgets about the islands and/or when an Argentine government becomes especially desperate to generate domestic political support.

The third type of conflict is more numerous but less immediately likely to result in fighting: boundary and territorial disputes compounded by the question of access to natural resources. Conflicts between Argentina and Chile and between Peru and Ecuador are only the most obvious of recent examples. The Essequibo dispute between Venezuela and Guyana may be more cause for concern because it is compounded by a third factor: the absence of any significant bilateral ties that might serve as a

shared stake diminishing the risk of conflict. Even if none of these conflicts is likely to result in fighting, one or more may; the continuing
skirmishing between Peru and Ecuador testifies to this possibility. And
even if fighting does not occur, these conflicts remain sources of uncertainty and bases for diverting scarce economic resources to purchase
arms.

There are no easy recipes for resolving any of these three types of
conflict. Their variety underscores the diversity within Latin America. It
also suggests a variety of different conflict-resolution strategies that Latin
American states, nonhemispheric actors, and the institutions in which
they participate might pursue.

Because internal and interstate conflicts are closely intertwined in
Central America, they can only be resolved through parallel sets of discussions—between domestic political forces, between individual Central
American states and neighboring countries, and among Central American
countries and other states with a direct interest in the resolution of
emerging conflicts. This approach was eventually pursued in the case of
Nicaragua, but the effort was halting and too late. States in the region—
for example, the Contadora group of Panama, Mexico, Venezuela, and
Colombia—should take the lead in such efforts.

This is not the place for a detailed discussion of U.S. policy toward
Central America. But given the relatively greater (if declining) U.S. influence there, the United States' actions will continue to matter more in
Central America than elsewhere in Latin America. There will also be
more opportunity for an OAS role in Central America than elsewhere in
the region. Certainly it would be helpful if Guyana and Belize could join
the OAS (they are currently excluded from membership by the charter
provision denying membership to states disputing boundaries with preexisting OAS members) and if the Caribbean states became more active in
inter-American institutions.

For the United States, parallel negotiations concerning Central America would reflect a clear calculation of real U.S. security interests that is
so often lacking in discussions of the area. United States security interests
in Central America are real but narrow: preventing more Soviet or Cuban
troop deployments, bases, or facilities with a clear military purpose. Provided that this U.S. objective could be achieved (through a negotiated
agreement with Cuba and the Soviet Union or through parallel statements of self-restraint provided that the other state did likewise, with
these understandings recognized or joined by states in the region), the
United States could afford to be less immediately preoccupied with the
precise political orientation of particular regimes.[19] Apart from Cuban
and Soviet activities, the United States frankly has little strategic interest
in what form of government emerges in El Salvador. The United States

should not shrink from making clear its preference for democracy, but it should also be prepared in the context of parallel discussions to pledge to respect existing governments, whatever their political orientation.

For more traditional interstate conflicts, the watchword should be openness to any mediating mechanism that has a chance of working effectively. Again, the first responsibility lies with the parties themselves. For some conflicts, groups of eminent citizens from the countries involved can lay the basis for solution, both by suggesting possible formulas and by beginning to change the political atmosphere so that a settlement will not be equated with treason. Even if the OAS is reoriented toward security and peacekeeping, its credibility in the wake of the Falklands/Malvinas conflict will remain low. After the South Atlantic war, Latin Americans began to discuss new security groupings *independent* of the United States. However, those discussions foundered on divisive issues such as which countries to include and which to exclude. It may also be that the region's smaller states are more concerned about being left alone with other Latin American states than about their by-now familiar position vis-à-vis the United States. A need will remain for some inter-American institution, and the OAS has the virtue of already existing.

Nonetheless, a first necessity is the creation of some structure for discussions of the Falklands/Malvinas case. The United Nations Secretary General may be able to play a creative role in this instance, particularly if the current incumbent (Javier Pérez de Cuellar, of Peru) means to enhance the role of his office. His effort before the 1982 South Atlantic war was constructive even if it was not ultimately successful in averting armed conflict.

It should not be beyond the imagination of Latin American states to design novel approaches to territorial disputes. For example, territorial claims might be separated from resource exploitation issues. Two decades ago Uruguay and Argentina settled their dispute over La Plata River by agreeing to one boundary for navigational purposes and another for political and administrative purposes. States might freeze boundaries where they are, with the state that foregoes its territorial claim compensated by receiving a larger share than it otherwise might of any resource zone at issue. Or states might agree to joint resource exploitation, as was part of the initial papal recommendation for the Beagle Channel.

The most promising way to limit arms races is to reduce the tensions that provoke them. Nevertheless, several arms control strategies should be followed. These efforts should be led by Latin American states themselves. They might begin by agreeing not to introduce certain categories of weapons into the region or to destabilize existing arms balances. This would be particularly important for Argentina and Chile, the Central American states, and to some degree the Andean countries. Latin American states and their arms suppliers could also begin discussions regarding their respective policies and areas of possible restraint. This would be useful notwithstanding the increased number of arms suppliers and the fact that some Latin American states (notably Brazil and Argentina) are both suppliers and recipients.

Precedents for such efforts exist. For example, in the 1974 Declaration of Ayacucho, the Andean countries plus Argentina and Panama sought to create conditions that would limit arms purchases and end arms acquisitions for offensive purposes. Although not much came of this effort, it was a significant attempt by Latin American states to limit arms races. Similarly, in January 1984 five Central American states (including Nicaragua) agreed to conduct an inventory of existing armaments in order to help end arms flows across their borders.

At a minimum these discussions would increase the transparency of military activities in Latin America, which are now often shrouded in secrecy and mistrust. Paradoxically, the decline of the United States' military presence in the region may have decreased the flow of information concerning military activities. For example, when the United States had a large military-assistance presence in Latin America, both its relations with local military establishments and its information about them were much better than now. The United States was thus in a position to convey information, extend its good offices, or suggest to one state that a neighboring country's acquisition of advanced fighter planes reflected an interest in placating a disgruntled air force more than an increased military threat across its borders.

Direct discussions between states concerning their military activities would provide reassurance and reduce the risk of conflict through misunderstanding. A number of confidence-building measures (formal or informal) might result from these discussions: advanced notification of military maneuvers, invitations for observers to attend those maneuvers, agreements not to stage maneuvers in sensitive areas, and so forth. There is no reason for Latin American countries to do less than what has been possible for the North Atlantic Treaty Organization (NATO) and the Warsaw Pact in the heart of heavily armed Europe.

Finally, the danger of nuclear proliferation in the region will continue to be cause for concern but not for alarm. Temptations to develop nuclear weapons options will remain (whether because of general frustration or the quest for prestige), especially for Argentina. But these temptations should remain relatively weak unless other, specific motivations are present. As with arms buildups, the best hope of averting nuclear proliferation lies with efforts by Latin American states themselves to reduce the mutual suspicions that might provoke such a development. In this regard the Brazilian-Argentine nuclear agreement is a model.

It would require only a few additional steps by several countries to bring the Treaty of Tlatelolco into force. This would be a useful means of increasing confidence, even if Brazil and Argentina continue to assert the right to "peaceful" nuclear explosions. More helpful still would be Argentina's willingness to place all its nuclear facilities (those developed domestically as well as those that have been imported from abroad) under international safeguards. These safeguards are not foolproof, but they would be a manifestation of Argentina's commitment not to increase uncertainty (and thus concern) among its neighbors. Certainly it would be difficult to justify any expansion in nuclear trade with Argentina by the United States or other nuclear suppliers until *all* Argentine facilities are placed under appropriate international safeguards.

In all of these approaches to interstate conflict resolution, the United States is likely to be more effective when it prods disputants from behind the scenes than when it takes a more prominent, public role. The exception is Central America, where the long history of U.S. involvement and current U.S. commitment will necessarily make this role more visible. Elsewhere, however, the U.S. role in helping to arrange papal mediation of the Beagle Channel dispute is a better model. The decline in the United States' presence and influence in Latin America is sometimes a frustration for policymakers. As previously noted, this shift may paradoxically increase the risks of interstate conflict in several ways. But on balance this decline is probably good, both for Latin American countries and for the United States. In any case it is a fact. Efforts to reverse this decline (for example, by promoting arms sales to restore the United States to a preeminent position as hemispheric arms supplier, so as to regain leverage) surely would be counterproductive.

John F. Kennedy School of Government
Harvard University

Notes

1. Compiled from data in *The Military Balance, 1976–1977* and *1977–1978* (London: International Institute for Strategic Studies, 1976 and 1977).
2. These conclusions are based primarily on two studies: Jorge I. Domínguez, "Ghosts from the Past: War, Territorial, and Boundary Disputes in Mainland Central and South America since 1960," unpublished paper, Harvard University, May 1977; and Wolf Grabendorff, "Interstate Conflict Behavior and Regional Potential for Conflict in Latin America," *Working Papers* No. 116, Latin American Program, The Wilson Center, Washington, D.C., 1982.
There is considerable overlap between the two sets of cases examined, but the two authors use somewhat different definitions. Domínguez limits his analysis to

conflict over boundaries and territory, and he excludes the Caribbean. He also focuses on relatively defined episodes of conflict; for example, conflict between Argentina and Great Britain over the Falkland/Malvinas Islands is divided into two episodes. Grabendorff examines a broader range of interstate conflict, and he includes conflicts between the United States and Latin American countries. He does not break long-standing conflicts into episodes, so Argentine-British conflict is one instance.

The cases are: *Domínguez*—Argentina-Uruguay, 1963–1964, 1967–1968, and 1972–1973; Argentina-Chile, 1963, 1964, 1965, and 1967–1971; Argentina–Great Britain, 1964–1975 and 1975–1977; Argentina-Paraguay, 1964–1967; Paraguay-Brazil, 1962–1966, 1970–1975; Paraguay-Bolivia, 1969–1975; Bolivia-Chile, 1962, 1967–1970, 1973–1975, and 1975 on; Chile-Peru, 1974 on; Bolivia-Peru, 1976 on; Ecuador-Peru, 1960–1961 and 1976–1977; Argentina-Brazil, 1970 on; Guyana-Suriname, 1969 on; Guyana-Brazil, 1976 on; Venezuela–Great Britain, 1962–1966; Venezuela-Guyana, 1966–1967 and 1968–1970; Venezuela–Trinidad and Tobago, 1975; Venezuela–Dutch Antilles, 1972 on; Venezuela-Colombia, 1966–1970 and 1970 on; Colombia-Nicaragua, 1971 on; Nicaragua-Honduras, 1960–1962; Nicaragua–Costa Rica, 1970–1974 and 1976 on; El Salvador-Honduras, 1967, 1969, and 1970–1976; Guatemala–Great Britain, 1963, 1970–1972, and 1974 on.

Grabendorff—Argentina-Brazil after 1825; Argentina–Great Britain after 1833; Chile-Argentina after 1881; Chile-Bolivia after 1879; Colombia-Venezuela after 1834; Costa Rica-Nicaragua, 1948–1956; Cuba–United States after 1960; Dominican Republic-Haiti after 1949; Dominican Republic–United States, 1961–1965; Guatemala–Great Britain, 1859–1981; Guatemala–United States, 1951–1954; Honduras–El Salvador, 1967–1980; Honduras-Nicaragua after 1957; Nicaragua-Colombia since 1979; Nicaragua–United States since 1980; Mexico–United States since 1864; Panama–United States since 1903; Peru-Chile since 1889; Peru-Ecuador since 1882; and Venezuela-Guyana since 1899.

The lack of attention to these issues a half a decade ago is illustrated by Domínguez's comment that when he presented his paper the audience regarded it as "lapidary poetry" of little relevance and (alone of all his research) he did not publish it. Indeed, there has been scant study of Latin American foreign policies (not to mention security issues such as interstate conflict), especially by Latin Americans and especially until recently. A few exceptions in the period before the late 1970s are: Gregory F. Treverton, *Latin America in World Politics: The Next Decade*, Adelphi Papers No. 137, (London: International Institute for Strategic Studies, 1977); Luigi R. Einaudi, ed., *Beyond Cuba: Latin American Takes Charge of Its Future* (New York: Crane, Russak and Co., 1974); and Ronald G. Hellman and H. Jon Rosenbaum, eds., *Latin America: The Search for a New International Role* (New York: Wiley, 1975).

3. For arguments along these lines, see Grabendorff, "Interstate Conflict," p. 4. See also Jerome Slater, *The OAS and United States Foreign Policy* (Columbus: Ohio State University Press, 1967); Tom J. Farer, "Limiting Intraregional Violence: The Costs of Regional Peacekeeping," in Tom J. Farer, ed., *The Future of the Inter-American System* (New York: Praeger, 1979).

4. One suggestive index is that the Inter-American Peace Committee of the Organization of American States was activated thirty-four times between 1948 and 1965 but only once thereafter, during the Honduras–El Salvador war. In 1970 it was replaced by the Inter-American Committee on Peaceful Settlement, which has not been activated.

5. There are many examples of this argument. On the national security doctrine, see Manuel Antonio Garretón and Genaro Arriagada, "Doctrina de seguridad nacional y régimen militar," *Estudios Sociales Centroamericanos* 7, No. 20 (1978): 129–53; Wayne A. Selcher, "The National Security Doctrine and Policies of the Brazilian Government," *Parameters* 7, No. 1 (Spring 1977): 10–24. On the external implications of these policies, see Alexandre S. C. Barros, "The Diplomacy of National Security: South American International Relations in a Defrosting World," in Hellmann and Rosenbaum, eds., *Latin America: The Search for a New International Role;* David F. Ronfeldt and Luigi R. Einaudi, "Conflict and Cooperation Among Latin American States," in Einaudi, ed., *Beyond Cuba.*

6. For instance, of the twenty conflicts in the Grabendorff study, six were ideological but four involved the United States. Grabendorff, "Interstate Conflict," p. 5ff.

7. Only seven of Domínguez's forty-one territorial conflicts were Central American (he did not consider the Caribbean), but eleven of the twenty conflicts Grabendorff examined involved at least one Central American or Caribbean state.

8. Domínguez, "Ghosts from the Past," p. 22ff.

9. For a military analysis of the conflict, see *Defense and Foreign Affairs Daily,* 6 February 1981.

10. For a variety of Latin American perspectives on the war and its implications, see *Estudios Internacionales,* 60 (October–December 1982), especially Carlos Moneta's discussion of Argentine miscalculations, p. 376ff. For a British assessment of the war, see Lawrence Freedman, "The War of the Falkland Islands, 1982," *Foreign Affairs* 61, No. 1 (Fall 1982): 196–210.

11. For a good summary of arguments concerning the spread of nuclear weapons (one that concludes that nuclear proliferation may not be a bad thing), see Kenneth N. Waltz, *The Spread of Nuclear Weapons: More May Be Better,* Adelphi Papers No. 171 (London: International Institute for Strategic Studies, 1981).

12. These data are from the Stockholm International Peace Research Institute, *1982 SIPRI Yearbook of World Armaments and Disarmament* (Stockholm, 1982), pp. 145, 153. Needless to say, all these comparisons are no more than approximations.

13. The arms exports discussed in this and the following paragraph are reported in Jozef Goldblat and Victor Millan, "Militarization and Arms Control in Latin America," ibid.

14. There has been much recent attention to Cuba's role and its relations with the Soviet Union. For example, see two chapters in a volume that is not reflexively anti-Cuban or anti-Soviet: Morris Rothenburg, "The Soviets and Central America," pp. 131–48, and Joseph Cirincione and Leslie Hunter, "Military

Threats, Actual and Potential," pp. 173–92, in Robert S. Leiken, ed., *Central America: Anatomy of Conflict* (New York: Pergamon Press, 1984).

15. The best-known (though not most widely read) work is General Golbery do Couto e Silva, *A Geopolítica do Brasil* (Rio de Janeiro: Livraría José Olympio, 1967). His work is, however, relatively sanguine about the dangers of interstate conflict, calling explicitly for the maintenance of existing boundaries. For a review of geopolitical writings, see John Child, "Geopolitical Thinking in Latin America," *Latin American Research Review* 14, 2 (Summer 1979): 89–111.

16. This includes my own predictions, although they were prudently hedged; Treverton, *Latin America in World Politics,* p. 39ff.

17. The discussion here and in the following paragraphs draws on a number of sources, including Treverton, *Latin America in World Politics,* in its basic picture and strategic analysis. For recent summaries of the state of nuclear programs in the region, see "Latin American Nuclear Technology," *International Herald Tribune,* 30–31 October 1981, and Goldblat and Millan, "Militarization and Arms Control." On the West German-Brazilian deal, see Hartmut Krugman, "The German-Brazilian Nuclear Deal," *Bulletin of Atomic Scientists* 37, 2 (February 1981): 32–36. For an interesting interview with Vice Admiral Carlos Castro Madero, the head of Argentina's nuclear program, see "Situación nuclear argentina," *Estrategia* (Buenos Aires) 69 (1981): 55–61. For a basic discussion of the strategic implications of this case, see Stephen M. Gorman, "Security, Influence, and Nuclear Weapons: The Case of Argentina and Brazil," *Parameters* 9, No. 1 (Spring 1979): 52–65. The discussion also draws on the author's own observations in Argentina and Brazil in 1982 and 1983.

18. Norman D. Arbaiza, *Mars Moves South: The Future Wars of South America* (Jericho, N.Y.: Exposition Press, 1974), argues that a wave of wars is likely, and that this development would not necessarily be bad.

19. The U.S.-Soviet understandings over Cuba of 1962, 1970 and 1979 are suggestive in this regard. The United States in effect agreed not to try to overthrow Castro in return for Soviet commitments not to introduce nuclear weapons into Cuba. This approach was recommended by the Woodrow Wilson Center's 1982–1983 Inter-American Dialogue; see *The Americas at a Crossroads* (Washington, D.C.: Woodrow Wilson International Center for Scholars, April 1983), p. 44.

20

Economics and Security: Contradictions in U.S.–Latin American Relations

Sergio Bitar

Shifts in economic power between Latin America and the United States have not been accompanied by similar changes in security relations. This imbalance has caused increasing divergence between Latin America's strategic interests and the limits imposed by U.S. security objectives in the hemisphere. Whereas the United States has given priority to its security aims in Latin America, Latin America has stressed its development goals.

This divergence has usually been resolved in favor of U.S. objectives. The United States' supremacy and Latin America's economic vulnerability have been the principal reasons for the subordination of Latin American aims to those of the United States. However, the degree of subordination is changing. Latin America's increased economic capacity has created new leverage. At the same time, the decline in the United States' relative economic power has limited the U.S. government's ability to impose its own criteria on Latin American governments. Both processes have produced conditions leading to a less asymmetrical realignment in strategic interests.

Strategic Divergence: The Historical Record

During the 1930s the United States actively promoted its economic expansion in Latin America with the goal of displacing European economic interests, which until then had been preponderant in the region. In doing so, the United States pursued the policy articulated by Theodore Roosevelt in 1904, in which the Monroe Doctrine and Manifest Destiny converged (the "Roosevelt corollary"). European countries were warned that the United States considered itself responsible for the internal conduct of Latin American governments.[1]

In the period immediately prior to World War II, the United States reaffirmed its decision to limit the presence of European powers in the region, particularly Germany. It was essential to reduce Fascist and Nazi influence in the Western Hemisphere and to obtain Latin American support for the United States. Thus the United States sought the creation of a hemispheric military agreement in order to confront possible extracontinental attacks. The militaries of North and South America reached an agreement along these lines during World War II and formalized it in 1947 with the signing of the Inter-American Treaty of Reciprocal Assistance (the Rio Treaty).

By the time the treaty was signed, however, world conditions had changed. The United States' principal enemy was now the Soviet Union, and inter-American agreements were to be used to combat Soviet influence and international communism. Other U.S. strategic aims in Latin America became less important. The United States had emerged from World War II as an undisputed global economic and military power. Europe was economically destroyed by the war, and U.S. economic predominance in Latin America was thus unrivaled. The Soviet Union's ability to reach Latin America through Communist parties (at that time considered to be a mere extension of the Soviet Union) made it the United States' principal rival for influence in the region.

Latin America did not share these concerns. After World War II, the region's top priority was economic growth as a basis for resolving problems of unemployment and poverty. In negotiations with the United States between 1946 and 1950, Latin America insisted upon its need for economic support, suggesting a Marshall Plan for the region. The United States responded that it did not have the necessary resources because they had been committed to European reconstruction. George Marshall, the U.S. Secretary of State, declared at the Rio Conference in 1947 that a special economic development plan for Latin America was not possible.[2]

Security issues had become the U.S. government's principal priority in Latin America. In the immediate postwar period the United States perceived, and made explicit for the first time, the relationship between U.S. security interests in the region and the domestic political stability of each Latin American country. Moreover, U.S. government representatives began to link political stability with the containment of communist activity. They also made it clear that a Latin American government's possibility of receiving economic aid depended upon its anticommunist zeal.[3]

A strong possibility of intervention was inherent in this policy. By defining U.S. security interests in terms of the political stability of each Latin American country, the United States legitimated its presence in Latin American domestic affairs. Latin American delegates to the Bogotá Conference in 1948 made this point forcefully. The United States' delegation to the conference fought for a strong anticommunist draft agreement linking U.S. security goals to Latin American domestic affairs. Several Latin American delegations foresaw the risk of intervention and rejected this draft, pointing out that the region's problems were caused by poverty and exploitation rather than supposed external sources of social and political agitation.[4]

The tensions between the United States' security and political stability objectives and Latin America's goals of economic development and nonintervention persisted in the 1950s. During this period the United States was sometimes accused of exerting economic pressures in an attempt to impose its own criteria on domestic or international policy decisions in Latin America.[5] The contradictions between U.S. security objectives (which included the security of U.S. private investment) and Latin Americans' control over their own development were also evident in official exchanges. For example, the Tenth Inter-American Conference in Caracas in 1954 is chiefly remembered for John Foster Dulles's response to an inquiry regarding U.S. economic assistance to Latin America; he replied that he had come to talk about communism, not about aid.[6]

The acute neglect of Latin America's interests in inter-American affairs was caused by the region's weakness vis-à-vis the United States. At the end of World War II Latin America was economically fragile, with low overall production levels, limited financial resources, and major problems of poverty and unemployment. In contrast, the United States was at the height of its economic hegemony. At least until the 1960s, there was no other economic power that could even partially rival its position. During the postwar period Latin America turned toward "inward-oriented" development and delegated responsibility for its external security to the United States, while at the same time attempting to secure some economic advantages in exchange. Thus Latin America's strategic contradictions with the United States have been a constant concern since World War II.

Economics and Security from the Latin American Perspective

Latin America has two kinds of security concerns: extracontinental and regional military threats, and domestic socioeconomic and political problems. However, threats to Latin America's territorial integrity from extracontinental forces have not been a high priority. Except for the 1982 crisis between Argentina and Great Britain over the Falkland/Malvinas Islands, there have not been any conflicts of this kind during the post-World War II period. Inter-American security agreements are directed against attacks by the Soviet Union. But it is clear that defense against such a threat is beyond Latin America's military capacity. In the event of a military conflict with the Soviet Union, the responsibility for hemispheric defense would of necessity rest entirely on the United States.

Threats to territorial integrity in Latin America have stemmed primarily from border disputes. There are various conflict-resolution mechanisms at the Latin American, inter-American, and global levels that decrease the probability of military clashes between neighboring countries. It is unlikely that new threats will arise in this area; the principal challenge is to prevent long-standing disputes from recurring. Thus military threats are less important in Latin America's security concerns than they are for the United States.

Economic factors, however, have become increasingly important for regional security. First, Latin American security has always been linked to autonomy, understood as the ability to retain control over basic economic and political decisions. For this reason Latin America has long defended the concepts of nonintervention and self-determination. At the same time, Latin America has advocated control over its own basic economic activities and the creation of less dependent foreign economic relations. These two Latin American concerns—nonintervention and economic autonomy—are central aspects of the region's relationship with the United States.

Second, Latin American security historically has been closely linked to domestic political unity, social progress, and economic development. It is a widely shared belief in Latin America that the resolution of social conflicts and the creation of political stability depend on the ability to attain rapid economic growth, decrease unemployment, improve living conditions, and incorporate the vast majority of the population into national life. Latin American proposals regarding hemispheric security have repeatedly emphasized concern with economic development. This was apparent in the Declaration of Bogotá of 1948; the creation of the United Nations Economic Commission for Latin America (1948) and the Inter-American Development Bank (1956); the nationalization of basic resources; the formation of the Latin American Economic System (SELA, 1975); and innumerable efforts to coordinate Latin American actions and initiatives with those of other developing countries. Latin America has consistently tried to strengthen its economic power and reduce its vulnerability through regional economic integration, trade agreements, financial collaboration, the collective defense of raw-material prices, the regulation of transnational corporations, and so forth.

Most of these initiatives were opposed (overtly or covertly) by the United States. From proposals for a Marshall Plan for Latin America in the 1940s to codes of conduct for transnational corporations in the 1970s, Latin America's efforts to protect its economic sovereignty have encountered U.S. opposition, based on the United States' own definition of its security concerns in the region.

The link between security and economics in Latin American perceptions led to the idea of Latin American economic security—national development and collective protection against external economic pressures inspired by U.S. military or ideological objectives. Thus in a 1960 common statement in Bogotá, Latin American representatives sought to include the idea of economic and social development in the concept of hemispheric collective security.[7] In the San José (Costa Rica) Protocol modifying the Charter of the Organization of American States (OAS), the idea of collective economic security appeared as a purely Latin American objective. After the 1982 Falklands/Malvinas conflict, in the wake of economic sanctions applied by the European Economic Community against Argentina, support for this position grew.[8]

Economic factors have thus held a prominent and enduring position in formulations of Latin American security. Nonetheless, there have been two important differences within the region concerning the way in which the relationship between economics and security is structured. The first difference concerns the relative priority attached to economic issues vis-à-vis means of maintaining internal order. Even in the extreme case of so-called national security doctrines, which were developed and implemented by military dictatorships in Southern Cone countries in the 1970s, both economic development and national autonomy are identified as key objectives. However, these doctrines give greater emphasis to internal subversion as a threat to security than to economic and social backwardness.

The second difference concerns which economic models are considered most appropriate for achieving development and autonomy. These approaches range from complete market freedom and an open-door policy toward foreign investment, to developmentalism and economic reform programs, to plans for socialized economies with central planning. Alternation among these different approaches has weakened national and regional capabilities to pursue a stable path toward economic development. However, all these models share an emphasis on the importance of economic factors in achieving medium- and long-term security.

Growing interdependence between Latin America and the world economy has underlined Latin American concerns regarding the need for economic strength. Proposals for a new international economic order and efforts to protect Latin American countries from the effects of economic policies implemented by the United States and other industrialized countries underline the conviction that the region's internal and external security depends increasingly on Latin America's relative economic weight and its capacity for joint decision making. From statements by Argentina's foreign minister in 1947 to the president of Brazil's address before the U.N. General Assembly in 1982, there has been a growing Latin

American conviction that economic security is a crucial dimension of national and regional security.

U.S. Economic Interests and U.S. Security in Latin America

From the Latin American perspective, it has always been difficult to understand what the U.S. government considers to be a threat to its security. The U.S. government historically has defended the economic interests of certain large transnational firms, disguising them as security concerns. It has been argued that the nationalization of a U.S.-owned corporation might constitute a threat to U.S. access to strategic materials. It has also been held in some U.S. circles that nationalizations and other measures promoting national economic autonomy increase state intervention, and that this could damage the private sector in Latin American countries and might even constitute a risk for democracy and the western world. Some have asserted that economic nationalism inevitably moves a government leftward and that it may even encourage closer ties with the Soviet Union. It also has been argued that policies such as these encourage inefficiency and are contrary to the national interest of Latin American countries. In other words, numerous actions undertaken in Latin American countries—which are internal matters—have encountered interference by the United States that is rationalized in terms of U.S. security concerns.

But what threats to U.S. security interests might realistically arise in Latin America? Let us first consider economic issues. The United States has repeatedly emphasized the need to ensure supplies of strategic raw materials. This concern first surfaced in the United States during World Wars I and II and, for a brief time, during the Korean War. But once these conflicts ended, the concern vanished. The 1973–1974 oil embargo by the Organization of Petroleum Exporting Countries (OPEC) revived this subject, but ways were devised to overcome the threat of disruption in petroleum imports.[9] More recently, some analysts have argued that the United States is very dependent on imports of certain strategic minerals and that a supply disruption would threaten national security.[10] This fear has caused the U.S. government to adopt policies opposing the formation of cartels or agreements among producer countries, because such arrangements might result in supply disruptions or impose higher prices on the United States.

However, these fears have been exaggerated. The United States does not depend on Latin America for any essential product to any significant degree. Except in a few cases (among which are bauxite, columbium, fluorite, and strontium), the United States does not depend on Latin

American countries for more than 50 percent of its strategic mineral imports.[11] In all of these cases the United States has abundant stocks to cover any emergency. Morever, there is no precedent of two or more Latin American countries acting together to block raw-material exports to the United States. On the contrary, after the nationalization of U.S. firms, Latin American countries have been even more inclined to export to the United States in order to increase foreign exchange earnings and obtain a larger share of the U.S. market.

An analysis of U.S. government behavior shows that the supply of mineral raw materials from Latin America has not been a serious security concern. The United States has been primarily interested in maintaining low prices; it has been somewhat less concerned with securing supplies. The United States' perception of a security threat is linked to the possible emergence of a "communist" presence rather than to specific economic questions.[12]

An examination of other issue areas presents similar conclusions. In foreign trade, Latin America's importance as a trading partner has decreased for the United States. In 1980 the region represented about 16 percent of total U.S. exports and imports.[13] This trade is distributed among numerous products, countries, and firms, and trade disputes with Latin America are highly unlikely to constitute a security threat to the United States.

With regard to foreign direct investment, although the volume of resources committed by the United States remains high in absolute terms, in recent years Latin America has declined in its relative importance as a focus of U.S. direct foreign investment. In the early 1980s Latin America represented about 12 percent of total U.S. investment abroad.[14] This proportion is low in comparison with other regions, and U.S. investments in Latin America are distributed among various sectors, firms, and countries. New U.S. affiliates for the most part have been established in manufacturing activities with advanced technologies, which are of great importance to Latin American countries. But eventual economic conflicts with some Latin American countries over investment issues do not threaten U.S. security.

Latin America may present a major problem for U.S. financial interests because of its impact on U.S. banks. In the early 1980s the nine largest U.S. banks' exposure in Latin America amounted to more than 150 percent of their capital.[15] Nonetheless, the banks also have made very large loans to East European socialist countries and other industrialized countries, and they do not seem to perceive the risk attached to debt obligations to be any greater when it is a question of regimes with different ideologies. Indeed, current financial tensions to a large extent derive from world economic recession, not from political intentions. And because Latin American debtor countries' vulnerability is also high, it is unlikely that they would choose financial issues as an area in which to challenge the United States.

Latin America's impact on the international economic order is also relevant in this regard. The main economic requirement for U.S. security is an open world economic system, to which Latin America does not constitute a threat. The domestic economic measures that a Latin American country might adopt would not affect the system as a whole. No single Latin American country has enough weight to reshape the international economic order, and none has any interest in breaking its international economic ties—unless it is forced to do so in order to survive a boycott or military attack. If anything, recent developments have increased Latin America's interdependence with the international economic order.

In the military sphere, there are no forces in Latin America capable of placing U.S. security in jeopardy. Nor do U.S. strategic planners believe that Latin America would provide any meaningful military support in a direct confrontation with the Soviet Union.[16] The European theater is different in this regard because West European countries have a direct role in defending that continent.

If in reality Latin America does not pose a significant economic or military threat to U.S. security, what do U.S. foreign policymakers *perceive* to be security threats in the region, and why do they do so?

The Security of Latin America from the U.S. Perspective

Under normal conditions, when U.S.–Latin American relations present no immediate security crises, the U.S. government has often acted to defend specific economic interests. The Department of State and other foreign policy institutions have been more receptive to the concerns of transnational companies under such circumstances.[17] But in crisis conditions when broader U.S. interests were perceived to be in jeopardy, the United States has intervened in Latin America, either openly or covertly. In these situations U.S. actions were not motivated by economic considerations or by the interests of specific firms. Neither Guatemala in 1954, the Dominican Republic in 1965, Chile in 1973, nor Nicaragua since 1981 posed major threats to U.S. economic interests. To the extent to which economic issues were present in these situations, they involved no more than several corporations.

To explain U.S. governmental actions in Latin America, one must consider the United States' strategic interests throughout the world. The United States' fundamental concern is its global rivalry with the Soviet

Union. All other security issues are evaluated in this context. The United States' policy goal in developing countries is to prevent the Soviet Union from winning any advantage. Some analysts have even suggested that the United States should concentrate its efforts on containing subversion rather than expanding its nuclear arsenal.[18] The U.S. government has emphasized the importance of political stability in developing countries on the assumption that stability reduces opportunities for Soviet influence. This emphasis is especially intense in Latin America due to the United States' great influence in the region. The United States is even less willing to accept risks in the Western Hemisphere than elsewhere, which means less autonomy for Latin America.[19]

The U.S. government understands that security threats do not originate *in* Latin America; rather, they occur *through* Latin America. Events in the region do not necessarily pose security threats in their own right. Instead, U.S. concern is with Soviet actions that take advantage of unstable circumstances, perhaps using a Latin American country as a base from which to attack the United States.

The priority that the United States gives to its relations with the Soviet Union is not new. It dates from the early post-World War II period. But the projection of that global rivalry on U.S.–Latin American relations has grown increasingly intense over time. The Cuban revolution dramatically changed the United States' perception of its postwar position in the hemisphere. After 1959 the United States considerably increased its pressure on Latin America so as to prevent any similar occurrence in the future. At about the same time, toward the end of the 1960s, the Soviet Union achieved overall strategic military parity with the United States. Technological, economic, and military progress also gave the great powers rapid access to all parts of the world. The Soviet Union now has the capability to project military force into Latin America.[20] As a result of these factors, U.S. security policy has been increasingly—indeed, almost exclusively—concerned with the Soviet Union.

Psychological factors have also become increasingly important as a basis on which to measure the relative power of the United States vis-à-vis the Soviet Union. Because relative power cannot be tested in an all-out military clash between the two powers, limited competition on specific fronts has assumed a new importance. In this sense, the impressions that other countries and domestic public opinion hold regarding the U.S. government's capacity to contain the Soviet Union have become an integral part of its power. Perceptions regarding relative strength can increase or diminish that strength, regardless of the actual state of military preparedness. The "national will" to face challenges, and the ability to project this will, are in themselves major components of U.S. power.

One belief informing U.S. foreign policy is that the Soviet Union places a high value on national will and on the firmness of the United States and its allies. Thus it becomes important to demonstrate U.S. resolve by specific actions. Many U.S. analysts believe that the Soviet Union seeks to paralyze western leaders through the threat of nuclear war, and so they argue that this campaign must be resisted by exercising great willpower and by initiating a psychological counteroffensive. In addition, the U.S. government must combat the Soviet argument that the world capitalist system will inevitably collapse by illustrating the superiority of the capitalist system and the failure of the Soviet economic model. Because the U.S.-Soviet rivalry involves subjective issues such as these, considerable importance is attached to the perception of the United States' relative strength or weakness.

The U.S. perception of threat depends, in turn, on a subjective evaluation of the Soviet Union's intentions and capabilities. This evaluation is influenced by the tendency in the United States to magnify Soviet power, making it appear uncontainable and highly efficient. In the last decade there has been a marked change in the prevailing U.S. attitude toward the Soviet Union, which (according to analysts such as George Kennan) has been induced by government officials favoring a hard line on largely subjective bases.[21]

The convergence of these factors—the global nature of U.S.-Soviet rivalry and the subjective grounds on which differences in power are perceived—has had important consequences for Latin America. The region has come to be viewed as simply one more area in the global confrontation between great powers. Thus the U.S. government seeks to demonstrate to its allies, its enemies, and domestic public opinion that it is capable of successfully containing any threat occurring through Latin America. Accordingly, U.S. credibility throughout the world depends on how well it imposes its policies in Latin America so as not to project an image of weakness.

Instability: Poverty or Subversion?

Because the United States' principal concern is with threats occurring *through* Latin America, its goal is to prevent the emergence of conditions that would favor Soviet influence. This objective is expressed in the search for internal "stability" in each Latin American country. The United States does not pretend that Latin America should play an active military role in a global conflict with the Soviet Union. Rather, it should avoid disturbances that might distract U.S. military attention. Latin America must remain "stable." The region's contribution to U.S. security is, therefore, its passivity.

This conception of "stability" is linked psychologically and culturally to the principles of law, order, and gradualism that characterize political practice within the United States. Order and tranquility are considered to be positive factors for business activity. The dominant economic interests in the United States generally assume that any disruption of that order is the work of subversive elements linked to external forces.

The United States' understanding of the way in which "stability" is achieved has great impact on Latin America. In this regard, two points of view coexist in the United States: (1) that political and social instability has domestic causes, such as poverty and oppression; and (2) that instability is provoked by subversive groups with foreign support, principally from the Soviet Union and Cuba. These two views are often merged in different proportions, depending upon the observer's ideological perspective, the Latin American country in question, and the kind of crisis at issue. Different policies derive from each point of view. From the first perspective, economic and social development is necessary to ensure political stability; economic assistance and respect for human rights are the most appropriate means through which to achieve this goal. In contrast, the second perspective emphasizes the role of subversive elements and proposes the use of police, military, and ideological weapons to combat them. This second perspective also favors the formation of political alliances with Latin American groups such as the military, the land-owning oligarchy, and the national business elite, whose interests coincide with U.S. priorities abroad.

Each U.S. administration has combined these two approaches in different proportions, giving rise to a double-faceted policy toward Latin America. However, in recent years the policy emphasis on economic and social development has decreased, and the priority given to combating subversion has risen. This shift strengthens the military and police aspects of the security question. The reasoning behind U.S. policy can be articulated in the following manner: although poverty and repression are at the root of political instability, these problems are centuries old and have deep cultural, institutional, economic, and social bases. There is little that the United States can do to correct this situation in the immediate future. Poverty-stricken masses have always existed, but open political conflicts and social struggles have not broken out because of this. Therefore, if Latin America's economic and social problems are to persist for a long time, and if their solution ultimately depends on far-reaching transformations that are more the responsibility of each Latin American country than of the United States, then it is better for the U.S. government to concentrate its resources on resisting subversive forces.[22]

This preference for counterinsurgency also arises from institutional and financial factors. First, each U.S. presidential administration has only a limited time in which to implement its policies. This period is not long enough to effect the economic development of Latin America. Long-term policy results offer few political or electoral returns for an incumbent administration. Nor can a particular administration be blamed for a crisis that is the consequence of decades of repression and poverty. Second, the U.S. government's capacity to allocate financial resources to Latin America is increasingly limited because of restrictions imposed by domestic economic demands, the enormous budget deficit, the dispute over funds for defense and social security, and Congress's active role in monitoring the use of such funds. Third, due to Latin America's economic size, enormous sums would be required to implement any policy that would yield rapid results. Even the smallest Central American countries would absorb substantial resources.

It follows, therefore, that problems of economic and social development—the fight against poverty, unemployment, the concentration of income and wealth, and economic dependence—are not and cannot be the top priority for U.S. security policy in Latin America. Thus U.S. efforts to maintain political stability in the region rely more on political, ideological, and counterinsurgency actions than on economic and social measures. The U.S. government believes that the former offer greater chances for immediate influence.

This view of security issues in Latin America ultimately rests on the conviction that political stability and social order are necessary prerequisites for private enterprise; they are conditions that encourage domestic savings and foreign investment. Because in this view stability precedes development, disorder and subversion must be avoided. However, this approach risks halting structural, social, and political change, which is necessarily accompanied by some degree of conflict and social mobilization. It favors the status quo rather than progressive change.

The Subordination of Latin America's Economic Interests to U.S. Security Interests

When defined in this way, U.S. security goals clash with Latin American economic objectives. Because economic issues have a major influence on Latin American security, the region's security interests diverge significantly from those of the United States. This divergence reflects different perspectives regarding the nature of change in Latin America.

Those responsible for the formulation of U.S. foreign policy perceive that socioeconomic change in the region results in the loss of U.S. control over Latin American countries. Some see social change leading to growing polarization, and polarization producing an environment that could attract a Soviet and/or Cuban presence. When an armed uprising against a dictatorship occurs, the common reaction of the dominant elite in the United States is to assume a connection between the insurgent forces and Marxism-Leninism. If the armed revolt should be successful, the strong concern is that the new rulers might establish a "totalitarian" regime with ties to the Soviet Union and Cuba and with an internationalist commitment to encourage subversion in other countries. The United States thus pursues policies intended to prevent such developments, but which in practice produce a self-reinforcing cycle of self-fulfilling prophecy. Even when social change occurs in a democratic context without armed struggle, some U.S. policymakers may fear that politics will eventually become polarized. If a strong Communist party and/or other Marxist groups are present, it is presumed there is a high probability that they will finally resort to violence. It is also assumed that even an elected "Marxist" government will in time be rejected by the people, and therefore the government will attempt to maintain power through the use of force. Consequently, it is necessary to act before this process is far advanced.

Chile constitutes an important example of this phenomenon. The Nixon administration's attempt to prevent Allende's election and its later involvement in his overthrow were undertaken without knowing what policies his government would pursue. There was no subversion or foreign military presence in Chile at the time. The Allende government came to office through elections; the Chilean army was strong and held political beliefs that opposed orthodox socialism; and there were well-established political parties in the opposition. Nevertheless, the U.S. government feared the precedent that the Allende administration's pursuit of socioeconomic change in a democratic context might set for other countries in Europe and Latin America. One cannot dismiss the strong possibility that Nixon's reaction may also have been due to his desire to show the corporate and banking communities his firm determination to prevent the nationalization of U.S. business interests in Latin America.[23]

A similar perception of change is implicit in the so-called domino theory. This image suggests that the example of one country must necessarily shape events in another, thus acquiring further momentum. It does not distinguish among cases: armed struggle, socioeconomic change effected by democratic means, or progressive military regimes. The domino theory has been applied to cases as divergent as Nicaragua under the Sandinistas, Chile under Allende, and Peru under Velasco, although this interpretation has been sustained most vigorously with regard to Nicaragua.

These widely held perceptions in the United States have important economic consequences for Latin America because they link economic transformations in the region with U.S. security concerns. Major changes in Latin America in financial or industrial ownership, in state activities, and in the role of the private sector or foreign capital are perceived in U.S. circles as a threat to the United States' security interests.

This link between economic and security issues may be manifested in various ways. Profound economic transformations (especially changes in the ownership of the means of production) may be associated with a polarization of social forces. Increasing polarization might later result in political, military, and ideological conflicts that would threaten U.S. security. In addition, broad economic transformations in Latin America may affect the functioning of the world economic system. It is essential for the United States to maintain an open international economic system based on private enterprise and the market. The international system, in turn, rests on national economies based on the same principles. Therefore, although the direct U.S. economic interests at stake may be limited, the country in question small, and its links to the international capitalist economy unaltered, domestic economic changes are to be discouraged because of the precedent that they might establish.

From this perspective, U.S. security depends on preventing fundamental economic transformations in Latin America. Of course, the definition of what constitutes a "fundamental" transformation is based less on economic considerations than on a political evaluation of the Latin American government undertaking the measure. For example, the nationalizations of the banking system in Mexico (1982) and petroleum in Venezuela (1976) were viewed with concern, but these actions were not considered to be part of a process of radical social and political change. These countries thus enjoyed greater freedom of action in this regard.

Preventing Structural Change

In the final analysis, the United States' foreign policy toward Latin America is intended to prevent structural transformations. The means available to accomplish this goal include military, ideological, political, and economic policies. Some general comments on these other subjects are necessary to place the question of economic policies in proper perspective.

In military affairs, the United States has attempted to strengthen its relations with Latin American armed forces through training and joint study programs, specialized courses in the United States (and in Panama until 1984), trips abroad for Latin American officers, and personal contacts. The most important development in this area has been the proliferation of "national security doctrines" throughout the region. As a result, Latin American militaries are less concerned with defense against external aggressors than with combating internal enemies. This emphasis became especially pronounced following the Cuban revolution, and during the 1960s national security doctrines evolved to reflect differences among Latin American armed forces. Direct links between the Pentagon and Latin American officers have focused principally on imposing political regimes whose essential function is to fight domestic insurgency.

Latin American armed forces have at their disposal human and material resources disproportionate to any realistic external threat. The concept of internal security embedded in national security doctrines opened up new perspectives to the military, creating much broader opportunities and providing new justifications for exercising political power. These options diverted even more military attention toward political issues and paved the way to military dictatorships. In many cases, even under democratic regimes, the armed forces have become a kind of parallel government.

The United States has also promoted alliances with those sectors of the national economic elite that support large private holdings and foreign capital and that pursue a significant reduction in the role of the state. In Chile, Argentina, and Uruguay during the 1970s, the alliance between the military and the economic elite produced brutally repressive regimes and the application of rigidly monetarist, free-market economic schemes that in the end harmed the national interest.

United States efforts to prevent change in Latin America also involve ideology. This is because the United States perceives its rivalry with the Soviet Union to be, in part, an ideological struggle. Indiscriminate ideological campaigns against "communism" become particularly damaging to Latin America when they advocate extremist ideas, or concepts that become extremist in the hands of national ruling minorities. One example of this phenomenon is the criticism now being directed against the Catholic church, which some senior U.S. government officials have suggested is an ally of Marxism.[24] Ideological attacks have also had an effect on economic issues by creating a negative image of the state, administrative controls, import substitution, the regulation of foreign investment, and even agreements concerning regional economic integration.

In the political sphere, the United States has pursued a number of policies intended to slow or inhibit change in Latin America, ranging from attempts to affect electoral campaigns, to so-called covert actions, to the conditioning of governments' foreign policies. For example, the U.S. government often conditions economic relations on Latin American countries' manifestations of friendship, including their voting patterns in international organizations.[25] The U.S. government has also exerted pressure concerning Argentina's grain sales to the Soviet Union, Brazil's relations with Angola, and the exclusion of Ecuador and Venezuela (as OPEC members) from the U.S. Generalized System of Preferences.

The United States' efforts to prevent change in Latin America set boundaries on the region's autonomy. United States governmental policy toward the region defines a framework within which Latin American countries' conduct is considered routine, and beyond which countries enter into conflict with U.S. security interests and are therefore subject to pressures or reprisals. United States policies limit the range of domestic Latin American economic choices concerning issues such as forms of ownership and relations with U.S. banks and corporations; affect particular political and social forces' opportunities to participate in government; and reduce Latin American countries' foreign policy options. For example, with varying degrees of intensity, the United States opposes producer-country agreements to defend the price of raw materials, tariff barriers, agreements among debtor countries intended to obtain more favorable terms of financing, relations with socialist countries, participation in the nonaligned country movement, the procurement of military supplies from non-U.S. sources, and so forth. Although the effectiveness of these actions depends upon the size of the Latin American country and the timing of their application, these different dimensions together constitute a limiting threshold for Latin American political, economic, and military initiatives.

To what extent does this limiting threshold really reflect U.S. security interests? There are four kinds of developments that may be considered a threat to the United States: Soviet military bases or a Soviet or Cuban military presence in other Latin American countries; an internal political struggle in which leftist forces have independent military capabilities and may be assumed to have military connections with the Soviet Union and/or Cuba; situations in which there is a strong, dominant Communist party in a governing political coalition, or in which such a party may come to power by electoral means; and international policies that are systematically hostile to the U.S. government.

Because situations such as these allow the U.S. government to hold a broad range of interpretations, it is of utmost importance to define the threshold in U.S.–Latin American security relations more precisely. However, because the United States' goal is to prevent the emergence of threatening situations, an administration often reacts before specific facts and trends are fully known. Rapid responses require that the U.S. government hold a "theory" about the possible evolution of events. It is at this level that subjective views regarding potential security threats become important. The security threshold thus remains uncertain for Latin America, and the region's relative autonomy depends upon a particular U.S. administration's ideological orientation.

The fact that this threshold is blurred constrains Latin America's behavior precisely because it is uncertain when the United States may react forcefully to perceived security threats and what means it may employ.

This uncertainty causes Latin American governments to proceed with extreme caution. One might argue that uncertainty is an integral part of U.S. security policy insofar as it constitutes a deterrent.[26]

Limits on U.S. Capabilities to Impose Its Security Criteria

United States security goals are constrained by the means available to pursue them. Because these means are finite, the United States must be selective in identifying its objectives. Discussions in the United States regarding the most appropriate security strategy have varied greatly in nature. In general, the breadth of U.S. security objectives in Latin America has depended on the health of the U.S. economy and its strength relative to other industrialized countries. After its apogee in the 1950s and 1960s, U.S. economic power has declined in relation to the magnitude of world problems. In a multipolar, interdependent international economic system, there are more interactions and reciprocal limitations. And in a U.S. domestic context characterized by slow growth and disputes concerning social security, budget deficits, and international responsibilities, available resources are limited. Consequently, the United States cannot give all developing countries equal priority, and it cannot afford to become involved in all conflicts.

In addition to these economic constraints, other factors reduce the United States' leverage in Latin America. The ongoing debate in the United States regarding security objectives is one such factor. The neoconservative position, which dominated this debate in the early 1980s, advocates an attempt to regain the power that the United States enjoyed in the immediate post-World War II period. From this perspective, any further loss of U.S. influence is understood as a significant security threat. This position has been criticized for its excessive emphasis on subjective perceptions of security interests, an attitude that some have labeled "national insecurity."[27] Others have questioned the wisdom of attempting to recoup past influence in a new international situation in which power is much less concentrated. Such efforts might erode the United States' position even further.[28]

Other participants in this debate object to the neoconservative position's disproportionate emphasis on East-West conflict and exaggerated estimates of Soviet power. The Soviet Union does not have the economic capacity to provide massive foreign assistance to developing countries, especially to Latin America. The ideological appeal of the Soviet/East European socialist model has also decreased considerably in Latin America. Nor is a Soviet presence irreversible, as demonstrated by the cases of Egypt, Somalia, and other countries that first established close ties with the Soviet Union and later broke them. Similarly, those revolutions that have led to the creation of Soviet-style political regimes have occurred in quite backward societies. The increasing social complexity of most developing countries, as well as their closer ties to the international capitalist economic system, make it increasingly unlikely that they will undergo broad structural transformations along the lines of the classic model of peasant revolution. It is even more unlikely that the country in question could cut itself off entirely from the international economy.

Some critics of the neoconservative position identify poverty and repression as the principal causes of political instability in Latin America, and they reject the emphasis that U.S. foreign policy places on counterinsurgency actions. Those who hold this position propose a clear distinction between national processes of social and political change and aggressive actions by the Soviet Union as sources of instability. They believe that this distinction is an essential basis for a realistic U.S. security policy toward Latin America.[29]

Critics of the neoconservative position argue that an alternative U.S. security policy should give greater attention to economic factors. This policy would be based on two principles: the need to further Latin America's independence vis-à-vis the United States rather than attempting to retain traditional control; and the importance of emphasizing economic relations rather than East-West considerations in U.S.–Latin American relations.[30]

To the extent to which U.S. policies confuse security with control and the maintenance of past relationships, any significant advance in Latin American autonomy will be seen as a threat to U.S. security. In contrast, a less hegemonic U.S. posture that recognizes changes in relative economic power would reduce tensions and encourage the development of a more mature hemispheric relationship. The growing interrelationship between Latin American economies and the economies of the United States and other developed capitalist countries makes extremely unlikely a political-economic rupture that would bring Latin America under Soviet influence. This closely woven network of economic ties with Latin America provides the United States with a system of coordination and cooperation that is a much more effective guarantee of U.S. security interests in the region than political and ideological pressures that attempt to enforce a rigid East-West alignment.

In addition to these considerations, two other factors limit the application of traditional U.S. security criteria in Latin America. The first concerns West European allies' perceptions of western security interests in the region. Western Europe's positions on security issues also differ from the neoconservative perspective currently dominant in the United States. Europeans are less inclined to believe that social and political change in developing countries automatically constitutes a security threat. They argue that it is better to adjust to processes of change—at the same time shaping their direction—than to oppose them. Moreover, West European analysts attach greater importance to the economic dimensions of security questions. From this point of view, the risk of conflict increases if economic relationships are not mutually beneficial. This is especially true in the case of developing countries that suffer from asymmetrical, dependent international economic relationships.

Western Europe's strategic interests are furthered by multipolar international relations because superpower hegemony is reduced. Thus western Europe encourages the emergence of medium-sized powers in order to improve its own relative position in international affairs. This strategic interest favors a more autonomous role for Latin America. European activities toward this end may expand Latin America's leverage vis-à-vis the United States.

Second, advances in military technology have reduced the importance of possible Soviet bases near U.S. territory. This fact somewhat weakens the argument that it is essential to prevent any Soviet presence in the region due to the risk that such a position could be used to launch a direct attack against the United States. Because the capability of launching a strategic attack depends less and less on geographical proximity, it is more difficult to justify preventive U.S. intervention in Latin America. Thus circumstances are now more favorable for differentiating clearly between real U.S. military security interests in Latin America and U.S. objectives of nonmilitary control over the region. This distinction is an important basis for defining a specific security threshold, which would expand Latin America's scope for autonomous action.

Economic Strength and Security in Latin America

Without underestimating the importance of nuances and variations throughout the Western Hemisphere, one can conclude that there are important differences in U.S. and Latin American perspectives on security issues. The dominant perspective in the United States gives priority to military, political, and ideological considerations, while the Latin American perspective emphasizes economic concerns. From the U.S. perspective, external factors (especially the Soviet Union) are most important, while Latin American conceptions of security stress domestic economic problems and international economic constraints. The first approach identifies subversion as the source of political instability, while the second sees it as the result of social and political mobilization. The U.S. perspective tends to favor the maintenance of the status quo, while the Latin American approach accepts social participation and political change.

The subordination of Latin America's strategic interests to those of the United States was largely due to a severe imbalance in economic power. Consequently, improving Latin America's strategic position depends on its becoming stronger economically. Latin American countries have undertaken a number of collective initiatives intended to achieve greater relative power, including both economic agreements and some forms of political coordination. Attempts at regional economic integration, joint industrial programing, financial and commercial agreements, laws regulating foreign investment, and the coordination of foreign economic policies in international forums are all examples of such actions in the economic field. The defense of principles of nonintervention and self-determination have also helped limit U.S. intervention in Latin American countries' internal affairs.

However, these measures have not fully succeeded in transforming economic potential into economic power. Latin America has enlarged its productive base, but when each country acts alone it cannot realize the full significance of this change. There is no collective Latin American vision of economic security, and Latin American perceptions of the region's subordination have scarcely been altered. Collective actions by Latin American countries are rare, and few Latin Americans think of the region in Latin American terms.[31]

A collective strategy to defend national and regional interests must be accompanied by efforts to strengthen relative economic power. A shift in relative power might then allow Latin America to achieve greater autonomy vis-à-vis the United States. Latin America's attempts to strengthen its international economic position should focus on measures that correct the basic asymmetry of the region's economic relations with industrialized countries; establish a multipolar global economic framework; and strengthen developing countries' coordination mechanisms, especially those multilateral organizations in which they have the most influence.

The goal of a collective economic security strategy is to reduce Latin America's vulnerability vis-à-vis external economic phenomena. This means increasing the region's relative economic power in a context of growing interdependence. In order to effect change of this kind, Latin America must first build a more solid economic structure, one with a more diversified industrial and technological base and closer regional integration of trade, finance, and technology. Latin America must also strengthen institutional mechanisms for the coordination and defense of each Latin American country against military, economic, and/or political aggression from outside the region.

Because Latin America's security requires more independence and greater economic autonomy vis-à-vis the United States, it cannot separate economic problems from security issues. Latin America has traditionally limited security concerns to purely military questions, which are to be addressed by the armed forces. As a result, security relations with the United States are handled through Latin American officers' direct dealings with the Pentagon, while civilian rulers concentrate on economic and political issues. This differentiated responsibility has weakened civilian rule because the military has in fact shifted its priority to "internal security," a doctrine that legitimates military participation in politics and economics. And as previously noted, the Latin American armed forces' concern with domestic political stability relegates responsibility for extra-continental defense to the U.S. military.

In contrast, the U.S. government makes no such distinction among its military, economic, ideological, and diplomatic policies. It addresses security issues in the broadest possible context. Despite the fact that the United States no longer has a real Latin American economic policy, it persists in a hemispheric security policy that asserts political trusteeship over Latin America. The paradox is that the United States has a global policy on economic issues and a hemispheric policy with regard to security. It gives absolute priority to the latter in U.S.–Latin American relations.

Latin America should do likewise for both domestic (ensuring democratic stability) and external (increasing its relative power) reasons. Linking economic and security issues would increase Latin America's bargaining leverage and place the region in a more balanced position vis-à-vis the United States. Latin America should develop new conceptions of security, subordinating military and public-order questions to goals such as democracy, autonomy, and economic development. Practically no one in Latin America questions the United States' legitimate security concerns; these are quite real. But Latin America must also clearly define its own concept of collective security in order to prevent U.S. economic interests, or those of Latin American elites, from being disguised by the rhetoric of security interests. When this happens, the strategic objectives of the general population are blocked.

International economic change and Latin America's own development have made economic problems an important part of regional security. Economic issues have acquired greater significance in Latin America's international affairs, especially in its relations with the United States. In this context, Latin America would make better use of its relative economic strength if it succeeded in transforming its potential into real capacity. This would accelerate the readjustment that is necessary between Latin America's strategic interests and those of the United States. In other words, it is essential to establish a new quid pro quo that is more favorable to Latin

America. This is the basis for a less conflictual relationship between Latin America and the United States. Its realization depends not on concessions but on the fulfillment of the region's economic potential through greater political unity and economic coordination.

Woodrow Wilson International Center for Scholars
Washington, D.C.

Notes

This essay was initially written during 1983 when the author was a Fellow at the Woodrow Wilson International Center for Scholars, Smithsonian Institution, Washington, D.C.

1. See R. McCall, "From Monroe to Reagan," in Richard Newfarmer, ed., *From Gunboats to Diplomacy* (Baltimore: Johns Hopkins University Press, 1984).

2. Marshall argued that what capital was available for foreign aid would have to be directed toward western Europe. Consequently, the Latin American share of U.S. aid between 1946 and 1960 never exceeded 4.8 percent; F. Parkinson, *Latin America, the Cold War, and the World Powers, 1945–1973* (Beverly Hills, Ca.: Sage Publications, 1974), p. 14. David Green, writing on the same period, argues that George Marshall's explanation was an excuse because "it was clear in the American Delegation's later report (1948) that such large-scale governmental aid probably would not have been forthcoming even if there were no European Recovery Program." David Green, *The Containment of Latin America* (Chicago: Quadrangle Books, 1971), p. 285.

3. Parkinson, *Latin America, the Cold War, and the World Powers*, pp. 14, 43.

4. Ibid., p. 16.

5. For evidence of U.S. efforts to pressure Brazil to support its position in the United Nations in exchange for U.S. economic aid, see ibid., p. 24.

6. See Green, *The Containment of Latin America*, p. 286.

7. See Margaret Daly Hayes, "Collective Security and the Global Balance," *Governance in the Western Hemisphere*, Aspen Institute (New York, May 1982).

8. Sistema Económico Latinoamericano (SELA), *Proyecto de estrategia para perfeccionar la seguridad económica colectiva* (Caracas) (June 1982).

9. For an analysis of how these preoccupations developed in the United States, see Stephen D. Krasner, *Defending the National Interest* (Princeton: Princeton University Press, 1978), pp. 48–51.

10. This is the case for bauxite, chromite, cobalt, columbium, tantalum, manganese, nickel, strontium, and tin. See U.S. Department of the Interior, Bureau of Mines, *Mineral Commodity Summaries* (Washington, D.C.: U.S. Government Printing Office, 1983), various pages and tables.

11. Ibid. Except in the case of bauxite, the quantities involved are relatively small. These minerals are used principally in alloys.

12. As Krasner notes, "The cases analyzed in this book suggest that there has

been a clear rank-ordering of goals for American policy related to foreign raw material investment. In order of decreasing importance, the ranking has been: (1) maximize the competitive structure of the market and thereby reduce prices; (2) increase security of supply; (3) secure general foreign policy objectives." Krasner, *Defending the National Interest,* pp. 277, 330–31.

13. See Sergio Bitar, "Latin America and the United States: Changes in Economic Relations During the Seventies," *Working Papers* No. 127, Latin American Program, Woodrow Wilson International Center for Scholars, Smithsonian Institution (Washington, D.C., 1983), p. 4.

14. Calculations based on data from the U.S. Department of Commerce, Bureau of Economic Analysis, Washington, D.C., 1982. See also Sergio Bitar, "Corporaciones transnacionales y las nuevas relaciones de América Latina con Estados Unidos," *Economía de América Latina,* 11 (Mexico) (1984): 118, table E.

15. Calculations based on Board of Governors, U.S. Federal Reserve Board, "Country Exposure Lending Survey," Washington, D.C.; estimate of banking capital based on data in William R. Cline, "External Debt: System Vulnerability and Development," *Columbia Journal of World Business* 17, No. 1 (Spring 1982): 10.

16. See Jorge I. Domínguez, "The United States and Its Regional Security Interests: The Caribbean, Central, and South America," *Daedalus* 109, No. 4 (Fall 1980): 117.

17. See Abraham F. Lowenthal and Gregory Treverton, "The Making of U.S. Policies Toward Latin America: Some Speculative Propositions," *Working Papers* No. 4, Latin American Program, Woodrow Wilson International Center for Scholars, Smithsonian Institution (Washington, D.C., 1976), pp. 3–6.

18. William Colby, former director of the Central Intelligence Agency, notes: "A nuclear arsenal is not the real threat from the Soviet Union. Subversion is more dangerous. It is not with MX missiles that we are going to stop communist subversion in the Third World, including Latin America and Africa." *El Nacional* (Caracas), 8 December 1982, p. A7.

19. For a view that reflects the Reagan administration's perceptions of the issues in the early 1980s, see Constantine Menges, "The United States and Latin America in the 1980s," in Prosser Gifford, ed., *The National Interest of the United States* (The Wilson Center, Smithsonian Institution, University Press of America, 1981), pp. 55–61.

20. This improvement in the Soviet position during the 1960s is examined by John Gaddis, *Strategies of Containment* (New York: Oxford University Press, 1982), p. 286.

21. George F. Kennan, "America's Unstable Soviet Policy," *Atlantic Monthly* 250, No. 5 (November 1982): 80.

22. For a clear exposition of this logic, see Vermont Royster, "Thinking Things Over," *Wall Street Journal,* 25 May 1983, p. 30.

23. For details on the Nixon-Kissinger policy toward Chile and some explanations of its origins, see Seymour Hersch, "The Price of Power," *Atlantic Monthly* 250, No. 6 (December 1982): 31–58.

24. See Colman McCarthy, "The Depuzzling of George Bush," *Washington Post,* 13 March 1983.

25. See *Washington Post,* 8 March 1983, p. A14.

26. With regard to the Nixon-Kissinger strategy, Gaddis argues: "The idea was to show that the U.S. could act if it chose to, and thereby to create questions in the minds of adversaries as to whether it would or not. Uncertainty itself became a deterrent." *Strategies of Containment,* p. 301.

27. See Abraham F. Lowenthal, "Ronald Reagan and Latin America: Coping with Hegemony in Decline," in Kenneth A. Oye et al., eds., *Eagle Defiant* (Boston: Little, Brown, 1983), pp. 311–35.

28. Kenneth A. Oye, "International Systems Structure and American Foreign Policy," in Oye et al., *Eagle Defiant,* p. 29.

29. This perspective informs *The Americas at the Crossroads,* report by Inter-American Dialogue, Woodrow Wilson International Center for Scholars (Washington, D.C., April 1983). See also Roger Hansen, "National Security in the 1980s," in Roger Hansen, ed., *U.S. Foreign Policy and the Third World* (New York: Praeger, 1982), p. 7.

30. On these points, see, respectively, Margaret Daly Hayes, "Collective Security and the Global Balance," and Richard E. Feinberg, *The Intemperate Zone: The Third World Challenge to U.S. Foreign Policy* (New York: W. W. Norton), chapter 5.

31. For a discussion of this problem, see Enrique Iglesias, "International Economic Cooperation: A View from Latin America", in Ricardo Ffrench-Davis and E. Tironi, eds., *Latin America and the New International Economic Order* (New York: St. Martin's Press, 1982), pp. 223, 228.

21

COMMENT: Security in the Western Hemisphere

Margaret Daly Hayes

> It is especially the demonstration of seemingly irresistible mili-
> tary power which exerts a strange fascination over the minds
> of those who are given to hasty prophesies rather than to cau-
> tious analysis.
>
> —Hans J. Morgenthau[1]

Security is a dimension of the United States' relations with Latin America
that is little understood and today much maligned. In one of the essays in
this section, Cole Blasier observes that "security as a concept has so many
meanings, misuses, and controversial associations that the term itself has
become a problem in U.S.–Latin American relations." Sergio Bitar notes
that in the post-World War II environment, both the U.S. and Latin
American governments have viewed political stability as a component of
security. But, he argues, the United States views stability as containment
of communist activities and avoidance of change, while Latin Americans
regard economic development as necessary for stability. Blasier argues
that security, for Latin Americans, is akin to political autonomy. Bitar
suggests that security is much more complex, including economic and
political systemic concerns. Blasier explains that U.S. responses to events
in the Western Hemisphere are colored by fears of possible Soviet military threats to the region, or of political threats deriving from Soviet ties
with Latin American governments. However, he argues that the historical
record shows that neither threat has been seriously credible in "security"
crises in Latin America in the post-World War II period. Bitar observes
that it is not the physical threat but the ideology of regimes that is of
concern to the United States. Gregory Treverton examines the historical
record of and future prospects for interstate conflict in Latin America.
Although he considers different states' increasing capabilities and opportunities for conflict, he hardly discusses security.

In short, these three essays present many different and noncomplementary understandings of what "security" is. Yet, for all this discussion, there is no agreement on a definition of security, security interest, or what might constitute threats to security.

A chief cause of confusion in the discussion of national security interests is the absence of any clear and accepted definition of security itself. Dictionary definitions include concepts such as "freedom from fear, care, doubt, anxiety, or danger," or "safe, sure, certain, confident, or undisturbed."[2] The international relations literature is replete with studies of perceptions of security threats, but it does not define what constitutes a state of security.[3]

National security is defined only in its most simplistic form as freedom from physical (that is, military) threats. National security also entails the defense of economic interests and the promotion of a world order that is compatible with national interests and goals and that is accepting of national values and ideology.[4]

Security is not an absolute; rather, it is a matter of degree. It implies confidence, opportunity, and capability in dealing with events. Security is the end result of a country's successful coping with its political, economic, and geographic environment. Threats, challenges, crises, and routine change all influence the degree of security that a country perceives itself to enjoy. The more supportive a country's environment is, the more secure that country is. The more the environment challenges a country's physical or managerial capabilities, or is hostile to national goals and interests, the more insecure that country is. Except in situations of direct military threat, security is a state of mind.

Even if the concept of security defies concrete definition, analysts have not hesitated to examine different countries' security policies. Two of the three essays in this section deal extensively with the state of U.S. security concerns in Latin America. Bitar's examination of different perceptions of security is one of the most successful analyses available of differences in U.S. and Latin American emphases in the security relationship. Much of his argument is very persuasive. Blasier addresses the controversial question of external threats to hemispheric security, but he adopts too narrow a definition of U.S. security interests. Treverton deals capably with an illusive topic, but he fails to include security as one of the factors that will influence the potential for intrahemispheric conflict.

If one of the key difficulties in dealing with "national security" is the absence of agreement concerning what the concept means and how to measure it, Bitar's effort is successful because he systematically seeks to penetrate myth and rhetoric by weighing evidence for and against specific assertions. Blasier is less successful because he is less rigorous with historical evidence. Treverton is straightforward in his examination of his subject, but his basic conclusion—that conflict is more likely in Latin America in the future—may be based on the questionable assumption that the Falklands/Malvinas conflict between Argentina and Great Britain is comparable to other boundary disputes in the region.

There is broad agreement among the three essays regarding those factors that influence security policies in the region. For example, the authors agree that rivalry between the United States and the Soviet Union is the dominant factor explaining U.S. foreign policy initiatives and reactions both in the Western Hemisphere and elsewhere in the world. They agree that the United States has little or no tolerance for the emergence of Soviet-allied regimes in the Western Hemisphere, and they all concur that U.S. fears that insurgencies will produce pro-Soviet regimes have often resulted in overreactions to political events in the region. The authors agree that U.S. reactions have presumed the worst outcome in situations in which the outcome was still undetermined, and that in some cases such reactions by the United States may have produced self-fulfilling prophesies. Finally, the authors agree that U.S. policy has not been especially successful in fostering a political order in Latin America that is supportive of long-term U.S. policy goals. Despite U.S. efforts to direct Latin American responses, from the U.S. perspective the countries of the region remain frustratingly independent of the "colossus of the north."

The three essays under discussion here also have several shortcomings. They exaggerate U.S. attitudes toward the Soviet threat in the hemisphere, while underplaying possible Soviet support for insurgency in the region. None of the authors examines thoroughly Soviet intentions in Latin America. Although the historical record is cited for its "lessons," there is no effort to compare historical circumstances to present-day conditions, circumstances, and policies. The authors are sometimes reluctant to ask whether the United States has security interests in Latin America and what those interests are. Finally, none of the papers considers the merits of "hard-line" conservative thinking that sees a Soviet-Cuban conspiracy in the region.

The authors offer a number of insights into the factors that influence perceptions of security and the making of security policy. Blasier observes correctly that official U.S. interpretations of events are often shaped by domestic political considerations. Bitar notes that Latin Americans have always had difficulty understanding exactly what the United States regards as threats to its security. However, he recognizes that although the United States and Latin America have differed historically in their interpretations of security, the focal point for both has been stability. The United States has emphasized ideological issues, while Latin Americans have focused on economic development as a prerequisite for political stability. At the same time, Bitar acknowledges that the question of political stability (freedom from internal subversion) has sometimes received an inordinate amount of Latin American attention, often to the neglect of economic concerns.

Although it often seems that U.S. policy has been directed at protecting U.S. economic interests in Latin America, Bitar notes that the "definition of what constitutes a 'fundamental' transformation is based less on economic considerations than on a political evaluation of the Latin American government undertaking the measure." This point is absolutely key to understanding the United States' approach to radical and potentially radical regimes in the region.

The Premises of Security Policies

Several premises appear to underlie the authors' discussion of security concerns and U.S. security policies in the Western Hemisphere. These include: the United States fears military threats from the region; the United States insists on the preservation of the status quo in the region; Latin America is ineluctably revolutionary; the Soviet Union has limited and largely benign interests in the region; revolutions are always justified—they are morality plays pitting "good guys" (the revolutionaries) against "bad guys" (the incumbents); and finally, the United States could easily disengage itself from Latin American affairs. The following sections examine each of these premises as a basis for a better understanding of security issues in the hemisphere.

A Military Threat to the Hemisphere?

Defense of territory is clearly a key security value for all states. Bitar notes that for Latin American countries, defense against external threat is not as high a priority as are other security concerns because defense of the hemisphere has long been regarded as the responsibility of the United States. Although Treverton sees reasons for greater concern about conflict between Latin American states in the future, most border disputes in the hemisphere can be managed through the region's conflict-resolution mechanisms. Because of the comparatively low priority they accord territorial defense, Latin Americans have been able to concentrate their attention on questions of political and economic development.

Blasier notes that, with the exception of the 1962 Cuban missile crisis, there has been no military threat to the United States from Latin America. Certainly no Latin American country poses a credible military threat to the United States. Indeed, a key element of U.S. foreign policy toward the region has been to exclude external powers that might pose a direct challenge. A careful examintation would show that, despite the rhetoric, direct military threats to the territory of the United States have not been the foremost U.S. security concern. Even in an era of increasing Soviet operation in and around the region, analysts recognize that the Soviet presence poses little direct military threat to the United States. Rather, the Soviet presence ties up resources that could be used elsewhere, because U.S. military and diplomatic forces must be engaged in the region in order to discourage further expansion of Soviet activities.[5] It is, of course, conceivable that at some future time a military threat could emerge within the region. However, a large number of wrong turns would be necessary for such a situation to evolve. One of the tasks of foreign policy is to avoid making errors that lead down that road.

A Threat to the Status Quo?

It is in every country's interest to cope successfully with its changing environment. It is also in every country's interest that its environment be nonthreatening and responsive to its interests and goals. In some cases it is possible to impose responsiveness through the use, or the threat, of military force. The Soviet Union employs this approach in its relations with bordering countries. For the most part, however, countries seek responsiveness through less dramatic (and far less costly) means of suasion.

The historical record of U.S. interventions in Latin American affairs appears to support the argument that the United States resists change in the region. This belief has become so prevalent that the National Bipartisan Commission on Central America (the Kissinger Commission) felt compelled to insist in the introduction to its 1984 report that "indigenous reform, even indigenous revolution, is not a security threat to the United States. But the intrusion of aggressive outside powers exploiting local grievances to expand their own political influence and military control is a serious threat to the United States, and to the entire hemisphere."[6] The presumption that the United States requires hegemony over and subjugation of the countries of the Western Hemisphere is based on a misunderstanding of the United States' preference for the status quo. In a world of practical politics, the political status quo does not mean continuation of backward political systems or inequitable economic practices. It need not concern the internal political order at all. Morgenthau, writing on the politics of the status quo, argued that "the policy of the status quo aims at the maintenance of the distribution of power (among nations) which exists at a particular moment in history. . . . Minor adjustments in the distribution of power, however, which leave intact the relative power positions of the nations concerned, are fully compatible with a policy of the status quo."[7] Because the United States is already the dominant power in the hemisphere, and not credibly challenged in that position, it has no reason to resist internal political, economic, and social changes that improve the well-being of Latin American citizens.

In earlier decades the United States enjoyed overwhelming economic superiority over Latin American countries. This is no longer the case. Although U.S. influence remains pervasive, the United States is no longer the only partner available to Latin American countries. Many, if not most, Latin American states have learned to manipulate foreign investment in their own interest. United States private economic interests in Latin America have become less significant as many U.S. firms close operations or reduce their presence in the region. Although the international market may not always be favorable to Latin American interests, this is a phenomenon that does not necessarily carry political overtones.

It is not economic change but the ideological character of the regimes undertaking change that is of greatest concern to the United States. Indeed, it is increasingly recognized that economic change is the sine qua non for political stability in Latin America. This point has been argued at least since the 1950s when President Dwight D. Eisenhower sent his brother, Dr. Milton Eisenhower, to the region to report on economic conditions. The Alliance for Progress represented one such policy response. Projects such as the recent Caribbean Basin Initiative incorporate current understanding of what problems need to be tackled and what remedies can be useful. The Kissinger Commission's "Marshall Plan" for Central America reflects the continuing belief that economic development is one of the key underpinnings of a secure political environment.

The tremendous emphasis placed on the concept of hegemony (understood in this context to mean an insistence on the internal, pro-U.S. status quo) overestimates the permanence of historical patterns and fails to recognize the continuing U.S. interest in progressive political outcomes in Latin America. The United States' position as a superpower does not guarantee it the ability to manipulate a world environment. Henry A. Kissinger has argued that the United States "is no longer in a position to operate programs globally. It has to encourage them. It can no longer impose its preferred solution; it must seek to evoke it."[8] The principal challenge to the United States in pursuing its interests in the Western Hemisphere is to evoke responses that are consistent with both U.S. and Latin American interests. It remains to be determined how that can best be done.

On Revolutions and Political Threat

If the United States does not reject change, why is the United States so concerned with leftist revolutions in Latin America? The United

States' overriding security interest in the region is to encourage and maintain a compatible political order. For this reason the main focus of U.S. security policy is on political instability in Latin America. The authors of the essays in this section recognize that U.S. security concerns are motivated by the United States' global role as a superpower and that the Soviet Union is the United States' most important concern. Bitar observes correctly that developing countries are perceived to be the key scene of confrontation between the superpowers. He also argues, correctly, that the United States believes the Soviet Union will take advantage of instability around the world in order to enhance its own position in the global balance of power. Whereas Latin American countries tend to define political stability in terms of internal political problems, the United States (as a global power) defines political stability in terms of both support for the prevailing international system and ideological compatibility. The more steadfastly Latin American countries align themselves with the United States, the more satisfactory is the situation from the United States' perspective. This is a purely pragmatic conclusion. Instability in Latin America, as elsewhere in the world, creates opportunities for Soviet incursions. The "threat" to the United States is not from Latin America; it is *through* Latin America, but *from* the Soviet Union and its like-minded ideological supporters. Bitar recognizes that the Soviet threat is political and psychological rather than military. In addition, it is a global issue rather than a regional problem.

Although acknowledging Soviet political intentions in the hemisphere, Blasier seeks to demonstrate that in several different security crises in the past the Soviet Union posed no political threat to the United States. He implies that these cases parallel the current situation in Central America, but the discussion of Central America in his essay fails to substantiate this interpretation. Neither formal diplomatic relations with the Soviet Union nor the existence of pro-Soviet Communist parties in many Latin American countries alone constitutes a credible threat to the United States or full justification for U.S. concerns about Soviet meddling in Latin American affairs. Blasier's essay distinguishes between pro-Soviet Communist parties (that is, orthodox Communist parties linked to Moscow) and other (often more extreme) leftist parties. But such a distinction begs the question.

It is true that orthodox Communist parties in Latin America have traditionally been weak and poorly organized. However, this does not preclude either their use as a façade by leftist radicals or their conversion to more militant policies.[9] The relevant actors in the political drama of instability are the leftist cadres, parties, quasi parties, and other political fronts and organizations that are sympathetic to the Soviet Union, other countries antagonistic to the United States, or to Marxist-Leninist ideology and that are willing to accept Soviet (or other countries') aid (overt or covert) to promote their political goals. These other groups, in addition to orthodox Communist parties, are the necessary focus of U.S. policymakers' security concerns.

Nicaragua (the most visible non-Communist leftist government in the hemisphere, according to Blasier) is a case in point. Few would claim that all Sandinistas are orthodox Communists. What is of concern is the fact that a radical Marxist-Leninist cadre has assumed (or sought to assume) direction of Nicaragua's political, economic, and foreign policies; that Cuban, Soviet, and East European advisors occupy key positions in the Nicaraguan government; that Nicaragua has armed itself beyond those levels necessary for its own territorial defense; and that the Nicaraguan government has adopted a radical, anti-U.S. foreign policy that includes both supporting subversion and exporting it to neighboring countries. In short, it is not by labels but by actions that the Sandinista regime should be judged.

There are several factors not discussed in the essays in this section that account for U.S. concern regarding leftist revolutions in Latin America. First, the experience of Cuba does not encourage confidence in the outcome of revolutions. It will never be resolved whether U.S. reactions to the Cuban revolution pushed Castro into the arms of the Soviets, as some analysts argue. Regardless of how it became that way, Cuba today is a militant Marxist-Leninist state whose activities are contrary to the interests of the United States. Cuba has trained and organized guerrilla forces; it has served as a base for Soviet operations in the hemisphere (operations that continue to increase in frequency and scale); and it has served as a catalyst for anti-U.S. sentiment in Latin America and among developing countries generally. If the United States has sometimes appeared to take actions that further antagonize relations with Cuba, a dispassionate analysis of Cuban responses to U.S. initiatives over time might show that Cuba also has demonstrated a limited interest in rapprochement with the United States.[10]

Second, the historical record of leftist revolution in the region shows that a revolution frequently leads to changes in the political alliances of the country in which it occurs, and sometimes to a regime that holds a messianic dedication to the export of revolution.[11] Equally important, given the historical weakness of the orthodox left in Latin America, there is a demonstrated tendency for extremists to capture the leadership of a revolution (recently demonstrated in Nicaragua and Grenada) or to upset the leadership of a more moderate left (as in Allende's Chile). Despite protestations to the contrary, a leftist revolution is rarely independent of East-West divisions. Revolutionaries rely on one bloc or the other for political and financial support. Indeed, the revolutionary left increasingly aligns itself with the Soviet Union, Cuba, Libya, or other sponsors whose motives for supporting revolutions are (or should be) suspect.

The Soviet Threat

Given the stakes entailed in superpower competition in developing countries, and the historical importance of a strong U.S. position in the hemisphere for the global balance of power, it would be in the United States' interest that there be no Soviet involvement in the Western Hemisphere at all, even if that involvement were benign. Of course, it is impossible for the United States to bar sovereign Latin American states from establishing relations with the Soviet Union if they choose to have them. But it is in the United States' interest to limit Soviet involvement to the least offensive areas, and simultaneously to promote more constructive relations between Latin American countries and the United States.

On the basis of his analysis of four historical cases (Guatemala, 1954; Cuba, 1960–1961; the Dominican Republic, 1965; Chile, 1970–1973), Blasier seeks to understand the source of errors in U.S. perceptions of past threats and lessons for reacting to current problems in Central America and the Caribbean. Although it may be true that those who ignore the lessons of history are destined to repeat past mistakes, it is not always the case that the circumstances and attitudes of thirty years ago (for example, Guatemala in the late 1940s and early 1950s) are instructive in the present environment. Blasier may accurately describe the tenuous Soviet link to leftists in Latin America in the 1950s, but he errs in not examining that linkage today.

By the tone of his analysis, Blasier seems to suggest that the present level of Soviet activities in the region should not be a source of major concern either for the United States or for Latin American countries. However, by not questioning Soviet intentions, Blasier projects an overly benign and perhaps naive attitude toward the Soviet Union, its purpose in expanding its relations with countries in the Western Hemisphere, and the nature of constraints on its behavior. Although critical of the United States' role in the region, Blasier observes that "the Soviet Union has pursued flexible and pragmatic strategies regarding Latin America ever since Castro came to power in 1959"; "Soviet policy toward the rest of Latin America shows the same cautious, steady, and flexible qualities that it has demonstrated toward Cuba and Nicaragua"; "the Soviet Union will continue to develop its relations with democratic countries in Latin America."

Blasier's analysis fails to examine Soviet policy in sufficient depth. He does not ask to what end the Soviets pursue their "pragmatic strategies" in Latin America, nor does he question whether some "small and politically vulnerable countries" deserve to be the opportunistic targets of armed revolts. Other analysts see a much more focused intent in the Soviet Union's interest in Latin America. Robert S. Leikin has observed that "the Soviet Union has quietly become a significant factor in Latin American affairs," moving "out of cunning, not out of restraint." Although Soviet probes in Latin America do not signify an independent threat to U.S. security, they are more serious precisely because they are components of and subordinate to the Soviet Union's global strategy.[12] Ambassador William H. Luers, a specialist on both the Soviet bloc and Latin America, notes that "Soviet policy toward Latin America has become more focused and activist over the past twenty years," and he argues that a more aggressive recent Soviet posture in Central America "is the product of Soviet perceptions of the conditions in the region, of U.S. capacities and policies, and a more bold, military emphasis to Soviet competition with the United States outside the NATO area. A major factor urging and assisting this Soviet posture is its superclient Cuba, which seems to have convinced Moscow after over twenty years of debate that the promotion of violent revolution in Central America is a wise and relatively low risk policy."[13]

The evaluation of Soviet activities in the Western Hemisphere should not be separated from evaluations of Soviet activities elsewhere in the world. Robert Legvold has argued that Soviet opportunities for influence in developing areas outside the Western Hemisphere were especially great in 1979 for four reasons. First, the collapse of historic leaderships in Africa and Asia (situations comparable with that in Central America after the fall of Somoza) opened new opportunities for Soviet initiatives. Second, regimes and liberation movements in developing countries had come to rely on the Soviet Union for military protection and for military and economic aid. Third, insurgencies actively sought Soviet assistance. Finally, a basic fact of superpower rivalry is that the "Soviet Union stands to gain from ferment any place it is now less favored than the United States." Thus, Legvold observes, "More than we often acknowledge, the Soviet Union finds one of its major missions in reinforcing the constraints on our [U.S.] policy—in neutralizing or counterbalancing our power, particularly in areas of instability where our role has been the most obtrusive."[14]

Another scholar of Soviet foreign policy, Donald Zagoria, states that "wherever the Soviet Union can intrude in the Third World defending 'just' and 'legitimate' causes, helping to undermine 'reactionary,' 'feudal,' or white minority regimes, and casting the United States as the defender of an unpopular status quo, they will do so. To expect the Soviets to give up such a promising field of endeavor where they can hope to expand their influence while supporting 'just' causes is unrealistic."[15]

The question remains: Does this new Soviet strategy pose a security problem for the United States and its Latin American neighbors? Zagoria argues that it does, particularly for middle-sized powers that have historically looked to the United States for leadership and support. He notes that the danger is not so much that the Soviet Union will achieve hegemony in developing countries but "that the spread of communism and Soviet power will upset tenuous regional balances of power, lead to intensified regional instabilities, and make even more difficult the settlement of a variety of regional clashes that could lead to war."[16] In short, it is the impact of present Soviet activities in the Western Hemisphere on the larger regional and global scene that is the principal U.S. concern. In an interdependent world, individual cases cannot be examined only in isolation.

The Prospects for Disengagement

A final premise underlying the three essays in this section is that U.S.–Latin American relations would be more positive if the United States would disengage itself in certain ways from the region, foreswearing both the use of military force and other means of influencing the course of events in Latin America. Blasier proposes that the United States declare limits to its actions in the region—ruling out Soviet military bases and nuclear weapons on the one hand and U.S. armed intervention and political interference in the region on the other. Bitar notes that there are empirical "limits" to U.S. flexibility in responding to change in Latin America. At a minimum, these limits preclude: Soviet military bases or a Soviet or Cuban military presence; Soviet/Cuban supported guerrilla movements; strong Communist parties dominating governments; and systematically anti-U.S. foreign policies. Bitar also suggests that Latin Americans would like greater clarity concerning limits on their actions *beyond* these boundaries. Treverton recommends that the United States negotiate limits to certain actions (no military bases or troop deployments) with the Cubans or Soviets. With agreed-upon limits, the United States could then "afford to be less immediately preoccupied with the precise political orientation of particular regimes."

There clearly is room for improvement in the form and substance of U.S.–Latin American relations. Even if awareness and understanding of the region have improved dramatically in the United States, there will always be room for refinements. No two countries' foreign policies will ever exactly suit each other. National interests are never precisely the same; a "special relationship" need not always be a felicitous one. Nonetheless, these three authors' proposals do not suggest a new and useful framework for improving U.S. policy toward Latin America. The prohibitions against Soviet military bases and Soviet nuclear weapons in the hemisphere are already central tenets of U.S. foreign policy, understandings arrived at in the context of the Cuban missile crisis. They represent the maximum point beyond which vital U.S. security interests are engaged, and there is general acceptance of these limits between the two superpowers. There is no parallel understanding on the question of Cuban support for revolution in the hemisphere, even though this was also at issue in the aftermath of the 1962 missile crisis. Moreover, it is not in Cuba's interest to agree on limits to its activities as a revolutionary state.

In an international climate characterized by political, military, economic, and ideological rivalry between the United States and the Soviet Union, it is not practical to negotiate unilateral restraints on behavior. Successful negotiations require that each party have equal interests in the outcome. The United States' interests in the political balance in the Western Hemisphere are infinitely greater than Soviet interests. Given competition between the two superpowers in developing countries, the Soviet Union has little incentive to desist from efforts to reduce U.S. influence in areas in which it is great. On the contrary, it is very much in the Soviet Union's interest to press U.S. tolerance *to* the limit—all the while being careful not to stretch that tolerance *beyond* the limit.

A corollary disincentive to negotiations is a lack of confidence between the Soviet Union and the United States and between the United States and Cuba. Because neither party trusts the other to keep its word, there is little incentive to negotiate serious agreements. Similar levels of distrust make negotiations among Central American countries difficult, as the Contadora nations (Colombia, Mexico, Panama, and Venezuela) have discovered.

Finally, no negotiations or public statements of limits to interests will, or should, lead the United States to withdraw attention from ongoing political and economic change in Latin America. The United States has become engaged in crises in the region precisely because it has ignored the area for long periods of time between crises. Many steps are required to establish a hostile military base, install a weapons system, undermine a political process, or distort an economic program. No one step in itself may be threatening to U.S. interests in the region, but the cumulative effect may be so. Bitar notes correctly that the goal of U.S. policy is to avoid a *gradual drift* toward communism. This policy is appropriate not because change is inimical to U.S. interests but because the cost of reversing such a development would be very high. In the present situation in Central America, the United States' interest is engaged not only in preventing drift toward radical leftism but also in promoting and pressuring for progressive changes by established regimes. Critics of U.S. policy often fail to acknowledge this aspect of U.S. governmental approaches to regional problems.

Conclusion

As noted at the beginning of this comment, a principal problem in recent discussions of "security" has been the absence of an accepted definition of "security" and "security interests." A formulation of U.S.

interests in the Western Hemisphere that interprets U.S. security broadly in terms of the national interest (not merely in military terms) might include the following consideration: It is in the United States' national interest that there exist in the hemisphere stable, friendly, prosperous states that permit the free movement of goods and services through the region; that respect the political integrity of their neighbors; and that do not offer support to the United States' global political rivals.[17] A close examination of any Latin American country's national interest would likely reveal a similar set of priorities.

United States security is increased the more closely that regional conditions approximate the description offered above. However, the United States can accept situations that do not exactly fit this model more easily than is often admitted. Because political instability and economic underdevelopment are essentially internal Latin American issues that do not necessarily have regionwide or extrahemispheric consequences, U.S. security interests are not threatened by policies aimed at addressing these problems. There has been little formal "policy" elaborated concerning Latin American development processes. The "hegemonic" U.S. approach of the early twentieth century and even of the 1950s no longer reflects governmental or private sector attitudes regarding U.S. economic relations with Latin America. Only when internal change threatens to produce political regimes inimical to broad U.S. interests (such as regional stability and amicable bilateral relations) must the United States resist such change. Change in a Latin American country's overall political alignment is not in the United States' interest, and the greater the projected change, the less acceptable it is. These are the simple truths of practical politics.

Different presidential administrations have interpreted U.S. interests in the Western Hemisphere in different ways—although consistently within the same general framework. Presidents and policymakers have reacted more or less strongly to political and economic changes in Latin America. The inconsistency of U.S. response is in large part due to the lack of consensus on the nature of U.S. security interests in the region. Until there is greater agreement on this issue, both North Americans and Latin Americans will continue to be confused by U.S. (and Latin American) security policies.

Director, Washington Office
Council of the Americas
Washington, D.C.

Notes

1. Hans J. Morgenthau, *Politics Among Nations: The Struggle for Power and Peace,* 5th ed., rev. (New York: Knopf, 1973), p. 157.

2. See *Webster's New Universal Unabridged Dictionary* (New York: Simon and Schuster, 1983).

3. The international relations literature has focused principally on rivalries between states in which military force is a salient factor. But military force is not the only factor in assessing security or power, as Morgenthau notes. If war (or the use of military force) is an extension of politics, as Clausewitz suggests, then most security relations continue to be conducted by political, not military, means.

4. This description draws heavily on the discussion in Donald E. Neucheterlein, *National Interests and Presidential Leadership* (Boulder, Colo.: Westview, 1978), chapter 1, where the author attempts to define the various dimensions of the national interest.

5. Bruce W. Watson, *Red Navy at Sea: Soviet Naval Operations on the High Seas, 1956–1980* (Boulder, Colo.: Westview, 1982).

6. National Bipartisan Commission on Central America ("The Kissinger Commission") *Report* (Washington, D.C.: U.S. Government Printing Office, 1984), p. 5.

7. Morgenthau, *Politics Among Nations*, p. 41.

8. Henry A. Kissinger, *American Foreign Policy*, rev. ed. (New York: W. W. Norton, 1974), p. 93.

9. For a detailed discussion of this argument, see Margaret Daly Hayes, "Coping with Problems That Have No Solutions: Political Change in El Salvador and Guatemala," in *Confrontation in the Caribbean Basin: International Perspectives on Security, Sovereignty, and Survival,* ed. Alan Adelman and Reid Reading (Pittsburgh: Center for Latin American Studies, University Center for International Studies, 1984).

10. For a more detailed discussion, see Margaret Daly Hayes, *Latin America and the U.S. National Interest: A Basis for U.S. Foreign Policy* (Boulder, Colo.: Westview, 1984), chapter 3.

11. Cuba is, of course, the principal example. Chile might have been. Nicaragua has shown signs of following in Cuba's footsteps. The Bishop government in Grenada called itself revolutionary, but it came to power in a coup d'état. Bishop certainly changed his country's political allegiance, and a more radical and pro-Soviet successor government might have been encouraged to proselytize its ideology throughout the region.

12. Robert S. Leiken, "Eastern Winds in Latin America," *Foreign Policy* 42 (Spring 1981): 94–113.

13. William H. Luers, "The Soviets and Latin America: A Three Decade U.S. Policy Triangle," *Washington Quarterly* 7, 1 (Winter 1984): 4.

14. Robert Legvold, "The Super Rivals: Conflict in the Third World," *Foreign Affairs* 57, No. 4 (Spring 1979): 758–59, 770.

15. Donald S. Zagoria, "Into the Breach: New Soviet Alliances in the Third World," *Foreign Affairs* 57, No. 4 (Spring 1979): 733–54.

16. Ibid., pp. 740–41.

17. See Hayes, *Latin America and the U.S. National Interest,* for further development of this theme.

22

COMMENT: The United States and Latin America: The Question of Security

Rafael Hernández

In the course of more than 150 years, relations between the United States and Latin America have accumulated such a residue of problems that no important issue can be posed in simple, schematic terms. Security issues—by nature polemical even at a purely conceptual level—have the special virtue of drawing this torrent of concerns to one's immediate attention, linking economic, politico-diplomatic, and specifically military factors. If one accepts the proposition that "war is the continuation of politics by other means," and that politics is in turn a kind of essential economics, then an analysis of security issues must consider at least minimally the interrelations among these different factors, which are usually examined individually. This is not simply a methodological consideration. What is at issue is the capacity of theory to be something more than a form of "quantum mechanics" in which objective conclusions become simple ideological assumptions. Vindicating objective analysis is (or could be) a means of reestablishing a rationality that is day by day devalued as an international currency.

Concepts and Ideas Concerning "Hemispheric Security"

If something like the concept of "security" exists in the body of strategic doctrine that inspires different U.S. administrations, it corresponds only to a binary logic that merits serious consideration because of the United States' economic and military power. Thus one asks: Is it possible that the whole structure of hemispheric relations for a global power such as the United States can rest on something so imponderable as "the threat of Soviet attack against the Western Hemisphere"? Not even the Roman Empire, in a much less complex world, rested on such a simple notion. What is at issue is not the Soviet Union's potential military presence or its actual political activity in Latin America, but the United

States' hegemonic dominance over the region. United States hegemony does not face a military threat from any quarter, but it *is* affected by internal social change in different Latin American countries. It is true that the United States faces a crisis of hegemony in Latin America, but this is the result of many diverse factors that do not stem from a confrontation with the Soviet Union and communism (as the binary logic of ideological discourse suggests). However, before turning to an examination of these factors, it is useful to evaluate in more detail the assumptions that underlie U.S. security policies toward Latin America.

The idea of an "external military presence in the Western Hemisphere" is an important example of the way in which ideological considerations color the U.S. debate on strategic issues. What is a "military presence" in the age of fourth-generation intercontinental ballistic missiles, submarine-launched ballistic missiles with a range of eight thousand kilometers, and antisatellite weapons in outer space? In *strategic terms,* the limited Soviet military presence in the Caribbean is irrelevant in this context, especially if one takes into account that there are many other available sites at sea or on other continents from which the Soviet Union can conduct a nuclear action. Moreover, U.S. military power in the Western Hemisphere (especially in the Caribbean Basin) is so overwhelming that it is unrealistic to discuss the two superpowers' military presence on this continent in the same terms. The "national security" imperative has led the United States to establish a massive military presence much closer to the Soviet Union's own frontiers (including U.S. military installations in Europe, the Middle East, and the Far East) in the "other" hemisphere. In short, the only ominous "hemispheric" presence in Latin America (including the threat posed by nuclear weapons) is that of the United States.

The "external" character of this perceived threat is also paradoxical, given that it includes Cuba and Nicaragua (although no longer Grenada, where in 1983 the "actual military presence" of the United States replaced the "potential military presence" of the Soviet Union). In the terms of this peculiar U.S. geopolitical discourse, Cuban military advisors in Nicaragua constitute an "external military presence in the hemisphere," while the British fleet operating near the Malvinas Islands is a legitimate defender of their sovereignty and an ally both within and beyond the hemisphere. It is doubtful that even President James Monroe would have engaged in such a contradictory application of his own doctrine. What is certain is that Cuba's relations—and those of Peru, Argentina, and other nonsocialist countries in Latin America—with the Soviet Union do not convert these countries into an "external force" in the same part of the world in which they have forged their histories, in many cases beginning earlier than the founding of the United States. Thus the notion of "hemisphere" has different connotations for the United States and for Latin American countries. From the U.S. perspective, it includes western Europe (and one wonders if it stretches as far as Poland) but excludes some Latin American countries. From the Latin American perspective, the idea of a *hemispheric* community of interests (one that would include both the United States and Latin America) is contrary to the essence of Latin American political thought from Bolívar and Martí to Allende and Bishop.

The development of modern societies in Latin America (both in terms of the emergence of popular sectors and the configuration of their progressive, democratic leadership) has occurred in permanent counterpoint to different U.S. administrations. Vargas, Quadros, and Goulart in Brazil; Cárdenas in Mexico; Perón in Argentina; Velasco Alvarado in Peru; and Torrijos in Panama (to mention only those leaders who are deceased) all faced major challenges from the United States. On the other hand, the United States' political and economic subjugation of Latin America has given rise to the emergence and perpetuation in power of regressive groups (oligarchies and military cliques) that have no relation to the self-determination and sovereignty of nation-states. Examples include Pinochet in Chile, Castillo Armas in Guatemala, Somoza in Nicaragua, Batista in Cuba, and numerous generals in Bolivia—to mention only the classic examples of U.S.-inspired "hemispheric community."

Thus the United States has not demonstrated historically that it is capable of determining what is in the best interests of Latin American countries. Nor have U.S. interventions to "correct" Latin American leaders promoted the stabilization and democratization of these societies. For precisely these reasons, the majority of Latin American governments opposed the recent recurrence of U.S. military intervention in the region (especially after the 1982 Malvinas conflict and the invasion of Grenada). Some countries (particularly Argentina, Guyana, Suriname, Trinidad and Tobago, and Nicaragua) have expressed concern regarding the possibility of U.S. military action against them. Indeed, a list of the United States' covert actions, indirect incursions, and direct military interventions in the hemisphere would include the majority of Latin American countries.

The corollaries to this curious U.S. formulation of "external military presence in the Western Hemisphere" are also peculiar. First, despite the concern that is often raised regarding the specter of "another Cuba," it is clear that the only factor that actually restricts political options or radicalizes the political process in Latin American countries is U.S. hostility to change. Only through ignorance of actual circumstances could the United States have perceived "another Cuba" in Grenada. If another "American tragedy" is now developing in El Salvador, it will be part of the bitter harvest of U.S. policy rather than the result of the "export of Castroistcommunist revolution." After all, what did the United States seek by opposing the Cuban revolution in 1959 and early 1960—acting against a popular movement that punished war criminals, promulgated a moderate agrarian reform, and diversified its foreign relations? All these actions occurred without expropriating the Cuban bourgeoisie, nationalizing foreign investments, or restricting political pluralism. Did U.S. actions in Cuba seek to prevent "another Guatemala" by supporting counterrevolutionary forces in a de facto act of war (March 1960), eliminating Cuba's share of the U.S. sugar-import quota (July 1960), and mounting an intense international propaganda campaign, along with maintaining heavy-handed diplomatic pressures on the revolutionary government? The history of U.S. policy toward Cuba in the first years of the revolution—not to mention the Playa Girón (Bay of Pigs) fiasco and the threat of a direct attack in 1962—is an exemplary lesson of where the "logic" of U.S. policy toward a Latin American country leads.

A second corollary is that "the strategic importance of the Caribbean Basin" for the United States justifies its large-scale military presence in the area. It is frequently claimed that in the event of an all-out confrontation between the United States and the Soviet Union that escalates to the nuclear level, U.S. supply lines through the Caribbean could be interrupted, with severe economic consequences. This line of reasoning (which might be called "the Day-After syndrome") casts the United States as a defenseless nation at the mercy of a handful of wicked developing countries at the service of the Soviet Union. These countries ostensibly have the capability of closing the Caribbean Sea and the Panama Canal, thereby cutting off supplies and strangling the U.S. economy—*which has survived a Soviet nuclear attack*. The silliness of this scenario does not merit comment.

In the rhetorical repertoire born of politics as consecrated by successive U.S. administrations, "to fall under communist or Soviet influence" is just as dangerous as "another Cuba in the hemisphere." In the zero-sum logic applied to inter-American relations, this necessarily implies a hostile attitude toward the United States. Nonetheless, the historical record clearly shows that economic—and even military—ties with the Soviet Union do not in themselves produce either a communist regime or integration into the socialist camp. Peru and Argentina are both cases in point. Why these ties sometimes cause an aggressive U.S. response, and why such linkages are tolerated in other cases, is one of the mysteries of U.S. policy toward Latin America. In general, it appears that it is not so much ties with the Soviet Union or a supposedly hostile predisposition against the United States that constitutes a threat to U.S. national security, but the essential nature of the regime in question and the character of social change occurring in the country. Thus the Nicaraguan agrarian reform and the development of tourist infrastructure in Grenada became platforms for the Soviet Union because of a series of speculations that produce the absurd conclusion that the national integrity of the United States can be threatened from a Central American jungle or a Caribbean island with fewer inhabitants than the Bronx.

The last element of the United States' "hemispheric-security" policy to be examined here is the tendency to explain aggressive U.S. government policies as a response to a fundamental bias in the perceptions about politics found among U.S. citizens. That is, the U.S. government is supposedly obligated to pursue aggressive policies toward some Latin American countries because of the natural anti-Soviet or anticommunist tenor of U.S. public opinion. It is true that U.S. public opinion has been shaped with this end in mind, and it is also true that political debate creates opportunities for "hawks" to accuse their opponents of weakness in confronting the "communist challenge." However, neither consideration justifies "official errors" (such as hostile U.S. actions against Guatemala, Cuba, and the Dominican Republic), explaining U.S. policy in terms of erratic efforts by a series of presidents to maintain the United States' influence in the region. If one assumes that this is the U.S. perception, then one has only touched the tip of the iceberg.

The recent case of Grenada demonstrates that the U.S. government does not *follow* domestic public opinion. Rather, it makes political bets, calculating that military victory will be easy and will allow it to win public support at low cost. To the extent that specific political actions can be presented to the public as triumphs, the government is able to "construct" domestic consensus. This occurs not as the result of anti-Soviet or anticommunist public pressure but as the stimulus and manipulation of "America is great" chauvinism in pursuit of clear political goals (in the case of Grenada, goals associated with the proximity of the 1984 electoral campaign).

For its part, the long history of U.S.-Cuban relations since 1959 shows that even during the period of détente between the United States and the Soviet Union (when their economic and cultural exchanges expanded, and when there was even progress in strategic negotiations—for which there existed a corresponding domestic political consensus), U.S. administrations failed to lift the economic blockade against Cuba or to normalize diplomatic relations. There was only a modest reduction in hostilities during a brief period of the Carter administration. Did the resistance that U.S. administrations displayed regarding this issue result from the public's visceral anticommunism? Or is it that Cuba (like Grenada and Nicaragua) is a small country in "this hemisphere" that does not merit the normal dialogue the United States conducts with "Soviet-bloc countries" in eastern Europe? If the latter is the case, then one must try to understand why U.S. "public opinion" has become more anti-Soviet regarding Cuba or Nicaragua than regarding the Soviet Union itself (or why it has become less anticommunist regarding China). Perhaps it is possible to present an alternative explanation of U.S. policy toward Latin America that is somewhat less puzzling.

Some Alternative Approaches to Security Issues

The idea of "national security" is a spectral image projected by the real political mechanisms through which the U.S. political elite exercises its hegemony. This hegemonic system has both "internal" (domestic) and "external" (international) dimensions, and although its development is characterized by contradictions and crises, it is interlocked as a whole. Logically, then, the foreign policy agenda constitutes part of the domestic political process. Similarly, domestic political confrontations result in diplomatic-military actions outside the United States that in themselves are manifestations of the hegemonic system.

This perspective, far from reflecting a mechanistic philosophy, permits a dynamic understanding of the formulation of specific policies by the U.S. political elite. In the context of this discussion, the term "government" is used as a shorthand reference to this elite—with the clear understanding that this term does not refer to any particular U.S. presidential administration. What is important is not merely what the occupant of the White House says, or what the U.S. Constitution stipulates concerning the appropriate spheres of executive branch activity; rather, what counts are those factors that shape the systematic exercise of real power and the objective logic of this process.

From this frame of reference, the U.S. government's hegemonic assumption in Latin America is not an aberration. Indeed, it is the logical consequence of the exercise of hegemonic domination by elite groups within the United States. Does this necessarily mean that U.S. policy toward the region is immutably marked by such a hegemonic presumption? This merits careful consideration.

It is, of course, meaningful to speak of U.S. hegemony and its practical political mechanisms in U.S.–Latin American relations. But it is false to assume that there is a *single* U.S. policy toward the region, or that this policy is formulated through a monolithic mechanism generically called "the U.S. government." For example, at present different power-holders within the United States confront the problem of Central America both by considering various alternative scenarios and by actually implementing diverse policies. The unfolding of U.S. policy in "layers" often has been viewed merely as an incongruity of the system. But from the perspective outlined here, the existence of multiple U.S. policies constitutes a basic propensity of the system. If these policies fit together well at the level of overall U.S. policy, it is not because of any mechanical convergence; rather, it is precisely because they represent accurately a complex power structure. Banks and corporations, civil and military bureaucratic groups, and political leadership factions *simultaneously* pursue direct military intervention in Central America, indirect intervention through regional actors, and coercive diplomatic action. These different policies promote destabilization and seek to achieve the financial, military, and political isolation of the progressive groups and revolutionary forces involved in the conflict. In the case of Central America, an alternative policy could arise only if groups emerging from these "layers" are capable under intense pressure of acting *in their own interest* to promote a nonmilitary hegemonic approach. This might happen if these groups confront a domestic political crisis like, for example, that produced by protracted U.S. involvement in Vietnam.

An axiom can be derived from this discussion: the policies that emanate from the U.S. system will admit change in U.S. hegemony only inasmuch as such change is necessary to protect the particular interests of those power-holders involved. This apparent paradox has become reality whenever the U.S. government has pragmatically chosen a "minimum" yet viable course that avoids the pursuit at all costs of illusory "maximum" returns, but which at least proves profitable. This has been the case each time that the U.S. government has chosen negotiation to resolve problems involving the expropriation of foreign investments; dialogue to end a crisis; or agreement to ensure a timely retreat. In short, this has happened when the U.S. government has obtained a Zimbabwe rather than a Cuba.

This same point can be made in business terms: the tendency of those groups affected by a given issue to stress policy options involving force runs the high risk of creating expectations of maximum gain in an uncertain regional "market," which closes off nonmilitary options (such as the approach pursued by the Carter administration in Nicaragua in 1979) by letting pass the time for investing in alternatives based on negotiations. These same expectations then increase the value of options involving force. This dynamic has been reinforced recently by the favorable domestic political consensus *created* by the U.S. invasion of Grenada and by U.S. military action in the Middle East.

However, the equation that relates *military options* and *domestic consensus* is basically parabolic. Even if the military dimensions of a crisis contribute to greater domestic political consensus for a time, after a certain point these options stop reinforcing themselves politically. The relationship then becomes reversed, and military options erode the consensus they previously created. This parabolic relationship was very apparent in the U.S. war in Vietnam (although at the time, the shift to the negative side of the curve was not as predictable or as certain as this image might suggest). The truth is that the "law of hegemony" in its "maximum gain" form has a strong—and dangerous—inertial effect on those groups affected, frequently leading them to "nonreimbursable" losses for the system as a whole.

A second general point is that U.S. hegemony in Latin America faces growing resistance. In contrast to what one might think, the United States' policy toward Cuba is not a special case in this regard. Rather, this case reveals better than any other example the challenges that confront U.S. hegemony in the region. This goes beyond the question of whether the ghost of communism haunts Latin America, or whether the peoples of Latin America are rising up against the U.S. empire. It is *not only* a question of popular reaction, nor is it *just* communism. Any dispassionate observer of contemporary Latin America must recognize that diverse political leaders and ideologies not generally linked to insurrection and violence have been significantly affected by the lesson of Cuba over the last quarter-century. Cuba is an exemplary case of disruption in the hegemonic system. Cuba changed its relation to this system in extremis. But, at the same time, Cuba represents a limiting case in the crisis facing the United States' hegemonic assumption in the region. As such, Cuba has demonstrated the range of actions and reactions that a Latin American country puts into play when it deals with the U.S. government as a sovereign equal. Cuba has also shown how vulnerable the hegemonic system's own inelasticity makes it when a Latin American country attempts to achieve a degree of autonomy. Even though Latin American political leaders are far from ending general dependency relations with the United States on the basis of an independent national development project, Latin American leaders of the 1980s nonetheless have reassessed their relations with the U.S. government. They have identified their own interests and they have initiated a more diversified foreign policy as part of an effort to improve their international negotiating position.

The ineptitude with which the U.S. government has confronted Cuba reveals a bundle of mistaken ideas and erroneous perceptions that increasingly complicates U.S. relations with other Latin American countries. Moreover, the United States' current ties with Argentina, Brazil, Mexico, Colombia, and Venezuela (to cite only the principal cases) also show that it has failed to maintain healthy collaborative relations (in the broadest political sense) with governments in the region. Latin American leaders have come to see more and more that their own interests are not served by yielding to U.S. influence.

Given that the U.S. government has lacked the capacity to cooperate politically with most Latin American governments, and given that it has failed to foresee the direction of social change in the region (for example, in Nicaragua and Grenada in 1979), the United States' most pragmatic response would be to establish a policy of accommodation that would not exclude Latin American domestic processes of sociopolitical change from the western orbit. A policy of this kind would establish incentives to maintain Latin American states' prowestern alignment. Cases such as Grenada (not to mention countries in regions such as Africa) show that revolutionary governments are not so temperamental or antagonistic regarding prowestern ties as has sometimes been suggested. By casting all issues in terms of "national security" concerns, the U.S. government loses an opportunity to benefit from the practical importance of economic relations.

It is relevant to ask whether the United States' relations with Latin America pose a serious economic threat to U.S. national security. The problem involves more than recording how many strategic raw materials pass through the Caribbean or other sea routes used by U.S. shippers. For example, Latin American petroleum is certainly important to the United States; imports from the region have tended to increase as a share of total U.S. petroleum imports, and the Caribbean islands are an important link in the international chain of U.S. oil shipping. But this does not imply that the best means of guaranteeing security of supply is to saturate the Caribbean Basin with military forces. Apart from the monumental costs involved, the concentration of U.S. military power in the area would likely impede commercial shipping in an era when U.S. vessels are no longer the only ones to pass through the Antilles. Even if the deployment of military forces was sufficiently proportionate to the density of international ship traffic in the area, would this ensure that Mexico, Venezuela, and Trinidad and Tobago would continue to sell petroleum to U.S. oil companies? Or will the U.S. Marines guarantee that social change in these countries does not threaten U.S. "national security"? There would seem to be some other strategy that would better serve the interests of the hegemonic system, but this has not been the approach followed by the U.S. government. Instead of pursuing a constructive policy that would accept a lower rate of profit, the United States has been inclined toward inflexibility—with the risk that the prospects for disruption in the system increase.

The United States' extension of its policy toward Cuba is both plainly evident and particularly significant in an era of intensified intraregional ties. Actions such as the landing of a military force on a Caribbean island or in a South Atlantic archipelago reverberate throughout Latin America, erasing traditional geopolitical frontiers such as "Caribbean Basin" and "Southern Cone."

The crisis in Central America is the clearest example of how the same mechanisms that formulate U.S. policy toward Cuba also dominate the handling of a regional conflict that directly or indirectly involves the great majority of Latin American countries. And precisely when the hegemonic system confronts such critical problems in the region, the U.S. government emphasizes its peculiar understanding of "national security" in its relations with Latin America. In doing so, it reveals the persistence of the "Cuba syndrome" when its policy should demonstrate a greater flexibility.

Finally, it is important to consider the position of Latin American countries within the parameters of the regional hegemonic crisis. Latin American countries' socioeconomic structures and political systems are too complex to be described in terms of forms of government without reference to social variables. Such a typology is misleading because it ignores tendencies toward continuity or change in the political system. There are two basic dynamics in contemporary Latin American political systems and ongoing political processes: systems that move toward further opening and systems that remain closed under tight authoritarian control. This characterization refers both to those forces (classes, sectors and social strata, political groups and organizations, economic interests) that promote change and those that seek to preserve the status quo. It is not accidental that these two tendencies are linked to U.S. groups in the hegemonic system. This key linkage, in turn, defines the essential characteristics of the two tendencies. Most U.S. factions link themselves more closely with authoritarian elements, without recognizing that only those forces favoring change have sufficient dynamics to stabilize political participation in countries experiencing the powerful effects of social transformation.

The ties that most U.S. groups have to conservative forces in Latin America reveal both their bias and their lack of a minimum plan to encourage political openings (and resolve crises of political "closure") in the region. Throughout the twentieth century Latin American societies have moved toward an economic modernity with improved income distribution, a political modernity based on a new kind of democracy, and a social modernity that is more egalitarian and participatory. These changes surely cannot be consolidated within the existing parameters of Latin American capitalism, and it is even doubtful that they can be effected within the context of reformed capitalism. Very probably—and from the perspective that informs this comment, inevitably—this ultimate modernity is called socialism. If this is the case, how will those U.S. groups with ties to Latin America respond? What is the United States' *minimum plan* for a Latin America in transformation? This is the challenge that U.S. power-holders have confronted since the Eisenhower administration. The United States' response has frequently been characterized by simplification and the most absurd references to ideology, depicting the complexity of Latin American social processes as a movement from "West" to "East."

Even if all Latin Americans do not agree concerning the merits of socialism, they share a new sense of reality regarding their "hemispheric neighbor." The disenchanted realism of Latin American political leaders and popular movements cannot be easily addressed by liberal proposals informed by "good will." For their part, the U.S. government and U.S. power-holders are not inclined toward a "new deal" for Latin America. Their perception of recurrent hegemonic crises in the region is to see an opponent behind each democrat and a Marxist behind each opponent.

For this reason, it appears as if force might be the only effective means of guaranteeing dialogue with the United States. In order to be able to negotiate, one must hold a position of strength; the interlocutors are the belligerents. Thus Central America now offers a historic lesson to other Latin American countries, just as Cuba did earlier: only those who will fight for their rights can (and deserve to) enjoy them. The hegemonic system will give ground only if it is forced to do so by necessity. In more "businesslike" terms, a negotiator only accepts an agreement that offers less than ideal benefits if he is in danger of suffering greater losses. Will the United States suspend hegemonic operations before its Latin America stock is permanently devalued? Time is running out.

Centro de Estudios sobre América
Havana, Cuba

Notes on the Contributors

SERGIO BITAR is an economist, author, and consultant. He served as minister of mining in Chile in 1973, and he has worked as general manager of a private manufacturing company and as a consultant to the Sistema Económico Latinoamericano (SELA) in Caracas, Venezuela. During 1975–1976 Mr. Bitar was a visiting fellow at the Harvard Institute for International Development, and during 1982–1983 he was a fellow at the Latin American Program of the Woodrow Wilson International Center for Scholars, Smithsonian Institution, in Washington, D.C. He has written extensively on U.S.–Latin American economic relations, U.S. international economic policy and its implications for Latin America, Latin American industrialization, and the political economy of Chile. His publications include *La política de EEUU en América Latina: Documentos de la Administración Reagan* (1984); *Chile: Experiment in Democracy* (1985); and *Venezuela: The Industrial Challenge* (1986).

COLE BLASIER is professor of political science at the University of Pittsburgh, founder of the University's Center for Latin American Studies, and president-elect of the Latin American Studies Association. He has been a resident scholar at the Institute of Latin America in Moscow, and he initiated the U.S./USSR Exchange in Latin American studies. Professor Blasier previously served as a U.S. foreign service officer in Belgrade, Bonn, and Moscow. He has also studied or taught at universities in Chile, Colombia, and Mexico. His extensive writings on the foreign policies of the United States, the Soviet Union, and Cuba include *The Hovering Giant: U.S. Responses to Revolutionary Change in Latin America* (1976); *Cuba in the World* (coeditor, 1979); and *The Giant's Rival: The USSR and Latin America* (1983).

ROBERTO BOUZAS is a senior researcher in international relations at the Facultad Latinoamericana de Ciencias Sociales (FLACSO) in Buenos Aires, Argentina. Since 1981 he has also served as a consultant to the Permanent Secretariat of the Sistema Económico Latinoamericano (SELA) on U.S.-Latin American economic relations. Between 1980 and 1984 he was deputy director of the Instituto de Estudios de Estados Unidos at the Centro de Investigación y Docencia Económicas (CIDE) in Mexico City. Professor Bouzas, an economist, has written extensively on U.S. economic policy and U.S.–Latin American economic relations. His publications include "La política económica de la administración Reagan (Bases para un desorden futuro)," in *La política internacional de los años 80: Una perspectiva latinoamericana,* ed. Helio Jaguaribe (1982); "La economía norteamericana y América Latina: Complementaridad y conflicto en una fase de crisis," in *Argentina, Brasil e Mexico face a crise internacional dos anos 1980s,* ed. Roberto Bouzas and Carlos Plastino (forthcoming); and "U.S. Trade, Investment, and Financial Policies Toward Latin America: From the Alliance for Progress to the Caribbean Basin Initiative," in *Latin American Views on U.S. Policy,* ed. Heraldo Muñoz and Robert Wesson (forthcoming).

RAFAEL BRAUN is professor of Christian ethics at the Universidad Católica Argentina and director of the journal *Criterio* in Buenos Aires. He was president of the Centro de Investigaciones Filosóficas in Buenos Aires and is a member of the editorial board of *Revista Latinoamericana de Filosofía.* Professor Braun has written extensively on political theory and bioethics. His publications include *El régimen militar, 1966–1973* (coauthor, 1973); "La teoría de la guerra en los Elements of Law de Hobbes," *Revista Latinoamericana de Filosofía* (1975); "Los limites del pluralismo," in *Pensar la república,* ed. Carlos A. Floria and Marcelo Montserrat (1977); "Los valores básicos," in *Futuro político de la Argentina,* ed. Virgilio R. Beltrán (1978); and "Matar y dejar morir," *Revista Latinoamericana de Filosofía* (1982).

MARGARET E. CRAHAN is Henry R. Luce Professor of Religion, Power, and the Political Process at Occidental College and a board member of the Inter-American Institute of Human Rights of the Organization of American States. She previously served as director of the Woodstock Theological Center's human rights project and as a member of the Latin American Studies Association's executive council. Professor Crahan, whose professional training is in Latin American history, has conducted research in a number of Latin American countries and in Europe and has written extensively on Spanish colonial administration, church-state relations, religion and politics, twentieth-century Cuba, and African cultural heritage in the Caribbean. Her publications include *Africa and the Caribbean: Legacies of a Link* (coeditor, 1979); *Human Rights and Basic Needs in the Americas* (editor, 1982); *Power and Piety: The Political Dimension of Religion in Latin America* (forthcoming); and *Cuba: Social Transformations, 1763–1958* (forthcoming).

MARGARET DALY HAYES is director of the Washington, D.C., office of the Council of the Americas. Between 1981 and 1984 she served as the senior Western Hemisphere specialist for the U.S. Senate Foreign Relations Committee. Dr. Hayes has taught at the Johns Hopkins University School of Advanced International Studies, and she was associate director of the school's Center of Brazilian Studies. Dr. Hayes was a principal consultant to the National Bipartisan (Kissinger) Commission on Central America. She has also worked as a consultant to the Inter-American Dialogue, the United States Information Agency, the U.S. Department of State's Foreign Service Institute, the National Defense University, and the Inter-American Defense College. Dr. Hayes's research focuses primarily on U.S.–Latin American relations, U.S. security interests in the Western Hemisphere, and regional political affairs. Her publications include *Latin America and the U.S. National Interest: A Basis for U.S. Foreign Policy* (1984).

GIUSEPPE DI PALMA is professor of political science and chairman of the Department of Political Science at the University of California at Berkeley. He specializes in comparative and western European politics. His recent work has focused on regime change and the problem of regime performance in postdictatorial democracies. Professor Di Palma is the author of *Apathy and Participation: Mass Politics in Western Societies* (1970); *The Study of Conflict in Western Society* (1973); *Surviving Without Governing: The Italian Parties in Parliament* (1977); and *The Central American Impasse* (coeditor with Laurence Whitehead, 1985).

FERNANDO FAJNZYLBER is regional adviser on industrial development for the United Nations Economic Commission for Latin America and the Caribbean (ECLAC) and the United Nations Industrial Development Organization (UNIDO) in Santiago, Chile. His professional training is in engineering and economics, with a specialization in industrial economy. His publications include *Sistema industrial e exportação de manufacturas* (1970); *Estrategia industrial e empresas internacionais* (1970); *Las empresas transnacionales: Expansión internacional y proyección en la industria de México* (coauthor, 1976); and *La industrialización trunca de América Latina* (1983).

RICHARD E. FEINBERG is vice-president of the Overseas Development Council (ODC) in Washington, D.C., and adjunct professor of international finance at the Georgetown University School of Foreign Service. Between 1977 and 1979 he served as the Latin American specialist on the U.S. Department of State's policy planning staff. Dr. Feinberg has also worked as an international economist in the U.S. Department of the Treasury and with the U.S. House of Representatives Banking Committee, and he has held several fellowships. He has written extensively on U.S. foreign policy, Latin American politics, and international economics, including *Subsidizing Success: The Export-Import Bank in the United States Economy* (1982); *Central America: International Dimensions of the Crisis* (editor, 1982); and *The Intemperate Zone: The Third World Challenge to U.S. Foreign Policy* (1983). Dr. Feinberg is also coeditor of the ODC's U.S.–Third World Policy Perspectives series, whose current volumes include *Adjustment Crisis in the Third World* (1984) and *Uncertain Future: Commercial Banks in the Third World* (1985).

WINSTON FRITSCH is associate professor of economics at the Pontifícia Universidade Católica do Rio de Janeiro and at the Universidade Federal do Rio de Janeiro. He is also dean of the Centro de Ciências Sociais of the Pontifícia Universidade Católica do Rio de Janeiro. Professor Fritsch was previously director of the faculty of economics and business administration at the Universidade Federal do Rio de Janeiro. He has written extensively on international economics, macroeconomic policy, and the history of twentieth-century Brazilian economic policy. His recent publications include "O futuro das relações comerciais Brasil-Estados Unidos," in *Brasil–Estados Unidos na transição democrática,* ed. Monica Hirst (1985); and *Latin American and Caribbean Countries in the World Trade System: Past Problems and Future Problems* (coauthor, forthcoming).

RAFAEL HERNÁNDEZ is a senior research fellow and director of the Departamento de Norte América at the Centro de Estudios sobre América in Havana, Cuba. He is also an associate professor at the Instituto Superior de Relaciones Internacionales in Havana and a member of the editorial board for *Cuadernos de Nuestra América*. Professor Hernández previously held positions in the history of philosophy and in literature at the Universidad de La Habana. He has written extensively on U.S.–Latin American relations, U.S. foreign policymaking toward Cuba, Cuban development and the Cuban state, and Cuban migration to the United States in the 1970s. His publications include "Indicadores del desarrollo económico cubano," *Foro Internacional* (1977); "La política inmigratoria de Estados Unidos y la revolución cubana," *Avances de Investigación* (1980); and "La estructura de clase de la comunidad cubana en el exterior," *Cuadernos de Nuestra América* (coauthor, 1983).

JAMES R. KURTH is professor of political science at Swarthmore College. Between 1983 and 1985 he was a visiting professor of strategy at the Naval War College. Professor Kurth has published extensively on U.S. foreign and defense policies and on European and Latin American politics. His recent publications on Latin America include "Industrial Change and Political Change: A European Perspective," in *The New Authoritarianism in Latin America,* ed. David Collier (1979); "The United States in Central America: Hegemony in Historical and Comparative Perspective," in *Central America: The International Dimensions of the Crisis* ed. Richard E. Feinberg (1982); and "The New Realism in U.S.–Latin American Relations: Principles for a New U.S. Foreign Policy," in *From Gunboats to Diplomacy: New U.S. Policies for Latin America,* ed. Richard Newfarmer (1984).

CARLOS MASSAD is special adviser to the executive secretary of the United Nations Economic Commission for Latin America and the Caribbean (ECLAC, Santiago, Chile) and professor of economics at the Universidad de Santiago de Chile. Professor Massad taught economics at the Universidad de Chile for many years, and between 1959 and 1964 he was director of the University's Instituto de Investigaciones Económicas. He has also served as vice-president and president of the Banco Central de Chile (1964–1970), as executive director of the Internationl Monetary Fund, and as a member of the World Bank's research advisory panel. His publications include *Macroeconomía* (1979); *Nociones de economía* (1980); and *Análisis económico: Introducción* (1983).

KEVIN J. MIDDLEBROOK is assistant professor of political science at Indiana University at Bloomington. Between 1983 and 1984 Professor Middlebrook was a Mellon Foundation visiting research fellow at the Center for U.S.–Mexican Studies, University of California at San Diego. Between 1982 and 1983 he served as a senior consultant to the Woodrow Wilson International Center for Scholars' Inter-American Dialogue. Professor Middlebrook has held several research fellowships on Latin America, and he has written on political liberalization and state-labor relations in Mexico, U.S.-Mexican energy relations, Andean regional economic integration, and agrarian reform under military government in Peru.

His recent publications include "The State and Organized Labor in Brazil and Mexico" (coauthor), in *Brazil and Mexico: Patterns in Late Development,* ed. Sylvia A. Hewlett and Richard S. Weinert (1982); "International Implications of Labor Change: The Mexican Automobile Industry," in *Mexico's Political Economy: Challenges at Home and Abroad,* ed. Jorge I. Domínguez (1982); and "Political Liberalization in an Authoritarian Regime: The Case of Mexico," in *Prospects for Democracy: The Transition from Authoritarian Regimes,* ed. Guillermo O'Donnell, Philippe Schmitter, and Laurence Whitehead (1986). He is currently finishing a book on the political economy of state-labor relations in Mexico since 1940.

GABRIEL MURILLO CASTAÑO is professor of political science and chairman of the Facultad de Ciencia Política at the Universidad de los Andes in Bogotá, Colombia. He has been a visiting professor at several universities in the United States, and he has also served as a consultant to international organizations such as UNESCO and the International Labor Organization (ILO). He has written extensively on international labor migration, inter-American relations, poverty and the informal sector, and Andean border studies. His most recent publications include *Migrant Workers in the Americas: A Comparative Study of Migration Between Colombia and Venezuela and Between Mexico and the United States* (1984); "Effects of Emigration and Return on Sending Countries: The Case of Colombia," *International Social Science Journal* (1984); "La articulación del sector informal y el sector formal de la economía urbana," in *Ciudades y sistemas urbanos* (1984); and "El tratamiento de la migración laboral internacional en la agenda de las relaciones interamericanas de la segunda mitad de los años ochenta," *Cuadernos Semestrales de Estados Unidos: Perspectiva latinoamericana* (1985).

RICHARD O'BRIEN is chief economist of American Express Bank Ltd. and editor of the *AMEX Bank Review* in London. He has been a consultant to the World Bank and to the United Nations International Development Organization (UNIDO). Mr. O'Brien's work in international banking has focused particularly on the analysis of country-risk questions. His recent publications include "Private Bank Lending to Developing Countries," *World Bank Staff Working Paper* (1981); "Roles of the Euromarket and the IMF in Financing Developing Countries," in *Adjustment and Financing in the Developing World,* ed. Tony Killick (1982); and "International Debt: Banks and the LDCs," *AMEX Bank Review,* Special Paper No. 10 (1984).

JOHN S. ODELL is associate professor of international relations at the University of Southern California. During 1984–1985 he worked at the Office of the U.S. Trade Representative and the Institute for International Economics in Washington, D.C., as a Council on Foreign Relations fellow. His research is concerned with the behavior of governments in international economic matters. Professor Odell is the author of "The Politics of Debt Relief: Official Creditors and Brazil, Ghana, and Chile," in *Debt and Less Developed Countries,* ed. Jonathan Aronson (1979); "Latin American Trade Negotiations with the United States," *International Organization* (1980); *U.S. International Monetary Policy: Markets, Power, and Ideas as Sources of Change* (1982); and "The Outcomes of International Trade Conflicts: The U.S. and South Korea, 1960–1981," *International Studies Quarterly* (1985).

GUILLERMO O'DONNELL is academic director of the Kellogg Institute and Helen Kellogg Professor of International Studies at the University of Notre Dame. Professor O'Donnell, a native of Argentina, holds joint appointments in the departments of government and sociology at Notre Dame, and he is a senior researcher at the Centro Brasileiro de Análise e Planejamento (CEBRAP) in São Paulo, Brazil. He has taught political science at a number of universities in both Latin America and the United States. Between 1974 and 1975 he was a fellow at the Institute for Advanced Study, Princeton University, and between 1982 and 1985 he was vice-president of the International Political Science Association. Professor O'Donnell has served on the advisory boards of numerous academic journals and research institutions, and he has held a number of distinguished fellowships. His publications on Latin American politics include *Modernization and Bureaucratic Authoritarianism: Studies in South American Politics* (1973); *El estado burocrático-autoritario: Argentina 1966–1973* (1982); *Prospects for Democracy: The Transition from Authoritarian Regimes* (coeditor, with Philippe Schmitter and Laurence Whitehead, 1986); and *Contrapuntos: Autoritarismo y democracia* (forthcoming).

CARLOS RICO is director of the Instituto de Estudios de Estados Unidos and professor of international relations at the Centro de Investigación y Docencia Económicas (CIDE) in Mexico City. Between 1983 and 1984 he was a visiting research scholar at the Center for U.S.-Mexican Studies, University of California at San Diego. Professor Rico has held visiting positions in international relations at several other universities in Mexico, and he has also served as a consultant to the Secretaría de Relaciones Exteriores in Mexico, the Inter-American Dialogue, and the Ford Foundation. He has written extensively on U.S. foreign policy toward Latin America, Mexican foreign policy, and U.S.-Mexican relations. His publications include "Las relaciones mexicano-norteamericanas y los significados de la 'interdependencia,'" *Foro Internacional* (1978); "El impacto de la crisis de consenso sobre la toma de decisiones en política exterior de Estados Unidos," *Cuadernos Semestrales de Estados Unidos: Perspectiva latinoamericana* (1981); "La frontera mexicano-norteamericana, la retórica de la 'interdependencia' y el problema de las asimetrias," in *La frontera del norte,* ed. Roque González Salazar (1981); and "The Future of Mexican-U.S. Relations and the Limits of the Rhetoric of 'Interdependence,'" in *Mexican-U.S. Relations: Conflict and Convergence,* ed. Carlos Vázquez and Manuel García y Griego (1983).

MICHAEL S. TEITELBAUM is a program officer at the Alfred P. Sloan Foundation in New York. Dr. Teitelbaum, a demographer, has held academic appointments at the Office of Population Research, Princeton University, and at Nuffield College, Oxford University. He has also served as staff director of the Select Committee on Population, U.S. House of Representatives, and on the professional staffs of the Ford Foundation and the Carnegie Endowment for International Peace. Dr. Teitelbaum has published essays in journals such as *Population Studies, Foreign Affairs,* and *Science,* and he is the author of *The British Fertility Decline: Demographic Transition in the Crucible of the Industrial Revolution* (1984); and *The Fear of Population Decline* (coauthor, 1985).

EDELBERTO TORRES-RIVAS is general secretary of the Facultad Latinoamericana de Ciencias Sociales (FLACSO) and professor of sociology at the Universidad de Costa Rica in San José, Costa Rica. He is also director of *Polémica,* a quarterly journal dedicated to the Central American crisis. Professor Torres-Rivas, a native of Guatemala, previously was director of *Estudios Sociales Centroamericanos* and director of the Central American Program in Social Science (Confederación Universitaria Centroamericana). His publications include *Las clases sociales en Guatemala* (1962); *Interpretación del desarrollo social centroamericano: Proceso y estructuras de una sociedad dependiente* (1977); *Problemas en la formación del estado nacional en Centroamérica* (1983); and *Democracia y sociedad en Centroamérica* (forthcoming).

GREGORY F. TREVERTON is a lecturer in public policy and a senior research associate at the Center for Science and International Affairs, John F. Kennedy School of Government, Harvard University. He previously served as staff member for western Europe on the U.S. National Security Council (1977–1978), assistant director of the International Institute for Strategic Studies (London), and a principal consultant to the National Bipartisan (Kissinger) Commission on Central America. Professor Treverton has also worked as a consultant to the Ford Foundation and as a professional staff member on the U.S. Senate Select Committee on Intelligence Activities (1975). His publications include *Latin America in World Politics: The Next Decade* (1977); *Energy and Security* (editor, 1980); *The Nuclear Confrontation in Europe* (coeditor, 1985); and *Making the Alliance Work: The United States and Western Europe* (1985).

LAURENCE WHITEHEAD is an official fellow in politics at Nuffield College, Oxford University, and teaches at the University's Latin American Centre. During 1985–1986 he was acting program director at the Center for U.S.-Mexican Studies at the University of California at San Diego. Professor Whitehead has undertaken research in Bolivia, Chile, and Mexico and at the Latin American Program of the Woodrow Wilson International Center for Scholars in Washington, D.C. He is coeditor (with Guillermo O'Donnell and Philippe Schmitter) of a four-volume study entitled *Prospects for Democracy: The Transition from Authoritarian Regimes* (1986). His other publications include *Inflation and Stabilisation in Latin America* (coeditor, 1980); and "Explaining Washington's Central American Policies," *Journal of Latin American Studies* (1983).

HOWARD J. WIARDA is resident scholar and director of the Center for Hemispheric Studies at the American Enterprise Institute for Public Policy Research in Washington, D.C., and professor of political science at the University of Massachusetts at Amherst. Professor Wiarda is also a research associate of the Center for International Affairs at Harvard University. He has served as a lead consultant to the National Bipartisan (Kissinger) Commission on Central America, editor of the journal *Polity,* and director of the Center for Latin American Studies at the University of Massachusetts at Amherst. Professor Wiarda has also held a number of research fellowships. He has written extensively on Latin America and on U.S. foreign policy, including *Politics and Social Change in Latin America: The Distinct Tradition* (editor, 1974); *The Continuing Struggle for Democracy in Latin America* (editor, 1980); *Corporatism and National Development in Latin America* (1981); *Human Rights and U.S. Human Rights Policy* (1982); *In Search of Policy: The United States and Latin America* (1984); *Rift and Revolution: The Central American Imbroglio* (editor, 1984); *Ethnocentrism in Foreign Policy: Can We Understand the Third World?* (1985); and *Latin American Politics and Development* (coeditor, 1985).

OTHER STUDIES